FROM WEIMAR TO HITLER

FROM WEIMAR TO HITLER

Studies in the Dissolution of the Weimar Republic and the Establishment of the Third Reich, 1932–1934

Edited by Hermann Beck and Larry Eugene Jones

berghahn

NEW YORK · OXFORD

www.berghahnbooks.com

First published in 2019 by
Berghahn Books
www.berghahnbooks.com

© 2019, 2020 Hermann Beck and Larry Eugene Jones
First paperback edition published in 2020

Library of Congress Cataloging-in-Publication Data
Names: Beck, Hermann, editor. | Jones, Larry Eugene, editor.
Title: From Weimar to Hitler: Studies in the Dissolution of the Weimar
Republic and the Establishment of the Third Reich, 1932-1934 / edited by
Hermann Beck and Larry Eugene Jones.
Description: First edition. | New York: Berghahn Books, 2019. | Includes
bibliographical references and index.
Identifiers: LCCN 2018040249 (print) | LCCN 2018047227 (ebook) | ISBN
9781785339189 (ebook) | ISBN 9781785339172 (hardback: alk. paper)
Subjects: LCSH: Germany--History--1918-1933. | Germany--Politics and
government--1918-1933. | Germany--History--1933-1945. | Germany--Politics
and government--1933-1945. | National socialism--History. | Social
change--Germany--History--20th century.
Classification: LCC DD251 (ebook) | LCC DD251 .F76 2019 (print) | DDC
943.085--dc23
LC record available at https://lccn.loc.gov/2018040249

British Library Cataloguing in Publication Data
A catalogue record for this book is available from the British Library

ISBN 978-1-78533-917-2 hardback
ISBN 978-1-78920-848-1 paperback
ISBN 978-1-78533-918-9 ebook

Contents

✚ Abbreviations

ADGB	Allgemeiner Deutscher Gewerkschaftsbund/General German Trade Union Federation
AEG	Allgemeine Elektrizitäts-Gesellschaft/General Electric
AHS	Adolf Hitler Spende der deutschen Wirtschaft/Adolf Hitler Donation of the German Economy
AKD	Arbeitsgemeinschaft kathoischer Deutscher/Alliance of Catholic Germans
BDM	Bund Deutscher Mädel/League of German Girls
BKA	Bund katholischer Deutscher "Kreuz und Adler"/League of Catholic Germans Cross and Eagle
BVP	Bayerische Volkspartei/Bavarian People's Party
CPD	Christlicher Pfadfinderschaft Deutschlands/Christian Pathfinders of Germany
DAF	Deutsche Arbeitsfront/German Labor Front
DHV	Deutschnationaler Handlungsgehilfen-Verband/German National Union of Commercial Employees
DNVP	Deutschnationale Volkspartei/German National People's Party
DVP	Deutsche Volkspartei/German People's Party
DT	Deutsche Turnerschaft/German Gymnastic Federation Deutsche Turnerschaft
ERwJ	Evangelischer Reichsverband weiblicher Jugend/Protestant Reich Organization of Female Youths
GB	Großdeutscher Bund/Greater German Confederation
GcG	Gesamtverband der christlichen Gewerkschaften Deutschlands/Federation of German Christian Trade Unions
GHH	Gutehoffnungshütte
HJ	Hitlerjugend/Hitler Youth
IHK	Industrie- und Handelskammer/Chamber of Industry and Trade
KJVD	Katholischer Jungmännerverband Deutschlands/Catholic Young Men's Association of Germany

KPD   Kommunistische Partei Deutschlands/Communist Party of Germany

KVP   Konservative Volkspartei/Conservative People's Party

NSBO   Nationalsozialistische Betriebszellenorganisation/National Socialist Factory Cells Organization

NSDAP Nationalsozialistische Deutsche Arbeiterpartei/National Socialist German Workers' Party

NSKK   Nationalsozialistische Kraftfahrkorps/National Socialist Automobile Corps

OSAF   Oberste SA-Führung/High Command of the SA

RddJ   Reichsausschuss der deutschen Jugendverbände/Reich Committee of German Youth Associations

RDI   Reichsverband der Deutschen Industrie/National Association of German Industry

RjF   Reichsjugendführung/Reich Youth Leadership

RLB   Reichs-Landbund/National Rural League

RSI   Reichsstand der deutschen Industrie/Reich Estate of German Industry

SA   Sturm-Abteilungen der NSDAP/NSDAP Storm Detachments

SAJ   Sozialistische Arbeiterjugend/Socialist Labor Youth

SAP   Sozialistische Arbeiterpartei/Socialist Workers' Party

SPD   Sozialdemokratische Partei Deutschlands/Social Democratic Party of Germany

SS   Schutzstaffel der NSDAP/NSDAP Protection Squadron

 # Introduction

THE NAZI SEIZURE OF POWER IN HISTORICAL AND HISTORIOGRAPHICAL PERSPECTIVE

Hermann Beck and Larry Eugene Jones

How did it happen that Adolf Hitler was able to gain access to the levers of power on 30 January 1933 and transform the German state into a one-man, one-party dictatorship that would wreak havoc with Germans, Jews, and the international order for the next ten years? No question has consumed the historians of modern German history more than this. Was Hitler's appointment as chancellor an accident—what some have called a *Betriebsunfall*—or the inevitable and necessary outcome of long-term historical processes over which specific historical actors had no effective control? Was there any way in which individuals like Reich president Paul von Hindenburg, Franz von Papen, and Kurt von Schleicher could have averted this outcome? Or were they morally culpable for having made possible what the renowned German historian Friedrich Meinecke called "The German Catastrophe"? In other words, were these developments driven by historical imperatives that precluded intervention by individual historical agents, or were these individuals either directly or indirectly responsible for the tragic events of 30 January 1933? If so, who were these individuals, what did they hope to accomplish, what did they do, and to what extent did they succeed or fail? Equally important, what did they do after the fateful events of 30 January 1933? Did they resist, or did they adapt and accommodate? If they resisted, why did they accomplish so little? If they accommodated, what effect, if any, did this have on the regime with which they had made their private peace? Or did they fall victims to the illusion that they could avert the worst and make the best of what was a horrible situation to begin with? Was there a conservative containment strategy? If so, was it in any way whatsoever coordinated, or was it simply a series of haphazard measures that stood little chance of success? Why, in the final analysis, did Germany's conservative elites prove so inept in responding to the threat that National Socialism presented to their vital interests and status in German society? Or were they more interested in accommodating to the demands of the regime than in containing the dynamism of the Nazi movement?

These are only a few of the myriad questions that confront the historian who tries to make sense of the events of 30 January 1933. No single volume—and certainly not one as modest in its design as this—can adequately address, let alone answer, all of these questions. This book rests upon the premise that Hitler's appointment as chancellor on 30 January 1933 and the Nazi seizure of power that followed were neither inevitable nor unavoidable. To be sure, historians have learned that if these events are to be properly understood, they must be placed in a broader historical perspective. Perhaps, as some historians have done, it is necessary to go back as far as the political transformations of the late nineteenth century, or to the founding of the Second Empire, or even to the romantic and nationalist revolt against the eighteenth-century Enlightenment with its cosmopolitanism, its belief in the primacy of human reason, and its affirmation of universally valid propositions like the concept of natural law and the doctrine of human rights. This position has certainly had its more recent exemplars as, for example, in George Mosse's assertion in his classic work on *The Crisis of German Ideology* that Hitler—or something like Hitlerism—would most likely have come to power in Germany even if the world economic crisis had never taken place. In other words, the cultural imperatives with all of their *völkisch* and antiliberal concomitants were so powerful in Germany that the collapse of Weimar democracy and the triumph of Nazism or something like it were inevitable.[1] A similar argument, though not from the perspective of cultural and intellectual history but from that of political history, came from Fritz Fischer and the school of young historians that rallied behind his banner. Extrapolating from theses that he had first developed in his monumental book *Germany's Aims in the First World War*, Fischer argued that there was a direct line of continuity from the constellation of elites that existed in Germany on the eve of World War I to the "alliance of elites" that resurfaced in the last years of the Weimar Republic and that turned to Hitler and his movement for their support in a crusade against the remnants of Weimar democracy.[2] In a similar vein, Hans-Ulrich Wehler and the so-called Bielefeld School that had crystallized around him and Jürgen Kocka in the 1970s and 1980s traced the rise and eventual triumph of National Socialism to certain deformities in Germany's social and economic development, the persistence of Germany's preindustrial elites, and the political weakness of Germany's liberal bourgeoisie first in the Second Empire and then, even more tragically, in the Weimar Republic.[3] Whatever their differences—and they were indeed profound—Mosse, Fischer, and Wehler all shared one thing in common: namely, the conviction that Germany's experiment in democracy was doomed to failure by the sheer weight of tradition and that it stood little, if any, chance of survival.

To be sure, the teleological determinism of these arguments was not without its critics.[4] As early as 1935, the British historian Robert Thomson Clark had argued that Hitler's appointment as chancellor was the culmination of a concatenation of events such that had one event turned out differently, then Hitler would never have come to power.[5] Karl Dietrich Bracher's explanation for the failure of Weimar democracy in his classic study *Die Auflösung der Weimarer Republic* employed a structural mode of analysis that focused on the systemic breakdown that occurred in the latter years of the Weimar Republic as a result of its inability to mediate the increasingly bitter conflict between the different sectors of the German economy. Bracher goes on to argue, however, that the state of political paralysis that existed in Germany since at least the fall of 1929 created a situation in which the agency of individual historical actors was suddenly invested with much greater causal efficacy than might otherwise have been the case. In the final analysis, it was how these actors behaved that would determine whether or not the Weimar Republic would survive the crisis that had descended upon it with such fury at the very end of the 1920s. Bracher thus rescues the principle of individual agency and moral responsibility from the more deterministic models of historical analysis associated with Fischer and Wehler. In Bracher's opinion, responsibility for Hitler's appointment as chancellor rests squarely on the shoulders of the camarilla around Reich president Paul von Hindenburg, a group that included the likes of Franz von Papen and Kurt von Schleicher.[6]

The principle of individual moral responsibility also plays an important role in the writings of Hans Mommsen, Heinrich August Winkler, and Henry Turner Jr. Although Mommsen and Bracher shared much in common and were outspoken critics of the more restorationist tendencies that made themselves felt in the German historical profession after 1945, Mommsen was extremely critical of the central role that Bracher assigned to Hitler both in the series of events that culminated in the Nazi assumption of power in 1933 and in the subsequent policies of the Third Reich. Mommsen's critique of Bracher was informed not just by his rejection of the totalitarian theory of the Nazi state but also by his concern that Bracher's Hitler-centrism had the practical effect of exculpating the German people of any responsibility for the crimes of the Third Reich. For Mommsen, the pattern of complicity in these crimes was much broader than intentionalists like Bracher were prepared to admit. Mommsen was particularly critical of the role that Germany's conservative elites had played in the series of events that culminated in Hitler's appointment as chancellor and how they allowed themselves to be duped into believing that they could control Hitler once he was in power.[7] Though careful not to associate himself with Mommsen's thoroughgoing embrace of structural functionalism, Winkler agrees that Hitler's appointment as chancellor and all that followed were in no way unavoidable and points to the wide range of responses that were available to Germany's conservative elites as they wrestled with the collapse of Weimar democracy. This was particularly true in light of the crisis within the NSDAP after the party's heavy losses in the November 1932 Reichstag elections and the subsequent split between Hitler and the NSDAP's Reich organization leader Gregor Strasser. That the camarilla around Hindenburg opted for the "Hitler solution" was a matter of choice and by no means the only option available to them in the last months of the Weimar Republic.[8] Henry Turner Jr. is even more explicit in this regard. Not only does Turner raise a series of nagging questions about the validity of Fischer's thesis about the "alliance of elites"[9] but he reminds us in his book *Hitler's Thirty Days to Power* that the NSDAP was on the verge of collapse right up until the moment of Hitler's fateful meeting with Papen on 4 January 1933. Even then there were still opportunities to avert a Hitler chancellorship if only Schleicher and his colleagues in the Reich defense ministry had found the resolve to act. In the final analysis, Turner argues, ultimate responsibility for Hitler's installation as chancellor lay with a small circle of men whose actions — or, in the case of Schleicher, inaction — helped elevate Hitler from his well-deserved obscurity to the leadership of the most powerful nation on the European continent.[10]

The second premise that stands at the heart of this book is that the Nazi seizure of power was not a single event that happened on 30 January 1933 but a process that extended over a longer period of time and involved more than Hitler's installation as chancellor. At the very least, this process extended from Franz von Papen's appointment as chancellor in early June 1932 to the Röhm Purge two years later. In this respect Bracher has identified four specific stages in the Nazi seizure and consolidation of power.[11] The first ran from the installation of the Hitler cabinet on 30 January 1933 through the Decree of the Reich President for the Protection of the People and State that Hindenburg enacted on the day after the Reichstag fire on the night of 27–28 February. During this phase Hitler and the Nazi leadership were still somewhat tentative and probing the legal and political parameters of what they could do within the restraints imposed upon them by the terms under which Hitler assumed the chancellorship. The decree of 28 February represented a fundamental assault on the legal protection that all Germans enjoyed under the Weimar Constitution and cleared the way for what would happen in the second phase of the Nazi consolidation of power. This phase lasted from the beginning of March through the middle of the summer of 1933 and was marked by the passage of the Enabling Act (Ermächtigungsgesetz) on 24 March, the systematic dismantling of what still remained of German democracy with the dissolution of all political parties save the NSDAP, the suppression of organized labor, and the coordination (*Gleichschaltung*) of the individual state governments. A particularly important feature of this phase was the systematic deployment of state-sanctioned violence against enemies of the regime, including functionaries of the conservative forces that had joined Hitler in his government of "national concentration."[12] Outmaneuvering their conservative allies at every turn, the Nazis were able to establish what amounted to a one-party dictatorship with little, if anything, in the way of organized resistance.

The third phase in the Nazi seizure of power began with Hitler's announcement in mid-July 1933 that the Nazi revolution had accomplished its objectives with the destruction of the Weimar state and that it was now time for a period of consolidation and renewal. This held obvious implications for Hitler's storm troopers (Sturm-Abteilungen der NSDAP or SA), the paramilitary wing that had been the principal agent of the Nazi revolution and now found itself relegated to the sidelines at least for the foreseeable future. The second half of 1933 was characterized by a relative calm that stood in sharp contrast to the preceding six months; a new normal had settled upon the country. But by the end of the year, there were signs of increasing unrest, particularly within the SA, whose leader Ernst Röhm began to make vague allusions to a "second revolution" in which the social promise of the Nazi revolution would be finally fulfilled. Rumors of a "second revolution" in which the destruction of the Weimar state was to be followed by a redistribution of wealth and property had an unnerving effect on Hitler's conservative allies and threatened to undermine their loyalty to the regime.[13] Nowhere was this more apparent than at the upper echelons of Germany's military establishment, where Röhm's plans for a "people's army" created through the amalgamation of the Reichswehr and SA had aroused particular concern.[14] As tension began to build through the late spring and early summer of 1934, Hitler and his closest supporters were finally forced into action by a speech that Franz von Papen, the vice chancellor in the Hitler cabinet and the putative leader of the conservatives who had allied themselves with Hitler, delivered at the University of Marburg on 17 June. Here Papen gave voice to the growing fears of Germany's propertied classes about the rumors of a "second revolution," drew public attention to the discrepancy between the promise and practice of the Nazi revolution, and announced that it was time to transform the Nazi revolution into a "conservative revolution" based upon a reaffirmation of the spiritual values that lay at the heart of Germany's national greatness. Papen's speech forced Hitler's hand, and on 30 June 1934 Hitler and a small circle of associates launched a two-pronged strike against the SA and those conservatives who had conspired to remove Hitler from office in what came to be known as Hitler's "Night of the Long Knives."[15]

Though first formulated more than a half century ago, Bracher's periodization of the Nazi seizure and consolidation of power still serves as a useful framework for the presentation of the chapters contained in this volume. The first three chapters by Larry Eugene Jones, Joseph Bendersky, and Martin Menke belong to what one might call the prehistory of the Third Reich and focus on three individuals who were deeply involved in the series of events that culminated in Hitler's appointment as chancellor. In his chapter on Kurt von Schleicher, Larry Eugene Jones argues that Schleicher was convinced that Germany could survive the present crisis only if its political establishment reached some sort of accommodation with the Nazis. The assumption underlying Schleicher's *Zähmungskonzept* was that the responsibilities of government participation would not only deprive the Nazis of the advantages they enjoyed in opposition but would also exert a moderating effect upon the NSDAP, as had previously been the case with the Social Democrats. A Nazi presence in the national government would provide Germany's conservative elites with the mantle of popular legitimacy they needed to carry out a revision of the Weimar Constitution along conservative lines. At the same time, Schleicher remained irreconcilably opposed to any solution to the political stalemate in the last months of the Weimar Republic that would have elevated Hitler to the chancellorship. In an attempt to overcome Hitler's opposition to his party's participation in the national government despite its heavy losses in the November 1932 Reichstag elections, Schleicher cultivated close ties with Gregor Strasser, the leader of the Nazi Party organization and a man generally regarded as the leader of the NSDAP's more moderate elements. But Schleicher did not, according to Jones, seek to provoke a secession on the NSDAP's left wing, and Strasser's decision to resign his party offices in early December 1932 represented a severe setback to Schleicher's hopes of strengthening the Nazi moderates. In the meantime, Schleicher was outmaneuvered by his own protégé Franz von Papen, who entered into negotiations with Hitler behind his back in early January 1933 and played the decisive role in the series of events that eventually led to the Nazi party leader's appointment as chancellor.

One of the most controversial figures in the politics of the late Weimar Republic is the renowned jurist and legal theorist Carl Schmitt. In his chapter on Schmitt, Joseph Bendersky takes issue with those of Schmitt's critics who make him and his constitutional theories culpable for Hitler's appointment as chancellor. To the contrary, Bendersky argues that Schmitt was strongly opposed to dismissing the Weimar Constitution and parliament in favor of a presidential dictatorship. At the same time, Schmitt recognized that the system of parliamentary government as embodied in the Weimar Constitution was no longer capable of providing the strong, effective government that was necessary if Germany was to survive the deepening economic and political crisis that had descended upon it in the early 1930s. On the basis of Schmitt's recently published diaries and his correspondence with Ernst Rudolf Huber, Bendersky reconstructs the relationship that developed between Schmitt and Schleicher in the second half of 1932 and the role that Schmitt played in providing Schleicher with legal justifications for the temporary suspension of certain provisions of the Weimar Constitution in order to achieve a modicum of political stability. At no point, however, did Schmitt advocate abandoning the Weimar Constitution in favor of a dictatorship. Even his advocacy of a "negative no-confidence vote" was always within the legal confines of the constitution and the political legitimacy of Hindenburg. Like Schleicher, Schmitt desperately hoped to prevent Hitler from gaining power and was deeply disturbed when that did not prove the case. Schmitt did his best to keep his distance from the new regime through its first months in office and did not endorse the principle of dictatorial rule, as an article he wrote on the Enabling Act in April 1933 clearly revealed.

A further factor that contributed to the collapse of the Weimar Republic was the weakness of those parties that remained loyal to the republican system of government. Martin Menke turns his attention to this question in his chapter on Ludwig Kaas, the chairman of the German Center Party (Deutsche Zentrumspartei) since December 1928. A compromise candidate whose primary virtue was that he was not associated with any of the factions that were vying for control of the Center, Kaas was, Menke argues, woefully unprepared for the chairmanship at the time of his election to the party leadership and never rose to the demands that it placed upon him over the course of the next four years. This could be seen in his frail health and his frequent absences from Berlin at critical points in the Center's efforts to rescue German democracy from the challenge of the more radical political parties on the left and right. Throughout all of this, Menke argues, Kaas remained unequivocally committed to the principle of constitutional government and never once wavered in his support for the Weimar Republic. At the same time, however, the concept of *Sammlung* that served as the fundamental principle of Kaas's political strategy remained hopelessly vague and never provided the appeal across class and party lines that would have been necessary to salvage the Weimar Republic from the forces of political radicalism. Nowhere was this more apparent than in the transition from Weimar democracy to the Third Reich, a period during which the Center found itself relegated to the political sidelines before being banished from the political stage in the summer of 1933. Acting partly out of his fear of Nazi violence and partly because he felt that all national-minded forces should unite, Kaas supported the Enabling Act and was instrumental in persuading a majority of the Center's Reichstag delegation to vote for it in March 1933. Kaas was therefore at least partly responsible for the uncertain and vulnerable situation in which the German Catholic Church found itself once the regime failed to live up to the terms of the Concordat with the Vatican.

The next chapter by Winfried Becker also examines the predicament of political Catholicism in the first months of the Third Reich, though not from the perspective of the Center but from that of its Bavarian counterparty, the Bavarian People's Party (Bayerische Volkspartei or BVP). The BVP was the mainstay of the Bavarian state government and, as such, was determined to resist takeover from Berlin with all the resources at its disposal. But its position became increasingly vulnerable on the heels of the Reichstag elections of 5 March 1933 and a concerted campaign by Nazi authorities at the state and national levels to strip the Bavarian government of its power. This "party revolution from below," as Martin Broszat has characterized it, manifested itself primarily in widespread grassroots violence that had taken shape in response to Hitler's repeated exhortations from 10 March on to maintain peace and order. In his detailed reconstruction of the events in Bavaria, Becker documents the haplessness of state authorities when confronted with the threat of brute force in Bavaria and the duplicity of authorities in Berlin. As Becker demonstrates, not even cabinet officers in the Bavarian government or city councilors who belonged to the BVP were safe from the wave of violence that descended upon Bavaria in March 1933. German Jews, including the leader of the Munich Israelite community (*Kultusgemeinde*) Rabbi Leo Bärwald, were treated with special brutality. In the meantime, efforts on the part of Bavaria's representatives in Berlin to initiate negotiations that would have led to the peaceful transfer of power under conditions that would have afforded the BVP a measure of protection from the wave of violence that had been unleashed against their party met with obfuscation and procrastination. Their situation was rendered all the more untenable by the calculated and systematic breach of the constitution in Bavaria and the complacency with which the bulk of the Bavarian population reacted to Nazi violence and the mistreatment of state government officials.

Becker's chapter brings into sharp relief two important themes that characterized the Nazi seizure of power in 1933 and 1934. The first of these was the systematic use of violence against those institutions or individuals that either stood in the way of the NSDAP and the SA in the Nazi consolidation of total power or were seen as opponents that needed to be brought into line. Attacks against Jews were closely connected to the *leitmotif* of violence in the Nazi consolidation of power and were no doubt in part designed to intimidate those who stood on the sidelines from opposing the regime. The stigmatization and exclusion of German and foreign Jews thus served as a lightning rod that greatly strengthened the internal cohesion of German society in the first months of the Third Reich. The second theme addresses the enormous popularity and appeal of the new regime. Nazi promises to rehabilitate cherished German traditions, to rescue the nation from communism, and to unify the people in a national community reminiscent of August 1914 lured even otherwise rational individuals into a false sense of hope or complacency. A case in point is the leadership of the German business community, the topic of Peter Hayes's chapter "German Big Business and the Nazi Revolution." While most German business leaders were caught off guard by Hitler's appointment as chancellor in January 1933, they were quickly brought into line, contributing massive sums of money to the NSDAP's campaign in the March 1933 Reichstag elections and eventually acquiescing to Nazi pressure to remove Jews—in some cases with great reluctance—from positions on their managerial boards. Much of this took place under an umbrella of campaigns against "corruption" and bribery and charges of tax evasion. A particularly critical moment in the acquiescence of big business was the forcible occupation of corporate and business headquarters by the SA in the spring of 1933 in an action that apparently did not enjoy Hitler's blessing but that nevertheless carried with it the implicit threat of violence if the German business community continued to waver in its support for the regime. Hitler's subsequent intervention to put an end to the SA occupation of businesses and factories reassured Germany's business leadership of the Nazi party leader's commitment to the principle of free enterprise and greatly facilitated their acceptance of the regime.

Research on antisemitism at the beginning of Nazi rule has generally concentrated on the boycott of April 1933 and the antisemitic legislation that followed, while the widespread antisemitic violence of the late winter and spring of 1933 has received comparatively little attention. Hermann Beck focuses on attacks that were directed against the approximately eighty thousand East European Jews residing in Germany in 1933. Antisemitic acts in the first months of Nazi rule ranged from the forced cancellation of debts and the destruction of goods and property to physical violence, kidnapping, aggravated robbery, bodily assault, and outright murder. Adding to the demoralization of Germany's Jewish population were rituals of humiliation, such as "pillory marches," in which victims were paraded through the streets in degrading conditions. German officials, who knew very well what was going on, minimized and excused attacks—reactions fed by their own prejudice and the desire to please their new Nazi masters. Members of the bureaucracy frequently went so far as to find fault with the victims by fabricating offenses that had allegedly caused the attacks, thus protecting the perpetrators. Such behavior on the part of officials signaled to the attackers that they had free rein and made it obvious that Jews not could expect any help from those who administered the country in the event of future crimes.

Nazi efforts to secure a popular consensus and to create a national community (*Volksgemeinschaft*) that transcended the divisions of class, confession, and region rested not just upon propaganda but also upon the systematic and intentional use of violence. Bruce Campbell's chapter on the role of the SA in the Nazi seizure and consolidation of power focuses on the organization within the Nazi movement that was primarily responsible for the use of violence as a means of forging a popular consensus in support of the regime and its totalitarian aspirations. Campbell's investigation stresses among other things political pressures such as the constant mobilization from 1930 on that left SA men at all levels burnt out, filled with resentment, and eager for revenge. Complicating the position of the SA were difficulties in controlling defections from its ranks, paradoxically coinciding with an influx of new members before 1933 that concealed the full extent of the defections and thus produced an overall balance sheet that showed rapid growth. Yet while the SA was the foremost organ of Nazi violence, its leaders often saw themselves as rivals to the Nazi party leadership in terms of power and tangible rewards. The leaders of the NSDAP party organization, on the other hand, often saw the SA as a threat to their own control of the party and pressured Hitler to take action aimed at reining in its radicalism. Campbell goes beyond analyzing the external factors that shaped the SA's behavior by delving into the personal characteristics of the SA rank and file to identify the importance of "primary male group" bonding and the fundamentally local nature of politics in the Weimar Republic as an explanation for SA violence. As Campbell explains, all of these contributed to the extent and nature of the SA violence that facilitated the National Socialist takeover in 1933–34.

The second major theme running through the chapters on the period after 30 January 1933 consists of the attractions and popularity of the new regime. The call for greater social equality and a new society free of class conceit and imbued with concern for the greater good of all contributed to what Fritz Stern once called "the temptation of National Socialism."[16] Few concrete measures toward this end were ever implemented, but the egalitarian tone that dominated National Socialist discourse and propaganda during 1933 and 1934 could not fail but to leave its mark on the popular perception of the regime.[17] This egalitarian appeal accounted for a good deal of the regime's popularity. An invigorating feeling of a newly forged *Volksgemeinschaft*, a national community reminiscent of the spirit of domestic solidarity in August 1914 when ranks had closed against a sea of enemies, took hold across the nation. As Protestant bishop Otto Dibelius, soon to become an opponent of the regime, said in a radio address to an American audience in which he rationalized the boycott of 1 April 1933, "Today the German Reich is united and firmly joined together as never before in our history."[18] Newly gained strength and self-assurance emanated from that knowledge, and the new government was credited with bringing it about. The early propaganda of the regime shrewdly emphasized the creation of an internally united and rejuvenated nation, an element that accelerated the breakup and demise of Germany's political parties, driven by the argument that multiple political parties were but an obstacle on the road toward a united national will.

The inspiration of the "Ideas of 1914" and the longing for some sort of national community that transcended the divisions of class, confession, and region resonated far beyond the ranks of the NSDAP and its affiliated organizations. That such an appeal had a universal purchase on the hearts and minds of those Germans who stood well outside the orbit of the NSDAP could be seen in the ranks of one of Nazism's most determined opponents, the Social Democratic Party of Germany (Sozialdemokratische Partei Deutschlands or SPD). As Stefan Vogt argues in his chapter on the Social Democratic intellectuals and politicians associated with the *Neue Blätter für den Sozialismus*, there were even Social Democrats who maintained that National Socialism, notwithstanding the obvious danger that it posed to German democracy and the welfare of the German working class, was a legitimate expression of the German national will and that some facets of it were worthy of support. The *Neue Blätter für den Sozialismus* was a journal that served as a platform for the promotion of a nationalist revision of socialist theory and politics, and its protagonists believed that patriotism was the great common denominator of the German people and that the truly socialist and national elements of the Nazi movement could be filtered out and separated from those elements in the NSDAP that were responsible for the repressive and essentially antisocialist rhetoric associated with its public profile. In the final analysis, Vogt argues, the ideological convictions of this group's members led them to adopt an assessment of the Nazi movement that was too optimistic, a factor that later prevented them from developing an effective strategy for its defeat and containment.

If the editors and writers of the *Neue Blätter für den Sozialismus* were slow to recognize the danger of National Socialism and the threat it posed to the welfare of the German working class, this was not, as William Patch argues in his chapter on the German trade union movement from 1930 to 1933, the case with leaders of organized labor. Patch's chapter addresses both the appeal that National Socialism held for some trade unionists in the transition from democracy to dictatorship in 1932–33 and the role that SA violence played in compelling the main trade union federations to set aside their differences in the search for unity in the struggle against Nazism and its antagonism toward the German trade union movement. Patch begins by challenging the argument that long-term oligarchic tendencies on the part of union leaders predisposed them to reach an accommodation with the Nazi regime and argues instead that union leaders worked strategically with political parties and government officials to address the priority of their rank-and-file membership of alleviating unemployment at the same time that they sought to rally their followers around national causes. The attempts of union leaders to "reconcile 'national' and 'social' values, i.e., patriotism with a commitment to egalitarian social reform" in order to accommodate the Nazi regime, however, were undermined by the latter's determination to take over the workers' movement. In the final analysis, internal union democracy fell victim to last-minute efforts by union leaders—driven by fear, opportunism, or pure naïveté—to tie the fate of their unions to the more radical interpretations of "nationalism" and "socialism" proffered by the NSDAP. Efforts on the part of the free, Christian, and liberal labor unions to close ranks in the face of the Nazi threat were ultimately outstripped by the regime's determination to destroy both organizational democracy and organizational freedom, with the result that the unions were unceremoniously dissolved in the late spring of 1933 and subsequently incorporated into the German Labor Front (Deutsche Arbeitsfront or DAF).

The next three chapters deal with efforts to build bridges between the German churches and the Nazi regime. In 1933 the German Protestant Church was subdivided into twenty-eight state churches or *Landeskirchen*. Drawing upon the example of the Hamburg State Church, Rainer Hering shows just how deeply politics penetrated all facets of life, not the least of which was the organizational life of German Protestantism. Hering focuses in particular on the introduction of the *Führerprinzip*—the leadership principle popularly associated with Hitler and the NSDAP—in the German Protestant Church. The focal point of Hering's chapter is the office of the state bishop (*Landesbischof*) that Nazi officials created as a corrective to the revolutionary changes that had taken place in the organization of German Protestant life with the founding of the Weimar Republic. The forms of governance that had been introduced into the church during the Weimar Republic had had a democratic effect on the church hierarchy and a levelling effect on the church's position in society. The "revolution in the church" that took place with the introduction of the *Führerprinzip* and other changes prompted by the Nazis reestablished a hierarchy in the church's organizational structure and thus brought the church into line with the authoritarian organization of the Nazi state. In illustrating the theological and political divisions that Nazi intervention created within the ranks of German Protestants, Hering brings into sharp focus the precarious conditions in which church leaders attempted to salvage what they could of the church's status and influence and the compromises that they had to make in order to do so. The first state bishop of Hamburg, Simon Schöffel, as well as his successor Franz Tügel, not only vilified Weimar and the whole concept of democracy in an attempt to break bread with the Nazis but also went to great lengths to create a purported symbiosis between Protestant theology and the goals of National Socialism. Liberal critics had no ground on which to stand in the new Germany. Hering emphasizes that the church's internal reforms and accommodation with the National Socialist state were not in any way predetermined but rather depended on the actions of individuals who were driven by very different motivations.

A different perspective on developments within the Protestant Church in the months that followed Hitler's appointment as chancellor is to be found in the chapter by Edward Snyder on Friedrich von

Bodelschwingh, director of the Bethel Institutes in Bielefeld and one of German Protestantism's foremost social policy theorists. Snyder's chapter casts new light on the pressures to which the leaders of Germany's Protestant Church found themselves subjected with Hitler's succession to power. A conservative who sympathized with many of the Nazi positions on racial hygiene and the Weimar state, Bodelschwingh saw in the Nazi rise to power an opportunity to create a politically and socially united German nation. At the same time, he actively opposed the agitation of the so-called German Christians for a more radical reform of Lutheran theology and liturgy and feared that this might lead to a rupture between church and regime. It was this fear that ultimately led Bodelschwingh in the spring of 1933 to stand for election as the first Reich bishop of the newly created German Protestant Reich Church (Deutsch-Evangelische Reichskirche). With strong support from those elements within the church that opposed the radicalism of the German Christians, Bodelschwingh was elected by a narrow margin in late May 1933 only to find himself immediately embroiled in a conflict with the German Christians that led him to resign the office he had assumed less than a month earlier. Bodelschwingh's resignation, Snyder argues, was significant because it signaled the collapse of efforts to keep the church from falling under control of the state and set in motion the series of events that culminated in the establishment of the Confessing Church under Martin Niemöller and Dietrich Bonhoeffer later that fall. More importantly, it revealed just how divided German Protestants were on an entire host of issues, not the least of which was their position on the so-called Jewish question and the relationship between church and state. In the final analysis, it was the Jewish question and the introduction of the Aryan clause that marked the fork in the road within the Protestant Church. Here, in contrast to a small minority of more courageous church men like Bonhoeffer, Bodelschwingh sought to avoid controversy and proved reluctant to confront the state over this and other issues.

In many respects, the situation of the Protestant Church in the early stages of the Third Reich was not significantly different from that of its Catholic counterpart. Here the major problem facing the regime was the fact that the vast majority of German Catholics did not share the widespread enthusiasm of German Protestants for the establishment of the Third Reich. It was against the background of these developments that a small handful of Catholic conservatives under the leadership of Franz von Papen, Hitler's vice chancellor and the putative leader of those conservative forces that sought to contain the radicalism of the Nazi movement, launched the Alliance of German Catholics

(Arbeitsgemeinschaft katholischer Deutscher or AKD) in the spring of 1933 in an effort to build a bridge between German Catholics and the Nazi regime. But, as Larry Eugene Jones and Kevin Spicer demonstrate in their chapter on the AKD, this effort was ultimately doomed to failure not just by Papen's own ineptitude but also by the deep-seated and mutual mistrust that existed between the regime and authorities of the Catholic Church. Despite support from elements of the Catholic intelligentsia and the Catholic nobility, the AKD never succeeded in developing that groundswell of popular support upon which Papen and the leaders of the Nazi regime had been counting. At the same time, increasing friction over the regime's failure to respect the legal protections that the institutions of Catholic associational life presumably enjoyed under Article 31 of the Reich Concordat of 20 July 1933 underscored just how superfluous the AKD had become in the eyes of Hitler and his associates. The AKD's fate was effectively sealed by the late spring of 1934, and it was discretely shut down by state authorities in the aftermath of the Röhm Purge.

The final two chapters by André Postert and Katharine Kennedy deal with the reception of the Nazi revolution by German youth and the impact the Nazi revolution had upon the instruction they received in history and social studies in elementary and secondary schools throughout the country. As Postert illustrates in his chapter on the political coordination of German youth, the advent of the new state was greeted enthusiastically by a large segment of young Germans throughout the country. The Hitler Youth (Hitlerjugend or HJ) exerted a strong natural attraction on rival German youth organizations of all sorts—political, *bündisch*, denominational, and sporting clubs—and did not hesitate to use coercion to force their incorporation into its own organizational structure. The vitality of the new Nazi state exercised a powerful appeal on young Germans from all sectors of society, including those who had been previously organized under the auspices of rival political movements. The new state's popularity stemmed less from any sort of overt identification with the ideological goals of the Nazi movement than from the Hitler Youth's vigor and opposition to old, entrenched structures and from the idealism of its commitment to the goal of uniting all Germans in a genuine *Volksgemeinschaft* in which social, confessional, and regional divisions were finally overcome. Yet while Postert emphasizes the need to recognize the passion with which large segments of the younger generation greeted the rise of National Socialism, he also points out that the enthusiasm of 1933 clearly eclipsed that of later years and that by 1935 much of the excitement of the first two years of Nazi rule had begun to fade as membership figures peaked and increasing apathy toward the regime's recruitment efforts became apparent.

That enthusiasm in 1933 was stronger and that measures taken then were more radical than in subsequent years is a point that Katharine Kennedy also emphasizes in her contribution on the Nazi penetration of the German school system. The reshaping of elementary school curricula began in the spring of 1933, as several German states suspended their usual history curriculum in March 1933 in order to offer nazified narratives of Germany's recent history aimed at exalting National Socialism and delegitimizing the Weimar Republic. In response to the educational policies of the new regime, some states hastily cobbled together supplementary booklets for use in the classroom that depicted the new racial state, the cult of the leader, and the obsession with national community that lay at the heart of the Nazi worldview. Kennedy's colorful account highlights how Nazi symbols, rituals, and festivals entered elementary schools in 1933 and quickly became defining aspects of the school year that actively encouraged an aestheticized attachment to National Socialism. In schools, as in other spheres of social life, the policies propagated during the period of the Nazi seizure of power often proved more radical than those in the years that followed.

*   *   *

The chapters assembled in this volume show that Hitler's rise to power and his appointment as chancellor of the German nation in January 1933 were made possible by the ineptitude and disunity of Germany's political elites and by the inability of those forces loyal to the Weimar Republic to develop an effective strategy for the containment of the Nazi threat. Schleicher's ill-fated "taming strategy" was based on the premise that giving the Nazis a share of power would require them to behave more responsibly at the same time that it would provide Germany's conservative elites with the mantle of popular legitimacy they needed to carry out an authoritarian reorganization of the German state system. In this respect, Schleicher sought the cooperation of Germany's most distinguished legal theorist Carl Schmitt, who worked closely with the Reichswehr in developing legal strategies for decoupling the exercise of executive authority from the vicissitudes of constantly shifting parliamentary coalitions in the Reichstag. But such schemes received little support from the leaders of Germany's republican parties who, like the Center's Ludwig Kaas, remained strongly committed to the principles of constitutional government and were deeply suspicious of plans for even a temporary suspension of the

Weimar Constitution and the transfer of power to an executive authority that was no longer responsible to the Reichstag. It could have been
of little solace to Kaas that when Hitler assumed the chancellorship,
his appointment was consistent with the letter, if not the spirit, of the
Weimar Constitution. All that remained was the desperate hope that
the conservatives who had installed Hitler in power would be able to
control the dynamism of the Nazi movement and harness it to their
own political agenda.

That this hope would prove illusory became abundantly clear in the
weeks that followed Hitler's appointment as chancellor. What ensued
was the marginalization of Hitler's conservative allies and the devastatingly rapid consolidation of power in the hands of the Nazi elite.
This was accomplished by a combination of violence and coercion
coupled with willing complicity and eager enthusiasm on the part of a
German public that embraced Hitler as the messiah who would redeem
Germany from the cloud of defeat and despair that had descended
upon it in 1918. That all of this took place under the Damocles sword
of physical retribution and incarceration for those who disagreed with
their new masters makes it difficult to gauge just how much of this
excitement was genuine. Yet, even where the passionate eagerness as
exhibited by parts of the youth movement was absent, there was still a
hopeful desire by elements of the trade union movement, Catholic conservatives, Protestant church leaders, and even the Social Democratic
pundits who wrote for the *Neue Blätter für den Sozialismus* to seek commonalities and accommodation with the regime. These commonalities,
often misconstrued or exaggerated by opportunistic or fearful individuals, were generally sufficient to stifle determined resistance.

By the end of 1933 the changes in the German state and society
were all-encompassing and irreversible. Federal traditions with deep
roots in German history that reached back over centuries had been
eliminated and replaced by a centralized state that flew in the face
of Germany's historical development since the Reformation and was
more reminiscent of revolutionary France. The multifaceted nature of
German society and organizations, from political parties, big business,
and trade unions to the churches and religious associations, had been
brought into line. In many respects, the period of the Nazi seizure
and consolidation of power would prove more radical than what followed during the years of peace between 1934 and 1938. The wave of
antisemitic violence that swept through Germany in the spring of 1933
met with no opposition and seemingly few misgivings on the part of
German civil society. Neither the civil administration nor the churches
nor the conservative elites that had placed Hitler in power were willing

to risk their place in the new Nazi state for the sake of the Jews. For many, the issue of antisemitism would prove to be the decisive litmus test of how they would relate to the regime in general. The process by which the Nazis seized and consolidated power between 1932 and 1934 would do much to define the essential features of Nazi society and the Nazi state for the millions of Germans who would either embrace it or, what was much less likely, reject it.

Acknowledgments

The editors of this volume would like to take this opportunity to express their gratitude to Marion Berghahn and the editorial staff at Berghahn Books for their encouragement, support, and counsel in bringing this project to a successful conclusion. We are particularly grateful to Chris Chappell and Amanda Horn for their support in the early stages of this project and to Soyolmaa Lkhagvadorj for her help in editing and preparing the manuscript for publication. We would also like to express our gratitude to the Wallstein Verlag and J. H. Dietz Verlag for permission to include the chapters by Rainer Hering and Stefan Vogt, respectively, in this volume.

Hermann Beck is professor of history at the University of Miami. He is author of *The Origins of the Authoritarian Welfare State in Prussia: Conservatives, Bureaucracy, and the Social Question, 1815–1870* (1995, 1998) and *The Fateful Alliance: German Conservatives and Nazis in 1933; The Machtergreifung in a New Light* (2008, 2010), and he has published numerous articles in leading American and European journals, including the *Historische Zeitschrift*, *The Journal of Modern History*, and *The Journal of Contemporary History*. He recently completed a book-length manuscript on "Before the Holocaust: Anti-Semitism and the Reaction of German Society during the Nazi Seizure of Power."

Larry Eugene Jones is professor of history at Canisius College in Buffalo, New York, where he specializes in the history of modern Germany and the Holocaust. He also edited *The German Right in the Weimar Republic: Studies in the History of German Conservatism, Nationalism, and Antisemitism* (2014). He is the author of *Hitler versus Hindenburg: The 1932 Presidential Elections and the End of the Weimar Republic* (2016) and is currently working on a new book tentatively titled *The German Right, 1918–1930: Political Parties, Organized Interests, and Patriotic Associations in the Struggle against Weimar Democracy*.

Notes

1. For the essential elements of Mosse's argument, see George L. Mosse, *The Crisis of German Ideology: Intellectual Origins of the Third Reich* (New York: Grosset and Dunlap, 1964), 254–93.

2. Fritz Fischer, *From Kaiserreich to the Third Reich: Elements of Continuity in German History, 1871–1945*, trans. Roger Fletcher (Boston: Allen and Unwin, 1986), esp. 97–99.

3. In this respect, see Hans-Ulrich Wehler, *Entsorgung der deutschen Vergangenheit. Ein polemischer Essay zum "Historikerstreit"* (Munich: Beck, 1988), as well as the fourth volume of Wehler's *Deutsche Gesellschaftsgeschichte: Vom Ende des Ersten Weltkrieges bis zur Gründung der zwei deutschen Staaten 1918–1949* (Munich: Beck, 2008), esp. 580–89.

4. For example, see Larry Eugene Jones, "Why Hitler Came to Power: In Defense of a New History of Politics," in *Geschichtswissenschaft vor 2000: Perspektiven der Historiographiegeschichte, Geschichtstheorie, Sozial- und Kulturgeschichte; Festschrift für Georg G. Iggers zum 65. Geburtstag*, ed. Konrad H. Jarausch, Jörn Rüsen, and Hans Schleier (Hagen: Magrit Rottmann Medienverlag, 1991), 256–76. In a similar vein, though with different conclusions, see Geoff Eley, *Nazism as Fascism: Violence, Ideology, and the Ground of Consent in Germany, 1930–1945* (London and New York: Routledge, 2013), 13–22.

5. Robert Thomson Clark, *The Fall of the German Republic: A Political Study* (London: Allen and Unwin, 1935), 9–13.

6. Karl Dietrich Bracher, *Die Auflösung der Weimarer Republik: Eine Studie des Machtverfalls in der Demokratie*, 3rd ed. (Villingen-Schwarzwald: Ring-Verlag, 1960), esp. 686–732. For the classic statement of this argument, see Theodor Eschenburg, "The Role of Personality in the Crisis of the Weimar Republic: Hindenburg, Brüning, Groener, Schleicher," in *Republic to Reich: The Making of the Nazi Revolution*, ed. Hajo Holborn (New York: Pantheon Books, 1972), 3–50.

7. Hans Mommsen, *The Rise and Fall of Weimar Democracy*, trans. Elborg Forster and Larry Eugene Jones (Chapel Hill and London: University of North Carolina Press, 1996), 490–544. For a more pointed critique of the role that Germany's conservative elites played in the appointment of the Hitler cabinet, see Hans Mommsen, "Die deutschen Eliten und der Mythos des nationalen Aufbruchs von 1933," *Merkur: Deutsche Zeitschrift für europäisches Denken* 38 (1984): 97–102, and "Die nationalsozialistische Machteroberung: Revolution oder Gegenrevolution," in *Europäische Sozialgeschichte: Festschrift für Wolfgang Schieder*, ed. Christof Dipper, Lutz Klinkhammer, and Alexander Nützenadel (Berlin: Duncker and Humblot, 2000), 41–56.

8. Heinrich August Winkler, *Weimar 1918–1933: Die Geschichte der ersten deutschen Demokratie* (Munich: Beck, 1993), 535–94.

9. Henry Ashby Turner Jr., "'Alliance of Elites' as a Cause of Weimar's Collapse and Hitler's Triumph?," in *Die deutsche Staatskrise 1930–1933:*

Handlungsspielräume und Alternativen, ed. Heinrich August Winkler (Munich: Oldenbourg, 1992), 205–14.

10. Henry Ashby Turner Jr., *Hitler's Thirty Days to Power: January 1933* (Reading, MA: Addison-Wesley, 1966), esp. 163–83.

11. Karl Dietrich Bracher, "Stages of Totalitarian Integration (*Gleichschaltung*): The Consolidation of National Socialist Rule in 1933 and 1934," in *Republic to Reich,* ed. Holborn, 109–28. For a fuller elaboration of Bracher's argument and periodization of the Nazi consolidation of power, see his chapter "Stufen der Machtergreifung," in Karl Dietrich Bracher, Wolfgang Sauer, and Gerhard Schulz, *Die nationalsozialistische Machtergreifung. Studien zur Errichtung des totalitären Herrschaftssystems in Deutschland 1933/34* (Cologne and Opladen: Westdeutscher Verlag, 1960), 31–219.

12. In this respect, see Hermann Beck, *The Fateful Alliance: German Conservatives and Nazis in 1933; The* Machtergreifung *in a New Light* (New York and Oxford: Berghahn Books, 2008), 219–52.

13. On Röhm, see the excellent biography by Eleanor Hancock, *Ernst Röhm: Hitler's SA Chief of Staff* (New York: Palgrave McMillan, 2008), esp. 140–66.

14. On the German military and its role in the series of events that led to the Röhm Purge in the summer of 1934, see the classic study by Klaus-Jürgen Müller, *Das Herr und Hitler: Armee und nationalsozialistisches Regime 1933–1940* (Stuttgart: Deutsche Verlagsanstalt, 1969), 88–141, as well as the more recent monograph by Immo von Fallois, *Kalkül und Illusion: Der Machtkampf zwischen Reichswehr und SA während der Röhm-Krise 1934* (Berlin: Duncker and Humblot, 1994).

15. On Papen, the Marburg speech, and the conspiratorial activities of the Papen vice chancery, see the definitive study by Rainer Orth, *"Der Amtssitz der Opposition"? Politik und Staatsumbaupläne im Büro des Stellvertreters des Reichskanzlerz in den Jahren 1933–1934* (Cologne, Weimar, and Vienna: Böhlau, 2016), esp. 345–450.

16. Fritz Stern, "National Socialism as Temptation," in Fritz Stern, *Dreams and Delusions: The Drama of German History* (New Haven and London: Yale University Press, 1999), 147–91.

17. Hermann Beck, "The Antibourgeois Character of National Socialism," *Journal of Modern History* 88 (2016): 572–609.

18. "Die nach Amerika gerichtete Rundfunkrede des Herrn Generalsuperintendenten Dibelius vom 4. April 1933," Evangelisches Zentralarchiv Berlin, 51, EII e 8, 4.

Bibliography

Beck, Hermann. "The Antibourgeois Character of National Socialism." *Journal of Modern History* 88 (2016): 572–609.

——. *The Fateful Alliance: German Conservatives and Nazis in 1933; The* Machtergreifung *in a New Light.* New York and Oxford: Berghahn Books, 2008.

Bracher, Karl Dietrich. *Die Auflösung der Weimarer Republik: Eine Studie des Macht-verfalls in der Demokratie*, 3rd ed. Villingen-Schwarzwald: Ring-Verlag, 1960.

———. "Stufen der Machtergreifung." In Karl Dietrich Bracher, Wolfgang Sauer, and Gerhard Schulz, *Die nationalsozialistische Machtergreifung: Studien zur Errichtung des totalitären Herrschaftssystems in Deutschland 1933/34*, 31–219. Cologne and Opladen: Westdeutscher Verlag, 1960.

———. "Stages of Totalitarian Integration (*Gleichschaltung*): The Consolidation of National Socialist Rule in 1933 and 1934." In *Republic to Reich: The Making of the Nazi Revolution*, edited by Hajo Holborn, 109–28. New York: Pantheon Books, 1972.

Clark, Robert Thomson. *The Fall of the German Republic: A Political Study*. London: Allen and Unwin, 1935.

Eley, Geoff. *Nazism as Fascism: Violence, Ideology, and the Ground of Consent in Germany, 1930–1945*. London and New York: Routledge, 2013.

Eschenburg, Theodor. "The Role of Personality in the Crisis of the Weimar Republic: Hindenburg, Brüning, Groener, Schleicher." In *Republic to Reich: The Making of the Nazi Revolution*, edited by Hajo Holborn, 3–50. New York: Pantheon Books, 1972.

Fallois, Immo von. *Kalkül und Illusion: Der Machtkampf zwischen Reichswehr und SA während der Röhm-Krise 1934*. Berlin: Duncker and Humblot, 1994.

Fischer, Fritz. *From Kaiserreich to the Third Reich: Elements of Continuity in German History, 1871–1945*. Translated by Roger Fletcher. Boston: Allen and Unwin, 1986.

Hancock, Eleanor. *Ernst Röhm: Hitler's SA Chief of Staff*. New York: Palgrave McMillan, 2008.

Jones, Larry Eugene. "Why Hitler Came to Power: In Defense of a New History of Politics." In *Geschichtswissenschaft vor 2000: Perspektiven der Historiographie-geschichte, Geschichtstheorie, Sozial- und Kulturgeschichte; Festschrift für Georg G. Iggers zum 65. Geburtstag*, edited by Konrad H. Jarausch, Jörn Rüsen, and Hans Schleier, 256–76. Hagen: Magrit Rottmann Medienverlag, 1991.

Mommsen, Hans. "Die deutschen Eliten und der Mythos des nationalen Aufbruchs von 1933." *Merkur: Deutsche Zeitschrift für europäisches Denken* 38 (1984): 97–102.

———. *The Rise and Fall of Weimar Democracy*. Translated by Elborg Forster and Larry Eugene Jones. Chapel Hill and London: University of North Carolina Press, 1996.

———. "Die nationalsozialistische Machteroberung: Revolution oder Gegen-revolution." In *Europäische Sozialgeschichte: Festschrift für Wolfgang Schieder*, edited by Christof Dipper, Lutz Klinkhammer, and Alexander Nützenadel, 41–56. Berlin: Duncker and Humblot, 2000.

Mosse, George L. *The Crisis of German Ideology: Intellectual Origins of the Third Reich*. New York: Grosset and Dunlap, 1964.

Müller, Klaus-Jürgen. *Das Heer und Hitler: Armee und nationalsozialistisches Regime 1933–1940*. Stuttgart: Deutsche Verlagsanstalt, 1969.

Orth, Rainer. *"Der Amtssitz der Opposition"? Politik und Staatsumbaupläne im Büro des Stellvertreters des Reichskanzlerz in den Jahren 1933–1934*. Cologne, Weimar, and Vienna: Böhlau, 2016.

Stern, Fritz. "National Socialism as Temptation." In Fritz Stern, *Dreams and Delusions: The Drama of German History*, 147–91. New Haven and London: Yale University Press, 1999.

Turner, Henry Ashby, Jr. *Hitler's Thirty Days to Power: January 1933*. Reading, MA: Addison-Wesley, 1966.

——. "'Alliance of Elites' as a Cause of Weimar's Collapse and Hitler's Triumph?" In *Die deutsche Staatskrise 1930–1933: Handlungsspielräume und Alternativen*, edited by Heinrich August Winkler, 205–14. Munich: Oldenbourg, 1992.

Wehler, Hans-Ulrich. *Entsorgung der deutschen Vergangenheit: Ein polemischer Essay zum "Historikerstreit."* Munich: Beck, 1988.

——. *Deutsche Gesellschaftsgeschichte: Vom Ende des Ersten Weltkrieges bis zur Gründung der zwei deutschen Staaten 1918–1949*. Munich: Beck, 2008.

Winkler, Heinrich August. *Weimar 1918–1933: Die Geschichte der ersten deutschen Demokratie*. Munich: Beck, 1993.

 1

Taming the Nazi Beast
Kurt von Schleicher and the End of the Weimar Republic
Larry Eugene Jones

The systemic breakdown of the late Weimar Republic created a situation in which the actions of specific individuals were suddenly invested with much greater causal agency than they would otherwise have ever possessed. This was especially true in the case of Kurt von Schleicher, the political mastermind of the German Reichswehr and the most important player behind the scenes between 1930 and 1933. Schleicher's personality and political machinations have long intrigued historians, and he remains a controversial figure in the last years of the Weimar Republic, with assessments of his career and accomplishments ranging from the hagiographic and exculpatory to the devastatingly critical by scholars of great stature such as Henry Ashby Turner Jr., who was planning to write a full-length biography of Schleicher before his untimely death in December 2008.[1] This chapter takes a fresh look at Schleicher's aspirations and policies from the fall of the Brüning cabinet in the late spring of 1932 through Hitler's appointment as chancellor on 30 January 1933. It focuses in detail on the two months of December 1932 and January 1933 when Schleicher served as chancellor in what was a desperate attempt to prevent the apparatus of the German state from being handed over to Adolf Hitler and his supporters in the leadership of the National Socialist German Workers' Party (Nationalsozialistische Deutsche Arbeiterpartei or NSDAP). The chapter not only draws upon the archival materials that were available to historians when the first detailed studies of his political career appeared in the early and mid-1960s but also makes use of new materials that have surfaced only in the last decade or so. From this will emerge a more balanced assessment of Schleicher's failure in the last months of the Weimar Republic to keep the Nazis from the reins of power than either his apologists or his detractors have been willing or able to provide.[2]

Schleicher's Taming Strategy

When Schleicher was appointed chief of the newly created Office of Ministerial Affairs (Ministeramt) in the Reich ministry of defense in January 1929, his overriding objective was to provide Germany with the most modern and effective military in Europe despite the limitations of size and armaments that had been placed upon it by the Versailles Peace Treaty. In this respect, however, Schleicher realized that the government could not dispense with the mantle of popular legitimacy if it were to mobilize the resources necessary for the modernization of the German army, and he was fully prepared to work within the framework of Germany's new republican government to accomplish his objectives. While this is not to suggest that Schleicher was somehow a *Vernunftrepublikaner* in the fashion of Gustav Stresemann or Friedrich Meinecke, it is nevertheless important to stress that his conservatism had little in common with the arch-conservatism of Prussia's prewar military elite and was actually more profoundly influenced by the writings of young conservative intellectuals like Arthur Moeller van den Bruck, Edgar Julius Jung, and Heinrich von Gleichen than by those conservatives whose view of the world was rooted in the old imperial order.[3] More importantly, Schleicher was quick to recognize that the Social Democrats of the Weimar era were different from the Social Democrats of the old imperial order and that the acceptance of governmental responsibility in Prussia and elsewhere had had a moderating effect upon their policies and actions. But Schleicher's hopes that the Social Democrats might underwrite his efforts to rearm and build up the German army were dashed by Philipp Scheidemann's revelations in December 1926 about the Reichswehr's secret arrangement with the Red Army.[4] Schleicher remained nonetheless impressed about the moderating effect that governmental responsibility had had upon the Social Democrats and used this as a model for how he would go about dealing with the National Socialists four years later.[5]

Schleicher had been following Hitler's career ever since the early 1920s and once described him in a conversation with the left-wing publicist Artur Zickler at the end of 1922 as a "schizophrenic windbag full of undigested ideas, a born asocial with inferiority complexes and delusions of grandeur, obsessed with a fixed sense of mission, egocentrically devious, revengeful, and disloyal."[6] But with the NSDAP's dramatic breakthrough in the 1930 Reichstag elections and its continued success into the first months of 1931, Schleicher felt that he and his associates could no longer afford to dismiss Hitler as a political

incompetent who did not have to be taken seriously and began to formulate the general outlines of a strategy for "taming" the Nazi beast.
The underlying premise of Schleicher's *Zähmungskonzept* was twofold,
first that the radicalism of the Nazi movement could be mitigated by
saddling it with political responsibility and second that the NSDAP's
entry into the government would deprive it of the obvious advantages
it enjoyed as an opposition party.[7] At the same time, bringing the Nazis
into the government would provide Germany's conservative elites with
the mantle of popular legitimacy they needed to carry out a fundamental revision of Germany's constitutional system, a revision that had
already begun under the aegis of Reich president Paul von Hindenburg
with the appointment of Heinrich Brüning, the parliamentary leader of
the German Center Party, as chancellor in March 1930. The Brüning cabinet, extending as it did from the left-liberal German Democratic Party
(Deutsche Demokratische Partei) to the moderate conservatives on the
left wing of the German National People's Party (Deutschnationale
Volkspartei or DNVP) and entrusted with special emergency powers
that Article 48 of the Weimar Constitution had invested in the office of
the Reich president, was indeed Schleicher's brainchild and bore the
clear imprint of his political calculus.[8]

The idea of taming the Nazis by bringing them into the government was not particularly new and had already been aired by no less
a figure than Count Kuno von Westarp, the former chairman of the
right-wing German National People's Party and a strong supporter of
the Brüning cabinet.[9] The idea had also gained traction within the ranks
of Germany's industrial elite, where it was seen as a way of keeping the
more radical elements on the NSDAP's left wing in check.[10] But it was
not until after the Austro-German banking crisis in the summer of 1931,
when pressure from the Reich president and his immediate entourage for a reorganization of the Brüning cabinet began to build,[11] that
Schleicher took up active pursuit of this strategy. This coincided with an
attempt by the Nazi party leader Adolf Hitler to ingratiate himself with
Germany's political leadership, no doubt with an eye to the upcoming
presidential elections that were scheduled for the spring of 1932. It
was against the background of these developments that Schleicher first
met with Hitler on 26 September 1931 and then arranged a meeting
between the Nazi party leader and the Reich president on 10 October,
the day before the anti-republican German Right was scheduled to hold
a major rally against the Brüning cabinet in the small central German
resort town of Bad Harzburg.[12] These and subsequent contacts between
the Reichswehr, the Reich president's office, and the Nazi party leadership in the fall of 1931 and early 1932 persuaded Schleicher and other

government leaders that Hitler was indeed sincere about his stated goal of pursuing the conquest of power by legal means and legal means only. From the perspective of Schleicher and his associates—and to a certain extent from that of Brüning as well—the principal obstacle to an understanding with the radical right was not Hitler but DNVP party chairman Alfred Hugenberg and the more militant elements within the NSDAP.[13]

All of this augured well for the success of Schleicher's taming strategy, at least in the initial stages of its implementation. But what had originally seemed a promising overture to the Nazi party leader quickly fell apart in the events leading up to the 1932 presidential elections. Brüning, Schleicher, and the presidential entourage had hoped that Hindenburg could be spared the rigors of a national reelection campaign by a special vote in the Reichstag that would extend the Reich president's term of office. In the initial stages of the negotiations, Hitler and Hugenberg indicated that they might be amenable to such a solution but that their support was conditional upon Brüning's dismissal as chancellor and the formation of a new national government that included the forces of the national opposition.[14] When Hindenburg replied that under no conditions would he accept the terms that the leaders of the radical right had attached to their support of a parliamentary initiative to extend the Reich president's term of office, Hitler and Hugenberg declared in separate statements on 11 January 1932 that the proposed maneuver violated provisions of the Weimar Constitution and that they could not support it.[15] On 22 February—a week after Hindenburg had declared himself a candidate for reelection to the Reich presidency—Hitler announced his own candidacy in a move that sabotaged the unity of the Harzburg Front and permanently damaged Hitler's relations with the non-Nazi elements of the national opposition.[16] To Schleicher, who had been following the Nazi party leader's rise to prominence since the early 1920s, Hitler's behavior before and during the ensuing presidential campaign definitively dashed whatever hopes he might have had of an understanding with the Nazis. When asked how he would vote in the upcoming election, Schleicher replied,

> Hindenburg is the only candidate who is in a position to defeat Hitler. Since I am convinced that Hitler is as suited for the presidency as the hedgehog for a face towel and because I fear that his presidency would lead to civil war and ultimately to Bolshevism, the decision about [the candidate] for whom I will vote is in this case not difficult. ...[17]

This did not mean, however, that Schleicher had abandoned his strategy of trying to tame the Nazis by saddling them with the burden of governmental responsibility. To the contrary, the strong gains that the NSDAP recorded in the state parliamentary elections that took place in much of Germany on 24 April 1932 only underscored—at least from Schleicher's perspective—the imperative of bringing the Nazis into the government at the earliest possible opportunity. To accomplish this, Schleicher would have to force the resignation of the two men who stood in the way of a rapprochement with the Nazis, Chancellor Heinrich Brüning and Wilhelm Groener, Brüning's defense minister and Schleicher's long-time mentor. By the end of May 1932 both had been driven from office.[18] The painful irony in all of this was that the resignations of Brüning and Groener left Schleicher greatly weakened at precisely the moment he sought to broker an arrangement with the NSDAP. Groener had always served as an effective filter through which Schleicher's ideas reached the Reich president, while Brüning had functioned for the most part as a trusted and loyal instrument of Schleicher's strategic initiatives. Without them Schleicher would become increasingly exposed to the intrigues of his enemies in the presidential entourage, namely Hindenburg's son Oskar and Otto Meissner, chief of staff in the Office of the Reich Presidency.

In the meantime, Schleicher had begun to set the stage for a change of political course by meeting secretly with Hitler on two occasions in the late spring of 1932. Here Schleicher struck a deal—or, at least, so he thought—with the Nazi party leader whereby the NSDAP would tolerate either a reorganized Brüning cabinet or an entirely new government in return for a suspension of the ban against the SA and new national elections, thereby effectively sealing the fate of the Brüning cabinet.[19] Schleicher then proceeded to install a relative unknown in Franz von Papen as Brüning's successor. Schleicher's choice of Papen continues to baffle historians as to why someone of Schleicher's political sophistication would pick a political neophyte and outsider like Papen for the chancellorship. What Schleicher had chosen in Papen was not only someone whose strategic assessment of the domestic political situation conformed to his own but whose lack of a genuine political constituency made him more pliable to manipulation from the Bendlerstraße. The choice of Papen was further predicated upon the twofold assumption that he would receive the support of the Center Party and that the National Socialists would honor their pledge to Schleicher. This strategy, however, began to unravel when first the Center responded to the formation of the new government with a blistering rebuff that caught both Papen and Schleicher off guard[20] and then later when the Nazis began to equivocate on Hitler's agreement with Schleicher that their party would tolerate a new right-wing cabinet.[21]

Schleicher and the Papen Gambit

Neither the dissolution of the Reichstag and the call for new elections nor the decision to lift the ban against the SA and other paramilitary organizations nor the removal of the Prussian state government in the infamous coup of 20 July 1932 was sufficient to secure the support or toleration of the NSDAP. Schleicher met with Hitler and Gregor Strasser, chief of the NSDAP Reich Organization Leadership (Reichs-Organisations-Leitung der NSDAP), on 5 August and allowed Hitler to expound upon what he would do if he were placed in charge of the government. As chancellor, Hitler would seek authority from the Reich president to form a new cabinet in which Strasser would assume the post of Reich minister of internal affairs and Papen that of foreign minister while the other ministers and the state secretaries would remain in office. At the same time, Hitler reassured Schleicher that he had no intention of violating the constitution or undertaking major constitutional revisions.[22] Although Schleicher later reported to the cabinet that Hindenburg showed little inclination to grant Hitler the far-reaching powers he was demanding for himself and his party,[23] the Nazi party leader nevertheless seems to have left the meeting with Schleicher with the impression that his appointment as chancellor was imminent.[24]

In the decisive meeting between Hitler and Hindenburg on the afternoon of 13 August, the Nazi party leader responded to the Reich president's query as to whether or not his party was prepared to join the Papen government with the blunt answer that participation and cooperation with the existing cabinet was out of the question.[25] In the hallway outside Hindenburg's office, Hitler subsequently assailed Papen, who had met with the Nazi party leader before his audience with Hindenburg and who had been present at the meeting itself, for having set him up for an embarrassing personal rebuff at the hands of the Reich president. He then proceeded to ask what would happen in the event that a majority in the Reichstag passed a motion of no confidence in his cabinet when it reconvened at the end of the month. Papen's immediate response was that there would be no such vote in the Reichstag, that he would send its members home after the necessary formalities had taken place, and that all of this only confirmed what he had been saying all along, namely that at the moment effective parliamentary government was no longer possible. As Papen explained to a small group of supporters in Neubabelsberg on 16 August, "There was no majority for positive work, only for negation. That gave the Reich president and him the moral justification [they needed] for their course of action."[26]

The outcome of the meeting, which lasted scarcely twenty minutes, and the subsequent exchange between Hitler and Papen in the hallway outside Hindenburg's office constituted a clear and unequivocal rejection of Schleicher's taming strategy and the assumptions upon which it was based. This marked the beginning of a rift between Papen and Schleicher that would become increasingly pronounced in the weeks to come. For although Schleicher and his entourage remained committed to the inclusion of the NSDAP and possibly even Hitler in the national cabinet,[27] Papen seemed to be falling more and more under the influence of hard-liners in his cabinet like Baron Wilhelm von Gayl, the Reich minister of internal affairs.[28] The propagation of Papen's "New State" as a remedy to the shortcomings of the modern democratic state by Walther Schotte and other right-wing publicists[29] undercut Schleicher's own aspirations of building a broad popular consensus in support of German rearmament. Relations between Papen and Schleicher were further strained by the latter's frustration over the slow pace of progress in the disarmament negotiations in Geneva and particularly with the failure of the German delegation to secure French consent to the principle that if other European powers would not disarm to the level of Germany, then Germany had the right to equality in armaments with other European countries. The fact that Papen tended to side with his foreign minister Konstantin von Neurath and the German foreign office in matters like this constituted a real conflict of interest that has escaped the attention of all but the most astute of Schleicher scholars.[30] In the short term, however, Schleicher had no choice but to play the Papen card to the end. It was with this in mind that Schleicher assembled a team of constitutional lawyers under the nimbus of the famed jurist Carl Schmitt to draft a series of measures that would make it possible for the government to deal with the Nazi threat once and for all. Working in close collaboration with Eugen Ott, one of Schleicher's most trusted aides in the ministry of defense, a trio of legal experts—Ernst Rudolf Huber, Carl Bilfinger, and Erwin Jacobi—labored through the night of 27–28 August in Schmitt's Berlin apartment to put the finishing touches on a series of specific measures that included a ban against the NSDAP, the arrest of Hitler and other Nazi leaders, and the immediate dissolution of the Reichstag without new elections as stipulated by Article 25 of the Weimar Constitution. At the same time, they worked on the draft of a statement to the nation that Reich president Hindenburg would issue to justify these actions.[31]

On 30 August Schleicher, Papen, and Gayl traveled to Hindenburg's estate at Neudeck to present the Reich president with the results of their deliberations about what needed to be done to combat the threat of Nazism. Hindenburg approved their recommendations and issued Papen authority to dissolve the Reichstag without scheduling new elections within the sixty days stipulated by the Weimar Constitution.[32] All of this would depend on Papen's ability to pull this stratagem off when the Reichstag resumed its official business on 12 September. And therein lay the rub. For when Papen assumed the podium after the Reichstag had elected its new president and executive committee to read the president's proclamation announcing its dissolution without calling for new elections within the time frame specified by the Weimar Constitution, he was rudely pushed aside by Hermann Göring, who in his capacity as the newly elected president of the Reichstag immediately called for a vote on a no-confidence motion in the Papen government that the Communists had introduced. Despite the specter of vehement, yet pitiable protests from the chancellor and his staff, Göring proceeded to take the vote, which returned a humiliating 512–42 vote against Papen and his cabinet[33] After this spectacle and the loss of public face that it entailed, it is hard to imagine that Schleicher too did not lose the last vestige of confidence he had once placed in the chancellor he had effectively placed in office a scant three and a half months earlier. Papen was simply no longer viable as an instrument for the containment of the Nazi threat.

Schleicher and the Strasser Gambit

It was against the background of these developments and the unremitting public ridicule to which the Nazi propaganda apparatus subjected Papen, his political philosophy, and his program[34] that Schleicher began to explore other alternatives. The first of these involved either somehow elevating Crown Prince Wilhelm of Hohenzollern to the Reich presidency or restoring him to the throne that his father had abdicated in November 1918.[35] Schleicher's friendship with the crown prince dated back to their days in the cadet school at Plön. After the end of the war Schleicher continued to correspond with the crown prince throughout the Weimar Republic and built up a relationship of trust that led Schleicher to vet the possibility of Wilhelm's candidacy for the Reich presidency at a private dinner with Chancellor Heinrich Brüning in early February 1932.[36] Schleicher hoped that Wilhelm's candidacy would either deter Hitler from running for the Reich presidency or keep him from being elected if he became a candidate. But once Hindenburg decided to stand for reelection himself, Schleicher had no choice but to temporarily shelve the idea of the crown prince's candidacy, only to resurrect it in the political crisis that gripped Germany in the fall of 1932.[37] It was also at this time that Schleicher began to develop an interest in Gregor Strasser. As Reich Organization Leader of the NSDAP, Strasser was arguably the second most influential figure in the Nazi party leadership behind Hitler. But Strasser, who had attracted widespread interest in circles outside the party for the moderate tone of a speech that he had delivered before fifteen thousand Nazi workers in the Berlin Sports Palace on 20 October,[38] had supposedly grown weary of Hitler's all-or-nothing tactics, and after the debacle of 13 August he was thought to be open to a possible accommodation with groups outside the NSDAP. It is not clear on the basis of existing evidence when Schleicher first met with Strasser or even if he met with him during the political stalemate of the late fall of 1932.[39] What is clear, however, is that after the heavy losses the NSDAP sustained in the November 1932 Reichstag elections, Strasser became the focus of widespread speculation across the political spectrum with respect to a fresh realignment of political forces that would include the more moderate elements of the Nazi Party.[40]

The November elections were followed by a flurry of negotiations that failed to break the stalemate that had existed before the elections.[41] Despite the fact that the NSDAP had suffered the loss of more than two million votes and thirty-six seats in the Reichstag, Hitler remained adamantly opposed to any accommodation with the existing political system and categorically rejected his party's participation in a coalition government that rested upon a broad parliamentary majority.[42] Only the stubborn loyalty of the Reich president kept Papen in office. But in the final analysis not even this could protect Papen against Schleicher's exasperation over the chancellor's inability to break out of the impasse in which he found himself trapped. Unable to reach an accommodation with the NSDAP, Papen still enjoyed the support of the DNVP and some of the smaller parties between the NSDAP and Center. But, as negotiations in the second half of November clearly revealed, he stood no chance of putting together a parliamentary majority with or without Nazi support. The question then was whether or not the Reich president was prepared to grant Papen the authority to dissolve the Reichstag without calling for new elections within the sixty-day limit specified by the Weimar Constitution in accordance with the strategy that had been agreed upon on 30 August. Such a stratagem, however, now encountered strong reservations from Schleicher, who had instructed Ott to conduct a "war game" to assess the risks and consequences of such an action. The conclusion was that the assumption of dictatorial powers even on a temporary basis would most likely provoke mass demonstrations and protests on both the left and the right that the Reichswehr would not be able to contain.[43]

At the conclusion of a series of high-level meetings at the very beginning of December 1932, Schleicher summoned Ott before the cabinet to present the results of the war-game exercise he had been commissioned to conduct on the consequences of invoking presidential emergency powers to dissolve parliament and postpone new elections until the following spring. After hearing that the Reichswehr would have a difficult time maintaining peace and civil order, Schleicher announced that he could not risk the unity of the Reichswehr for the sake of a cabinet to which "nine-tenths of the German people" were opposed. In doing so, Schleicher effectively sabotaged the idea of a *Kampfkabinett* that would immediately declare a state of emergency and use presidential emergency powers to rule in defiance of the Reichstag and the Weimar Constitution. Schleicher's refusal to commit the Reichswehr to such a course of action effectively sealed the fate of the Papen chancellorship and left the chancellor with no alternative but to declare his efforts to form a new government at an end. Exasperated by all the intrigues, a frustrated Reich president promptly turned to Schleicher and made him responsible for forming a new government.[44] Schleicher was not at all comfortable with assuming the responsibilities of the Reich chancellorship. His métier had always been to work informally behind the scenes through the vast network of personal contacts he had built up over years of service. At the same time he lacked the public profile and personal charisma to compete with the likes of Hindenburg and Hitler. But as an officer in the Reichswehr he felt he had no alternative but to obey a direct order from his commander in chief, and with great reservations he reluctantly accepted the chancellorship on 2 December 1932.

Much has been made of Schleicher's *Querfront* strategy, by which he presumably sought to base his government upon an axis that stretched from the trade union elements on the right wing of the SPD through the Center, Bavarian People's Party (Bayerische Volkspartei), and other middle parties to the left wing of the NSDAP around Gregor Strasser.[45] There is, however, no reliable evidence to support the thesis that Schleicher actually hoped either to win the support of the Social Democrats or to provoke a secession on the left wing of the NSDAP.[46] Schleicher's overtures to the leaders of the socialist labor movement at the end of November 1932 are best understood as an attempt to preempt a major demonstration against his chancellorship in the eventuality that he actually became chancellor.[47] And while they met with a promising response from SPD stalwarts like Otto Braun and Rudolf Hilferding as well as from leaders of the socialist labor movement, Schleicher was never able to overcome the residual distrust these elements felt toward Germany's military leadership and the bitterness they felt toward Schleicher for his role in the coup against the Prussian government in July.[48] And Schleicher's negotiations with Strasser, the putative leader of the NSDAP's left wing, in late November and early December 1932 were motivated not by the desire to split the Nazi Party in two but rather by the hope that Hitler and the Nazi party leadership could be persuaded to participate—or at the very least tolerate—the government he was putting together. In no way whatsoever, as we shall see, was Strasser's decision to resign his seat in the Reichstag along with all of his offices in the Nazi Party organization on 8 December 1932 part of a plan by Schleicher to split the NSDAP in two. To the contrary, Strasser's resignation was actually a severe blow to Schleicher in that it deprived him of an influential and trustworthy voice at the upper echelons of the Nazi party leadership.

In a postwar interview with the journalist Heinrich Egner, Strasser's widow Else recalled that after the November elections Hitler had given his consent to her husband's participation, along with that of other Nazi party members, in a future Schleicher cabinet with Strasser assuming the post of vice chancellor. Strasser was given the task of working out the details of such an arrangement, and after they had been finalized Hitler would come to Berlin to give it his stamp of approval. But Hitler failed to show up at the appointed meeting place on the morning of 30 November, having disembarked from the night train to Berlin at Jena to catch another train to Weimar, where Hermann Göring, a staunch opponent of the NSDAP's participation in a Schleicher cabinet, was waiting for him. Strasser traveled to Weimar on his own but suffered a bitter setback at a meeting of the Nazi party leadership later in the day.[49] Frustrated by Hitler's sudden and inexplicable change of mind, Schleicher dispatched Ott to Weimar in a last desperate attempt to persuade the Nazi party leader to reconsider his abrupt withdrawal from the efforts to form a new government by offering him the vice chancellorship and his party the number of cabinet posts commensurate with its electoral strength.[50] Spurred on by Goebbels, Hitler not only cited chapter and verse as to why the NSDAP should not join Schleicher's cabinet but argued that Schleicher should decline the chancellorship if for no other reason than the disastrous effect it would have on the unity of the Reichswehr.[51] For Schleicher, however, it was too late to turn back, and he had no choice but to accept his appointment as chancellor without having first secured what he thought to be indispensable pre-requisites for his success in office.

For Strasser this turn of events could only have come as a devastating disappointment. Back in Berlin he and Wilhelm Frick met with Schleicher in a purely official capacity on 5 December to learn that the chancellor planned to dissolve the Reichstag if the Nazis refused to tolerate his cabinet.[52] Aside from this one meeting, there is no evidence whatsoever of any direct or indirect contact between Schleicher and Strasser through the first week of December 1932.[53] Throughout all of this Strasser continued to hope that Hitler might reconsider his hard-line position against Nazi participation in the Schleicher cabinet, but he was unable to gain traction with either Hitler or other party leaders. For Hitler any accommodation with Schleicher or his cabinet was out of the question. As he exclaimed at a meeting of the NSDAP Reichstag delegation on 6 December: "A great movement has never triumphed by taking the path of compromise."[54] For Strasser, on the other hand, Hitler's categorical refusal to consider even the possibility of a coalition government under Schleicher was the last straw. On the morning of 8 December Strasser informed Paul Schulz and other close associates of his decision to resign all of his party offices except for his Reichstag mandate, which he would retain because of the immunity from prosecution it afforded him.[55] On short notice Strasser then called a meeting of the ten men who reported directly to him as state inspectors of the NSDAP party organization. Here he informed his closest collaborators in the party organization that he had written a letter to Hitler announcing the decision he had reached the day before. Strasser then proceeded to outline in great detail his reasons for doing so. First and foremost, Strasser cited the irreparable breach that had developed in his relations with Hitler. At the heart of the breach lay the fact that the Nazi party leader had become fixated on becoming chancellor without realizing that this had been blocked by opposition from all directions ever since he had rejected the offer of the vice chancellorship in August. In the meantime, Hitler had squandered the opportunities for an illegal seizure of power, something that Strasser would have supported had the Nazi party leader given the order, by his inability to act decisively. And all through this the suffering of the great mass of the movement's followers continued to mount. Their suffering, Strasser claimed, was too great, and he could no longer wait for what seemed at best something that lay in the distant future.[56]

Before the meeting Strasser had composed a letter to Hitler informing the Nazi party leader that the differences between their respective viewpoints had made it impossible for him to fulfill his responsibilities as a deputy and speaker for the party and that he was therefore resigning all his party offices, including his Reichstag mandate. Strasser reaffirmed his unshaken commitment to the goals and ideals of the Nazi movement but rejected a tactic whereby the party's chances of success and ultimate triumph "depended solely upon hopes of chaos as wrong, dangerous, and not in Germany's national interest." At the same time, Strasser reassured Hitler that he had no intention of allowing himself "to become the middle point of oppositional efforts or of discussions thereof," and for that reason he would be leaving Berlin and Germany for a longer period of time.[57] Leaving it to Schulz and two other party associates to transmit the letter and news of his resignation to Hitler,[58] Strasser left for Munich later that evening, where he met with his wife Else and departed for a two-week vacation in northern Italy.[59] In the meantime, Hitler and Schleicher would have to deal with the fallout from Strasser's action. For Hitler and the Nazi party leadership, whose fears of a Strasser-Schleicher conspiracy may have been fueled by an ill-advised inquiry from the British journalist Sefton Delmer,[60] Strasser's decision to withdraw from the political limelight only confirmed the deep-seated animosity that Goebbels, Göring, and other members of the Hitler entourage had developed toward the party's Reich organization leader and was immediately seized upon in an effort to unite a badly divided party behind allegations of treachery and collusion with enemies of the party.[61] For Schleicher, on the other hand, Strasser's resignation signaled the virtual collapse of his taming strategy. It had never been Schleicher's intention to split the NSDAP but to do everything in his power to win the party over to a more responsible course of action. There is no evidence that Schleicher had any contact with Strasser in the days leading up to the latter's decision to retire from active political life, and it was clear to Strasser's closest confederates that the decision to resign his offices in the NSDAP was his and his alone.[62] Still, the Strasser card was the only one that Schleicher had left to play, though it was far from clear whether it would still carry the weight that it might have previously.

Schleicher's Last Chance

Schleicher received a brief respite from the partisan political strife that had done so much to poison German political life when the Council of Elders, or *Ältestenrat*, of the Reichstag assented to the government's request to postpone the opening of the Reichstag until the end of January 1933. Schleicher proceeded to present a generally upbeat status report of where he and his government stood at a meeting of the German high command in mid-December,[63] and in his radio address to the German nation on 15 December he struck a clearly conciliatory note when he reassured the nation, as he had done in an earlier address shortly after the Prussian coup of 20 July,[64] that a permanent solution to the crisis in which Germany found itself did not lie in the establishment of a military dictatorship. Schleicher then went on to identify the creation of work for Germany's unemployed as his government's highest priority in a gesture addressed to both the Social Democrats and the left wing of the NSDAP.[65] In the meantime, Hitler and the Nazi party leadership were still struggling to recover from the effects of Strasser's resignation, and—perhaps even more importantly—the party treasury was running dry. The situation within the NSDAP was in fact so desperate that one could legitimately ask whether or not it would survive into the new year.[66] By the end of 1932 Schleicher and his associates had every reason to believe that the Nazis had been visibly weakened by the desertion of Strasser and that they themselves were well on the way to providing, at least in the short term, the political stability that Germany needed to address the economic and fiscal problems that continued to beleaguer the nation.

Finally, there were promising signs that Schleicher's overtures to Strasser were beginning to bear fruit. Strasser did not return to Berlin in the first week of January 1933 but had been kept apprised of the situation in the NSDAP by Schulz and former party associates like Hans Reupke.[67] One can also assume that Strasser had been in touch with Schleicher during his absence from Berlin, but there is no specific evidence in either the Schulz diaries or other contemporary sources to that effect. In any event, Strasser met secretly with Schleicher in the house of the dentist Hellmuth Elbrechter on the evening of 3 January after having met with Brüning earlier in the day.[68] In his meeting with Strasser, Schleicher indicated that he was prepared to hand over the chancellorship to Strasser in a move that enjoyed Brüning's full support. But because Hindenburg was opposed to such a move, he offered Strasser the vice chancellorship and his appointment as Reich commissar in Prussia as an alternative.[69] Strasser then met with the Reich president on the morning of 6 January and reported that the meeting had gone well, although nothing concrete had emerged from it.[70] At this point things were beginning to look up for Schleicher, complicated only by the unsettling news of Papen's secret meeting with Hitler in Cologne two days earlier. As late as the second week of January the entourage around Schleicher, as the tenor of a letter from his press secretary Erich Marcks to the historian Siegfried Kähler clearly suggested, was still optimistic about the chancellor's prospects of mastering the political crisis.[71] But Schleicher, who had kept close track of developments within the NSDAP through reports from the SA's Franz von Hörauf that had been forwarded to him by Crown Prince Wilhelm,[72] tended to discount the importance of the Hitler-Papen meeting and apparently accepted Papen's account of the meeting that he was acting in Schleicher's best interests by trying to mediate an understanding with the Nazi party leader.[73] Presumably Papen was now doing precisely what Schleicher had hoped he would do when he first tapped him for the chancellorship in the summer of 1932. Although Schleicher may have questioned the wisdom of Papen's decision to meet with the Nazi party leader, he refused to ascribe much significance to the meeting and failed to recognize the threat that the rapprochement between Papen and Hitler posed to his own political future until it was too late to do much about it.[74]

By the end of the second week of January, however, things began to unravel for Schleicher. Perhaps most importantly Strasser had met with Hindenburg for a second time on 11 January only to hear from the president's own mouth that Schleicher would be his last Reich chancellor.[75] Schleicher still hoped that Strasser could be persuaded to accept a position in his cabinet but did not think that Strasser would be able to bring much with him. Referring to the failure of the DNVP secession in 1929–30, Schleicher observed, "The experiences that one had with Treviranus must have been chilling." Even if Strasser were to enter the cabinet, Schleicher continued, "he would not leave the NSDAP but remain in it in order to shape it positively."[76] What this suggests is that even at this late state of the game, Schleicher was not thinking of using Strasser to provoke a secession on the left wing of the NSDAP. Schleicher's goal had always been and remained one of winning the NSDAP over to the support of the government as a way of taming the National Socialists and transforming them into responsible participants in the political process. But his chances of doing this were growing dimmer with every passing day. Even Strasser's closest associates in the NSDAP realized that the prospects of transforming the NSDAP along the lines envisaged by Schleicher and Strasser were hopeless as long as fanatics like Goebbels and Göring continued to dominate Hitler.[77] And Brüning, who had temporarily overcome his pique against Schleicher to join forces with him in the struggle to keep Hitler from gaining power,[78] had become thoroughly exhausted by Schleicher's constant intrigues and bitterly advised Strasser that Schleicher was simply using him to accomplish his own ends; for his own good he should settle his differences with Hitler as gracefully and honorably as possible.[79] All of this placed Strasser in an incredibly difficult situation and made it virtually impossible for him to find a way out of the dilemma in which he found himself.[80]

While Strasser was trying to assess his own prospects in the second and third weeks of January 1933, Papen and his staff were hard at work doing their best to subvert Schleicher's negotiations with Strasser.[81] At the same time, Schleicher's position began to deteriorate rapidly as the result of a coordinated offensive by Hugenberg and his allies in the German agricultural community. On 13 January the National Rural League (Reichs-Landbund or RLB), the largest and most influential of Germany's agricultural interest organizations, published a resolution sharply attacking the government's farm policy in an attempt to set in motion the chain of events that would lead to the fall of the Schleicher cabinet.[82] But as annoying as these developments may have been, they were quickly overshadowed by what Schleicher learned from the crown prince about the most recent developments within the NSDAP. On 13 January Wilhelm had forwarded to Schleicher a detailed report from Hörauf about the meeting between Papen and Hitler filled with speculation about the former chancellor.[83] Although Hörauf's report tended to downplay the threat this posed to the Reich chancellor, it could only have unnerved Schleicher at a time when he was just beginning to face a more concerted challenge from the DNVP and RLB. Schleicher's real concern was that Papen might use his influence with Hindenburg to undermine his own standing with the Reich president, thus leaving him easy prey to the machinations of Papen, Otto Meissner, and Hindenburg's son Oskar. Although Schleicher continued to hope that Strasser might still be persuaded to join his cabinet,[84] he felt himself forced more and more on the defensive, so much so in fact that for him the only solution to the deepening political crisis lay in the dissolution of the Reichstag and the postponement of new elections beyond the time specified in the Weimar Constitution.[85] But when Schleicher proposed this to the Reich president on the morning of 23 January, Hindenburg replied that he would take the proposal to dissolve the Reichstag under advisement but refused to sanction a postponement of new elections on the grounds that this would constitute a breach of the constitution.[86]

Though temporarily reassured by the Reich president's statement that he would authorize the dissolution of parliament and call for new elections if the Reichstag's Council of Elders should vote to reconvene the Reichstag on 31 January, Schleicher was well aware of the negotiations that were taking place behind his back and did not fully trust Hindenburg's words of encouragement.[87] In the meantime, Papen and his supporters continued to lay the foundation for a new government that would elevate Hitler to the Reich chancellorship as head of a new cabinet that would include himself as vice chancellor as well as the DNVP's Alfred Hugenberg and other representatives of the non-Nazi right on the assumption that their presence in the cabinet would be sufficient to contain the radicalism of the Nazi movement.[88] Not even the intervention of Baron Kurt von Hammerstein-Equord, the commander in chief of the German army who met with Hindenburg on 26 January in an attempt to salvage Schleicher's chancellorship, could persuade the Reich president to alter his political course. All Hammerstein could get from Hindenburg was the assurance that he had no intention of entrusting "that Austrian corporal Hitler" with the responsibilities of the Reich defense minister or the chancellorship.[89] By the time that Hindenburg received Schleicher on 28 January and summarily rejected his request for emergency powers that would have allowed him to dissolve the Reichstag without calling for new elections, the Reich president had finally warmed to the idea of a Hitler chancellorship and dismissed the sitting chancellor with little more than token expressions of gratitude for Schleicher's service.[90] Schleicher accepted his dismissal as chancellor with a stoic equanimity that reflected his exhaustion and lack of a viable alternative. At this point the only chance of preventing a Hitler chancellorship lay in declaring a state of military emergency and imposing a military dictatorship along the lines of the war-games exercise that Ott had conducted in November. But on the afternoon of 29 January when Schleicher, Hammerstein, Wilhelm Adam as chief of the Troup Office, and Baron Erich von dem Bussche-Ippenburg from the Office of Army Personnel met in Hammerstein's office to discuss what might still be done to block Hitler's appointment as chancellor, the four generals, including Schleicher, concluded that the Reichswehr was too weak to sustain itself for any length of time in a two-front war against the Communists and Nazis and that it was best to do nothing at this point in time and await further developments.[91]

Conclusion

Hitler's appointment as chancellor was based on the premise that the conservatives who occupied most of the posts in the new cabinet would be able to contain the dynamism of the Nazi movement and harness it to their own political agenda. As one of Hugenberg's confederates expressed it, "Hitler sits in the saddle, but Hugenberg holds the whip."[92] All of this represented a perversion of Schleicher's taming strategy for the simple fact that Papen, the key conservative in the new government, would prove totally incapable of containing Nazism and would soon find himself reduced to the status of junior partner in the Nazi-conservative alliance. Moreover, Schleicher's taming strategy had always assumed that the Reichswehr could be entrusted with the task of enforcing the terms of the taming strategy upon a restive and undisciplined Nazi Party. Schleicher had assumed that he would stay on as minister of defense, a position from which he could ensure Nazi compliance with the terms of his taming strategy, but, as it would quickly become apparent, this solution was totally unacceptable to Hitler and Papen. But when the Reich president turned to Werner von Blomberg, one of Schleicher's most determined opponents at the upper echelons of the Reichswehr leadership and a man who was not a Nazi but who was mesmerized by Hitler's charismatic personality, and appointed him to the post as defense minister in the new Hitler cabinet that was presented to the public on the morning of 30 January 1933,[93] Schleicher's hopes that the military might somehow contain the threat of Nazism were definitively dashed in a turn of events that signaled the complete and irrevocable collapse of his taming strategy.

Aside from the brief moment at the end of 1931 and the beginning of 1932 when Schleicher had deluded himself into believing that Hitler might actually honor his pledge to pursue the conquest of power according to the principle of legality, Schleicher regarded Hitler as the single greatest threat to the welfare of the German nation and was determined to do everything possible to keep him from attaining power. At the same time, however, Schleicher and his associates realized that, with the dramatic growth of the NSDAP in the last years of the Weimar Republic, it was imperative to find some way of integrating the party—or at least what Schleicher considered the more valuable elements within it—into the existing state structure. There was in Schleicher's mind no way that Germany could possibly survive the crisis that had descended upon it with all its fury in the early 1930s without reaching some sort of accommodation with the Nazis whereby they would accept a measure of responsibility for whatever would have to be done to restore fiscal and economic stability. But in his single-minded pursuit of this goal, Schleicher alienated key supporters—most notably Groener, Brüning, and even the supercilious Papen as well as Hindenburg—to the point where by the beginning of 1933 he found himself totally isolated with the exception of his loyal supporters in the ministry of defense and the Reichswehr. In the meantime, Hitler had only become more emboldened by the overtures of men like Papen and Schleicher to the point where he learned how to play one against the other and exploit their animosity toward one another in service of his own political ambitions. Perhaps the bitterest irony of all was that the government that eventually assumed power on 30 January 1933 was based on the very taming strategy that Schleicher had advocated ever since the NSDAP's emergence as a mass political party, but with the crucial difference that with Schleicher out of the picture and the Reichswehr neutralized with the appointment of Blomberg, there was little prospect that Papen and his conservative cronies would be able to defuse the radicalism of the Nazi beast and harness its dynamism to their own political agenda.

Larry Eugene Jones is professor of history at Canisius College in Buffalo, New York, where he specializes in the history of modern Germany and the Holocaust. He also edited *The German Right in the Weimar Republic: Studies in the History of German Conservatism, Nationalism, and Antisemitism* (2014). He is the author of *Hitler versus Hindenburg: The 1932 Presidential Elections and the End of the Weimar Republic* (2016) and is currently working on a new book tentatively titled *The German Right, 1918–1930: Political Parties, Organized Interests, and Patriotic Associations in the Struggle against Weimar Democracy*.

Notes

1. This represents an expanded and revised version of a paper that was originally presented at the 38th Annual Conference of the German Studies
   Association in Kansas City, Missouri, 19 September 2014. It is deeply
   indebted to the insightful analysis by Peter Hayes, "'A Question Mark
   with Epaulettes'? Kurt von Schleicher and Weimar Politics," *Journal of
   Modern History* 52 (1980): 35–65, which remains the best concise overview
   of Schleicher's political activities.
2. The secondary literature on Schleicher is far too voluminous to be listed
   here. Above all, see Thilo Vogelsang, *Reichswehr, Staat und NSDAP: Beiträge
   zur Deutschen Geschichte 1930–1932* (Stuttgart, 1962), and Francis L. Carsten,
   The Reichswehr and Politics, 1918–1933 (Oxford: Oxford University Press,
   1966), 296–308, 325–50, as well as the numerous articles by Wolfram Pyta
   cited below. More problematic in its reading of Schleicher's political strategy is the recent monograph by Irene Strenge, *Kurt von Schleicher: Politik im
   Reichswehrministerium am Ende der Weimarer Republik* (Berlin: Duncker and
   Humblot, 2006).
3. Schleicher enjoyed particularly close ties to Heinrich von Gleichen, chairman of the German Lords' Club (Deutscher Herrenklub) and a relentless critic of Weimar party democracy. See the extensive correspondence
   between the two in the unpublished Nachlass of Kurt von Schleicher,

Bundesarchv-Militärarchiv Freiburg (hereafter cited as BA-MA Freiburg), NL Schleicher, vols. 7 and 77.

4. In this respect, see Josef Becker, "Zur Politik der Wehrmachtabteilung in der Regierungskrise 1926/27," *Vierteljahrshefte für Zeitgeschichte* 14 (1966): 69–78.

5. Hayes, "Question Mark with Epaulettes," 40–44.

6. Artur Zickler, "Erinnerungen über antifascistische Strömungen in deutschen Kreisen des Militärs und des Bürgertums from 1922 bis 1945," 3 July 1945, Bundesarchiv Berlin (hereafter cited as BA Berlin), SGY 30/1052. The author is indebted to Rainer Orth for directing him to this source.

7. On Schleicher's "taming strategy," see Karl Dietrich Bracher, *Die Auflösung der Weimarer Republik: Eine Studie des Machtverfalls in der Demokratie*, 3rd ed. (Villingen-Schwarzwald: Ring-Verlag, 1960), 423–31, as well as Hayes, "Question Mark with Epaulettes?" 43–49. On the "taming strategy" in general and on its failure to keep Hitler from power, see Gotthard Jasper, *Die gescheiterte Zähmung: Wege zur Machtergreifung Hitlers 1930–1934* (Frankfurt a.M.: Suhrkamp Verlag, 1986).

8. On Schleicher's role in the formation of the Brüning cabinet, see the recollection of a meeting with Brüning and other government officials in the Berlin home of Schleicher's close associate Baron Friedrich Wilhelm von Willisen on 29 December 1929, in Gottfried Reinhold Trevianus, *Das Ende von Weimar: Heinrich Brüning und seine Zeit* (Düsseldorf and Vienna: Econ-Verlag, 1968), 114–15. For Brüning's recollection of this meeting, see Heinrich Brüning, *Memoiren 1918–1934* (Stuttgart: Deutsche Verlags-Anstalt, 1970), 150–52.

9. Count Kuno von Westarp, "Was nun?," *Volkskonservative Stimmen*, no. 36 (20 September 1930).

10. August Heinrichsbauer, *Schwerindustrie und Politik* (Essen-Kettwig: West-Verlag, 1948), 40–42.

11. On this point, see Schleicher to Körner, 1 August 1933, BA Berlin, R 601, 403/601–3. See also Schleicher's letter to the editorial board of the *Vossische Zeitung*, 30 January 1934, Institut für Zeitgeschichte Munich (hereafter cited as IfZ Munich), NL Schleicher, Bestand ED 74, 1.

12. A protocol of this meeting, prepared by Meissner and dated 10 October 1931, has survived in BA-MA Freiburg, NL Eberhardt, 35. On Schleicher's contacts with Hitler prior to this meeting, see Hanshenning Holtzendorff, "Die Politik des Generals von Schleicher gegenüber der NSDAP 1930–1933: Ein Beitrag zur Frage Wehrmacht und Partei," 22 June 1946, BA-MA Freiburg, NL Holtzendorff, 5/8–15, here 8. For Schleicher's opinion of the Nazi party leader, see his disparaging references to Hitler from October 1931 cited by Anton Hoch and Hermann Weiß, "Die Erinnerungen des Generalobersten Wilhelm Adam," in *Miscellanea: Festschrift für Helmut Krausnick zum 75. Geburtstag*, ed. Wolfgang Benz (Stuttgart: Deutsche Verlags-Anstalt, 1980), 32–62, esp. 39, and the remarks recorded by retired general Magnus von Eberhardt, "Verschiedene Aussprüche aus Deutschlands schwerster Zeit," n.d., BA-MA Freiburg, NL Eberhardt, 25. For further details, see Larry Eugene Jones, *Hitler versus Hindenburg: The 1932 Presidential Elections and*

the End of the Weimar Republic (Cambridge: Cambridge University Press, 2016), 111–12.

13. See the comments by Brüning as recorded in the diary of Hans Schäffer, 9 January 1932, in IfZ Munich, NL Schäffer, 19/58–59, as well as Groener's optimistic assessment of Hitler in his remarks in the minutes of the meeting of the Reichswehr command, 11 January 1932, BA-MA Freiburg, NL Liebmann, 2/8–12, reprinted in Thilo Vogelsang, "Neue Dokumente zur Geschichte der Reichswehr 1930–1933," *Vierteljahrshefte für Zeitgeschichte* 2 (1954): 414–15. That Groener would quickly revise his opinion of Hitler in light of the Nazi party leader's subsequent behavior is apparent from his two letters to retired major general Gerold von Gleich, 24 and 26 January 1932, BA-MA Freiburg, NL Groener, 36/38–42.

14. On the negotiations to extend Hindenburg's term of office by parliamentary initiative, see the memorandum prepared by Hermann Pünder, 8 January 1932, and subsequently amended, 11 January 1932, BA Berlin, R 43 I, 583/222–28. On the deliberations of the radical right, see Quaatz, "Betrifft: Wahl des Reichspräsidenten durch den Reichstag," n.d. [January 1932], Bundesarchiv Kolbenz (hereafter cited as BA Koblenz), NL Quaatz, 17. See also Jones, *Hitler versus Hindenburg*, 119–48.

15. See Hugenberg to Brüning, 11 January 1932, BA Koblenz, NL Pünder, 97/266–67, also in BA Koblenz, NL Hugenberg, 36/37–38, and Hitler to Brüning, 12 January 1932, BA Koblenz, NL Pünder, 87/265.

16. For a detailed reconstruction of the developments on the radical right, see Volker R. Berghahn, "Die Harzburger Front und die Kandidatur Hindenburgs für die Reichspräsidentenwahlen 1932," *Vierteljahrshefte für Zeitgeschichte* 13 (1965): 64–82, as well as the more recent study by Jones, *Hitler versus Hindenburg*, 149–204.

17. Schleicher to Rigal, 27 February 1932, BA-MA Freiburg, NL Schleicher, 30/11–12. For an even more devastating assessment of Hitler's political qualifications, see Schleicher's comments as recorded in Schäffer's diary, 29 January 1932, IfZ Munich, NL Schäffer, 19/137–46.

18. There can be little doubt that Schleicher was the driving force behind the resignations of both Groener and Brüning. For further details, see Vogelsang, *Reichswehr, Staat und NSDAP*, 184–202.

19. On the negotiations between Schleicher and Hitler, see the entries for 28 April and 9 May 1932, in *Die Tagebücher von Joseph Goebbels*, ed. Elke Fröhlich, Teil 1, Bd. 2/II (Munich: J. P. Saur, 2004), 270–71, 276–77. For the terms of this agreement, see Gayl's memoir on his experiences as a member of the Papen government, n.d., BA Koblenz, NL Gayl, 53, as well as the memorandum by Ott and Bredow, "Aufzeichnung betreffs Treubruch der nationalsoziaistischen Führung durch Angriffe gegen das Präsidialkabinett v. Papen," 16 September 1932, BA-MA: NL Schleicher, 22/141–43.

20. On the reaction of the Center Party, see Georg Schreiber, *Brüning — Hitler — Schleicher: Das Zentrum in der Opposition* (Cologne, 1932), 27–34. Papen's frustration over the Center's reaction to his installation as chancellor is reflected in a letter to Diego von Bergen, 6 June 1932, USHMM Washington, RG-76.001M, Reel 7, Pos. 627, Fasc. 144, Bl. 46–50.

21. On developments within the NSDAP, see the entries for 7, 9, and 13–15 June 1932, in *Goebbels Tagebücher*, ed. Fröhlich, Teil 1, Bd. 2/II, 298–99, 302–4.

22. In this respect, see Reiner's report of a conversation with Planck on Schleicher's meeting with Hitler and Strasser in Schäffer's diary, 10 August 1932, IfZ Munich, NL Schäffer, 23/730–31.

23. Report by Schleicher at a ministerial conference, 10 August 1932, BA Berlin, R 43 I, 1457/276–78.

24. The optimism that existed at the upper echelons of the Nazi party leadership is clearly reflected in the entries for 5–11 August 1932, in *Goebbels Tagebücher*, ed. Fröhlich, Teil 1, Bd. 2/II, 333–38.

25. For the official record of the meeting, see the memorandum of 13 August 1932, BA Berlin, R 43 I, 1309/215–19. Both the presidential palace and the NSDAP had different versions of what transpired at this meeting. For example, see the text of the communiqué that Hitler, Frick, and Röhm released to the press, 13 August 1932, and appended to Hitler's letter to Schleicher, Meissner, and Planck, 13 August 1932, BA Berlin, NS 51, 222/104–8, as well as Planck's response of 14 August 1932, BA Berlin, R 43 I, 1309/231–33. On the reasons for Hindenburg's behavior, see Wolfram Pyta, *Hindenburg. Herrschaft zwischen Hohenzollern und Hitler* (Berlin: Siedler Verlag, 2007), 716–20.

26. See Papen's report on his altercation with Hitler in the minutes of a conversation with Jacob Goldschmidt, Fritz Springorum, Ernst Brandi, and Hans Humann in Neubabelsberg, August 16, 1932, in the unpublished Nachlass of Theodor Reismann-Crone, Stadtarchiv Essen, 15. See also Papen's report on the meeting between Hindenburg and Hitler at a ministerial conference, 15 August 1932, BA Berlin, R 43 I, 678/234–38.

27. Notes prepared by Bredow for Schleicher for a meeting of the Reichswehr High Command, 15 August 1932, BA-MA Freiburg, NL Bredow, 2/90–91.

28. For Gayl's views on constitutional reform, see his detailed memorandum, "Gesichtspunkte für den Staatsneubau," 22 August 1932, BA Koblenz, NL Gayl, 37/40–47. For an indication of Schleicher's dissatisfaction with Gayl and his political course, see Leipart's report on his conversation with Schleicher to the executive committee of the General German Trade Union Federation (Allgemeiner Deutscher Gewerkschaftsbund or ADGB), 28 November 1932, in *Die Gewerkschaften in der Endphase der Republik 1930–1933*, ed. Peter Jahn, Quellen zur Geschichte der deutschen Gewerkschaftsbewegung im 20. Jahrhundert, vol. 4 (Cologne: Bund-Verlag, 1988), 766–69.

29. In this respect, see Walther Schotte, *Der neue Staat* (Berlin: Neufeld and Henius, n.d. [1932]).

30. The notable exception here is Edward W. Bennett, *German Disarmament and the West, 1932–1933* (Princeton, NJ: Princeton University Press, 1979), 176–96.

31. In this respect, see the letter from Huber to Schmitt, 28 August 1932, as well Huber's autobiographical sketch from 1961–62 in *Carl Schmitt—Ernst Rudolf Huber: Briefwechsel 1926–1981; Mit ergänzenden Materialien*, ed. Ewald Grothe (Berlin: Duncker and Humblot, 2014), 107, 562–64. On Schmitt's contacts with Ott and the ministry of defense, see the entries in his diary for 25, 27–29,

and 31 August 1932, in Carl Schmitt, *Tagebücher 1930–1934*, ed. Wolfgang Schuller (Berlin: Akademie-Verlag, 2010), 210–12. For further details, see Wolfram Pyta, "Die Staatsnotstandsplannung unter den Regierungen Papen und Schleicher," in *Die deutsche Staatskrise 1930–1933*, ed. Heinrich August Winkler (Munich: Oldenbourg, 1992), 155–82, esp. 163–66.

32. Transcript of the conversation in Neudeck, 30 August 1932, BA-MA Schleicher, 22/147–57.

33. On the events of 12 September 1932, see Heinrich August Winkler, *Weimar 1918–1933: Die Geschichte der ersten deutschen Demokratie* (Munich: C. H. Beck, 1993), 522–24.

34. For example, see Reichspropagandaleitung der NSDAP, *Reichskanzler von Papen im Lichte seiner Politik* (Munich: Zentral-Parteiverlag Frz. Eher Nachf., 1932).

35. Much of the following is based upon a preliminary draft of a far more detailed analysis of Schleicher's relationship with the crown prince and Strasser by Rainer Orth and Wolfram Pyta, "Eine konservative Troika gegen Hitler: Kurt von Schleicher, Gregor Strasser, and Crown Prince Wilhelm." The author would like to express his deep gratitude to the authors of this article for having shared with him the results of their research.

36. For further details, see Heinrich August Winkler, *Weimar 1918–1933: Die Geschichte der ersten deutschen Demokratie* (Munich: C. H. Beck, 1993); Heinrich Brüning, *Memoiren 1918–1934* (Stuttgart: Deutsche Verlags-Anstalt, 1970), 520. The meeting can be placed at 2 February 1932 by Brüning's daily notes, Harvard University Archives, Cambridge, Massachusetts, Brüning Papers, HUGFF 93.35, Box 1. For Brüning's motives in meeting with the crown prince, see his letter to Ostrau, 22 March 1961, ibid., Acc. 13634, Box 1, Folder 5.

37. For example, see the remarks of Erwin Planck, state secretary in the Reich chancery, in a conversation with Hans Schäffer, 28 October 1932, IfZ Munich, NL Schäffer, 24/945–46.

38. Gregor Strasser, *Das wirtschaftliche Aufbauprogramm der NSDAP: Eine Rede gehalten vor 15000 nationalsozialistischen Betriebszellenmitgliedern am 20. Oktober 1932 im Berliner Sportpalast* (Berlin: Verlag und Druck von Hempel und Co. G.m.b.H., 1932).

39. The most reliable source of information on Strasser's political activities in the last month of 1932 is the recently published biography of Strasser's adjutant Paul Schulz by Alexander Dimitrios, *Weimar und der Kampf gegen "rechts": Eine politische Biographie*, 3 vols. in 4 (Ulm, 2009). There is no evidence in the numerous excerpts from Schulz's diary from the fall and early winter of 1932 of any contact between Schleicher and Strasser before the end of November.

40. Comments by Planck in a conversation with Schäffer, 28 October 1932, IfZ Munich, NL Schäffer 24/944.

41. For further details, see Vogelsang, *Reichswehr*, 318–34; Winkler, *Weimar*, 536–56; and Pyta, *Hindenburg*, 743–66.

42. Transcripts of meetings between Hindenburg and Hitler, 19 and 21 November 1932, BA Berlin, R 43 I, 1309/443–49, 453–65.

43. Eugen Ott, "Ein Bild des Generals Kurt von Schleicher," *Politische Studien* 10 (1959): 360–71, esp. 367–69. For further details on plans for a military state of emergency in the late fall of 1932, see Wolfram Pyta, "Vorbereitungen für den militärischen Ausnahmezustand unter Papen/Schleicher," *Militärgeschichtliche Mitteilungen* 51 (1992): 385–428.

44. Meissner's memorandum from 2 December 1932 on Hindenburg's conversation on the previous day with Schleicher and Papen, BA Berlin, R 601, 405/486–88. See also the entry for 2 December 1932, in the diary of Count Lutz von Schwerin-Krosigk, IfZ Munich, ZS/A-20, vol. 4.

45. For the most uncritical statement of this thesis, see Axel Schildt, *Militärdiktatur mit Massenbasis? Die Querfrontkonzeption der Reichswehrführung um General von Schleicher am Ende der Weimarer Republik* (Frankfurt a.M. and New York: Campus Verlag, 1981), esp. 116–82.

46. Henry Ashby Turner Jr., "The Myth of Chancellor von Schleicher's *Querfront* Strategy," *Central European History* 41 (2008): 673–82.

47. On Schleicher's overtures to the socialist labor movement, see Leipart's report to the ADGB executive committee, 28 November 1932, in Jahn, *Gewerkschaften in der Endphase*, 766–69.

48. By far the most detailed analysis of Schleicher and his overtures to the leaders of the SPD and socialist labor movement is to be found in Pyta, "Vorbereitungen," 385–428; Schildt, *Militärdiktatur mit Massenbasis?*, 138–50, 166–73; Turner, "Myth of Chancellor von Schleicher's *Querfront* Strategy," 673–82; and Wolfram Pyta, "Verfassungsumbau, Staatsnotstand und Querfront: Schleichers Versuche zur Fernhaltung Hitlers von der Reichskanzlerschaft August 1932 bis Januar 1933," in *Gestaltung des Politischen. Festschrift für Eberhard Kolb*, ed. Wolfram Pyta and Ludwig Richter (Berlin: Duncker and Humblot, 1998), 173–97, esp. 186–91. See also Heinrich Muth, "Schleicher und die Gewerkschaften 1932: Ein Quellenproblem," *Vierteljahrshefte für Zeitgeschichte* 29 (1981): 189–215, and Richard Breitman, "On German Social Democracy and General Schleicher 1932–33," *Central European History* 9 (1976): 352–78.

49. Heinrich Egner, "Verzerrungen der Erinnerung an Straßers Rücktritt," *Landshuter Zeitung*, 25 January 2006, in Sammlung Egner, Institut für Zeitgeschichte, Munich, Bestand ED 911, 1/41. On the meeting in Weimar, see also Hinrich Lohse, "Der Fall Strasser," in the Archiv der Forschungsstelle für Zeitgeschichte Hamburg (hereafter cited as AFZ Hamburg), 18, as well as the entry for 1 December 1932, in *Goebbels Tagebücher*, ed. Fröhlich, Teil 1, Bd. 2/III, 70–71.

50. For further details, see Ott, "Bild des Generals von Schleicher," 369–70.

51. Entry in Goebbels diary, 2 December 1932, in *Goebbels Tagebücher*, ed. Fröhlich, Teil 1, Bd. 2/III, 72.

52. Entry in Goebbels diary, 6 December 1932, ibid., Teil 1, Bd. 2/III, 75.

53. The absence of any such evidence in the most important source of information on Strasser's activities during this time, namely the Schulz diary, can possibly be explained by the fact that Schulz was strongly opposed to Strasser's participation in a Schleicher cabinet and was therefore not privy to information about Strasser's negotiations with Schleicher. In this

respect, see Schulz to Reinhardt, 27 April 1933, and to Buch, 21 September 1933, both in the records of the Oberstes Parteigericht der NSDAP, formerly held at the Berlin Document Center (hereafter cited as BDC), Personalakte Schulz.

54. Quoted by Lohse, "Der Fall Strasser," AFZ Hamburg, 18.

55. Egner, "Verzerrungen der Erinnerung an Straßers Rücktritt," *Landshuter Zeitung*, 25 Jan. 2006, in Sammlung Egner, IfZ Munich, Bestand ED 911, 1/41.

56. The text of Strasser's remarks is to be found in Lohse, "Der Fall Strasser," AFZ Hamburg, 20–22.

57. Strasser to Hitler, 8 December 1932, Harvard University Archives, Brüning Papers, Acc. 19098, Box 4, Folder 24. The handwritten draft of Strasser's letter can be found in Alexander Dimitrios, *Weimar und der Kampf gegen "rechts:" Eine politische Biographie*, 3 vols. in 4 (Ulm: Schulz, 2009), 3:306–11. For further information on Strasser's motives, see his letter to Curt Korn, 21 January 1933, IfZ Munich, NL Korn (F28), 1/88. The author would like to thank Martin Großmann of the Institut für Zeitgeschichte for having provided him with a copy of this letter.

58. Entries in Schulz's diary, 8–9 December 1932, quoted in Dimitrios, *Weimar*, 2:435–37.

59. Egner, "Schwerer Abschied in die politische Abstinenz," *Landshuter Zeitung*, 6 February 2006, in Sammlung Egner, IfZ Munich, Bestand ED 911, 1/42.

60. Sefton Delmer, *Trail Sinister: An Autobiography*, 2 vols. (London: Secker and Warburg, 1961–62), 1:168–70.

61. For example, see the text of Hitler's remarks at a special meeting of the state inspectors, 8 December 1932, as recorded in Lohse, "Der Fall Strasser," AFZ Hamburg, 25–28, as well as the entry for 9 December 1932, in *Goebbels Tagebücher*, ed. Fröhlich, , Teil 1, Bd. 2/III, 77–78.

62. For example, see Schulz to Lehmann, 12 June 1933, BA Berlin, NS 26/1375.

63. See Schleicher's remarks at a meeting of the Reichswehr command, [13–15] December 1932, BA-MA Freiburg, MSg 1/1667/28–32, reprinted in Thilo Vogelsang, "Neue Dokumente zur Geschichte der Reichswehr 1930–1933," *Vierteljahrshefte für Zeitgeschichte* 2 (1954): 426–30.

64. For the text of Schleicher's radio address, see "Die Aufgaben und die Lage der Reichswehr," 26 July 1932, BA-MA Freiburg, RH 12–5/43.

65. Kurt von Schleicher, *Das Programm der Regierung: Rundfunkrede des Reichskanzlers vom 15. Dezember 1932* (Berlin: Reichszentrale für Heimatsdienst, 1932), 3–5.

66. On the situation within the NSDAP, see Dietrich Orlow, *The History of the Nazi Party, 1919–1933* (Pittsburgh, PA: University of Pittsburgh Press, 1969), 287–98, and Wolfgang Horn, *Führerideologie und Parteiorganisation in der NSDAP* (Düsseldorf: Droste Verlag, 1972), 369–78.

67. For example, see the summary of a letter from Reupke to Strasser, 9 December 1932, in the records of the Oberstes Parteigericht der NSDAP, BDC, Personalakte Reupke.

68. Entry in Schulz's diary, 3 January 1933, quoted in Dimitrios, *Weimar*, 2:738–39.

69. Entry in Schulz's diary, 4 January 1933, ibid., 2:739.
70. Entry in Schulz's diary, 6 January 1933, ibid., 2:739.
71. Marcks to Kähler, 8 January 1933, reprinted in Otto Jacobsen, *Erich Marcks: Soldat und Gelehrter* (Göttingen, n.d. [1971]), 57.
72. In this respect, see Wilhelm to Schleicher, 13 December 1932, BA-MA Freiburg, NL Schleicher, 23/10–19, and Hörauf to Wilhelm, 21 and 23 December 1932, and 13 and 21 January 1933, ibid., 46–52, 58–58a.
73. For the best scholarly analysis of this meeting, see Heinrich Muth, "Das 'Kölner Gespräch' am 4. Januar 1933," *Geschichte in Wissenschaft und Unterricht* 37 (1986): 463–80, 529–41, and Henry Ashby Turner Jr., *Hitler's Thirty Days to Power: January 1933* (Reading, MA: Addison-Wesley, 1996), 37–47.
74. For Schleicher's reaction to the meeting between Papen and Hitler, see his remarks at a press conference, 10 January 1933, IfZ Munich, NL Schäffer, 33/16–18.
75. Entry in Schulz's diary, 12 January 1933, quoted in Dimitrios, *Weimar*, 2:739.
76. Schleicher's comments at a ministerial conference, 16 January 1933, BA, R 43 I, 1459/4. What Schleicher proposed was perfectly consistent with the strategy recommended by Franz Hörauf, Schleicher's source of information on developments within the NSDAP. See Hörauf to Crown Prince Wilhelm, 13 December 1932, BA-MA Freiburg, NL Schleicher, 23/10–10a.
77. For example, see Reupke to Strasser, 28 and 21 January 1933, records of the Oberstes Parteigericht der NSDAP, BDC, Personalakte Reupke.
78. In this respect, see the affidavits that Brüning provided for Elbrechter, 10 January 1953, Harvard University Archives, HUGFP 93.10, Box 8, Folder 20, and Schulz, 17 January 1952, ibid., Box 36, Folder 10.
79. Entry in Schulz's diary, 19 January 1933, quoted in Dimitrios, *Weimar*, 2:739–40.
80. On Strasser's dilemma, see also Lohse, "Der Fall Strasser," AFZ Hamburg.
81. Papen's efforts in this regard have been convincingly reconstructed in the recent monograph by Rainer Orth, *"Der Amtssitz der Opposition"? Politik und Staatsumbaupläne im Büro des Stellvertreters des Reichskanzlers in den Jahren 1933–1934* (Cologne, Weimar, and Vienna: Böhlau-Verlag, 2016), 256–62.
82. For further details, see Bernd Hoppe, "Von Schleicher zu Hitler: Dokumente zum Konflikt zwischen dem Reichslandbund und der Regierung Schleicher in den letzten Monaten der Weimarer Republik," *Vierteljahrshefte für Zeitgeschichte* 45 (1997): 629–57, esp. 645–51.
83. Wilhelm to Schleicher, 13 January 1933, with enclosure, BA-MA Freiburg, NL Schleicher, 23/49–52.
84. Schleicher's comments at a ministerial conference, 16 January 1933, BA Berlin, R 43 I, 1459/1–9.
85. The alternatives Schleicher was considering were outlined in a memo dated 20 January 1933 from the defense ministry that was attached to the minutes of the ministerial conference, 16 January 1933, BA Berlin, R 43 I, 1459/15–17.
86. Memorandum on Hindenburg's audience with Schleicher, 23 January 1933, BA Berlin, R 601, 405/572–73.

87. In this respect, see the entry in the diary of Heinrich Gaertner, 26 January 1933, in the Politisches Archiv des Auswärtigen Amts, Berlin, R 26698.
88. On the final stages of the negotiations that culminated in Hitler's appointment as chancellor, see Winkler, *Weimar*, 378–94, and Turner, *Hitler's Thirty Days*, 109–61.
89. On this meeting, see Hammerstein's memorandum of 28 January 1935, BA-MA Freiburg, NL Hammerstein, 2/3–6, and Bussche-Ippenburg, "Aktenvermerk," 7 April 1951, BA-MA Freiburg, NL Busche-Ippenburg, 3. There are conflicting accounts between these two sources as to whether the meeting took place on 26 or 27 January or—what is the more likely possibility—whether there were in fact two meetings, the first of which was between Hammerstein and Hindenburg and the second of which also included Busche-Ippenburg.
90. Memorandum on Hindenburg's audience with Schleicher, 28 January 1933, BA Berlin, R 601, 405/573–74. See also the entries in the diary of Schwerin von Krosigk, 25–28, 1933, IfZ Munich, NL Schwerin-Krosigk, Zs/A-20, 4/12–14.
91. Busche-Ippenburg to Ott, 30 January 1951, IfZ Munich, NL Ott, ZS/A-32/12.
92. Entry in Quaatz's diary, 17 January 1933, BA Koblenz, NL Quaatz, 17. For further details, see Larry Eugene Jones, "'The Greatest Stupidity of My Life': Alfred Hugenberg and the Formation of the Hitler Cabinet, January 1933," *Journal of Contemporary History* 27 (1992): 63–87.
93. On Blomberg's appointment, see Kirstin A. Schäfer, *Werner von Blomberg—Hitlers erster Feldmarschall: Eine Biographie* (Paderborn: Ferdinand Schöningh, 2006), 97–100.

Bibliography

Becker, Josef. "Zur Politik der Wehrmachtabteilung in der Regierungskrise 1926/27." *Vierteljahrshefte für Zeitgeschichte* 14 (1966): 69–78.
Berghahn, Volker R. "Die Harzburger Front und die Kandidatur Hindenburgs für die Reichspräsidentenwahlen 1932." *Vierteljahrshefte für Zeitgeschichte* 13 (1965): 64–82
Bracher, Karl Dietrich. *Die Auflösung der Weimarer Republik: Eine Studie des Machtverfalls in der Demokratie*, 3rd ed. Villingen-Schwarzwald: Ring-Verlag, 1960.
Breitman, Richard. "On German Social Democracy and General Schleicher 1932–33." *Central European History* 9 (1976): 352–78.
Brüning, Heinrich. *Memoiren 1918–1934*. Stuttgart: Deutsche Verlags-Anstalt, 1970.
Carsten, Francis L. *The Reichswehr and Politics, 1918–1933*. Oxford: Oxford University Press, 1966.
Delmer, Sefton. *Trail Sinister: An Autobiography*, 2 vols. London: Secker and Warburg, 1961–62.
Dimitrios, Alexander. *Weimar und der Kampf gegen "rechts": Eine politische Biographie*, 3 vols. in 4. Ulm: Schulz, 2009.

Fröhlich, Elke, ed. *Die Tagebücher von Joseph Goebbels*, Teil 1, Bd. 2/II. Munich: J. P. Saur, 2004.

Grothe, Ewald, ed. *Carl Schmitt—Ernst Rudolf Huber: Briefwechsel 1926–1981; Mit ergänzenden Materialien*. Berlin: Duncker and Humblot, 2014.

Hayes, Peter. "'A Question Mark with Epaulettes'? Kurt von Schleicher and Weimar Politics." *Journal of Modern History* 52 (1980): 35–65.

Hoch, Anton, and Hermann Weiß. "Die Erinnerungen des Generalobersten Wilhelm Adam." In *Miscellanea: Festschrift für Helmut Krausnick zum 75. Geburtstag*, edited by Wolfgang Benz, 32–62. Stuttgart: Deutsche Verlags-Anstalt, 1980.

Hoppe, Bernd. "Von Schleicher zu Hitler: Dokumente zum Konflikt zwischen dem Reichslandbund und der Regierung Schleicher in den letzten Monaten der Weimarer Republik." *Vierteljahrshefte für Zeitgeschichte* 45 (1997): 629–57.

Horn, Wolfgang. *Führerideologie und Parteiorganisation in der NSDAP*. Düsseldorf: Droste Verlag, 1972.

Jacobsen, Otto. *Erich Marcks: Soldat und Gelehrter*. Göttingen, n.d. [1971].

Jahn, Peter, ed. *Die Gewerkschaften in der Endphase der Republik 1930–1933*. Quellen zur Geschichte der deutschen Gewerkschaftsbewegung im 20. Jahrhundert, vol. 4. Cologne: Bund-Verlag, 1988,

Jasper, Gotthard. *Die gescheiterte Zähmung: Wege zur Machtergreifung Hitlers 1930–1934*. Frankfurt a.M.: Suhrkamp Verlag, 1986.

Jones, Larry Eugene. "'The Greatest Stupidity of My Life': Alfred Hugenberg and the Formation of the Hitler Cabinet, January 1933." *Journal of Contemporary History* 27 (1992): 63–87.

——. *Hitler versus Hindenburg: The 1932 Presidential Elections and the End of the Weimar Republic*. Cambridge: Cambridge University Press, 2016.

Muth, Heinrich. "Schleicher und die Gewerkschaften 1932: Ein Quellenproblem." *Vierteljahrshefte für Zeitgeschichte* 29 (1981): 189–215.

——. "Das 'Kölner Gespräch' am 4. Januar 1933." *Geschichte in Wissenschaft und Unterricht* 37 (1986): 463–80, 529–41.

Orlow, Dietrich. *The History of the Nazi Party, 1919–1933*. Pittsburgh, PA: University of Pittsburgh Press, 1969.

Orth, Rainer. *"Der Amtssitz der Opposition"? Politik und Staatsumbaupläne im Büro des Stellvertreters des Reichskanzlers in den Jahren 1933–1934*. Cologne, Weimar, and Vienna: Böhlau-Verlag, 2016.

Pyta, Wolfram. "Die Staatsnotstandsplannung unter den Regierungen Papen und Schleicher." In *Die deutsche Staatskrise 1930–1933*, edited by Heinrich August Winkler, 155–82. Munich: Oldenbourg, 1992.

——. "Verfassungsumbau, Staatsnotstand und Querfront: Schleichers Versuche zur Fernhaltung Hitlers von der Reichskanzlerschaft August 1932 bis Januar 1933." In *Gestaltung des Politischen: Festschrift für Eberhard Kolb*, edited by Wolfram Pyta and Ludwig Richter, 173–97. Berlin: Duncker and Humblot, 1998.

——. "Vorbereitungen für den militärischen Ausnahmezustand unter Papen/ Schleicher." *Militärgeschichtliche Mitteilungen* 51 (1992): 385–428.

——. *Hindenburg: Herrschaft zwischen Hohenzollern und Hitler*. Berlin: Siedler Verlag, 2007.

Schäfer, Kirstin A. *Werner von Blomberg—Hitlers erster Feldmarschall: Eine Biographie.* Paderborn: F. Schöningh, 2006.

Schildt, Axel. *Militärdiktatur mit Massenbasis? Die Querfrontkonzeption der Reichswehrführung um General von Schleicher am Ende der Weimarer Republik.* Frankfurt a.M. and New York: Campus Verlag, 1981.

Schleicher, Kurt von. *Das Programm der Regierung: Rundfunkrede des Reichskanzlers vom 15. Dezember 1932.* Berlin: Reichszentrale für Heimatsdienst, 1932.

Strenge, Irene. *Kurt von Schleicher: Politik im Reichswehrministerium am Ende der Weimarer Republik.* Berlin: Duncker and Humblot, 2006.

Treviranus, Gottfried Reinhold. *Das Ende von Weimar: Heinrich Brüning und seine Zeit.* Düsseldorf and Vienna: Econ-Verlag, 1968.

Turner, Henry Ashby, Jr., *Hitler's Thirty Days to Power: January 1933.* Reading, MA: Addison-Wesley, 1996.

——. "The Myth of Chancellor von Schleicher's *Querfront* Strategy." *Central European History* 41 (2008): 673–82.

Vogelsang, Thilo. "Neue Dokumente zur Geschichte der Reichswehr 1930–1933." *Vierteljahrshefte für Zeitgeschichte* 2 (1954): 426–30.

——. *Reichswehr, Staat und NSDAP: Beiträge zur Deutschen Geschichte 1930–1932.* Stuttgart: Deutsche Verlags-Anstalt, 1962.

 2

AUSNAHMEZUSTAND, STAATSNOTSTANDSPLAN, AND ERMÄCHTIGUNGSGESETZ
Reappraising Carl Schmitt's Political Constitutionalism and the Demise of Weimar

Joseph W. Bendersky

In his postwar commentary, Carl Schmitt described his *Legalität und Legitimität* (1932) as "a despairing attempt to rescue the presidential system, the last chance of the Weimar constitution," from a jurisprudence that would permit the destruction of that system through legal democratic means. Moreover, he asserted that during Weimar's final crisis he had "never engaged in the prattle about a *Staatsnotstand*."[1] In the scholarly atmosphere of the 1950s such statements were almost universally dismissed as mendacious, even shameless, self-exculpations. A Schmitt *Festschrift* created a scandal.[2] The interpretive canon of the era manifested one variant or another of Schmitt as a conservative revolutionary, who undermined Weimar in favor of an authoritarian "New State," justified the 1932 Prussian *Staatsstreich*, and then supported Hitler's seizure of power. Schmitt's writings and activities as Nazi *Kronjurist* were supposedly the apotheosis of his political and legal theory. Such a thinker lacked credibility; his ideas were dismissed as of limited value or inherently dangerous. Forty years of subsequent research, driven by an increasing richness of new documentation, as well as more detached perspectives, has drastically transformed the interpretive landscape of Schmitt scholarship. The former intellectual pariah is now one of the most studied thinkers around the world.[3] Nonetheless, most contentious discussions of Schmitt inevitably pivot toward the few years before and after the Nazi seizure of power.

By now, an abundance of evidence convincingly supports those interpretations encapsulated recently by Reinhard Mehring: "Schmitt rejected handing over power to Hitler" and pursued the presidential system as an instrument to prevent it.[4] Despite such evidence, new variations of the old theme of Schmitt as part of the German "Intelligenz und Bildung" that pursued the "subversion of legal democracy" continue to surface.[5] One still encounters references among major scholars that Schmitt's legal theory led to his "welcoming Hitler's seizure of power."[6] Such lingering views affect the historical record, as well as the intense current debates on Schmitt's thought occurring among scholars in the fields of political, legal, and social theory. This is of particular importance in the Anglophone world where often both the key secondary German research and the extensive archival documentation from Schmitt's papers are either neglected or linguistically inaccessible to scholars and their readership. Although Schmitt's voluminous correspondence and copious diaries (and other archival sources) are essential to understanding the diverse historical and political contexts in which he formulated his ideas, the debates often occur solely on the basis of English translations of his published works from which his alleged political motives and goals are inaccurately extrapolated.[7]

However, even the well-documented literature presenting a more favorable view of Schmitt's role at the end of Weimar lacks clarity on the key issue of the *Staatsnotstandspläne*, the plans for the Hindenburg government to declare a "state of emergency" in 1932 and early 1933. Depicting Schmitt as a central figure in the conceptualization and promotion of such plans, these pioneering studies either overlook or contradict Schmitt's postwar disassociation with any *Staatsnotstand*.[8] This issue is further complicated by the detailed recollections about the plan of Ernst Rudolf Huber, the young jurist who assisted Schmitt at that time. A major historical source on this subject, Huber invoked the term *Notstandsplan*.[9] Indeed, "state of emergency" has been the longstanding standard terminology in the historical literature describing the various proposals of Franz von Papen and Kurt von Schleicher in 1932–33. Yet even a cursory reading of Schmitt's publications and proposals from this period would show that he consistently thought and wrote in terms of *Ausnahmezustand* (state of exception) and not *Notstand*.

Such distinctions are no mere linguistic quibbling. They go to the very core of Schmitt's political and legal thought, as well as the political and constitutional strategy he counseled as Weimar faced its final crises. Interpreting Schmitt's advice to the presidential government in terms of *Staatsnotstand* creates, at a minimum, a crucial misunderstanding and, in its most distorted form, culminates in assertions that the proposals emanating from his theories meant that he advocated the transition from "the rule of law to rule by decree."[10] Here, the truism "the devil is in the details" is more than appropriate. An in-depth inquiry into the specifics and intricacies of Schmitt's writings at the time and his actual advice on the commonly labeled "emergency plans" reveals his struggle to keep the policies and strategies of the presidential system within the confines of both constitutionalism and the popular legitimacy of the

Reich president. These are paradigmatic examples of the very essence of his legal and political thought, as he confronted and attempted to adjust his ideas to the rapidly changing circumstances and dangers of 1930–33. We find a similar desperate effort, though in a much more threatening situation with an increasingly limited scope of potential thought and action, in his analysis of the *Ermächtigungsgesetz*.

Commissarial Dictatorship in an *Ausnahmezustand*

From his earliest writings on the subject during World War I, Schmitt used the concept of *Ausnahmezustand* to indicate an "exceptional situation" requiring extraordinary executive responses to a present danger. The purpose was always the security of the state, preservation of the existing constitutional order, and reestablishment of normalcy within the country. He was categorically clear about the extensive latitude and legal limitations on such executive actions. Under wartime martial law, a military commander could, if a threat demanded it, temporarily suspend constitutional laws or institute *Massnahmen* (temporary measures) required by the situation but not covered by current statutes. A commander could not enact *Gesetze* (laws), as such permanent legal statutes remained the constitutional prerogative of the legislature. Once a crisis was resolved, all *Massnahmen* were nullified and suspended laws reinstated in their original form. Since *Massnahmen* and suspensions were inherently limited to specific actions for a limited period, a commander could never suspend the entire constitutional order, for it was the very legal system that granted him the authority to act to ensure its preservation.[11] In his classic 1921 study *Die Diktatur*, Schmitt formalized this concept into his definition of a "commissarial dictator." Deriving his authority solely from the current constitutional order, a commissar could only act within that constitutional framework, which he had been commissioned to defend. While temporarily instituting "measures" and suspending particular laws, he could not enact laws or suspend the constitution. Schmitt contrasted this "commissarial dictator" with a "sovereign dictatorship" exemplified by the Leninist dictatorship in the Soviet Union (with allusions to Communist aspirations across Europe). The latter sought not to preserve but to eliminate the existing constitutional order in favor of a true constitution; as such, it represented the dramatic transition to an entirely new political and legal system. Schmitt now identified the powers of the Reich president under Article 48 as those of a commissarial dictator, acting temporarily to confront a crisis, thereby defending the existing constitutional order from collapse or destruction. This by no means implied an "absolute form of rule, but an exclusively republican and constitutional method of preserving freedom."[12]

At the constitutionalists' conference in 1924, Schmitt presented his first fully developed analysis of presidential authority under Article 48 as that of a commissarial dictator. Article 48 authorized a president to implement *Massnahmen* and suspend parts of the constitution to confront a serious crisis and reestablish order and security. Most jurists advocated immediate passage of a federal law specifying and limiting presidential action under Article 48 in order to preclude an abuse of such power. Schmitt, however, argued that a president needed extensive powers in an *Ausnahmezustand*; efforts to precisely define and restrict his freedom of action were contrary to that article's spirit. Precise statutory limitations could hinder a president from taking the necessary action to meet unforeseen crises, thereby undermining the very purpose of that constitutional provision. Schmitt also held that a president could suspend more constitutional articles than those delineated in Article 48, if necessitated by the dangers of a particular crisis. Since a president derived his authority from that constitutional system his emergency actions were intended to preserve, his powers and scope of action were not unlimited. All such measures were temporary in time and scope; neither could one alter the constitution. And certain constitutional institutions were immune from infringement or suspension under Article 48: the presidency, Reichstag, and government. The Reichstag retained all of its authority, including that of rescinding emergency decrees, which for Schmitt served as the check on the abuse of presidential power.[13]

Schmitt's interpretation of Article 48 reflected the essence of his entire approach to constitutional theory and practice. A constitution must not be interpreted merely in the abstract, or in terms of the wording of its specific articles. Constitutional interpretation and application must always relate to the realistic "concrete situation." Furthermore, any constitutional provision should be interpreted in relationship to the fundamental principles of the entire constitutional system; in Weimar this meant a republican form of government. For these reasons, even the extensive powers he granted the president remained within the confines of the legality and legitimacy of the Weimar Constitution. Schmitt's interpretation of Article 48 was neither an attempt to institute a reactionary authoritarian government nor an effort by conservative elites to undermine Weimar democracy. Schmitt was emphatic that one could not "abrogate" or "revise the constitution," or "transform the republic into a monarchy" under Article 48.[14] He had introduced this interpretation while Friedrich Ebert, a Social Democratic founder of the republic, was Reich president. Ebert had employed Article 48 on numerous occasions to ensure Weimar's survival during its early years of turmoil. Hugo Preuss, framer of the constitution, concurred that in an *Ausnahmezustand* a president must "retain as much unrestricted freedom to act as possible," and "the constitutional dictator of Article 48 will have to play an even greater role than previously in protecting the Reich and its unity."[15]

Even after Hindenburg assumed the presidency, Schmitt devoted a brief but significant section of the 1927 edition of *Die Diktatur* to the "Distinction of *Staatsnotsrecht*" from the authority of Article 48. *Staatsnotrecht* was the right of a "state to preserve its own existence" in an extreme unforeseen case, as happens in war or other drastic circumstances that could lead to the total collapse of the existing order. It must not be confused with presidential authority under Article 48 because such a response to a *Notstand* occurs beyond constitutional authorization and procedures. Moreover, *Staatsnotrecht* could be invoked by any "state organ" that had the power to act, including the Reich government against a presidential coup. In contrast, all actions under Article 48 derived their legality from the constitution and always remained within its jurisdiction. Thus, Article 48, Schmitt emphasized, contained or implied no aspect of the extraconstitutionality of *Staatsnotrecht*. Schmitt merely mentioned the issue, "rarely discussed in constitutional literature," of whether those acting on behalf of the state in a *Notstand* could suspend or alter the constitutional order. However, he was adamant that "no such right existed under Article 48."[16]

That the Weimar Constitution must be interpreted in light of the "concrete situation" of political realities in which it functioned, as well as the dangers these might pose, was an essential aspect of his constitutional theory. With this in mind, he introduced in 1929 the basic features of his theory that—not the Supreme Court but—the Reich president was the "guardian of the constitution." Elected directly by the people for a seven-year term, the president's popular legitimacy and independent authority allowed him to serve as a stabilizing political force against the volatility of Reichstag party politics. The president was not above other branches of government but firmly embedded in the constitutional system as a "neutral third." He was both the symbolic and actual democratic representative of the German people as a unified whole, in contrast to the individual segments of it exhibited in the divisive and often paralyzing political parties.[17]

Within a year Schmitt's interpretation took on particular importance when the onset of the Great Depression quickly destroyed the economic and political stability of the late 1920s. With the collapse of the Grand Coalition in March 1930 and its replacement by the presidential cabinet of Heinrich Brüning, Schmitt was engaged to provide a *Gutachten* on the constitutionality of issuing financial decrees as emergency measures under Article 48. Following his longstanding latitudinarian interpretation of the constitution and presidential power, Schmitt fully supported the constitutionality of these financial measures as within the legal competence of the president, since the dire economic crisis constituted a serious threat to order and security. Although Schmitt had clearly expanded Article 48 to cover an "economic *Ausnahmezustand*," he was categorically clear that this did not represent a step toward a presidential dictatorship or authoritarian state. "A limitless, uncontrolled competency [of the president] is not being advocated," since the Reichstag could assert its prerogative to suspend any decree. But a Reichstag incapable of exercising its own constitutional obligation to govern "should not be allowed to incapacitate a republican government."[18]

However, the stunning Nazi electoral breakthrough in September 1930 and subsequent Reichstag paralysis significantly transformed the political dynamics of Germany forever. A severely depressed Schmitt felt "a coming catastrophe," even impending "civil war."[19] In this atmosphere of increasing uncertainty and extremism, Schmitt expanded his preliminary thesis on the "guardian of the constitution" into a major theoretical study. This crucial question, he argued, could be properly addressed only in terms of the "concrete constitutional situation" of the time rather than in a purely theoretical and legalistic manner. His interpretation was compelled by "necessity." The Weimar constitutional order, and with it the fate of the German state and nation, was increasingly endangered, on the one hand, by the fratricidal politics of the "pluralistic *Parteienstaat*" and, on the other, by the "inner political neutrality of the state" toward those groups and parties seeking the destruction of the existing order by legal means. Thus, the survival of the Weimar Constitution, and perhaps also the German state itself, depended upon the recognition of, and proper response to, these political perils. He emphasized that a state and constitution could not remain neutral toward threats to their own existence emanating from revolution or manipulation of the democratic constitutional system. The presidency was the one institution constitutionally authorized, and with sufficient popular legitimacy and state power, to fend off an impending Nazi or communist revolution, or complete collapse and civil war. The presidential oath to uphold the constitution obligated the president to defend that system of government against overt and insidious threats to it. His command of the army and authority granted under Article 48 also accorded him the necessary power to meet such threats.[20]

These ideas were the cornerstone of Schmitt's constitutional advice about the presidential system until 1933, and of the warnings he promoted through lectures and publications. While granting the president wide latitude in interpreting the constitution and issuing emergency decrees, Schmitt felt strongly that the legitimacy and political effectiveness of the president depended upon his remaining within the fundamental principles of the constitutional order. For these reasons, Schmitt rejected the authoritarian "New State" visions of the Conservative Revolutionary movement. Events would show, however, that his theories and advice never had the impact he intended on the three presidential chancellors he served. Whether with Brüning, Franz von Papen, or Kurt von Schleicher, Schmitt was a behind-the-scenes advisor whose theories and arguments were used or ignored by the real powerbrokers within the various presidential coteries. Among these circles, Schmitt was closest to Schleicher's aides Majors Erich Marcks and Eugen Ott, as well as State Secretary Johannes Popitz. Schmitt's diaries reveal the deep trust he had in these men, who were among the very few who escaped his cynical deprecations. Above all, Schmitt's constitutional arguments and political advocacy strongly supported the various strategies of the Schleicher circle to prevent the collapse of the government and a Nazi seizure of power.[21]

As the failure of Brüning's chancellorship, the rising strength and violence of the Nazis and Communists, and depths of the Depression created a probability of complete political collapse or civil war, Schmitt foresaw yet another danger for Weimar and the German state. The extraordinary numerical expansion of the Nazi Party and its electoral constituency, together with discussions of coalition governments with Hitler, would, Schmitt feared, open the way for a Nazi legal acquisition of power. Thus, the central thrust of his 1932 *Legalität und Legitimität* warned against this prospect, again offering a counter to it through the popular legitimacy and constitutional authority of the president. No system, he argued, could remain neutral toward its own existence. To allow movements whose expressed goal was the destruction of the constitutional system to acquire power legally was suicidal. Therefore, the president was obligated as "guardian of the constitution," and had the legal authority under Article 48, to take action against antidemocratic forces. This included the right to deny such forces the "equal chance" to acquire power legally. Schmitt explicitly focused on the Nazis and Communists, arguing that their legality or illegality should not be determined by isolated individual constitutional articles (e.g., freedom of speech or assembly) but rather from the perspective of the continued existence of the entire constitutional system. A narrow literal constitutional interpretation, with "neutrality" toward the nature and objectives of anticonstitutional parties, would open the way for groups to manipulate the democratic process in order to achieve any "aspired goal … Soviet Republic, National Socialist Reich … monarchy of the old style … and another constitution." Schmitt specifically cited the presidential decree of 13 April 1932, which banned Nazi storm troopers and SS members from wearing uniforms and insignia in public and from organized activity in the public arena, as an example of the necessary and legal action he endorsed.[22]

Ausnahmezustand or Papen's *Staatsnotstandsplan*, August 1932

Shortly after completing his book on 10 July 1932, Schmitt was surprised by news of Papen's Prussian coup of 20 July, which he learned about from reading the press.[23] The Papen government then engaged him to defend its Prussian action before the Supreme Court. Although unsympathetic with Papen's goal of undermining Social Democratic power, Schmitt, in agreement with the Schleicher coterie, believed the action was necessary in order to prevent civil war and the NSDAP from seizing power in Prussia and with it legal control over the large and powerful state police.[24] Behind all the legalities and rhetoric, he perceived the real question as the "National Socialists and Communist Party." It would be suicide for the Weimar constitutional order, he argued, "to give the equal chance to a party which is the enemy of the state."[25] The Weimar electorate, however, provided the NSDAP and KPD the majority in the Reichstag elections of 31 July. Germany now faced the possibility of total paralysis. The two radical parties could obstruct formation of any parliamentary majority while simultaneously impeding the presidential system by rescinding all emergency decrees.

Papen's various proposals for dissolving the newly elected Reichstag without scheduling new elections, revising the constitution in the interim, and possibly banning the NSDAP and KPD are well known. However, Schmitt's involvement in such schemes remained unknown until they were revealed by his assistant Ernst Rudolf Huber at a 1986 conference following Schmitt's death. Huber had already briefly described the general outlines of this revelation in a 1961/62 unpublished memoir. Secretly summoned to Berlin by Schmitt in "August" 1932, Huber was met by Ott and other officers and taken to Schmitt's apartment to work out the details of legal documents justifying a Papen-Schleicher plan to ban the NSDAP, arrest its leaders, and "put an end to this entire nightmare by force." These also included a presidential appeal to the German people justifying these actions. But the dissolution of the Reichstag on 12 September, with new elections scheduled for 6 November, had deferred any such plans, though for months Huber anxiously anticipated their implementation. Significantly, in this memoir Huber never even alluded to the concept of *Notstand*, instead referring only to "emergency decrees" as "*Massnahmen*" or measures under Article 48, all of which were quite consistent with Schmitt's concept of *Ausnahmezustand* and his postwar disclaimer on *Notstand*.[26] It was only in his 1986 paper that Huber invoked the commonly used term *Notstandsplan*. But the content of Huber's presentation as well as subsequent conference discussion regarding the *Notstandsplan* clearly indicated that all such actions were envisaged in Schmittian terms of *Ausnahmezustand* based on Article 48 and within, not in disregard of, the existing constitutional framework.[27] Although the Schmitt-Huber correspondence corroborates Huber's meeting with Ott in Berlin, no other documentation has survived substantiating his memory of the details of the plan.[28] There is no archival copy of the Papen-Schleicher emergency plan, and Huber's copies of what he and Schmitt had composed were lost during the war.

Interrelated with the *Notstandsplan* is the question of Schmitt's involvement in attempts at reactionary constitutional revision promoted by Papen and Interior Minister Wilhelm von Gayl, which they had revived after dissolving the Reichstag on 12 September. Since such plans were inherently inconsistent with Schmitt's constitutional theory and his political assessments of the crisis situation, they caused him much consternation. In August, Huber had unsuccessfully attempted to raise the issue of constitutional revision with him, but Schmitt was preoccupied with the immediate situation, not the future.[29] When on 25 September Ott informed him that Papen wanted a draft of a constitution, Schmitt noted he was "terrified by the task, but felt secure and competent in dealing with state law." A few nights later Schmitt wrote that he was "in despair and tired, ridiculous that I am supposed to write a new constitution, then hopeful again." Yet on 4 October press reports that the government already had a draft of a new constitution caught him by surprise. "I know nothing about this," he jotted in his diary, "I feel ridiculous." If it were not for Ott, he "would simply jump off with a great weight." On 2 November, Ott informed him that the constitutional question would be postponed for the future.[30] It is unknown whether Schmitt ever did compose any constitutional revisions. No documents exist of that nature; nor are there references to it beyond these brief diary entries, showing great reluctance on his part. There are no inklings of what revisions might entail or the process for instituting these. In *Legalität und Legitimität* that he published in August, Schmitt had taken a strong stand against fundamental constitutional change through Article 48 or a two-thirds amending vote under Article 76. He had long argued that only the German people could alter the democratic nature of the constitution that they had inaugurated in 1919. Whatever Schmitt might have tried to compose under Papen's directives, he did so with much trepidation and obviously was unable to bring it to fruition. To the extent that he attempted anything on constitutional revision, Schmitt was acting as a lawyer engaged for a particular task in the same way he defended Papen's government before the Supreme Court. In that trial he also felt caught in a "ridiculous" predicament over which he almost resigned.[31] Within a few days of Papen's dismissal on 17 November, Schmitt again publicly warned against "new constitutions" and "constitutional experiments." With the popular legitimacy and legality of the president based upon the existing constitution, Schmitt stated, "It is better first of all not to establish authority through new institutions ... [but rather] the government should utilize all constitutional means, but all constitutional means, at its disposal."[32]

Schleicher's appointment as chancellor on 3 December greatly bolstered the hopes of Schmitt and Huber about an anticipated decisive action to restore order and fend off a Nazi seizure of power. "If Schleicher is what we hope him to be," Huber wrote to Schmitt, "... then the general will find you indispensable." Schmitt responded that the "Prussian general staff is the most marvelous collective in the world; it has survived defeat and victory, but now faces the new task of saving the Reich."[33] Nonetheless, Schmitt soon became chronically depressed through December and January as he watched the faltering of Schleicher's various strategies for outmaneuvering the Nazis while attempting to restore stability through negotiations with the antagonistic political factions and economic recovery programs. During these months Schmitt remained in close contact with Marcks and Ott, who still consulted him on constitutional matters, especially regarding proposals for revived emergency plans.[34] Aware of the Papen-Hitler intrigues to oust him, Schleicher proposed such a plan to Hindenburg in late January 1933.

Schmitt's Constitutional Alternative to *Staatsnotstand*, January 1933

The evidentiary gap regarding the August 1932 emergency plan makes the archival documents relevant to this January 1933 plan crucial for understanding Schmitt's actual constitutional and political position. They go to the very heart of his thinking and his appraisal of the "concrete situation." Nonetheless, these documents have received insufficient attention in Anglophone discussions of Schmitt and the collapse of Weimar. Before the revelatory documentary discoveries in the Schmitt Nachlass in the 1990s, published and expertly analyzed by Lutz Berthold, only one document was known. A two-page memorandum from the defense ministry dated 20 January 1933 outlined the advantages and disadvantages of three alternatives for Schleicher maintaining the chancellorship and dealing with an intransigent Reichstag dominated by Nazis and Communists.[35]

The first alternative would dissolve the Reichstag before an impending no-confidence vote and suspend new elections, with the advantage of excluding parliament. But the opposition would declare this a breach of the constitution and the government illegal; with the Center Party joining the resistance, the government would need to defend itself against party agitation. An alternative would be the forced adjournment of the Reichstag on the grounds of its incapacity to govern and that new elections would unlikely change the party makeup of that body. This approach would provide a breathing space while avoiding the legal questions and political opposition of postponing elections. But a forced adjournment also deviated from the constitution; strong resistance from the NSDAP, Center, and democratic parties would be expected. Also avoiding a Reichstag dissolution and new elections, the third alternative proposed not recognizing a no-confidence vote of the paralyzed Reichstag and having the government remain in power through presidential authority. The justification was that a "negative no confidence vote" should not be allowed to overthrow a necessary and viable government while the Reichstag could not provide a governing alternative in such a dire political and economic situation. More constitutionally defensible, keeping the Reichstag in session would continually expose the incompetence of the political parties to the entire population. The disadvantage was that the parties could use the Reichstag as a forum for agitation, though this would be less dangerous once the parties lost the power of a no-confidence vote. If serious conflict developed between the parties and the government, the alternative of a Reichstag dissolution still remained an option for the government.[36]

As it turns out, that defense ministry memorandum was a condensed version of the six-page document discovered in Schmitt's papers that was definitely inspired and probably composed by Schmitt. Schmitt had conveyed this to Schleicher probably in mid-January through the historian Horst Michael, a young conservative activist whom Schmitt had often used as a liaison with the coterie around Hindenburg and Schleicher. Although this document does not specifically identify Schmitt as its author, it was from its opening statement Schmittian to the core: "How can one preserve a viable presidential government against the obstruction of a Reichstag unwilling to function, with the goal 'to protect the constitution'?"[37] Unlike the defense ministry memorandum version, Schmitt categorized the options as "two alternatives," which he analyzed meticulously in terms of their constitutionality and realistic political feasibility in the "concrete situation" of January 1933. He warned that the first alternative—forced adjournment or Reichstag dissolution with suspended elections—posed a "maximum of constitutional violation." The "milder way" of nonrecognition of a no-confidence vote required a "minimal constitutional violation" and an "authentic interpretation" of Article 54, the relevant constitutional provision.[38]

Schmitt was categorically clear that there were "hardly any constitutional arguments (*Staatsnotstand*, etc.)" supporting the first option. Therefore, this approach would rest solely upon three "sound political arguments," which he described very briefly. A Reichstag incapable of functioning while making it impossible for the government to work violated its constitutional obligation, engaged in constitutional sabotage, and disrupted public order and security. Two previous attempts had already proven that new elections would not alter the makeup of the Reichstag, and the economy required tranquility. He then juxtaposed twelve detailed counterarguments that "considerably weakened" these political arguments and would delegitimize the government in the eyes of the people by making it appear that "the government resorted to a *Notstandsverfahren*" merely to save itself. Indeed, Schmitt interjected, "a no confidence vote … is not a *Staatsnotstand*." The exclusion of the Reichstag went beyond the necessity required by the situation; it would cut off government contact with the representatives of the people; the Reichstag's incapacity to function could no longer be demonstrated; and the Center Party would strongly oppose it (unless it was included in the government). This option was "the *ultima ratio*" after exhausting all other means, and then used only with a specific date pledged for the Reichstag to reconvene. It also contradicted Schleicher's declaration against the advisability of a dictatorship, "robbing him of his best moral position." It would create unforeseeable outcomes and more instability than necessary while disrupting the economy and the economic recovery program that would determine the government's success or failure. This option "goes far beyond the constitutional-political goal."[39]

Any deviation from the constitution, Schmitt emphasized, must be founded upon constitutional grounds, compelling circumstances, and the consent of public opinion. "This goal is not the transfer of popular representation to the executive ... but a strengthening of the executive" through "an authentic interpretation of the power of a no confidence vote" under Article 54. If the current government followed the second option, Schmitt proposed the Reichstag would be incapable of undermining it with a "negative no confidence vote." This option was a "sensible corrective of a constitutional article through which the constitution would be saved and restored without excluding popular representation" by adjourning or dissolving the Reichstag. It was a necessary constitutional-political path that could acquire widespread public support, avoiding the danger of veering widely away from the goal of protecting the constitutional order. By refusing to recognize an obstructionist "negative no confidence vote," the government could remain in power, demonstrating its competence while exposing the incapacity of the Reichstag. Moreover, it forced the "opposition" to remain within the bounds of legal procedures. So long as the Reichstag remained in session, the parties could not engage in unrestricted agitation but would be forced to confront each other in that institution. The public would witness this party paralysis, in contrast to the government's constructive activities. It would preclude the Center Party's objections to the first alternative and "clearly differentiate itself from the *Notstandsverfahren* of the German Nationalists." Consistent with "Schleicher's declaration against a dictatorship," the second option would likewise demonstrate his true motives.[40]

Schmitt understood the potential problems that could arise with the second option if the Reichstag agitated against the government through "dangerous laws" and resolutions against the use of Article 48 or adherence to a literal interpretation of Article 54. But he quickly countered these objections. Party agitation would be much worse outside the confines of the Reichstag, and one could anticipate "dangerous laws," with Reichstag dissolution always an option. With legal opinions supporting the right and obligation of a functioning government to remain in power after a negative no-confidence vote, the position of the government would also be significantly strengthened if the Reich president explicitly endorsed the government. Schmitt invoked the metaphor of option two as a cauldron in which the opponent's position could be exposed and bombarded while the government remained under cover.[41]

Schmitt concluded with an implementation strategy (*Stichworte*) involving a "Political Proclamation of the Reich President" read by the chancellor after a no-confidence vote. The proclamation Schmitt composed blamed the plight of the German people directly on the Reichstag's failure to fulfill its constitutional obligations, necessitating the president to govern by emergency decrees since 1930. Since recent attempts at forming a majority government had again failed, it would be "disastrous" if this paralyzed Reichstag would incapacitate a functioning government, "arbitrarily rescind my emergency decrees," and in such "irresponsible manner leave the most important segments of the economy and finance in a lawless situation." His responsibility to the German people would no longer allow the president to leave their ordered public life unprotected against political party strife. His "constitutional oath" obligated him to "safeguard the constitution of the Reich," which he would do through all "necessary measures." Another dissolution of the Reichstag and new elections would only cause further disruption of domestic peace and the economy. And the current paralyzed Reichstag did not have the right to interfere with these "necessary measures" or remove an effective government. A Reichstag that failed to meet its own constitutional obligations and attempted to prevent a government from conducting necessary work was one that "I no longer consider a popular representative in the sense of the Reich constitution."[42]

Schmitt's handwritten "*Stichworte* for Political Argumentation" supplementing the presidential proclamation is a distilled version of his theoretical standpoints and political advice since the inception of the presidential system, as elaborated throughout 1932. He addressed the "abuse of legal" rights and procedures by those political parties utilizing them as "poisonous weapons" and "tactical instruments" to undermine the state and constitution. Since no state or constitution could survive in such an atmosphere, the government's current use of Article 48 amounted to a "kind of self-defense" in which it was compelled to invoke all of its legal options against this "abuse of legality." Schmitt compared such party assaults under the cover of legality to foreign affairs where military force against a weaker power is used without a declaration of war in order to avoid being designated as a peacebreaker. With implicit reference to the Nazis and Communists, Schmitt warned of certain parties, though enemies of each other, that would unite in a no-confidence vote so as to undermine parliamentary government itself. In this "poisoned atmosphere" it was the government's mission to regain a position where a meaningful order—based upon law and the constitution—could be reinstituted against such assaults. In this regard, the Reich president was both the "Guardian of the Constitution" and the "Guardian of the Fundamental Existence of the People and the Reich" against such "pathological conditions."[43]

In eschewing a *Staatsnotstand* Schmitt was not abandoning the use of force to suppress the Nazis and Communists when necessary. Such potential suppression was inherent in his concept of denying the "equal chance" to anticonstitutional parties attempting to acquire the power of the state through the legal democratic process. And he had consistently supported presidential measures under Article 48 against both extremist parties. However, he understood the imperative of keeping all strategies and actions within the confines of legality, thus his emphasis on "preserving the constitution" that permeated all alternative plans and political argumentation reinforcing them. The entire presidential system rested upon the legal authority granted by the constitution and the popular legitimacy of Hindenburg. Possession of such legal authority also conferred control over the power of the state, or what Schmitt had called the "political premiums" of incumbency (e.g., Article 48, army, state bureaucracy), all of which were not only vital to deal with the current crisis but were essential to containing and, if necessary, suppressing the NSDAP and KPD. If the government resorted to a *Staatsnotstandsplan* it risked losing the constitutional foundation for its existence and with it the sanction for its actions bestowed by the possession of "legality." As Schmitt affirmed in his postwar statement on *Staatsnotstand*, he had rejected that recourse, because "with it the legality of the constitution would only be surrendered to its enemies." As the government lost the sanction of legality, the radical parties, though intent upon destroying the entire legal system, would assume the stance as defenders of it.[44]

Schmitt added that in January 1933 he "was of the opinion that the legal possibilities, bound up with the premiums of the legal possession of power, were still in no way exhausted."[45] In addition to the popular legitimacy enjoyed by Hindenburg, the presidential government also retained such "political premiums" as the power of the state apparatus, army, and police. And all of Schmitt's political assessments and constitutional advice presumed that Schleicher would remain chancellor in control of this state and military power. Schmitt believed it essential that Schleicher retain this control during the election period in the event of a Reichstag dissolution. Otherwise, the presidential system would abandon the "political premiums" to other forces, which most likely would use the sanction of legality and possession of state power for its particular party interests, or even to destroy the entire constitutional system.

Unknown to Schmitt, as his constitutional-political document worked its way through the Schleicher circle, ultimately abridged into the defense ministry memorandum, it lost not only much of its original detail but also the saliency and imperative of his arguments regarding legality. The defense ministry memorandum neglected entirely Schmitt's emphasis on the popular legitimacy of the Reich president; it never even alluded to Schmitt's core focus on defending the constitution. Schmitt was also unaware that Ott, perhaps in consultation with Schleicher, had rejected his critique of a *Staatsnotstand* and had on 20 January endorsed "Option 1" — Reichstag dissolution and suspended elections.[46] When Schmitt had lunch with Ott on 26 January, he apparently did not yet know that three days earlier Schleicher had already attempted to convince Hindenburg to dissolve the Reichstag without new elections. Schmitt was surprised when a "hopeful [Ott] wanted to push ahead with dissolution." Schmitt jotted in his diary that Ott "did not want to listen to what I had to say, found it too theoretical, and had no time for such things. I feel pushed aside."[47]

The following night a despondent Schmitt met with an equally depressed Marcks, who informed him that the "Hindenburg Myth is over," that Schleicher would resign and be replaced by either Papen or Hitler. To Schmitt, this was a "horrible situation." Over the next few days, Schmitt was "fearful of coming political events."[48] Hitler's fateful appointment on 30 January meant that the various Schleicher strategies and maneuverings to contain the Nazis had failed. All of Schmitt's arguments against allowing Hitler the "equal chance" to acquire power legally and thereby assume the mantle of legality and the "political premiums" of the power of the state had been ignored. More immediately, it would allow Hitler, not Schleicher, to control the conditions of the upcoming Reichstag elections and use the power of the state against his opponents, both communist and democratic. Schmitt jotted in his diary: "Furious over the stupid, ludicrous Hitler."[49] Schmitt shared Marcks's despair over the "end of the last German legend and the political passivity of Hindenburg." Seriously concerned over his personal future, as well as that of Germany, Schmitt considered "an escape plan" to Switzerland or Italy, "to disappear into nothingness."[50] On 20 March, Chief of Staff Kurt von Hammerstein, an ardent anti-Nazi who had warned Hindenburg against a Hitler chancellorship, explained the details of that appointment to Schmitt and Ott. Schmitt said to Hammerstein, "There is only one kind of death for a government, suicide."[51]

The Enabling Act as *Staatsnotrecht* and "Supra-Legality"

Three days later, the Reichstag passed the Enabling Act, confirming Schmitt's prognosis that Weimar was indeed committing suicide. That very day Otto Liebmann, editor of the *Deutsche Juristen-Zeitung*, requested an article from Schmitt on this act, which he completed the next day, and Liebmann rushed into print.[52] When Schmitt declared that act an "expression of the victory of the National Revolution," he was not welcoming the Nazi seizure of power. Instead, he provided a sober and insightful analysis of the magnitude of the political and legal transformation manifested in that constitutional amendment. Schmitt showed far more foresight than those conservatives confident that they could outmaneuver Hitler. He also saw through the illusions of the Catholic Center Party's faith in worthless Nazi promises of guaranteeing basic rights. He did not share the misguided hopes of those reassured that the act granted this extraordinary authority and power to the government for a mere four years. Neither was he convinced by comparisons with earlier experiences with enabling acts during the war and the crises of the early republic, acts that had fulfilled their objectives and then lapsed as the system returned to its former constitutional functionality. Schmitt showed that, in its legal composition, the new Enabling Act was unique. And, in its political implications, it presented a fait accompli of enormous and probably irreversible consequence. That is why he declared the Enabling Act "[a] significant turning-point in constitutional history!"[53]

That act, he argued, differed in three fundamental ways from all previous examples of a parliament delegating such power. First, it created a "new Reich legislator." In addition to the Reichstag, the people, and emergency authority under Article 48, German constitutional law now recognized the "Reich government" (i.e., the cabinet) as a legislative body. Furthermore, that newly created "Reich government legislator" could go beyond instituting temporary "emergency decrees" as all earlier governments had done under previous enabling acts. A revolutionary aspect of the new act was that this "Reich legislator" could, more importantly, pass laws in the "formal legal sense," with all of the permanence that implies.[54] The second unique characteristic of the new law was that it allowed the government not only to infringe upon individual constitutional provisions—as previous enabling acts had done—but also to create constitutional laws that would replace previous ones. The government had thus endowed itself with the power to fundamentally alter the constitution. Although Schmitt did not state so explicitly in this article, he recognized that henceforth no part of the Weimar Constitution was legally immune from radical transformation or destruction. The only exceptions were those constitutional entities specifically excluded from revision under the Enabling Act (e.g., the office of the Reich president).[55]

Finally, the tersely worded new law was not "definable and measurable" by particular content circumscribing its authority, as had been the case with similar acts. On the contrary, the provisions of this act granted the government "unlimited authority for four years." When such undefined authority is considered in conjunction with both the legislative authority and constitutional granting authority of the Reich government, it created a serious difficulty for interpreting this law, as well as for any possibility of constitutional review. Again, though not mentioned in his article but argued in *Legalität und Legitimität*, Schmitt, the realist, was very concerned about the new government legally instituting new laws or constitutional provisions that removed even the time restraint of four years, or the implementation of laws or amendments that politically made such restraints irrelevant.[56]

Schmitt's brief section on the "legal foundations" of the Enabling Act must be read in light of the fact that the process of its passage and its provisions were antithetical to Schmitt's legal theory and his recent advice concerning the presidential system. Against the opinion of almost all Weimar jurists, Schmitt had long ardently held that such fundamental transformation of the constitutional system could not be done through a mere constitutional amendment under Article 76. He had also opposed constitutional change in the midst of the current crisis, as well as cautioned against resorting to *Notstand* alternatives. On 23 March, all those battles were lost. His statements on the act's legality were a fatalistic acquiescence to the de facto political-constitutional realities of its passage. Never revealing any of his reservations, Schmitt addressed its legality in matter-of-fact statements devoid of the analyses in the rest of his article. While never referencing his own theoretical opposition to such a process, Schmitt took a veiled swipe at a major critic of his earlier position on the limits of constitutional change: "The law is based first of all formally on Art. 76 of the Reich Constitution. According to the prevailing interpretation of Art. 76, especially that of [Gerhard] Anschütz, the authority for constitutional change had no limits whatsoever." Thus, no further discussion of the "problem of the limits of Article 76 was necessary." The law was also "an expression of the victory of the National Revolution." Just as the courts had recognized new powers arising from the "collapse of November 1918" they must now consider a "National Revolution" from the same standpoint. Schmitt, however, never specified what he meant by the "National Revolution." At a minimum, he probably thought in terms of the results of the Reichstag elections on 5 March 1933 that provided a Conservative-Nationalist-Nazi majority. Finally, he tersely stated that there existed a "new legal circumstance" in the form of "*Staatsnotrecht,*" as denoted in the title "The Law to Alleviate the Distress [*Not*] of the People and the Reich." Here too, he offered no elaboration or clarification; it was a mere unspoken recognition that the government had moved further in the direction of *Staatsnotstand* than he privately thought was constitutionally justified by either necessity or political prudence.[57]

Previously, the presidential system's deliberations regarding a *Staatsnotstand* were aimed at containing Hitler; now it would be invoked in collaboration with him. The fox was already in the henhouse. The system was in the process of being subverted from within. Schmitt now had to deal with both the reality of the new law, as well as the fact that the Nazis were already wielding extraordinary state power in a variety of ways. The Wilhelmstrasse, he had privately noted, "was full of SA."[58] Thus, even though Schmitt had developed serious reservations about Hindenburg's mental capacity and political judgment, he understood that the president remained the crucial entity in restraining the Nazis. Only Hindenburg had the popular legitimacy, the legal authority, and command of the forces necessary to act as this counterweight. That was also the opinion of Schmitt's close confidant, the Prussian official Johannes Popitz, then serving in the cabinet. The office of the president, backed by the army and state bureaucracy, was the last constitutional instrument to salvage the German state and traditional society from its own suicide and a radical transformation under the Nazis. Therefore, Schmitt's article emphasized the "reserved rights of the Reich president." In contrast to the debatable institutional reserved rights of the Reichstag, all existing presidential authority and powers were explicitly guaranteed within the Enabling Act. Schmitt underscored the most significant of these reserved presidential rights, which were immune from any alteration under the otherwise unlimited law-giving and constitutional-changing prerogatives granted the cabinet under the Enabling Act. These specified "reserved rights" were also those most applicable and necessary to containing the Nazis: "exceptional powers under Article 48, supreme command of the army, the right to appoint officials, dissolve the Reichstag, and appoint and dismiss the Reich chancellor."[59]

Equally important, the extraordinary authority of the Enabling Act was granted specifically to the "existing Reich government." That authority would lapse if that cabinet were "dissolved" or replaced by another one. However, to Schmitt, individual members of the current cabinet did not, in themselves, constitute the "identity" or substance of that body. The removal of specific individuals would, therefore, not signal the dissolution of the cabinet. Schmitt acknowledged that the "political leadership" in the current cabinet was determined by the chancellor. But the "identity" and substance of the existing cabinet was also determined by a series of other defining aspects. Here again, Schmitt intentionally specified these: the trust of the Reich president and the participation and support of those men who received a popular vote of confidence in the plebiscitary election of 5 March. Schmitt also included in the defining characteristics of the cabinet the collaboration of state ministers, citing the two groups with which he was politically and personally connected, the finance and defense ministries. In one of the most important components of his entire analysis of the Enabling Act, one certainly aimed at restraining any further Nazi usurpation of power, Schmitt wrote, "The replacement of these [latter professional ministers] with *Parteileute* would constitute a change in the political character of the current Reich government." How far such change in political leadership of the cabinet would be required before it constituted a change in the cabinet's identity—and thus the loss of its extraordinary powers—was a political question for the future.[60]

Under the circumstances of March 1933, Schmitt continued to accentuate the necessity of "national unity" and "political will." While never explicitly referring to the Nazi Party, and always cloaking his critical attitude in familiar disdain for the "pluralistic *Parteienstaat*," he was clearly rejecting options involving a party line. He concluded his article by noting the enormous tasks and responsibilities for the "German people and their history" involved in the exercise of these new powers. He did not look to Hitler or the Nazi Party. He never had done so. Quite the contrary, now as before, the traditional-minded conservative Schmitt spoke not of the party but of the "renewal" of the "State." Along with this would go the "cleansing and rejuvenation of constitutional law and constitutional theory."[61] It would, however, be a renewal made far more difficult and precarious due to Nazi political strength and popularity. And no matter how he interpreted the Enabling Act, he realized it could potentially undermine not only what was left of Weimar but also the traditional German state with which he identified, as represented by the president, traditional ministers, and the army.

A few days after hastily submitting his article, Schmitt elaborated his thoughts on the relationship between *Staatsnotrecht* and the Enabling Act. Speaking before a conference of legal scholars in Weimar, he argued that *Notrecht* implied the need for the "state" to reestablish a "normal situation" and the "right to defend its own existence." In his diary he identified the subject of his lecture as the "Right of sovereignty and [the] Enabling Act." This question could not be understood in terms of legality and illegality. A state is not only a legality but also a reality ("*faktisch*"); "it is power." Through the National Revolution of the 5 March elections the people bestowed "legitimacy" on the new government in order to "create a normal situation." It was the "triumph of legitimacy over legality, the triumph of facts over pure legalistic validity." Months of discussion about "extra-constitutional *Notstand*," including that of the Center Party and SPD, had taken the country away from the legal path and toward the "sphere of supra-legality." Then the revolutionary Enabling Act conferred "legality" on such "supra-legal" proposals and consequent actions, thus extending the legal foundations of contemporary state life far beyond the Reich constitution. That act had also settled the controversial question of the juridical recognition of a "political *Staatsnotstandsrecht*" by embodying "a rare example of limitless empowerment" that signified an "extraordinary turning point" in the constitutional history of all states. The only legal aspects of the constitution immune from such limitless power were the rights of the Reich president. Otherwise, no matter what legal scholars might argue, the "old legality-state" had been supplanted by the reality of a "Reich government" functioning on the basis of a political leader with the "plebiscitary trust" of the people.[62]

Throughout his lecture, Schmitt referred to the failed, and now irrelevant, constitutional theories of his great adversaries, particularly Gerhard Anschütz, Walter Jellinek, and Richard Thoma. While on the surface Schmitt only critiqued their stand on "supra-legality" and "political *Staatsnotrecht*," he also subtly chided them for their responsibility in bringing constitutionalism to this point. What he could not openly state in light of recent Nazi hegemony was that their legal positivism (with its neutrality toward the legal access to power and insistence on the omnipotence of the legislature's right of unlimited constitutional change) had left the constitution vulnerable to its enemies. They had long ridiculed his political constitutionalism. They had dismissed his conviction that a constitution must be interpreted in light of its fundamental principles, toward which it could not remain neutral. They had rebuffed his theory of the limitation on the Reichstag's right to amend the constitution. In contrast, he had insisted that a constitution be interpreted in terms of the political realities of the "concrete situation." He had urged denying the "equal chance" to anticonstitutional movements. These jurists had denigrated his ideas on the *Ausnahmezustand,* Article 48, and the president as the "guardian of the constitution." Yet to him, these were necessary to the defense of the Weimar state and constitution.[63]

Schmitt was not abandoning law in favor of political power or rule by decree. An accurate assessment of Schmitt's role at the end of Weimar requires an understanding of his distinction between *Ausnahmezustand* and *Staatsnotstand.* Into 1933, he perceived Weimar's final crisis in terms of an *Ausnahmezustand,* not *Staatsnotstand.* His advice to the Schleicher circle regarding a "negative no confidence vote" kept governmental actions within the legality of the constitution and the political legitimacy of the Reich president. When he reluctantly conceded the necessity of a "minimal constitutional violation," it was as a necessary defense against those who would destroy the constitution and the rule of law itself. When this might involve Reichstag adjournment or suspension of elections, he insisted that these must be accompanied by a specified date for reassembly or new elections. In January 1933, even the Social Democratic leader Otto Braun was willing to compromise on the suspension of elections after a Reichstag dissolution.[64] A *Staatsnotstand* Schmitt would concede only as a truly unavoidable *ultima ratio.* Neither this nor a conservative revolutionary "New State" ever constituted a part of his plans. Whether Schleicher and Hindenburg could have played the role Schmitt had hoped remains a point of historical dispute. Neither was the outcome certain if they had heeded his advice. But these would be failures of personality, politics, and an incessantly evolving crisis, not Schmitt's political constitutionalism.

Joseph W. Bendersky is professor of German history at Virginia Commonwealth University and book review editor for *Holocaust and Genocide Studies.* He is author of *A Concise History of Nazi Germany* (2014); *The "Jewish Threat": Anti-Semitic Politics of the U.S. Army* (2000); and *Carl Schmitt: Theorist for the Reich* (1983). He has also published a translation and scholarly edition of Carl Schmitt's *On the Three Types of Juristic Thought* (2004). His recent work includes "Schmitt's Diaries," *The Oxford Handbook of Carl Schmitt* and "Trajectories in the Study of National Socialism," *German Studies Review* (October 2016), and "Carl Schmitt and the Weimar Right."

Notes

1. Carl Schmitt, "Afterword (1958)," *Legality and Legitimacy*, trans. Jeffrey Seitzer (Durham, NC: Duke University Press, 2004), 95, 100.
2. In this respect, see Hans Barion, Ernst Forsthoff, and Werner Weber, eds., *Festschrift für Carl Schmitt zum 70. Geburtstag* (Berlin: Duncker and Humblot, 1959); Adolf Schule, "Eine Festschrift," *Juristenzeitung* 14, no. 22 (20 November 1959): 729–31; Erich Kaufmann, "Carl Schmitt und seine Schule: Offener Brief an Ernst Forsthoff," *Deutsche Rundschau* 84, no. 11 (October 1958): 1013–15.
3. The most complete bibliography is the five-hundred-page list by the French rightist intellectual Alain de Benoist, *Carl Schmitt: Internationale Bibliographie der Primär- und Sekundärliteratur* (Graz: Ares, 2010). For a historiographical examination of the various interpretations, see Joseph W. Bendersky, "From the *Führerstaat* to God and Abu Ghraib: The Strange Path of Carl Schmitt in the English-Speaking World," in *Carl Schmitt: Análisis Crítico*, ed. H.E. Herrera (Valparaíso: Universidad de Valparaíso, 2012), 23–61.
4. Reinhard Mehring, *Carl Schmitt: A Biography*, trans. Daniel Steuer (Cambridge: Polity Press, 2014), 271–72.
5. Dirk Blasius, *Carl Schmitt: Preußischer Staatsrat in Hitlers Reich* (Göttingen: Vandenhoeck and Ruprecht, 2001), 12–14, 23, 71. See also John P. McCormick, "Identifying or Exploiting the Paradoxes of Constitutional Democracy?," introduction to Schmitt, *Legality and Legitimacy*, xlii–xliii.
6. David Dyzenhaus, "Introduction: Why Carl Schmitt?" in *Law as Politics: Carl Schmitt's Critique of Liberalism*, ed. David Dyzenhaus (Durham, NC: Duke University Press, 1998), 3.
7. Some of the most important secondary literature related to Schmitt in 1930–33 neglected in these Anglophone debates includes Wolfram Pyta and Gabriel Seiberth, "Die Staatskrise der Weimarer Republik im Spiegel des Tagebuchs von Carl Schmitt," *Der Staat* 38 (1999): 423–48, 594–610; Lutz Berthold, *Carl Schmitt und der Staatsnotstandsplan am Ende der Weimarer Republik* (Berlin: Duncker and Humblot, 1990); and Gabriel Seiberth, *Anwalt des Reiches: Carl Schmitt und der Prozess "Preußen contra Reich" vor dem Staatsgerichtshof* (Berlin: Duncker and Humblot, 2001). Particularly egregious, yet influential, disregard of these and other German-language studies is in the introductions to the English translations of several of Schmitt's most important works. These introductions distort and decontextualize Schmitt's role at the end of Weimar before the reader can confront Schmitt's arguments on their own terms and with accurate historical information on his actual positions and activities. For example, in his introduction to Schmitt's pivotal *Legality and Legitimacy*, McCormick cites Berthold's book but then totally ignores the documentation in it regarding Schmitt and emergency plans, providing instead a historically inaccurate and incomplete version not only of Schmitt but of events at the end of Weimar. Other examples can be found in Tracy Strong's foreword to Schmitt's *Political*

Theology: Four Chapters on the Concept of Sovereignty, trans. George Schwab (Chicago: University of Chicago Press, 2005), vii–xxxiii; and *The Concept of the Political*, trans. George Schwab (Chicago: University of Chicago Press, 2007), ix–xxxi.

8. The major exception to such incomplete or imprecise treatment is Berthold's *Carl Schmitt und der Staatsnotstandsplan*, to whose documentary discoveries and historical interpretation my current chapter is greatly indebted. Pyta and Seiberth's "Die Staaatskrise der Weimarer Republik" does not fully explore the distinctions between *Ausnahmezustand* and *Notstand*. Neither does Andreas Koenen, *Der Fall Carl Schmitt: Sein Aufstieg zum "Kronjuristen des Dritten Reiches"* (Darmstadt: Wissenschaftliche Buchgesellschaft, 1995). Mehring, *Carl Schmitt*, devotes only two imprecise paragraphs to the emergency plans. See also Wolfram Pyta, " Die Staatsnotstandsplannung unter den Regierungen Papen und Schleicher," in *Die deutsche Staatskrise 1930–1933: Handlungsspielräume und Alternativen*, ed. Heinrich A. Winkler (Munich: R. Oldenbourg, 1992), 155–82; and "Verfassungsumbau, Staatsnotstand und Querfront: Schleichers Versuche zur Fernhaltung Hitlers von der Reichskanzlerschaft August 1932 bis Januar 1933," in *Gestaltungskraft des Politischen: Festschrift für Eberhard Kolb*, ed. Wolfram Pyta and Ludwig Richter (Berlin: Duncker and Humblot, 1998), 173–97.

9. Ernst Rudolf Huber, "Carl Schmitt in der Reichskrise der Weimarer Endzeit," in *Complexio Oppositorum: Über Carl Schmitt*, ed. Helmut Quaritsch (Berlin: Duncker and Humblot, 1988), 33–70.

10. McCormick, introduction to Schmitt's *Legality and Legitimacy*, xxxvi.

11. Carl Schmitt, "Diktatur und Belagerungszustand: Eine staatsrechtliche Studie," *Zeitschrift für die gesamte Strafrechtswissenschaft* 38 (1916): 138–61; and "Die Einwirkungen des Kriegszustandes auf das ordentliche straf-prozessuale Verfahren," *Zeitschrift für die gesamte Strafrechtswissenschaft* 38 (1917): 783–97.

12. Carl Schmitt, *Die Diktatur: Von den Anfängen des modernen Souveränitätsgedanken bis zum proletarischen Klassenkampf* (Berlin: Duncker and Humblot, 1978), 6–7, 13–37, 146, 204–5.

13. See Carl Schmitt, "Die Diktatur des Reichspräsidenten nach Artikel 48 der Weimarer Verfassung," Anhang in *Die Diktatur*, 213–59.

14. Ibid., 238–42; Carl Schmitt, *Constitutional Theory*, trans. Jeffrey Seitzer (Durham, NC: Duke University Press, 2008), 77, 104–11.

15. Hugo Preuss, "Reichsverfassungsmässige Diktatur," *Zeitschrift für Politik* 13 (1924): 101.

16. Schmitt, *Die Diktatur*, 234–35.

17. Carl Schmitt, "Der Hüter der Verfassung," *Archiv des öffentlichen Rechts*, XVI (March 1929): 161–237.

18. Carl Schmitt, "Verfassungsrechtliche Gutachten über die Frage, ob der Reichspräsident befugt ist, auf Grund des Art. 48 Abs. 2 RV. Finanzgesetzvertretende Verordnungen zu erlassen" (28 July 1930), in the unpublished records of the Reichskanzlei, Bundesarchiv Berlin-Lichtenfelde, Bestand R 43 I (hereafter cited as BA Berlin, R 43 I), 1870/286–310.

19. Carl Schmitt, *Tagebücher 1930–1934*, ed. Wolfgang Schuller and Gerd Giesler (Berlin: Akademie Verlag, 2010), 59, 62.

20. Carl Schmitt, *Der Hüter der Verfassung*, 2nd ed. (Berlin: Duncker and Humblot, 1969), 16, 32–33, 40, 88–89, 132, 139, 158–59.

21 . See Carl Schmitt–Erich Marcks correspondence and Schmitt–Eugen Ott correspondence, Schmitt *Nachlass*, Nordrhein-Westfälischen Hauptstaatsarchiv, Düsseldorf, Bestand RW 265 9024–33, 10741–46 (hereafter cited as NRWHStA Düsseldorf, NL Schmitt). See also Mehring, *Carl Schmitt*, 252–72.

22. Schmitt, *Legality and Legitimacy*, 27–36, 48–49, 71.

23. Schmitt diary, 20–27 July 1932, in *Tagebücher 1930–1934*, ed. Schuller and Giesler, 201–3.

24. Mehring, *Carl Schmitt*, 259–60.

25. Carl Schmitt, "Die Verfassungsmässigkeit der Bestellung eines Reichskommissars für das Land Preußen," *Deutsche Juristen-Zeitung* 37, no. 15 (1 August 1932): 958.

26. Huber, "Lebensbericht, 1961/62," in Carl Schmitt and Ernst Rudolf Huber, *Briefwechsel, 1926–1981*, ed. Ewald Grothe (Berlin: Duncker and Humblot, 2014), 562–64. In this memoir Huber mistakenly cited the date for these events as September rather than August, which he later corrected.

27. Huber, "Carl Schmitt in der Reichskrise der Weimarer Endzeit," 33, 37, 40–42, 46–50, 58–59, 62–68.

28. Huber to Schmitt, 23 and 28 August 1932; Schmitt to Huber, 23 August 1932, Schmitt and Huber, *Briefwechsel*, 105–7.

29. Huber, "Carl Schmitt in der Reichskrise der Weimarer Endzeit," 59, 66–67.

30. Entries in Schmitt diary, 25 September, 4 October, and 2 November 1932, in *Tagebücher 1930–1934*, ed. Schuller and Giesler, 219, 222, 229.

31. Entries in Schmitt diary, 9 September, 15 and 17 October 1932, in ibid., 219, 224–25.

32. Carl Schmitt, "Gesunde Wirtschaft im starken Staat," *Mitteilungen des Vereins zur Wahrnung der gemeinsamen wirtschaftlichen Interessen in Rheinland und Westfalen*, 1933, N. F., Heft 21, 30–31.

33. Correspondence between Huber and Schmitt, 3–18 December 1932, in Schmitt and Huber, *Briefwechsel*, 115–18, 124–26.

34. See various Schmitt diary entries for these months, in *Tagebücher 1930-1934*, ed. Schuller and Giesler, 240–58.

35. See "Vortragsnotiz aus der Wehrmachtsabteilung," in Berthold, *Carl Schmitt und der Staatsnotstandsplan*, 78–79. It is the archival copy of this document that Henry A. Turner Jr. used in his meticulous examination of this final period. When drawing his inferences and conclusions, Turner was aware of neither the original version and related documents nor Schmitt's authorship of these plans. See *Hitler's Thirty Days to Power: January 1933* (Reading, MA: Addison-Wesley, 1996), 118–33.

36. "Vortragsnotiz aus der Wehrmachtsabteilung," 78–79.

37. "Horst Michaels 'Papier,'" in Berthold, *Carl Schmitt und der Staatsnotstandsplan*, 80–85.

38. Ibid., 80.

39. Ibid., 80–82.
40. Ibid., 82–85.
41. Ibid., 84.
42. "Entwurf einer politischen Kundgebung des Reichspräsidenten," in Berthold, *Carl Schmitt und der Staatsnotstandsplan*, 86.
43. "Stichworte für die politische Argumentation," in Berthold, *Carl Schmitt und der Staatsnotstandsplan*, 87–88.
44. Schmitt, "Afterword (1958)," *Legality and Legitimacy*, 100.
45. Ibid.
46. See "Vortragsnotiz aus der Wehrmachtsabteilung," 79. See also Turner, *Hitler's Thirty Days to Power*, 119.
47. Schmitt diary, 26 January 1933, in *Tagebücher 1930–1934*, ed. Schuller and Giesler, 255–56.
48. Ibid., 27 January 1933, 256.
49. Ibid., 31 January 1933, 257.
50. Ibid., 2 February 1933, 260.
51. Ibid., 3 March 1933, 271–72.
52. Ibid., 23–24 March 1933, 272–73.
53. Carl Schmitt, "Das Gesetz zur Behebung der Not von Volk und Reich," *Deutsche Juristen-Zeitung* 38, no. 7 (1 April 1933): 455.
54. Ibid.
55. Ibid., 456.
56. Ibid.
57. Ibid., 456–57.
58. Schmitt diary, 22 March 1933, in *Tagebücher, 1930–1934*, ed. Schuller and Giesler, 272.
59. Schmitt, "Das Gesetz zur Behebung der Not von Volk und Reich," 457.
60. Ibid., 457–58
61. Ibid., 458.
62. Carl Schmitt, "Das Staatsnotrecht im modernen Verfassungsleben: Aus einem Vortrage, gehalten Ende März in Weimar," *Deutsche Richterzeitung* 25 (1933): 254–55. See also the entry in Schmitt diary, 27 March 1933, in *Tagebücher, 1930–1934*, ed. Schuller and Giesler, 274.
63. Schmitt, "Das Staatsnotrecht im modernen Vefassungsleben," 254–55. See also Schmitt's postwar commentary on this legal positivism and the end of Weimar in "Afterword (1958)," *Legality and Legitimacy*, 95–101.
64. Turner, *Hitler's Thirty Days to Power*, 83–84.

Bibliography

Bendersky, Joseph W. *Carl Schmitt: Theorist for the Reich*. Princeton, NJ: Princeton University Press, 1983.

——. "Carl Schmitt and the Weimar Right." In *The German Right and the Weimar Republic: Studies in the History of German Conservatism, Nationalism, and Antisemitism*, edited by Larry Eugene Jones, 268–90. New York: Berghahn Books, 2014.

Berthold. Lutz. *Carl Schmitt und der Staatsnotstandsplan am Ende der Weimarer Republik*. Berlin: Duncker and Humblot, 1999.

Blasius, Dirk. *Carl Schmitt: Preußischer Staatsrat in Hitlers Reich*. Göttingen: Vandenhoeck and Ruprecht, 2001.

Huber, Ernst Rudolf. "Carl Schmitt in der Reichskrise der Weimarer Endzeit." In *Complexio Oppositorum: Über Carl Schmitt*, edited by Helmut Quaritsch, 33–70. Berlin: Duncker and Humblot, 1988.

Koenen, Andreas. *Der Fall Carl Schmitt: Sein Aufstieg zum "Kronjuristen des Dritten Reiches."* Darmstadt: Wissenschaftliche Buchgesellschaft, 1995.

Mehring, Reinhard. *Carl Schmitt: A Biography*. Translated by Daniel Steuer. Cambridge: Polity Press, 2014.

Pyta, Wolfram. "Die Staatsnotstandsplannung unter den Regierungen Papen und Schleicher." In *Die deutsche Staatskrise 1930–1933: Handlungsspielräume und Alternativen*, edited by Heinrich Winkler, 155–82. Munich: R. Oldenbourg, 1992.

———. "Verfassungsumbau, Staatsnotstand und Querfront: Schleichers Versuche zur Fernhaltung Hitlers von der Reichskanzlerschaft August 1932 bis Januar 1933." In *Gestaltungskraft des Politischen: Festschrift für Eberhard Kolb*, edited by Wolfram Pyta and Ludwig Richter, 173–97. Berlin: Duncker and Humblot, 1998.

Pyta, Wolfram, and Gabriel Seiberth. "Die Staatskrise der Weimarer Republik im Spiegel des Tagebuchs Carl Schmitt." *Der Staat* 38 (1999): 423–48, 594–610.

Schmitt, Carl. *Der Hüter der Verfassung*. Berlin: Duncker and Humblot, 1969.

———. *Die Diktatur: Von Anfängen des modernen Souveränitätsgedanken bis zum proletarischen Klassenkampft*. Berlin: Duncker and Humblot, 1978.

———. *Legality and Legitimacy*. Translated by Jeffrey Seitzer. Durham, NC: Duke University Press, 2004.

———. *Tagebücher, 1930–1934*. Edited by Wolfgang Schuller and Gerd Giesler. Berlin: Akademie Verlag, 2010.

Schmitt, Carl, and Ernst Rudolf Huber. *Briefwechsel 1926–1981*. Edited by Ewald Grothe. Berlin: Duncker and Humblot, 2014.

Seiberth, Gabriel, *Anwalt des Reiches: Carl Schmitt und der Prozess "Preußen contra Reich" vor dem Staatsgerichtshof*. Berlin: Duncker and Humblot, 2001.

Turner, Henry A., Jr. *Hitler's Thirty Days to Power: January 1933*. Reading, MA: Addison-Wesley, 1996.

 3

LUDWIG KAAS AND THE END OF THE GERMAN CENTER PARTY

Martin Menke

"I remain unable to bear the health burdens an intensive and effective party leadership requires at the moment and which our common cause deserves." With these words, Center Party leader Monsignor Ludwig Kaas announced his resignation from his party office in a letter to his deputy party leader Joseph Joos on 2 June 1932. In his letter of resignation, Kaas noted that only the urgent pleas of friends and colleagues had kept him from resigning a year earlier.[1] Yet despite Kaas's acknowledgment of his inability to lead the Center Party during Weimar's last year, he remained in office until April 1933.[2] His successor Heinrich Brüning assumed the party chairmanship in May 1933 only to preside over the party's dissolution.

For such a significant figure in the history of the late Weimar Republic, Kaas has received relatively little scholarly attention. Aside from one hagiographic three-volume biography,[3] he makes little more than cameo appearances in the biographies of others or in monographs relating to Weimar and the Nazi seizure of power. In evaluating Kaas's role as leader of the German Center Party (Deutsche Zentrumspartei), historians have focused on his frequent absences, his obstinate refusal to cooperate with the Papen cabinet, and his role in the passage of the Enabling Act to paint a fairly critical picture of the Center Party leader as someone whose actions inadvertently helped the Nazis seize and consolidate power. While some of this criticism is no doubt valid, much of it is unfair and must be reevaluated. His commitment to a vision of German politics in which the Weimar Republic either recovered or was at least transformed into something more successful by a gathering of all cooperative and willing forces under the rubric of what Kaas called *Sammlung* proved ultimately ineffective. The concept of *Sammlung* and its application by Kaas to his discussions with potential political partners, particularly the German National People's Party (Deutschnationale Volkspartei or DNVP) and even the National Socialist German Workers' Party (Nationalsozialistische Deutsche

Arbeiterpartei or NSDAP), deserve a careful review, as does his leadership of the party from December 1928 through his departure for Rome in April 1933.

Kaas's political views were well formed before his election to the Center Party chairmanship. He was born in Trier in 1881 and entered the seminary upon graduating school. He earned doctoral degrees in canon law and theology and initially harbored no political ambitions. In 1919 Kaas was elected to the National Assembly for his hometown of Trier. He viewed the world through the lens of Catholic theology and thought in legal terms. Within the Center Kaas would become one of its several foreign policy experts. Despite his lack of charisma and innate political intuition, Kaas would lead the party effectively through his first years as party chairman. Throughout his tenure as party chairman, Kaas remained deeply committed to the Catholic faith and to the church's teachings on the nature of the state and church-state relations. He was no less committed to the existing constitutional order and in particular to the processes for constitutional revision. And lastly, Kaas emphasized the importance of law and diplomatic agreement as the basis of conflict resolution.

The Weaknesses of an Accidental Leader

Kaas's election as Center Party chairman was something of an accident. He did not campaign for the chairmanship and had not sought the office. At the time of his election, the party was badly divided, and his election received strong support from those constituencies within the Center that feared that the election of either Adam Stegerwald or Joseph Joos, both closely identified with the interests of the working class, would only accelerate the party's internal disintegration. But Kaas immediately tried to soothe the bitterness the Center's working-class elements felt over Stegerwald's rejection by offering him the chairmanship of the party's Reichstag delegation, a position Stegerwald accepted and held until his appointment as Reich minister of labor in April 1929.[4] For his own part, Kaas had not been groomed for the party leadership and was constitutionally ill-suited to deal with the rough and tumble of party in-fighting. The effectiveness of his leadership was further undercut by frequent absences from Berlin, during which times he left others such as Joos and Heinrich Brüning to lead the party. Kaas was conspicuously absent during two of the most important crises in the late Weimar Republic and early Nazi period, first when he traveled to Rome during the formation of the Brüning cabinet in March 1930 and then to his domicile at Sterzing/Vipiteno in South Tyrol in August and September of 1932 when the crisis over the cabinet of Franz von Papen was drawing to a head. But the leaders of the Center's Reichstag delegation adhered to a well-established pattern of decision-making and did their best to negotiate the crises that their party faced during Kaas's absences from Berlin. While this seemed to have had little effect upon how the Center voted and behaved, Kaas's record of attendance suggests that he may not have enjoyed his new role. As his letter of resignation to Joos suggests, Kaas seems to have considered his party office a burden.

The second area of weakness in Kaas's political profile lay in the extent to which he relied upon the concept of *Sammlung* in the articulation of his political views. The concept of *Sammlung* was rooted in a long tradition of Catholic teaching about the nature of community and one's duty to support the state constructively, as German Catholicism's leading political theologian of the time, Father Joseph Mausbach,[5] had explained in 1922. Kaas had evoked the concept of *Sammlung* as early as 1925, when in a speech before the Reichstag he called for the "cooperation and coalition of all reasonable and moderate political forces, which in the long run will be the only force able to surmount the impending unavoidable challenges in order to shape Germany's destiny." According to Kaas, this would "require the isolation of the incorrigible forces on the political extremes."[6] Five years later, while addressing the Center Party leadership on 27 July 1930, Kaas appealed for a "move from interest politics to a reasonable and authentic community of the people." Kaas announced that he was willing to lead the Center into a "new, larger, and creative synthesis as long as this political community of the people reflected good statesmanship."[7] A year later, Kaas declared that "*Sammlung* is the imperative of the hour, not incitement and discrediting [attacks]. All those who are willing and capable of supporting a self-confident, peaceful yet activist foreign policy are called to cooperate."[8] For Kaas, *Sammlung* was the appeal to all reasonable, moderate, and well-intentioned Germans who rejected political extremism and who were willing to work together, much like what the French called *ralliement*, for the welfare of the entire country. Above all, it required a willingness to engage in self-sacrifice in political service to the people. *Sammlung* would become the leitmotif of Kaas's political vision.

With the collapse of Hermann Müller's government in March 1930, it would seem as if Kaas's concept of *Sammlung* defied political reality. As Kaas himself conceded, the Reichstag was no longer capable of legislating since the Nazi and Communist parties rejected cooperation out of hand, while the Social Democrats remained aloof from the coalition that had rallied behind the government of the new chancellor, Kaas's party colleague and associate Heinrich Brüning. In the Reichstag elections that followed the dissolution of the Reichstag in the summer of 1930, many voters abandoned political compromise and functional government altogether as ideological extremism and populist anger moved to center stage. Throughout all of this, Kaas persisted in his appeal for *Sammlung* as the only solution to Germany's problems. Only a broadly based political coalition, Kaas argued, could rebuild Germany.[9] But Kaas was particularly disappointed by the DNVP's failure to respond to his appeal for *Sammlung*, which was directed as much to the moderate elements within the right-wing DNVP as it was to the Social Democrats. The election of film and press magnate Alfred Hugenberg to the DNVP chairmanship in the fall of 1928 and the subsequent exodus of the DNVP's more moderate elements over the course of the next year and a half could only have come as a bitter disappointment to Kaas and represented a severe setback to his policy of *Sammlung*. In January 1930 Kaas had rejected Hugenburg's call for the creation of a united anti-Marxist front and reaffirmed his commitment and the commitment of his party to finding a solution to Germany's social, economic, and political problems on the basis of the existing constitutional order.[10] Then, in the summer of 1931, Kaas called for the *Sammlung* of Germany's constructive forces on the broadest possible basis as a precondition for launching a new diplomatic offensive aimed at a reduction of Germany's reparations burden and shaking off the burden of the Versailles Treaty.[11] On 27 August Kaas took part at Brüning's invitation in the chancellor's meeting with Hugenberg to determine whether or not the DNVP might be willing to participate in a new right-wing government that Reich president Hindenburg and his chief political strategist, the Reichswehr's Kurt von Schleicher, were anxious to install in power. The meeting, however, ended in a complete failure as Hugenberg rejected Brüning's proposal out of hand and refused to break ties with Hitler and the NSDAP.[12]

The fact of the matter was that the various parties in the Reichstag were drifting further and further away from each other to the benefit of the extremist parties on the left and the right. At the same time, the rejection of Kaas's concept of *Sammlung* by the two largest opposition parties, the NSDAP and KPD, and the DNVP's sharp move to the right under Hugenberg made it more and more difficult to consider *Sammlung* a realistic option for saving the Weimar Republic. While the concept of *Sammlung* as articulated by Kaas was essential if the Weimar Republic was to survive, the diminishing commitment of Germany's political leadership to the very principle of parliamentary democracy undermined the likelihood of translating this goal into practice. This, however, was not just a failure of Kaas or the Center Party but is something that could be said of most of Weimar's parties as they faced the same leadership and policy challenges.

Kaas as Center Party Leader

Kaas's ascendancy to the Center Party chairmanship in December 1928 also underscored the challenges the concept of *Sammlung* faced even within the Center Party. At the time, the party was deeply divided, and the decision to settle for a last-minute compromise candidate who had never been in any leadership position in the party or in the government was in itself a sign of weakness rather than strength. Without the sincere commitment Kaas identified as crucial to the success of the concept, *Sammlung* could create an outward show of unity that in reality no longer existed. For his own part, Kaas did not actively seek the chairmanship, but as in the case of his nomination to the National Assembly in 1919, he believed he could not refuse. Kaas's election nevertheless had the effect of reaffirming the confessional values that lay at the heart of the Center's political and historical identity and thus acted as an antidote to the poisonous effect that a decade of social and economic conflict had had upon the party's internal coherence.[13] The increasingly prominent role that clerics like Kaas began to play in the leadership of Germany's Catholic parties was part of a general trend to find candidates who by definition stood above the clash of antagonistic social interests and who were assumed to be self-sacrificing and sincere. This happened because the various factions in the party had become so hardened to each other that the candidates put forth by one side or another would almost invariably encounter rejection from the other side.

Kaas's attendance record in the Reichstag, however, suggests that he did not enjoy his new role. After his election as party chairman, Kaas irregularly attended the meetings of the Reichstag and of the Center Party deputies. Between the fall of 1929 and the summer of 1930, Kaas did not attend meetings of the Reichstag for months at a time, missing the sessions in which Brüning presented his new government along with the emergency measures with which he sought to respond to the deepening world economic crisis. When the newly elected Reichstag convened in October 1930, he was present for the duration of that parliament until the middle of May 1932. The parliamentary record for the only two sessions of the Reichstag that was elected in June 1932 lists Kaas as excused for ill health when he retreated to Sterzing for recuperation. In August he attended the meetings of the Center's Reichstag delegation leadership committee, but not those of the delegation as a whole. He even missed the vote of confidence on the newly appointed government of Franz von Papen at the beginning of June 1932. Kaas managed to attend all three sessions of the Reichstag elected in November 1932 and was present for both sessions of the Reichstag that was elected in March 1933. Compared with the other Center Party deputies, no other deputy missed as many votes as Kaas did.[14]

There were two principal reasons for Kaas's repeated absences: One was poor health, which he used to explain his absences in 1929 and early 1930.[15] The other generally unannounced reason for Kaas's poor attendance record lay in his other professional life as liaison between the German bishops and the nuncio.[16] After Kaas's death in 1952, Eugenio Pacelli, by then Pope Pius XII, claimed that Kaas had been a dear and close friend.[17] Perhaps Kaas had expected more from this friendship than was realistically possible. When Pope Pius XI recalled Pacelli to Rome on 9 December 1929 and then made him a cardinal on 16 December, Kaas soon followed the former nuncio to Rome. After Pius XI appointed Cardinal Pacelli as his cardinal secretary of state on 7 February 1930, Kaas traveled to Rome to conduct negotiations in an official capacity for the creation of a separate military bishop.[18] Whether or not Kaas hoped to parlay his stay into a Vatican position remains unclear, but if he did, Kaas's hopes for Rome must have come to naught, for by July 1930 he had returned to Berlin. Again Kaas cited his poor health as the reason for his long absence.[19] But privately he made no secret of his desire to be relieved of the party chairmanship.[20] With no new position waiting for him in Rome, and since the party could ill afford a new leadership crisis with elections so close at hand, Kaas returned to Berlin and resumed his responsibilities as party chairman.

Kaas's prolonged absences appear to have had scant effect on the Center Party and its parliamentary representatives. There was little sign of any decline in the activity, unity, or effectiveness within the party's Reichstag delegation. In fact, during Kaas's tenure as party chair, but especially until the 1930 elections, the Center's Reichstag deputies remained active and vocal. Furthermore, the discussions in the Center Party Reichstag delegation indicate there was no particular deference to Monsignor Kaas as party leader. Responsibility for the party's organizational affairs resided in the hands of deputy party leader Joseph Joos, while Brüning, one of the party's economic and fiscal experts, led the party's political affairs first as leader of the Center Party Reichstag delegation and then in his capacity as Reich chancellor. In fact, Kaas had insisted on Brüning's assistance as a condition for assuming the party leadership in 1928. Thus, it seems the party was left less adrift than one might assume. And it is very likely that Kaas's extended absence in 1930 allowed Brüning to transition more smoothly from the position of chairman of the Center Party Reichstag delegation to that of the Reich chancellor without any loss of authority among the deputies.

Kaas and the Shifting Fronts of 1932

As the Weimar Republic continued to unravel in the early 1930s, Kaas delivered one of his more important public speeches, *Nicht rück-warts — vorwärts!*, in the summer of 1931 in which he acknowledged the depth of Germany's economic and emotional depression. Kaas warned against the radical political forces tearing apart the country by making it impossible to elect a functioning parliament. Giving his full support to Brüning, Kaas reminded readers that ever since 1918, the Center Party had made great sacrifices to preserve Germany. Kaas's commitment to Brüning's policies would bring neither Brüning nor the Center Party any popularity, but the Center had to assume a role no other party was willing to assume: to provide balance and mediation, to avoid extremism, and to be constructive. While the Center Party was engaged in constructive work for the last twelve years, the NSDAP and the KPD had only sought to exploit conflicts for their own gain. Once again emphasizing the concept of *Sammlung* to defend cooperation with the SPD, Kaas claimed that "anyone who lets anti-Marxism prevent cooperation with constructive forces in Germany might be a party leader, but never a statesman."[21] While Kaas had no innovative solutions to offer, he clearly rejected the refusal of Germany's right-wing parties to cooperate with the SPD against the NSDAP. Kaas's remarks revealed the dilemma in which the Center found itself: if the other parties could learn to cooperate with each other, then Germany could be governed by parliamentary means. But until such time, the Center did not have the option of withdrawing from the government in order to force the other parties to act responsibly. Throughout the Weimar period, the Center had negotiated compromises time and time again, with the result that the radical parties on both the left and the right were left free to oppose all government measures without ever having to assume responsibility for their actions.

In the spring of 1932, Kaas and Brüning fought to secure Reich president Paul von Hindenburg's reelection against NSDAP leader Adolf

Hitler and Ernst Thälmann from the KPD, only to see Hindenburg repay Brüning for his loyalty by dismissing him as chancellor and placing governmental responsibility for the first time in the history of the Weimar Republic in the hands of the nationalist right. Hindenburg, who blamed Brüning for the fact that his reelection as Reich president had been secured with the support of those political forces for which he felt the least innate sympathy, demanded his resignation as chancellor on 29 May. Two days later Hindenburg asked Franz von Papen, a Westphalian aristocrat who stood on the Center's extreme right wing, to form a new cabinet.

The role of Kaas in all of this remains ambiguous. Two weeks before Brüning's dismissal, Kaas had had a long conversation with Papen in which the future chancellor had recognized the hopelessness of Brüning's political situation while Kaas expressed support for the call that Papen had made the previous November—here Kaas was referring to a speech that Papen had delivered the previous November in Dülmen—for the appointment of a presidential cabinet without formal ties to any of the political parties. Kaas even went so far as to characterize Schleicher, the driving force behind Papen's installation as chancellor, as an honorable man without political ambitions for himself.[22] In a postwar conversation, former *Germania* journalist Walter Hagemann went so far as to claim that in 1932 Kaas had come to consider Brüning an obstacle to German stability because of his refusal to form a coalition with the DNVP.[23] There is, however, little evidence to support such a claim. Not only is there not so much as a single utterance by Kaas, either at this point or in the years before and after, to indicate that Kaas had lost his faith in Brüning, but Kaas had been present at a meeting between Brüning and Hugenberg in the late summer of 1931 to witness the DNVP leader's unequivocal rejection of any cooperation whatsoever with the Brüning cabinet.[24] From this point on Brüning refused to consider any further overtures in the direction of the DNVP.

Papen later claimed that he had consulted Kaas before seeing the Reich president and had reassured Kaas that he had no intention of accepting the offer of the chancellorship.[25] Even when Papen explained in a brief meeting with Kaas after having seen Hindenburg that the Reich president had appealed to his sense of honor and duty with such passion that he could no longer refuse, Kaas supposedly accepted Papen's explanation.[26] In the second of the two letters that Kaas was to write on 2 June—this one to Brüning—the Center Party chairman expressed glowing praise for the former chancellor and his firm hope that Brüning would be the one to replace him as the new party leader.[27] Nothing in Kaas's letter suggested that from his perspective there was any sign of the rift between the two men that Brüning later alleged. All of this, however, was to change when the list of Papen's cabinet members with six nobles and three former members of Hugenberg's DNVP was published the following day. Kaas felt betrayed by Papen, whom he described as the "'Ephialtes' of the Center."[28] The new cabinet's first policy statement further outraged Kaas and the Center Party. Papen decried the class warfare, cultural bolshevism, atheism, and Marxist thinking that was undermining the national community. With much of this Kaas would have agreed, but Papen's claim that the "Christian forces in the state had proved too willing to compromise for the sake of political parity" proved unacceptable. Papen further claimed that "a clear decision must be made to determine which forces are willing to help construct a new Germany on the basis of the inviolable principles of the Christian worldview."[29] This amounted to a disavowal of the Center's politics since 1918 and an ultimatum that the Center break with the political middle and moderate left at the risk of finding itself excluded from government.

Papen remained a bête noire for Kaas until February 1933. Whether there was any direct connection between the appointment of the Papen cabinet and Kaas's letter of resignation quoted at the beginning of this chapter remains a matter of speculation. Even before the change of governments had taken place, there was speculation that Kaas would not continue as Center Party chairman. Indeed, the notes that Wilhelm Bormann took of the meeting of the Center Party executive committee on 8 June 1932 described Kaas as "half sick and in weak voice."[30] While Kaas was indeed ill, one also has to wonder if he did not consider Papen's appointment an affront and a betrayal of the Center Party for which he as its leader should take responsibility. Kaas in fact devoted a third of his letter to Joos to the lack of cooperation across the political spectrum for the sake of the common good. Kaas seemed to think that *Sammlung* remained the best possible strategy for recovery but was bitterly disappointed by Papen and his disregard for the plight of the Center.

Kaas in the Last Months of Weimar

Despite claims of poor health, Kaas campaigned vigorously for the Center Party in the different elections that took place in 1932. Kaas was a frequent and ardent speaker, and Papen was the target of his ire as often as was Hitler.[31] The July 1932 Reichstag elections produced the best result ever for the NSDAP in free elections. While the Center held its own and actually managed to improve upon its performance in the 1930 Reichstag elections, other parties, especially the DNVP, suffered tremendously. But after the elections, Kaas subsequently took ill again and remained unavailable for the Reichstag deliberations following the July 1932 elections.[32] His Center Party colleagues were dismayed that he chose this moment to retreat to his house in Sterzing, South Tyrol.[33] According to Brüning, Kaas's physicians questioned his mental health and well-being, but the evidence stems from Brüning's postwar letters, the veracity of which is often difficult to determine, especially when statements about Kaas are concerned.[34] On the other hand, Kaas's absences from Berlin after the NSDAP had won its greatest electoral victory seemed highly irresponsible, especially as the new cabinet negotiations were expected to be complicated and difficult. Reporting on a Center Party leadership conference on 5 August 1932, the *Bayerischer Kurier* reported, "The Center's chairman Monsignor Kaas has been seriously ill for some time [and that to] recuperate, he currently is spending time in the South [in Sterzing]. Reichstag deputy Joseph Joos is acting on behalf of the ill chairman."[35] Kaas may very well have been ill, or perhaps distraught at the electoral outcome, but to leave the capital and even the country at this critical juncture bordered on irresponsibility.

Given the results of the July elections, a small minority in the Center Party leadership recommended cooperation with the Papen government in hopes of achieving stability. Most of the Center Party's leadership sought instead to persuade the NSDAP to behave like a "normal" political party by assuming government responsibility. The party leadership argued that one could no longer exempt the NSDAP from responsibility and leave it free to obstruct the government with impunity.[36] Extensive negotiations failed, in large part because the NSDAP and Hitler insisted on the chancellor's post and the most influential ministries.[37] Complicating the situation even further was the fact Kaas was not willing to include Papen in any of his party's future plans.[38] In fact, there was speculation that Kaas's intransigence toward the Papen government had aroused such strong opposition within the Center that it might cost him the chairmanship.[39] Throughout this period, Kaas returned to Berlin only once to attend a meeting of the executive committee of the Center Reichstag delegation on 12 September for the purpose of discussing the party's options at the opening of the new Reichstag. He was not recorded as present for any other meetings of the Center Party or the Reichstag during that parliamentary session or even that same day. Other long-serving party members such as Brüning, Joos, and Thomas Esser assumed responsibility for making policy decisions. At the opening session of Reichstag, Reichstag president Hermann Göring and Reich chancellor Franz von Papen competed for the rostrum in what became a much-celebrated demonstration of the chancellor's political ineptitude. With the votes of the Center, the Reichstag passed a vote of no confidence in the Papen cabinet before the chancellor could present Göring with Hindenburg's order to dissolve the Reichstag.[40]

On the same day that Kaas spoke in Münster, Papen wrote a letter to Franz von Galen indicating that several times he had asked both Kaas and Brüning for a meeting, but to no avail.[41] The Center refused to cooperate with Papen. In fact, Kaas bitterly criticized the Papen government.[42] Four days later *Germania* reported serious riots in Berlin, Leipzig, and Bochum. The increasingly desperate economic situation in which Germany found itself in the fall of 1932 was no longer a matter for abstract discussion of principles; there was evidence of suffering every day.[43] At this point, the same Catholic conservatives who had welcomed Kaas in 1928 began to lose faith in him because he had not fulfilled their expectations of a turn to the right by the Center Party, a goal that he himself had never articulated.[44] Catholic conservatives like Count Franz von Galen, a Westphalian noble who in April 1932 had been elected to the Center's delegation to the Prussian Landtag, urged Kaas to cooperate with Papen, but they were bitterly disappointed by the entire tenor of his speech in Münster.[45] Fundamental differences in their respective views of Germany's political order separated Kaas from the Catholic conservatives. Galen and others sought a solution that might involve curbing constitutional guarantees; Kaas and the Center were not willing to violate the constitutional order to establish a new government.

In the November elections, the Center sustained its share of the vote, while that of the NSDAP declined for the first time. Papen subsequently invited Kaas and Joos to discuss the formation of a new cabinet. While Kaas insisted there was no "personal animosity" between Papen and himself, he refused to consider negotiations with other parties before being instructed to do so by the Reich president, a process the constitution required. Furthermore, Kaas and Joos demanded on behalf of the Center Party that the cabinet resign to "clear the way for new options."[46] Papen's cabinet remained unacceptable. On 18 November 1932 Hindenburg discussed the formation of a future cabinet with both Kaas and DNVP chairman Alfred Hugenberg. Kaas once again reclaimed the concept of *Sammlung* as the basis of Center Party policy.[47] As the situation clearly revealed, the electorate was too deeply divided for a coalition cabinet. While Kaas continued to reject Papen as chancellor, he recognized the necessity of securing the NSDAP's participation in the government. In the meeting with Hindenburg, Kaas admitted that it was time to end parliamentary government and to appoint an authoritarian cabinet of a few trusted leaders who might possibly receive the support of a parliamentary majority. The apparent contradiction between this statement and Kaas's definition of authoritarian government outlined in a speech of 17 October resolves itself if one considers Kaas's insistence on fidelity to the constitution. Kaas believed that an anticonstitutional regime would be illegal and immoral, but an authoritarian regime supported by a parliamentary majority might lead to constitutional reforms that would provide a more stable basis for German government. In his desire for constitutional reforms, Kaas was not alone. Kaas had not abandoned the Weimar Republic, yet he recognized that the electorate was incapable of electing strong majority governments. Throughout the meeting Kaas repeatedly insisted on remaining within constitutional bounds, and even went so far as to remind Hindenburg of his oath to uphold the constitution.[48]

Hindenburg subsequently offered Hitler the opportunity to form a cabinet based on the support of a majority in the Reichstag. The NSDAP, however, refused to participate in any coalition government that did not provide it with control of the most important levers of government.[49] It was at this point that Hindenburg turned to Kaas on 24 November and asked the Center Party chairman to see if he might be able to form a cabinet supported by a parliamentary majority. Late in the afternoon on 25 November, Kaas reported to the Reich president that he was deeply distressed to report that neither the DNVP nor the NSDAP was willing to join the government, which meant that it was impossible to form a cabinet with parliamentary backing. The Center still refused to work with Papen, while Brüning, whose reappointment as chancellor Kaas had recommended, was unacceptable to the Reich president. Given Kaas's use of the phrase "cause for sincere mourning" to describe his failure to form a new coalition cabinet, he knew that his efforts might very well have been the last chance to form a cabinet with constitutional legitimacy.[50]

As yet unaware of the outcome of Kaas's negotiations with Hitler, Papen's cabinet met to discuss the future course of action. Eventually, they saw only two options remaining: either a cabinet appointed by Hindenburg and supported by the German army or the chancellorship of Hitler. The latter was to be avoided at all costs.[51] Thus, the appointment of Hitler as chancellor was not only not inevitable but, it seems that, in late 1932, all non-Nazi forces seemed to agree that Hitler should never become chancellor. On 3 December Hindenburg asked Schleicher to form a cabinet that included all members of the previous government with the exception of Papen and Reich minister of the interior Wilhelm Gayl. In the months before his appointment, Schleicher had asked several legal scholars for reports concerning the legality of a prolonged suspension of the Reichstag and a revision of the constitution by plebiscite. While some of the scholars, among them Catholic political philosopher Carl Schmitt, supported Schleicher's aims, they did not come to fruition. In the end, Schleicher's cabinet could not overcome the challenges that Germany faced without breaching the constitutional order, for which there was insufficient support. Schleicher's cabinet could not remedy the economic crisis, end the almost civil war–like conditions in the streets, or resolve the parliamentary impasse.

On 16 January 1933 Schleicher held a conference of his cabinet ministers in which he explored exit strategies from the fundamental crisis of government Germany faced. For the chancellor, the most important question was the NSDAP's attitude toward the government. Would it cooperate with the cabinet, tolerate it, or oppose it? Schleicher did not think there was much chance of collaboration.[52] Instead, he envisioned a coalition from the Center to the Strasser wing of the NSDAP, to which, however, Hugenberg remained opposed out of fear that the SPD would ride the Center's coattails to power. According to Schleicher, Kaas was willing to forego Center Party representation in the cabinet as long as the participating parties agreed to constructive politics. Schleicher thought, however, that one would have to include a representative from the Center in the next cabinet. He also claimed that if the Center raised complaints about the postponement of parliamentary elections, this would be for the sake of appearance and nothing more. Schleicher concluded by reflecting on the reality of German politics in early 1933: One could no longer rule Germany without significant support from the people, and one could not form a cabinet based on a parliamentary majority without the cooperation of Adolf Hitler. One could only wish that the mood of the electorate would soon swing in favor of those parties that supported the cabinet. Schleicher's wishful thinking, in many ways similar to that of Kaas, would not come to fruition. Contrary to Schleicher's beliefs, the Center's opposition to a long prorogation of the Reichstag was rooted in deeply held convictions.

As late as 20 January 1933, Kaas and the Center Reichstag delegation reaffirmed their commitment to constitutional change conforming to the law by refusing to countenance a presidential decree authorizing an indefinite adjournment of the Reichstag.[53] In late 1931 Kaas had briefly participated in a conversation between Schleicher and Brüning in which Schleicher had floated the idea of a constitutional experiment that would have included dissolution of the Reichstag without calling for new elections within the period stipulated by the Weimar Constitution.[54] At that meeting Kaas voiced no opinion, and the matter passed without consequence. That incident and his reference to an authoritarian government are the only instances in which Kaas came even close to considering unconstitutional measures. Unlike Schleicher, Kaas refused to violate the constitutional order to achieve the reforms Kaas and most Germans desperately sought.[55] On 26 January Kaas wrote to Schleicher that a postponement of Reichstag elections was not only constitutionally but also morally and politically impossible.[56] By this time, however, Schleicher had lost the confidence of the Reich president, and Hindenburg was already well on his way to appointing Hitler as chancellor of a new government and entrusting him, among other things, with the authorization to order the dissolution of the Reichstag. Hopefully new elections on 5 March 1933 would bring the clarity that Germany's political leaders so desperately sought.

Kaas and the Hitler Cabinet

What occurred between 26 January and 23 March 1933 to convince the Center Party and particularly Kaas to support the Enabling Act? The Enabling Act, though technically constitutional, undermined any hopes of preventing a period of anticonstitutional rule and empowered a party that refused to abjure violence. What convinced Kaas to redefine his commitment to Weimar's constitutional order and to urge his colleagues to support this anticonstitutional but not unconstitutional bill?

At first, Kaas sought to find some accommodation with Hitler's cabinet of national concentration that assumed office on the morning of 31 January 1933. Kaas met with Hitler on 31 January to explore the possibility of cooperation. While Hitler emphasized his personal achievement in becoming chancellor, Kaas dismissed the chancellor's personal achievement and asked about the new cabinet's program, about which little had been revealed.[57] Without responding directly, Hitler offered Kaas cabinet posts for the Center Party in the Prussian cabinet in return for the Center's support for the Reich cabinet. Afterward Hitler claimed that he had asked for the Center's agreement to a one-year adjournment of parliament but that Kaas would agree only to a two-month adjournment—and even that only on the condition Hitler provide constitutional guarantees in response to questions to be posed by the Center.[58] Hitler used Kaas's hesitancy and his demand for assurances and clarifications to claim that the Center would not be supporting his cabinet and made it clear he no longer wished to engage the Center Party as a meaningful force in German politics. In practice, Hitler would only pretend to embrace the Center's demands when he needed its vote, as in the case of the Enabling Act.

Kaas, however, did not comprehend Hitler's intentions. On 2 February 1933, Otto Meissner, state secretary in the Office of Reich Presidency, sent Kaas a letter to warn that publishing the details of his exchange with Hitler about the Center's conditions for supporting the Hitler cabinet would jeopardize further discussions. Meissner obviously sought to shift the blame for the collapse of talks from Hitler to Kaas.[59] The Center Party leader, however, did know enough to mistrust Hitler, with the result that Kaas not only posed his questions in writing but also released them to the press.[60] This supposed breach of confidentiality allowed Hitler to shift the blame for the failure of talks to Kaas. On 6 February Hans Heinrich Lammers, head of the Reich chancery, informed Hindenburg that talks with the Center had failed.[61] Lammers also claimed there had been no time to negotiate with the Bavarian People's Party (Bayerische Volkspartei or BVP), a claim that was patently untrue. Already on 4 February the Bavarian minister president Heinrich Held had written to Hindenburg to warn against possible plans to disempower the state governments.[62] As the government's actions confirmed, Hitler tolerated neither opposition nor compromise.

Kaas now had to consider the Center's future course. The party could oppose the Hitler cabinet the way he had opposed the Papen cabinet, but the situations were incomparable. One was a right-wing cabinet committed to changing Germany, but without the willingness to employ violence. The other was a radical cabinet whose paramilitary forces had proved all too willing to sow terror. Also, there was a difference between traditional Prussian anti-Catholicism and the NSDAP's paganism. On 5 February Kaas addressed the Center Party's executive. Since the Reich president had dissolved the Reichstag, Kaas vowed that the Center would embark upon the new electoral campaign as a free and independent party. Kaas added that the Center was willing to cooperate with all forces willing to engage in the recovery of Germany. Perhaps Kaas's personal outrage contributed to his vehement critique of the new government as a minority government formed without negotiations that included all parties, without parliamentary support, and without a program. He reaffirmed that the Center continued to promote *Sammlung* and the cooperation of all forces ready to labor for Germany's recovery. Kaas rejected the NSDAP's accusations against the Weimar-era political parties. The Center would have to defend itself constantly against claims that it had betrayed Germany to the Western allies. Kaas ended his speech by claiming that for fourteen years, the Center had served Germany well, despite the NSDAP's incessant claims to the contrary.[63] Beyond emphasizing the Center's record and exposing the NSDAP's lies, Kaas seemed to have no strategy adequate to respond to the NSDAP's ensuing terror. The Center and Kaas faced stark choices. The Center could either pursue a course of constructive cooperation aimed at improving whatever government existed, or it could withdraw and let those bearing responsibility see how they could stabilize German politics and, above all, the life of average Germans. This second option, however, the Center could not do and had never done. Its values demanded that it remain constructive and prevent potential anarchy and civil war. To this Kaas remained committed.[64]

Kaas, the Center, and the Enabling Act

The campaign for the 5 March 1933 Reichstag elections was more brutally contested than any other in Weimar's history. On 15 February the Center's newsletter *Das Zentrum* warned that "one cannot combat Bolshevism with nationalist phrases and a racial ideology which itself constitutes a heresy and will plunge the people into error and perdition. Necessary is a Christian renewal of the foundations of state, society and economy."[65] On 19 February the government banned the newspapers related to the Center for three days.[66] Then, a scant nine days later, the Reichstag fire triggered a sustained wave of violent persecution of communists, conservatives, Jews, and Catholics throughout Germany. Leading Center politicians such as Brüning, Adam Stegerwald, and Carl Ulitzka were threatened and even assaulted while campaigning.[67] And yet, despite the terror, the Center Party's voters remained loyal as the German electorate as a whole denied the NSDAP the parliamentary majority it had sought. The NSDAP would have to cooperate with the DNVP and the forces that had come together in the Combat Front Black-White-Red (Kampffront Schwarz-Weiß-Rot) to gain a parliamentary majority. Not even that, however, would suffice to enact constitutional changes.

Kaas seized the opportunity to try to regain a small measure of influence over the government—if only to protect Catholic values—and sought a meeting with Vice Chancellor Franz von Papen that took place the day after the election. According to Papen's report to the cabinet, Kaas visited him without informing the rest of the Center Party leadership. Supposedly, Kaas came to "draw a line with the past" and to offer the new government "the cooperation of the Center Party." At no point in his report did Papen mention an enabling law or a concordat.[68] Kaas was not the only Center Party leader reaching out to the NSDAP. According to Göring, he had been approached by Fritz Grass, one of the leaders of the Prussian Center, with an offer of Center Party cooperation as long as the Prussian government ceased making personnel changes that would adversely affect Catholic civil servants. Göring responded that if the Center refused to support the government, then all civil servants who belonged to the Center Party would be dismissed. Otherwise, he suggested to his colleagues in the Reich cabinet, it would be best to politely ignore the Center from here on out.[69] The NSDAP leadership concluded from all of this that members of the Center themselves were increasingly worried about their futures, as were many Germans.

A week later, the situation had changed dramatically. At a ministerial conference on 7 March 1933 Hitler explained that the passage of the Enabling Act with a two-thirds majority in the Reichstag no longer posed a problem. Reich minister of the interior Wilhelm Frick added that the nonsocialist parties had signaled their willingness to cooperate. This did not mean, however, that the Center or the other parties consciously supported the new cabinet's plans. Not even Papen seemed to have understood the momentous changes that were in store for Germany's political parties; he was so naïve as to suggest that keeping the political parties abreast of planned changes might help integrate German political Catholicism into the new political order.[70] Nor do the minutes of the ministerial conference shed any light on what might have transpired in the conversation between Kaas and Papen. In any case, Kaas believed the door to limited cooperation with the Reich government had been reopened. Not only were other Center Party officials seeking contact with the Reich government, but one of Germany's leading newspapers, the *Frankfurter Zeitung*, commented within days on the possibility of Center support for an Enabling Act.[71] Given the national distribution of the *Frankfurter Zeitung*, Kaas's negotiations with the government had not remained secret. As the *Frankfurter Zeitung* noted, all politically aware Germans recognized the burden that now rested so heavily on the Center as the party whose support would determine the fate of the Enabling Act in the Reichstag and, with it, the future of Germany's itself.[72]

The next step in the negotiations was a meeting on 20 March 1933 between Hitler, Frick, and three Center Party leaders: Kaas, Stegerwald, and Albert Hackelsberger. As Hitler reported at a ministerial

conference later in the day, "The Center Party leaders had acknowledged the need for an enabling act and had merely voiced the request
that a small body be established to receive regular information about
government measures." The chancellor added that the Center's support would yield a great prestige victory abroad.[73] According to Kaas's
own report to the Center Party leadership, Hitler had emphasized the
anti-Marxist thrust of the Enabling Act and assured the Center Party
officials that "the rights of the Reich President, the Federal Council
[Reichsrat], and the Reichstag would be substantially preserved."[74]
One might be forgiven for thinking these were accounts of two different meetings. Kaas, however, had no illusions about the cabinet's
intentions. Reporting to the Center Party Reichstag delegation, he
warned that the party's political strategies and tactics would be limited for the near future and that the defense of religious concerns
would become the party's primary concern. Nonetheless, he argued
that the Center "must strive with all means to return to a constitutional basis [of governing]." He added that he hoped "the bourgeois
circles represented in the current cabinet might at least prevent the
worst from happening."[75]

Others in the Reichstag were not quite so complacent about the
regime's intentions and its trustworthiness. Instead they sought to
create last-minute safeguards against a National Socialist dictatorship.
As Brüning recalled some years later, "On the morning of 21 March
[DNVP Reichstag delegation chairman Ernst] Oberfohren approached
me before the ceremonies in the Potsdam Garrison Church, and on
the same day I had a message from another influential member of the
DNVP asking me to meet Hugenberg at his house that night. It was
agreed at that evening meeting that I should draft an amendment to the
proposed Enabling Bill that would guarantee civil and political liberties, and that this amendment should be introduced in the Reichstag,
for tactical reasons, by the DNVP. The amendment was drafted by Dr.
[Johannes] Bell and myself with two other members of the Center Party
and delivered to the DNVP."[76] Kaas apparently was aware of this last-
ditch legislative proposal, which would have represented an improve-
ment over the guarantees Hitler had promised to put in writing. Yet
one has to wonder why Kaas failed to mention this promise during
the debate in the Center Reichstag delegation on 22 March. Here Kaas
spoke of efforts to strengthen the rights of the Reich president and to
define more narrowly some of the terms in the bill, which he would
pursue in a meeting with Hitler scheduled for the afternoon.[77] But there
is no mention of the arrangement with the DNVP in the minutes of the
Center Reichstag delegation.

Kaas returned from the meeting with Hitler quite distraught. The Reich president's prerogatives were to be curtailed and the duration of the law much longer than originally indicated. On a number of other points, Hitler gave only ambiguous or evasive answers to Kaas's concerns. In the end, according to Kaas, Hitler warned that the government's measures would be implemented one way or another, either by means of an Enabling Act or by declaring a state of emergency.[78] Upon Kaas's request that these guarantees be put in writing, Hitler promised only that the Center would be involved in formulating the bill that would implement these guarantees. This, however, never occurred.

On the following morning with the first reading of the Enabling Act scheduled for later in the day, Bell—himself one of the longest-serving members in the Center Reichstag delegation and an important figure in defending the Center against the "stab-in-the-back" legend—and Hackelsberger visited Frick to help formulate the bill's final text with special attention to the concerns of the Center. Bell and Hackelsberger, however, had little, if any, success in influencing the draft of the bill despite Hitler's assurances that the Center would be involved its final details. In the subsequent meeting of the Center Reichstag delegation, Kaas reviewed Hitler's assurances and warned that both rejection and adoption of the bill bore immeasurable dangers. Kaas announced that he would not recommend how deputies should vote.[79] At the same time, Kaas recognized that the way in which individual deputies voted might put them at severe risk, with the result that all deputies would have to agree to all vote one way or the other.[80] It was with this in mind that Kaas urged deputies to think of their spouses and children.[81] Kaas obviously understood the gravity of the decision facing the Center, having lamented earlier in the day that the vote for the Enabling Act was even more difficult than the vote for the Versailles Peace Treaty.[82] Nonetheless, he personally supported the bill as the best that could be achieved to maintain the semblance of constitutional order. Rather than advocate authoritarian solutions for Germany's parliamentary crisis, Kaas sought to restrict the government's power. The fears of many deputies, not only in the Center Party, that a failure to adopt the proposed bill would result in immediate violence not just in the Reichstag but throughout Germany demonstrates that Kaas's concerns were indeed legitimate.

As the deputies left their caucus in the Reichstag for the plenary session in the Kroll Opera House across the square, Brüning warned that there were no guarantees that the NSDAP would stand by the assurances it had promised. One could not rely on Hindenburg, Brüning continued, to serve as an effective check on the government. While Kaas had emphasized the lack of alternatives and the need to avoid collapse at all costs, Brüning emphasized the lack of safeguards and the moral hazard involved in this momentous decision. Both politicians were correct in their assessment, but whereas Kaas remained true to the long practices of the Center Party and to his own understanding of remaining within constitutional frameworks, Brüning had come to realize that the constitutional safeguards were too weak to be reliable.[83]

In the Reichstag session, Hitler presented the draft Enabling Act. His comments included all of the safeguards the Center had demanded as a precondition for the party's support as well as an unexpected statement expressing a desire for improved relations with the Holy See. When Hitler assured the Center's deputies of his interest in preserving existing concordats, he seemed to be meeting the Center's demands. New was Hitler's promise to maintain constructive relations with the Holy See, but it was merely one statement in a lengthy passage on the future of German foreign policy. Nonetheless, it seemed Hitler had gone further than previous chancellors in expressing a concrete desire for an agreement with the Holy See.

Following Hitler's surprising speech in the afternoon of March 23 and the concessions that he had apparently made to the concerns of the Catholic Church and its defenders, the deputies from the Center returned to their deliberation of the bill. At no point in these deliberations, however, did they discuss or mention the possibility of a Reich concordat between the Nazi regime and the Holy See.[84] There was and never had been a quid pro quo of a concordat for the Enabling Act. Moreover, Kaas did not use the possibility of such a quid pro quo to convince the deputies to support the Act—in contrast to the emphasis he placed on Hitler's guarantees, something that Johannes Schauff, first elected to the Reichstag in 1932, bitterly criticized. "[Kaas]," Schauff wrote some time later, "knew how to render support [for the bill] palatable by using overly wise arguments to emphasize the many promised conditions and safeguards."[85] This statement is revealing for several reasons. First, it indicates that Kaas had to work hard to convince his fellow deputies to support the bill and that they would not follow blindly. Second, the reason for Kaas's eventual success lay in the promises that had been made for the preservation of minimal democratic vestiges. Judging by Schauff's statements, he did not believe Kaas's argumentation to be sincere. Kaas's notion of *Sammlungspolitik*, of a broad German movement against the political left and with strong corporatist structures, had completely unraveled in the wake of Hitler's appointment as chancellor.[86] Kaas's credibility was deeply shaken. Schauff believed that Kaas wanted to liquidate the Center to facilitate the integration of German Catholics into the new order.[87] Furthermore, in Schauff's opinion, Kaas was too much the canon lawyer and church diplomat to consider the Center Party beyond its usefulness to the church. As the debate dragged on, Josef Wirth asked for a straw poll of the deputies' intention to vote. Although the majority supported the Enabling Act, a significant minority did not. Nonetheless, "after further discussion about the result of the straw poll, the consensus of the deputies, in consideration of the future of the party, was to follow the majority and to vote for the Enabling Act." Kaas was then authorized to make a statement on behalf of the delegation.[88] In his own remarks, Kaas welcomed the chancellor's speech earlier in the afternoon. In the final analysis, all but two absent Center deputies voted in favor of the bill.

An Ignominious End

In an article that appeared anonymously in the *Kölnische Volkszeitung* on 5 April, Kaas defended his party's vote for the Enabling Act as the logical corollary to the appeal he had issued at Münster for the *Sammmlung* of all national forces without regard to party affiliation into a united front dedicated to the positive reconstruction of the German nation. At the same time, Kaas reassured the party faithful that the promises that Hitler had made in his speech to the Reichstag—though not in the formal written statement Kaas had requested—eliminated the threat of a radical break with established constitutional practice and guaranteed a constitutional transition to the new political order.[89] While Kaas believed he had safeguarded constitutional processes, Karl Bachem, a Center Reichstag deputy from Cologne, later wrote that while the decision to support the Enabling Act was in keeping with Kaas's *Sammlungspolitik*, it was the very antithesis of the Center's tradition of constitutionalism, justice, and freedom.[90] Kaas, however, still considered the Center necessary as guardian of Catholic rights. On 7 April Kaas departed for Rome and ran into his old nemesis Franz von Papen while in transit. When Papen suggested that after the passage of the Enabling Act the Center was no longer necessary, Kaas replied that firm guarantees were still needed for the preservation of Germany's Catholic culture.[91] While the idea of a concordat had played no role whatsoever in the decision-making process that led the Center Reichstag delegation to affirm its support of the Enabling Act, Kaas was eager to capitalize on Hitler's comments about his desire for improved relations with the Holy See. It was only natural that the conversation between Kaas and Papen would turn to the question of a concordat between the new regime in Berlin and the Holy See. According to both men, this was the first time they discussed a concordat. Whether or not this is true is impossible to determine, as there is no evidence either way. The fact that they spoke at all indicates that the rift of the previous summer had not been too deep to bridge.

Kaas's career as Center Party leader ended ignominiously. He left Berlin shortly after the vote on the Enabling Act, returned, and then left again on 7 April. His resignation as party chairman was almost an after-thought, declared from afar, without a word of apology or explanation. He left it to Brüning, Joos, Hackelsberger, and others to lead the party in the critical ten weeks from late April until the beginning of July. Even in late May 1933 Kaas continued to stress that in Germany "the existing government should be supported with [available] means."[92] In Rome Kaas sought to garner a position as concordat negotiator, which neither the German bishops nor the Reich government desired.[93] That Kaas nonetheless crafted the first draft of the Vatican's concordat proposal underscored the trust that Pacelli held in his former advisor. As early as 1930, Pacelli had let the German ambassador to the Holy See, Diego von Bergen, know that Kaas would be most welcome as government-appointed negotiator.[94] Now, however, Kaas's role during the negotia-tions was an unofficial but public one. In congratulating Pacelli on the successful conclusion of the Concordat, the bishop of Trier Franz Rudolf Bornewasser praised Kaas for his contributions to the agreement. At the same time, Bornewasser lamented that "unfortunate current conditions prevent Kaas from returning to his home."[95] Pacelli replied that Kaas had come to Rome on his own initiative and that only on 23 June had Cardinal Adolf Bertram of Breslau suggested to Pacelli that Kaas might be considered the episcopate's confidant. Since Kaas had delivered the first rough draft in April, this was somewhat disingenuous of Pacelli, especially since Pacelli also wrote that he had hoped Kaas would remain in Rome longer as the execution of the Concordat was causing difficul-ties.[96] For his part, Kaas was bitterly disappointed with the final terms of the Concordat and bore a strong sense of personal responsibility for the vulnerable situation in which the German Catholic Church found itself after the regime failed to live up to the terms of its agreement with the Vatican. As Kaas expressed it in February 1934, "We simply thought we were dealing with honorable men."[97]

Conclusion

Contemporaries and scholars alike have pointed to the difficulties in assessing Kaas's role as Center Party chairman. His task was challenging; the times were extremely difficult. How under these circumstances does one define success? Most but not all scholars consider him a failure, but by what standard? Charges that Kaas "sold out" the Center Party or that he was only a disengaged absentee leader are unsustainable. On the other hand, there is much positive to note. Kaas understood his own strengths and weaknesses and recruited competent help to strengthen his leadership. The administrative work of leading the party he delegated to Joos. In legislative matters Kaas sought Brüning's assistance and busied himself with larger policy questions. Initially Kaas also focused heavily on his competing career in the church, but once it became clear that he would not be called to Rome by his former mentor, Cardinal Pacelli, he devoted himself fully to his task as party leader. The Center endured and persevered, in some instances because of Kaas's leadership, at a time when most other German parties were hemorrhaging support in one election after another. Most importantly, the Center did not fracture, something that had seemed possible in 1928. It supported the Brüning government through two difficult years and contributed to the reelection of President von Hindenburg. And throughout all of this, Kaas insisted the Center Party remain committed to constitutional government and the defense of civil rights.

As a party leader at the end of the Weimar Republic, Kaas sought to rally leaders of other parties by his appeals to *Sammlung*. What initially was a concrete appeal for a grand coalition stretching from the DNVP to the SPD eventually became a *cri de coeur* that Germans might recognize that only self-sacrificing cooperation across party lines could rescue Germany from impending chaos. Kaas's relationship with the DNVP shifted. Initially rejecting the DNVP's sharp turn to the right under Hugenberg, Kaas was later at times willing to engage with the DNVP as long as plans excluded Franz von Papen, a man whom Kaas had branded the "Ephialtes of the Center." His refusal to work with Papen, despite the urging from the right wing of his own party, further narrowed options to prevent the rise of Hitler in the fall of 1932. Excluded from negotiations for a new cabinet in January 1933 and then facing the bitter reality of a national government under Hitler's leadership, Kaas sought to save what remained to be saved, both for his party's constituents and also for German constitutional government. Kaas's efforts to safeguard the rights of the Reichstag and the constitutional order were sincere, even in the discussions surrounding the Enabling Act. But it was precisely here that Kaas experienced his greatest failure. For in urging his party to support the Enabling Act so as to preserve if not the semblance of constitutional government itself, then at least the semblance of a constitutional transition to a new political order, he was responsible for helping make possible the very thing he was trying to prevent. And therein lay the tragedy of Ludwig Kaas.

Martin Menke is professor of history and political science at Rivier University in Nashua, New Hampshire, where he also serves as chair of the Department of History, Political Science, and Criminal Justice. Menke has published in the *Catholic Historical Review, Kirchliche Zeitgeschichte,* and the *Journal of Church and State,* and most recently "Multiple Caesars? Germany, Bavaria, and German Catholics in the Interwar Period" in *Beyond the Borders of Baptism: Catholicity, Allegiances, and Lived Identities* (edited by Michael L. Budde, 2016). He is currently working on a manuscript on the German Center Party from 1917 to 1933.

Notes

1. Kaas to Joseph Joos, 2 June 1932, in Harvard University Archives, Cambridge, Massachusetts, Brüning Papers (hereafter cited as Harvard University Archives, Brüning Papers), Acc. 13034, Box 1, Folder 2. I would like to thank Larry Eugene Jones not only for having shared this document and other materials related to this chapter but also for his careful editing and insightful review of this chapter as it made its way to publication.
2. Ludwig Volk claimed that Kaas did not resign because party leaders feared a repeat of the 1928 party elections. See Ludwig Volk, *Das Reichskonkordat vom 20. Juli 1933: Von den Ansätzen in der Weimarer Republik bis zur Ratifizierung am 10. September 1933* (Mainz: Matthias-Grunewald-Verlag, 1972), 42.
3. Georg May, *Ludwig Kaas: Der Priester, der Politiker und der Gelehrte aus der Schule von Ulrich Stutz,* 3 vols. (Amsterdam: Verlag B. R. Grüner, 1981).
4. On these developments, see Karsten Ruppert, *Im Dienst am Staat von Weimar: Das Zentrum als regierende Partei in der Weimarer Demokratie 1923–1930* (Düsseldorf: Droste, 1992), 347–57, and Bernhard Forster, *Adam Stegerwald (1874–1945): Christlich-nationaler Gewerkschafter, Zentrumspolitiker, Mitbegründer der Unionsparteien* (Düsseldorf: Droste, 2004), 455–64.
5. Josef Mausbach, *Christliche Staatsordnung und Staatsgesinnung* (Mönchen-Gladbach: Volksvereinsverlag, 1922).
6. *Stenographischer Bericht über die Verhandlungen des Reichstags,* 19 May 1925, 385: 1910.
7. Speech by Kaas before the information conference of the Center executive committee, 27 July 1930, ACDP Sankt Augustin, VI-051, 280/1–2.
8. Ludwig Kaas, *Nicht rückwärts—vorwärts! Rede* (Berlin: Zentralverlag, 1931), 5. A copy may be found in Bundesarchiv Berlin (hereafter cited as BA Berlin), R 43 I, 2659/17–29.
9. Ibid.

10. Kaas to Hugenberg, 7 January 1930, in the unpublished Nachlass Otto Schmidt-Hannover, BA Koblenz (hereafter cited as BA Koblenz, NL Schmidt-Hannover), 73.

11. Kaas, *Nicht rückwärts—vorwärts!*, 8–10.

12. Entry in the diary of Reinhold Quaatz, 27 August 1931, in Quaatz's unpublished Nachlass, BA Koblenz, 17, reprinted in Hermann Weiß and Paul Hoser, eds., *Die Deutschnationalen und die Zerstörung der Weimarer Republik: Aus dem Tagebuch von Reinhold Quaatz 1928–1933* (Munich: Oldenbourg, 1989), 143–45.

13. In this respect, see the correspondence between Franz and Clemens August von Galen from 1928, in the Nachlass of Franz von Galen, Vereinigte Westfälische Adelsarchive, Münster (hereafter cited as VWA Münster), 227. On the role of confession as a unifying factor in the Center Party, see Karsten Ruppert, "Die weltanschaulich bedingte Politik der Deutschen Zentrumspartei in ihrer Weimarer Epoche," *Historische Zeitschrift* 285 (2007): 49–97.

14. Records of the roll-call votes in the *Stenographische Berichte über die Verhandlungen des Reichstags 1930–33*. See also May, *Ludwig Kaas*, 214–21, esp. 221. Without evidence, May claims that Kaas wanted to remain in Rome but decided that his responsibilities in Germany obliged him to return. May, *Kaas*, 216.

15. Kaas to Hugenberg, 7 January 1930, BA Koblenz, NL Schmidt-Hannover, 73.

16. Ludwig Volk, *Das Reichskonkordat vom 20. Juli 1933 vom 20. Juli 1933: Von den Ansätzen in der Weimarer Republik bis zur Ratifizierung am 10. September 1933* (Mainz: Matthias-Grunewald-Verlag, 1972), 37–38.

17. Fritz Buschmann, "Graue Eminenz in Berlin und Rom: Ludwig Kaas— Fraktionsvorsitzender der Zentrumspartei im Deutschen Reichstag und Berater des Papstes Pius XII," conversation of 29 May 1986, in the unpublished Nachlass of Fritz Buschmann, Institut für Zeitgeschichte, Munich (hereafter cited as IfZ Munich), MS 2108, 2.

18. Ludwig Volk claims that Kaas traveled to Rome on behalf of the foreign office on a mission to secure a bishop for the armed forces, which would make him exempt from the hierarchical authority of any metropolitan bishop and directly responsible only to the Holy See. In that case, would Kaas not have asked for leave from the Reichstag? See Ludwig Volk, "Die unverzeihlichen Sünden des Prälaten Kaas: Was Heinrich Brüning nicht verwinden konnte." in Ludwig Volk, *Katholische Kirche und Nationalsozialismus: Ausgewählte Aufsätze*, ed. Dieter Albrecht (Mainz: Mathias-Grunewald-Verlag, 1987), 323.

19. *Germania*, 29 July 1930, no. 347.

20. *Vossische Zeitung*, 9 May 1933, no. 219, BA Berlin, R 5–VI, 716/17. See also Ruppert, *Im Dienst am Staat von Weimar*, 356–57.

21. Kaas, *Nicht rückwärts—vorwärts!*, 6–11, the quote on 9.

22. Papen to Schleicher, 21 September [(*sic*) May] 1932, Bundesarchiv-Militärabteilung (hereafter cited as BA-MA Freiburg), NL Schleicher, 22/149–49a.

23. Walter Hagemann, Zeugenschriften 1656, 7 May 1958, IfZ Munich.

24. Entry in the diary of Reinhold Quaatz, 27 August 1931, BA Koblenz, NL Quaatz, 17.

25. Government statement on Kaas's discussion with Papen about a possible chancellorship, 7 June 1932, BA Berlin, R 43 I, 2659/117–18. Franz von Galen claimed on 2 August 1932 that Kaas and Papen had spoken for five minutes before Papen accepted Hindenburg's offer. Galen to Riex, 2 August 1922, VWA Münster NL Galen, 44. In the private papers of Franz von Galen, there is an account of Papen's talks with Kaas and Hindenburg that matches Kaas's later claims. The document lists no author but is dated 7 June 1932. No title, first line begins, "Es ist nicht mehr ausführlich über Brünings Rücktritt zu sprechen." This was most likely the draft of an article that Galen had written for subsequent publication.

26. For Kaas's own account of his negotiations with Papen, see Bormann's notes on his report to the Center executive committee, 8 June 1932, in the unpublished Nachlass of Wilhelm Bormann, Archiv für Christlich-Demokratische Politik, Sankt Augustin (hereafter cited as ACDP Sankt Augustin), NL Bormann, I-392, 9, reprinted in Martin Schumacher, "Zwischen 'Einschaltung' und 'Gleichschaltung': Zum Untergang der Deutschen Zentrumspartei 1932/33," *Historisches Jahrbuch* 99 (1979): 268–303, 291–93.

27. Kaas to Brüning, 2 June 1932, Harvard University Archives, Brüning Papers, Acc. 13034, Box 1, Folder 2.

28. In the Papen cabinet, there was one Graf, four Freiherren, two "vons," and three commoners.

29. Government statement, 4 June 1932, in *Akten der Reichskanzlei: Das Kabinett von Papen: 1. Juni bis 3. December 1932*, ed. Karl-Heinz Minuth, 2 vols. (Boppard am Rhein: Harald Boldt Verlag, 1989), 1:13–14.

30. Bormann's notes on the meeting of the Center executive committee, 8 June 1932, ACDP Sankt Augustin, NL Bormann, I-392, 9, reprinted in Schumacher, "Zwischen 'Einschaltung' und 'Gleichschaltung,'" 290.

31. Appeal of Kaas to Center Party voters, 26 June 1932, in BA Berlin, NS 5–VI-714/96. See also various newspaper clippings in the file on Ludwig Kaas in the press archives of the Reichs-Landbund, BA Berlin, R 8034 III, 225/19. The party placed him second only to Brüning on the list of national candidates. See the *Vossische Zeitung*, 2 July 1932, no. 315.

32. Once again Joos "ran" the party. He was willing to travel to Neudeck to see Hindenburg in order to prevent an unconstitutional government. See *Germania*, 1 September 1932, no. 163.

33. Herbert Hömig, *Brüning: Politiker ohne Auftrag: Zwischen Weimarer und Bonner Republik* (Paderborn: Ferdinand Schöningh Verlag, 2005), 28.

34. Ibid.

35. *Bayerischer Kurier*, 5 August 1932, no. 218, in the unpublished Nachlass of Herbert Frank, IfZ Munich, ED 414, vol. 211.

36. Ibid. See also Joos to Galen, 2 August 1932, VWA Münster, NL Galen, 45. Galen had written to Joos and the leader of the Prussian Center Party Steger to urge support for the Papen government in opposition to the

NSDAP. See Galen to Joos, 2 August 1932, ibid., and Steger, 2 August 1932, ibid.

37. Minutes of the executive committee of the Center Reichstag delegation, 29 August 1932, in *Die Protokolle der Reichstagsfraktion und des Fraktionsvorstandes der Deutschen Zentrumspartei 1926–1933* (hereafter cited as *Zentrumsprotokolle II*), ed. Rudolf Morsey (Mainz: Mathias Grünewald, 1969), 581–82.

38. Galen to Joos, 2 November 1932, VWA Münster, NL Galen, 45/100–107.

39. For example, see Kurt von Lersner to Schleicher, 27 July 1932, BA-MA Freiburg, NL Schleicher, 22/66–68.

40. Minutes of the executive committee of the Center Reichstag delegation, 29 August 1932, in *Zentrumsprotokolle II*, 581–82. According to Hömig, Brüning had urgently requested that Kaas return from Sterzing. See Herbert Hömig, *Brüning, Politiker ohne Auftrag*, 38. See also Föhr's notes on the meetings, 13 September 1932, in the unpublished Nachlass of Ernst Föhr, Erzbischöfliches Archiv Freiburg (hereafter cited as EAB Freiburg), NL Föhr, Na 73/1, as well as the report in the *Münsterscher Anzeiger*, 13 September 1932, no. 975.

41. Papen to Galen, 17 October 1932, VWA Münster, 45.

42. *Germania*, 18 October 1932, no. 290.

43. *Germania*, 24 October 1932, no. 296.

44. There is a parallel here to the larger conclusion Larry Eugene Jones draws about Protestant conservatives' disappointed view of Hindenburg in 1932. See Larry Eugene Jones, *Hitler versus Hindenburg* (Cambridge: Cambridge University Press, 2016), 314.

45. On Galen, see Joachim Kuropka, "Aus heißer Liebe zu unserem Volk und zu unserer hl. Kirche: Franz Graf von Galen als Politiker," *Oldenburger Jahrbuch* 107 (2007): 101–25, esp. 113–17.

46. Planck's memorandum of a conversation with Kaas and Joos, 16 November 1932, in *Das Kabinett Papen*, ed. Minuth, 2:944–45.

47. Meeting of the Center Reichstag delegation, 29 November 1932, in *Zentrumsprotokolle II*, 598–600.

48. Memorandum by Undersecretary Otto Meissner on a conversation between the Reich president and Kaas, 18 November 1932, in *Das Kabinett Papen*, ed. Minuth, 2:973–74.

49. Fritz Grass, "Aufzeichnung," 26 November 1932, NL Lauscher, reprinted in Rudolf Morsey, "Die Deutsche Zentrumspartei," in *Das Ende der Parteien 1933: Darstellungen und Dokumente*, ed. Erich Matthias and Rudolf Morsey (Düsseldorf: Droste Verlag, 1960), 425. See also Meissner to Hitler, 24 November 1932, in *Das Kabinett Papen*, ed. Minuth, 2:998–1000.

50. Minutes by Meissner of a meeting of Kaas and Hindenburg, 25 November 1932, ibid., 2:1023–25.

51. Report by Papen at a ministerial conference, 25 November 1932, ibid., 2:1013.

52. Report by Schleicher at a ministerial conference, 16 January 1933, in *Akten der Reichskanzlei: Das Kabinett von Schleicher. 3. Dezember 1932 bis 30. Januar 1933*, ed. Anton Golecki (Boppard: Harald Boldt 1986), 234.

53. Minutes of the executive committee of the Center Reichstag delegation, 20 January 1933, in *Zentrumsprotokolle II*, 606–7. See also Christoph Hübner, *Die Rechtskatholiken, die Zentrumspartei und die katholische Kirche in Deutschland bis zum Reichskonkordat von 1933: Ein Beitrag zur Geschichte des Scheiterns der Weimarer Republik* (Berlin: Lit Verlag, 2014), 710.

54. Herbert Hömig, *Brüning: Kanzler in der Krise der Republik; Eine Weimarer Biographie* (Paderborn: Ferdinand Schöningh, 2000), 387.

55. Monsignor Ernst Föhr, one of the leading Center Party figures in Baden, noted on 13 September 1932 at a meeting of the Center Party Reichstag deputies that the Papen government had violated the constitutional order by its measures against Prussia. Likewise, the dissolution of the Reichstag to prevent it from abrogating emergency decrees and preventing votes of no confidence were also denounced as violations of the constitution. EBA Freiburg, NL Föhr, NA73/1.

56. Kaas to Schleicher, 26 January 1933, BA Berlin, R 43 I, 1865/403–5. For an account of conversations the leaders of the Center and Schleicher conducted with the DNVP and NSDAP in January 1933, see "Die Wühlarbeit der Krisenmacher," *Das Zentrum* 4, nos. 1–2 (January–February 1933): 3. Joseph Bendersky has argued that Germany's politicians should have understood that the way to block Adolf Hitler's rise to power was to accept unconstitutional measures in January 1933 and that the failure to use emergency decrees against Hitler permitted him later to institute his own after the Reichstag fire. See Joseph W. Bendersky, *Carl Schmitt: Theorist for the Reich* (Princeton: Princeton University Press, 1983), 185. This, however, seems to ignore Kaas's conviction that only a strict adherence to constitutional processes could guarantee responsible change. It also ignores the Center's position since 1917, that the constitutional order must be upheld and that the Center's fateful task is to preserve government at all costs rather than withdraw from government and let the anti-republican parties assume responsibility.

57. Protocol of a conversation between representatives of the Center Party and Hitler, 31 January 1933, in the unpublished Nachlass of Ludwig Kaas, BA Koblenz, 3/1–6.

58. Ministerial conference, 31 January 1933, *Akten der Reichskanzlei: Die Regierung Hitler; 30. Januar bis 31. August 1933*, ed. Karl-Heinz Minuth (Boppard: Harald Boldt 1983), part 1, 5–8.

59. Lammers to Vockel, 2 February 1933, ibid., 33.

60. *Kölnische Volkszeitung*, 1 February 1933, no. 32.

61. Lammers to the Bureau of the Reich President, 6 February 1933, in *Die Regierung Hitler*, ed. Minuth, 46–47.

62. Held to Hindenburg, 4 February 1933, ibid., 45.

63. In this respect, see Bormann's handwritten notes on the meeting of the Center executive committee, 5 February 1933, ACDP Sankt Augustin, NL Bormann, I-392, 9, reprinted in Schumacher, "Zwischen 'Einschaltung' und 'Gleichschaltung,'" 299–31, as well as the report in *Germania*, 6 February 1933, no. 37.

64. In this regard, Bendersky's criticism of the Center is valid. Perhaps Weimar would have achieved stability had the Center withdrawn from govern-

ment in one of the many earlier crises and thus forced the non-NSDAP right to take government responsibility in an emergency. See Bendersky, *Schmitt*, 189.

65. *Das Zentrum* 4, nos. 3–4 (15 February 1933): 96.
66. *Germania*, 19 February 1933, no. 49. After Wilhelm Marx intervened with Hermann Göring, the government lifted the ban the following day.
67. *Germania*, 23 February 1933, no. 54.
68. Ministerial conference, 7 March 1933, in *Die Regierung Hitler*, ed. Minuth, 161.
69. Göring at the ministerial conference, 7 March 1933, ibid., 162.
70. Papen at the ministerial conference, 15 March 1933, ibid., 215.
71. *Frankfurter Zeitung*, 9 March 1933, no. 182, reprinted in Rudolf Morsey, ed., *Das "Ermächtigungsgesetz" vom 24. März 1933* (Göttingen: Vandenhoeck and Ruprecht, 1968), 28.
72. *Germania*, 19 March 1933, no. 78. For a fuller discussion of the Center Party and the Enabling Act, see Martin Menke, "Misunderstood Civic Duty: The German Center Party and the Enabling Act," *Journal of Church and State* 51 (2009): 236–64.
73. Hitler's reports in the ministerial conference, 20 March 1933, in *Die Regierung Hitler*, ed. Minuth, 239.
74. Meeting of the executive committee of the Center Reichstag delegation, 20 March 1933, in *Zentrumsprotokolle II*, 622.
75. Minutes of the Center Reichstag delegation, 20 March 1933, ibid., 623.
76. Brüning, untitled document, Harvard University Archives, Brüning Papers 93.35, Box 4, Folder 3.
77. Minutes of the Center Reichstag delegation, 22 March 1933, in *Zentrumsprotokolle II*, 624.
78. Minutes of the executive committee of the Center Reichstag delegation, 22 March 1933, ibid., 629.
79. Minutes of the Center Reichstag delegation, 23 March 1933, ibid., 630.
80. Clara Siebert, MdR, in Morsey, *Ermächtigungsgesetz*, 137.
81. According to a sworn statement by Heinrich G. Ritzel, 30 August 1961, IfZ Munich, NL Schauff, ED 346, 24, Kaas implored Ritzel to support the Enabling Act to protect his family. Ritzel supposedly responded by imploring Kaas to vote against the Enabling Act since the monsignor had no family.
82. Minutes of the executive committee of the Center Reichstag delegation, 20 March 1933, in *Zentrumsprotokolle II*, 622.
83. Draft of the minutes of the Center Party Reichstag delegation, 23 March 1933, BA Koblenz, NL Kaas, 4/2–4.
84. Rudolf Morsey, "Das Ende der Zentrumspartei 1933," in *Das Reichskonkordat: Forschungsstand, Dokumente, Kontroverse*, ed. Thomas Brechenmacher (Paderborn: Ferdinand Schöningh, 2007), 51. Cesare Orsenigo, the papal nuncio in Berlin, also noted that he hoped Kaas's efforts to secure Center Party support for the Enabling Act "will have an effect on the government, especially regarding the concordats." See Orsenigo to Pacelli, 24 March 1933, in *Die Kirchlichen Akten über die Reichskonkordatsverhandlungen 1933*, ed. Ludwig Volk (Mainz: Ferdinand Schöningh, 1969), 3–5.

85. Johannes Schauff, "Dezember 1934: Aus meiner beruflichen und politischen Arbeit," *Pulheimer Beiträge zur Geschichte und Heimatkunde* 9 (1985): 94.
86. For details on Kaas's supposed affinity for fascist regimes, see Klaus Scholder, "Altes und Neues zur Vorgeschichte des Reichskonkordats,." *Vierteljahrshefte für Zeitgeschichte* 26 (1978): 535–70, and Gerhard Besier and Francesco Piombo, *Der Heilige Stuhl und Hitler-Deutschland: Die Faszination des Totalitären* (Stuttgart: Deutsche Verlagsgesellschaft, 2004), 191.
87. Schauff, "Dezember 1934," 92. Despite his bitter criticism of Kaas, Schauff remained close to Kaas. Kaas helped the Schauff family resettle in Rome upon their return from Brazil after the war.
88. Minutes of the Center Reichstag delegation, 23 March 1933, in *Zentrumsprotokolle II*, 631–32.
89. For the text of Kaas's article "Der Weg des Zentrums," see Josef Becker, "Zentrum und Ermächtigungsgesetz," *Vierteljahrshefte für Zeitgeschichte* 9 (1982): 195–210, esp. 202–7.
90. Morsey, *Ermächtigungsgesetz*, 84.
91. Protocol by Perlitus of conversation between representatives from the Center and Hitler, 31 January 1933, BA Koblenz, NL Kaas, 3/1–6. See also the introduction by Morsey in "Ludwig Kaas, 'Tagebuch 7.-20. April 1933,'" ed. Rudolf Morsey, in *Stimmen der Zeit* 166 (1959 60), 424, as well as Robert Leiber, "Reichskonkordat und Ende der Zentrumspartei," *Stimmen der Zeit* 167 (1960): 220.
92. Remarks by Kaas at a luncheon of German clerics, 19 May 1933, as recorded in the notes of Bishop Wilhelm Berning of Osnabrück for the period of 15–27 May 1933, reprinted in *Die Kirchlichen Akten*, ed. Volk, 32.
93. Volk, *Reichskonkordat*, 204–5.
94. Ibid., 45.
95. Bishop of Trier to Pacelli, 30 July 1933, in the United States Holocaust Memorial Museum, RG-76.001M, Reel 1, Pos. 645, Fasc. 165.
96. Pacelli to Bornewasser, 16 August 1933, ibid., Reel 1, Pos. 645, Fasc. 165.
97. Excerpt from the memoirs of Alois Eckert from 1964, in *Die Kirchliche Akten*, ed. Volk, 354.

Bibliography

Beck, Hermann. *The Fateful Alliance: German Conservatives and Nazis in 1933; The Machtergreifung in a New Light*. New York and Oxford: Berghahn Books, 2008.

Becker, Josef. "Zentrum und Ermächtigungsgesetz." *Vierteljahrshefte für Zeitgeschichte* 9 (1982): 195–210.

Becker, Winfried, ed. *Die Minderheit als Mitte: Die Deutsche Zentrumspartei in der Innenpolitik des Reiches 1871–1933*. Paderborn: Ferdinand Schöningh, 1986.

———. "Die Deutsche Zentrumspartei gegenüber dem Nationalsozialismus und dem Reichskonkordat 1930–1934: Motivationsstrukturen und Situationszwänge." *Historisch-Politische Mitteilungen der Görresgesellschaft* 7 (2000): 1–37.

Besier, Gerhard, and Piombo, Francesco. *Der Heilige Stuhl und Hitler-Deutschland: Die Faszination des Totalitären*. Stuttgart: Deutsche Verlagsgesellschaft, 2004.

Brechenmacher, Thomas, ed. *Das Reichskonkordat 1933: Forschungsstand, Kontroversen, Dokumente*. Paderborn: Ferdinand Schöningh, 2007.

Golecki, Anton, ed. *Akten der Reichskanzlei: Die Regierung Hitler; 30. Januar bis 31. August 1933*. Boppard: Harald Boldt, 1983.

Hömig, Herbert. *Brüning: Kanzler in der Krise der Republik: Eine Weimarer Biographie*. Paderborn: Ferdinand Schöningh, 2000.

———. *Brüning: Politiker ohne Auftrag; Zwischen Weimarer und Bonner Repubik*. Paderborn: Ferdinand Schöningh, 2005.

Hübner, Christoph. *Die Rechtskatholiken, die Zentrumspartei und die katholische Kirche in Deutschland bis zum Reichskonkordat von 1933: Ein Beitrag zur Geschichte des Scheiterns der Weimarer Republik*. Berlin: Lit Verlag, 2014.

Jones, Larry Eugene. "Franz von Papen, Catholic Conservatives and the Establishment of the Third Reich, 1933/34." *Journal of Modern History* 83 (2011): 272–318.

———. *Hitler versus Hindenburg: The 1932 Presidential Elections and the End of the Weimar Republic*. Cambridge: Cambridge University Press, 2015.

Junker, Detlef. *Die Deutsche Zentrumspartei und Hitler 1932/33: Ein Beitrag zu Problematik des politischen Katholizismus in Deutschland*. Stuttgart: Klett-Verlag, 1969.

Kuropka, Joachim. "Aus heißer Liebe zu unserem Volk und zu unserer hl. Kirche: Franz Graf von Galen als Politiker." *Oldenburger Jahrbuch* 107 (2007): 101–25.

Leiber, Robert. "Reichskonkordat und Ende der Zentrumspartei." *Stimmen der Zeit* 167 (1960): 218–23.

May, Georg. *Ludwig Kaas: Der Priester, der Politiker, der Gelehrte aus der Schule von Ulrich Stutz*, 3 vols. Amsterdam: B. R. Grüner, 1981–82.

Menke, Martin. "Good Catholics—Good Germans." *Kirchliche Zeitgeschichte* 14 (2006): 1–16.

———. "Misunderstood Civic Duty: The German Center Party and the Enabling Act." *Journal of Church and State* 51 (2009): 236–64.

Morsey, Rudolf. "Die Deutsche Zentrumspartei." In *Das Ende der Parteien 1933: Darstellungen und Dokumente*, edited by Rudolf Morsey and Erich Mathias, 279–453. Düsseldorf: Droste Verlag, 1960.

———. "Adenauer und Kaas (1929–1931)." In *Adenauer-Studien*, edited by Rudolf Morsey, 1:226–42. Mainz: Mathias Grunewald Verlag, 1974.

———. *Der Untergang des politischen Katholizismus: die Zentrumspartei Zwischen christlichen Selbstverständnis und "Nationaler Erhebung" 1932/33*. Stuttgart: Belser Verlag, 1977.

———. "Das Ende der Zentrumspartei 1933." In *Das Reichskonkordat: Forschungsstand, Dokumente, Kontroverse*, edited by Thomas Brechenmacher, 37–54. Paderborn: Schöningh, 2007.

———. ed. "Ludwig Kaas, 'Tagebuch 7.-20. April 1933.'" *Stimmen der Zeit* 166 (1959–60): 422–30.

———. ed. *Das "Ermächtigungsgesetz" vom 24. März 1933*. Göttingen: Vandenhoeck and Ruprecht, 1968.

———. ed. *Die Protokolle der Reichstagsfraktion und des Fraktionsvorstandes der Deutschen Zentrumspartei 1926–1933*. Mainz: Mathias Grunewald Verlag, 1969.

Patch, William L. *Heinrich Brüning and the Dissolution of the Weimar Republic*. Cambridge: Cambridge University Press, 1998.

Petzold, Joachim. *Franz von Papen: Ein deutsches Verhangnis*. Berlin: Buchverlag Union, 1995.

Pyta, Wolfram. *Hindenburg: Herrschaft Zwischen Hohenzollern und Hitler*. Berlin: Siedler Verlag, 2007.

Ruppert, Karsten. *Im Dienst am Staat von Weimar: Das Zentrum als regierende Partei in der Weimarer Demokratie 1923–1930*. Düsseldorf: Droste Verlag, 1992.

———. "Die weltanschauliche Bedingungen der Politik der Deutschen Zentrumspartei in ihrer Weimarer Epoche." *Historische Zeitschrift* 285 (2007): 49–97.

Scholder, Klaus. "Altes und Neues zur Vorgeschichte des Reichskonkordats." *Vierteljahrshefte für Zeitgeschichte* 26 (1978): 535–70.

Schumacher, Martin. "Zwischen 'Einschaltung' und 'Gleichschaltung': Zum Untergang der Deutschen Zentrumspartei 1932–33." *Historisches Jahrbuch* 99 (1979): 268–303.

Schumann, Dirk. *Politische Gewalt in der Weimarer Republik 1918–1933: Kampf um die Straße und Furcht vor dem Bürgerkrieg*. Essen: Klartext Verlag, 2001.

Volk, Ludwig. *Das Reichskonkordat vom 20. Juli 1933: Von den Ansätzen in der Weimarer Republik bis zur Ratifizierung am 10. September 1933*. Mainz: Mathias Grunewald Verlag, 1972

———. ed. *Die Kirchlichen Akten über die Reichskonkordatsverhandlungen 1933*. Mainz: Ferdinand Schöningh, 1969.

———. *Katholische Kirche und Nationalsozialismus: Ausgewählte Aufsätze*. Edited by Dieter Albrecht. Mainz: Mathias Grunewald Verlag, 1987.

 4

THE NAZI SEIZURE OF POWER IN BAVARIA AND THE DEMISE OF THE BAVARIAN PEOPLE'S PARTY
Winfried Becker

The progressive destabilization of Germany's political institutions in the late Weimar Republic had the effect of creating a power vacuum that prepared the way for the decisive breakthrough of political radicalism in the early 1930s. This was most apparent at the national level where the rivalry of competing political forces produced a stalemate that made it increasingly impossible to forge a consensus on the conduct of national policy. That the Weimar Republic was a federal state, however, has received surprisingly little attention in the discussions about the preconditions for the National Socialist seizure of power. What is often overlooked is the fact that a number of middle-sized states, or *Länder*, like Bavaria, Baden, Württemberg, and Saxony, as well as smaller states like Oldenburg and the Hanseatic cities, continued to function on the basis of more or less stable parliamentary majorities right up until the installation of the Hitler cabinet on 30 January 1933. Nowhere was this more apparent than in Bavaria, where events from the end of January to the end of April 1933 revealed just how the newly installed Nazi regime systematically stripped legitimate political institutions of the German federal state of power and thus rendered them ineffective. In the administrative bureaucracy that the National Socialists conquered in the first months of 1933, there was a virtual revolution that in the case of Bavaria had clear precedents in the contentious relationship between Bavaria and the Reich long before the establishment of the Third Reich.

The Bavarian People's Party and the Defense of States' Rights

Known as the "Free State" or "People's State of Bavaria" since 1918, Bavaria had been reduced from a kingdom and federal state in the Second Empire to a mere state, or *Land*, of the "decentralized unitary state" of the Weimar Republic. According to the Weimar Constitution, the exercise of sovereign power no longer rested, as it had in the

Bismarckian Empire, on treaties between the governing dynasties but upon the sovereign will of the people. Bavaria had been obliged to renounce the special privileges it had enjoyed in the Second Empire, namely, its sovereignty over rail and water transportation, postal and telegraph communications, and military command in times of peace. At the same time, whatever remained of the sovereignty of individual states over the police had been greatly weakened by repeated exemptions in favor of the central government in Berlin. By the same token, the Federal Council (Reichsrat) that served as the representative of the individual states could only delay but not permanently prevent legislation passed by the Reichstag from being enacted into law.

The Bavarian People's Party (Bayerische Volkspartei or BVP) saw itself not only as a proponent of Bavarian autonomy and Bavaria's special interests but also as the defender of what remained of the federal principle in Germany's state structure. Formerly the Bavarian branch of the German Center Party (Deutsche Zentrumspartei), the BVP had broken away from its mother party in the revolutionary upheaval of November–December 1918, in part out of bitterness over the unitarian course the Center and its national leadership had pursued in the last years of the war, in part out of rejection of the revolution itself.[1] The BVP was committed to preserving and strengthening the unique and independent character of the Bavarian state at a time when the Bavarian monarchy no longer existed. The BVP stood "on the basis of the Christian world view" and was committed to the equal representation of the interests of all large professional groups, the peasantry, the worker, the white-collar employee, the civil service, the artisanry, commerce, retail, and industry. The two programs the BVP had promulgated in Bamberg first in 1920 and then again in 1922 called for a reform of the national constitution along federalist lines. Although the BVP Reichstag delegation had operated separately from the Center since 1920, its chairman Johann Leicht successfully managed to reconcile differences between the two parties.[2]

From 1919 to 1933 the BVP was consistently the strongest political force in Bavarian political life with approximately 35 percent of the electorate and an average of fifty-three to fifty-four delegates in the Bavarian Landtag. After a series of civil servant cabinets that held power from 1920 to 1924, the BVP moved to center stage for the six years from 1924 to 1930 when the BVP's Heinrich Held headed a series of cabinets that enjoyed the support of a parliamentary majority. After the resignation of the Bavarian Peasants' League (Bayerischer Bauernbund) from the Bavarian government in July 1930 deprived his cabinet of its parliamentary majority, Held continued to lead his government on a caretaker basis through the last years of the Weimar Republic, although its position vis-à-vis the national government in Berlin was weaker than it had been before 1930. Held was a passionate champion of states' rights but often found little support for his position. Held ultimately fell back on the Bismarckian model that had conceded the right of an independent existence to Bavaria and other middle-sized German states. But there were also powerful nationalist impulses in Bavarian political culture, as in the case of Minister President Gustav von Kahr in the early 1920s and Justice Minister Franz Gürtner from the right-wing German National People's Party (Deutschnationale Volkspartei or DNVP). In the early years of the Weimar Republic, the Bavarian right had sought to build up the "Order Cell of Bavaria" into a bastion against what many Bavarians saw as the rising tide of Bolshevism in Berlin.[3] In December 1928, when Wilhelm Sollmann from the Social Democratic Party (Sozialdemokratische Partei Deutschlands or SPD) proposed dissolving the states by popular referendum, the BVP was joined by the DNVP, Bavarian Peasants' League, and the newly emergent National Socialist German Workers' Party (Nationalsozialistische Deutsche Arbeiterpartei or NSDAP) in a united front defending Bavaria "against the red unitary state."[4]

From September 1930 to July 1932 the number of Nazi delegates in the Reichstag increased from 107 to 230 in a trend that could be seen in state elections throughout Germany. In April 1932 the NSDAP established itself as the strongest party in Prussia and Anhalt with 43.2 and 40.9 percent of the popular vote respectively as opposed to 1.8 and 2.1 percent in 1928, while in Bavaria the NSDAP's 32.5 percent share of the popular vote lagged behind that of the BVP by only a tenth of a point. In none of the state elections between 1930 and 1933 did the NSDAP achieve an absolute majority of the popular vote. Its gains, however, had less to do with the success of the tactic of legality that Hitler had adopted following his return to political life in 1925 than with the conditions under which they were achieved. In 1932 there were five elections that followed one another in relatively quick succession. This was accompanied by the descent into what amounted to a virtual civil war and unremitting civil unrest. Tumultuous parades and marches, wild speeches and abusive taunts, SA units at the ready, the disruption and breakup of election rallies of rival parties, beatings and violent threats right up to the door of the polling stations—all of that belonged to the repertoire of Nazi campaign agitation in the spring, summer, and fall of 1932.

Karl Stützel, the Bavarian minister of interior and a member of the BVP, reacted to the increasing brutality of the political climate from 1930 on with a firm hand. At first his efforts were directed primarily against the Communists, but then he began to target the NSDAP on such a massive scale that Wilhelm Frick, chairman of the NSDAP Reichstag delegation, introduced a motion branding the action of the Bavarian government as unlawful.[5] Stützel protested vigorously against the decision to lift the ban on wearing political uniforms and against the way in which the provisions for combatting political excesses that were contained in a series of presidential emergency decrees from June to December 1932 had been softened to appease the National Socialists. At the same time, Stützel complained bitterly that the Reich minister of the interior had encroached upon the police powers of the individual states.[6] The Bavarian Council of Ministers even went so far as to consider lodging a formal complaint against Reich minister of the interior Wilhelm Gayl for having usurped the authority of the police to permit public political assemblies and parades, thereby assuming control over the police of the individual German states.[7]

Papen's coup of 20 July 1932 against the legally installed Prussian government struck at the very roots of the constitutional state. Bavaria joined the legal action that Prussia brought against the central government in the Reich Court in Leipzig, but the court paid little more than lip service to the principle of states' rights. In its decision of 25 October 1932 the court ruled that the Reich commissar—in this case, Papen—was authorized to temporarily assume the responsibilities of the Prussian cabinet ministers. According to this ruling, sovereignty in Prussia was held in limbo, to be shared between the Reich commissar and the legitimate Prussian government led by the SPD's Otto Braun until the latter had been completely removed from power. Fritz Schäffer, the BVP national party chairman, subsequently entered into negotiations with Papen on behalf of a constitutional reform that would have strengthened the powers of the Federal Council and required its approval for use of the special emergency powers that Article 48 of the Weimar Constitution had vested in the office of the Reich president. In return, Schäffer was prepared to accept closer ties between Prussia and the Reich as long as the rights of the individual states and the existing constitutional order were respected.[8] Schäffer insisted upon the preservation of the rights of popularly elected legislatures in the face of authoritarian, corporatist, or "organic" reforms. In the meantime, Brüning and several BVP spokesmen were actively exploring the possibility of a coalition government between the Center or BVP and the NSDAP as a way of preventing future actions like the one that had just taken place in Prussia.[9]

The collapse of the Brüning government left the BVP and Center with little in the way of political options. In February 1932 BVP circles in Berlin believed that a Hitler-Brüning cabinet was indeed possible but feared that this government would sooner or later fall apart so that "then only a National Socialist dictatorship or chaos remained."[10] From their perspective, the transition to a Hitler-Papen-Hugenberg cabinet was not so much a disturbing turn of events as a continuation of the instability and uncertain future to which they had become accustomed. Conservatives like Baron Franz von Gebsattel and BVP Reichstag deputy Count Eugen von Quadt zu Wykradt und Isny as well as aristocratic and business circles that stood close to the BVP dismissed Held's protests against the excesses of the Reich in defense of the constitutional *Rechtsstaat* as "unfruitful legalistic whining." What they advocated was a rapprochement with Papen and greater distance from the Center and its strong trade union wing.[11] Held, on the other hand, continued to fear that Papen's authoritarian course posed a new threat to Bavarian autonomy vis-à-vis the Reich and found himself moving more and more closely to the BVP's sister party, which felt nothing but total revulsion for the "apostate" Papen.

After Hitler's appointment as chancellor on 30 January 1933, the BVP came under increasingly heavy pressure from the Hitler cabinet and began to fear for the loss of its power in Bavaria. On 7 February the new Reich minister of the interior Wilhelm Frick impressed upon Franz Sperr, the Bavarian envoy in Berlin, the need to form a governmental coalition in Munich that rested upon a broad parliamentary majority. In sharp contrast to its behavior before 1933, the NSDAP delegation to the Bavarian Landtag now seemed serious about negotiating. The BVP party chairman Fritz Schäffer even appeared open to the possibility of a coalition with the NSDAP in preliminary talks with Hitler and the chairman of the NSDAP delegation to the Bavarian Landtag, Rudolf Buttmann, and was prepared to offer the NSDAP the ministries of justice and finance in the Bavarian government. Schäffer, however, stressed that he had no authority from Held to negotiate on his behalf and remained doubtful as to whether the NSDAP was truly interested in cooperation.[12] The BVP overtures met with traditional Nazi disdain toward Catholic parties.[13]

The NSDAP's demands for a role in the Munich government cut across efforts from within the Bavarian Landtag to place the state government on a broader political foundation. Here the goal was to form a new governmental coalition and at the same time initiate a reform of the Bavarian constitution that would strengthen the powers of the minister president and cabinet. The minister president, up to now only a *primus inter pares*, would receive increased new powers, such as the right to dismiss ministers or to remain in office until the passage of a constructive no-confidence vote that would install a new government in office. The BVP also wanted to insure that partners in a future majority coalition would show proper respect for the "Christian worldview." Despite the NSDAP's commitment to "positive Christianity," its hostility toward the church, its racial theory, its thinly veiled socialism, and its openly unitarian conception of the state were incompatible with the basic values of the BVP.[14]

It was against the background of these developments that the leaders of the Bavarian government and BVP began to consider whether the appointment of Crown Prince Rupprecht as general state commissar or king could prevent the establishment of National Socialist rule in Bavaria.[15] The Wittelsbach monarchy was popular throughout Bavaria. All parties including the Social Democrats were receptive to its restoration. At the burial of Prince Alfons von Bayern on 13 January 1933 a large crowd of demonstrators made no secret of their attachment to the lost monarchy. The widespread popularity of the Wittelsbachs reflected a confluence of particularist and national patriotism that was typical of Bavaria's political culture. Nationalist and business circles as well as those who embraced the call for authoritarian reform hoped for a symbiosis of the blue and white of Bavaria and the black, white, and red of the old imperial order under a restored Wittelsbach monarchy. But with Held and the Bavarian council of ministers there were reservations of all kinds. After all, the Weimar Constitution prescribed for all states the republican form of government. Held asked himself whether and how the crown prince could take a pledge to the constitution and the principle of fundamental rights. In the meantime, the Wittelsbach claimant to the throne, Crown Prince Rupprecht, was careful to avoid an open conflict with the national government. When Prince Eugen von Öttingen-Wallerstein and Baron Alfons von Redwitz went to Berlin to test the terrain for a restoration of the Bavarian monarchy, they received a sharp rebuff from Hindenburg. That their project met with a favorable response from Konstatin von Neurath, Lutz Schwerin von Krosigk, and Franz Gürtner—all ministers in the Papen cabinet who dreamed of restoring the Prussian monarchy—was of little political consequence.[16] On the negative side, efforts at a restoration of the Wittelsbach monarchy only confirmed the distrust that both the national conservatives and the National Socialists felt with respect to the leaders of the Bavarian political establishment.

Held saw his constitutional and political credo severely challenged by Hitler's assumption of power. In a memorandum for Hindenburg on 28 January, Held warned against using the so-called state of emergency for "anti-constitutional experiments," called upon the Reich president to protect "the constitutional rights of the individual German states," and offered the help of the smaller German states in overcoming the economic crisis.[17] After the Nazi assumption of power, individuals and groups that suddenly found themselves the targets of persecution chose Bavaria as a place of refuge. Shortly after Hitler assumed the chancellorship, liberal intellectuals, Social Democrats, and members of the Central Association for German Citizens of the Jewish Faith (Centralverein deutscher Staatsbürger jüdischen Glaubens) had sought refuge in Bavaria.[18] The fact that Stützel had thus far blocked all actions that threatened the state, had exercised the powers of his office with great circumspection, and had reprimanded those civil servants with sympathy for National Socialism spared Bavaria the turmoil that could be seen in most other parts of the Reich.

In the meantime, the individual states found it increasingly difficult to maintain a common front against the incursions of National Socialism. Bavaria's political leadership was cognizant of the way in which Hesse had acquiesced to pressure from Vice Chancellor Papen and the former diplomat Kurt von Lersner to accept a Reich commissar and to remove the Social Democratic minister of the interior Wilhelm Leuschner.[19] Sperr reported to the cabinet ministers Neurath, Gürtner, and Schwerin von Krosigk that the states were deeply disturbed by the fact that the Reich chancellor seemed well on his way to the creation of a "fascist Third Reich" and in Prussia had "already achieved in part a fascist monopoly of power."[20] He referred in particular to the most recent speeches of Hitler, Frick, and Hermann Göring, the latter even going so far as to instruct Prussian civil servants to follow orders that contradicted existing laws, to treat the SA and SS as a surrogate police force, and to exempt them from criminal prosecution. Sperr asked the three ministers to keep the Reich president informed about the most recent developments and to encourage him to take appropriate action "against the National Socialists with the help of the Reichswehr." All of this, however, ended in bitter disappointment when four days later Hindenburg acquiesced in what proved to be a fateful weakening of his position. On 28 February 1933 he enacted the Decree for the Protection of the People and State passed by the Hitler cabinet in response to the Reichstag fire the preceding night. Ostensibly for the purpose of restoring public safety and order, this decree granted the national government the authority to temporarily usurp the police powers of the individual German states. With this decree the Hitler cabinet had been entrusted with the dictatorial authority that had previously been reserved to the Reich president.

The Reichstag elections of 5 March 1933 represented the first step toward the coordination (*Gleichschaltung*) of the individual German states into the structure of the Nazi state. Although the NSDAP's performance in the March elections in Bavaria lagged behind its successes in the rest of the Reich, it still surpassed the BVP by a considerable margin of sixteen percentage points. The Nazi victory resulted in large part from the support of those in the cities and countryside who had not previously voted but also from strong gains in Protestant as well as Catholic areas that had previously remained immune to the Nazi appeal.[21] The Nazis were also aided by the restrictions that the Decree of the Reich President for the Protection of the German People from 4 February 1933 and the emergency decree of 28 February placed upon the freedom of expression, particularly in the radio and press. The BVP was hurt by a sharp drop-off in the subsidies that it had previously received from the Bavarian business community, in large part as a result of dissatisfaction with Held's democratic political course.

The Nazi Assault and the Removal of Minister President Held

After the BVP's devastating defeat in the March 1933 Reichstag elections, authorities in Munich were deluged with alarming reports from Sperr in Berlin. Among other things, Sperr reported that Papen had asked him about the possibility of dissolving the Bavarian Landtag. Hindenburg, on the other hand, made it clear that Bavaria had to understand the implications of the Reichstag elections for the composition of its own Landtag while indicating that under no circumstances would new national elections take place.[22] More alarming still were the warnings and threats of Hitler. The Reich chancellor continued to fume over the enormous danger of Marxism—something that he pledged to destroy without mercy—and boasted of the "powerful revolution" that was sweeping through Germany. The BVP, Hitler argued, had failed to recognize the changing times but disavowed any intention of wanting to launch attacks from the Reich. But "pressure from below," he warned, could become so strong that intervention as in the case of Hamburg, Baden, and Württemberg would be unavoidable.[23]

Confronted with threats like these, the BVP came to see negotiations with the NSDAP as the only way out of the impasse in which it found itself. Hopefully it would be able to achieve acceptable results through an agreement with the more moderate elements in the Bavarian Nazi Party around Rudolf Buttmann, chairman of the NSDAP delegation to the Bavarian Landtag. On 7 March the Bavarian council of ministers decided to ask the BVP's Georg Stang in his capacity as president of the Bavarian Landtag to intensify efforts for a reorganization of the Bavarian government. The following day the BVP Landtag delegation appointed Fritz Schäffer, the BVP national party chairman, and Georg Wohlmuth, chairman of the BVP delegation, to a four-man committee that also included Anton Scharnagl, deacon of the Munich cathedral, and Alois Hundhammer from the Christian Peasant Union. Their assignment was to enter into serious negotiations aimed at expanding the base of the existing governmental coalition on terms that were compatible with the fundamental principles of the BVP and to seek new state elections in the event that efforts to form a new government failed.[24] The delegation still believed that the substance of the BVP was intact and entertained realistic hopes that the party could improve its performance in the event of new state elections. On 6 March BVP Reichstag deputy Hans Ritter von Lex met with the NSDAP's Buttmann and school inspector Josef Bauer and agreed that seats in the Bavarian council of ministers should be divided between the BVP and NSDAP according to a ratio of two to three. The following day Hitler assented to this agreement in Berlin.[25]

On 8 March the BVP general secretary Anton Pfeiffer mistakenly assumed that in the next several days the NSDAP would decide how it would resolve the south German problem by unilaterally assuming control of the ministries of the interior in the various south German states.[26] Later that evening Hitler announced to a circle of his confederates the decision to proceed with the illegal and unconstitutional takeover of power in Bavaria. As Goebbels noted in his diary, "It has been decided that tomorrow Bavaria is the next in line." Serious resistance, Goebbels continued, was not expected from either the BVP or Held and would in any event be pointless. Bavaria's destiny, Goebbels concluded, "hangs by a thread. No other government has even been in the position to do what the leader intends to do. He can afford to do this because the Bavarian people stands on his side."[27]

Around 10:30 on the evening of 8 March, Sperr received a telephone call from Stützel informing him that Adolf Wagner, the NSDAP district leader in Bavaria, would be departing from Berlin for Munich by express train at 9:37 the following morning.[28] Upon his arrival the SA would march to the Bavarian ministries of foreign and internal affairs as well as to the headquarters of the Munich police in a display of force that would lead to the resignation of the Bavarian government. Sperr immediately notified the office of the Reich presidency but was referred to Hitler as the person responsible for dealing with the situation in Munich. The Reich chancellor agreed to intercede with Wagner, but his adjutant Wilhelm Brückner, who had supposedly tried to reach Wagner at the train station, later reported that he had been unable to reach him before he departed for Munich. Later in the morning Sperr was able to reach Frick, the Reich minister of the interior, who agreed to pass on Sperr's request that Hitler stop the SA action and appoint NSDAP delegates for cabinet negotiations with the BVP without further delay. Frick, however, informed Sperr that the NSDAP was demanding for itself the minister presidency and the ministries of internal affairs and finance but would concede the ministry of culture to the BVP. No new elections, Frick continued, would take place after the municipal elections that were scheduled for Prussia on 12 March. The Bavarian Landtag would be reconstituted according to the results of the recent Reichstag elections by means of a special enabling act.

At 11:45 that morning Sperr received a phone call from Joseph Bleyer, state counselor in the Bavarian ministry of foreign affairs, that authorized him to announce that the BVP was prepared to concede the three cabinet posts to the NSDAP and to press for the immediate appointment of NSDAP delegates for cabinet negotiations with the BVP. Earlier that morning Held and other government officials in Munich had agreed that the Bavarian government should resist the SA with all the force at its disposal but without bloodshed and the use of firearms. Shortly thereafter at 12:30 Wagner appeared in the company of SA chief of staff Röhm and SS leader Heinrich Himmler in Held's office to demand the immediate appointment of retired general Franz Xaver Ritter von Epp as general state commissar entrusted with full state authority.[29] A national conservative member of the NSDAP since 1928, Epp was widely respected in nationalist and Catholic circles. Then, imitating Hitler's own style, Wagner slammed his riding crop down on the table. Held took offense at Wagner's crass behavior and responded that he would not be intimidated by the armed forces that had assembled at the central railroad station, on the Nymphenberger Strasse, and before the "Braunes Haus." When Held insisted that he did not have authority to entrust a state commissar with full governmental powers, Röhm retorted that he was acting on orders from Hitler and Frick and that the national government would appoint Epp as Reich commissar for Bavaria if he were not appointed to the position of general state commissar by 3:00 that afternoon.

The situation in Munich continued to deteriorate through the early afternoon of 9 March as armed SA units stood at the ready in a transparent threat to use force if the Bavarian government did not accede to the national cabinet's demands. Telegrams that Held sent to Berlin imploring the Reich president and Reich chancellor to intervene in order to avoid bloodshed and offering to facilitate a reorganization of the state government under National Socialist leadership had no effect. Government officials in Berlin continued to disavow any intent to intervene in Munich and insisted that intervention would be necessary only in the absence of "good will." Sperr immediately misread this as a disavowal of Röhm and reported it to Held, who had been meeting with his council of ministers since 2:30 that afternoon. Held and his cabinet were determined that they would not be pressured into appointing Epp as state commissar, but they indicated that as a compromise they would accept Epp's election as minister president by the Landtag when it reconvened on 11 March. The council of ministers also called upon the Reichswehr to assist the state police in doing what was necessary to keep the SA under control and ordered the acting commanding officer in Bavaria, Colonel Alfred Wäger, to report to the ministry of foreign affairs. But when Wäger turned to the ministry of defense in Berlin for approval to come to the aid of the Bavarian government, he was immediately advised that the Reichswehr should stay out of domestic political matters and in no case undertake any action against the SA and SS.[30]

When after the expiration of Röhm's ultimatum Epp appeared in the Bavarian ministry of external affairs at 3:40 that afternoon, Held refused to appoint him as state commissar because he had not yet received an answer to the telegram he had sent to the Reich chancellor and Reich president earlier in the morning. In the meantime, officials in Berlin added to the confusion in Munich with a trail of misinformation that left Held and his associates in the dark as to what was actually happening. After a conversation between Hitler and Hindenburg around 5:00 that afternoon, Hindenburg's chief of staff Otto Meissner notified Sperr that the Reich president and cabinet did not want to intervene in Bavaria without just cause, that it did not intend to appoint a Reich commissar, and that it would not deploy the Reichswehr or declare a military state of emergency in Bavaria. In the same breath, Meissner expressed doubt as to whether or not the Bavarian government was still in control of the situation and criticized it for not having already taken decisive action. Sperr protested strongly that a sharp response on the part of the Bavarian government would have inevitably led to bloodshed and that in any case the situation in Munich was under control.[31] In the meantime, the Bavarian council of ministers had voted to acquiesce in the election of a National Socialist minister president and had forwarded this decision to Hitler and Hindenburg.[32] All of this would suggest that the Bavarian government could stop for a moment to catch its breath.

Held immediately informed Röhm about the information that Sperr had received from Meissner. The SA chief of staff, apparently acting on the authority of a telegram that Frick had sent to the minister of the interior around noon so that it would be ready for publication in the event that Held did not give in to Berlin's demands, responded that in the meantime Epp had been appointed Reich commissar in Bavaria.[33] Later that evening Frick took matters into his own hands by announcing Epp's appointment as the Reich commissar in Bavaria in a speech in Frankfurt and warned that other states risked similar action if their governments did not act responsibly. The situation assumed an even more ominous tone when around 6:45 that evening Dr. Alban Haas from the Bavarian legation was summoned to a press conference in Berlin where "something special" was to be announced. That "something special" turned out to be Epp's appointment as Reich commissar for Bavaria.

Upon learning of Epp's appointment, Sperr confirmed the report with the government press office, which provided him with the contents but not the precise wording of Frick's telegram to Held. In the telegram Frick justified Epp's appointment on the grounds that public safety and order in Bavaria could no longer be protected in light of the public disturbances that had been provoked by the "political transformations that were taking place throughout Germany."[34] To Sperr and his colleagues in Munich the pretext was completely fabricated, the action an open breach of the constitution. Held, however, did not receive Frick's telegram announcing Epp's appointment until 8:45 that evening. Was this simply an oversight as Frick claimed or a tactic of wearing down the opposition? In any event, Epp appeared with his full entourage at the Promenadeplatz in Munich fifteen minutes later, presented Held, Stützel, and Schäffer with Frick's telegram, and demanded the immediate transfer of responsibility for all governmental business.

Ever the consummate jurist, Held proceeded to transfer to Epp the powers for the maintenance of public safety and order as specified in Frick's decree, including full police powers, but not all governmental powers. Between 10:00 and 12:00 that night Held sent protest telegrams to Frick, Hitler, and Hindenburg, complaining in particular about the legality and justification of Frick's decree for the simple reason that peace and order in Bavaria were already secure. Held appealed to Hindenburg to repeal the decree because it stood in conflict with what he understood as the express will of the Reich president and instructed Sperr to meet with the Reich president the first thing the following morning. But Meissner refused to arrange an audience with Hindenburg on the grounds that the appointment of a Reich commissar for Bavaria had taken place on the authority of the national cabinet and not on that of the Reich president. Meissner reassured Sperr that Hindenburg would arrange a meeting between Sperr and the Reich chancellor, a meeting that never took place despite Sperr's efforts to receive an appointment. Nor would it have helped had Sperr been able to meet with Vice Chancellor Franz von Papen, for as he learned from Enoch von Guttenberg, the state leader of the Bavarian League for Homeland and King (Bayerischer Heimat- und Königsbund), Papen too felt that he had been left out of the entire action.

Upon assumption of police powers in Bavaria, Epp reassured Held that he accepted personal responsibility for the safety of the cabinet ministers, the protection of their property, and the security of their homes. But that very evening a wave of SA and SS terror descended upon unpopular ministers and members of the BVP, journalists and newspaper editors, and Social Democratic politicians.[35] The fortunate ones were those who were able to leave their homes beforehand. Held, for example, found refuge with friends and associates, while the Social Democrat Erhard Auer escaped with Wilhelm Hoegner to Salzburg across the Austrian border. Fritz Schäffer, on the other hand, was rousted out of his home and taken to the "Braunes Haus," where he was rudely interrogated for several hours. Stützel was pulled out of his bed by SA men who took him out of his apartment in his night shirt, beat him on the head with a steel rod, and threatened him with execution in the "Braunes Haus" because he had supposedly wanted to unleash armored cars against the SA. The BVP city councilor Josef Ostermaier was beaten by the SA in his bedroom, then driven throughout the city in his nightshirt before being taken to the "Braunes Haus," where he was beaten with a whip and thrown unconscious into the street. Twelve SA men rousted Sebastian Schlittenbauer, general secretary of the Bavarian Christian Peasant Union (Bayerischer Christlicher Bauernverein), threatened him with execution, berated him as a "traitor of the peasants," and set him loose on an open road south of Munich. The Catholic publicist Fritz Gerlich was assaulted in the offices of his journal *Der Gerade Weg*, taken into "protective custody," severely beaten on two occasions, dismissed from his post in the state archives, and eventually murdered in Dachau in 1934. The SA broke into the house of Rabbi Leo Bärwald, took him to a forest in north Munich, put him up against a tree, and repeatedly conducted mock executions by shooting in accordance with the sentence he had received in the "Braunes Haus." Here, as in the state of Baden, the sheer number of such incidents would be justified by the Nazi legal expert Hans Frank as an expression of the "great excitement" and "righteous bitterness of the masses," something that required no excuse or apology.[36]

On the night of 9–10 March Epp proceeded to appoint a series of state commissars: Hans Frank for the ministry of justice, Adolf Wagner for the ministry of the interior, Ludwig Siebert for the ministry of finance, Ernst Röhm and Hermann Esser for special assignments, and Heinrich Himmler as chief of the Munich police. Epp held the first meeting of his "usurpation cabinet" the next morning at precisely the same time that Held was meeting with the legitimate council of ministers for the last time. Held read the text of the telegrams he had sent to Berlin, reported on the mistreatment of Stützel, and rebuked state commissar Esser for attending the meeting without proper authorization. Held then returned to his office only to find it occupied by the SA and was forced to clear out of his official residence by the end of the day. Suffering from a heart condition and diabetes, Held suddenly found himself without a permanent and secure place to live. He was, however, able to get a passport at police headquarters, and on 15 March he left for Lugano, where his oldest son Joseph had gone for his own good health. Before leaving for Lugano, Held wrote a letter to his close associate Bleyer that was typed on the afternoon of 14 March but dated 15 March in which he simply announced his resignation as minister president effective immediately. But at the insistence of the Bavarian minister of the interior Stützel and BVP deputies Alfons Maria Probst, Josef Müller, and Otto Graf,[37] Held wrote a second letter to Bleyer during the night from 14 to 15 March but dated 14 March in which he announced that on the advice of his doctor he had begun a period of convalescence and was appointing Bleyer to temporarily assume the responsibilities of the minister presidency.[38] Although this letter had been written after the letter containing the short notice of Held's resignation, it had been dated a day earlier and was delivered to Bleyer by Graf on the morning of 15 March. Graf informed Bleyer that Held had changed his decision to resign his office and that his letter of 15 March was therefore no longer relevant.

At approximately 7:00 on the evening of 15 March, Bleyer handed Epp a letter in which he informed the Reich commissar that because of long-standing illness and exhaustion Held had resigned the office of minister president as well as the ministries of economics and labor. Furthermore, the conduct of the state's business was to be transferred to the Reich commissar and his "constitutional representatives." In doing this, Bleyer completely ignored Held's letter of 14 March that had been handed to him by Graf and that contained the retraction of Held's resignation. Bleyer's action was highly problematic in that the resignation of a minister president was legally binding only if it was directed to the entire council of ministers, not just to a civil servant as Bleyer was. Moving quickly to exploit the official act of Bleyer, Epp released a statement on 16 March announcing that he had assumed responsibility for the conduct of all state matters.[39] He subsequently transferred unlimited ministerial responsibility to the state commissars Wagner, Siebert, and Frank and appointed Hans Schemm to head the ministry of culture. He further confirmed Esser, Röhm, and Georg Luber as state commissars, though without ministerial portfolios. To justify these measures, Epp cited Held's supposed resignation, Frick's decree of 9 March, and the Bavarian constitutional charter from 1919 that allowed the formation of a "cabinet of the whole," or *Gesamtministerium*, to take measures necessary to secure peace and order in the face of threatened or real danger. On 17 March Epp's "commissary state ministers" met for the first time as a new *Gesamtministerium* and declared the ministers of the Held cabinet as deposed.

From Lugano Held carried out what in retrospect can only be regarded as a hopeless "rear-guard action" against the Nazis for the usurpation of the constitutional powers of the Bavarian government. On 16 March Held rescinded his resignation of the previous day and challenged Epp's usurpation of power with reference to Paragraph 66 of the Bavarian state constitution that entrusted the sitting government with the conduct of state affairs until a new government had been formed by the Bavarian Landtag.[40] For Held it was not so much a question of his own person as one of constitutional principle. He had already indicated to the BVP Landtag delegation on 8 March that the impending cabinet negotiations with the NSDAP meant that he would have to place the powers of his office in other hands.[41] What mattered most to Held was that Bleyer as his delegated temporary successor continue to exercise the powers of his office according to the provisions of the Bavarian constitution even though this would place Bleyer in a dangerous position vis-à-vis the new power holders. For Bleyer, however, it was intolerable that two governmental authorities could exist side by side and insisted that he had given Held a way out of a hopeless situation on terms that preserved his self-respect and dignity.[42] With a heavy heart, Held reluctantly acknowledged what Bleyer had done on his behalf and ended his stay in Switzerland to return to his home in Regensburg, where his wife Maria had suffered a nervous breakdown. Harassed by the regime and local Nazi authorities, Held turned down an offer of emigration to the United States and eventually succumbed to cancer in 1938.

The establishment of Nazi authority in Bavaria after 9 March 1933 was accompanied by disinformation and intimidation. In a statement to the press on 10 March, the government press spokesman Walter Heide in Berlin totally misrepresented the situation in Bavaria by reporting that the Bavarian government had asked the national government for protection in the interests of maintaining peace and order but had then refused to appoint Epp to the post of general state commissar as the government in Berlin had recommended.[43] Röhm and Hitler further clouded the issue by asserting that Held had voluntarily acceded to Epp's appointment as Reich commissar and had even sought the consent of the Bavarian Council of Ministers.[44] The two Nazi leaders continued to insist that Stützel had authorized the use of firearms against the SA in an attempt to justify not only the reprisals that had already taken place but to threaten new ones if warranted. The Nazis even circulated the rumor that Held would be standing trial for high treason.

The Final Transfer of Power and the Coordination of the Landtag

The BVP delegates to the Landtag and Reichstag could only have witnessed the dismissal of the Bavarian government and the rejection of their overtures on behalf of cabinet negotiations with the NSDAP with a sense of impotence and futility.[45] They were deluged with reports that city officials and parliamentary deputies who belonged to the BVP had been dismissed or arrested, that denunciations, acts of revenge, and "assaults in the schools" were widespread. The BVP party leadership began to fear that it was losing control over "local actions" like these, but its complaints with the new Bavarian minister of the interior Adolf Wagner were pointless. The BVP press was encouraged to remain firm but at the same time to withhold its criticism for fear of being banned. In the meantime, the BVP's youth and combat organization, the so-called Bavarian Watch (Bayernwacht) experienced physical confrontations with the National Socialists that left dead and wounded in their wake.[46] The attitude of the Catholic clergy and the Bavarian bishops to whom the BVP leadership had traditionally shown homage seemed to be leaning toward giving the party a free hand to cooperate with the National Socialist government in most areas except for Christian cultural policy, an area to which it would retreat and defend.[47]

Here, however, there were two problems. If the BVP were to abandon the political arena, then it would be rewriting its own history as a party whose sense of purpose had evolved from defending the prerogatives of the church and the freedom of religious conscience into that of uniting diverse social forces under the umbrella of a universal ideology around which its politics were oriented. If this were the case, then the only recourse would be a return to the sacristy. Second, it would soon become clear that the wave of national revolutionary terror that had been unleashed throughout Germany would not stop at the doors of the sacristy. It was no idle warning when Hans Frank, the newly appointed Nazi minister of justice in Bavaria, threatened the suspension of Bavaria's Concordat with the Holy See in the event that the Catholic Church did not make the necessary transition and seek a rational relationship with the "national movement."[48] Similarly, in the conversations that the BVP Reichstag deputy Hans von Lex held in Berlin with Hitler, Frick, and Röhm on 13–14 March, the Reich chancellor rejected the BVP's claim over cultural policy with the response that he did not want to subject his party to a reawakened "Furor Protestantikus."[49] Hitler made no attempt to conceal his contempt for the "old" parties, parliaments, and parliamentarians. Rather than enter into serious negotiations with the BVP's so-called front generation over ministerial seats, Hitler threw up a smoke screen and abruptly broke off talks. In a moment of unbridled opportunism, Lex offered the BVP's support for the use of "the most severe methods" against the "infection" of Marxism in the defense of "Christian culture." To be sure, Lex held the use of terror as incompatible with "our Christian conscience," but apparently not preventative measures by the new power holders such as taking up to a thousand Social Democratic functionaries into "protective custody." That Lex was even part of the conversation was due in large part to Buttmann's strategy of trying to break the BVP's backbone by bringing into the government the "young rebels [*junge Frondeure*]" who were spreading through the party like a "fungus."[50]

As the crisis in the BVP reached its high point in the spring of 1933, tensions between rival groups in the party became more and more pronounced. An open letter to Schäffer from young party members calling themselves the "Tatkreis" criticized the politics of the last years and prompted a lengthy discussion in the BVP delegation to the Bavarian Landtag on 15 March. The "Catholic youth and the Catholic young voters" complained bitterly about the liberal and capitalist forces within the party for having placed tactical considerations ahead of long-term goals and for having distanced itself from the church. Targets of this criticism were the BVP's Business Advisory Committee (Wirtschaftsbeirat der Bayerischen Volkspartei) and its chairman Franz August Schmitt as well as Lex, BVP party chairman Schäffer, and Count Quadt zu Wykradt und Isny. In place of the liberal policies the party had pursued for the past decade, the "Young Catholics" demanded a revitalization of Catholic values and the "orientation [of the party] behind the older generation [of political leaders] who had experienced the era of the Center in Bavaria and whose sense of politics was based

on fundamental principles rooted in faith."[51] Here the letter was referring to the leadership cadre around Leicht, Held, and Wohlmuth.
Wohlmuth, whom the Landtag delegation congratulated on the occasion of his sixty-eighth birthday on 3 April 1933, warned of the external and internal dangers that faced the party but spoke passionately
against its dissolution because its energies would still be needed in the
future.[52]

More than anything else, two factors accounted for the BVP's
strength in the past. In the first place, the party was firmly anchored in
Bavaria's dense and multifaceted Catholic milieu. Its social foundation
constituted the basis of its passive resistance in the Third Reich, that
resistance of proscribed organizations or "disaggregated unities" that
expressed itself in nonconformity, dissent, refusal, and distance from
the Nazi regime.[53] Second, the BVP identified itself with the Bavarian
state and thought of itself as a political and state-supporting force. This
stood in sharp contrast to the Prussian Center Party, which, despite the
way in which it as a confessional minority party was rooted in Prussia's
Catholic milieu, still could not identify itself with the Prussian state.

Less than a month had passed since the Bavarian government had
been unceremoniously stripped of its powers before a second act on the
part of the national government targeted Bavaria once again—this time
the Landtag—and robbed it of whatever remained of its freedom and
independent existence. The Provisional Law for the Coordination of the
States with the Reich of 31 March 1933 dissolved the duly elected parliaments of all German states with the exception of Prussia and reconstituted them according to the results of the March Reichstag elections.
The BVP's candidates for the reorganized Landtag were selected by
party chairman Schäffer upon the recommendation of the state party
leadership in what was a token concession to the leadership principle.
Of the 103 new deputies, 51 belonged to the NSDAP, 30 to the BVP, 17 to
the SPD, and 5 to the German National Front (Deutschnationale Front),
while the KPD was no longer represented. The NSDAP and German
Nationalists now enjoyed a narrow parliamentary majority with 56
seats in the Landtag.[54] To the BVP the reorganization of the Bavarian
legislature represented a "colossal sacrifice."[55] The prospect of new
elections in which the BVP hoped to benefit from a dramatic reversal in
public opinion as a result of the regime's unpopular acts and persecution
of political dissidents had vanished. As one report from Munich read,
"The dictatorship continues to have its way, but the number of clenched
fists continues to grow."[56] As did the number of those taken into "protective custody," a figure that Hans Frank put at six to seven thousand
as of the beginning of April. In March the Landtag had been repeatedly

occupied by the SA and SS. And the Second Law for the Coordination of the States with the Reich from 7 April further consolidated the position of the NS government in Bavaria. The new law authorized the appointment of Reich governors (*Reichsstatthalter*) who were responsible for making certain that the guidelines promulgated by the Reich chancellor were followed. Epp was appointed Reich regent of Bavaria effective immediately and summoned Ludwig Siebert, the former lord mayor of Lindau, to the post of Bavarian minister president.

The third coup after Held's dismissal and the two coordination laws was the Bavarian Enabling Act of 29 April 1933, the Law for the Relief of the Bavarian People and State. In order to secure passage of the Reich Enabling Law the previous month, Hitler had prevailed upon Frank to put pressure on the BVP leadership circle around Wohlmuth and Held. The BVP's response was that consent to the Enabling Act would produce serious conflicts of conscience: "It would be asking one to place his head on the chopping block for the next four years."[57] In announcing his party's support for the Enabling Act to the Reichstag on 23 March, Lex attached to his party's "Yes" the reservation that no government or individual person could be freed from the constraints of Christian moral law. When the BVP agricultural specialist Michael Horlacher returned to Munich after the fateful vote in Berlin, he proceeded to get drunk out of heartache over this "bitter hour of the German people."[58]

Hermann Esser celebrated the ceremonious reopening of the Landtag on 28 April as the conclusion of the first stage in the struggle that Adolf Hitler had begun a decade before.[59] From a purely legal perspective, the contents of the Bavarian Enabling Act that was approved the following day did not go significantly further than the provision in the coordination law of 31 March stipulating that the state governments had the power to issue laws that deviated from the constitution. The symbolic significance of the Enabling Act, however, was enormous. For it was the BVP, NSDAP, and German National Front that had granted the government absolute power to take measures and issue laws that stood outside the authority granted to it by the constitution. In doing so, they sanctioned the elimination of Bavaria's popularly elected legislature and with it the parliamentary foundation of Bavarian autonomy that the BVP leadership had always supported. Only the Social Democrats—their spokesman was Albert Rosshaupter—rejected the new law.[60] Schäffer and Hans Müller, the uninspiring new parliamentary chairman of the BVP, affirmed their willingness, though with reservations about the special status of Christian schools and worldview, to cooperate in the national regeneration of the German people. The Bavarian Christian Peasant Union under the leadership of Alois Hundhammer struck a decidedly national tone when Hundhammer assured Hitler of his loyal support "in the difficult struggle for the internal and external emancipation of the German people."[61] But hopes of survival through accommodation or collaboration proved deceptive. At the end of June BVP deputies, functionaries, and spokesmen were taken into "protective custody,"[62] and on 1 July the Bavarian Christian Peasant Union was unceremoniously dissolved. On 4 July the BVP's own minister of economics Count Eugen von Quadt zu Wykradt und Isny, who only the day before had applied for membership in the NSDAP and hoped to join the Nazi delegation to the Bavarian Landtag as a guest or *Hospitant*, signed the statement announcing the dissolution of the BVP. Those who had been taken into "protective custody" in the Stadelheim prison—Schäffer, Probst, Stang, and Anton Pfeiffer—had also signed the statement shortly beforehand in order to secure the release of those BVP functionaries and deputies who had been arrested in the police action against political Catholicism.

Conclusion

The NSDAP party headquarters were located in Munich and remained there through the end of World War II. It could only have annoyed Hitler that Munich was also the home of another party, the Bavarian People's Party, a party whose fundamental principles were rooted in the Christian traditions and culture of the state and that fused the awareness of what it meant to be a Bavarian with a commitment to the federal separation of powers for all of Germany. Hitler stood fundamentally opposed to the inherited culture of Germany's political parties, and his relationship to Bavaria was sentimental, superficial, and without a sense of its history.[63] The coordination of Bavaria into the structure of the Nazi state cut a deep swath in the federal fabric of Weimar Germany. Hitler, Frick, Röhm, and Wagner used the powers afforded them by the Decree of the Reich President for the Protection of the People and State and by the threat of an SA rebellion to depose the legitimate government of Bavaria. With their consent to the Bavarian Enabling Act, the democratic parties—with the exception of the Social Democrats—succumbed to regime pressure and abdicated their political responsibilities well before their official dissolution. The Nazi conquest of power was not caused by the loss of the special rights that Bavaria had enjoyed in the Second Empire or by the abdication of the monarchy but resulted from the calculated and systematic breach of the Weimar Constitution by martinets without a sense of conscience or responsibility. To be sure, the constitution of 1919 was never an ideal custodian of the federal principle. But had it been respected, then the constitutional autonomy of Bavaria—and with it Bavaria's democratic institutions—could have been safe from destruction.

In the final analysis, the Bavarian government failed to mount as effective a response as it would have liked to the misuse of the dictatorial powers that Article 48 had vested in the office of the Reich president. The ever vigilant troika of Held, Stützel, and Sperr reacted quickly to the threats that Hitler's accession to power posed to the federal structure of the German state and fought energetically for the preservation of the constitutional state. In doing so, they represented the true interests of the state that Hitler and Frick, in consort with their illegal auxiliaries in the SA, SS, and Stahlhelm, were determined to smash in the name of the national revolution. Bavaria's political leaders not only had abstract juristic principles on their side but also the support of a well-ordered state system. Criticism of Held that his defense was based too much on legal principle and lacked effective force behind it is misleading. To be sure, the prospects of effective resistance in Bavaria in the spring of 1933 were worse than they had been in Prussia at the time of the Papen coup some eight months earlier.[64] Nevertheless Held responded as vigorously as the powers of his office allowed and was fully prepared to deploy the police forces at his disposal against Nazi paramilitary units had that not run the risk of an open civil war. What was perhaps most astonishing about the situation in Bavaria, however, was the incredible lethargy with which contemporaries responded to the forced resignation of the minister president and his entire cabinet, the mistreatment of officials and innocent civilians, the occupation of the Landtag, and the acts of violence by the SA and SS. All of this was only compounded by the stupidity with which a large mob cheered the hoisting of the Hakenkreuz flag to the dome of the Landtag on 9 March.

The use of the police in a situation like this would only have made Nazi propaganda all the more effective and provided Frick with all the justification he needed to have those who had given the orders to resist arrested and shot on the spot. Here one can only ask whether the deployment of armed police might have unleashed a civil war in order to open the eyes of the public to the true nature of National Socialism and perhaps prevented the far greater calamity of allowing the National Socialists to occupy the entire state apparatus. Resistance against the Nazi regime, as Sperr later conceded, could have succeeded if it could have counted on the support of the Wehrmacht and parts of the Munich police.[65] But Sperr and Held were bitterly disappointed in the hopes they had placed in the Reich president and the armed forces under his command. Hindenburg remained a factor of great uncertainty even to those in the SA, but in the final analysis he allowed himself to be completely outmaneuvered by Hitler in the fateful events of 9 March. For the self-styled revolutionaries in the SA, only Hindenburg's retirement as Reich president and the expulsion of the German Nationalists from the national cabinet would create for Hitler the "ceasarist position" he presumably deserved.[66]

The conduct of the BVP can only be properly understood if viewed from a variety of perspectives and in the context of the circumstances under which the party was forced to operate. The talks between Schäffer and Nazi negotiators over a possible coalition after the events of 30 January 1933 were futile in light of the dramatically different assumptions and goals of the two parties. When the BVP delegation to the Bavarian Landtag tried to find a way out of the painful situation in which it found itself after the March elections by entering into cabinet negotiations with the NSDAP, this path was immediately blocked by Held's dismissal as Bavarian minister president. Negotiations between the BVP and NSDAP became superfluous before they ever really started. And even if these negotiations had succeeded in creating a broadly based parliamentary coalition, the government in Bavaria as well as its counterpart in Baden could almost certainly have counted on the immediate appointment of a police or Reich commissar by the authorities in Berlin.[67] To be sure, Schäffer demonstrated a surprisingly great eagerness to cooperate with the NSDAP in the task of national reconstruction in April 1933.[68] Yet he hardly spoke for the entire leadership of the BVP. The circle around Wohlmuth, Leicht, and Held continued to enjoy widespread confidence throughout the party, something that both Frank and Hitler had to take into account. Rarely would the differences of opinion in the BVP reach the level of what some have called a "process of internal decay."[69] Though resigned and intimated, the BVP delegation to the Bavarian Landtag continued to harbor hopes of a future recovery and new electoral victories. The BVP represented an important and powerful force of political Catholicism in the second largest state in the Weimar Republic. That alone is sufficient to explain the extraordinary furor with which the new Reich chancellor and his minister of the interior joined forces with a rebellious SA for a two-pronged attack on "Black Munich."

Winfried Becker is professor emeritus for modern and contemporary history at the University of Passau. He has published on a wide range of topics extending from the Westphalian Peace Congress and the institutions of the Holy Roman Empire to the history of National Socialism and postwar Germany. His most important publications include *Georg von Hertling (1843–1919)*, vol. 1 (1981), and *Frederic von Rosenberg (1874–1937): Diplomat vom späten Kaiserreich bis zum Dritten Reich, Außenminister der Weimarer Republik* (2011). He is currently working on various projects related to the history of political Catholicism in Germany, Bavaria, and Western Europe as well as on the continuation of his Hertling biography.

Notes

1. On the founding of the BVP, see Claudia Friemberger, *Sebastian Schlittenbauer und die Anfänge der Bayerischen Volkspartei* (St. Ottilien: Eos-Verlag, 1998), 48–64, and Florian Breitling, *Georg Wohlmuth: Geistlicher, bayerischer Politiker und Kirchenkämpfer aus Eichstätt zwischen Königreich und Republik* (PhD diss., Passau, 1987), 187–91.

2. On Leicht's role in the BVP, see the detailed study by Christian Maga, *Prälat Johann Leicht (1868–1940): Konservativer Demokrat in der Krise der Zwischenkriegszeit; Eine politische Biographie des Vorsitzenden der Reichstagsfraktion der Bayerischen Volkspartei in Berlin* (PhD diss., Würzburg, 1990), esp. 64–68.

3. Heinz Hürten, "Revolution und Zeit der Weimarer Republik," in *Handbuch der bayerischen Geschichte*, vol. 4: *Das neue Bayern von 1800 bis zur Gegenwart*, part 1: *Staat und Politik*, ed. Alois Schmid et al. (Munich: C. H. Beck, 2003), 439–98, esp. 483–87. On the BVP in the Weimar Republic, see Winfried Becker, "Ein bayerischer Sonderweg? Die Bayerische Volkspartei und die Republik von Weimar," in *Die Herausforderung der Diktaturen: Katholizismus in Deutschland und Italien 1918–1943/45*, ed. Wolfram Pyta, Carsten Kretschmann, Giuseppe Ignesti, and Tiziana Di Maio (Tübingen: Max Niemeyer Verlag, 2009), 62.

4. Robert Probst, *Die NSDAP im Bayerischen Landtag 1924–1933* (Frankfurt a.M.: Peter Lang, 1998), 171.

5. Motion by Frick, 14 October 1931, in *Verhandlungen des Reichstags* (Berlin: J. Sittenfeld, 1932), vol. 451, Anlagen, no. 1195.

6. Thomas Fürst, *Karl Stützel: Ein Lebensweg in Umbrüchen. Vom Königlichen Beamten zum Bayerischen Innenminister der Weimarer Zeit (1924–1933)* (Frankfurt a.M.: Peter Lang, 2007), 359–60, 340–410. For the object of Stützel's complaints, see *Reichsgesetzblatt* I, 1932, 297–99 (14–16 June 1932), 339–40 (28 June 1932), and 548–50 (19 December 1932).

7. Minutes of the Bavarian Council of Ministers, 30 June 1932, in *Die Protokolle des Bayerischen Ministerrats 1919–1945: Das Kabinett Held IV. Mai 1932–März 1933*, ed. Walter Ziegler (Munich: Kommission für Bayerische Landesgeschichte, 2010), 61–71.

8. Otto Altendorfer, *Fritz Schäffer als Politiker der Bayerischen Volkspartei (1888–1945)*, 2 vols. (Munich: Hanns-Seidel-Stiftung e. V., 1993), 2:632–41.

9. Christiane Reuter, *"Graue Eminenz der bayerischen Politik"*: *Eine politische Biographie Anton Pfeiffers (1888–1957)* (Munich: Kommissionsverlag UNI-Druck, 1987), 56–57.

10. Gebsattel to Reusch, 12 February 1932, Rheinisch-Westfälisches Wirtschaftsarchiv, Cologne (hereafter cited as RWWA Cologne), Abt. 130, Nachlass Paul Reusch, 400101293/3. The author would like to thank Larry E. Jones for having provided him with copies of this letter and other materials from the Reusch Nachlass.

11. For detailed reports on the political situation in Bavaria, see Gebsattel to Reusch, 30 November 1932, and 7 March 1933, RWWA Cologne, NL Reusch, 400101293/3.

12. Anonymous memorandum on the coalition negotiations, [n.d.], in the Archiv für Christlich-Soziale Politik, Munich (hereafter cited as ACSP Munich), NL Josef Müller, V 11.

13. See the notes on a conversation between Schäffer and Papen, 5 February 1933, ACSP Munich, NL Müller V 11, as well as the lengthy document prepared by Baron Karl von Imhoff on Held's meeting with Hitler, 1 March 1933, reprinted in Falk Wiesemann, *Die Vorgeschichte der nationalsozialistischen Machtübernahme in Bayern 1932/1933* (Berlin: Duncker and Humblot, 1975), 294–303, esp. 301–2.

14. Alois Hundhammer, *Die staatsbürgerlichen Vorträge von Alois Hundhammer aus den Jahren 1930 und 1931*, ed. Oliver Braun (München: Institut für Bayerische Geschichte, 2005), 149–75.

15. For further information on efforts to restore the Wittelsbach dynasty in Bavaria in the spring of 1933, see Christina M. Förster, *Der Harnier-Kreis: Widerstand gegen den Nationalsozialismus in Bayern* (Paderborn: Ferdinand Schöningh, 1996), 101–20; and Dieter J. Weiß, *Kronprinz Rupprecht von Bayern (1869–1955): Eine politische Biografie* (Regensburg: Verlag Friedrich Pustet, 2007), 266–72.

16. "Monarchistische Bestrebungen," 24 February 1933, ACSP Munich, NL Müller, V 11. See also Sperr an Held, 24. February 1933, ibid. For further details, see Wiesemann, *Vorgeschichte*, 231–36.

17. Sperr, Aide memoire for Hindenburg, 28 January 1933, ACSP, Munich, NL Müller, V 11. See also Elke Fröhlich, "Sperr als Offizier und Gesandter," in *Franz Sperr und der Widerstand gegen den Nationalsozialismus in Bayern*, ed. Hermann Rumschöttel and Walter Ziegler (Munich: Verlag C. H. Beck, 2001), 70–71.

18. Fürst, *Stützel*, 439–42.

19. Note by Sperr, 7 February 1933, ACSP Munich, NL Müller, V 11.

20. Sperr to Held, 24 February 1933, Bayerische Gesandschaft, Nr. 475, with Göring's speech before the Prussian governors on 15 February 1933, in an attachment identified as a letter from "Brutus," n.d., ACSP Munich, NL Müller, V 11.

21. Mathias Rösch, *Die Münchner NSDAP 1925–1933: Eine Untersuchung zur inneren Struktur der NSADP in der Weimarer Republik* (München: R. Oldenbourg Verlag, 2002), 375–79; see also Martin Hille, "Zur Sozial- und Mitgliederstruktur der Passauer NSDAP in den zwanziger und dreißiger

Jahren," in *Passau in der Zeit des Nationalsozialismus: Ausgewählte Fallstudien*, ed. Winfried Becker (Passau: Universitäts-Verlag, 1999), 9–42.

22. On Sperr's meetings with Papen, Hindenburg, and Hitler, 7–8 March 1933, see his letter to Held, 8 March 1933, Bayerische Gesandtschaft, Nr. 589, ACSP Munich, NL Müller, V 11.

23. Hitler's remarks in his meeting with Sperr, 8 March 1933, as reported in Sperr to Held, 8 March 1933, ibid.

24. Minutes of the BVP Landtag delegation, 8 March 1933, ACSP Munich, LTF, BVP-Protokolle, 4/154–57.

25. Memorandum over the coalition negotiations, n.d., ACSP Munich, NL Müller, V 11.

26. Pfeiffer's remarks at a meeting of the BVP Landtag delegation, 8 March 1933, ACSP Munich, LTF, BVP-Protokolle, 4/154–57.

27. Entry in Goebbels's diary, 8 March 1933, in *Die Tagebücher von Joseph Goebbels*, Sämtliche Fragmente Teil I, Bd. 2. 1931–1936, ed. Elke Fröhlich (Munich: K. G. Saur, 1987), 389. See also Wiesemann, *Vorgeschichte*, 275, and Fröhlich, "Sperr als Offizier und Gesandter," 51–82, 77–78.

28. On the events of 9 March in Munich and Berlin there are three major sources: a documentary report that Held prepared shortly after the events and subsequently published by Winfried Becker, "Die nationalsozialistische Machtergreifung in Bayern: Ein Dokumentarbericht Heinrich Helds aus dem Jahr 1933," *Historisches Jahrbuch* 112 (1992): 412–35, and the two reports by Franz Sperr, his "Vormerkungen für den 8. und 9. März 1933, 8.–10. März," and [Franz Sperr] "Aufzeichnung der Vorgänge vom 8.–10. März 1933," n.d., all three in ACSP Munich, NL Müller, V 11, nos. 5, 11, and IV. See also Sperr's recollection of these events from March 1947 in *Die Protokolle des Bayerischen Ministerrats*, ed. Ziegler, 310–14, as well as the commentary on these recollections by Gerhard Hetzer, "Archivalische Quellen zu Franz Sperr," in *Sperr und der Widerstand*, ed. Rumschöttel and Ziegler, 208–14.

29. Bernhard Grau, "Die Reichsstatthalter in Bayern: Schnittstelle zwischen Reich und Land," in *Staat und Gaue in der NS-Zeit. Bayern 1933–1945*, ed. Hermann Rumschöttel and Walter Ziegler (Munich: Verlag C. H. Beck, 2004), 139. See also Fürst, *Stützel*, 458.

30. Personal recollection of Schäffer, n.d., ACSP Munich, NL Müller, V 11.

31. Sperr, "Aufzeichnung der Vorgänge vom 8.–10. März 1933," ACSP Munich, NL Müller, V 11.

32. Ibid.

33. Becker, "Die nationalsozialistische Machtergreifung," 432.

34. Frick to Held, 9 March 1933, Reichsminister des Innern, no. I A 2030/9.3, ACSP Munich, NL Müller, V 11.

35. Held's protocol on the events of the night of 9–10 March 1933, ACSP Munich, NL Müller, V 11. See also Josef Müller, *Bis zur letzten Konsequenz: Ein Leben für Frieden und Freiheit* (Munich: Süddeutscher Verlag, 1975), 373–78, for the general atmosphere, 40–47, and *Fritz Gerlich—ein Publizist gegen Hitler: Briefe und Akten 1930–1934*, ed. Rudolf Morsey (Paderborn: Ferdinand Schöningh, 2010), 268–79, as well as the recent study by

Rudolf Morsey, *Fritz Gerlich (1883–1934): Ein früher Gegner Hitlers und des Nationalsozialismus* (Paderborn: Ferdinand Schöningh, 2016), 261–65.

36. On the events in Baden, see Jürgen Schmiesing, *1933—die Gleichschaltung des politischen Katholizismus in Baden: Ein Beitrag zur Geschichte der national-sozialistischen Machtübernahme* (Karlsruhe: KIT Scientific Publishing, 2013), 10.

37. Memorandum by an unknown author on the events related to Held's resignation as Bavarian minister president, n.d., ACSP Munich, NL Müller, V 11.

38. Held to Bleyer, 14 March 1933, ACSP Munich, NL Müller, V 11, no. 6. See also the correspondence between Held, Bleyer, and Epp, in *Die Protokolle des Bayerischen Ministerrats 1919-1945*, ed. Ziegler, 325–35. For further information on Held's dilemma, see Winfried Becker, "Heinrich Held (1868–1938): Aufstieg und Sturz des bayerischen Parlamentariers und Ministerpräsidenten," *Zeitschrift für bayerische Landesgeschichte* 72 (2009): 807–91, 860–74, and Barbara Pöhlmann, *Heinrich Held als Bayerischer Ministerpräsident (1924–1933): Eine Studie zu 9 Jahren bayerischer Staatspolitik* (PhD diss., München, 1996), 235–40.

39. Notarized statement by Esser in the records of the Staatskanzlei, Bayerisches Hauptstaatsarchiv, Munich (hereafter cited as BHStA Munich), 5255, 92–93.

40. Held to Bleyer, 16 March 1933, BHStA Munich, Staatskanzlei, 5255/89.

41. Minutes of the BVP Landtag delegation, 8 March 1933, ACSP Munich, LTF, BVP-Protokolle, 4/154–57.

42. Held to Bleyer, 16 March 1933, BHStA Munich, Staatskanzlei 5255/89.

43. Press conference at noon, 10 March 1933, ACSP Munich, NL Müller, V 11.

44. On 14 March 1933 Röhm informed Lex that Held had said to him that he, the minister president, would "most emphatically" recommend Epp's appointment as the general state commissar to the Bavarian Council of Ministers. See Walter Dierker, "'Ich will keine Nullen, sondern Bullen': Hitlers Koalitionsverhandlungen mit der Bayerischen Volkspartei im März 1933," *Vierteljahrshefte für Zeitgeschichte* 50 (2002): 143–45.

45. Notes on the meetings of the BVP Landtag delegation, 13–15, 23–24, 29–30 March 1933, ACSP Munich, LTF-BVP Protokolle, 4/158–68.

46. Memorandum by Lex, 8 April 1946, BA Koblenz, NL Ritter von Lex, 16, reprinted in *"Das Ermächtigungsgesetz" vom 24. März 1933: Quellen zur Geschichte und Interpretation des "Gesetzes zur Behebung der Not von Volk und Reich,"* ed. Rudolf Morsey (Düsseldorf: Droste Verlag, 2010), 147.

47. Faulhaber to the Bavarian state minister, 5 July 1933, *Akten deutscher Bischöfe über die Lage der Kirche 1933–1945*, ed. Bernhard Stasiewski et al., 6 vols. (Mainz: Matthias-Grünewald-Verlag, 1968–83), 1:259, 251.

48. Conversation in the ministry of justice, 20 March 1933, ACSP, NL Müller, V 11.

49. In a meeting with Lex on 14 March 1933 Hitler categorically and repeatedly rejected the BVP's key demand that it retain responsibility for matters related to the churches and schools even under a Bavarian minister president under Hitler's control. See the protocol of Lex's meeting with Hitler, 14 March 1933, in Dierker, "Ich will keine Nullen," 143–48.

50. Dierker, "Ich will keine Nullen," 120.
51. "Bayerische Jugend hab acht," *Junge Front/Michael*, 2 April 1933, no. 14.
52. Meeting of the BVP Landtag delegation, 3 April 1933, ACSP Munich, LTF, BVP-Protokolle, 4/167–68.
53. In this respect, see Winfried Becker, "Begriffe und Erscheinungsformen des Widerstands gegen den Nationalsozialismus," *Neue Folge* 12 (1989): 11–42.
54. *M.d.L. Das Ende der Parlamente 1933 und die Abgeordneten der Landtage und Bürgerschaften der Weimarer Republik in der Zeit des Nationalsozialismus: Politische Verfolgung, Emigration und Ausbürgerung 1933–1945; Ein biographischer Index*, ed. Martin Schumacher (Düsseldorf: Droste Verlag, 1995), 20*–24*.
55. Conversation in the Bavarian ministry of justice, 20 March 1933, NL Müller, V 11.
56. Gebsattel to Reusch, 17 and 24 March 1933, RWWA Cologne, Abt. 130, NL Reusch, 400101293/3.
57. Conversation in the Bavarian ministry of justice, 20 March 1933, NL Müller, V 11.
58. Johann Kirchinger, *Michael Horlacher: Ein Agrarfunktionär in der Weimarer Republik* (Düsseldorf: Droste Verlag, 2011), 449–50.
59. "Die feierliche Eröffnung des Bayerischen Landtags," *Bayerische Staatszeitung*, 29 April 1933, no. 99.
60. "Zum Bayerischen Ermächtigungsgesetz," 7–10, ACSP Munich, NL Müller, V 11. See also Joachim Lilla, *Der Bayerische Landtag 1918/19 bis 1933: Wahlvorschläge — Zusammensetzung — Biographien* (Munich: Eos Verlag, 2008), XXXVf.
61. Report in the *Bamberger Volksblatt*, 24 April 1933, in "Zum Bayerischen Ermächtigungsgesetz," 6–7, ACSP Munich, NL Müller, V 11. See also Oliver Braun, *Konservative Existenz in der Moderne: Das politische Weltbild Alois Hundhammers (1900–1974)* (Munich: Hanns-Seidel-Stiftung, 2006), 221–27.
62. Günter Buchstab, Brigitte Kaff, and Hans-Otto Kleinmann, eds., *Verfolgung und Widerstand 1933–1945: Christliche Demokraten gegen Hitler* (Düsseldorf: Droste Verlag 1986), 29–33.
63. Walter Ziegler, *Hitler und Bayern: Beobachtungen zu ihrem Verhältnis* (Munich: Verlag C. H. Beck, 2004), 41, 72–94. See also; Rösch, *Münchner NSDAP*, 79–138.
64. Statement of fact by Magnus Heimannsberg, 26 September 1957, Historisches Archiv der Stadt Köln, NL Leo Schwering, 176, 2.
65. Winfried Becker, "Franz Sperr und sein Widerstandskreis," in *Franz Sperr und der Widerstand gegen den Nationalsozialismus*, ed. Rumschoettel and Ziegler, 106–14.
66. Paul Stengel to J. Müller notes on conversations with Müller and others, 18 March 1933, ACSP, NL Müller, V 11.
67. Michael Braun, *Der Badische Landtag 1918–1933* (Düsseldorf: Droste Verlag, 2009), 498. This was similar to the situation in Saxony. See Andreas Wagner, *"Machtergreifung" in Sachsen: NSDAP und staatliche Verwaltung 1930–1935* (Cologne: Böhlau Verlag 2004), 141–47.

68. Klaus Schönhoven, "Der politische Katholizismus in Bayern unter der NS-Herrschaft 1933–1945," in *Bayern in der NS-Zeit*, ed. Martin Broszat et al., 6 vols. (Munich: Oldenbourg Verlag, 1977–83), 5:550.
69. Probst, *NSDAP im Bayerischen Landtag*, 193.

Bibliography

Altendorfer, Otto. *Fritz Schäffer als Politiker der Bayerischen Volkspartei (1888–1945)*, 2 vols. Munich: Hanns-Seidel-Stiftung e. V., 1993.

Becker, Winfried. "Begriffe und Erscheinungsformen des Widerstands gegen den Nationalsozialismus." *Jahrbuch für Volkskunde*, no. 12 (1989): 11–42

———. "Die nationalsozialistische Machtergreifung in Bayern: Ein Dokumentarbericht Heinrich Helds aus dem Jahr 1933." *Historisches Jahrbuch* 112 (1992): 412–35.

———. "Franz Sperr und sein Widerstandskreis." In *Franz Sperr und der Widerstand gegen den Nationalsozialismus in Bayern*, edited by Hermann Rumschöttel and Walter Ziegler, 106–14. Munich: Verlag C. H. Beck, 2001.

———. "Ein bayerischer Sonderweg? Die Bayerische Volkspartei und die Republik von Weimar." In *Die Herausforderung der Diktaturen: Katholizismus in Deutschland und Italien 1918–1943/45*, edited by Wolfram Pyta, Carsten Kretschmann, Giuseppe Ignesti, and Tiziana Di Maio, 39–63. Tübingen: Max Niemeyer Verlag, 2009.

Braun, Oliver. *Konservative Existenz in der Moderne: Das politische Weltbild Alois Hundhammers (1900–1974)*. Munich: Hanns-Seidel-Stiftung, 2006.

Breitling, Florian. *Georg Wohlmuth: Geistlicher, bayerischer Politiker und Kirchenkämpfer aus Eichstätt zwischen Königreich und Republik*. PhD diss., Passau, 1987.

Buchstab, Günter, Brigitte Kaff, and Hans-Otto Kleinmann, eds. *Verfolgung und Widerstand 1933–1945: Christliche Demokraten gegen Hitler*. Düsseldorf: Droste Verlag 1986.

Dierker, Walter. "'Ich will keine Nullen, sondern Bullen': Hitlers Koalitionsverhandlungen mit der Bayerischen Volkspartei im März 1933." *Vierteljahrshefte für Zeitgeschichte* 50 (2002): 111–48.

Förster, Christina M. *Der Harnier-Kreis: Widerstand gegen den Nationalsozialismus in Bayern* (Paderborn: Ferdinand Schöningh, 1996).

Friemberger, Claudia. *Sebastian Schlittenbauer und die Anfänge der Bayerischen Volkspartei*. St. Ottilien: Eos-Verlag, 1998.

Fröhlich, Elke. "Sperr als Offizier und Gesandter." In *Franz Sperr und der Widerstand gegen den Nationalsozialismus in Bayern*, edited by Hermann Rumschöttel and Walter Ziegler, 51–82. Munich: Verlag C. H. Beck, 2001.

Fürst, Thomas. *Karl Stützel: Ein Lebensweg in Umbrüchen; Vom Königlichen Beamten zum Bayerischen Innenminister der Weimarer Zeit (1924–1933)*. Frankfurt a.M.: Peter Lang, 2007.

Grau, Bernhard. "Die Reichsstatthalter in Bayern: Schnittstelle zwischen Reich und Land." In *Staat und Gaue in der NS-Zeit. Bayern 1933–1945*, edited by

Hermann Rumschöttel and Walter Ziegler, 130–69. Munich: Verlag C. H. Beck, 2004.

Hetzer, Gerhard. "Archivalische Quellen zu Franz Sperr." In *Franz Sperr und der Widerstand gegen den Nationalsozialismus in Bayern,* edited by Hermann Rumschöttel and Walter Ziegler, 208–14. Munich: Verlag C. H. Beck, 2001.

Hille, Martin. "Zur Sozial- und Mitgliederstruktur der Passauer NSDAP in den zwanziger und dreißiger Jahren." In *Passau in der Zeit des Nationalsozialismus: Ausgewählte Fallstudien,* edited by Winfried Becker, 9–42. Passau: Universitäts-Verlag, 1999.

Hundhammer, Alois. *Die staatsbürgerlichen Vorträge von Alois Hundhammer aus den Jahren 1930 und 1931.* Edited by Oliver Braun. München: Institut für Bayerische Geschichte, 2005.

Hürten, Heinz. "Revolution und Zeit der Weimarer Republik." In *Handbuch der bayerischen Geschichte,* vol. 4: *Das neue Bayern von 1800 bis zur Gegenwart,* part 1: *Staat und Politik,* edited by Alois Schmid et al. (Munich: C. H. Beck, 2003), 439–98.

Kirchinger, Johann. *Michael Horlacher: Ein Agrarfunktionär in der Weimarer Republik.* Düsseldorf: Droste Verlag, 2011.

Maga, Christian. "Prälat Johann Leicht (1868–1940): Konservativer Demokrat in der Krise der Zwischenkriegszeit; Eine politische Biographie des Vorsitzenden der Reichstagsfraktion der Bayerischen Volkspartei in Berlin." PhD diss., Würzburg, 1990.

Morsey, Rudolf. *Fritz Gerlich (1883–1934): Ein früher Gegner Hitlers und des Nationalsozialismus.* Paderborn: Ferdinand Schöningh, 2016.

———. ed. *"Das Ermächtigungsgesetz" vom 24. März 1933: Quellen zur Geschichte und Interpretation des "Gesetzes zur Behebung der Not von Volk und Reich."* Düsseldorf: Droste Verlag, 2010.

———. ed. *Fritz Gerlich—ein Publizist gegen Hitler: Briefe und Akten 1930–1934.* Paderborn: Ferdinand Schöningh, 2010.

Müller, Josef. *Bis zur letzten Konsequenz: Ein Leben für Frieden und Freiheit.* Munich: Süddeutscher Verlag, 1975.

Probst, Robert. *Die NSDAP im Bayerischen Landtag 1924–1933.* Frankfurt a.M.: Peter Lang, 1998.

Reuter, Christiane. *"Graue Eminenz der bayerischen Politik": Eine politische Biographie Anton Pfeiffers (1888–1957).* Munich: Kommissionsverlag UNI-Druck, 1987.

Rösch, Mathias. *Die Münchner NSDAP 1925–1933: Eine Untersuchung zur inneren Struktur der NSADP in der Weimarer Republik.* München: R. Oldenbourg Verlag, 2002.

Schönhoven, Klaus. "Der politische Katholizismus in Bayern unter der NS-Herrschaft 1933–1945." In *Bayern in der NS-Zeit,* 6 vols., edited by Martin Broszat et al., 5:541–646. Munich: Oldenbourg Verlag, 1977–83.

Schumacher, Martin, ed. *M.d.L. Das Ende der Parlamente 1933 und die Abgeordneten der Landtage und Bürgerschaften der Weimarer Republik in der Zeit des Nationalsozialismus: Politische Verfolgung, Emigration und Ausbürgerung 1933–1945; Ein biographischer Index.* Düsseldorf: Droste Verlag, 1995.

Stasiewski, Bernhard, et al., eds. *Akten deutscher Bischöfe über die Lage der Kirche 1933–1945.* 6 vols. Mainz: Matthias-Grünewald-Verlag, 1968–83.

Weiß, Dieter J. *Kronprinz Rupprecht von Bayern (1869–1955): Eine politische Biografie.* Regensburg: Verlag Friedrich Pustet, 2007.

Wiesemann, Falk. *Die Vorgeschichte der nationalsozialistischen Machtübernahme in Bayern 1932/1933.* Berlin: Duncker and Humblot, 1975.

Ziegler, Walter. *Hitler und Bayern: Beobachtungen zu ihrem Verhältnis.* Munich: Verlag C. H. Beck, 2004.

———. ed. *Die Protokolle des Bayerischen Ministerrats 1919–1945: Das Kabinett Held IV. Mai 1932–März 1933.* Munich: Kommission für Bayerische Landesgeschichte, 2010.

 5

GERMAN BIG BUSINESS AND THE NATIONAL REVOLUTION, 1933–34

Peter Hayes

For the leaders of Germany's largest corporations, the appointment of the Hitler-Papen government of national revival heralded a period of uncertainty. At various moments in 1931–32 numerous prominent executives had favored persuading part or all of the NSDAP to support and/or participate in a cabinet led by someone other than Hitler, but only a handful of ranking businessmen ever had endorsed his appointment as chancellor. Franz von Papen's patrons among the barons of heavy industry believed that he was still negotiating during January 1933 to get Hitler to play second fiddle, and they welcomed the progress they thought Papen was making. Conversely, in the waning days of the month, the principal business manager of the National Association of German Industry (Reichsverband der deutschen Industrie or RDI) advised its vacationing chairman, who concurred, that a continuation of the Schleicher cabinet seemed the best available option for the present.[1] The announcement of the new government on the morning of 30 January thus surprised most members of the nation's corporate elite and left them wondering what to expect.

Many eminent bankers and industrialists, including Ernst Brandi and Karl Haniel from the Ruhr region, shared Papen's confidence that the conservatives who occupied three-quarters of the seats in the new Hitler cabinet would "tame" or "frame in" Hitler. But other executives, such as Otto Wolff of the metals industry and Hermann Bücher of Germany's General Electric (Allgemeine Elektrizitäts-Gesellschaft or AEG), remained concerned about the potential economic effects of the Führer's expressed dedication to antisemitism, autarky, agricultural tariffs, and the "primacy of politics" in economic decision-making.[2] The appointment of Alfred Hugenberg, the intransigently pro-agrarian leader of the German National People's Party (Deutschnationale Volkspartei or DNVP), as both economics and agriculture minister also aroused deep misgivings in some commercial quarters. Accordingly, the initial reaction of the RDI's presidium to the new government was

a call for clarification of its economic program and proof that "disturbances of domestic order and social peace would be avoided." Paul
Reusch's guideline for the editorial stance of the newspapers controlled
by his conglomerate, the Gutehoffnungshütte (GHH), captured the
prevailing attitude of watchful waiting: "Goodwill, but not too much
enthusiasm."[3]

Events soon made clear that German big business was in no position to demand explanations from the new government or to negotiate
with it over policy. In the run-up to the parliamentary elections set for 5
March, the executives got a foretaste of the "revolution running amok"
that the rest of the first half of 1933 would bring.[4] Euphoric at the rise
of their Führer, emboldened Nazis, "of whom no one had known anything," as Fritz Roessler, the supervisory board chair of the chemicals
and precious metals firm later known as Degussa, reported, "popped
up on all sides."[5] Many of these zealots began insisting on wearing
their party uniforms to and from work and in offices, getting Jews and
"double earners" (women with employed husbands) fired and unemployed Nazis hired instead, replacing previously elected workers' representatives with exponents of the "National Revolution," obtaining
corporate funds for various party projects and organizations, and generally infusing plants and workplaces with the NSDAP's militant spirit.

Along with these grassroots encroachments on managerial authority and efficient operations, Germany's leading industrialists quickly
encountered greatly reduced deference to their power and status at the
top level of the state. The emblematic occasion was a meeting at the
Reichstag president's palace in Berlin on 20 February 1933, to which
Hermann Göring attracted two dozen commercial leaders with the
promise that "the Reich Chancellor will explain his policies." After
keeping the invitees waiting for about half an hour, Hitler delivered a
ninety-minute monologue that depicted the impending election as the
culmination of the long Manichean struggle for the soul of Germany
between his movement and the "decomposing forces" of communism.
He concluded with the blunt warning that "if the election does not
decide, the decision simply will have to be brought about by other
means." Apparently taken aback by this filibuster culminating in a
threat of civil war, Gustav Krupp von Bohlen und Halbach, the head of
the RDI, discreetly pocketed his prepared statement calling for a clear
"demarcation line between the state and the economy" and briefly and
politely thanked Hitler. Göring then seized the opportunity to promise
that the upcoming vote would make no difference to the composition
of the current cabinet, which would continue in office indefinitely, since
"the election of 5 March would certainly be the last one for the next ten

years, probably even for the next hundred years." Having offered the assembled executives no reassurances regarding policy but only the peremptory demand that they choose sides, the two Nazi leaders then abruptly departed, leaving Hjalmar Schacht behind to conduct a shakedown for campaign contributions. He extracted pledges of three million marks for the Nazis and their electoral allies from the ambushed and browbeaten attendees.[6]

Pressure and Placation

The importuning of business leaders by low- and high-ranking Nazis only grew more insistent in the aftermath of their qualified victory on 5 March. Claiming a mandate by virtue of the Nazis' 44 percent share of the popular vote and the 8 percent for the so-called Papen Bloc, but frustrated by Hitler's failure to win an outright majority, party activists redoubled their efforts to bring corporate policies into line with Nazi ideology. The usual spearheads of these efforts were chapters of the 260,000-member-strong National Socialist Factory Cell Organization (Nationalsozialistische Betriebszellenorganisation or NSBO), known as "the SA of the factories."[7] In many instances, their demands had the backing of newly (or even self-) appointed Nazi government officials or of state agencies. Thus, in March, the arrest and dispatch to a concentration camp of the non-Nazi works council members at the Robert Bosch plant in Stuttgart cleared the way for the installation of more politically palatable workforce representatives.[8] At the main offices of the Allianz insurance company and its affiliated Allianz Leben, NSBO, SA, and SS men simply barged into meetings of the works councils on 30 March, compelled the resignations of non-Nazis, and announced a list of their replacements.[9] So extensive were disruptions of this and other sorts that Hitler felt compelled to declare as early as 10 March that "harassment of individual persons, obstructions of cars or disturbances of business categorically must cease," words that the harried managers of the Economics Policy Section (Wirtschaftspolitische Abteilung) of IG Farben passed on to the concern's factories and offices.[10]

The sincerity of Hitler's calls for restraint is doubtful, however, in view of his decree of 4 April retroactively legalizing the Nazi takeovers of factory councils and his simultaneous connivance in a putsch directed at the leadership of the RDI.[11] After Paul Reusch and other magnates quashed an effort by the Führer's principal industrial backer, Fritz Thyssen, to undermine Krupp's position atop that organization in late March, the Nazis turned on his closest advisors. Just as Carl

Friedrich von Siemens and Krupp were calling on the chancellor on the morning of 1 April, Otto Wagener, at the time the leader of the NSDAP's economic policy section, appeared at the RDI headquarters in Berlin and demanded the immediate dismissal of two of the three principal business managers, their replacement by one representative of the NSDAP and another of the DNVP, and the removal of all Jews from the presidium. Accounts vary as to whether Wagener arrived in the company of storm troopers or merely threatened to do so later, but the effect was the same either way. Once Krupp learned two days later that Hitler would not rescind or disavow his follower's demands, the RDI chief concluded on his own authority and without consulting his organization's board members that he had no choice but to comply. The personnel changes occurred on 5 April, and Krupp silenced several outraged colleagues who urged him to reconsider at a meeting of the presidium the following day by threatening to resign.[12] In solidarity with the Jews thus ousted from that body, several non-Jewish dissenters from Krupp's course also withdrew. One of them, Georg Müller-Oerlinghausen of the textile industry, penned a fervent dissent to Krupp on 13 April that laid out industry's options with eloquence and courage, but in vain:

> Too many positions already have been abandoned unnecessarily and their previous occupants brought scorn upon themselves by running after the ruling party. No one has less respect for lack of courage than the decisive figures of the new regime ...
>
> As long as the way forward is as unclear as it is today ... we cannot and must not take sides, if we want to preserve even a spark of self-respect. ... Political opposition would be sheer madness for a business association, but blandly falling in behind the economic utopia of the dominant party would be suicide. We [i.e., the RDI] exist to preserve freedom of opinion and to persuade the authorities of its necessity. ... The RDI can and must never be drawn into agreement with the unheard of penalizing and oppression of German Jewry if it still wants to claim any moral standing. Should this attitude mean that the RDI loses the possibility, temporarily or for a longer period, of gaining a hearing from key political leaders, then we will have to endure that fate, sure in the knowledge that we tried to do what was best.[13]

Krupp chose pragmatism over principle, and so did most other corporate leaders as similar events took place across Germany on the local level. Representative of the trend was the takeover by Nazi activists of the Chamber of Industry and Trade (Industrie- und Handelskammer or IHK) in Frankfurt on 1 April. They expelled the elected executive committee and installed Dr. Carl Lüer, a party member since 1927 and at the time a vigorous proponent of the "aryanization" of the Frankfurt stock exchange, as the IHK president. Local corporate leaders, including Ernst Busemann of Degussa, promptly formed an electoral committee to ratify these changes and complete the expulsion of Jews from the organization.[14] The phrases "in order to avoid worse" and "in response to the given or prevailing conditions" became the standard, oft-invoked justifications for compliance with Nazi demands to "coordinate" organizations and their personnel with the new regime's ideology. Adaptive impulses also propelled an influx of business leaders into the NSDAP by the time it declared a moratorium on new applications in early May. Fragmentary records suggest that, allowing for some variation by industry and region, roughly a third of the board members of the largest German firms signed up during the spring.[15]

The first day of April 1933 has gone down in German history as the infamous date of the Nazi boycott of Jewish businesses and professional offices, but historians often fail to note that it was also a central date in the capitulation of German industry to Nazi power. Equally often forgotten is the extent to which legal harassment of business leaders supplemented political agitation in bringing about that capitulation. Peter Langer argues that the regime's strong-arm tactics transformed Paul Reusch from a confidently outspoken to a compliant industrialist between March and May of 1933. The display of force began with the arrests of the editors of the GHH's newspapers in Munich, the appointment of Nazi commissars as replacements, and the dismissal of Jewish employees, followed by the confiscation of GHH's stock in its publishing company and the detention of its lawyers, whereupon Reusch meekly agreed not to contest the confiscation further in order to obtain their release.[16] Intimidating Robert Bosch, the aged head of the eponymous firm in Stuttgart, was more difficult, but the regime made that effort in April with the office search and arrest of Paul Distelbarth, one of the old industrialist's confidants.[17] At the Vereinigte Glanzstoff-Fabriken, whose Dutch ownership stake aroused suspicion among Nazis, allegations of tax evasion led to searches of the homes of three leading executives, Fritz Blüthgen of the supervisory board and Carl Benrath and Willy Springorum of the managing board, the arrest of the latter two, and the resignations of all three by early May, after which more party-friendly figures were appointed.[18]

Simultaneously, Philipp Reemtsma, the cigarette magnate whom the Nazis disliked for both his willingness to work with the SPD in local government during the Weimar Republic and his competition with Nazi-owned smoking products, and Günther Quandt, the owner of the Accumulatoren Fabrik AG, a major battery producer and the former husband of Joseph Goebbels's wife Magda, got caught up in the campaign that Hanns Kerrl, the new Prussian justice minister, launched against alleged instances of corruption and bribery under the "Weimar System." Reemtsma's firm began appearing in newspaper accounts of suspected firms in April, arrest orders for five of his managers went out in June, raids followed on his offices, and the Gauleiter of Schleswig-Holstein called for his replacement with a commissar. Though Reemtsma was not taken into custody, the investigation hung over his head for months, and he could only get it resolved by ultimately bribing Hermann Göring to quash the proceedings in return for three million Reichsmark.[19] Quandt and his principal managers, on the other hand, were arrested, interrogated by Kerrl's delegates, and held for weeks, while a veteran Nazi named Heinrich Stahmer took over as commissar of the Accumulatoren Fabrik. The case attracted such attention that, when Quandt paid a bail of over one million U.S. dollars in June, the *New York Times* ran a headline to that effect. He remained under house arrest until September, when he resumed his corporate functions, but legal proceedings did not come to a close until two years later.[20]

In short, genuine personal vulnerability combined with Krupp's pragmatic calculations to make most industrial leaders eager to express solidarity with the new regime by the time it inaugurated 1 May as the Day of National Labor in celebration of the emergent "people's community." In the run-up to the festivities, the head of IG Farben's Leverkusen works called on "all colleagues and associates to join the rally on this day of demonstration and thus prove our will to cooperate."[21] At the combine's Hoechst site, the plant leader invoked the spirit of national unity of August 1914 and closed his May Day speech with three shouts of "Heil" to Hindenburg and Hitler.[22] But at the concern's headquarters in Frankfurt, the managing board member responsible for personnel issues, Erwin Selck, sounded a more cautionary note. After reminding his listeners of the delicacy of social and economic structures and of "how easily they can be torn by inexperienced hands," he emphasized that "the success or failure of this beautiful movement depends considerably on whether upright men or petty spirits lead it. ... We must hope that in all the vital positions the right men gradually will appear. On that depends everything."[23] Remarks of this sort indicate that a somewhat condescending and naïve sense of duty prompted high-ranking executives to make common cause with Nazism in the spring of 1933. So do Fritz Roessler's writings later that year, in which he told himself that "one should not stand grumbling on the sidelines, even if one feels momentarily superfluous, but should recognize the good in the [Nazi] movement, ignore the human deficiencies associated with every revolution, and do one's bit so that this wild-grown juice becomes wine."[24]

Placating the new regime at both the national and local levels was the predominant business policy by the late spring of 1933, but it could take various forms. In the face of insistent agitation to hire "old fighters" and dismiss politically unacceptable employees and board members, some firms and employers were more pliable than others. The Karstadt department store purged its boards and workforces of Jews even before the 1 April boycott, as a means of being exempted from it, as its competitor, Leonard Tietz, did two weeks later.[25] In Berlin, AEG and a subsidiary that it co-owned, Osram GmbH, the principal German manufacturer of light bulbs, sought to relieve party pressure by voluntarily applying to their workforces the Hitler government's decrees of April removing certain categories of non-Aryans from the civil service and capping the Jewish proportion of students in *Gymnasien* and universities at 1.5 percent.[26] But Carl Friedrich von Siemens initially stood his ground against party demands, telling their bearer that "the staffing of senior positions was his responsibility as head of the firm, in which he would let no one interfere."[27] Even within the same company, conduct varied: Ludwig Hermann at IG Farben's Hoechst plant seems to have acceded enthusiastically to party pressure to fire communists and less eagerly to removing Jews, but to have put up more resistance on economic grounds to taking on additional party members.[28] Fritz Gajewski at the Wolfen factory, on the other hand, showed flexibility about hirings but not about firing Jews, and he deflected NSBO demands to that effect by having one of his aides adroitly reply that "if the parliamentary system is going to be abolished in the Reich, it cannot be the purpose of National Socialism to introduce it into our factory." He even resolutely defended a senior manager he did not like, Eduard Curschmann, from party attacks on political grounds and consistently refused to dismiss Jews.[29] As late as May, both Carl Bosch of IG Farben and Hans Walz of Robert Bosch tried to convince Hitler and his economic advisor Wilhelm Keppler, respectively, that "aryanization" would have disastrous consequences for Germany's economic welfare, international standing, and scientific progress, but both men were rebuffed.[30]

By June of 1933, the month that Germany became a one-party dictatorship, the country's business elite had been as thoroughly outmaneuvered as its political parties and other once-independent institutions. All autonomous business associations had disappeared into the new Reich Estate of German Industry (Reichsstand der deutschen Industrie or RSI) nominally headed by Krupp, and the new Adolf Hitler Donation of the German Economy (Adolf Hitler Spende der deutschen Wirtschaft or AHS) had institutionalized the regular flow of corporate donations, pegged at 0.5 percent of a firm's labor costs, to the NSDAP. The former development seemed to rule out the vague desire of some Nazi factions to establish an "estate based" (*ständisch*) economic structure, and the latter to limit the party's constant supplications, even at the price of establishing a new, but predictable, annual political tax on firms. The falls of both Hugenberg in the economic ministry and Otto Wagener in the NSDAP, followed by the appointment of Kurt Schmitt of Allianz as economics minister, combined with these changes to presage a return to more orderly commercial conditions.

At least that was the impression that IG Farben's leaders sought to make on the representatives of the DuPont corporation who called in Frankfurt in July, apparently to explore divesting their shares in the German conglomerate. Bosch reassured the American executives that things were looking up: "In the beginning, Hitler did not consult industrial leaders, but in recent weeks he has shown his stability by curbing the more extreme element of the party and bringing the industrial leaders into consultation." Several other members of Farben's boards seconded Bosch's judgment that "in the end sane views will prevail" and offered upbeat assessments of even the regime's Jewish policy.[31] Whether feigned or genuine, the optimism of Farben's leaders was not universally shared. An American diplomat reported at almost exactly the same time, "The owners of large factories are thoroughly unnerved as to the durability of their present position in firms. They fear measures that make a mockery of any form of legality and that will rob them of control over their businesses."[32] But Paul Reusch echoed Bosch's view in a letter to Hans Luther during July, and that evaluation became more widespread during the summer of 1933.[33] In early September, Eduard Hilgard of Allianz told a meeting in Berlin, "For the private economy, which appeared strongly endangered in the first period of the revolution, there are no more grounds for fear today."[34]

Sacrificing the Jews

Satisfied that industry had been brought into line and was committed to generating an economic revival that alone could guarantee the Nazi regime's continuation, the party did, indeed, ease up its pressure on business during the latter half of 1933 in most respects.[35] Moreover, as the economic revival that had begun in late 1932 continued to gather strength, the costs to industry of acceding to Nazi hiring demands declined, thus reducing a major ground for conflict. Finally, as the first benefits of Nazism's emphasis on autarky and rearmament emerged, firms quickly took advantage, as exemplified by Paul Reusch's enthusiastic willingness to put financial backing behind Schacht's creation of the Metallurgical Research Corporation (Metallurgische Forschungsgesellschaft) to fund arms expenditures, and by IG Farben's eager embrace of government measures that stimulated its production of synthetic fibers and magnesium and rescued the firm's investment in making gasoline from coal.[36]

But pressure on industry did not relax in all respects, and the price of increasing security for corporations in the new Reich remained cooperation in achieving not only its economic goals but also its racial ones. The principal casualties of the modus vivendi that gradually developed between the corporate world and the Nazi regime were the Jewish owners, board members, executives, and employees of the nation's leading firms and banks, many of whom were forced out of their positions during the National Revolution. One indication of their rate of attrition is Martin Münzel's study of the managing and supervisory boards of the top twenty companies in each of fifteen economic sectors—three hundred firms in all. He calculates that more than one-third of the Jews in the managerial group and one-quarter of the supervisory directors lost their positions during the first six months of Nazi rule, and that the proportions rose to 56 and 50 percent respectively by mid-1934.[37] In Berlin-based firms, by the same author's calculations, the toll was even higher, affecting fully two-thirds of the Jews on managing boards, as well as one-half of those on supervisory bodies by mid-1934.[38]

Such results attest not only to the relentlessness of Nazi Party pressure but also to the half-hearted defense of Jews put up by even sympathetic corporate leaders. Two highly illustrative cases in point stand out: the conduct of the Deutsche Bank toward Jews on its own boards and those of companies in which the bank had a major stake; and the development and fate of discussions among prominent industrialists during the summer of 1933 regarding ways of mitigating the regime's antisemitic policies. That the Dresdner Bank removed a Jew, Wilhelm Kleemann, from its managing board shortly after Hitler took office; a few months later added to that body Erich Niemann, an old flying mate of Hermann Göring, who concentrated on harassing Jewish clients of the bank into selling the firms they owned; and fired half of its 540 Jewish employees before the end of the year was not surprising in view of the fact that the state had acquired the majority of the bank's shares during the Depression.[39] Because the state's ownership stake in the Commerzbank was indirect and perhaps because its managing and supervisory board chairs were among the few industrialists who publically advocated Hitler's appointment as chancellor in 1932, that financial institution could afford to move more slowly in shedding its smaller number of Jewish employees and directors.[40] But the Deutsche Bank was neither under government control nor politically well-connected in 1933, facts that make its decision to exhibit "anticipatory obedience" regarding the removal of Jews particularly revealing.

The non-Jewish members of the Deutsche Bank's managing board told Hjalmar Schacht, the new Reichsbank president, early in April 1933 that they were prepared to remove their two observant Jewish colleagues, even though Schacht assured them that the matter could wait, and then peremptorily announced these executives' departures without the usual simultaneous promotion to the supervisory board. Dismissals of Jewish directors and senior staff followed at the bank's branches in Breslau and Essen. Even though bank records include a few expressions of regret over individuals' fates, the usual purpose of such remarks was to preserve an appearance of decency. As one managing board member wrote to another in January 1934, "Times may someday change, and we must for the sake of the bank make sure that no one can ever offer the reproach that the highest administrative bodies contributed to the fact that the non-Aryans had to leave the shop."[41]

The behavior of the Deutsche Bank's representatives in or at the head of the supervisory boards of other enterprises in 1933 reflected the same concern, along with the assignment of absolute priority to protecting sales against threats of commercial boycotts by Nazi Party members or government agencies. Representative of Deutsche Bank policy was its response to pressures applied to three construction firms during 1933, Johannes Jesserich AG, Hochtief AG, and Philipp Holzmann AG. In each case, potential or actual exclusion from the right to bid on government contracts was the lever used to compel the dismissal of Jews, and in each case the Deutsche Bank's delegate mounted rearguard defenses of the ousted figures but also drove hard severance bargains with many of them in order, as one bank executive noted in July 1933, "to cover my own back," presumably with regard to suspicious and hostile party or government observers.[42]

In view of the array of formal and covert pressures banks and firms confronted, the fact that no common front against persecution developed is disappointing in retrospect, but not surprising. Moreover, those few voices raised in defense of Jews betrayed notable ambivalence, a fact that attests to the fateful weakness of anti-antisemitism in Germany in early 1933.[43] Even business leaders who opposed blanket discrimination, such as Fritz Roessler of Degussa and Kurt Schmitt of Allianz, expressed dislike of some supposed Jewish traits or types and believed that Jews had acquired such prominence in Germany that they needed to "be pushed back."[44] Indicative of the partial acceptance of bigotry even among its would-be opponents is a letter that Carl Friedrich von Siemens circulated to his aides in April. Though written in compliance with the regime's request for business leaders to counteract supposedly "sensational" foreign accounts of the situation of Jews in Germany, the text tallied closely with views the author expressed in private during the following months.

On the one hand, Siemens's text requested understanding for two ugly aspects of what was happening in Germany, thus more or less endorsing them: the incarceration of numerous intellectual and "well-mannered communists" (*Edelbolschewisten*), including "a very large percentage of Jews ... primarily newly immigrated ones"; and the desire of "popular feeling" to reduce the number of Jews in the legal and medical professions, which "had grown quite extraordinarily in the postwar years under socialist influence, to a healthy proportion that approximates the population mix." On the other hand, Siemens condemned the drive to oust Jews from the private economy as a "deplorable movement ... traceable largely to selfish motives," and regretted that "partially justified efforts ... had degenerated into excesses and caused emotional suffering to the German Jews who are deeply rooted in our Fatherland and have served in war like the best other Germans." Extending "the sincerest sympathy" to these countrymen, Siemens concluded by observing that "all right-thinking people hope that this period of exaggerated antisemitism will soon belong to history."[45]

Siemens no doubt thought that his willingness to meet the Nazis halfway on the subject of antisemitism, to concede that some Jews had gone too far in Germany, would make his reservations more persuasive. But to National Socialist ears, his position amounted to nothing more than sentimental and squeamish special pleading on behalf of people like him. The effect of Siemens's consciously defiant description of Jews as "other Germans," to take a telling instance, was undone by his references to "partially justified efforts" and "exaggerated antisemitism." Who was Siemens to draw the line between legitimate and excessive discrimination? Nor was that the end of Siemens's compromising vocabulary. In another passage that remarked on the failure of upright German Jews to distance themselves adequately in previous years from the leftist activities of "their racial comrades [*ihrer Rassengenossen*]," he chose a phrase loaded with multiple meanings that gave still more of the argument away.[46] The temporizing tone of Siemens's remarks betrayed hesitancy about the place of Jews in German life and thus drained business's objections to discrimination of conviction.

The same fatal flaw undercut an initiative to stem the tide of Nazi antisemitism that took shape between May and August of 1933 on the part of a group of prominent Jewish bankers and lawyers and several of the nation's front-rank corporate leaders, including Krupp, Siemens, and Carl Bosch. At their first meeting on 23 May, they discussed a nineteen-page draft proposal that Max Warburg of the eponymous bank in Hamburg had prepared on the "race question"; by the time they reconvened on 28 June, that document had been pared to fewer than five full pages. The participants were divided about the efficacy of submitting it to anyone in the government but nevertheless asked two of the lawyers to present a presumably final text, which circulated in early August. From the beginning, the discussions and drafts had an almost unworldly quality. Each iteration concentrated on two unrealistic goals: correcting the inflated figures in circulation (some of them spread by the RDI) about the "overrepresentation" of Jews in various walks of German economic life, and persuading the regime to leave the livelihood of each "patriotic non-Aryan" undisturbed for the present in return for a "regrouping" (*Umschichtung*) of the professional distribution of German Jews in the future through greater agricultural and manual training of the next generation. To be sure, the authors challenged the regime by portraying the prevailing concentration of Jews in commerce and the professions as the product of history and culture, not race and conspiracy, and by arguing that attacks on the economic rights of "non-Aryans" were bound to have adverse consequences for "Aryans" as well. But the expressed goal "of bringing the views of the national government to fulfillment," just over time rather than immediately, was obsequious and an extension of the behavior that Müller-Oerlinghausen had condemned so resoundingly in April. Whether the authors ever submitted the final version to Economics Minister Kurt Schmitt is unclear; it had a negligible effect on events in any case.[47]

As these examples show, throughout 1933 German big business followed a strategy of ingratiation—what one scholar has characterized as "Krupp's *Anbiederungskurs*"—that increasingly entailed the sacrifice of Jewish colleagues to achieve the commercial or personal priorities of their non-Jewish peers.[48] Some executives complied with Nazi antisemitism reluctantly, as Carl Bosch did when he transferred two close and valued Jewish aides to posts in the United States and Switzerland.[49] Others acted more opportunistically, choosing to "howl with the wolves." Günther Quandt, for example, became active in driving Jews from professional groups in Berlin and in firing them from his enterprises and those to which he was tied.[50] Most non-Jewish corporate magnates simply abdicated responsibility for their Jewish confreres, arranging quiet exits when possible, and precipitate ones when pressured. Siemens expressed the governing philosophy when he embarrassedly confessed to a departing Jewish employee, "If I pursued opposition for the sake of a few, I would place the existence of the entire firm as risk."[51] By the end of the year, even Paul Reusch, who thought the persecution of the Jews disastrous for Germany's reputation abroad, was resigned to the failure of "influential circles" to bring about a change of policy, despite the appearance of several official decrees that purported to shield Jews in commerce from restrictions on their other activities.[52]

Besides, pressure on Jewish business owners was beginning to create attractive opportunities for other corporations at a time when even non-Jewish executives reluctant to take advantage of would-be sellers could let the prevailing market conditions do that for them. Thus, Degussa paid 9.3 million marks in two stages during 1933–34 for the stock that Alfred Koppel, a Protestant of Jewish heritage, held in the Degea AG (also known as the Auergesellschaft), much of whose business was with the German military. The purchase price came to approximately 133 percent of the stock's face value, yet by virtue of the owner's eagerness to sell at a time when asset values were still depressed, Degussa obtained property that it considered worth some 14 million marks.[53] Although some bankers and corporate executives feared that "aryanization" would have damaging side effects as competent owners gave way to politically connected novices, other executives and firms may have recognized that recovering property values would be offset by mounting pressure to sell in the future, and thus that bargains awaited.[54] In short, Nazi persecution of Jewish executives and Jewish-owned commercial operations not only proved impervious to counterarguments but also presented temptation to the people who tried to make them. The combination eroded resistance.

Into the Third Reich

Various surviving sources suggest that around the turn of 1933–34, the roller coaster ride of party-business relations during 1933 took still another dip. After the tumultuous and anxious initial months, followed by senses of relief and resignation as political pressures grew more manageable and appeasable and the economy appeared to improve, business leaders expressed renewed worries about the durability of those trends. Fritz Roessler gave voice to one sort of concern in December 1933 when he wrote that the government has tackled work creation with wonderful energy and optimism and without consideration of the costs. But is it not ... constructing ... highways and administrative buildings ... that are unproductive for the present and likely to have value only in the remote future and without thinking where the money will come from when the bills are due? Are we not entering a publicly indebted economy of the worst sort? The present forced relief through road and canal construction can be sustained financially for only a few years. Then the hundreds of thousands thus employed will be without jobs once more, probably at a time when business still cannot take them on.[55]

Similarly, in early February, Swiss vice-consul Franz-Rudolf von Weiss told his minister at home that "among influential economic personages ... the stormy tempo of development arouses concern" and then quoted the misgivings of both Peter Klöckner, a steel manufacturer in Duisburg, and Georg Zapf, the head of the supervisory board of Felten and Guilleaume, a major producer of cables and electrical equipment in Cologne. The latter man apparently likened the emergent Nazi economy to "a mockup or a sham [*eine Atrappe*]; the exterior makes an excellent impression, but the interior leaves a lot to be desired."[56] And in April 1934 Reusch referred in a note to a subordinate to "the false boom [*Scheinkonjunktur*] ... that we are presently living through" and expressed doubt that it would last.[57] An equivalent instance of political sobering up is evident in a report sent home by the Danish envoy to Berlin, Herluf Zahle, on 17 January 1934 that included this passage, "In propertied circles, large land owners and big businessmen, the general enthusiasm for National Socialism is beginning to cool off. They believed that they could lead the movement if they joined it, but they did not succeed."[58] An apt illustration of how badly they had failed at taming the party, at least at the rhetorical level, is the remark of Gauleiter Adolf Wagner that the *Frankfurter Zeitung* quoted on 19 January 1934: "In the banks still sit today the same cutthroats as before ... I admit openly that I would rather see a not too limited selection of these gentlemen in Dachau than thousands of lesser people."[59]

During the first half of 1934, a series of new decrees codified the terms of business-state relations in the emerging Third Reich. Employers acquired the upper hand in determining wages, working conditions, and employee representation in the factories, but subject to the approval of thirteen regional trustees of labor, nearly all of whom were longtime, committed National Socialists. Schmitt carried out a reorganization of economic interest groups that dissolved the RSI and shunted Krupp aside in favor of a new leader—or Führer—of the economy, Philipp Kessler of the electrical industry, who was responsible to the economics minister alone.[60] As consolation for these changes, which in Krupp's opinion marked "the transition from a free and private association system to a sort of economic administrative apparatus with a compulsory character," firms' obligatory contributions to the AHS decreased from 0.5 to 0.3 percent of labor costs.[61] By the time the dust settled, Krupp had failed to achieve a single one of the three objectives that Werner Abelshauser believes underlay his *Anbiederungskurs*. He had not maintained a unified business stance on economic policy, he had not prevented the growth of government interventionism in the economy, and he had not managed to moderate Nazi racial policy.[62] Recognizing his failure, he tried to resign from his remaining national position as head of an economic group in the new organizational structure, and though he was rebuffed, he became increasingly inactive.[63] That he recognized his own failure is apparent in his self-pitying comment to a Swiss banker in late 1934, in which he expressed that, as a result of the new decrees, the regime's perceived favoritism toward small business, and the arbitrary actions of party figures, "we [big businessmen] are worse off here than the natives in Timbuctoo."[64]

Just as in mid-1933, when Kurt Schmitt succeeded Hugenberg as economics minister, another figure trusted by big business succeeded the exhausted Schmitt in mid-1934 and reassured the corporate world that its interests were being protected.[65] Hjalmar Schacht would last longer in office by improvising stopgap solutions to Germany's inability to afford the program of armaments and autarky that Hitler pursued, but the ministerial term of the "Old Wizard" ended similarly in late 1937. Like Schmitt, Schacht did his part to turn the nation's economy and its leaders to the purposes of the regime, then tried to make it see the need for a course correction, only to be dismissed for his pains. The Third Reich redoubled its bet on an economic program of militarized Keynesianism and thus fulfilled the prediction that Wagener had made to Krupp in that fateful first week of April 1933: that industry's profits from rearmament and autarky henceforth would more than offset losses in foreign markets.[66]

Cowed by Nazi bullying in 1933–34, constrained by an increasingly tight system of regulations and rationing, and corrupted by the rewards of untrammeled government spending and plunder, German big business became during the ensuing decade, according to one commentator, like "the conductor of a runaway bus who has no control over the actions of the driver but keeps collecting the passengers' fares right up to the final crash."[67] That simile is arresting, but incomplete; the conductor also kept using some of the fares to arm and fuel the bus, thus assuring that the ultimate collision would be all the more explosive.

Peter Hayes is professor of history and Theodore Zev Weiss Holocaust Educational Foundation Professor Emeritus at Northwestern University. In addition to his two studies of corporations in Nazi Germany, *Industry and Ideology: IG Farben in the Nazi Era* (1987) and *From Cooperation to Complicity: Degussa in the Third Reich* (2004), he has also edited two significant anthologies, *The Oxford Handbook of Holocaust Studies*, with John K. Roth (2013) and *How Was It Possible? A Holocaust Reader* (2015). His most recent book is *Why? Explaining the Holocaust*, which appeared with W. W. Norton in 2017. He is currently writing a synthetic work on German big business, the Nazi economy, and the Holocaust with Stephan Lindner.

Notes

1. In this respect, see Peter Langer, *Macht und Verantwortung: Der Ruhrbaron Paul Reusch* (Essen: Klartext, 2012), 545–46; Werner Abelshauser, *Ruhrkohle und Politik: Ernst Brandi 1875–1937* (Essen: Klartext, 2009), 66–71, 77–78; Henry Ashby Turner Jr., *German Big Business and the Rise of Hitler* (New York: Oxford University Press, 1985), 319; and Harold James, *Krupp: A History of the Legendary German Firm* (Princeton, NJ: Princeton University Press, 2012), 187–88.
2. Turner, *Big Business*, 327. See also Langer, *Macht und Verantwortung*, 552; R. J. Overy, *War and Economy in the Third Reich* (Oxford: Oxford University Press, 1994), 124–26; Eckart Conze, "'Titan der modernen Wirtschaft': Otto Wolff (1881–1940)," in *Otto Wolff: Ein Unternehmen zwischen Wirtschaft und Politik*, ed. Peter Danylow and Ulrich S. Soenius (Berlin: Siedler, 2005), 129–32; and Astrid von Pufendorf, *Die Plancks: Eine Familie zwischen Patriotismus und Widerstand* (Berlin: Propyläen, 2006), 379.
3. For further details, see Peter Hayes, *Industry and Ideology: IG Farben in the Nazi Era* (New York: Cambridge University Press, 2001), 83, and Langer, *Macht und Verantwortung*, 549.
4. Heinz Höhne, *"Gebt mir vier Jahre Zeit": Hitler und die Anfänge des Dritten Reiches* (Berlin: Ullstein, 1996), 87–124.
5. Peter Hayes, "Fritz Roessler and Nazism: The Observations of a German Industrialist, 1930–37," *Central European History* 20 (1987): 70.
6. For further details, see Hayes, *Industry and Ideology*, 82–86, and Werner Abelshauser, "Gustav Krupp und die Gleichschaltung des Reichsverbandes der Deutschen Industrie, 1933–1934," *Zeitschrift für Unternehmensgeschichte* 47 (2002): 8–9.
7. Stephan H. Lindner, *Inside IG Farben: Hoechst during the Third Reich* (New York: Cambridge University Press, 2008), 64–65.
8. Joachim Scholtyseck, *Robert Bosch und der liberale Widerstand gegen Hitler 1933–1945* (Munich: Beck, 1999), 137.
9. Gerald D. Feldman, *Allianz and the German Insurance Business, 1933–1945* (New York: Cambridge University Press, 2001), 61–62.

10. Lindner, *Inside IG Farben*, 65.
11. On the decree, see Feldman, *Allianz*, 63.
12. On this putsch and its aftermath, see Abelshauser, *Ruhrkohle und Politik*, 42–45; Abelshauser, "Krupp und die Gleichschaltung," 10–16; Langer, *Macht und Verantwortung*, 568–72; and Turner, *Big Business*, 335–36, as well as Günter Brakelmann, *Zwischen Mitschuld und Widerstand: Fritz Thyssen und der Nationalsozialismus* (Essen: Klartext, 2010), 43–45; and Reinhard Neebe, *Großindustrie, Staat und NSDAP 1930–1933* (Göttingen: Vandenhoeck and Ruprecht, 1981), 181–88.
13. Neebe, *Großindustrie*, 187.
14. Peter Hayes, *From Cooperation to Complicity: Degussa in the Third Reich* (New York: Cambridge University Press, 2004), 27–28, 52.
15. See Hayes, *Industry and Ideology*, 102–3, and the literature cited therein.
16. Langer, *Macht und Verantwortung*, 573–77, 593, 595–618.
17. Scholtyseck, *Bosch*, 126.
18. Ludwig Vaubel, *Glanzstoff, Enka, Aku, Akzo: Unternehmensleitung im nationalen und internationalen Spannungsfeld 1929 bis 1978*, 2 vols. (Haan: Fiebes and Schimpf, 1986), 1:32–33, and 2:3–32.
19. Tina Jacobs, *Rauch und Macht: Das Unternehmen Reemtsma 1920–1961* (Göttingen: Wallstein, 2008), 88–93, 115–22.
20. Scholtyseck, *Aufstieg der Quandts*, 253–61. Threats of legal action remained a potent form of Nazi intimidation of industrialists in subsequent months, as treason charges became the lever that prompted Otto Junkers to sign his company over to the Reich in October 1933 and a prosecution for tax evasion that began in January 1934 was launched against Otto Wolff, who had provided former chancellor Kurt von Schleicher with a home in Berlin after he left office. See Adam Tooze, *The Wages of Destruction* (New York: Penguin, 2006), 126, and Conze, "'Titan der modernen Wirtschaft,'" 132–35.
21. Hayes, *Industry and Ideology*, 94.
22. Lindner, *Inside IG Farben*, 66.
23. Hayes, *Industry and Ideology*, 96.
24. Hayes, *Cooperation to Complicity*, 26.
25. For example, see Rudolf Lenz, *Karstadt: Ein deutscher Warenhauskonzern 1920–1950* (Stuttgart: Deutsche Verlags-Anstalt, 1995), 143, 154–55, 176–83, and Helmut Genschel, *Die Verdrängung der Juden aus der Wirtschaft im Dritten Reich* (Göttingen: Musterschmidt, 1966), 74, as well as the contemporary account in *Jüdische Rundschau* 38, nos. 30/31 (13 April 1933): 149.
26. "Einzelfälle von Maßnahmen gegen jüdische Angestellten," n.d. [May 1933], and "Zu den Akten: Osram," 22 May 1933, Leo Baeck Institute Archive, New York (hereafter cited as LBIA-NY), Hans Schäffer Papers, AR 7177, Box 1A, and Landesarchiv Berlin, ehemaliges Stadtarchiv, Rep. 231: Osram GmbH KG (hereafter cited as LAB-STA), Akten O.424, O.449, O.1059, as well as Wilfried Feldenkirchen, *Siemens, 1918–1945* (Munich: Piper, 1995), 361–62
27. Feldenkirchen, *Siemens*, 557n.162.
28. Lindner, *Inside IG Farben*, 68–70, 155–57.

29. In this respect, see Peter Löhnert and Manfred Gill, "The Relationship of I.G. Farben's Agfa Filmfabrik Wolfen to its Jewish Scientists and to Scientists Married to Jews, 1933–1939," in *The German Chemical Industry in the Twentieth Century*, ed. Jon E. Lesch (Dordrecht: Kluwer Academic, 2000), 130, and Rainer Karlsch, "Fritz Gajewski (1885–1965)—charismatischer Manager in einem multidivisionalen Konzern?," in *Studien zur Geschichte der Filmfabrik Wolfen und der IG Farbenindustrie AG in Mitteldeutschland*, ed. Rainer Karlsch and Helmut Maier (Essen: Klartext, 2014), 100, 107–14.

30. For further details, see Scholtyseck, *Bosch*, 125, and Hayes, *Industry and Ideology*, 92, as well as the entry for 28 June 1933 in the diary of Hans Schäffer, LBIA-NY, A28/7, Box 3, 65–67.

31. Hayes, *Industry and Ideology*, 100.

32. Scholtyseck, *Aufsteig der Quandts*, 255.

33. Langer, *Macht und Verantwortung*, 592–94.

34. Feldman, *Allianz*, 81.

35. See Höhne, *"Gebt mir vier Jahre Zeit,"* 254–55.

36. For further details, see Langer, *Macht und Verantwortung*, 590–92, 650–55, and Hayes, *Industry and Ideology*, 113–20.

37. Martin Münzel, *Die jüdischen Mitglieder der deutschen Wirtschaftselite 1927–1955: Verdrängung, Emigration, Rückkehr* (Paderborn: Schöningh, 2006), 182. For similar results based on a narrower sample of firms, see Martin Fiedler, "Die 'Arisierung' der Wirtschaftselite," in *"Arisierung" im Nationalsozialismus*, ed. Irmtrud Wojak and Peter Hayes (Frankfurt a.M.: Campus, 2000), 69–71.

38. Martin Münzel, "Die Verdrängung jüdischer Vorstands- und Aufsichtsratmitglieder aus Berliner Großunternehmen im NS-Staat," in *"Arisierung" in Berlin*, ed. Christof Biggeleben, Beater Schreiber, and Kilian J. L. Steiner (Berlin: Metropol, 2007), 101.

39. Klaus-Dietmar Henke, ed., *Die Dresdner Bank im Dritten Reich* (Munich: Oldenbourg, 2006), vol. 1: Johannes Bähr et al., *Die Dresdner Bank in der Wirtschaft des Dritten Reiches*, 87, 90–93, and vol. 2: Dieter Ziegler et al., *Die Dresdner Bank und die deutschen Juden*, 13, 24, 48, 113.

40. For further details, see Thomas Weihe, "Die Verdrängung jüdischer Mitarbeiter und der Wettbewerb um Kunden im Nationalsozialismus," in *Die Commerzbank und die Juden 1933–1945*, ed. Ludolf Herbst and Thomas Weihe (Munich: Beck, 2004), 46–50; Christopher Kopper, *Bankiers unterm Hakenkreuz* (Munich: Carl Hanser, 2005), 50–51; Christopher Kopper, *Zwischen Marktwirtschaft und Dirigismus: Bankenpolitik im "Dritten Reich" 1933–1939* (Bonn: Bouvier, 1995), 135–36, 221, 223; and Turner, *Big Business*, 241–43, 303.

41. Peter Hayes, "The Deutsche Bank and the Holocaust," in *Lessons and Legacies III: Memory, Memorialization, and Denial*, ed. Peter Hayes (Evanston, IL: Northwestern University Press, 1999), 75–77. See also Harold James, "Die Deutsche Bank und die Diktatur 1933–1945," in Lothar Gall et al., *Die Deutsche Bank 1870–1995* (Munich: Beck, 1995), 336–39; and Kopper, *Zwischen Marktwirtschaft und Dirigismus*, 132–35.

42. For further details, see Hayes, "Deutsche Bank and the Holocaust," 78–79, and Pohl, *Holzmann*, 201, 208, 212.

43. For an argument that this weakness was more decisive to political outcomes in Germany in 1932–33 than the breadth of antisemitism, see Peter Hayes, *Why? Explaining the Holocaust* (New York: W. W. Norton, 2017), 65–66, 91–92.

44. In this respect, see Hayes, *Cooperation to Complicity*, 25–26, and Feldman, *Allianz*, 57–58.

45. Circular letter from Siemens, 8 April 1933, Siemens-Archiv, Munich (hereafter cited as SAA Munich), 4/Lf 676, 3, 6–7.

46. Ibid., 3.

47. The documentation on this is extensive. For example, see Max Warburg to Carl Bosch, 18 May 1933, and the first draft by Warburg, 19 June 1933, in the BASF Unternehmensarchiv, Ludwigshafen, W1, and Krupp to Siemens, 6 August 1933, with the third draft attached, SAA Munich, 4/Lf 676, as well as Schäffer to Melchior, 20 August 1933, LBIA-NY, AR 7177, Hans Schäffer Papers, Box IA, and entries for 12, 17, and 23 May 1933, and 28 June 1933, in Schäffer's diary, LBIA-NY, A28/7, Box 3, 42–49, 65–67. Avraham Barkai, "Max Warburg im Jahre 1933: Mißglückter Versuch zur Milderung der Judenverfolgung," in *Juden in Deutschland: Emanzipation, Integration, Verfolgung und Vernichtung*, ed. Peter Freimark, Alice Jankowski, and Ina S. Lorenz (Hamburg: Christians, 1991), 390–405, provides a broadly accurate account of this episode but is unreliable on details because he could not consult Schäffer's diary. The best recent examination is Abelshauser, "Krupp und die Gleichschaltung," 16–19. I have come to understand the context of this initiative differently and thus to assess it more harshly than I did in Peter Hayes, "State Policy and Corporate Involvement in the Holocaust," in *The Holocaust and History: The Known, the Unknown, the Disputed, and the Reexamined*, ed. Michael Berenbaum and Abraham J. Peck (Bloomington: Indiana University Press, 1998), 199.

48. Langer, *Macht und Verantwortung*, 584.

49. Hayes, *Industry and Ideology*, 93.

50. Scholtyseck, *Aufstieg der Quandts*, 314–15.

51. Feldenkirchen, *Siemens 1918–1945*, 557n.162.

52. Langer, *Macht und Verantwortung*, 632. See also Karl A. Schleunes, *The Twisted Road to Auschwitz* (Urbana: University of Illinois Press, 1970), 114.

53. Hayes, *Cooperation to Complicity*, 79–83.

54. For an expression of such fears regarding "aryanization," see Harold James, *The Deutsche Bank and the Nazi Economic War against the Jews* (New York: Cambridge University Press, 2001), 50. Similarly, Albert Fischer has shown that such measures as Hjalmar Schacht undertook to slow the pace of "aryanization" stemmed solely from pragmatic concerns; see Albert Fischer, *Hjalmar Schacht und Deutschlands "Judenfrage"* (Cologne: Böhlau, 1995).

55. Hayes, *Cooperation to Complicity*, 25.

56. Gedrückte Stimmung in Köln, dispatch from Franz-Rudolf von Weiss, Swiss vice consul, to Paul Diniert, 3 February 1934, in *Fremde Blicke auf das "Dritte Reich": Berichte ausländischer Diplomaten über Herrschaft und Gesellschaft in Deutschland 1933–1945*, ed. Frank Bajohr and Christoph Strupp (Göttingen: Wallstein, 2011), 399.

57. Langer, *Macht und Verantwortung*, 633.
58. Dispatch from Herluf Zahle, Danish envoy in Berlin, 17 January 1934, in *Fremde Blicke*, ed. Bajohr and Strupp, 396.
59. Muenzel, *jüdischen Mitglieder*, 142.
60. Hayes, *Industry and Ideology*, 120–21; Höhne, *"Gebt mir,"* 175–78
61. See Abelshauser, "Krupp und die Gleichschaltung," 23, and Hayes, *Industry and Ideology*, 121.
62. Abelshauser, "Krupp und die Gleichschaltung," 3.
63. Ibid., 24.
64. Overy, *War and Economy*, 134.
65. On Schmitt's mounting frustration and physical collapse, see Feldman, *Allianz*, 100–102.
66. For the prediction, see Brakelmann, *Zwischen Mitschuld und Widerstand*, 44. On the self-destructive evolution of Nazi economic policy, see Peter Hayes, "The Economy," in *The Oxford Illustrated History of the Third Reich*, ed. Robert Gellately (New York: Oxford University Press, 2018), 189–212, and Tooze's magisterial *Wages of Destruction*.
67. Richard Grunberger, *The 12-Year Reich: A Social History of Nazi Germany 1933–1945* (New York: Holt, Rinehart and Winston, 1971), 184.

Bibliography

Abelshauser, Werner. "Gustav Krupp und die Gleichschaltung des Reichsverbandes der Deutschen Industrie, 1933–1934." *Zeitschrift für Unternehmensgeschichte* 47 (2002): 3–26.

———. *Ruhrkohle und Politik: Ernst Brandi 1875–1937*. Essen: Klartext, 2009.

Bajohr, Frank, and Christoph Strupp, eds. *Fremde Blicke auf das "Dritte Reich": Berichte ausländischer Diplomaten über Herrschaft und Gesellschaft in Deutschland 1933–1945*. Göttingen: Wallstein, 2011.

Barkai, Avraham. "Max Warburg im Jahre 1933: Mißglückter Versuch zur Milderung der Judenverfolgung." In *Juden in Deutschland: Emanzipation, Integration, Verfolgung und Vernichtung*, edited by Peter Freimark, Alice Jankowski, and Ina S. Lorenz, 390–405. Hamburg: Christians, 1991.

Brakelmann, Günter. *Zwischen Mitschuld und Widerstand: Fritz Thyssen und der Nationalsozialismus*. Essen: Klartext, 2010.

Conze, Eckart. "'Titan der modernen Wirtschaft': Otto Wolff (1881–1940)." In Peter Danylow and Ulrich S. Soenius, *Otto Wolff: Ein Unternehmen zwischen Wirtschaft und Politik*, 99–151. Berlin: Siedler, 2005.

Feldenkirchen, Wilfried. *Siemens 1918–1945*. Munich: Piper, 1995.

Feldman, Gerald D. *Allianz and the German Insurance Business, 1933–1945*. New York: Cambridge University Press, 2001.

Fiedler, Martin. "Die 'Arisierung' der Wirtschaftselite." In *"Arisierung" im Nationalsozialismus*, edited by Irmtrud Wojak and Peter Hayes, 59–83. Frankfurt a.M.: Campus, 2000.

Fischer, Albert. *Hjalmar Schacht und Deutschlands "Judenfrage."* Cologne: Böhlau, 1995.

Genschel, Helmut. *Die Verdrängung der Juden aus der Wirtschaft im Dritten Reich.* Göttingen: Musterschmidt, 1966.

Hayes, Peter. "Fritz Roessler and Nazism: The Observations of a German Industrialist, 1930–37." *Central European History* 20 (1987): 58–79.

——. "State Policy and Corporate Involvement in the Holocaust." In *The Holocaust and History: The Known, the Unknown, the Disputed, and the Reexamined,* edited by Michael Berenbaum and Abraham J. Peck, 197–212. Bloomington: Indiana University Press, 1998.

——. "The Deutsche Bank and the Holocaust." In *Lessons and Legacies III: Memory, Memorialization, and Denial,* edited by Peter Hayes, 71–89. Evanston, IL: Northwestern University Press, 1999.

——. *Industry and Ideology: IG Farben in the Nazi Era.* New York: Cambridge University Press, 2001.

——. *From Cooperation to Complicity: Degussa in the Third Reich.* New York: Cambridge University Press, 2004.

——. *Why? Explaining the Holocaust.* New York: W. W. Norton, 2017.

Henke, Klaus-Dietmar, ed. *Die Dresdner Bank im Dritten Reich,* 4 vols. Munich: Oldenbourg, 2006.

Höhne, Heinz. *"Gebt mir vier Jahre Zeit": Hitler und die Anfänge des Dritten Reiches.* Berlin: Ullstein, 1996.

Jacobs, Tina. *Rauch und Macht: Das Unternehmen Reemtsma 1920–1961.* Göttingen: Wallstein, 2008.

James, Harold. "Die Deutsche Bank und die Diktatur 1933–1945." In Lothar Gall et al., *Die Deutsche Bank 1870–1995,* 315–408. Munich: Beck, 1995.

——. *The Deutsche Bank and the Nazi Economic War against the Jews.* New York: Cambridge University Press, 2001.

——. *Krupp: A History of the Legendary German Firm.* Princeton, NJ: Princeton University Press, 2012.

Karlsch, Rainer. "Fritz Gajewski (1885–1965)—charismatischer Manager in einem multidivisionalen Konzern?" In *Studien zur Geschichte der Filmfabrik Wolfen und der IG Farbenindustrie AG in Mitteldeutschland,* edited by Rainer Karlsch and Helmut Maier, 91–130. Essen: Klartext, 2014.

Kopper, Christopher. *Zwischen Marktwirtschaft und Dirigismus: Bankenpolitik im "Dritten Reich" 1933–1939.* Bonn: Bouvier, 1995.

——. *Bankiers unterm Hakenkreuz.* Munich: Carl Hanser, 2005.

Langer, Peter. *Macht und Verantwortung: Der Ruhrbaron Paul Reusch.* Essen: Klartext, 2012.

Lenz, Rudolf. *Karstadt: Ein deutscher Warenhauskonzern 1920–1950.* Stuttgart: Deutsche Verlags-Anstalt, 1995.

Lindner, Stephan H. *Inside IG Farben: Hoechst during the Third Reich.* New York: Cambridge University Press, 2008.

Löhnert. Peter, and Manfred Gill. "The Relationship of I.G. Farben's Agfa Filmfabrik Wolfen to Its Jewish Scientists and to Scientists Married to Jews, 1933–1939." In *The German Chemical Industry in the Twentieth Century,* edited by Jon E. Lesch, 123–45. Dordrecht: Kluwer Academic, 2000.

Münzel, Martin. *Die jüdischen Mitglieder der deutschen Wirtschaftselite 1927–1955: Verdrängung, Emigration, Rückkehr.* Paderborn: Schöningh, 2006.

——. "Die Verdrängung jüdischer Vorstands- und Aufsichtsratmitglieder aus Berliner Großunternehmen im NS-Staat." In *"Arisierung" in Berlin*, edited by Christof Biggeleben, Beater Schreiber, and Kilian J. L. Steiner, 95–120. Berlin: Metropol, 2007.

Neebe, Reinhard. *Großindustrie, Staat und NSDAP 1930–1933: Paul Silverberg und der Reichsverband der Deutschen Industrie in der Krise der Weimarer Republik.* Göttingen: Vandenhoeck and Ruprecht, 1981.

Overy, R. J. *War and Economy in the Third Reich.* Oxford: Oxford University Press, 1994.

Pufendorf, Astrid von. *Die Plancks: Eine Familie zwischen Patriotismus und Widerstand.* Berlin: Propyläen, 2006.

Schleunes, Karl A. *The Twisted Road to Auschwitz.* Urbana: University of Illinois Press, 1970.

Scholtyseck, Joachim. *Robert Bosch und der liberale Widerstand gegen Hitler 1933–1945.* Munich: Beck, 1999.

Tooze, Adam. *The Wages of Destruction: The Making and Breaking of the Nazi Economy.* New York: Penguin, 2006.

Turner, Henry Ashby, Jr. *German Big Business and the Rise of Hitler.* New York: Oxford University Press, 1985.

Vaubel, Ludwig. *Glanzstoff, Enka, Aku, Akzo: Unternehmensleitung im nationalen und internationalen Spannungsfeld 1929 bis 1978.* 2 vols. Haan: Fiebes and Schimpf, 1986.

Weihe, Thomas. "Die Verdrängung jüdischer Mitarbeiter und der Wettbewerb um Kunden im Nationalsozialismus." In *Die Commerzbank und die Juden 1933–1945*, edited by Ludolf Herbst and Thomas Weihe, 43–73. Munich: Beck, 2004.

 6

Violence against *"Ostjuden"* in the Spring of 1933 and the Reaction of German Authorities

Hermann Beck

Already months after Hitler had become chancellor, the spiritual leader of German Jews, Leo Baeck, was forced to recognize that "the thousand-year-old history of German Jewry has come to an end."[1] His statement was prompted in part by the nationwide boycott of shops and lawyers' and doctors' offices, as well as the April 1933 antisemitic laws that excluded German Jews from the civil service, banned judges, attorneys, and public prosecutors from practicing law, and excluded doctors from the national health insurance organization. Accompanying these well-known antisemitic measures, however, were even more pernicious actions, not well documented in historical records, that underscore the truth of Baeck's assertion. Countless violent attacks, armed robbery, assaults by gangs of SA men that wounded and incapacitated victims, as well as blackmail, extortion, abduction into SA torture cellars and "wild" concentration camps, and outright murder meant that German and foreign Jews were threatened by torture and economic or physical annihilation already at the beginning of Hitler's reign.[2] Contemporaries were painfully aware of the attacks. In February 1946, for example, prompted by the soul-searching of the still raw wounds of the catastrophic events that accompanied total defeat, Konrad Adenauer wrote to a Catholic clergyman, "The Jewish pogroms of 1933 and 1938 occurred in full public view."[3] As Adenauer wrote, many acts of violence against foreign Jews did indeed take place in the plain light of day, as did the countless "pillory marches," during which victims were led by foot or on an oxcart through town, a humiliating experience that left those who suffered through it demoralized and broken. These attacks set in immediately after the March 1933 Reichstag elections and only gradually abated during the summer.

The enormous wave of violence first engulfed those Jews who lived in Germany without German citizenship. These were the most vulnerable and thus became the initial targets of personal acts of revenge carried out by members of the SA and SS. Among them, the so-called "*Ostjuden*" were especially affected—those Jews who had fled to Germany since the early 1880s from eastern Europe, mostly from tsarist Russia but also in part from Austrian Galicia, to escape persecution.[4] German Jews and Christians referred to these eastern European Jews who had immigrated to Germany (or got stuck there on their way to the United States) as "*Ostjuden*," a term that was always tinged with "something of the scornful German attitude toward eastern Europe."[5]

According to the June 1933 census, 98,747 foreign Jews lived in the German Reich, accounting for 19.8 percent of the Jewish population. Approximately 56,000 of them (57.2 percent) were Polish citizens and about 20 percent were stateless, mostly from Russia. In order of decreasing numbers, Austrians, Czechs, Hungarians, and Romanians followed.[6] More than 80 percent of foreign Jews in Germany would thus have been regarded as "*Ostjuden*," of which about 40,000 (38,919) had been born in Germany and a further 2,400 in the territories Germany lost after the First World War. In states that adhered to the *jus soli*—the "territorial" principle of citizenship (as opposed to Germany's *jus sanguinis* "blood" principle)—this group would have possessed German citizenship; in the German Reich many of them remained foreign nationals. Of foreign Jews in Germany, 74 percent (73,025) lived in Prussia (41,122 in Berlin and about 12,000–15,000 in the Ruhr area), a further 12,804 in Saxony, 4,640 in Bavaria, and 2,000 in Baden.[7] As a result of the immigration by "*Ostjuden*," the percentage of foreigners in the Jewish population in Germany rose from 7 percent (in 1900) to 19.1 percent (1925) and finally to 19.8 percent (1933). Apart from Berlin, the number of foreign Jews was high in Munich, Leipzig, and Dresden: in 1933 they constituted about 30 percent of the Jewish population in Berlin, 26.7 percent in Munich, 60.7 percent in Dresden, and a full 73.9 percent in Leipzig.[8] The fate of these "*Ostjuden*" has attracted some scholarly attention, notably with regard to the German Empire and the Weimar Republic; less, however, is known about the violence directed against this group in 1933.[9] This chapter is designed to help close the gap in the scholarly literature by analyzing the wide-ranging and diverse spectrum of violence against "*Ostjuden*," as well as the reaction of the German bureaucracy to the brutal attacks on foreign Jews, their families, and their businesses.

The majority of attacks on the "*Ostjuden*" are not registered in police files, since the police almost always refused to record violent attacks against non-German Jews and because victims feared reporting attacks. Reasons for refusing or failing to report offenses varied: either victims of attacks feared retribution from SA members working as so-called

Hilfspolizisten (auxiliary police) for the police force,[10] police squads contacted by telephone failed to appear to help the victims,[11] or the police simply refused to officially record statements from anyone with foreign citizenship.[12] In Wanne-Eickel in the Ruhr area, for example, the police went so far as to say to a Polish Jew that "foreigners [had] no right to police protection."[13] In 1933 police reactions were still not uniform and varied considerably by region. In Duisburg, for example, police even went so far as to prevent a degrading pillory march, many of which had occurred in other areas. Regardless of the reaction of local police, foreign Jews had the possibility of complaining to their embassies and consulates on German territory. Ironically, given their disadvantaged status as non-citizens, this means that occasionally attacks on non-German Jews are better documented than attacks on German Jews.

The following account deals mainly (but not exclusively) with Polish Jews, since violence against them is the most well documented. The attacks are divided into five categories: (1) physical violence and aggravated robbery; (2) economic/financial damages such as boycotts and the forced cancellation of debts, vandalism of property, and destruction of goods; (3) rituals of humiliation such as pillory marches and the setting of victims against each other; (4) violent kidnapping, mostly in connection with pressure on victims to give up their businesses and emigrate; and finally (5) aggravated bodily assault and murder. After cataloging the attacks, the chapter turns to an analysis of how officials dealt with them. Here the analysis clearly reveals antisemitic prejudices in action.

A Litany of Violent Attacks Already in Early 1933

More than two-thirds of violent attacks against non-German Jews were carried out against Polish nationals. On 5 April 1933, the Polish Embassy sent its fifth formal letter of complaint to the foreign ministry in Berlin, in which numerous violent attacks against Polish Jews who lived in the German Reich were recorded.[14] Since this chapter documents events that have largely remained unknown in the literature, the following recounts numerous examples of violence against Polish Jews to give an impression of how widespread antisemitic attacks were in the spring of 1933. A large number of them took place in Berlin's so-called *Scheunenviertel*, the area around the Dragonerstrasse, Schönhäuser Tor, Landsbergerstrasse, Alte Schönhauserstrasse, and Grenadierstrasse, where many Polish and other east European Jews lived. On 6 March, two uniformed men forced their way into Wolf Leibowitz's shop in Gellnowstraße 15, beat him up, and stole twelve suits and a coat. On 24

March, Israel Gernstein was attacked by two men in front of the synagogue at Grenadierstraße 37 and beaten up; Isaak Moses Kalb suffered
the same fate on the same date and in the same street—five people
assaulted him and forcibly cut off his beard. Gustav Ganz, Metzerstraße
14, was attacked and beaten up by two uniformed men on Linienstraße
8 and suffered a concussion as a result.[15] In Chemnitz on 25 March,
six Polish Jews were forced to wash communist slogans off the sides
of buildings and were beaten up as they did so. In Gelsenkirchen, five
men pushed their way into the apartment of Hersz Weissmann on 27
March and demanded that he "pay back" six hundred marks that one
of the five had paid him for furniture. On the following night, three
men again forced their way into Weissmann's apartment and again
demanded money. Since none was at hand, the men hit Weissmann's
fifteen-year-old son and stole two gold watches.[16] Also in Gelsenkirchen
on 28 March around 4:30 p.m., two uniformed men forced their way
into Josef Issler's shop, Hochstrasse 73, and demanded that he immediately close it down. Half an hour later, fifteen men raided Issler's private abode and beat both him and his son until they were unconscious.
Neighbors took them to a hospital. A similar fate befell Abraham Tanne
and Jakob Neimann, as well as Mojzes Erlich and his sister Cyla Erlich,
who were beaten up and had their valuables stolen.[17] In Leipzig, several
men in uniform grabbed Uszer Haim Schenker, Blücherstraße 33, on 26
March and beat him until he was bleeding heavily; Moszek Aron Syne
was called into a pub frequented by National Socialists on 22 March,
searched, and beaten up. Chaim Baruch Durst suffered the same fate:
on 12 March he was attacked by three men in his Munich apartment,
Agnesstraße 46, and beaten with rubber truncheons, after which his
attackers stole two hundred marks in cash, four prayer books, and
several official identification documents from him.[18] In Wiesbaden, I.
Schleider was attacked in his shop, Nerostasse 3, by half a dozen men
in uniform on 23 March and so brutally beaten up that he suffered a
double fractured skull and had to be brought to the hospital.[19]

This inventory of violent acts can be extended based on the reports
of the Polish Embassy. Already on 11 March 1933 the Polish Embassy
recorded about twenty violent attacks on Polish Jews in Berlin alone,
including raids on several Jewish-owned restaurants that served a predominantly Jewish clientele. During attacks on Jewish restaurants on
5 and 9 March in the Alte Schönhauserstraße that were carried out by
groups of SA men, guests were wounded with rubber truncheons, all
the furnishings destroyed, the food thrown on the floor, and a "fee"
imposed upon the owner for the subsequent search of the premises.[20]
On 8 March a Jewish-owned hotel was attacked by uniformed men,

the guests beaten and wounded with knives, the windows smashed, and the furniture demolished.[21] During attacks by bands of SA men on the Café Engländer in the Schönhäuser Allee on 9 March, guests were beaten so badly that they had to be taken to the hospital. When the SA descended upon the café again on 15 March, guests were forced to accompany the attackers to an SA meeting point, where they were searched, robbed, and "beaten unconscious with rubber truncheons."[22] One of the victims was taken to a nearby hospital. The Café New York in the Schönhauserstraße 59 was likewise raided several times. On 2 March 1933, a group of uniformed men went into the restaurant and took food from the buffet without paying; on 5 March, a different group of SA men threatened to throw a bomb into the café if it was not shut down, and during another attack on 15 March, guests were yet again beaten until they fell unconscious.[23] The Polish Embassy informed the official in charge of such matters in the German foreign ministry, Legationsrat Alexander von Bülow-Schwante,[24] that the perpetrators of the attacks were "exclusively SA and SS men in Hilfspolizei uniforms."[25]

Most of the attacks took place in Berlin, in 1933 the fourth largest city in the world after London, New York, and Tokyo, with more than 4.2 million inhabitants. As memoranda from the Polish Embassy to the German foreign ministry on 11, 18, and 27 March clearly indicate, however, violent attacks were intensifying in other German cities as well. Regional focal points of attacks on Polish Jews included Düsseldorf and Duisburg-Hamborn, each with a dozen reported attacks, as well as Essen, Köln, Gelsenkirchen, and Wanne-Eickel in the Prussian Rhine province. A multitude of further attacks took place in Saxony's large cities—Leipzig, Dresden, Chemnitz, and Plauen, as well as in Worms in Rhine-Hessen; in Wiesbaden, the capital of the Prussian province of Hessen-Nassau; in the Upper Silesian cities of Beuthen, Gleiwitz, and Hindenburg; as well as in the Silesian provincial capital Breslau. The upper Silesian industrial center, to which Beuthen, Gleiwitz, and Hindenburg belonged, was part of the so-called *Optionsgebiet*, in which a referendum was held in 1922 to decide whether the territory would be incorporated into Poland or remain part of the German Reich. Nazi attacks on Polish Jews in Upper Silesia undermined the 1922 convention on the protection of minorities.[26]

Economic Damages and Ruin

The direct physical attack was the most frequent but certainly not the only form of assault on "*Ostjuden*." Another type of aggression was aimed at inflicting economic damage or causing ruin, often initiated by envious competitors. In addition, victims were often prevented from offering their merchandise at markets, such as at a commercial fair in Deggendorf in Bavaria, where Polish Jews had rented stalls in full compliance with official regulations but were then informed by the local town council that they ought not to participate in the fair, since their personal security could not be guaranteed.[27] Rejections of applications to sell goods at markets and removal of market stalls were also issued at the behest of competing non-Jewish traders. In a letter to the Breslau police president of 17 June 1933, for example, the street trader Luise Rupprecht requested that her Jewish competitors be expelled from their places in the Breslau market. Adroitly using the jargon of the day, Rupprecht complained that "of all people, a Jewish trader of foreign race and doubtlessly also a communist has limited the few remaining opportunities we Germans have to earn money in this part of town."[28] Breslau's police president in March 1933 was the infamous Silesian SA leader and convicted murderer Edmund Heines, who had made Breslau famous nationwide for its anti-Jewish orientation. He was a man with an open ear for such requests. The petition was successful.

The removal from market stalls also became a formidable method of discrimination in Saxony. When the Austrian consulate general in Dresden complained to Saxon authorities that the Jewish Austrian citizen Berta Rosenbaum had been denied access to markets in the Saxon cities of Bautzen, Pirna, and Reichenbach even though she had the required permissions, the Saxon economics ministry responded that there existed no police regulations concerning the removal of Jewish traders; the order denying access was a "spontaneous" measure concerning public order and security.[29] The Austrian Consulate thereupon asserted that Frau Rosenbaum's rejection was solely based on the fact that she was Jewish and that it should be taken into consideration that she had lived in Saxony for over thirty years and now her entire livelihood was at stake.[30] A Polish complaint from early May 1933 makes it clear that Rosenbaum's case was no isolated incident but that hundreds were affected by similar actions. In more than twelve cities, "Polish merchants of the Mosaic religion" had been removed from city markets—forty in Halle, thirty in Dessau, and fifty-five in Erfurt.[31] Elsewhere, Christian merchants demanded in the presence of city officials that their Jewish counterparts be removed; in some cases the local police had prevented their participation in the markets.[32] Others received letters from state authorities, according to which "their presence in markets was denied because of their heritage" or they were "assigned to special, so-called Jewish rows" in the market-place.[33] Comparable actions occurred not only in Saxon cities such as Leipzig, Apolda, and Bautzen but also in southern German cities such as Landshut, Nürnberg, Karlsruhe, Freiburg, and Konstanz.[34] To justify the rejection of both foreign and German Jews from markets in Saxony, the Saxon interior ministry claimed that in some places "disturbances to public peace and order had already occurred" and that the "national population" was negatively predisposed toward "Jewish market traders, whether of German or foreign citizenship."[35] For this reason, the interior ministry asserted, it was unable to counteract police regulations against the Jewish traders, even if the papers of the persons concerned were in order.[36] It was emphasized that there were no special regulations for foreign Jews but that the measures pertained to all Jewish traders.[37]

Thus, already in the spring of 1933, "spontaneous" local ordinances and decrees annulled existing rights and legislation, even if these had been in place for decades. These "spontaneous" ordinances and decrees that were initiated on the spur of the moment replaced existing laws and affected Jewish daily life in Germany already months after 30 January 1933. In Ernst Fraenkel's terminology, the "Maßnahmenstaat" based on ad hoc local ordinances and decrees had partly superseded the statutes and legislation of the "Normenstaat" insofar as it applied to Jewish daily life as early as the spring of 1933.[38] To preserve the veneer of legality, Saxony's interior ministry emphasized repeatedly in orders to subordinate authorities to make it clear in their directives that Jewish traders were not to be excluded from markets "merely because they were Jews."[39] At the end of May 1933 the foreign office in Berlin entered the fray and, for reasons of expediency, insisted on a more legalistic position: all previous measures, such as the boycott of 1 April, had been directed solely against German Jews and excluded foreign business owners. It would be advisable to refrain from introducing measures against foreign Jews in future, since these "could give the Polish government cause for reprisals against German citizens or administrative harassment of the German minority in Poland."[40]

Here foreign Jews were clearly in a more advantageous position, since *raison d'état* forced German authorities to be more lenient in their case. How things actually looked at the local level, where the SA ruled and made decisions, was another question altogether. In July 1933, the Saxon interior ministry's directive regarding the "admittance of Jewish traders to public markets" was also modified to read, "[The] admission of foreign Jewish traders may be denied only in those cases in which business practices or the character of the claimant justify rejection."[41] Even though these new directives leave room for interpretation, foreign Jews still enjoyed certain advantages for fear of "countermeasures on the part of foreign governments against German citizens or members of German minorities."[42] Or, as the county office in Zwickau wrote to the interior ministry in Dresden, rejection of foreign traders "provides [added] unwelcome material to the charge of *Greuelpropaganda* [atrocity propaganda] abroad regarding agitation of Jews in the German Reich."[43] This theme of "atrocity propaganda" played an important role in the political discourse in the spring of 1933. Beginning in mid-March, soon after the onset of violent antisemitic attacks throughout Germany, the Western press, especially in England and the United States, reported in detail about events in Germany.[44] Under government auspices but with the willing cooperation of large parts of German society, a domestic front against foreign reports formed in Germany. The German press initiated a counter campaign, arguing that foreign press reports were either fabrications or else vastly exaggerated, and comparing them to the Allied "atrocity propaganda" during World War I, that is, to French and British propaganda in 1914/15 regarding German atrocities in Belgium and northern France.[45] Not only the (already fully censored) German press but also the churches, notably the Protestant Church, were in complete agreement that these "vastly exaggerated" reports about antisemitic attacks constituted just another anti-German plot. Who, some asked, had cared about the manifold injustices committed against the German minorities in Poland and Czechoslovakia?

Another type of violent transgression mentioned in Polish diplomatic reports involved extensive material damages: destruction of goods and merchandise and the annihilation of property. In March and April 1933, countless Jewish shop windows were smashed throughout the Reich.[46] Jahnka Rand's window, for example, in the Alleestraße 126 in Duisburg-Hamborn, worth seven hundred marks, was smashed on 27 March; on 22 March in Groß-Strelitz, fruit and vegetable stands had been thrown over by uniformed men, while other Jewish traders were forbidden to sell their merchandise.[47] In Hindenburg in Upper Silesia, a group of fifty uniformed men forced a heavy goods truck of the Jewish firm Ginsberg & Rosenberg off the street and turned it over, wrecking the truck and damaging the goods inside.[48] Another terse report of an incident, typical for this time, fails to adequately convey the potential tragedy behind it: in Hamborn, "in the marketplace an unknown person attacked Simon Leib Herszberg, Hagedornstraße 25, and turned over his basket with 500 eggs, while spewing out abuse."[49]

Rituals of Humiliation

The wanton and pointless destruction of property or carefully stacked-up goods in market stalls already contained elements of humiliation: perpetrators wanted to show the hated and reviled *"Ostjuden"* that they were now completely at the mercy of the arbitrary violence of attackers and that they should leave Germany and leave it fast. Over and above this, another category of anti-Jewish crime involved forms of personal degradation and served exclusively the attackers' goal of twisted amusement and visceral satisfaction. Even though official Polish reports only curtly summarized the nature of the attacks and refrained from detailed descriptions, several assaults can be classified in this category. The demolition of religious instruments and the shearing of beards are included in this category as specific ways of demoralizing and humiliating victims.

Toward this end Isaak Moses Kalb was assaulted by five people, two of them in uniform, on 24 March around 7:00 p.m. in the Grenadierstraße in Berlin. He was not only "badly beaten up" but also had to undergo the indignity of having his "beard cut off."[50] Similar incidents took place throughout March and April. On 9 March around 5:00 p.m. in the Dragonerstraße in Berlin, four uniformed men not only cut off the beard of the victim, Aron Schegel, and ripped his wallet from his hands, but they also beat him badly[51]; the following day in Düsseldorf, Salomon Laas had parts of his beard singed off.[52] A synagogue in the Blankenfelderstraße in Berlin was stormed on 1 April by uniformed men who wore armbands of the auxiliary police. The attackers sheared off the beard of one victim, searched everyone present in the synagogue, beat them with rubber truncheons, threatened them with revolvers, and then smashed the synagogue's entire inventory, including sacred religious instruments. At the end of all the tumult, the victims were forced to sing "nationalist" songs — "those who refused to do so were beaten up." It was practically de rigueur in this and similar attacks that the perpetrators went one step further and demanded a declaration from the victims that all present had been treated well.[53]

An even more infamous means of public humiliation, which recalled the "pillories" of the Middle Ages, was the so-called "pillory march" (*Prangermarsch*), whereby chosen victims were led through the streets of their hometowns either on foot or in a cart. Victims of pillory marches were mostly well-established Jewish Germans who owned businesses and were well-known in the community; they thus must have felt the public humiliation especially deeply. In the Germany of the 1930s, geographical mobility was limited due to the absence of economic opportunities and other factors, so that most inhabitants of German cities and towns rarely ventured beyond the confines of their home-towns or province. For this reason people knew each other all the better inside their respective familiar surroundings. The public running of the gauntlet of a "pillory march" therefore caused victims lasting personal and economic damage. In the case of foreign Jews, most of whom were not well-known in their places of residence, pillory marches were a less frequent, but not unknown, type of assault.

A report of the Polish Mission of 5 April 1933 recounts how Fischel Häusler was prepared for such a *Prangermarsch* on 25 March in Duisburg. At a Nazi Party meeting place, red paper flowers were stuck on his suit and a communist and black-red-gold flag pressed into his hands, upon which he was prepared to be forcibly marched through the streets of the city. The police were able to prevent this act at the last moment. David Schimmel and David Miller, however, could not be spared this humiliation: both were forced "to carry a black-red-gold flag that had been tied around their necks through the streets of Duisburg."[54] A still worse fate befell the Duisburg rabbi Jakob Bereisch, who was attacked by five uniformed men on 18 March in his apartment and beaten with rubber truncheons. The riot squad that had been called in declared that "it is not part of police duties to protect Jews."[55] Five days later, uni-formed men forced their way into his synagogue, wrapped Bereisch up in the republican black-red-gold flag, and chased him through several well-populated streets in Duisburg, all the way to the city theater.[56]

Another form of humiliation was devised by the SA in Worms, where on 9 March, Chaim and Milan Ormianer, as well as Hermann Grünebaum, were dragged to an SA meeting place and forced to "punch each other," as it was described in the report of the Polish Diplomatic Mission of 11 March.[57] Documents from another archival collection that deals with political disturbances during the seizure of power in general make it clear that this form of humiliation enjoyed special popularity with the SA in Worms: "In Worms SA men brought the Jewish leather merchants G. (father and son) and the Jewish gentlemen R. and Gl. to the 'Brown House' [where they] were forced to beat each other up under threat of being shot dead. Then they all had to sign a declara-tion in which they promised to keep quiet about the events that had occurred. Otherwise, they would be shot. The mistreated victims now lie in the Jewish hospital in Frankfurt am Main."[58] The same dossier records another, similar incident: "In Worms the Jewish merchants, the brothers K. were forced to punch each other under threat of being shot [if they refused]. They are [now] hospitalized in Mannheim suffering from serious injuries."[59] That these attacks are not recorded in the records of the Polish Diplomatic Mission is not significant, for not all assaults were officially reported, because victims correctly feared that an official complaint might result in making them the renewed targets of attacks.

Abductions and Forced Deportation

A further type of crime was the forced closing of shops and businesses in conjunction with the abduction and maltreatment of shop owners. In the March *aide-mémoires* of the Polish Diplomatic Mission there were dozens of such cases. A typical example of this type of attack reads as follows: "On the 13th of the month six uniformed men [in Hindenburg/ Upper Silesia] forced their way into the shop of Herszlik Saper and threatened him with the destruction of all his wares if he did not close his shop. Upon their departure one of them ripped out the telephone line."[60] Demands to close shops were frequently connected with the threat to destroy goods and merchandise and demolish the whole inventory of the shop if the victims refused to comply. Another case that was typical for its violence occurred in Berlin: "On the 20th of the month at around 4:00 pm two people ... in uniform and *Hilfspolizei* armbands went into the shop of the butcher Gedalli Scheck, Kielstraße 34. They demanded from the son of the aforementioned, Isaak Leib Scheck, that he immediately close the shop. ... [then] ... he was brought to the police station, Steinstraße 5. There he was made to kneel with his face against the wall in a special room and, at gunpoint, beaten with a rubber truncheon over his head and on his face. At around 7:00 pm he was let go, although under threat of death, if he were again to open his shop."[61]

These and similar attacks were often initiated by business owners who had close ties to the SA or NSDAP, considered victims disagreeable competitors, and now seized the opportunity offered by the political situation and their party connections to get rid of them. Thus, in attacks where victims were physically menaced unless they shut down their shops, they were usually known to the perpetrators, and the attack was "commissioned," so to speak. A frequently used pretext to lend weight to the threatened shop closure was that victims had not settled an alleged debt, and further demands for repayment could be avoided only if the shop was immediately shut down.[62] In a case in Duisburg in March 1933, in which a certain Joseph Mond had requested help from the police after receiving repeated threats, police officers claimed that they were "not in a position to take remedial action," so that Mond had no alternative but to close his shop.[63]

Throughout March, abductions, which were always accompanied by brutal maltreatment and theft, became ever more prevalent. Erwin Wellner, Immanuel Kirchstrasse 31 in Berlin, for example, was seized on 26 March by six people in uniform and taken to an empty apartment in the Prenzlauer Straße, where he was "beaten up and manhandled in an especially drastic way for two hours."[64] Chaim Juda Safier was carried off to the Nazi Party meeting place in the General-Pape Straße in Berlin on 30 March after he had refused to yield to extortion and pay 850 reichsmark "protection money." He was held there for two days and "beaten up and mistreated." The report emphasized that the police presidium refused "to instruct the official medical officer of the district to examine the injured person."[65] Often victims were kidnapped directly out of their own apartments. A group of eleven uniformed men, for example, broke into Abraham Pinkus Seile's residence at Fürstenstraße 8 in Leipzig, threatened him at gunpoint, and took him away.[66] In a majority of cases, victims were let go on the same day or after a few days. It also happened, however, that relatives of kidnapping victims went for weeks without hearing any news. Lajbus Fauszlegier, as a case in point, was arrested on 23 March around 11:30 p.m. at the Café Dobberstein in Berlin and brought to the twelfth police precinct. On 1 April the police presidium reported in response to an inquiry that no trace of Fauszlegier was to be found anywhere; by 5 April his wife still had received no information as to his whereabouts or fate.[67]

The assault on Juda Tager on 20 March in Dresden is revealing regarding the mindset of the attackers; in his case a Dresden police station took down details of the incident. Tager was snatched from his apartment around midnight by three SA men and taken to an SA meeting place. He told the police afterward that he was placed with his face against the wall and asked which German woman he had already raped. Then he was told that he would be shot "on the count of three" if he did not reveal the name. When repeated attempts at this "procedure" failed to illicit a response from him, Tager was shown a Social Democratic Party flag and told that he had donated money to the cause of socialism. Throughout, he was repeatedly manhandled with bare fists and rifle butts. Finally he was told that he had to leave Germany forthwith or else the SA would come for him again. Tager, born in 1898, informed the police that he had been a resident of Germany since 1913 and, beginning in 1916, had fought for Austria in the World War, for which service he had received several official recognitions.[68] The police protocol indicated that Tager had blood-suffused eyes, a bloody nose, and suffered acute pain all over his body. His case illustrates the entrenched prejudices that lay behind the attacks and that had been disseminated in Nazi newspapers and magazines, such as the *Stürmer*. There, Jews were frequently viewed as "seducers" or even as "rapists" of German women and girls.[69] Responding to the complaint of the Polish Consulate in Leipzig about Tager's abduction, the Saxon foreign ministry asserted that investigations of this case had been initiated but that Tager had been arrested again on 19 April for being suspected of "having spread atrocity propaganda."[70] This flimsy accusation was often employed to excuse SA attacks. A letter of the Saxon interior ministry of 9 May made clear that Tager's complaint would not be further investigated, "since the alleged actions of the members of the SA, in so far as they can be classified as criminal acts, fall under the amnesty."[71]

It is striking that precisely on the day of the boycott, Saturday, 1 April 1933, numerous abductions, assaults, and other transgressions against foreign and German Jews took place. Despite all the protestations of the German press (which by then had been "brought into line" with Nazi policies), the day of the boycott was not as calm and bloodless as not only German newspapers but also Western diplomats reported to their governments.[72] In addition to the well-known *cause célèbre*—the murder of the Königsberg lawyer Friedrich Schumm in Kiel—there were countless further and in no way bloodless incidents. The Polish Diplomatic Mission, for example, reported two abduction cases in Berlin, where Mojzeszoni Ehrlich was carried off to a Nazi Party headquarters in the General-Pape Straße, robbed, and badly beaten up with rubber truncheons, after which he was forced to sign a statement that he had been treated well.[73] A similar fate befell Emanuel Weiss, who was taken to an SA meeting place in the Linienstraße in Berlin on that same day, where he was first roughed up and then, along with others, forced to sing "nationalist" songs.[74] National Socialist gangs obviously took advantage of the day of the boycott to attack or jail Jews all throughout the Reich. Several such cases that took place precisely on 1 April are also reported in the Hessian compensation claims files.[75] As David Abramowicz confirmed in his compensation claim file, he was attacked by three National Socialists in Hessen on the day of the boycott and badly injured—in addition to nose and sinus injuries, he suffered from a concussion. Paul Aron from Frankfurt was arrested on the same day on the charge of high treason for allegedly taking photos with the intent of supporting the propagation of "horror propaganda" abroad.[76]

Grievous Bodily Harm and Murder

From the records of foreign diplomatic missions it would appear that fewer foreign than German Jews were victims of murder and attempted murder. It is difficult to judge if this really was the case, since the number of attacks that went unreported, whether out of fear or because victims had no next of kin to report the crimes, is probably high. As indicated earlier, the written records are incomplete and, given that most crimes went unreported, faulty in the extreme in terms of providing reliable figures as to the total number of assaults against specific groups. The attack on Martes Abraham on 20 March in Köln can be classified as attempted murder. According to the Polish Diplomatic Mission, "two young people, one of them in uniform" and armed with revolvers, pushed their way into his apartment and threatened him. To escape his attackers, Abraham sprang out the window and lay—after a nine-meter fall—badly injured in the inner courtyard, where the attackers caught up with him and continued to hit him.[77] In Wiesbaden, eight SA men attacked the silk wares trader Salomon Rosenstrauch on 23 March in his store, beat him up, destroyed his furnishings, and ordered him to close his shop immediately—otherwise he would be killed. When Rosenstrauch, who suffered several broken ribs as a result of the attack, reopened his shop despite the threats weeks later, it became clear that the SA men had been in earnest. On 22 April several men appeared at Rosenstrauch's apartment and shot him. Apparently the murder was committed by his former attackers, who now carried out their threat.[78] On the very day of her husband's murder, Rosenstrauch's widow was ordered to the hospital to identify the body and asked to sign a declaration that her husband had died of a sudden heart attack. According to the statement in her compensation claim, she refused since she had seen that her husband's dead body showed distinct signs of violence.[79] Even though no charges were brought against Rosenstrauch's murderers (which would have aided his widow's claims for compensation after the war), the case was mentioned in short notices in the *Frankfurter Zeitung*, the *Deutsche Allgemeine Zeitung*, and the *London Evening Standard* on 24 April 1933.[80]

As testified by a further *aide-mémoire* of the Polish Diplomatic Mission of 22 May 1933, violent attacks and abductions of Polish Jews continued, if in reduced intensity, throughout April and May.[81] Forced shop closings also continued, whereby also cases from Württemberg—in Esslingen on the Neckar and Cannstatt near Stuttgart—were mentioned, as well as another murder case.[82] Mendel Zelig Haber, who had disappeared from Dortmund on 25 April and had been delivered to an SA guardhouse on 25 April, was pulled lifeless out of a side canal of the Dortmund-Ems Canal. Haber's body showed signs of gunshot wounds in his head, neck, and back, as well as numerous indications of severe maltreatment.[83]

As indicated by its enormous volume, antisemitic violence in 1933 was markedly different from that in the Weimar Republic: attacks were carried out with greater brutality since the police turned a blind eye and attackers could now be certain that they would get away with their crimes. During the republic, antisemitic crimes were reported to the police and legal proceedings instituted.[84] In addition, larger antisemitic attacks also did not go unnoticed since they drew the attention of the Social Democratic, Communist, and at times even the (left) liberal party press.[85] From the attackers' point of view, the *"Ostjuden"* were especially fair game. After 5 March 1933, members of the SA and other Nazi organizations used antisemitic attacks to "excel" within their peer group by demonstrating their "ferocity" and their allegiance to the Nazi cause. Sebastian Haffner, writing in 1939 after leaving his native Germany in 1938, emphasized that for the Nazis antisemitic violence functioned as a test of courage, a means of selection, and a bonding of the Nazi "in-group," "through the iron trammels of jointly committed crimes."[86] Around the same time, the head of the Frankfurt School in exile, Max Horkheimer, emphasized that antisemitic attacks were used "as a means of intimidating the population at large by showing that the system is ruthless and will stop at nothing. Politically speaking, pogroms are aimed at the onlookers."[87] More recently, Michael Wildt has argued that antisemitic attacks contributed to the creation of the *Volksgemeinschaft*, whereby those who belonged strengthened their internal coherence by prosecuting and attacking those who did not. The antisemitic policies of the regime, which found its most brutal expression in violence against Jews, also served to undermine traditional civil society and civil order and, by implication, helped blaze the trail for the Nazi state.[88]

The Reaction of German Authorities

The way authorities dealt with the violent attacks on *"Ostjuden"* can be clearly demonstrated in the case of the highly industrialized state of Saxony. With 346 inhabitants per square kilometer, it was the most densely populated state in the Reich (excepting city-states),[89] and it incorporated several large cities with a high proportion of *"Ostjuden,"* including Leipzig, Dresden, and Chemnitz.[90] In the predominantly Protestant state, the NSDAP was stronger than in the Reich overall; the same was true for Communists and Social Democrats: in the 5 March 1933 elections, the NSDAP received 43.9 percent of the vote (45.0 percent in Saxony); the SPD 18.3 percent (26.2 percent in Saxony) and the KPD 12.3 percent (16.5 percent in Saxony). More than 90 percent of Saxony's population was Protestant in 1925.[91] Numbers of reported attacks on east European Jews were high. A listing of arrests and cases of bodily injury of 24 April 1933, sent by the Saxon ministry for foreign affairs to the interior ministry with the request to review the information, records "fifty known arrests of Polish citizens—predominantly those of the Jewish race" and "twenty-five arrests of Czech citizens." Of the fifty cases "of bodily injury of Polish citizens ... police inquiries still have not led to the identification of perpetrators in any single case." The report conceded that "according to the information that reached us it cannot be denied that some cases have involved considerable mistreatment."[92] The Saxon foreign ministry asserted that it had "up to this point refrained from providing answers to queries in all cases to the Polish Consul, since any official reference to these matters—excepting denials—merely furnished foreign Consuls with further material to hinder the rejection of atrocity propaganda."[93] Here it becomes apparent that ultimately *raison d'état* dictated how the bureaucracy dealt with antisemitic attacks.

With increasing numbers of cases, the Saxon foreign ministry enacted guidelines "for the response to complaints levied by foreign consulates regarding the mistreatment of their citizens"[94]: these were to be characterized by "uniform interpretations." Police authorities were never to respond directly to complaints, but to first convey the results of police investigations to the interior ministry, which would then forward the results of its inquiry to the foreign ministry.[95] For complaints issued by the Polish Diplomatic Mission in Berlin, the complicated route through administrative channels did not end here: Saxony's foreign ministry was to forward its reports to the Reich interior ministry. In general, inquiries were to be "handled in a dilatory fashion"—that is, delaying tactics were to be applied to whole process.[96] In dealing with the brutal attacks on *"Ostjuden,"* Saxon officials found themselves caught between the Scylla of expected national solidarity with the perpetrators and the Charybdis of their own sense of justice, for they knew all too well that reports about the SA's brutal maltreatment of victims corresponded to the truth. In this dilemma, *raison d'état* prevailed. The authorities distorted the truth to protect the reputation of the Reich. For some officials it may have been an easy choice on account of their own prejudices. The post factum recording of the progression of events in assault cases by the police makes it clear that the brutality of the attacks was minimized and that victims were intimidated and put under pressure not to press their cases too strongly, so that they often downplayed what had happened to them.

Officials Minimize Attacks

This became apparent from a 5 April 1933 report of the Chemnitz police presidium to the Saxony interior ministry.[97] The merchant Littmann Grebler had been forced by the SA to scrape political graffiti off of the sides of buildings on 25 March. His statement reads as follows: "I have not been beaten. My wife, mentioned here, was in no way bothered. I have not reported the incident to the Consulate and also do not know who has."[98] The commercial assistant Markus Reich, born in 1898 in Galicia, was abducted on 8 March by the Dresden SA together with his brother Simon and other Polish Jews. While Simon Reich stated that he had been beaten by SA men, Markus Reich declared that "he had been treated very correctly and politely and thought highly of the SA men, who [even] in this excitable time had not said one impolite word to him."[99] It is obvious that Markus Reich wanted to protect himself with this soothing statement from revenge attacks by the SA. The hairdresser Alex Kamelhar, born in 1914, who had also been forced by the SA to rub communist political slogans off buildings, and whose hair, like that of others, was cut off, could not appear in person owing to "illness." Apparently he had been beaten up by the SA and lay in hospital. His mother made the following statement: "An SA man used very small scissors to cut off a portion of the hair on his head."[100]

Efforts to minimize attacks are all too apparent. The merchant Jakob Salomon Pfeffer, born in 1880 in Poland, admitted to being repeatedly hit "by several SA men" and had to be treated by a doctor, yet apologized for the Polish Consulate's complaint: "I did not turn to the Consulate and also cannot state on whose part this action was taken."[101] The police report mentioned that Pfeffer and his daughter, who was arrested with him, "are accused of high treason," that is, of being involved in politically subversive activities. This was clearly a trumped-up allegation, used to explain Pfeffer's injuries. The Polish Jews who had been attacked and arrested consisted of small shopkeepers, office workers, the owner of a bakery, and a hairdresser so that the assertion that "with respect to these people, the ... Chemnitz NSDAP has established that Jews support leftist political parties and finance their election campaigns" is absurd. Allegations such as these served only as a standing excuse and justification for the brutal attacks of the perpetrators. The all-pervasive fear that so obviously dictated the statements of the victims to the police was fully justified, since attackers were clearly not held accountable for their actions and might well strike again, as indicated by the usual conclusion to the aforementioned report: "Despite detailed investigations, the persons who assaulted Jews have not been apprehended."[102]

On 13 April, Hans Pfundtner, undersecretary of state in the Reich interior ministry, sent a further list with about fifteen "attacks against foreigners" to the state commissar for Saxony, Manfred von Killinger, regarding arrests and severe maltreatment in Saxon cities, and concluding with a comment typical for the mindset of the bureaucracy: "I respectfully request that these complaints be verified and the results of the investigation shared with me. At the same time, I request that it be examined to what extent undesirable, especially Jewish, foreigners can be deported."[103] In the eyes of the authorities the victims of attacks were evidently considered responsible for their own plight, so that deportation seemed the best solution, also to avoid unnecessarily provoking the SA by their very presence. The reports of Saxony's interior ministry, which "interpreted" police accounts of the incidents before transmitting them to the Saxon foreign ministry, consistently indicate that the attacks were explained in such a way as to provide excuses for the perpetrators. Flimsy reasons are cited that supposedly justified the attacks or explained them away as practically "within rights." Specific charges against the victims were fabricated and this construed incriminating evidence was put forward to excuse the attacks, exonerate attackers, and provide justification for their actions as a form of self-defense against communists, subversives, and other dubious elements.[104] Incriminating material against victims was also fabricated to enable officials to take the moral high ground when confronted by the complaints of Polish diplomats. Toward that end, the interior ministry often directly adopted the SA version of events.

Fabricated Charges against Victims

To give but a few examples from archival documents: In response to a complaint by the Polish Consulate in Leipzig about an attack on a synagogue in Dresden, the Saxon interior ministry stated in its report, "The Dresden police presidium declared that on the day in question it was suspected that in the synagogue in the Sporergasse 2 a political meeting was to be held."[105] Against the opposition of the police, the SA had then "brought the Jews to the *Volkshaus* [now an SA meeting place]," but "interrogations failed to produce incriminating materials ..."[106] The pretext that the raid was founded on a (supposedly Communist) meeting was clearly contrived by the SA to give their action a veneer of legality. In a 9 May report, the arrest of Josef and Chane Weiner was thus explained: "The husband Weiner had been charged with fomenting agitation among his Jewish co-religionists and communists against the regime." It soon came to light that "sufficient proof thereof could not be furnished."[107] The arrest of Sabina Haspel, born in 1907 in Galicia, was explained by virtue of the supposition that "in a letter that became known, [she] spread rumors of alleged violent acts against Jews."[108] During the Nazi takeover, spreading this particular rumor was not an unusual "crime."

Officials in the interior ministry were often confronted with reports of antisemitic attacks and knew very well that Sabina Haspel had been arrested solely because she was foreign born and Jewish. The aforementioned Juda Tager was accused of disseminating "atrocity propaganda" and "according to a credible witness ... [of having] spread the following seditious statement: ... 'In Chemnitz SA-men had cut off the beard of an old Jew. In the Dresden Brüdergasse they had threatened and extorted 200 Reichsmark from a sick Jew ...'"[109] That officials in the interior ministry considered Tager's action of making this information known a criminal act, though they knew perfectly well that the "seditious statements" corresponded to the truth, says much about their political independence. Despite the Reich interior ministry's frequent warnings to "diligently and promptly investigate [attacks] against foreign citizens that were allegedly committed by members of the SA and SS," the procedure among Saxon officials continued unaltered:[110] assaults were minimized and victims were incriminated with fabricated crimes. This didn't always work, as became clear in the case against Heinrich Leßmann, who was taken into "protective custody" because he "was about to flee to Poland ... [to] disseminate atrocity propaganda about the treatment of Jews in Germany" and who (allegedly) had also made disparaging remarks about Reichskanzler Hitler.[111] Of the eight witnesses supporting the accusations, seven withdrew their testimony after being summoned by the police. One witness by the name of Kiesauer claimed that Leßmann had said that "the Germans are pigs, just as is Hitler's party." Leßmann denied this charge, and when Kiesauer was interrogated again on 12 May, he conceded that he had been "mistaken." Leßmann was released the next day after the fabricated case against him collapsed.[112]

In cases where no plausible charges could be construed, other pretexts were put forward to provide reasons for arrests and shroud them in legality: "The police had to put Milewsky in protective cus-tody since the public mood against Jewish traders, especially against Milewsky himself, was so strong that transgressions against him were to be feared."[113] In cases where beatings had been exceptionally brutal, authorities asserted that the case happened "at a time of greatest national excitement,"[114] or, as the Saxon interior ministry commented on 22 June, "In reviewing the cases before us, it must be taken into account that all of them took place during the first weeks after the national revolution. Insofar as encroachments occurred, this is regret-table; yet with major political upheavals, such as came in the wake of the national revolution, this cannot be avoided completely even when authorities are fully alert."[115] Another method to excuse perpetrators was to discredit the "moral character" of the victim: "Löwenkron, Max, has been taken into protective custody on 11 April, released again on 9 May 1933 and consigned to the Dresden-Friedrichstadt hospital. … Löwenkron is a man suffering from a serious venereal disease."[116] This suggests that Löwenkron was hospitalized not because of injuries inflicted by the SA but because of a venereal disease that, in turn, was meant to indicate a questionable lifestyle. Occasionally, as far as the authorities were concerned, cases took care of themselves: "Steinitz, Anna, has poisoned herself with gas on 7 April 1933 in Chemnitz for unknown reasons. Therefore, she could not have been taken into cus-tody on 24 April 1933."[117]

In those rare instances where subordinate administrative branches acted in ignorance of instructions that prescribed standardized responses and replied directly to complaints by the Polish Consulate in Leipzig, the same pattern of argumentation is prevalent. The district office in Zwickau, for example, responded to the Polish Consulate in the case of the painter Moses Scheiner (who had been taken into "pro-tective custody") that Scheiner had been arrested because he "is under the well-founded suspicion of supporting communist subversion." Scheiner was also in personal danger "because he was very unpopu-lar in wide circles of Plauen's population due to existing suspicion of treasonous and subversive objectives and his affiliation with the *Judentum*."[118]

In August 1933, when the wave of antisemitic violence had passed its zenith and officials in both Saxony and the Reich had been confronted with hundreds of cases, a directive of Reich interior minister Frick regarding the "treatment of Polish Jews" summarized the matter: "Let me note that from the standpoint of my portfolio, I consider it necessary that Germany be freed as soon as possible from such eastern Jewish ele-ments who lack citizenship. By dint of personal conduct and business practices they are unworthy of German hospitality."[119] Even contemporary Prussian or Saxon officials (though bound by the strictures of a different mindset) may have wondered that this was an odd kind of "hospitality" that expressed itself in robbery, serious bodily harm, and attacks designed to humiliate the guests. The intra-bureaucratic correspondence as a whole leaves no doubt that the authorities tried to put blame for the attacks squarely on the shoulders of the victims. In the end, those Prussian and Saxon officials who so shrewdly manipulated the truth may have come to believe their own lies.

A memorandum of the German foreign office to the interior ministry of 22 June also throws light on the attitude of Polish authorities toward their Jewish subjects:[120] the Polish government desired "after the recent relaxation of tensions in German-Polish relations … to avoid new aggravations in mutual relations due to incidents with Polish Jews."[121] The Polish side thereby stressed that conflicts regarding the "Jewish question" in the spring "had to do with ill-treatment or other excesses that took place in the wake of revolutionary turbulence," whereas now the "destruction of the livelihood of Polish Jews in Germany" was at risk in view of the treatment of those Polish Jews "who travel from marketplace to marketplace in order to sell their wares," and their "expulsion … from Germany."[122] According to the foreign ministry, it was important for the Polish side that Polish Jews in Germany could maintain their already meager existence, and that Germany would not expel them merely because of passport law misdemeanors, such as failure to renew residence permits in time. In other words, Poland was interested in Germany retaining as many Polish Jews as possible, while the German side wanted to deport ever larger numbers of them.[123] In 1933, Polish authorities did not seem to be concerned primarily with protecting Jews from attacks by the SA. The priority for the Polish government was that Polish Jews could remain in Germany for economic reasons. Beginning in the summer of 1933, both sides seemed interested in a further relaxation of tensions, and the Polish side put forward mostly instrumental reasons for ending transgressions against Polish Jews in Germany: attacks "triggered strong repercussions with the Jewish population in Poland, so that it would become ever more difficult for the Polish government to work toward consolidating an easing of tensions."[124]

Conclusion

As it can safely be assumed that the estimated number of unknown cases was high, we may infer from the many hundreds of reported cases in the spring of 1933 alone that possibly as many as a thousand attacks on "*Ostjuden*" in the German Reich took place. Already weeks after Hitler became chancellor, eastern Jews were without protection or rights and exposed to the wanton brutality of the SA, since the police, for the most part, failed to intervene. The fact that there was a pogrom-like climate only weeks into Hitler's chancellorship points not only to the effectiveness of antisemitic indoctrination among Nazi formations but also to significant antisemitic residues in some parts of German society.

Authorities of the Reich and Länder knew quite well what was going on, but they did everything to minimize crimes and shield the perpetrators, thereby becoming willing accomplices of the attackers. The bureaucratic correspondence makes it appear as if victims triggered attacks against them by dint of their very presence in Germany. Readers of the files are left with the impression that the SA committed the crimes and the bureaucracy invented reasons to minimize and excuse them. By their early "successes" with attacks that went as far as murder, and the fact that they got off scot free, Nazi formations quickly understood that the bureaucracy was willing to cover up their encroachments. To the SA this was a distinct sign of encouragement and a signal to keep on going, for nothing would happen to them. This attitude of the bureaucracy toward the multitude of brutal antisemitic attacks in the spring of 1933 makes it painfully obvious that in the event of future antisemitic outrages, no help could be expected from the German authorities.

Hermann Beck is professor of history at the University of Miami. He is author of *The Origins of the Authoritarian Welfare State in Prussia: Conservatives, Bureaucracy, and the Social Question, 1815–1870* (1995, 1998) and *The Fateful Alliance: German Conservatives and Nazis in 1933; The Machtergreifung in a New Light* (2008, 2010), and he has published numerous articles in leading American and European journals, including the *Historische Zeitschrift*, *The Journal of Modern History*, and *The Journal of Contemporary History*. He recently completed a book-length manuscript on "Before the Holocaust: Anti-Semitism and the Reaction of German Society during the Nazi Seizure of Power."

Notes

1. On the occasion of the founding of the "Reichsvertretung der Juden in Deutschland" in September 1933, see Moshe Zimmermann, *Die Deutschen Juden 1914–1945* (Munich: Oldenbourg, 1997), 57.

2. With the exception of Richard Bessel, "The Nazi Capture of Power," *Journal of Contemporary History* 39 (2004): 169–88, esp. 176–79, the literature tends to focus more on the economic aspects of violence and exclusion, such as the boycott of 1 April 1933, than on the widespread physical violence. See Avraham Barkai, *"Wehr Dich!" Der Centralverein deutscher Staatsbürger jüdischen Glaubens 1893–1938* (Munich: Beck, 2002), 270–84; Armin Nolzen, "The Nazi Party and Its Violence against the Jews, 1933–1939," *Yad Vashem Studies* 31 (2003): 245–85; Michael Wildt, *Volksgemeinschaft und Selbstermächtigung: Gewalt gegen Juden in der deutschen Provinz* (Hamburg: Hamburger Edition, 2007), 101–38; Saul Friedländer, *Nazi Germany and the Jews: The Years of Persecution, 1933–1939* (New York: HarperCollins, 1997), 17–18; and Karl Schleunes, *The Twisted Road to Auschwitz* (Urbana: University of Illinois Press, 1970).

3. Konrad Adenauer, *Briefe 1945–1947*, ed. Hans Peter Mensing (Berlin: Siedler, 1983), 172.

4. See Werner Bergmann, *Geschichte des Antisemitismus* (Munich: Beck, 2004), 58–65, and Hugh Seton-Watson, "Two Contending Policies toward Jews: Russia and Hungary," in *Hostages of Modernization: Studies on Modern Anti-Semitism 1870–1933/1939*, ed. Herbert A. Strauss (Berlin, New York: De Gruyter, 1993), 3:948–60, esp. 953.

5. Esra Bennathen, "Die demographische und wirtschaftliche Struktur der Juden," in *Entscheidungsjahr 1932: Zur Judenfrage in der Endphase der Weimarer Republik*, ed. Werner A. Mosse (Mohr: Tübingen, 1966), 87–131.

6. Ibid., 98. See also Trude Maurer, "Ausländische Juden in Deutschland, 1933–1939," in *Die Juden im nationalsozialistischen Deutschland*, ed. Arnold Paucker (Tübingen: Mohr 1986), 189–210, esp. 189.

7. Maurer, "Ausländische Juden in Deutschland," 189; Zimmermann, *Die deutschen Juden*, 22–23.

8. Bennathen, 98. See Wilhelm Treue, "Zur Frage der wirtschaftlichen Motive im deutschen Antisemitismus," in *Deutsches Judentum in Krieg und Revolution 1916–1923*, ed. Werner E. Mosse (Tübingen: Mohr 1971), 387–409, esp. 399.

9. Steven Aschheim, *Brothers and Strangers: The East European Jew in German and German Jewish Consciousness* (Madison: University of Wisconsin Press, 1982); Jack Wertheimer, *Unwelcome Strangers: East European Jews in Imperial Germany* (New York: Oxford University Press, 1987); Trude Maurer, *Ostjuden in Deutschland 1918–1933* (Hamburg: Christians, 1986). Yfaat Weiss, "'*Ostjuden*' in Deutschland als Freiwild: Die nationalsozialistische Außenpolitik zwischen Ideologie und Wirklichkeit," *Tel Aviver Jahrbuch für Deutsche Geschichte* 23 (1994): 215–32; and Jerzy Tomaszewski, "Polish Diplomats and the Fate of Polish Jews in Nazi Germany," *Acta Poloniae Historica* 61 (1990): 183–204.

10. 15 March 1933, "Auswärtiges Amt an Preußisches Ministerium des Innern," Akten der Reichskanzlei, NSDAP, Bundesarchiv, Berlin-Lichterfelde (hereafter: BA Berlin), R 43 II, 1195/107.

11. Ibid., R43 II, 1195/108.

12. 23 March 1933, "Auswärtiges Amt an Reichsministerium des Innern," Akten der Reichskanzlei, NSDAP, BA Berlin, R 43 II, 1195/173.

13. 27 March 1933 "Polnische Gesandschaft an Auswärtiges Amt," BA Berlin, R43 II, 1195/204.

14. 5 April 1933, "Polnische Gesandschaft an Auswärtiges Amt," Akten der Reichskanzlei, Judentum: Stellung und Behandlung der Juden im nationalsozialistischen Deutschland, BA Berlin, R 43 II, 603/16–29. German foreign minister Neurath forwarded these complaints to Interior Minister Frick, demanding that an end be put to the attacks as they might "seriously endanger the reputation of the German government and the German nation abroad." See 6 April 1933, "Neurath an Frick," BA Berlin, R 43 II, 603/8–10.

15. 5 April 1933, ibid., R43 II, 603/17.

16. Ibid., 21, 23.

17. Ibid., 24.

18. Ibid., 25–26.

19. Ibid., 27.

20. 11 March 1933, "Polnische Gesandschaft an Auswärtiges Amt," Akten der Reichskanzlei, NSDAP, BA Berlin, R43 II, 1195/114–15.

21. Ibid., 117.

22. 23 March 1933, "Auswärtiges Amt an Ministerien," ibid., 166–68.

23. Ibid., 165–66, 168.

24. Vicco von Bülow-Schwante (1891–1970) was one of the experts on Jewish affairs in the foreign ministry. See Eckart Conze, Norbert Frei, Peter Hayes, and Moshe Zimmermann, *Das Amt und die Vergangenheit: Deutsche Diplomaten im Dritten Reich und in der Bundesrepublik* (Munich: Pantheon, 2012), 42–51.

25. 23 March 1933, "Auswärtiges Amt an Ministerien," ibid., 164.

26. In the Versailles Treaty, Upper Silesia was designated a German-Polish mixed-language area, the legal status of which would be decided by referendum. In 1921, 59.6 percent of the area's population opted for remaining in Germany and 40.3 percent for being part of Poland. At the behest of France, 3,200 square kilometers with about 950,000 inhabitants were awarded to Poland, including cities with a German majority such as Kattowitz (Katowice) and Königshütte (Chorzów), with 57 percent and 75 percent Germans respectively, that were surrounded by a predominantly Polish population. On 15 May 1922, Germany and Poland negotiated a bilateral convention on the protection of minorities. See R. Blunke, "The German Minority in Interwar Poland and German Foreign Policy—Some Reconsiderations," *Journal of Contemporary History* 25 (1990): 87–102.

27. 2 May 1933, "Polnische Gesandschaft an Auswärtiges Amt," Sächsisches Hauptstaatsarchiv Dresden (hereafter cited as SHStA Dresden), Judentum 1933–1935, Bestand 10717, 1723/22.

28. *Die Verfolgung und Ermordung der europäischen Juden durch das nationalsozialistische Deutschland 1933–1945*, vol. 1: *Deutsches Reich, 1933–1937*, ed. Rolf Gruner (Munich: Oldenbourg, 2008), 193–94.

29. 21 Apr. 1933 "Österreichisches Generalkonsulat an sächsisches Ministerium der auswärtigen Angelegenheiten," SHStA Dresden, Bestand 10717, 1723/1–3, esp. 3.

30. Ibid., 3.

31. 2 May 1933, "Polnische Gesandschaft an Auswärtiges Amt," ibid., 20–22.

32. Ibid., 20–21.

33. Ibid., 21.

34. Ibid.

35. Ibid., 22.

36. 27 May 1933, "Ministerium der auswärtigen Angelegenheiten an Reichsministerium des Innern," ibid., 25.

37. Ibid., 23.

38. Ernst Fraenkel, *Der Doppelstaat* (Hamburg: Europäische Verlagsanstalt, 1974). See also Wildt, *Volksgemeinschaft*, 133–37.

39. 15 June 1933, "Sächsisches Ministerium des Innern an Kreishauptmann-schaften und Polizeidirektionen," SHStA Dresden, Bestand 10717, 1723/31. See also Weiss, "'Ostjuden,'" 221.

40. 31 May 1933, "Auswärtiges Amt an Oberbürgermeister der Stadt Berlin," ibid., 28–29.

41. 15 July 1933, "Sächsisches Ministerium des Innern an Kreishauptmann-schaften," ibid., 35.

42. Ibid. See also Weiss, "'Ostjuden,'" 220–25.

43. 18 September 1933, "Kreishauptmannschaft Zwickau an das Ministerium des Innern," SHStA Dresden, Bestand 10717, 1723/42–45, esp. 45.

44. See, for example, the articles in the *New York Times* in March 1933: 21 March, "Terror in Germany"; 26 March, "Herr Hitler's Nazis Hear an Echo of World Opinion"; 27 March, "German Jailings Spread Terror;" and many others. For the British press reaction, see "The Persecution of Jews in Germany," Bayerisches Hauptstaatsarchiv Munich, Abt. V, Sammlung Varia 231.

45. While the essence of Allied charges regarding the shooting of Belgian civilians was true, German wartime atrocities came to be largely inter-preted as Allied propaganda beginning in the late 1920s. In 1928, the book by the British Labour MP Arthur Ponsonby, *Falsehood in Wartime* (London: G. Allen & Unwin, 1928), showed some of the atrocities to be deliber-ate fabrications. The book was quickly translated, went through several German editions, and shaped German public perception of Allied war propaganda, especially since German authorities had consistently main-tained that the Allied charges were invented. See John Horne, *German Atrocities 1914: A History of Denial* (New Haven and London: Yale Press, 2001), esp. 3, 369, 374, and 417.

46. Geheimes Staatsarchiv Preußischer Kulturbesitz Dahlem (hereafter cited as GStAPK Dahlem), I. HA, Innenministerium, Rep. 77/127, "Politische Ausschreitungen und Zusammenstöße." Monatsberichte, Beiheft 1b, 1932–1933.

47. 5 April 1933, "Polnische Gesandschaft an Auswärtiges Amt," R43 II, 603/25, 26.

48. Ibid., 27.

49. 27 March 1933, "Polnische Gesandschaft an Auswärtiges Amt," R 43 II, 1195/203.

50. 5 April 1933, "Polnische Gesandschaft an Auswärtiges Amt," R43 II, 603/17.

51. 23 March 1933, "Auswärtiges Amt an Ministerien," R43 II, 1195/ 165.

52. Ibid.

53. 5 April 1933, "Polnische Gesandschaft an Auswärtiges Amt," R43 II, 603/19.

54. Ibid., fol. 22–23.

55. 27 March 1933, "Polnische Gesandschaft an Auswärtiges Amt," R43 II, 1195/201.

56. Ibid., fol. 202.

57. 11 March 1933, "Polnische Gesandschaft an Auswärtiges Amt," R 43 II, 1195/118.

58. GStAPK Dahlem I. H.A. Rep. 90p, no. 71, "Ausschreitungen: März 1933," Vol. 2, fol. 47. At the beginning of the document it was noted (dated 25 April 1935), "The collated documents in the supplement … have been given to me today by Herr ORR Flothow, to whom they were given by Herr Staatssekretär Landfried during his time in office, with the instruction not to record them and also not to include them in the files. Signed: Schröder, Amtsrat." Surprisingly, the documents survived, despite the order not to include them in the official records.

59. "Ausschreitungen: März 1933," GStAPK Dahlem, I. H.A. Rep. 90p, no. 71, Heft 2, fol. 50.

60. 18 March 1933, "Auswärtiges Amt an Ministerien," BA Berlin, R43 II, 1195/172.

61. 27 March 1933, "Polnische Gesandschaft an Auswärtiges Amt," R 43II, 1195/200–201.

62. 23 March 1933, "Auswärtiges Amt an Ministerien," R 43II, 1195/170.

63. 27 March 1933, "Polnische Gesandschaft an Auswärtiges Amt," R 43II, 1195/202.

64. 5 April 1933, "Polnische Gesandschaft an Auswärtiges Amt," R43 II, 603/18.

65. Ibid., 18.

66. Ibid., 25–26.

67. Ibid., 15.

68. 21 March 1933, "Polizeipräsidium Dresden," SHStA Dresden, Beschwerden ausländischer Vertreterbehörden wegen Übergriffen an ihren jüdischen Staatsbürgern, Bestand 10717, 4846/83–85.

69. Daniel Roos, *Julius Streicher und "Der Stürmer"* (Paderborn: Schöningh, 2014).

70. 13 May 1933, "Ministerium der auswärtigen Angelegenheiten an Polnisches Konsulat," SHStA Dresden, Bestand 10717, 4846/86.

71. 9 May 1933, "Sächsisches Ministerium des Innern an Ministerium für auswärtige Angelegenheiten," ibid., 82. On the amnesty, see "Betrifft Gnadenerweise aus Anlaß der Beendigung der nationalsozialistischen

Revolution vom 22.7. 1933 in Verbindung mit der allgemeinen Verfügung des Justizministers vom 25. Juli 1933," GStA PK, Rep. 84a, no. 54771.

72. *Documents on British Foreign Policy 1919–1939,* 2nd series, Vol. V (London, 1956), 1–55; *Foreign Relations of the United States,* Vol. II (Washington, DC: Government Printing Office, 1949), 320–54; Abraham Ascher, *Was Hitler a Riddle? Western Democracies and National Socialism* (Stanford, CA: Stanford University Press, 2012), 15–144.

73. 5 April 1933, "Polnische Gesandschaft an Auswärtiges Amt," BA Berlin, R 43 II, 603/20.

74. Ibid., 20–21.

75. Of a total of 110,000 compensation claim files in Hessen, 6,000 were examined in detail in the 1990s for a research project on "Opposition and Persecution under National Socialism in Hessen." The databank set up for the purpose lists about twelve compensation claim files where claimants were persecuted between March and May 1933. I am grateful to Dr. Eichler of the Hessisches Hauptstaatsarchiv in Wiesbaden for this information.

76. Hessisches Hauptstaatsarchiv Wiesbaden, Entschädigungsakten, Abt. 518, no. 76, David Abramowicz; Abt. 518, no. 2980, Paul Aron.

77. 27 March 1933, "Polnische Gesandschaft an Auswärtiges Amt," BA Berlin, R 43 II, 1195/203.

78. Entschädigungsakten, Hauptstaatsarchiv Wiesbaden Abt. 518, no. 48634, Salomon Rosenstrauch.

79. Ibid.

80. Copy of the notice in Rosenstrauch's compensation claim file, ibid.

81. *Die Verfolgung und Ermordung der europäischen Juden durch das nationalsozialistische Deutschland, 1933–1945,* 1:160–62.

82. Ibid., 161.

83. Ibid.

84. Dirk Walter, *Antisemitische Kriminalität und Gewalt: Judenfeindschaft in der Weimarer Republik* (Bonn: Dietz, 1999), 97–151; 166–71; 200–44; Cornelia Hecht, *Deutsche Juden und Antisemitismus in der Weimarer Republik* (Bonn: Dietz, 2003), 101–345; Wildt, *Volksgemeinschaft,* 69–101; and Dirk Schumann, *Politische Gewalt in der Weimarer Republik 1918–1933* (Essen: Klartext, 2001), 199, 221, 238, 262, 333–34, 367.

85. Schumann, *Politische Gewalt,* 334.

86. Sebastian Haffner, *Germany: Jekyll & Hyde* (Berlin: Verlag 1900, 1996), 69–70.

87. Max Horkheimer, "Die Juden und Europa," *Zeitschrift für Sozialforschung* 8 (1939); quoted in Roger Griffin, ed., *Fascism* (Oxford: Oxford University Press, 1995), 272.

88. Wildt, *Volksgemeinschaft,* 26–68, 352–74.

89. *Statistisches Jahrbuch für das deutsche Reich,* ed. Statistisches Reichsamt (Berlin, 1933), 5. The Reich average was 140.6 inhabitants per square kilometer. With 5,196,000 inhabitants (1933), Saxony had an area of 14,986 square kilometers and was thus smaller than Baden, which had half as many inhabitants.

90. In 1933 Leipzig was the fifth largest (713,470 inh.), Dresden the seventh largest (642,143), and Chemnitz the seventeenth largest (350,734) of German cities in the Reich. See Hans-Ulrich Thamer, *Verführung und Gewalt: Deutschland 1933–1945* (Berlin: Siedler, 1986), 258. On the *"Ostjuden"* in Saxony, see SHStA Dresden, Bestand 10736, no. 11708, "Einwanderung und Ausweisung von *Ostjuden*," fol. 126.

91. *Statistisches Jahrbuch für das deutsche Reich,* 540–41, 18.

92. 24 April 1933, "Verhaftungen," SHStA Dresden, Bestand 10717, no. 4846.

93. Ibid.

94. 12 May 1933, "Entwurf an Innenministerium," SHStA Dresden, Bestand 10717, no. 4846, ibid.

95. Ibid.

96. 30 August 1933, "Reichsminister des Innern an Landesregierungen," SHStA Dresden, Bestand 10717, no. 4846. The Reich interior ministry also demanded "to be informed of all cases in which foreigners are taken into protective custody, so that the necessary material is immediately at hand to respond to diplomatic protests."

97. 5 April 1933, "Polizeipräsidium Chemnitz an Ministerium des Innern."

98. 5 April 1933, ibid.

99. 30 May 1933, "Sächsisches Innenministerium an Ministerium für auswärtige Angelegenheiten," ibid.

100. 5 April 1933, ibid.

101. Ibid.

102. Ibid.

103. 13 April 1933, "Reichsministerium des Innern an Killinger," SHStA Dresden, Bestand 10717, no. 4846.

104. 28 April, 9 May, 23 May, 27 May, 30 May, 22 June, 19 July, and 22 July 1933, "Sächsisches Ministerium des Innern an Ministerium der auswärtigen Angelegenheiten," SHStA Dresden, Bestand 10717, no. 4846. In all cases presented here, Polish Jews were assaulted, mistreated, and also often robbed.

105. 28 April 1933, ibid.

106. Ibid.

107. 9 May 1933, ibid.

108. 13 May 1933, ibid.

109. Ibid. In its report, Saxony's foreign ministry adopted the interior ministry's version almost verbatim.

110. 22 May 1933, "Sächsisches Ministerium des Innern an Ministerium für Auswärtige Angelegenheiten," SHStA Dresden, Bestand 10717, no. 4846.

111. 27 May 1933, "Sächsisches Ministerium des Innern an Ministerium für Auswärtige Angelegenheiten," ibid.

112. Ibid.

113. 30 May 1933, ibid.

114. Ibid.

115. 22 June 1933, "Sächsisches Ministerium des Innern an Ministerium für Auswärtige Angelegenheiten," SHStA Dresden, Bestand 10717, no. 4846.

116. 19 July 1933, ibid.

117. Ibid. On the suicides of German Jews in 1933, see Christian Goeschel, "Suicides of German Jews in the Third Reich," *German History* 25 (2007): 22–45, esp. 23–24.
118. 15 July 1933, "Kreishauptmannschaft Zwickau an polnisches Konsulat Leipzig," SHStA Dresden, Bestand 10717, no. 4846. Plauen had 113,860 inhabitants in 1933 (*Statistisches Jahrbuch*, 7).
119. 24 August 1933, "Reichsminister des Innern an preußischen Minister des Innern und sächsisches Ministerium der Auswärtigen Angelegenheiten," ibid.
120. 22 June 1933, "Auswärtiges Amt, abschriftlich dem Reichsministerium des Innern," ibid.
121. 22 June 1933, ibid.
122. Ibid. In the summer of 1933, the German side also emphasized that regarding the deportation of eastern Jews (which had been accelerated since March) "interstate relations with Poland" should be taken into account. 24 August 1933, ibid.
123. Already on 17 February 1933 an edict of the Prussian interior ministry to the police was issued whereby the standing order to refrain from deporting "*Ostjuden*" was rescinded. On 15 March a directive of the Reich interior ministry declared that further immigration of "*Ostjuden*" was to be avoided. Eastern Jews should also not be granted citizenship; those without valid residence permits were to be deported. See Joseph Walk, ed., *Das Sonderrecht für die Juden im NS-Staat* (Heidelberg: UTB, 1996), 3–4. On antisemitism in Poland, see William W. Hagen, "Before the 'Final Solution': Toward a Comparative Analysis of Political Anti-Semitism in Interwar Germany and Poland," *Journal of Modern History* 68 (1996): 351–81.
124. 22 June 1933, "Auswärtiges Amt, abschriftlich dem Reichsministerium des Innern," ibid.

Bibliography

Bankier, David, ed. *The Germans and the Final Solution: Public Opinion under Nazism*. Cambridge, MA: Blackwell, 1992.
Beck, Hermann. "Between the Dictates of Conscience and Political Expediency: Hitler's Conservative Alliance Partner and Anti-Semitism during the Nazi Seizure of Power." *Journal of Contemporary History* 41 (2006): 611–41.
——. *The Fateful Alliance: German Conservatives and Nazis in 1933; The Machtergreifung in a New Light*. New York and Oxford: Berghahn Books, 2008.
——. "Konflikte zwischen Deutschnationalen und Nationalsozialisten während der Machtergreifungszeit." *Historische Zeitschrift*, 292 (2011): 645–80.
——. "Anti-Semitic Violence 'from Below': Attacks and Protestant Church Responses in Germany in 1933." *Politics, Religion, and Ideology* 14 (2013): 395–412.

———. "Antisemitische Gewalt während der Machtergreifungszeit und die Reaktion der deutschen Gesellschaft." In *Die "Reichskristallnacht" in Schleswig-Holstein: Der Novemberpogrom im historischen Kontext*, edited by Rainer Hering, 141–91. Hamburg: Hamburg University Press, 2016.

Becker, Josef, and Ruth Becker, eds. *Hitlers Machtergreifung: Dokumente zum Machtantritt Hitlers*, 2nd ed. Munich: Deutscher Taschenbuch-Verlag, 1992.

Bessel, Richard. "The Nazi Capture of Power." *Journal of Contemporary History* 39 (2004): 169–88.

Broszat, Martin. *The Hitler State: The Foundation and Development of the Internal Structure of the Third Reich*. London: Longman, 1981.

Evans, Richard. *The Coming of the Third Reich*. New York: Penguin, 2004.

Feuchtwanger, Lion. *The Oppermanns*. New York: Carroll and Graf, 1983.

Friedländer, Saul. *Nazi Germany and the Jews: The Years of Persecution, 1933–1939*. New York: HarperCollins, 1997.

Gellately, Robert. *Backing Hitler: Consent and Coercion in Nazi Germany*. Oxford and New York: Oxford University Press, 2001.

Goeschel, Christian. "Suicides of German Jews in the Third Reich." *German History* 25 (2007): 22– 45.

Haffner, Sebastian. *Defying Hitler: A Memoir*. New York: Picador, 2002.

Hecht, Cornelia. *Deutsche Juden und Antisemitismus in der Weimarer Republik*. Bonn: Dietz, 2003.

Horne, John. *German Atrocities 1914: A History of Denial*. New Haven and London: Yale Press, 2001.

Isherwood, Christopher. *The Berlin Stories*. New York: New Directions, 2008.

Noakes, Jeremy, and Geoff Pridham. *Nazism: A Documentary Reader*, vol. 1: *The Rise to Power 1919–1934*. Exeter: University of Exeter Press, 1983.

Nagorski, Andrew. *Hitlerland: American Eyewitnesses to the Nazi Rise to Power*. New York: Simon & Schuster, 2012.

Nolzen, Armin. "The Nazi Party and Its Violence against the Jews, 1933–1939." *Yad Vashem Studies* 31 (2003): 245–85.

Ponsonby, Arthur. *Falsehood in Wartime*. London: G. Allen & Unwin, 1928.

Ryback, Timothy W. *Hitler's First Victims: The Quest for Justice*. New York: Knopf, 2014.

Schleunes, Karl. *The Twisted Road to Auschwitz*. Urbana: University of Illinois Press, 1970.

Schumann, Dirk. *Politische Gewalt in der Weimarer Republik 1918–1933*. Essen: Klartext, 2001.

———. "Gewalt als Methode der nationalsozialistischen Machteroberung." In *Das Jahr 1933*, edited by Andreas Wirsching, 135–56. Göttingen: Wallstein, 2009.

Stern, Fritz. "Germany 1933: Fifty Years Later." In Fritz Stern, *Dreams and Delusions: The Drama of German History*, 119–47. New Haven: Yale University Press, 1999.

Turner, Henry Ashby, Jr. *Hitler's Thirty Days to Power: January 1933*. New Haven and London: Yale University Press, 1996.

Walter, Dirk. *Antisemitische Kriminalität und Gewalt: Judenfeindschaft in der Weimarer Republik*. Bonn: Dietz, 1999.

Wildt, Michael. *Hitler's Volksgemeinschaft and the Dynamics of Racial Exclusion: Violence against Jews in Provincial Germany, 1919–1939*. New York and Oxford: Berghahn Books, 2012.

 7

THE SA IN THE *GLEICHSCHALTUNG*
The Context of Pressure and Violence
Bruce B. Campbell

The SA was the fundamental motor of the Nazi "seizure of power"[1] and *Gleichschaltung*: it was the main source of violence for overcoming resistance and intimidating social and political institutions into accepting Nazi rule, and it was the public face of the Nazi movement as it sought to win people over to the new regime. The Nazi Party (Nationalsozialistische Deutsche Arbeiterpartei or NSDAP) used violence as a conscious political tool and welcomed it as a positive force in human society. The SA was its main tool for the exercise of violence, at least until the NSDAP took over the state and gained control over the police, the military, and the courts. But the role of the SA in the *Gleichschaltung* was not a simple one, and its actions were as much influenced by context and the pressures that existed on the SA rank and file and leadership as by cold calculation or rational planning.

The goal of this chapter is to explain why SA violence took the intense and uncontrollable form that it did. It stresses several reasons for the particularly brutal and bitter nature of violence in 1933 and into 1934 that have either previously escaped scholarly attention or not gained enough of it. Many of these factors had their roots in the political competition of the period immediately prior to the *Gleichschaltung*. Above all, this chapter emphasizes the pressures of constant mobilization and conflict since 1930, which left SA men at all levels burnt out, as well as full of hatred and the desire for revenge. Other factors are cited as well. The SA and NSDAP had great difficulty controlling both the rapid growth of their respective organizations and constant defection prior to 1933.

The structural contradictions inherent in the role and position of the SA also encouraged violence. On the one hand, there was the contradiction between the SA's role as the organ of party violence and its growing imbrications with the state, a factor that made it difficult to rein in the SA and to separate it from the state and legitimate organs of violence. On the other hand, the tensions between the SA and the party resulting from the party's larger size and public role led to growing competition for influence, power, and resources, both within the party and over external resources such as state positions. This, too, served to exacerbate the propensity for violence. Finally, this chapter includes other important elements, such as the personal characteristics of SA members, the importance of "primary male groups" in explaining SA violence, and the fundamentally local nature of politics in the Weimar Republic, and thus of SA activities and violence. All of these contributed to the extent and nature of SA violence that underpinned the rapid and total National Socialist expansion of power in 1933 and 1934.

The Long-Term Context of Nazi Violence

The general context of German politics in the late 1920s and early 1930s helps to explain the events of 1933–34, not least because of significant continuity between those events and what had transpired in 1931–32. Since the German revolution of 1918, political violence was never far below the surface, increasing during times of greater economic and political crisis, such as during the inflation of 1922 and 1923, and decreasing in the period of relative stabilization from 1924 to 1928.[2] From at least 1929 to early 1933 there was a new radicalization of politics in Germany, due both to the effects of the Great Depression and the growth of the Nazi Party and its disruption of the political system. Physical and verbal violence, intimately connected, both increased during this period. The entire political debate grew ever more violent—including the concepts and language with which this debate was conceived and conducted. Forces on the left were not free of some responsibility in this development—particularly in the increased violence of discourse—but the NSDAP was the main culprit. It deliberately followed a policy of increasing the violence of the language of political debate, while it correspondingly increased the physical violence of political confrontation. This allowed it to gain ever more public attention and intimidate its opponents, all the while casting itself as both the victim of left-wing "terror" and the only real force for "order" holding it back.

The SA, as the primary executor of street violence and the most visible public face of the Nazi movement, was central to this process. Yet at the same time it was torn by conflicting impulses. Both the SA rank and file and its leadership desired power for the Nazi movement and the personal and institutional rewards that would bring. Promises made by both the party and SA leaderships fueled the continuing readiness of

SA members to sacrifice their free time and even risk injury and death on the streets. Yet the National Socialist strategy before 1933 could work only if it did not step over a fine legal limit that might lead to its interdiction. The so-called "legality strategy" of Hitler and his henchmen was predicated on going right up to that limit, but never crossing over it. Thus the SA was both encouraged in its violent impulses and constantly pulled back and held in check. The growing activity of the SA led to increasing violence, which the party was glad to use in small doses but to which it could never give free rein as long as it did not control the courts. The result was increasing frustration within the SA. By January 1933 this frustration was deadly, at precisely the time when all restraints were lifted.[3]

An important part of this context was the rapid expansion of both the SA and party membership.[4] The huge increase in the size of the NSDAP between 1932 and 1934 was more than mirrored by the growth of the SA. At the beginning of 1931, the SA had roughly 77,000 members.[5] Within three months the SA had gone over the 100,000-member mark and was numerically stronger than the Reichswehr for the first time.[6] By 15 December 1931 the SA had grown to 260,438—more than three times its strength of just one year earlier.[7] Growth continued during 1932, so that by January 1933 membership had increased to at least 427,538.[8] And this paled in comparison to its explosive expansion in 1933 and 1934: as of 1 January 1935, the SA officially numbered 3,543,099 men,[9] although this included many who were forcibly absorbed when nationalist paramilitary organizations, or *Wehrverbände*, were taken over by the SA during the *Gleichschaltung*. The benefit of this increased membership is clear: the larger the SA, the more political weight the NSDAP had and the greater the threat it could present to its opponents—and erstwhile allies. Yet the scale of the resulting problem faced by both the SA and NSDAP leadership is equally evident: how could all these men be organizationally and ideologically integrated into a cohesive and disciplined organization?

The stress provoked by the rapid expansion of both the SA and the NSDAP was all the greater since the process was not linear: while the SA expanded dramatically before 1933, thousands also left the organization at the same time.[10] This placed great stress on unit leaders at all levels who had to work hard to ensure basic uniformity and adherence to the tenets of National Socialism. But at the same time, as the SA became larger and better organized in this period, its members expected commensurate rewards within the party, state, and economy. In a sense, the more the SA grew, the more fragile it became as expectations and resentments grew with increasing numbers. Even after 1933 the NSDAP could not fulfill SA expectations fast enough to suit all its members.

Other internal challenges related to growth added to tensions and member burnout within the SA in the early 1930s. By 1930, new SA "recruits" were increasingly young men without military experience. They had to be taught the basics, including a sense of discipline and hierarchy often quite foreign to them. Discipline could and did suffer. While the rank and file could be trained locally, expansion led to a shortage of men capable of holding key positions as "noncommissioned officers" and lower-level unit commanders or "officers."[11] These positions were the backbone of any military or paramilitary organization; it was crucial that they be filled by men with the necessary military and organizational skills who were capable of leadership. Absorbing men who had occupied similar positions in other paramilitary organizations helped,[12] as did the establishment of regional and national schools for noncommissioned officers and unit commanders,[13] but leadership remained a major problem, as did discipline. In addition, the transition from an organization based on bands of local men to a centralized national organization made up of large regional divisions was particularly challenging. It brought the SA into greater contact with the regional and national party leadership and often provoked internal conflicts between different groups of elites, not least between the very different style and character of rural versus large urban SA units.[14]

Growing Mobilization, Stress, and Internal Tension

A growing split between the SA and the party apparatus became a major issue in the early 1930s and only worsened after Hitler's nomination as chancellor. There were many signs of restlessness within the SA as early as 1930. Many of the SA's earliest members had come out of the putschist underground and did not understand or fully accept Hitler's "legality" strategy; members of an avowedly antidemocratic movement frequently had a difficult time understanding and abiding by the rules of democratic politics. The party and SA leadership expected the SA to be violent and to respond violently to attacks, but within measure. The legality strategy required that nothing take place that would set off legal action against the NSDAP by the state. But where was the line? The balance was constantly shifting, as external events emphasized one or the other policy. As a result fear, danger, and frustration hounded ordinary SA men.

Much of the friction had immediate roots in issues of money and personal power. Key points involved financing and the relationship of the SA to the party, not least over lines of subordination. Both came to a head in 1930 and again in 1931 in the so-called Stennes Putsch, when Walther Stennes, leader of the Berlin SA, led an SA attempt to take over NSDAP offices in the capital in late March and early April 1931.[15] Though Stennes lost and was forced out of the party, the basic disagreements remained. The same set of issues, expressed in a much less dramatic and confrontational fashion, also led to the removal of Franz von Pfeffer[16] and his replacement as overall SA commander by Ernst Röhm.[17] The friction cooled but never ended and reemerged in force after 1933, when competition over jobs and other tangible rewards increased. SA men often felt as if they were fighting their own party, as well as the hated "system" for which they blamed a host of personal and public ills.

The Nazi movement had a culture of total commitment, born of romantic absolutism and wartime standards of political mobilization. The subsequent use of the term *Kampfzeit* for the period before 30 January 1933 speaks volumes about the moral universe within which SA men and ordinary party members found themselves. While many did not, of course, live up to this ethos, the SA and NSDAP pushed the idea of total commitment to the point of self-sacrifice.[18] Nazi Party and SA rules were clear that total commitment was expected, and that those deemed too half-hearted should be punished or expelled.[19] The cult of sacrifice and victimhood that the SA and NSDAP deployed as a weapon used the suffering of individual SA and NSDAP men not only to justify extreme acts against opponents but also to motivate even greater commitment from the living. How could one remain inactive in the face of the sacrifice of one's comrades?[20] It was expected that SA men participate in various kinds of "duty" (*Dienst*), which could add up to a massive time commitment. "Regular" SA "duty" was usually scheduled several times a week. SA propaganda expeditions, protection for Nazi rallies and speakers, and other organizational duties took place alongside the steady drumbeat of elections and plebiscites that ensued in the latter years of the Weimar Republic, all of which kept mobilization at a fever pitch. This climate of total mobilization and self-sacrifice made the SA and NSDAP a force to be reckoned with in German politics, but it also caused individual members to pay a very high price. Burnout, psychological problems, broken families, lost jobs, poverty, alcoholism, physical and mental wounds all took a heavy toll. They also all contributed to the severity and degree of violence in 1933: self-victimization can breed brutality.

While many of the events requiring SA participation may have been local or regional in scope—such as city council elections and rallies led by local party leaders—large numbers of SA men would often be drawn in from a much larger surrounding area for bigger rallies and events. The massing of large numbers of SA men for public marches was a characteristic tactic, and to this end the NSDAP and SA were very mobile. Public transport, but especially trains and civilian motor vehicles were used extensively and planned with general staff precision, often by former general staff officers who were now serving as SA commanders.[21] The party even had a separate paramilitary National Socialist Automobile Corps (Nationalsozialistisches Automobilkorps, later the Nationalistisches Kraftfahrkorps or NSKK) under SA control.[22] The ability to mobilize men from whole regions was highly effective for the party and often very exciting for the SA and party men involved, but it also considerably added to the work and fatigue of individual SA men and increased their exposure to physical danger.

One of the greatest stresses on the SA was its role at the front line of "enemy" violence. While the NSDAP and SA were often the responsible parties when it came to initiating violence, their opponents were also quite willing to respond in kind.[23] No matter who initiated violence, the rank and file of both sides bore its effects. Wounds, even death, were a constant reality, so much so that as early as the end of 1926 the SA had instituted its own compulsory life insurance system to compensate members who were hurt or killed. From 1930 this system, called the *NS-Hilfskasse*, was made obligatory for all NSDAP members.[24] The NSDAP policy of creating a cult of martyrs and emphasizing the suffering of its members likely only intensified the fear. The SA felt that it bore the brunt of the risks faced by party members and performed a greater share of the work. Its position on the front line of party activities led to tension, fatigue, and simple exhaustion after three or more years of intense political infighting, which by 1932 had reached a state of latent civil war in some places.[25] Many SA men were thus close to the burnout point by the spring of 1933.[26] Just as fatigue can weaken restraint, the constant National Socialist stress on their own victimization, combined with real stress and fear, led to a desire for payback and revenge.

Three further elements, important but difficult to measure, may help explain how stress affected the behavior of SA members. First were the lingering physical and emotional side effects of the Great War.[27] Many SA men of the war generation had been wounded, with all of the attendant physical and emotional trauma. Head wounds, close exposure to explosions, and the aftereffects of oxygen deprivation, or *Verschüttung*, often led to lasting traumatic brain injuries.[28] The long-term effects of post-traumatic stress disorder (PTSD), not well understood and not well treated at the time, were often considerable.[29] These included problems with anger management, aggression, a propensity to violence, and sudden mood swings.[30] PTSD could also be a factor among the cohort of younger men who did not serve in the war but who suffered trauma in the postwar fighting or in SA-initiated street fighting. Second, alcohol was important in the world of the SA and often played a role in the use of violence. As with many other clubs and political organizations, local SA units almost always frequented their regular bar, or *Sturmlokal*, where they met both formally and informally, often in a specially reserved back room. Such locations became centers of both private life and public activities for SA men and often served as epicenters of SA violence.[31] Alcoholism was a real problem for SA members and surfaces frequently in the investigations during the purges of the SA in 1934 and 1935.[32] Finally, a further source of violence in 1933 and 1934, particularly after the extremely rapid growth of the SA in the early 1930s and especially in 1933, can be postulated. While definitive numbers are lacking, it is highly likely that at least some of those who joined the SA in this period had previously been among the opponents of the Nazis, or at least sympathetic to them.[33] In other words, some of the perpetrators of violence in the *Gleichschaltung* may have had something to hide or needed to make up for past "sins" by showing particular zeal in attacking the SA's opponents. This is hard to document, but the sheer scale of SA growth makes it more than plausible.

All of this stress took place and was psychologically processed within a world of all-male primary groups separate from normal work and family contexts.[34] SA men tended to suffer more from unemployment than non-SA party members. In the most extreme cases, single, unemployed SA men lived full time in so-called "SA Homes" (*SA-Heime*) established mainly in big cities to house indigent SA men. Yet even married, gainfully employed SA men tended to spend more and more time together with their "comrades," if only because they spent so much time in SA "service." These male primary groups created intimate bonds among their members but also further intensified SA values of violence, courage, and sacrifice and mixed them with anger, victimization, and a sense of entitlement.

Contemporary bio-documents from SA men underscore the above analysis and reveal an explosive mixture of feelings of victimization, putative suffering and humiliation, and physical and verbal aggression.[35] They stylize themselves as victims, feel sorry for themselves, and emphasize their personal suffering and sacrifice for the Nazi Party, particularly the wounds incurred and loss of employment. And they do so in bombastic and pathetic terms. And yet at the same time, they feel a sense of entitlement as the "true" representatives of the nation, the "true" patriots.[36] Documents such as these illustrate the aggressive and combative ethos of the SA and lay bare a key psychological mechanism: the self-definition as victim so common to SA men. How better to justify the use of violence than to stress one's own suffering?

In short, a feeling of victimization, constant mobilization leading to fatigue and stress, physical threat and often injury, uncertainty due to a lack of clear boundaries, alcohol, unemployment (or the threat thereof), an ethos of sacrifice, lack of a stable family life, and submersion in a male world of violence and anger all provided a potent and toxic cocktail for SA members. SA men emphasized their own personal sufferings (whether or not they had objectively suffered at all) to justify making others suffer; tension, stress, and lack of sleep intensified hatreds. All of these factors together greatly lowered the threshold for violence.

The SA Role in the *Gleichschaltung*

SA violence was the defining element of the *Gleichschaltung* in 1933 and 1934.[37] Other party or nationalist organizations were also empowered to carry out violence in the name of the "National Revolution," but they were far smaller in number.[38] Much of what the SA did in 1933 and 1934 is well documented, though the sheer scale of the violence is often forgotten.[39] Much still remains unknown or unknowable. On the one hand, incessant demonstrations and marches, as well as a constant, uniformed presence in the streets maintained the image of the SA as the public symbol of the NSDAP's strength and the power of the new order. On the other hand, the SA conducted what can only be labeled state terror, not only against identifiable opponents of the regime but also against anyone who got in its way or who could even potentially stand in the way of establishing a one-party dictatorship.[40] Not what the SA did, but why its members did it with such brutality and manic energy is what needs to be explained. The answer lies in the permanent mobilization of SA men combined with the sudden end to legal and disciplinary restraints. After living so close to the edge for so long, the chance to act out without limits led to an explosion of violence.

When comparing SA violence before and after 30 January 1933, the overwhelming impression is continuity: the targets of violence, the willingness to see the violence extended to "innocent" bystanders, the type of violence, and even the attitude of SA members remains largely

202 • Bruce B. Campbell

the same. Already by 1932, SA men acted as if they were entitled to be representatives of state power.[41] After January 1933 the only major differences were less restraint on SA members' actions and much less interference by the police. From the SA perspective, the "work" of violence was seamless from 1932 to 1934—the only change after 30 January 1933 was that there was virtually no chance of punishment, and the SA could act on a grand scale.

After the already high level of political violence in 1932, a rapid escalation of violence ensued in the first four months of 1933. First, the euphoria and enthusiasm generated by the formation of the Hitler-Papen government on 30 January 1933 immediately led to an upswing in violence. Simultaneously, key early legal measures of the regime helped ensure that there would be little restraint on violent actions. These included the Decree of the Reich President for the Protection of the German People of 4 February 1933, first drafted during the Papen government in 1932, which not only instituted key restrictions on freedom of the press and public demonstrations but also began the process of legally justifying acts of state terror by giving the Reich minister of the interior wide powers of interpretation. This measure encouraged high levels of violence by empowering the Reich government to appoint state commissars (*Reichskommissare*) to take over the government of any state unable to maintain public order. The Nazis thus had a strong incentive to use violence to disrupt public order so as to "legitimate" their takeover of state governments.[42]

Events in Prussia, by far the largest of the German federal states, often established a pattern for the rest of Germany. The fact that Hermann Göring was Prussian minister of the interior allowed the Nazis to move quickly to remove barriers to SA terror. He immediately began to purge the Prussian police of those who had belonged to the Social Democratic Party (Sozialdemokratische Partei Deutschlands or SPD) and all others who might oppose the Nazis and appointed SS-*Gruppenführer* Kurt Daluege as his special plenipotentiary to comb out "untrustworthy" policemen.[43] Next, on 17 February, in the Circular Directive on the Promotion of the National Movement, Göring officially ordered police to work together with nationalist paramilitary organizations such as the SA and Stahlhelm. In the same order, he specifically told the police to make use of their firearms and promised to cover any policeman who killed a left-wing opponent.[44] Several days later, on 22 February 1933, Göring ordered the appointment of SA, SS, and Stahlhelm members as auxiliary policemen, or *Hilfspolizisten*.[45] The measure was soon extended to other German federal states. Although the auxiliary police existed only until August 1933, their establishment was a key step, for the SA could now officially act in the name of the state irrespective of whether or not a given group of SA men were actually auxiliary police, thus ensuring that the police would have great difficulties reining them in.

Violence further intensified after the Reichstag fire in the night of 27–28 February and in the prelude to the Reichstag elections of 5 March 1933. Yet the floodgates of SA violence were already open well before. The subsequent Decree of the Reich President for the Protection of the People and State of 28 February 1933,[46] which essentially suspended all civil rights, and the later so-called Enabling Act, or *Ermächtigungsgesetz*,[47] merely confirmed or justified what was already practice. The violence of the SA, once liberated, was difficult to control. This was a problem faced both by the party, as it sought to control the SA, and by the SA leadership itself, which was not always in a position to fully control local actions and which in any case had very little incentive to restrain violence since the SA's use of violence was important to the party.[48] The party and the SA hierarchy had sent a clear message—both directly through the issuing of orders and the creation of a legal climate of impunity, and indirectly through their incendiary rhetoric—that violence was not only permitted but also necessary to intimidate opponents and bring social and political institutions in line with the new Nazi-led government. The Nazis' conservative coalition partners were content to go along, at least until the violence began to be directed against them.[49]

Spontaneous versus Planned Violence, and the Importance of the Local

While SA and party strategy focused largely on the national level, and the violence it perpetrated in the *Gleichschaltung* had a national reach, it was at the local level that action most directly affected a large part of the rank and file. Most political violence in Germany at this time occurred between neighbors and colleagues.[50] Naturally, this increased the scope for acts that were motivated by factors other than the strictly political, such as personal rivalry, revenge, or theft. Local structures of power, still underresearched, were also fundamental in that they provided the framework within which violence was enacted and made sense to the participants.[51] The SA rank and file tended to view the ideological mobilization of the period and the use of violence through a local lens; this is confirmed by the fact that violence was not uniform across Germany. Local context and personalities could make a big difference in the degree of violence used by SA members to pursue their goals.[52] In general, the violence seems to have been worse in areas where the level of political conflict was very high before 1933 and in eastern Germany.

Given that violence was encouraged from the top, much of it was genuinely "spontaneous" in that the initiative came from the lowest levels. As individuals and in groups, SA men very often acted on their own initiative to pick specific targets and used a remarkable level of violence to settle personal and political scores. Certainly, despite the threat to both public order and internal discipline, at least in the beginning, the party leadership welcomed this spontaneous violence as essential to the "coordination" process. The *Gleichschaltung* occurred on a huge scale, far larger than could be planned in detail. The entire process depended on the widespread, low-level initiative of individual nationalists, SA men, and party members.[53] SA violence was like a wildfire, which burned on such a wide front and so thoroughly that it rapidly achieved an unstoppable momentum. "Spontaneous" violence—that perpetuated by individual SA and party members—provided fuel to this fire, making it burn with relentless force and intensity. Yet in many cases, ostensibly "spontaneous" local acts often presaged systematic national efforts.[54] Were these "pilot projects" truly spontaneous acts that were then copied nationally when they succeeded or simply actions by subordinates jumping the gun on impending measures ordered from above? Who learned from whom? Either way, these acts gave a feeling of inevitability to the National Socialist takeover.

Of course, much violence was planned and ordered from the very top down in a deliberate manner. Yet even then it might have any of several origins: top party figures such as Göring or SS leader Heinrich Himmler, who also took over state offices, had their own armed men whom they could command directly (or via a direct internal chain of command); they could also call on SA units via the SA chain of command.[55] NS district leaders, or *Gauleiter*, as well as other regional or local office holders in the party could call on SA and SS units to act on their behalf in the same way, and in most cases could also informally draw on SA units via their long-standing personal contacts with the local SA leadership.[56] National, regional, and local SA commanders could act on their own initiative to order or carry out their own violent acts from the top down. And even low-ranking SA officers (*Führer*) and noncommissioned officers (*Unterführer*) could order their subordinates to commit violent acts. In short, the climate created by the new "government of national concentration" encouraged violence; just who made the decision in any individual case is often less important than the fact that those in charge had decided that violence would be allowed. The use of very broad-gauged violence became practically a reflex for the SA; it easily spilled over into spontaneous attacks against Jews, foreigners, business interests, members of the bourgeoisie, and simple bystanders. The Nazis understood well that the terror often hit the innocent, but they were indifferent insofar as economic interests or foreign relations were not affected.[57] It was actually quite convenient for the National Socialist leadership to be able to downplay or condemn certain acts of violence as purely "spontaneous" and "regrettable," yet perhaps "understandable," acts (from a nationalist perspective) and selectively deny responsibility for them.

It is difficult to determine the exact amount of violence committed by the SA during the *Gleichschaltung*. Numbers of men arrested and sent to "protective custody" or *Schutzhaft* are one proxy,[58] but give only a very imprecise sense of the actual level of violence. Much of the violence was extralegal, and both the state agencies and the party had an incentive to downplay its scale. Individual perpetrators also often had an incentive to conceal or minimize their own actions, particularly when they involved theft, extortion, or torture. The legal system was not completely dismantled at this time, and legal challenges to SA terror could be made and even sometimes enjoy success (in part because everything was still in flux, in part because the NSDAP sought to maintain an appearance of legality to the outside world). Consequently (and likely out of long habit as well), local and regional SA commanders often sought to hide their acts from the legal system. The "wild" concentration camps and other detention and torture sites, which were practically inaccessible to the police and often unknown to them, were one major expression of this activity.[59] They numbered in the hundreds all over Germany and were often established by subordinate SA (or SS) units. Only later did these unofficial camps evolve into state-sponsored concentration camps, all of which were taken under SS control after the Röhm Purge of June–July 1934.[60] The institution that has become more characteristic of the Third Reich than any other was an invention of the SA during the spring of 1933.

Real Violence, Symbolic Violence, Intimidation, and Learning to Be a Nazi

In the euphoria and fear of 1933, the NSDAP had a fairly small window of time within which it could do almost anything to seize and consolidate power, including the perpetration of unimaginable acts. The task was nothing less than the destruction, cooptation, or neutralization of all of government and civil society. Given the time constraints under which it operated and the limited resources at the disposal of the Nazi party leadership, including the lack of qualified administrators and leaders, the *Gleichschaltung* depended on violence and state terror. Both were widespread and quickly developed a momentum that could not have been stopped except perhaps by the intervention of the armed forces in what would then surely have become a protracted civil war. The *Gleichschaltung* of social and political institutions was a coherent process of organized state violence that entailed paradoxically a very complex mix of spontaneity and planning at every scale imaginable. It involved real physical violence and brutality, but also a complex web of propaganda and symbolic violence. Yet intimidation and propaganda were as much or even more important in this context than the actual physical violence itself, because fear and ideological justifications spread by propaganda undercut the will to resist in all but the most resolute opponents or victims of Nazi terror. In a sense, the threat of violence was greater in scale—and perhaps ultimately more effective—in intimidating opponents than outright acts of violence.

The greatest advantage of unleashing the SA was not the actual damage it did to enemies but the threatening sense of fear it cast over all of German society. The simple possibility of violence certainly caused countless Germans to accept what was happening and refrain from anything that might provoke the Nazis and their allies. The effects of the threat of violence are hard to measure, for they essentially involved actions not taken. Nevertheless, there are some hints. Despite the mix of spontaneous and planned violence, there was a clear pattern: first the SPD and KPD and their organizations came under massive attack, and then, particularly after the Reichstag elections of 5 March 1933, it was the members of non-Nazi nationalist organizations ostensibly allied with the Nazis that became the objects of intimidation. The SA used real, tangible, and systematic violence against the left on a large scale, and this violence against real or potential opponents often enough spilled over into violence against Jews and other groups. But systematic violence was not usually used against "bourgeois" or middle-class organizations or institutions, where the violence exercised against the left, combined with scattered targeted acts where necessary, was usually sufficient to intimidate those with less organization and more ideological affinity for the NSDAP. Examples of this may be found in the *Gleichschaltung* of the many clubs or *Vereine* that were so characteristic of German middle-class society. While left-wing and working-class clubs usually experienced violent acts against their members as they were seized and shut down, middle-class associations that often contained significant numbers of members who already supported the Nazis and their conservative allies usually submitted to party pressure quietly, or even willingly.[61]

What made intimidation so effective was that the SA seemed to be everywhere. Constant propaganda, both on an individual and a mass scale, was a primary task for the SA during the *Gleichschaltung*. The first act of the SA on the evening of 30 January, the day of Hitler's installation as chancellor, was to organize mass torchlight marches through Berlin and other cities and towns. The role of the SA as living propaganda is an important aspect of the pall it cast over all of Germany. Even during the *Gleichschaltung*, the SA remained the public face of the NSDAP and played an important role in propaganda. Violence—being seen to "stand up to the left" and "defend" Germany—was just one but nevertheless essential component of its propaganda strategy. Another was the very characteristic "propaganda of the masses" in the form of SA marches and ceremonies. In this way National Socialist power and authority were projected into every corner of Germany, literally down the home streets of supporters and opponents alike. This allowed the Nazis to project an image of discipline and overwhelming, omnipresent strength. The SA choked off opposition not just through violence but by occupying and filling public space. Violence was propaganda, and propaganda generated violence; the two reinforced each other and could not be separated.

Another important role for the SA in the *Gleichschaltung*, again connected to the rapid expansion of its membership, was its socialization and acculturation function. For many latecomers to the Nazi movement, the SA was their first experience of belonging to and being active in a party organization—their first socialization as Nazis and members of the *Volksgemeinschaft*. By the late spring of 1934, this included, at least nominally, a significant percentage of German men between eighteen and forty-five years of age. Even for those on the left, the SA was often their main model for how one was to act as a part of the new order. For many, the SA epitomized the example of what life under National Socialism was supposed to be. Membership in the SA gave men a claim to being a part of the National Socialist movement, belonging to a community greater than the sum of its parts, while isolating them from all previous ties in society, be they to family, friends, or organizations. This sense of participating in a *Volksgemeinschaft*, by itself, was a powerful agent for the *Gleichschaltung* of German society. Theories of totalitarianism illustrate how fascist movements complemented the atomization of society—that is, the destruction of traditional social relationships— with efforts to whip up a sense of belonging to a larger movement; by including such a large portion of German society in its ranks, the SA had become a wholly new kind of tool for the coordination and indoctrination of an entire society, as well as a power to be reckoned with even apart from the party.[62]

A Structural Complication

An additional complication in assessing the role of the SA in the *Gleichschaltung* arises in the form of the progressive imbrication of the SA and other NS Party affiliates in the covert national defense and rearmament efforts of the Reichswehr. The Nazi assumption of power is often characterized as a violent invasion and occupation of the German state by the NSDAP—and this is surely true, in part. But there is also a counternarrative of the mutual penetration of the state and SA. This is not simply the rush of Nazi leaders to seize attractive state positions and jobs, although this was important and motivated much violence; it is also the placing of Nazi Party organizations such as the SA on a quasi-state footing in terms of financing and their often direct participation in state tasks, projects, and institutions. For the SA, this refers less to its temporary role as the "auxiliary police"—which was little more than a legal fig leaf covering state violence—and more to the expansion of its existing cooperation with the military, which grew out of the decision to begin covert rearmament in violation of the Versailles Treaty.

By the spring of 1933, the SA had become increasingly involved in covert military training. This built on a much older covert relationship between the SA and the Reichswehr, going back at least to 1931.[63] Some entire SA units, such as the SA *Feldjägerkorps*,[64] were transferred to state purposes and given police functions or even placed under direct state control. Within the SA, a separate organization, the Director of Training Activities (*Chef des Ausbildungswesens* or Chef-AW), was formed to conduct secret military training in cooperation with the armed forces.[65] The Chef-AW not only included the border-protection units already filled with SA men but was a much larger undertaking that existed all across Germany.[66] Other SA or SS units, such as the SS Leibstandarte and various SA guard units, were given quasi-state status.[67] As a result, the conflation and amalgamation of party and state occurred quickly. Although the military was not subject to the same level of *Gleichschaltung* as the state and civil society, it was unable—or unwilling—to remain aloof from the Nazi regime. Conversely, SA involvement in covert rearmament and border protection meant that it was impossible to control SA violence given the secrecy of the relationship between the SA and the Armed Forces and the growing sense that the SA was acting as an organ of state.

How to Control the Wildfire: Permanent Purge and Reorganization

But a wildfire can easily get out of control. Once the tidal wave of violence unleashed in the spring of 1933 had largely achieved its goal, it had to be reined in. Already by the late spring of that year, a combination of alcohol and impunity had turned many SA and SS men into a real public danger and threatened the internal discipline of the organization. The Röhm Purge of June–July 1934 sought to provide an answer. Much has been written about the motivation for the violent purge of the SA. However complex those reasons may have been,[68] these events and the motivations that lay behind them need to be placed in a larger context.

In a sense, the SA existed in a state of permanent purge between 1930 and 1935.[69] The SA began a systematic process of purging its own organization as early as 1932.[70] A second internal reorganization and self-purge was begun in the spring of 1933,[71] but this was not pursued as vigorously as needed to bring the SA back into line. A much more thorough and violent purge soon followed, this time conducted by the party with state help. It began with the arrest and murder of Ernst Röhm and a significant part of the higher SA leadership from 30 June to 2 July 1934.[72] It was at first quite chaotic due in large part to the complexity of the inner-party infighting behind it, but it then became more planned and institutional. This last purge, which lasted until early 1936, was conducted largely by the SA itself after July 1934. It was designed not only to remove "bad apples" of all kinds, including those who were simply burned out or militarily incompetent, but also to bring the SA down to a more manageable and sustainable size and thus complete its transition into an institution supporting the status quo. In this sense, the Röhm Purge was merely a violent episode in a much longer process.

After the events of 1932–34, some sort of a purge of the SA, violent or not, would have been necessary in any case. The fact that the party and SS also purged their own memberships between mid-1934 and 1936 is a reflection of this fact.[73] The differences in what was needed and expected of the SA as a revolutionary body seeking power outside of the state, and then as a semi-state/semi-private representative of state power were so vast that large-scale changes in structure and personnel were inevitable. The choice for Hitler and the SA and party leaderships in 1934 was not *if*, but *how* the transition was to take place and *how* this would be managed. The post-purge SA managed the transition from a revolutionary body seeking to subvert and combat the state into a semi-state institution dedicated to maintaining the new status quo very well in 1935 and 1936. It was not SA incompetence that forced the decision to purge it violently in 1934 but rather reasons specific to the inner workings of the National Socialist movement, such as its cliquishness, the importance of individual leaders and their personal rivalries, and the Nazi belief in violence as a positive force.

Conclusion

The *Gleichschaltung* depended upon the large-scale mobilization of Nazis and their supporters. It would not have been possible without widespread violence, which "lubricated" everything else. The SA, together with the then-subordinate SS and aided by nationalist allies, was the main agent of that violence. The ease with which it is possible to motivate humans to initiate or take part in violent acts alone cannot explain either the scale or the brutality of the violence during the NS *Gleichschaltung*. Nor can it be overlooked that fear, exhaustion, and sheer burnout played a major role in making the SA prone to extreme violence. By 1933, party and SA cadres alike were exhausted, worn thin, overextended, and on the edge of breakdown. This had a direct impact on the level of violence: it was a primal outbreak of a specific group of men who found themselves liberated from constraint, fear of violence to themselves, and fear of punishment. Moreover, outsider movements like the SA and NSDAP always have a high percentage of members who are social outsiders and marginal figures, often with psychological or moral weaknesses. A revolution that succeeds in destroying or significantly altering an existing society cannot be accomplished by those who have a stake in the existing order. At the same time, no revolution is successful unless it also attracts those who are well integrated and capable of running a modern state and economy. The success of the NSDAP in seizing power can be partially explained by the fact that by 1933 its movement encompassed both elements.[74] If the more unstable and marginal elements were eventually weeded out after July 1934, they were no less explosive than before; they had simply done their duty and could be safely eliminated afterward.

Second, the cliché "all politics is local" aptly describes the situation in Germany in the 1920s and 1930s. The fact that neighbors were often either political opponents or trusted allies served to increase the level of violence. The close proximity of opponents meant constant friction, especially when political disagreements inevitably became personal. Much of the most severe violence during the *Gleichschaltung* occurred when individual SA men or small groups decided to settle personal scores. Civil wars are often more brutal than conventional wars, and the usual explanation is that civil wars involve people who resemble each other and know each other intimately. This is certainly the case in the context of the latent civil war that existed in Germany in 1932 and 1933. The fact that often tangible benefits could be gained caused the violence to spread and intensify even more.

Still, the role of the SA in the *Gleichschaltung* should not be reduced to the perpetuation of violence alone. The SA was always the most public face of the Nazi Party. If it was responsible for vast and often random violence, it also provided a positive face for the party through constant propaganda and public marches and other similar mass events. The SA also gave many an opportunity to participate directly in the "national uprising" [*nationale Erhebung*] that spread through Germany in the first months of 1933. By expanding from roughly five hundred thousand men in early January 1933 to a maximum of over four million by the late spring of 1934, the SA integrated a large percentage of young male Germans (albeit often only temporarily and incompletely) into the Nazi movement. This, too, was a form of *Gleichschaltung*, particularly for those of a nationalist persuasion. Transferring large numbers of men already active in nationalist paramilitary organizations such as the Stahlhelm to the SA not only prevented them from becoming potential opponents of the Nazi takeover, it also gave many their first taste of actively participating in the Nazi movement.

Many of the factors that made the SA such a key organization in German politics between 1930 and 1934 also ultimately led to its purge by the party and eclipse by the SS. Neither the explosive growth and personal mobilization of the SA nor the level of violence it exercised were sustainable in the long term. By the time the Nazi Party was firmly in power, and all potential opponents were either destroyed or cowed, something had to change. Yet most of the contextual problems faced by the SA between 1929 and 1936 were shared by the entire NSDAP as a whole; the SA simply faced these problems in a more concentrated and visible form. As a result, the *Gleichschaltung* was not simply a process of asserting and deepening the power of the NSDAP vis-à-vis the state and civil society, but it also provided an ongoing mechanism for internal purges and the reordering of the entire NS apparatus. The party and its organizations had to undergo their own *Gleichschaltung* in the transition from an insurgent political movement into a state party. In a climate of easy violence, it is no surprise that this competition between different parts of the Nazi movement and different individuals within it was often violent, even murderous. The SA could be thoroughly and publicly purged not only to discipline and streamline the organiza-tion—it had gotten wildly out of hand—but also to make a public sacri-fice to the German nation, a promise of future order and stability under Nazi rule. It was ultimately this "social bargain" and not only the famil-iar one with the military that led to the Röhm Purge. Yet the SA was not innocent, not some sort of a sacrificial lamb on the altar of Hitler's ego. It was an eager and widespread participant in extreme violence and a fundamental component of a movement that saw violence not as a means to an end but as a positive moral force. There is no excuse for the actions of the SA just as there is no excuse for those party members and others who perpetrated no violence themselves, but merely tolerated and profited from the violence of others. The SA was a violent organiza-tion at a brutal time. Many factors helped to intensify the violence in which it was engaged, but none of them provide an adequate excuse for the way in which it behaved.

Bruce B. Campbell is the Class of 1964 Associate Professor of German Studies and German Studies program director at the College of William & Mary. Major works include *The SA Generals and the Rise of Nazism* (University Press of Kentucky, 1998, 2004) and two coedited volumes: *Death Squads in Global Perspective: Murder with Deniability* (with Arthur Brenner; St Martin's, 2000, 2002) and *Detectives, Dystopias and Poplit: Studies in Modern German Genre Fiction* (with Alison Guenther-Pal and Vibeke Petersen; Camden House, 2013). He is currently working on two books, one about radio and modernity in Germany, and the other a biography of the Freikorps leader and putschist Gerhard Rossbach.

Notes

1. The Nazis themselves liked to use the term *Machtergreifung* or "seizure of power." The reality of events, as this volume shows, was more complicated.
2. In general, see Dirk Schumann, *Politische Gewalt in der Weimarer Republik 1918–1933* (Essen: Klartext, 2001).
3. On the "legality policy" and the frustrations of the SA, see Robert H. Frank, "Hitler and the National Socialist Coalition 1924–1932" (PhD diss., Johns Hopkins University, 1969), chapter 10. See also Klaus Rüffler, *Vom Münchener Landfriedensbruch bis zum Mord von Potempa: Der "Legalitätskurs" der NSDAP* (Frankfurt/Berlin: Lang, 1994).

4. On the NSDAP, see Michael H. Kater, *The Nazi Party: A Social Profile of Members and Leaders 1919–1945* (Cambridge, MA: Harvard University Press, 1983).

5. Andreas Werner, "SA: 'Wehrverband,' 'Parteitruppe,' oder 'Revolutions-armee'? Studien zur Geschichte der SA und der NSDAP 1920–1933" (PhD diss., Friedrich-Alexander-Universität zu Erlangen-Nürnberg, 1964), 544. This figure should be treated as an estimate.

6. Werner, "SA," 544–45. This had more of a symbolic meaning than anything else, since the SA could not at all be compared to the Reichswehr in terms of training, discipline, or equipment.

7. For the source of these statistics, see Oberste SA-Führung (High Command of the SA, henceforth OSAF) Ib Nr. 316/32, 1 January 1932, BA Berlin, NS 23, 123, and OSAF, Abteilung I, 1 February 1932, BA Berlin, Sammlung Schumacher (Bestand R 187), Ordner 415. Werner, 550–51, gives a January 1932 figure of 290,941 men.

8. A *Schnellbrief* from the Oberste SA-Führung Command Office (*Führungsamt*) to the head of the SA *Reichsführerschule* (F2 Nr. 51328), 3 September 1935, BA Berlin, NS 23, 337, puts the strength of the SA in January 1933 at 427,538. This figure likely does not include either the SS or the Austrian SA. Werner, "SA," 551–52, gives a slightly different figure of 518,977.

9. NSDAP, Reichsorganisationsleiter der NSDAP, *Parteistatistik* (Munich: Hauptorganisationsamt, Amt Statistik, 1935), 3:70–71. As Heinrich Bennecke rightly points out, this figure is likely well under the spring 1934 maximum size of the SA, since many were purged or left voluntarily after the June–July 1934 Röhm Purge. Heinrich Bennecke, *Hitler und die SA*, (Munich and Vienna: Günter Olzog Verlag, 1962), 214.

10. Mathilde Jamin, "Zur Rolle der SA im nationalsozialistischen Herrschafts-system," in *Der "Führerstaat": Mythos und Realität; Studien zur Struktur und Politik des Dritten Reiches*, ed. Gerhard Hirschfeld and Lothar Kettenacker (Stuttgart: Klett-Cotta, 1981), 332.

11. The SA itself was very careful never to use the word "officer" (*Offizier*), but instead used the German word stem *"Führer"* (leader). This was at once the expression of a new concept of leadership and a careful effort to distinguish the SA from the army.

12. Bruce Campbell, *The SA Generals and the Rise of Nazism* (Lexington: University Press of Kentucky, 1998).

13. Special schools for SA leaders were first organized locally and regionally. These were put on a national basis early in 1931, with the foundation of the SA *Reichsführerschule*, and soon after a series of *"SA-Führer-Vorschulen."* See Werner, "SA," 555–64.

14. Dietrich Orlow, *The History of the Nazi Party, 1933–1945* (Pittsburgh, PA: Pittsburgh University Press, 1973), 141.

15. On the Stennes Putsch, see Werner, "SA," 461–85, 521–35; Robert H. Frank, "Hitler and the National Socialist Coalition 1924–1932" (PhD diss., Johns Hopkins University, 1969), chapters 8 and 11; Orlow, *History of the Nazi Party*, 210–34; Walther Stennes, ed., *Wie es zur Stennes-Aktion kam!* (Berlin: Hausdruck Walther Stennes, n.d.); and Charles Drage, *The Amiable Prussian* (London: Anthony Blond Ltd., 1958).

16. Actually Franz Pfeffer von Salomon. He was the brother of the nationalist writer Ernst von Salomon.
17. See Institut für Zeitgeschichte, Munich (hereafter cited as IfZ Munich), Zeugenschriften 177, Franz von Pfeffer [Franz Pfeffer von Salomon], vol. 1. See also Werner, "SA," 517–35, and Eleanor Hancock, *Ernst Röhm: Hitler's SA Chief of Staff* (New York: Palgrave MacMillan, 2008).
18. See Jay W. Baird, *To Die for Germany: Heroes in the Nazi Pantheon* (Bloomington: Indiana University Press, 1992).
19. For example, the *Dienstvorschrift für die P.O. der N.S.D.A.P.* states that party members must be ready to sacrifice themselves and everything they own: "Wer Nationalsozialist wird, tritt nicht irgendeiner Partei bei, sondern er wird damit Soldat der Freiheitsbewegung Deutschlands. Das bedeutet mehr, weit mehr, als seinen Beitrag zahlen und Mitgliederversammlungen besuchen. Er übernimmt damit die heilige Verpflichtung alles, was er hat, sich selbst und sein Gut, wenn es sein muss, Deutschland zu widmen. Nur wer das kann, soll Nationalsozialist werden." See NSDAP, der Führer, *Dienst-Vorschrift für die P.O. der N.S.D.A.P.* (Munich, 1932), 34, §88.
20. SA personnel questionnaires had a separate category for injuries and punishment incurred on behalf of the party as a formal measure of commitment and worth. See *"Personalfragebogen für die Anlegung der SA-Personalakte"* or the earlier *"SA-Führer-Fragebogen"* (which asked only about punishment, but contained a question under military service about wounds, which was usually also used for injuries incurred during political clashes by the SA men who filled it out). In general, see Baird, *To Die for Germany*.
21. Many SA leaders were former staff officers or had gained staff experience in the military. See Campbell, *SA Generals*, 72, 93.
22. Franz Seidler, "Das Nationalsozialistische Kraftfahrkorps und die Organisation Todt im Zweiten Weltkrieg: Die Entwicklung des NSKK bis 1939," *Vierteljahreshefte für Zeitgeschichte* 32 (1984): 625–36.
23. See Eve Rosenhaft, *Beating the Fascists? German Communists and Political Violence* (Cambridge: Cambridge University Press, 2008), and Timothy Scott Brown, *Weimar Radicals: Nazis and Communists between Authenticity and Performance* (New York and Oxford: Berghahn Books, 2016).
24. Werner, "SA," 408–15. See also Orlow, *History of the Nazi Party*, 82, 141–43, 203, 213, 220.
25. Though not by any means the first work to speak of 1932 in these terms, see Dirk Blasius, *Weimars Ende: Bürgerkrieg und Politik 1930–1933* (Göttingen: Vandenhoeck and Ruprecht, 2005).
26. This is a common theme in personal narratives and bio-documents produced by SA members. For example, see *Lebenslauf* of Walter Oscar Arthur Schmidt (born June 1903, Waldkirchen i.E.), 16, in NARA, microfilmed records received from the Berlin Document Center (hereafter cited as BDC), SA Personnel Files. Microfilm Publication A3341, Series "SA-Kartei," roll B195.
27. This theme is so important, and so underresearched, that it deserves its own monograph.
28. See the case of Josef Schmidt, fn. 36 below.

29. SA-*Standartenführer* Ernst Schmid (born 8 April 1894, Steinberg) is a good example of an SA leader who manifested symptoms of PTSD or some other neurological disorder. See his *Lebenslauf* of 25 September 1944 in BDC, now BA-Berlin.

30. On post-traumatic stress syndrome in general, see American Psychiatric Association (APA), *Diagnostic and Statistical Manual of Mental Disorders*, revised 4th ed. (Washington, DC: American Psychiatric Association, 2000); Board on Population Health and Public Health Practice, *Posttraumatic Stress Disorder: Diagnosis and Assessment* (Washington, DC: National Academies Press, 2006); and Cheryl A. Roberts, *Coping with Post-Traumatic Stress Disorder: A Guide for Families*. (Jefferson, NC: McFarland, 2011).

31. Sven Reichardt, *Faschistische Kampfbünde: Gewalt und Gemeinschaft im italienischen Squadrismus und in der deutschen SA* (Cologne, Weimar, Vienna: Böhlau Verlag, 2002), 435–75.

32. See, for example, the case of SA-*Gruppenführer* Herbert Fust (born 1 June 1899). In particular, see his SA Disciplinary Court (*Disziplinargericht*) file F44/M/34, in BDC, now BA-Berlin. There is room for much more research on alcohol and drug use within the SA.

33. This was a common accusation against the SA, though concrete proof is difficult to find in most cases.

34. See Andrew Wackerfuss, *Stormtrooper Families: Homosexuality and Community in the Early Nazi Movement* (New York: Harrington Park Press, 2015).

35. In general, see Bruce Campbell, "Autobiographies of Violence: The SA in Its Own Words" *Central European History* 46 (2013): 217–37.

36. See, for example, the SA personnel file of Josef Schmidt, in NARA, BDC, SA Personnel Files, Microfilm Publication A3341, Series "SA-P Akten," roll D241, file of Josef Schmidt (born 8 April 1894). See also his *Lebenslauf* of 25 September 1944.

37. Until July 1934 the SS was still organizationally part of the SA.

38. Aside from NS organizations such as the SA, SS, and NSKK, members of some nationalist paramilitary organizations such as the Stahlhelm were deputized in Prussia and some other federal states as "auxiliary policemen."

39. See Michael Wildt, *Volksgemeinschaft als Selbstermächtigung: Gewalt gegen Juden in der deutschen Provinz 1919 bis 1939* (Hamburg: Hamburger Edition, 2007).

40. This has been documented elsewhere in great detail; two books stand out: Michael Wildt, *Volksgemeinschaft als Selbstermächtigung: Gewalt gegen Juden in der deutschen Provinz 1919 bis 1939* (Hamburg: Hamburger Edition, 2007), and Dirk Erb, ed., *Gleichgeschaltet: Der Nazi-Terror gegen Gewerkschaften und Berufsverbände 1930 bis 1933; Eine Dokumentation* (Göttingen: Steidl, 2001). Both of these books compile large bodies of grassroots testimony from both perpetrators and victims of NS terror, but especially the latter. Too much of our understanding of the *Gleichschaltung* still comes mainly from state and Nazi Party records; the victims' perspectives are a needed corrective. For an important step in this direction, see Hermann Beck's use of

DNVP records and appeals of DNVP politicians to the Reich chancery in Hermann Beck, *The Fateful Alliance: German Conservatives and Nazis in 1933: The Machtergreifung in a New Light* (New York and Oxford: Berghahn Books, 2008).

41. See, for example, the actions of the SA in Frankenthal (Pfalz) in 1932, which gave the order "Stop, or we'll shoot" when chasing men who were caught painting anti-Nazi graffiti. In Erb, *Gleichgeschaltet*, 34–36. Given the fact that the SA already felt as if it represented the state in 1932, the debate over Hitler's "legality policy" takes on a new light.

42. Hans Mommsen, "Entstehung und Bedeutung des Ermächtigungsgesetzes vom 23. März 1933 (Vortrag, gehalten auf einer Veranstaltung des 'Gesprächskreises Geschichte' in der Friedrich-Ebert-Stiftung Bonn am 24. März 2003)," in *Gesprächskreis Geschichte*, Heft 53 (Bonn: Friedrich Ebert Stiftung, 2003), 11. See also Beck, *Fateful Alliance*, 119, 124–26.

43. This step paralleled similar purges of individual top civil servants elsewhere in Prussia, other states, and in the national government, long before the *"Gesetz zur Wiederherstellung des Berufsbeamtentums"* of 8 April 1933.

44. *"Runderlaß über 'Förderung der nationalen Bewegung,'"* 17 February 1933," in *Ministerialblatt für die Preußische innere Verwaltung* 1 (1933): 169, cited in Karl Dietrich Bracher, Wolfgang Sauer, Gerhard Schulz, *Die nationalsozialistische Machtergreifung: Studien zur Errichtung des totalitären Herrschaftssystems in Deutschland 1933/34* (Wiesbaden: Springer Fachmedien, 1960), 865.

45. See Hans Buchheim, "SA-Hilfspolizei, SA-Feldpolizei und Feldjägerkorps und diebeamtenrechtliche Stellung ihrer Angehörigen," in *Gutachten des Instituts für Zeitgeschichte*, vol. 1 (Munich: Institut für Zeitgeschichte, 1958), 335–40. See also Martin Schuster, "Die SA in der nationalsozialistischen 'Machtergreifung' in Berlin und Brandenburg 1926–1934" (PhD diss., Technische Universität Berlin, 2005).

46. *"Die Verordnung des Reichspräsidenten zum Schutz von Volk und Staat vom 28. Februar 1933,"* in *Reichsgesetzblatt* (hereafter cited as RGBl) 1933, Teil I, 83.

47. *"Gesetz zur Behebung der Not von Volk und Staat,"* in RGBl 1933, Teil I, 141.

48. SA terror is well documented in *Braunbuch über Reichstagsbrand und Hitler-Terror*, with a foreword by Lord Marley. *Bibliothèque de philosophie scientifique* (Basel: Universum Bücherei, 1933). See also Mathilde Jamin, *Zwischen den Klassen: Zur Sozialstruktur der SA-Führerschaft* (Wuppertal: Peter Hammer Verlag, 1984), 347ff, simple terror; 335ff, acts against businesses.

49. See Beck, *Fateful Alliance*, chapters 2 and 3.

50. For example, see Stefan Hördler, ed., *SA-Terror als Herrschaftssicherung: "Köpenicker Blutwoche" und öffentliche Gewalt im Nationalsozialismus* (Berlin: Metropol Verlag, 2013), which documents this in great detail for Berlin.

51. See Hördler, ed., *SA-Terror*, for a good example of what this approach can bring. A pioneering microstudy, Hördler's book shows just how large-scale national violence played out at a grassroots level. See in particular Hördler's chapter "Ideologie, Machtinszenierung und Exzess: Taten und Täter der 'Köpenicker Blutwoche,'" 83–104, and the chapter by Sven Reichardt, "Vergemeinschaftung durch Gewalt: Der SA-'Mördersturm 33'" in Berlin-Charlottenburg." Both in Hördler, ed., *SA Terror*, 110–29.

52. Beck, *Fateful Alliance*, 115.
53. See Schuster, "Die SA in der nationalsozialistischen 'Machtergreifung,'" 250–52. Schuster discounts "spontaneous" violence in the sense that he contends that all SA men were involved in the discovery and "punishment" of opponents and were ordered to act on their own initiative, even without specific orders.
54. For example, in Bitterfeld the *Gewerkschaftshaus* was forcibly occupied by SA units on 1 April 1933, one month before all union buildings were systematically occupied across Germany on 2 May 1933. See Erb, ed., *Gleichgeschaltet*, 15.
55. Himmler, of course, had the SS, and as he took on more and more police functions, also police units. Göring had the Prussian police, and he rapidly formed his own armed guard under their auspices. See Reinhard Stumpf, "Die Luftwaffe als drittes Heer: Die Luftwaffen-Erdkampfverbände und das Problem der Sonderheere 1933 bis 1945," in *Soziale Bewegung und Politische Verfassung: Werner Conze zum 31.12.75*, ed. Ulrich Englehardt, Volker Sellin, and Horst Stuck (Stuttgart: Klett Verlag, 1976), 857–94.
56. The PO (Politische Organisation) of the NSDAP and the SA had essentially parallel hierarchies. They were ordered to cooperate and work together, but party leaders were specifically forbidden to intervene in internal SA affairs. *Politische Leiter* (party members in leadership positions) were allowed to request SA assistance and action when they found it necessary, and both political and SA leaders were ordered to coordinate actions in their districts. See NSDAP, Oberste SA-Führung, *Dienstvorschrift für die SA der NSDAP* (Diessen vor München: Jos. Huber Verlag, 1932), 1:70–76. The degree of actual cooperation varied by location, time period, and, above all, the individuals involved. In most cases, party and SA leaders in a given area all knew each other quite well and often for much longer than they had belonged to the NSDAP.
57. Erb, ed., *Gleichgeschaltet*, 16–17.
58. Beck, *Fateful Alliance*, 115.
59. Most early "wild" concentration camps were established by the SA, but others were run by the SS, various state ministries of the interior, or the Gestapo. See note 60 below.
60. On the concentration camps, see Geoffrey P. Megargee and United States Holocaust Memorial Museum, *The United States Holocaust Memorial Museum Encyclopedia of Camps and Ghettos, 1933–1945* (Bloomington: Indiana University Press, 2009); and Wolfgang Benz and Barbara Distel, eds., *Der Ort des Terrors: Geschichte der nationalsozialistischen Konzentrationslager*, 9 vols. (Munich: Beck, 2005–9).
61. This is borne out by the example of radio hobby clubs in Germany, such as the *Gleichschaltung* of the *Funktechnischer Verein* (FTV) branch club in the Beuth-Schule. See "Aus den Vereinen..." in *Funk: Die Wochenschrift des Funkwesens* 11, no. 20 (12 May 1933): Programmteil, 1–4, and "FTV, Gruppe Beuth-Schule," in "Aus den Vereinen ...," ibid., no. 19 (5 May 1933): Programmteil, 1–4.

62. For example, see Hannah Arendt, *The Origins of Totalitarianism* (New York: World Publishers, 1958, 1951); Reinhard Bendix, "Social Stratification and Social Power," *American Political Science Review* 46 (1952): 357–75; and William S. Kornhauser, *The Politics of Mass Society* (Glencoe, IL: Free Press, 1959). For a critique of the "mass society" hypothesis, see Bernt Hagtvet, "The Theory of Mass Society and the Collapse of the Weimar Republic: A Re-Examination," in *Who Were the Fascists? The Social Roots of European Fascism*, ed. Bernt Hagtvet et al. (Bergen, Oslo, Tromso: Universitetsforlaget, 1980), 66–117 and Jürgen Falter, *Hitler's Wähler* (Munich: C. H. Beck, 1991).

63. Rudolf Absolon, *Die Wehrmacht im Dritten Reich*, 4 vols. (Boppard: Harald Boldt Verlag, 1969–79), 1:35–39. See also Jun Nakata, *Der Grenz- und Landesschutz in der Weimarer Republik 1918–1933: Die Geheime Aufrüstung und die deutsche Gesellschaft* (Freiburg: Rombach Verlag/Militärgeschichtliches Forschungsamt, 2002), and Heinrich Bennecke, *Die Reichswehr und der "Röhm-Putsch"* (Munich and Vienna: Günter Olzog Verlag, 1964). Bennecke is an indispensable voice here, but hardly objective, since he himself was an SA-*Obergruppenführer* and later a Wehrmacht officer.

64. See Hans Buchheim, "SA-Hilfspolizei, SA-Feldpolizei und Feldjägerkorps und die beamtenrechtliche Stellung ihrer Angehörigen," in *Gutachten des Instituts für Zeitgeschichte* 1: 335–40. See also Schuster, "Die SA in der nationalsozialistischen 'Machtergreifung,'" 226–30.

65. On the Chef-AW organization, see Thilo Vogelsang, "Der Chef des Ausbildungswesens (Chef AW)," in *Gutachten des Instituts für Zeitgeschichte* (Stuttgart: Deutsche Verlagsanstalt, 1966), 2:146–56; and Absolon, *Wehrmacht*, 1:10–113.

66. OSAF ChM. 181/33 Betr: Marine-Stürme der SA of 12 July 1933, and "Erfahrungsbericht über die Ausbildung in Nachrichtensport" (Geheim) (o.D.) [1933 or 34]; SA der NSDAP, Marinestandarte 7, Gr. Kurpfalz Br.B. Nr.64/35a geh betr: Ausbildung in Nachrichtensport (Geheim) of 12 April 35, both in BA Berlin, Sammlung Schumacher, Ordner 405, as well as FOa, "Das Nachrichtenwesen der S.A.," of 4 April 1938, BA Berlin, NS 23, 194.

67. Bernd Wegner, *Hitlers Politische Soldaten: Die Waffen-SS 1933–1945; Leitbild, Struktur und Funktion einer nationalsozialistischen Elite*. Sammlung Schöningh zur Geschichte und Gegenwart (Paderborn: Ferdinand Schöningh, 2008), 81–84. See also James J. Weingartner, "Sepp Dietrich, Heinrich Himmler, and the Leibstandarte SS Adolf Hitler, 1933–1938," *Central European History* 1 (1968): 264–84.

68. Many reasons have been put forward to explain the Röhm Purge. Hitler's need to win over the Reichswehr leadership has the most traction. For example, see David Jablonsky, "Röhm and Hitler: The Continuity of Political-Military Discord," *Journal of Contemporary History* 23 (1988): 367–86. But in the past, other specialists on the topic have cited personal intrigues among the top party leadership, as well as the fear of SA "social-ism" and hatred of homosexuals. On the role of personal intrigues, see Heinz Höhne, *Mordsache Röhm. Hitlers Durchbruch zur Alleinherrschaft 1933–1934* (Hamburg, Spiegel-Verlag/Rowohlt, 1984). On the fear of socialism,

see Bloch, *SA*, and Gallo, *Long Knives*; and on the hatred of homosexuals, Hans Rudolf Wahl, "'National-Päderasten?' Zur Geschichte der (Berliner) SA-Führung 1925–1934," *Zeitschrift für Geschichtswissenschaft* 56 (2008): 442–59.

69. Heinrich Bennecke, who was a leading member of the SA from the very beginning down to the bitter end, underscored the constant necessity in his experience of weeding out unfit SA men. See Heinrich Bennecke and Andreas Peschel, *Die SA in Sachsen vor der "Machtübernahme": Nachgelassenes von Heinrich Bennecke (1902–1972)* (Beucha-Markkleeberg: Sax Verlag, 2012), 34–40.

70. At the lifting of the SA ban in June 1932, the SA High Command required that all SA leaders be reconfirmed in their positions. OSAF IIa Nr. 1549/32, "Neuaufstellung der SA und SS. Führerbefehl Nr.1" of 1 July 1932, in BA Berlin, Schumacher Sammlung, Ordner 404.

71. Der Oberster SA-Führer, Chef Nr. 1227, Betrifft: "Auffassung über die Lage" of 1 June 1933, BA Berlin, NS 23, 125.

72. Characteristically, the party also used the situation to kill a number of other enemies, such as General Kurt von Schleicher, Gregor Strasser, and Edgar Jung. See Höhne, *Mordsache Röhm*, chapter 7 and appendix, 319–21.

73. Orlow, *History of the Nazi Party*, chapter 3.

74. See Campbell, *SA Generals*, for proof that the top levels of the SA leadership were often highly educated and socially well integrated.

Bibliography

Absolon, Rudolf. *Die Wehrmacht im Dritten Reich*. 4 vols. Schriften des Bundesarchivs, no. 16. Boppard am Rhine: Harald Boldt Verlag, 1969–79.

Bennecke, Heinrich. *Hitler und die SA*. Munich and Vienna: Günter Olzog Verlag, 1962.

———. *Die Reichswehr und der "Röhm-Putsch."* Munich and Vienna: Günter Olzog Verlag, 1964.

Bessel, Richard. *Political Violence and the Rise of Nazism: The Storm Troopers in Eastern Germany 1925–1934*. New Haven, CT: Yale University Press, 1984.

Bloch, Charles, *Die SA und die Krise des NS-Regimes 1934*. Frankfurt: Suhrkamp Verlag, 1970.

Brown, Timothy S. *Weimar Radicals: Nazis and Communists between Authenticity and Performance*. New York and Oxford: Berghahn Books, 2009.

Campbell, Bruce. "The SA after the Röhm Purge and the Institutionalized State of Emergency in the Third Reich." *Journal of Contemporary History* 28 (1993): 659–74.

———. *The SA Generals and the Rise of Nazism*. Lexington: University Press of Kentucky, 1998.

———. "Autobiographies of Violence: The SA in Its Own Words." *Central European History* 46 (2013): 217–37.

———. "Gewalt bis in die obersten Ränge: Die Höheren SA-Führer der SA-Gruppe Berlin-Brandenburg." In *Der SA-Terror als Herrschaftssicherung*

":*Köpinecker Blutwoche*" *und Öffentliche Gewalt im frühen Nationalsozialismus*, edited by Stefan Hördler, 62–82. Berlin: Metropol Verlag, 2013.

Cuomo, Glenn R. "The NSDAP's Enduring Shadow: Putting in Perspective the Recent Outing of Brown Octogenarians." *German Studies Review* 35 (2012): 265–88.

Erb, Dirk, ed. *Gleichgeschaltet: Der Nazi-Terror gegen Gewerkschaften und Berufsverbände 1930 bis 1933; Eine Dokumentation*. Göttingen: Steidl, 2001.

Fischer, Conan. "The Occupational Background of the SA's Rank and File Membership during the Depression Years, 1929 to mid-1934." In *The Shaping of the Nazi State*, edited by Peter D. Stachura, 131–59. London: Croom Helm, 1978.

———. "The SA of the NSDAP: Social Background and Ideology of the Rank and File in the Early 1930s." *Journal of Contemporary History* 17 (1982): 651–70.

———. *Stormtroopers: A Social, Economic and Ideological Analysis 1929–1935*. London: Allen and Unwin, 1983.

Frank, Robert H. "Hitler and the National Socialist Coalition 1924–1932." PhD diss., Johns Hopkins University, 1969.

Gallo, Max. *The Night of the Long Knives*. Translated by Liley Emmet. New York: Harper & Row, 1972.

Hancock, Eleanor. *Ernst Röhm: Hitler's SA Chief of Staff*. New York: Palgrave MacMillan, 2008.

———. "'Indispensible Outsider'? Ernst Röhm as Chief of Staff of the SA, 1931–1933." Paper presented at the annual meeting of the German Studies Association, Seattle, Washington, 11 October 1996.

Höhne, Heinz. *Mordsache Röhm: Hitlers Durchbruch zur Alleinherrschaft 1933–1934*. Hamburg: Spiegel-Verlag/Rowohlt, 1984.

Hördler, Stefan, ed. *Der SA-Terror als Herrschaftssicherung: "Köpinecker Blutwoche" und Öffentliche Gewalt im frühen Nationalsozialismus*. Berlin: Metropol Verlag, 2013.

Jamin, Mathilde. "Zur Rolle der SA im nationalsozialistischen Herrschafts-system." In *Der "Führerstaat": Mythos und Realität; Studien zur Struktur und Politik des Dritten Reiches*, edited by Gerhard Hirschfeld and Lothar Kettenacker, Veröffentlichungen des Deutschen Historischen Instituts London, no. 8, 329–60. Stuttgart: Klett-Cotta, 1981.

———. *Zwischen den Klassen: Zur Sozialstruktur der SA-Führerschaft*. Wuppertal: Peter Hammer Verlag, 1984.

Jones, Larry Eugene. "Nationalists, Nazis, and the Assault against Weimar: Revisiting the Harzburg Rally of October 1931." *German Studies Review* 29 (2006): 483–94.

Kater, Michael H. "Ansätze zu einer Soziologie der SA bis zur Röhm-Krise." In *Soziale Bewegungen und Politische Verfassung*, edited by Ulrich Engelhardt, Volker Sellin, and Horst Sture, 789–831. Stuttgart: Klett-Cotta, 1997.

———. "Zum gegenseitigen Verhältnis von SA und SS in der Sozialgeschichte des Nationalsozialismus." *Vierteljahresschrift für Sozial- und Wirtschaftsgeschichte* 62 (1975): 339–79.

Longerich, Peter. *Die braunen Bataillone: Geschichte der SA*. Munich: C. H. Beck, 1989.

Merkl, Peter H. *The Making of a Stormtrooper*. Princeton, NJ: Princeton University Press, 1980.

Reichardt, Sven. *Faschistische Kampfbünde: Gewalt und Gemeinschaft im italienischen Squadrismus und in der deutschen SA*. Cologne, Weimar, and Vienna: Böhlau Verlag, 2002.

Reiche, Eric G. "From 'Spontaneous' to Legal Terror: SA Police and the Judiciary in Nürnberg 1933–34." *European Studies Review* 9 (1979): 237–64.

Rosenhaft, Eve. *Beating the Fascists? The German Communists and Political Violence 1928–1933*. Cambridge: Cambridge University Press, 1983.

Rüffler, Klaus: *Vom Münchener Landfriedensbruch bis zum Mord von Potempa: Der "Legalitätskurs" der NSDAP*. Frankfurt and Berlin: Peter Lang, 1994.

Sauer, Bernhard. "'Goebbels' 'Rabauken': Zur Geschichte der SA in Berlin-Brandenburg." In *Berlin in Geschichte und Gegenwart: Jahrbuch des Landesarchivs Berlin 2006*, edited by Uwe Schaper, 107–64. Berlin: Gebrüder Mann, 2007.

Schuster, Martin. "Die SA in der nationalsozialistischen 'Machtergreifung' in Berlin und Brandenburg 1926–1934." PhD diss., Technische Universität Berlin, 2005.

Stumpf, Reinhard. "Die Luftwaffe als drittes Heer: Die Luftwaffen-Erdkampfverbände und das Problem der Sonderheere 1933 bis 1945." In *Soziale Bewegung und Politische Verfassung: Werner Conze zum 31.12.75*, edited by Ulrich Englehardt, Volker Sellin, and Horst Stucke, 857–94. Stuttgart: Klett Verlag, 1976.

Turner, Henry Ashby, ed. *Hitler aus nächster Nähe: Aufzeichnungen eines Vertrauten 1929–1932*. Frankfurt, Berlin, and Vienna: Ullstein, 1978.

Wackerfuss, Andrew. *Stormtrooper Families: Homosexuality and Community in the Early Nazi Movement*. New York: Harrington Park Press, 2015.

Wegner, Bernd. *Hitlers Politische Soldaten: Die Waffen-SS 1933–1945; Studien zu Leitbild, Struktur und Funktion einer Nationalsozialistischen Elite*. Paderborn: Ferdinand Schöningh, 1982.

Werner, Andreas. "SA: 'Wehrverband,' 'Parteitruppe,' oder 'Revolutionsarmee?' Studien zur Geschichte der SA und der NSDAP 1920–1933." PhD diss., Friedrich-Alexander-Universität zu Erlangen-Nürnberg, 1964.

Wildt, Michael. *Volksgemeinschaft als Selbstermächtigung: Gewalt gegen Juden in der deutschen Provinz 1919 bis 1939*. Hamburg: Hamburger Edition, 2007.

 8

NATIONALIST SOCIALISM AGAINST NATIONAL SOCIALISM?

Perceptions of Nazism and Anti-Nazi Strategies in the Circle of the *Neue Blätter für den Sozialismus*, 1930–34

Stefan Vogt

In November 1932, at a crucial moment in the German Social Democrats' fight against the National Socialists, Alexander Schifrin, the coeditor of their major theoretical journal, *Die Gesellschaft*, felt obliged to take issue with a specific position that had emerged inside the Social Democratic movement and crystallized in a circle around the journal *Neue Blätter für den Sozialismus*. Since the late 1920s, the circle and its journal had made increasingly strong demands to revise the ideology and policies of Social Democracy, and some of its members had gained influential positions within the party, the socialist trade unions, and even the Reichstag faction. Schifrin was convinced that the ideas developed in this circle were totally detrimental to the fight against the Nazis. "Those who promote a nationalist left socialism," Schifrin declared, "are in no way capable of adopting a firm anti-fascist position. Anti-fascism requires the awareness that socialism is separated from fascism by an abyss, the awareness that they are deadly enemies. A nationalist left-socialist ideology inhibits an emphasis on this antagonism. It leads directly to the idealization of fascism."[1]

Schifrin considered the circle to be one of the various left-wing factions that had grown within the Social Democratic Party (Sozialdemokratische Partei Deutschlands or SPD) during the last years of the Weimar Republic—a misconception that is echoed by a significant portion of the scholarly literature on the group. A closer look at the ideological and political position, as well as the history of the circle, reveals that it was actually a faction on the right wing of the Social Democratic movement.[2] In both cases, this misconception was based on the radical posture with which the circle's members presented their critique of the party leadership's policies, and especially on their call for a more radical strategy to confront Nazism. Against this backdrop, Schifrin's claim that the circle was in fact idealizing fascism carried particular weight.

It suggested a serious contradiction within the circle's attitude toward National Socialism, between the call for vigorously fighting Nazism and an ideological affinity with it. In this regard, Schifrin's critique was accurate. Their ideological convictions, especially their inclination to hold nationalist ideas, made the members of the circle arrive at a far too positive and optimistic assessment of the Nazi movement. Whereas the group's commitment to a synthesis of nationalism and socialism did not compel its members to collaborate with National Socialism[3] but rather increased their opposition to it and brought many of them into the resistance movement, it did prevent them from developing a viable strategy against Nazism and unwittingly made them contribute to the decline of the Weimar Republic. In order to make this argument, this chapter analyzes the perceptions and interpretations of Nazism by the circle, its suggestions for a socialist anti-Nazi strategy, and its immediate reactions to the Nazi assumption of power.

The circle around the *Neue Blätter für den Sozialismus* emerged during the Weimar Republic as a project of collaboration between younger political activists and a number of prominent intellectuals who were either members of or politically close to the SPD. The younger activists came mostly from the Hofgeismarkreis, the right wing of the Jungsozialisten, which was the young adult SPD organization. Among them were Franz Osterroth, August Rathmann, and Theodor Haubach. Others, such as Fritz Borinski, were former members of the bourgeois youth movement who had gravitated toward socialism. In both cases, these activists brought a strong nationalist conviction into their socialist commitment. Fritz Borinski, born in 1903, was an adult educator in the *Volkshochschule* movement and the founder of the Leuchtenburgkreis, a bourgeois youth movement group. After the Second World War, he became professor of education at the Free University of Berlin. Haubach, born in 1896, had studied with Karl Jaspers and Alfred Weber in Heidelberg, worked for the party press in Hamburg—where he also helped found the Reich Banner Black-Red-Gold (Reichsbanner Schwarz-Rot-Gold)—and was minister of the interior Carl Severing's press secretary in 1929 and Berlin police commissioner Albert Grzesinski's press secretary from 1930 to 1932. He is much better known, however, for his participation in the Kreisau Circle (Kreisauer Kreis) resistance in the 1940s, for which he was tried before the People's Court (Volksgerichtshof) and executed in 1945. August Rathmann, born in 1895, was trained as a carpenter and, beginning in 1921, employed as secretary of the General German Trade Union Federation (Allgemeiner Deutscher Gewerkschaftsbund or ADGB) in Bochum, where he met Franz Osterroth. From 1930 to 1933, he was the editor in chief of the *Neue Blätter für den Sozialismus*.

Osterrorth, born in 1900, came from a family of Social Democratic politicians, had also made his career in the party press, and became editor of the *Reichbannerzeitung* in Magdeburg in 1928. After the war, which he survived in exile in Czechoslovakia and Sweden, he was a leading member of the SPD program committee and a very active chronicler of the party's history.

After having left the Jungsozialisten over a conflict about the stance towards nationalism, the *"Hofgeismarer"* joined forces with prominent intellectuals such as Hermann Heller, Hendrik de Man, and Paul Tillich, who advocated ethical and religious concepts of socialism and were themselves interested in integrating nationalist ideas into socialist thinking. Heller, born in 1891, had worked in the *Volkshochschule* movement before becoming a professor at the German Academy for Politics (Deutsche Hochschule für Politik) in Berlin and, in 1932, at Frankfurt University. He was one of the leading scholars of law and political science in the Weimar Republic. Being Jewish, he was also one of the first among the members of the circle who had to emigrate in 1933. Hendrik de Man was a Belgian socialist intellectual and politician who had worked in Germany already before World War I, and again during the Weimar Republic. In 1933, he returned to Belgium to become the leader of the Parti Ouvrier Belge and in 1935 a government minister. Tillich was the most eminent of the intellectuals involved and the leader of the so-called Berliner Kreis, a group of religious socialist intellectuals that was founded in 1919. Born in 1886, he was a professor at Marburg and Frankfurt universities. After emigrating to the United States, he became the president of the Council for a Democratic Germany, a major organization of political exiles that tried to establish itself as the official representation of the German opposition. As a professor at the Union Theological Seminary in New York, Harvard, and the University of Chicago, he was one of the most influential Protestant theologians of his time. Some individual socialist activists and politicians, again mostly from the younger generation, also came on board, including Carl Mierendorff, born in 1897, who was a longtime friend of Theodor Haubach. Mierendorff began his political career in the trade unions and the party press, later became secretary of the Social Democratic Reichstag faction, as well as to the Hessian minister of the interior Wilhelm Leuschner, and was finally himself elected to the Reichstag in 1930. Together with Haubach, he was involved in the Kreisau Circle and the preparations for the 20 July 1944 plot against Hitler, but he was killed in 1943 in an Allied bombing raid. During the second half of the 1920s, contacts between these and other activists were consolidated into an increasingly cohesive organization. In 1930, the circle managed to launch its own journal, the *Neue Blätter für den Sozialismus*. It now was a force to be reckoned with within the Social Democratic camp, and Schifrin's attack testified to its growing importance.

It is not possible to present the ideological and political positions of the group here in detail. Suffice to say that, in addition to their conviction that socialism should become a "nationalist socialism," their main goal was to disentangle socialist theory from its liberal, rationalist, and materialist foundations, and thus from Marxism. Instead, socialism should be grounded on ethical and religious ideas and on an understanding of man and society in terms of *Lebensphilosophie*. This meant that the affirmation not only of the nation but also of concepts such as vitality, blood, and leadership should be part of the socialist worldview. "In these concepts," argued, for example, Paul Tillich, "the question is raised whether the understanding of life that socialism adopted from the bourgeois way of thinking does in fact damage or even destroy all things vital."[4] The members of the circle felt that incorporating irrationalism and vitalism into the socialist platform would not only rejuvenate socialism but also, and despite all political enmity, create a commonality with some of the ideologies and movements of the radical right. This, they were convinced, would also include parts of the National Socialist movement. It is immediately clear that such a conviction had to have important consequences for the ideas of the circle about the appropriate strategy against Nazism.

Nevertheless, the members of the circle of the *Neue Blätter für den Sozialismus* were particularly active and vocal in analyzing Nazism and proposing ways to fight it, even by Social Democratic standards. However, they were by no means the only Social Democrats to do this. Already since the Italian Fascists came to power in 1922, and much more so after the landslide victory of the National Socialists in the Reichstag elections of September 1930, there was an intensive debate within the Social Democratic movement about how to understand and confront these threatening developments.[5] Although afflicted with many misconceptions and wrong conclusions, this debate was unmatched — not only in its scope but also in its intellectual and political quality — by the corresponding efforts of liberals and conservatives. The perceptions of Nazism and the anti-Nazi strategies discussed in the *Neue Blätter für den Sozialismus* circle were thus parts of the movement's well-developed discourse with many of its strengths and weaknesses. Their discussions about Nazism, however, also developed some very distinctive features of their own. While this was already obvious during the 1920s, when these debates focused on Italian fascism, it became even clearer toward the end of the Weimar Republic, as German Nazism moved to the center of the stage.

Interpretations of Nazism in the Final Years of the Weimar Republic

Especially after the September 1930 Reichstag elections, the Social Democrats' debates concentrated on the analysis of National Socialism's social base. The dominant position was that the Nazi movement consisted mostly of members of the middle class who had experienced or who feared a loss in their social and economic status.[6] Despite being more and more proletarianized, however, these members of the middle class stuck to their bourgeois ideology and refused to join the socialist movement. Nazism, the argument went, was thus not a proxy or an agent, as the communists thought, but indeed an auxiliary force of capitalism. Most Social Democrats therefore did not see anything progressive in the ideology and politics of the Nazi movement. At the same time, however, they overlooked the ambivalent attitude of Nazism toward bourgeois society, which included both conservative and revolutionary elements. Already in June 1930, Carl Mierendorff, a prominent member of the circle of the *Neue Blätter für den Sozialismus*, suggested a different assessment. He urged taking the anti-bourgeois elements of Nazism seriously. "The successful mixture of racial and social resentment, of genuine economic interest and all kinds of hatred," Mierendorff wrote, "is the chemical basis for the penetrating power and the explosiveness of National Socialism."[7] He recognized that a specific version of anticapitalism was at work in the middle class, and he criticized the SPD for not having recognized Nazism as a political danger in its own right, apart from its function as a support for capitalism. This view, which was widely shared among the members of the circle of the *Neue Blätter für den Sozialismus*, set Mierendorff apart from most other Social Democrats who analyzed Nazism. Yet he concurred with the Social Democratic mainstream in the assessment that, despite their social decline and their anticapitalist ideology, the members of the middle class did still pursue genuinely antisocialist class interests. For Mierendorff, their class consciousness, including the type of anticapitalism they adhered to, was reactionary and therefore a "false" consciousness.[8]

This was exactly where most other members of the circle of the *Neue Blätter für den Sozialismus* came to a radically different conclusion. August Rathmann, for instance, believed that in the September 1930 elections "the bourgeoisie had been squarely defeated" and that these elections had produced, for the first time, a truly anticapitalist majority. "There is no doubt," he claimed, "that the vast majority of the voters of the National Socialists are anti-capitalists." Rathmann considered this anticapitalism to be authentic and therefore compatible with socialism. He was convinced that Nazism's success was based on an "enormous growth of an anti-capitalist tendency within a broad segment of the people, a tendency that hasn't yet been recognized by the socialist movement."[9] Rathmann was quick to add that this did not apply to the leadership of the National Socialists, who just used this tendency to accumulate power and to help capitalism regain ground that it had lost to the proletariat. This, however, would not make the anticapitalism of their followers any less authentic. The anticapitalist forces, who, according to the circle of the *Neue Blätter für den Sozialismus*, were a central part of the National Socialist movement but were abused by its leaders, had to be wrested from this movement and led toward their true socialist purpose. Or as Eduard Heimann put it, "Everything depends on whether we acknowledge the authentic anti-capitalist incentives of the National Socialist movement as a necessary addition to our own struggle, liberate these incentives from the reactionary grasp, and plant them in our own soil. It is only here that they can bear fruit, because here they belong and here they are indispensable."[10]

Heimann, who was the most eminent economist among the members of the circle of the *Neue Blätter für den Sozialismus*, developed this idea into a complete theory about the role of the middle class in the current political crisis. According to this theory, it was not individual members of the middle class suffering proletarianization that was at issue, but rather that the class as a whole was in social decline. In this process, the middle class would not dissolve but would remain a distinct social class. The clinging of the members of this class to their social identity was not judged negatively by Heimann as an ideological reaction to the actual loss of this identity, but positively, as anticapitalist class consciousness. This would also apply to the nationalist convictions and to the rejection of the liberal and rationalist worldview that were elements of this consciousness. The radicalization of the middle class, which indeed was a crucial factor in the success of the National Socialists, was thus converted from a reactionary threat into a promising advantage for socialism. Both the members of the circle of the *Neue Blätter für den Sozialismus* and the majority of the Social Democrats emphasized the role of the middle class as the basis of National Socialism. In contrast to the dominant view in the party, however, the members of the circle of the *Neue Blätter für den Sozialismus* were convinced that it was not necessary to show the members of the middle class their true interests, because the interests and sentiments that they articulated by following National Socialism were already authentically anticapitalist. Instead, Social Democracy should embrace these positions as a part of its own socialist agenda.[11] From the important insight about the significance of a specific anticapitalist attitude for the rise of National Socialism, the circle of the *Neue Blätter für den Sozialismus* had thus come to an extremely problematic conclusion. "It is not possible to prove to all these people that they are proletarians," wrote Eduard Heimann, "because they aren't. But it is possible to win them over for the fight against the rule of capital, because they are victims of this rule, just as the proletarians."[12]

The members of the *Neue Blätter für den Sozialismus* circle agreed with most other Social Democrats that, in order to understand National Socialism, it was essential to know its social base and especially to understand the reasons for its strong support from the middle class. They were able to improve this analysis by adding the important notion that anticapitalist sentiments among the members of the middle class were crucial for this support. Instead of problematizing these sentiments as a form of ideology, however, they regarded them as an expression of an authentic and legitimate class consciousness and therefore as a starting point for an alliance of the middle class with socialism. In this view, the rise of National Socialism was the result of the legitimate demand to overcome the rationalist and individualist, and thus alienated, social condition that was considered the core of capitalism. Even if National Socialism as a political force had to be fought, it still represented an intellectual development that was not only legitimate but also worthy of support by socialists. From this perspective, the National Socialist version of anticapitalism should not be criticized as "false consciousness" any longer, but rather acknowledged and endorsed. With this conclusion, the members of the circle of the *Neue Blätter für den Sozialismus* stood largely alone within Social Democracy. To be sure, many other Social Democrats also discussed ways to win back anticapitalist protest votes from the NSDAP, but this usually referred to proletarian and subproletarian voters. They almost always rejected, however, the motives of the middle classes in supporting National Socialism as being part of a reactionary ideology. Arguing directly against Eduard Heimann, the Social Democratic journalist Georg Decker made this unmistakably clear when he wrote in *Die Gesellschaft*, "It is most dangerous to depict the supposedly 'anti-capitalist' mobilization of the middle class, which in fact is much more 'anti-Marxist' and thus anti-proletarian than anti-capitalist, as the 'brother' of the socialist labor movement. Even more so at a time when we have to appeal to the intuitive rejection of this hostile development by the proletarians in order prevent it from penetrating the working class."[13]

The *Neue Blätter für den Sozialismus* after January 1933

Immediately after Hitler was appointed Reich chancellor on 30 January 1933, the Social Democrats began to feel the full force of the Nazi attack against democracy. By the end of February, most Social Democratic newspapers, including the *Vorwärts*, had been banned. After the 5 March Reichstag elections, many members and activists of the party became victims of persecution and physical violence, bringing the legal activity of the party to a de facto end even before it was explicitly outlawed in June. A significant number of the *Neue Blätter für den Sozialismus* circle members, especially those holding prominent positions in the SPD and its affiliate organizations, were also hit by this early wave of repression. The attacks only increased the involvement of the circle members in the party's fight against the National Socialists, as well as the internal SPD debates on how this fight should be carried out. One thing, however, made the circle stand out in this context: as opposed to all other Social Democratic journals and newspapers, the *Neue Blätter für den Sozialismus* was able to appear until June 1933.[14] This allows for an examination of the attitudes of the circle toward National Socialism during the first months of the Third Reich. To be sure, the analysis must remain extremely cautious. Considering the conditions of censorship and repression, it is not possible to draw direct conclusions based on what was written in the journal about what its authors actually thought. However, it should not be assumed either that everything that was printed after January 1933 had been vetted by the authorities. Up until June, the *Neue Blätter für den Sozialismus* was able to publish rather harsh and open criticisms of the new regime. Even if internal materials from the circle do not exist, a fairly reliable picture of its members' intellectual development during this period emerges.

At first sight, the authors of the journal were hardly ambiguous in their condemnation of the new regime. The editorial of the February issue declared that the "ultimate struggle for the foundations of democracy, and therefore for the preconditions for the rise of the working class and of socialism" had arrived. Social Democracy, the editorial argued, had therefore no choice but to adopt the more militant strategy against National Socialism that the members of the circle had called for over the last years.[15] This strategy involved a strong emphasis on nonviolent extraparliamentarian activities, tightened internal organization with firm leadership, and the use of mass psychology concepts.[16] After the elections of 5 March, by which time repression against Social Democrats had already escalated, journal authors became even more outspoken. The crucial fact, read one editorial, was not that democracy had been defeated but that it had been defeated by democratic means. Even if the principle of the rule of law should not be given up, "the labor movement has had it with the legal structure of bourgeois society."[17] Social Democracy should reinvent itself as the principal adversary of National Socialism, "take charge of the situation and defeat its enemy." Although these lines sounded almost like a call for violent resistance against Nazism, they had in fact a rather different objective. Their main target was Social Democracy itself. With Social Democracy being defeated by the National Socialists, the editorial went on, it was necessary to radically reconsider its ideological and organizational principles. "The relationship between party and state, between power and law, between democracy and leadership, between state and economy, between the nation and the world: drawing from previous experiences and mistakes, Social Democracy has to develop theoretical answers to these questions if it wants to be able to solve them practically."[18]

In accordance with their understanding of National Socialism, the authors of the *Neue Blätter für den Sozialismus* expected that these programmatic and strategic changes would help to win over the supposedly anticapitalist Nazi supporters for Social Democracy. They were convinced that these supporters would very soon be disappointed by the actual pro-capitalist policies that Nazi leaders pursued in order to maintain their alliance with bourgeois and conservative forces.[19] As a result, they hoped, the regime would lose its public support and therefore quickly fall apart. As it became clear that the new government was not as short-lived as the previous ones and that the Reichstag election of March 1933 did not bring any middle- or lower-class voters from the NSDAP to the SPD, the journal had to adjust its arguments. In order to retain their conviction that the rise of National Socialism was based on an authentic anticapitalist tendency that ultimately would benefit socialism, its authors now had to identify these anticapitalist traits inside the National Socialist regime. At the same time, they made an effort to portray anticapitalism as an autonomous orientation, independent of the regime, and relevant in its own right. In this vein, the author of an editorial in the April issue of the *Neue Blätter für den Sozialismus* detected an "ambivalence between revolution and reaction among the supporters of the ruling party" that "is also present within National Socialism itself."[20] This statement was not just a concession to censorship, as it also spoke of the reactionary side of the new regime and most openly addressed the "fact of dictatorship." Rather, the article's objective was to make use of "the socialist forces within the National Revolution" in order to realize socialism. "This realization," the article concluded, "remains the task of the working class. It will not be able to achieve it alone, but even less can it be taken off its shoulders by anyone's diktat or command."[21]

The brutal dissolution of the socialist trade unions on 2 May added urgency to the journal's search for socialist elements within the new regime. The authors of the *Neue Blätter für den Sozialismus* acknowledged that the strike against the trade unions turned the independent organization of the workers into a state-controlled element of the corporatist reorganization of society. However, the fact that it was carried out just one day after May Day was celebrated for the first time as an official state holiday also demonstrated to these authors that National Socialism could not escape the socialist dynamics within the society. The regime had taken over both the vast organization of the trade unions and also their members. "Some of these people may become party members," the editorial of the journal's May issue claimed. "They will most probably remain members of the unions. But most of all, they will remain workers in the factories, victims of the capitalist economy, and thus protagonists of every true socialist development."[22] If the trade unions were integrated into the new state, the members of the circle of the *Neue Blätter für den Sozialismus* reasoned, so would the elements from which socialism could be developed. The journal focused more and more on criticizing the insufficient fusion of national and social policies by the National Socialist regime. It demanded that National Socialism should live up to its socialist pretensions and go beyond a merely symbolic avowal of labor. "The government calls on the worker to contribute to the work of national reconstruction," the May editorial read. "But in case the architects, engineers, and foremen do not know, the workers in the factories, in the trade unions as well as in all organizations, in the National Socialist Party, and in the whole of working life will tell them: the plan for this reconstruction must be one of socialist reconstruction or this work will fail."[23]

Most interesting in this context were the comments in the *Neue Blätter für den Sozialismus* about the so-called *Friedensrede*, the foreign policy declaration that Hitler gave to the Reichstag on 17 May, and to the reaction of what was left of the Social Democratic Reichstag faction to it. In this speech, Hitler had declared that his government would respect the rights of other nations, refrain from acquiring offensive weapons, and join any nonaggression pact to which it would be invited.[24] Despite this dovish rhetoric, it was clear to most observers that the speech was purely tactical and did not represent the true intentions of the regime. The leadership of the Social Democratic Party, already in exile in Prague, vehemently rejected the speech, while the leadership of the Reichstag faction approved it. This approval provoked a serious conflict between the two groups and became a heavy liability to the Social Democrats' fight against Nazism. The members of the *Neue Blätter für den Sozialismus* circle were also critical of the Reichstag faction leadership. Their criticism, however, was not directed against the approval as such; they claimed that Social Democracy had always supported "a policy of national self-assertion, international coequality, general disarmament, and honest peacekeeping," which had comprised, after all, the main content of Hitler's speech.[25] Instead, they criticized the faction for not using its approval of the speech to influence the government in pursuing more socialist domestic policies. The need of the government to rally all political forces behind its foreign policy, the *Neue Blätter für den Sozialismus* claimed, would have been an opportunity to push for changes in the domestic realm. The preliminary goal should be to arrive at "a National Socialist Germany that is more socialist and less nationalist" and could thus serve as a starting point for further positive developments.[26]

Until the very last issue, and despite increasing censorship, the editorials of the *Neue Blätter für den Sozialismus* made every effort to maintain at least a rudimentary independent socialist standpoint that was distinguished from and critical of National Socialist policies. They were able to do this remarkably well. They advocated the idea of a nationalist socialism that could incorporate substantial parts of the National Socialist movement as well as certain elements of National Socialist policies. The conviction that this would be possible was not the result of Nazi repression or censorship, nor does it indicate a political or ideological turn taken after 30 January 1933. Rather, it was consistent with the circle's prior ideological positions and with its members' long-standing interpretation of National Socialism. The journal's articles published after that date did not represent the complete political views of the circle, since much of the sharp critique that they contained until January 1933 would not have passed censorship anymore, even though some of it still did. The articles, however, did represent the circle's views on the continued existence of socialist and anticapitalist elements within National Socialism and on the necessity to support them. The *Neue Blätter für den Sozialismus* circle members did not think that National Socialism had achieved a true synthesis of socialism and nationalism; as late as the April issue, a distancing footnote was added to an article that had so claimed.[27] Yet the possibility of such a synthesis was not ruled out, not even under the new regime, making it perfectly reasonable, members of the circle argued, to demand it from the National Socialists.

The most radical version of the claim that a socialist development would be possible on the basis of the National Socialist takeover of political power was not presented in the *Neue Blätter für den Sozialismus*, but in the *Gewerkschafts-Zeitung*, the official organ of the socialist trade unions. Its author, however, was Walther Pahl, a prominent member of the circle of the *Neue Blätter für den Sozialismus*.[28] Immediately after Hitler had assumed power, some trade union leaders, among them the ADGB president Theodor Leipart and several of his young assistants, explored ways to preserve their organization by distancing it from the SPD and by cooperating with the new regime. This process culminated in the decision to participate in the Nazi regime's official celebrations of "National Labor Day" on 1 May.[29] Two days before, on 29 April, Pahl wrote in the *Gewerkschafts-Zeitung* that this day would not symbolize a defeat but a victory of the working class, as it was now finally integrated into the nation. This, Pahl continued, had been the goal of the labor movement all along. "We are not separated from National Socialism by a different valuation of the nation and of socialism," he wrote, "only by a different prioritization. We wanted socialism first, in order to form the nation. National Socialism called for and now achieves the unity of the nation in order to build German socialism on this broad and solid basis."[30] The association of socialism with class struggle was not a matter of principle but only the result of external circumstances that socialism and National Socialism both strove to abolish. This, however, would require real political power. "The most important cause of the impossibility of accomplishing socialism has been the lack of undivided political power, which also gradually crushed the system of Weimar. This sort of political power exists today."[31] Therefore, Pahl concluded, National Socialism had the unique opportunity, but also the unique responsibility, to realize socialism. The content and the intent of this article was almost identical with the position put forward in the *Neue Blätter für den Sozialismus*, even if the call for collaboration with the new regime was made much more bluntly. The futility of this call, too, could not have been demonstrated more brusquely. One day after "National Labor Day," the trade unions had ceased to exist.

Resistance Activities 1933 to 1934

The fact that the new regime had no intention of cooperating with Social Democrats, even if they advocated a nationalist version of socialism, was soon personally demonstrated to many members of the *Neue Blätter für den Sozialismus* circle. Several of them, including Walther Pahl, were arrested or had to go underground. Those who worked for Social Democratic institutions or organizations, held public positions, or taught at universities soon lost their jobs. Many others—especially those who were Jewish or were considered Jewish by the Nazis—chose to emigrate. Some of them, such as Paul Tillich, continued to be politically active in exile. The only member of the circle who was working directly for the exiled Social Democratic Party, the Sopade, was Franz Osterroth, who had fled to Czechoslovakia at the beginning of 1934. He worked as a liaison between the party leadership in Prague and the border secretariat in Bodenbach, on the one hand, and illegal groups within Germany on the other. In this capacity, he made several trips to Germany where he met, among others, with his former comrades from the Hofgeismarkreis and members of the *Neue Blätter für den Sozialismus* circle.[32]

Some circle members discussed possibilities of keeping up some sort of organizational structure after the banning of the journal. August Rathmann reports on a meeting in Frankfurt am Main in March 1933 that was attended by Paul Tillich, Hendrik de Man, Adolf Löwe, Theodor Haubach, Alfred Protte—the publisher of the *Neue Blätter für den Sozialismus*—and himself. At this meeting, plans for the production and distribution of illegal publications were discussed, possibly even the publication of an underground journal. Rathmann contemplated such a project under the title *Der Überblick*, which, however, could not be realized due to the lack of financial means.[33] In some cities, such as Leipzig, the journal's *Leserkreise*—groups constituting an organized periphery of the *Neue Blätter* circle that met specifically to discuss the journal's articles—continued to exist for a while.[34] In accordance with the general practice of Social Democratic *Gesinnungsgemeinschaften* in Nazi Germany, those circles were probably low-key meetings to exchange political views and observations among trusted comrades and were not used as a basis for open resistance activities. It is not possible to determine to what extent the circle around the *Neue Blätter für den Sozialismus*, let alone those who sympathized with it or participated in the *Leserkreise*, were involved in various resistance activities. There were, however, three distinct resistance groups during the early years of the Third Reich that clearly represented a continuation of the circle's work from the Weimar Republic. These were parts of the illegal Reich Banner groups, the so-called Rote Stoßtrupp in Berlin, and the Rechberg-Gruppe in the Mannheim-Heidelberg area. The Reich Banner groups had emerged in various parts of Germany after the organization itself had been banned in March 1933. Theodor Haubach, who was one of the highest-ranking Reich Banner leaders still in Germany, coordinated and commanded a significant number of these groups. The Rote Stoßtrupp had already been founded in 1932 by three authors of the *Neue Blätter für den Sozialismus*: Rudolf Küstermeier, Franz Hering, and Curt Bley. The Rechberg-Gruppe was an independent Social Democratic resistance organization that was founded and led by Emil Henk, another member of the circle of the *Neue Blätter für den Sozialismus* and a close friend of Carl Mierendorff and Theodor Haubach. All three groups were typical of the first phase of Social Democratic resistance activities in that they were based on the organizational networks of Weimar Social Democracy and concentrated on mobilizing activists within their own political milieu.[35]

Former members of the Reich Banner were particularly active in the "official" Social Democratic resistance structures—those that worked under the supervision of the exiled party leadership in Prague. There were, however, also a number of illegal groups of the Reich Banner proper. The most comprehensive attempt to create a centralized structure of these groups was carried out and led by Theodor Haubach. Already in 1933, Haubach was involved in setting up a network of illegal groups in Hamburg that operated independently from the Sopade structures, included several hundred men (mostly former members of the *Schutzformation* elite units of the Reich Banner), and was organized in groups of five, each of which was active in a specific factory or neighborhood.[36] According to the Gestapo, the organization had gathered weapons, set up a radio station, and maintained contact with Reich Banner groups in Bremen and other cities.[37] Haubach soon moved the center of his activities to the capital of the Reich. The Gestapo concluded that by mid-1934, the illegal Reich Banner structures in Berlin had up to a thousand members and were organized in a military fashion and commanded by several *Gruppenführer* who were subordinate to Haubach.[38] This organization was independent from the "official" Social Democratic resistance structures and the exiled party leadership in Prague, which in Berlin was represented by the illegal district leadership or *Illegale Bezirksleitung*."[39] However, Haubach did cooperate intensively with the *Bezirksleitung*, having frequent conferences with its leaders to discuss resistance strategies, including the possibilities for an overthrow of the regime.[40] It was therefore no coincidence that his illegal network was dissolved by the Gestapo during its large-scale campaign against Social Democratic structures that began in late 1934, when Haubach was arrested, and ended with the dissolution of almost all illegal structures of the Social Democrats by mid-1936.[41]

According to the available sources—mostly Gestapo reports from illegal meetings—Haubach's Reich Banner organization was stricter and much more hierarchical than the informal network of the "official" Social Democratic resistance and set up in a quasi-military manner with clear chains of command. Haubach would make his men available for larger actions "on an ad-hoc basis," but he was convinced that the time had not yet come for this. Therefore, the illegal Reich Banner organization would refrain, for the time being, from any visible activity, including the production of printed materials. Haubach was convinced, however, that it was necessary immediately to set up an effective organization that was prepared to strike out when the time was right, such as the appearance of an internal crisis in the National Socialist regime. In June 1934, a Gestapo informer reported that Haubach had said he believed this would happen "in a few months." The capitalists and the conservatives would want to get rid of Hitler if he refused to comply with their demands. "They want to topple the Hitler of the SA, but they would accept the Hitler of the Reichswehr." Because Hitler would certainly go along with this, "the industry will soon become the true government in Germany and Hitler will be needed only as a decoration."[42] Haubach here rather precisely predicted the so-called Röhm Putsch, which took place only a few days later. However, his assumption that this would turn Nazi leaders into puppets of big capital and lead to a serious crisis of the regime proved utterly wrong. It underestimated the stability of the regime and its relative independence from traditional class conflicts, and it perpetuated a misinterpretation from the last years of the Weimar Republic. Obviously, Haubach still hoped to find socialist forces within National Socialism that would oppose the leadership's pro-capitalist policies. In this regard, his resistance activities in 1933 and 1934 clearly represented a continuation of his work in the circle of the *Neue Blätter für den Sozialismus*.

This was also the case for the Rote Stoßtrupp. During the last weeks of the Weimar Republic, its members decided to set up another journal, to be edited by Rudolf Küstermeier, that would also be published illegally.[43] The first issue of the *Der Rote Stoßtrupp*, as the journal was called, appeared underground already on 9 April 1933.[44] During 1933 twenty-eight issues, which appeared on a weekly basis and reached a circulation of more than fifteen hundred copies, were published. The journal was distributed not only in Berlin but also in other cities, where issues were sometimes even reprinted. The Rote Stoßtrupp group developed into a sizable network of activists all over the Reich; in Berlin it was especially densely organized and hierarchically structured.[45] A Gestapo report from October 1934 claimed that it had fully developed organizational structures in Berlin, Essen, Duisburg, and Düsseldorf, as well as over seven hundred small individual groups across the country and more than two thousand activists.[46] This could have been an exaggeration, but the truly impressive size of the Rote Stoßtrupp is also documented by the fact that the Gestapo arrested about 240 people when it finally smashed the organization in November 1933.[47] During its existence, the Rote Stoßtrupp refrained from militant action and from acquiring weapons, but it strove to prepare its followers for such action in the future. That meant building up the organization, mobilizing activists, and gathering as well as distributing suppressed information. For these purposes, the group established contacts with representatives of foreign media and informants in the institutions of the regime, including the *Hausmeister* of Hermann Göring's home in Berlin, who was a former Social Democrat.[48]

Because no copies of *Der Rote Stoßtrupp* have survived, it is possible to reconstruct the ideology of the organization only through the fragmentary pieces that are quoted in the court records. What emerges is an idiosyncratic mixture of neo-Leninism and nationalist socialism. In the first issue of the journal, an article with the title "Was tun?" introduces the organization as a "new movement" that would replace the old parties destroyed by the Nazis. "We are not committed any more to the dogma or the banner of a party," the article read. "We know only one flag: the red flag of socialism!"[49] The tone of the articles referred to here was consistently radical and anti-reformist. The stated goal was the creation of a united socialist front and the carrying out of a "proletarian revolution" that would lead to a "proletarian dictatorship."[50] In order to bring the revolution about, the Rote Stoßtrupp group wanted to initiate workers' protests against low wages and high prices, and also "against the persistent enslavement by foreign capitalist countries."[51] Obviously, it was still believed that the strategy of combining nationalist and socialist ideologies could pull the masses away from the regime. This was a clear continuation of the ideology of the *Neue Blätter für den Sozialismus* circle. Despite the claim that the organization would leave old party allegiances behind and overcome the schism in the labor movement, most of its activists, as well as most of the journal's readers, were Social Democrats.[52] The Rote Stoßtrupp group also reached out to left-wing splinter groups, especially the Socialist

Workers' Party (Sozialistische Arbeiterpartei or SAP).[53] This was in line with the neo-Leninist part of the organization's self-conception. However, it also maintained contacts with Otto Strasser's Black Front (Schwarze Front). This, again, attests to the persistence of nationalist-socialist ideas in the organization. The contacts to Strasser dated back to the last years of the Weimar Republic, when members of the *Neue Blätter für den Sozialismus* circle engaged in intensive debates with some representatives of the radical right, among whom activists from the Schwarze Front featured most prominently. Rudolf Küstermeier later claimed that he was among the few people who knew how to contact Otto Strasser in his exile in Austria. Strasser's journal, *Die Deutsche Revolution*, in turn, praised the *Rote Stoßtrupp* and reprinted excerpts from Küstermeier's book, *Die Mittelschichten und ihr politischer Weg*.[54] The idea of a common front of all truly socialist nationalists, which had been developed in the circle of *Neue Blätter für den Sozialismus*, was still alive in the Rote Stoßtrupp.

The third major resistance organization that developed out of the circle of the *Neue Blätter für den Sozialismus* was the Rechberg-Gruppe. "Rechberg" was the code name of Emil Henk, who had authored several articles in the journal. In October 1933 he set up the Rechberg-Gruppe in Heidelberg, together with Otto Calvi, who had also been in contact with the *Neue Blätter für den Sozialismus* circle. Most of its members came from the SPD youth organizations and the Reich Banner or were students at Heidelberg University.[55] The Rechberg-Gruppe was organized as a tightly structured conspiratorial circle and had branches in various places in the area, as well as affiliated groups in Frankfurt, Darmstadt, and Offenbach.[56] The liaison between the Rechberg-Gruppe in Heidelberg and the groups in the Frankfurt area was Willi Brundert, who was a former member of the Leuchtenburgkreis, an organization of the bourgeois youth movement that had merged with the *Neue Blätter für den Sozialismus* circle in 1930.[57] It is not just the close personal relationship between Henk and Theodor Haubach that suggests that the Rechberg-Gruppe also had links with Haubach's illegal Reich Banner organization. According to Henk, Haubach came to Mannheim in 1934 to catch up on the activities of the group and to discuss possibilities for joint actions against the regime.[58] Similar to both the Reich Banner organization and the Rote Stoßtrupp, the Rechberg Gruppe focused on the preparation for such an uprising in the near future and refrained from open activities in the present. Henk and his friends wanted to remain independent from the Sopade and the "official" Social Democratic underground, but they sought cooperation with them as well as with the SAP.

The ideological orientation of the Rechberg-Gruppe is, again, very difficult to determine. While there is no evidence that would place the group on the left fringe of Social Democracy, several factors suggest a programmatic affinity with the *Neue Blätter für den Sozialismus* circle. Not the least significant of these factors is the continuous relationship to Haubach and Mierendorff. It is, however, possible to get a glimpse of the ideology of the group itself. When in the summer of 1933 members of an illegal network of Social Democrats in Frankfurt and Offenbach, led by Johann Stoffers, shifted their allegiance from the Sopade to the Rechberg-Gruppe, they did so, according to the state attorney, in order "to create an organization that would confront National Socialism with a 'German socialism.'"[59] Such a statement by a Nazi law enforcement agency would, of course, be of almost no value unless supported by other sources. This, however, is the case. Georg Reinbold, the representative of the Sopade in the region, had no doubt that "Rechberg is nothing but the former Haubach-Mierendorff faction," by which he meant the *Neue Blätter für den Sozialismus* circle.[60] The escalating conflict between the Rechberg-Gruppe and the Sopade was fueled also by ideological differences. At a conference of several illegal socialist groups that took place in Neunkirchen in the Saarland in June 1934, the delegates of the Rechberg-Gruppe harshly criticized the Prague Manifesto in which Sopade had reinforced its commitment to Marxist theory. "With regard to the manifesto," Otto Calvi announced, "I want to make clear that, even if it is in some parts radical, we consider it an incredibly narrow-minded program, which we are not able to support." Fascism, another Rechberg delegate added, had shown that socialism was not only about economics and that it would be necessary to oppose "certain Marxist dogmatists."[61] The *Rechberg-Gruppe* also shared the belief of Haubach and Küstermeier that in the summer of 1934 the Nazi regime was about to enter into a serious crisis and could collapse before the end of the year.[62] This suggests that they, too, still pinned their hopes on the disappointment of the workers and the middle classes in National Socialist economic policies.

Conclusion

The information available about these three resistance groups is, of course, far from enough to draw a comprehensive picture of their ideology. It does, however, clearly correspond to the fact that, in terms of organization and membership, these groups represent a continuation of the *Neue Blätter für den Sozialismus* circle. Seen in this light, a continuous ideological thread that runs from the Weimar period all the way to the early years of Nazi rule becomes visible. This thread was the conviction that it was possible to lure the lower and middle classes away from the grip of National Socialism by offering them a nationalist socialism as an alternative. The members of the *Neue Blätter für den Sozialismus* circle believed that many of those who followed National Socialism did so because they considered it the most credible and powerful defender against the threats posed to them by capitalism. Taking the anticapitalist motivations of these people seriously was a major intellectual achievement of the circle. However, the members of the circle did more than this. They considered this form of anti-capitalism, including its irrational and nationalist components, to be legitimate, and they wanted Social Democracy to adjust itself to them. By doing this, the members of the *Neue Blätter für den Sozialismus* circle granted National Socialism, too, a certain degree of legitimacy. They believed that National Socialism gave the wrong answers but neverthe-less posed some of the right questions. They were convinced that it had ridden to power on an ideological wave that was, in principle, justified and had to be affirmed. The essence of this wave was a synthesis of socialism and nationalism. They hoped that this essence also could be found within parts of the National Socialist movement and even within some elements of the National Socialist regime. Their anti-Nazi strat-egy was based on faith that it was possible to extract this essence and direct it against the false synthesis offered by National Socialist leaders and, eventually, against the regime itself.

This, as it turned out, was a serious mistake. To be sure, those mem-bers of the Social Democratic resistance who did not agree with the circle's assessment also had no chance against the force of the regime's assault against any kind of left-wing opposition. The mistaken strategy of the *Neue Blätter für den Sozialismus* circle, therefore, played no part in the failure of the anti-Nazi resistance movement in 1933 and 1934. In a larger perspective, however, it did contribute to the weakening and dissolution of an emancipative alternative to the Nazi takeover in 1933. Precisely as Alexander Schifrin had claimed in November 1932, in its understanding of Nazism the circle had failed to draw a clear line between the forces of emancipation and the forces of barbarism. It did not see that the synthesis of socialism with nationalism was part of the problem rather than part of the solution. This does not mean, however, that the members of the *Neue Blätter für den Sozialismus* circle collaborated with the Nazis. The conviction that there was something true and legitimate about National Socialism led only very few of them to actively support the regime. For many others, it fueled the decision to participate in the anti-Nazi resistance, since they felt that National Socialism seriously distorted and abused a good and important idea. This fact, and the fact that some of them, such as Theodor Haubach and Adolf Reichwein, paid for their resistance with their lives, does not contradict the conclusion that their perception of National Socialism was fundamentally flawed. Rather, it adds another layer of complexity to the already complicated picture of the German resistance movement. The realization that some of the political and ideological concepts of the resistance groups were highly questionable should be a reason to critically engage with these concepts, but not one to deny respect for the courage of these men and women.

Stefan Vogt is a *Privatdozent* for modern history in the History Department and a *Wissenschaftlicher Mitarbeiter* at the Martin-Buber-Chair for Jewish Thought and Philosophy at Goethe University in Frankfurt am Main. He is the author of *Subalterne Positionierungen: Der deutsche Zionismus im Feld des Nationalismus in Deutschland 1890–1933* (2016) and of *Nationaler Sozialismus und Soziale Demokratie: Die sozialdemokratische Junge Rechte 1918–1945* (2006). In his current book-length project, "Colonialism and the Jews in Germany, 1880–1918," he investigates the relationship between antisemitism and colonial racism in the German Empire.

Notes

Parts of this chapter have been previously published in Stefan Vogt, *Nationaler Sozialismus und Soziale Demokratie: Die sozialdemokratische Junge Rechte 1918–1945* (Bonn: Dietz, 2006).

1. Alexander Schifrin, "Nationaler Linkssozialismus?," *Deutsche Republik* 7, no. 9 (26 November 1932): 267.
2. For a detailed analysis of the history, ideology, and politics of the circle, see Stefan Vogt, *Nationaler Sozialismus und Soziale Demokratie: Die sozialdemokratische Junge Rechte 1918–1945* (Bonn: Dietz, 2006). This chapter is based on parts of this book.
3. There are a few exceptions to this rule. Most well-known is Hendrik de Man who, after returning to his native Belgium in 1933, led the Parti Ouvrier Belge into collaboration with the German occupiers during World War II. There is a lack of critical studies on de Man, but see Peter Dodge, *Beyond Marxism: The Faith and Works of Hendrik de Man* (The Hague: Nijhoff, 1966). Another example is Walther Pahl, who became a well-read author of geopolitical and imperialist books and pamphlets during the Nazi period. On Pahl, see Karsten Linne, "Walther Pahl—eine Gewerkschafterkarriere," *1999* 5 (1990): 39–55.

4. Gustav Radbruch, Paul Tillich, and Hendrik de Man, "Der Sozialismus und die geistige Lage der Gegenwart," *Neue Blätter für den Sozialismus* 3, no. 1 (January 1931): 15. The article documents a radio discussion aired by the station *Deutsche Welle* on 10 November 1931.

5. There is still no adequate comprehensive analysis of the Social Democratic debate about fascism during the Weimar Republic. The best overview is Wolfgang Wippermann, *Zur Analyse des Faschismus: Die sozialdemokratischen und kommunistischen Faschismustheorien 1921–1945* (Frankfurt a.M.: Diesterweg, 1981), 9–58.

6. See, for example, Theodor Geiger, "Panik im Mittelstand," *Die Arbeit* 7, no.10 (October 1930): 637–54; Alexander Schifrin, "Gegenrevolution in Europa," *Die Gesellschaft* 8, no. 1 (January 1931): 1–21; Rudolf Breitscheid, "Die Überwindung des Faschismus," in *Sozialdemokratischer Parteitag in Leipzig 1931 vom 31. Mai bis 5. Juni im Volkshaus: Protokoll* (Leipzig: Vorwärts, 1931), 87–108; Rudolf Hilferding, "Unter der Drohung des Faschismus," *Die Gesellschaft* 9, no. 1 (January 1932): 1–12.

7. Carl Mierendorff, "Gesicht und Charakter der nationalsozialistischen Bewegung," *Die Gesellschaft* 7, no. 1 (January 1930): 494. See also Carl Mierendorff, "Lehren der Niederlage," *Neue Blätter für den Sozialismus* 1, no. 11 (November 1930): 481–84.

8. See Carl Mierendorff, "Was ist der Nationalsozialismus. Zur Topographie des Faschismus in Deutschland," *Neue Blätter für den Sozialismus* 2, no. 4 (April 1931): 149–54.

9. August Rathmann, "Antikapitalistische Politik," *Neue Blätter für den Sozialismus* 1, no. 10 (October 1930): 433, 435.

10. Eduard Heimann, "Warum SPD?" *Neue Blätter für den Sozialismus* 2, no. 12 (December 1931): 594. See also "Die Sieger von übermorgen," *Neue Blätter für den Sozialismus* 3, no. 10 (October 1932): 505–17; Walther Pahl, "Der Run zum Nationalsozialismus," *Sozialistische Monatshefte* 36, no. 9 (September 1930): 864–72.

11. For an expanded version of this theory, see esp. Eduard Heimann, "Sozialismus und Mittelstand," *Neue Blätter für den Sozialismus* 3, no. 7 (July 1932): 356–71.

12. Heimann, "Warum SPD?," 598.

13. Georg Decker, "Bekenntnisse der Sozialdemokratie," *Die Gesellschaft* 10, no. 2 (February 1933): 95.

14. It is not clear what made this exception possible. August Rathmann speaks vaguely of "left-wing nationalists" and *"Reichswehr* officers close to us," who protected the journal. See August Rathmann, "Gegen den Nationalsozialismus: Die Berliner Wochenzeitung 'Blick in die Zeit' 1933 bis 1935," in *Andreas Gayk und seine Zeit: Erinnerungen an den Kieler Oberbürgermeister,* ed. Jürgen Jensen and Karl Rickers (Neumünster: Wachholtz, 1974), 65. The circle seems, indeed, to have developed contacts with certain National Socialists, but it is unclear who exactly those National Socialists were and what kind of influence they could exert. On these contacts see Vogt, *Nationaler Sozialismus,* 149–51.

15. "Der Marsch durchs Brandenburger Tor," *Neue Blätter für den Sozialismus* 4, no. 2 (February 1933): 60.

16. See Theodor Haubach, "Die militante Partei," *Neue Blätter für den Sozialismus* 2, no. 5 (May 1931): 208–13. Haubach and others explicitly referred to fascism and National Socialism as models for this strategy.

17. "Berlin, den 12. März 1933," in *Neue Blätter für den Sozialismus* 4, no. 3 (March 1933): 114.

18. Ibid., 117.

19. See "Der Marsch durchs Brandenburger Tor"; Kurt Buchner, "Findet die akademische Jugend zum Sozialismus?" *Neue Blätter für den Sozialismus* 4, no. 3 (March 1933): 137–42.

20. "Im Zwielicht," *Neue Blätter für den Sozialismus* 4, no. 4 (April 1933): 161.

21. Ibid., 162.

22. "Gleichschaltung!" *Neue Blätter für den Sozialismus* 4, no. 5 (May 1933): 217.

23. Ibid., 218. See also August Rathmann, "Auf Sozialisten, schließt die Reihen!," *Neue Blätter für den Sozialismus* 4, no. 6 (June 1933): 319–21.

24. The text of the speech can be found in *Verhandlungen des Deutschen Reichstages*, vol. 457, 17B-54B.

25. "Pfingsten," *Neue Blätter für den Sozialismus* 4, no. 6 (June 1933): 271.

26. Ibid., 273.

27. See Kurt Behrens, "Um den Neubau des Staates," *Neue Blätter für den Sozialismus* 4, no. 4 (April 1933): 179–86.

28. Walther Pahl, "Der Feiertag der Arbeit und die sozialistische Arbeiterschaft," *Gewerkschafts-Zeitung* 43, no. 17 (29 April 1933): 259–62.

29. See "Der Bundesausschuß des ADGB zum 1. Mai," and "An die Mitglieder der Gewerkschaften!," *Gewerkschafts-Zeitung* 43, no. 16 (22 April 1933): 241.

30. Pahl, "Der Feiertag der Arbeit," 259.

31. Ibid., 261.

32. See Franz Osterroth, *Erinnerungen (II) 1934 bis 1975*, Archiv der Sozialen Demokratie Bonn (hereafter cited as AdSD Bonn), Nachlass Franz Osterroth, Box 1, 154. See also Osterroth, "Spezielle Bemerkungen nach einer dreiwöchigen Deutschlandreise (ca. Oktober 1934)," AdSD Bonn, PV-Emigration (Sopade), folder 86; "Bericht von Osterroth über das Ruhrgebiet und das angrenzende Westfalen," n.d., AdSD Bonn, PV-Emigration (Sopade), folder 86; and Franz Osterroth to Erich Rinner, 11 June 1935, 5 August 1935, 12 October 1935, and 2 December 1935, all in AdSD Bonn, Rinner-Korrespondenz, no. 28.

33. See "Plan einer Zeitschrift 'Der Überblick,'" no date, Schleswig-Holsteinische Landesbibliothek Kiel, Nachlass August Rathmann, Cb 155, box 2.277. See also August Rathmann to Walter Hammer, 13 November 1954, Institut für Zeitgeschichte München (hereafter cited as IfZ Munich), Nachlass Walter Hammer, ED 106, vol. 49; "Besprechung mit den Genossen List, Weber, Lehmann, Fröhbrodt am 29.7.1933 in Bodenbach," Bundesarchiv Berlin (hereafter cited as BA Berlin), SAPMO, Ry 20/II 145/54, 14–16; "Aufzeichnungen über die Aussprache in der W.-Baude am Sonnabend und Sonntag, den 7. und 8. Oktober 1933," BA Berlin, SAPMO, Ry 20/II 145/56, 71–75.

34. See ibid.; Fritz Borinski, *Erinnerungen (IV) 1925—Frühjahr 1933*, IfZ Munich, Nachlass Fritz Borinski, ED 340, Box 1, 1009.

35. On the early phase of Social Democratic resistance activities, see Michael Schneider, *Unterm Hakenkreuz: Arbeiter und Arbeiterbewegung 1933 bis 1939* (Bonn: Dietz, 1999), 783–1078.

36. See "Besprechung mit einem Hamburger Vertrauensmann am Sonntag, den 20. Mai 1934 in Bodenbach," BA Berlin, SAPMO, Ry 20/II 145/56, 116–18; Otto Grot, "Kommentar zum Widerstandsmanuskript, Anfang Februar 1983," Forschungsstelle für Zeitgeschichte Hamburg, Bestand SPD, File 832–5; "Gestapo-Bericht vom 18.6.1935, betr. Illegale SPD-Bewegung in Hamburg," BA Berlin, R 58/3328, 38–42.

37. See ibid.; "Gestapo-Bericht vom 28.3.1934, betr. Illegale Organisation des verbotenen Reichsbanners," BA Berlin, R 58/3370, 153–56; "Anklageschrift gegen Theophil Johannes Jazdziewski u. a. vom 22.12.1934," BA Berlin, R 3017 alt/R 60 II/63, 1–27.

38. See "Abschrift von Briefberichten," n.d., BA Berlin, R 58/2, 181–207. These were copies of reports to the Sopade that the Gestapo had found in October 1935. The Gestapo mistakenly called the organization "*Caubach-Gruppe*," see ibid., 194. See also "Gestapo-Bericht vom 7.6.1934," BA Berlin, R 58/3329, 63–64; "Abschrift eines von der illegalen SPD-Leitung Berlin unter dem 10.8.34 an den Prager Vorstand abgesandten Briefes," BA Berlin, R 58/3315, 8–13; "Gestapo-Bericht vom 15.8.1934," BA Berlin, R 58/3315, 19; "Bericht über die Zusammenkunft der illegalen SPD Gewerkschaften u. des Reichsbanners von der Bezirksleitung Berlin vom 31.5.1934," BA Berlin, R 58/3329, 52–56. The Gestapo might have exaggerated the size of the organization for its own purposes, but there is no reason to believe that the copies from the illegal material had been forged or tampered with.

39. See "Interview von Karl Ditt mit Otto Grot vom 18.2.1982," Forschungsstelle für Zeitgeschichte Hamburg, Bestand SPD, File 832–5; Grot, "Kommentar zum Widerstandsmanuskript."

40. See "Gestapo-Bericht vom 18.6.1935"; "Bericht über die Zusammenkunft"; "Gestapo-Bericht vom 20.6.1934, betr.: Besprechung der illegalen SPD-, Gewerkschafts- und Reichsbannerführer," BA Berlin, R 58/3315, 5–7; "Bericht über den Stand der illegalen Arbeit der SPD (Juli bis September 1935) vom 18.9.1935," BA Berlin, R 58/3334, 1–31; "Besprechung mit Paul [Hertz] am Sonnabend, dem 15. September 1934," BA Berlin, SAPMO, Ry 20/II 145/56, 139–40; Alfred Markwitz to Walter Hammer, 29 May 1955, IfZ Munich, NL Hammer, ED 106, 49. These conferences were also often attended by the leaders of the illegal socialist trade unions.

41. Social Democratic resistance activities resumed in the 1940s, especially in the context of the plot of 20 July 1944. Several members of the *Neue Blätter für den Sozialismus* circle, among them Carl Mierendorff, Theodor Haubach, and Adolf Reichwein, participated in the *Kreisauer Kreis*, making it to some degree a further element of continuity of the circle's work. See Vogt, *Nationaler Sozialismus*, 411–49.

42. "Gestapo-Bericht vom 20.6.1934," 5–6.

43. See Rudolf Küstermeier, *Der Rote Stoßtrupp*, 3rd ed. (Berlin: Landeszentrale für politische Bildungsarbeit, 1981), 3–6.

44. See Franz Hering, "Bericht über die Tätigkeit des Roten Stoßtrupps, Januar 1934," BA Berlin, SAPMO, Ry 20/II 145/56, 90–95.

45. See "Bericht des Genossen Strinz aus Berlin am 12.8.1933," BA Berlin, SAPMO, Ry 20/II 145/56, 63; "Bericht von Dr. R. Mischler vom 15.11.1933," BA Berlin, SAPMO, Ry 20/II 145/56, 60–62; "Gestapo-Bericht vom 15.11.1934: Zur Verfügung vom 12.11.1934," BA Berlin, R 58/448, 34–36; Küstermeier, *Der Rote Stoßtrupp*, 10–14.

46. See "Bericht über die Neuorganisation des Roten Stoßtrupp in Berlin und im rheinischwestfälischen Industriegebiet, ca. Oktober 1934," BA Berlin, R 58/448, 30–33.

47. Küstermeier, *Der Rote Stoßtrupp*, 18.

48. "Achtung! Rote Stoßtrupps!," *Der Rote Stoßtrupp*, 7 May 1933, no. 4, quoted in "Anklageschrift des ORA gegen Georg Zinn und andere," BA Berlin, R 3017, AZ: 8 J 1856/33, 3; Küstermeier, *Der Rote Stoßtrupp*, 11.

49. "Was tun?," *Der Rote Stoßtrupp*, 9 April 1933, no. 1, quoted in "Anklageschrift des GStA beim Kammergericht Berlin gegen Bruno Senftleben u. a.," reprinted in Küstermeier, *Der Rote Stoßtrupp*, 23–24.

50. *Der Rote Stoßtrupp*, 14 June 1933, no. 9, quoted in "Anklageschrift des ORA gegen Zinn und andere," BA Berlin, R 3017, AZ: 8 J 1856/33, 4; and 21 June 1933, no. 10, quoted in "Gestapo-Bericht vom 15.11.1934: Zur Verfügung vom 12.11.1934," BA Berlin, R 58/448, 35.

51. *Der Rote Stoßtrupp*, 7 June 1933, no. 8, quoted in "Anklageschrift des GStA beim Kammergericht Berlin gegen Bruno Senftleben u. a.," reprinted in Küstermeier, *Der Rote Stoßtrupp*, 24.

52. *Der Rote Stoßtrupp*, 7 May 1933, no. 4, quoted in "Gestapo-Bericht vom 15.11.1934," 35. See also Franz Hering, "Bericht über die Tätigkeit des Roten Stoßtrupps, Januar 1934," BA Berlin, SAPMO, Ry 20/II 145/56, 90.

53. See "Anklageschrift des ORA gegen Georg Zinn und andere," BA Berlin, R 3017, AZ: 8 J 1856/33, 5–6, quoting a written agreement between the Rote Stoßtrupp and the SAP. See also *Der Rote Stoßtrupp*, 14 June 1933, no. 9, quoted in "Anklageschrift des GStA beim Kammergericht Berlin gegen Bruno Senftleben," 24; Küstermeier, *Der Rote Stoßtrupp*, 8.

54. Ibid.; Johann von Bach, "Die Front der deutschen Revolutionäre," *Die Deutsche Revolution*, no. 23 (14 October 1934); Rudolf Küstermeier, "Sozialistische Aktion! Die Mittelschichten und der Sozialismus," ibid., no. 17 (2 September 1934).

55. Emil Henk, "Sozialdemokratischer Widerstand im Raum Mannheim," in *100 Jahre SPD in Mannheim: Eine Dokumentation* (Mannheim: SPD Kreis Mannheim, 1967), 70; Günter Braun, "Die Sozialdemokraten," in *Widerstand gegen den Nationalsozialismus in Mannheim*, ed. Erich Matthias and Hermann Weber (Mannheim: Edition Quadrat, 1984), 142.

56. "Anklageschrift des GStA Darmstadt gegen Wilhelm Ernst Rösler und andere vom 18.6.1935," BA Berlin, Bestand Nazi-Justiz, NJ 6500, 17–31; "Anklageschrift des GStA Karlsruhe gegen Emil Henk und andere vom 4.2.1934," BA Berlin, Bestand Nazi-Justiz, NJ 3334, 2–15; "Anklageschrift des

GStA Darmstadt gegen Georg Liebig und andere vom 8.7.1936," ibid., NJ 1205, 5–19; and "Anklageschrift des GStA Darmstadt gegen Theobald Sturm und andere vom 19.9.1936," ibid., NJ 5478, 2; Henk, "Sozialdemokratischer Widerstand," 70.

57. Ibid.

58. Henk, "Sozialdemokratischer Widerstand," 72. See also Georg Reinbold to Sopade, 14 August 1934, AdSD Bonn, Bestand PV-Emigration (Sopade), folder 90, no. 22; Georg Reinbold to Sopade, 15 October 1934, AdSD Bonn, Bestand PV-Emigration (Sopade), folder 90, no. 27; "Lagebericht über reformistische Organisationen (Januar 1935)," BA Berlin, R 58/416, 84–86.

59. "Anklageschrift des GStA Darmstadt gegen Theobald Sturm," BA Berlin, NJ 5478, 2.

60. Reinbold to Sopade, 14 August 1934. See also Reinbold to Sopade, 10 April 1934; note by Georg Reinbold, 23 April 1934, AdSD Bonn, Bestand PV-Emigration (Sopade), folder 91, no. 46; Georg Reinbold to Sopade, 5 November 1934, BA Berlin, SAPMO, Ry 20/II 145/56, 168–70; Georg Reinbold to Sopade, 3 April 1935, ibid., folder 91, no. 43.

61. "Neunkirchener Konferenz vom 2., 3. und 4. Juni 1934," BA Berlin, SAPMO, Ry 20/II 145/54, 91, 95.

62. Ibid., 92. See also Rechberg to Sopade, 27 July 1934, AdSD Bonn, Bestand PV-Emigration (Sopade), folder 90, no. 20.

Bibliography

Beck, Dorothea. "Theodor Haubach, Julius Leber, Carlo Mierendorff, Kurt Schumacher: Zum Selbstverständnis der 'militanten Sozialisten' in der Weimarer Republik." *Archiv für Sozialgeschichte* 26 (1986): 87–123.

Buchner, Bernd. *Um nationale und republikanische Identität: Die deutsche Sozialdemokratie und der Kampf um die politischen Symbole der Weimarer Republik.* Bonn: Dietz, 2001.

Friedrich-Ebert-Stiftung, ed. *Widerstand und Exil der deutschen Arbeiterbewegung 1933–1945.* Schriftenreihe der Bundeszentrale für politische Bildung 180. Bonn: Verlag Neue Gesellschaft, 1981.

Groh, Dieter, and Peter Brandt. *"Vaterlandslose Gesellen": Sozialdemokratie und Nation 1860–1990.* Munich: Beck, 1992.

Harsch, Donna. *German Social Democracy and the Rise of Nazism.* Chapel Hill: University of North Carolina Press, 1993.

Heer, Hannes. *Burgfrieden oder Klassenkampf: Zur Politik der sozialdemokratischen Gewerkschaften 1930–1933.* Neuwied: Luchterhand, 1971.

Lösche, Peter, and Michael Scholing. "Solidargemeinschaft im Widerstand: Eine Fallstudie über 'Blick in die Zeit.'" *Internationale wissenschaftliche Korrespondenz zur Geschichte der Arbeiterbewegung* 19 (1983): 517–61.

Mammach, Klaus. *Die deutsche antifaschistische Widerstandsbewegung 1933–1939.* Berlin/DDR: Dietz, 1974.

Martiny, Martin. "Die Entstehung und die politische Bedeutung der 'Neuen Blätter für den Sozialismus' und ihres Freundeskreises." *Vierteljahrshefte für Zeitgeschichte* 25 (1977): 317–419.

Matthias, Erich. "Die Sozialdemokratische Partei Deutschlands." In *Das Ende der Parteien 1933,* edited by Erich Matthias and Rudolf Morsey, 101–278. Düsseldorf: Droste 1960.

Mommsen, Hans. "Die Sozialdemokratie in der Defensive: Der Immobilismus der SPD und der Aufstieg des Nationalsozialismus." In *Sozialdemokratie zwischen Klassenbewegung und Volkspartei,* edited by Hans Mommsen, 106–33. Frankfurt a.M.: Athenäum, 1974.

Moraw, Frank. *Die Parole der "Einheit" und die Sozialdemokratie: Zur parteiorganisatorischen und gesellschaftspolitischen Orientierung der SPD in der Periode der Illegalität und in der ersten Phase der Nachkriegszeit 1933–1948.* Bonn: Dietz, 1973.

Pyta, Wolfram. *Gegen Hitler und für die Republik: Die Auseinandersetzung der deutschen Sozialdemokratie mit der NSDAP in der Weimarer Republik.* Düsseldorf: Droste, 1989.

Rohe, Karl. *Das Reichsbanner Schwarz Rot Gold: Ein Beitrag zur Geschichte und Struktur der politischen Kampfverbände zur Zeit der Weimarer Republik.* Düsseldorf: Droste, 1966.

Schneider, Michael. *Unterm Hakenkreuz: Arbeiter und Arbeiterbewegung 1933 bis 1939.* Bonn: Dietz, 1999.

Smith, Woodruff D. "The Mierendorff Group and the Modernization of German Social Democratic Politics, 1928–33." *Politics and Society* 5 (1975): 109–29.

Vogt, Stefan. *Nationaler Sozialismus und Soziale Demokratie: Die sozialdemokratische Junge Rechte 1918–1945.* Bonn: Dietz, 2006.

———. "Die Sozialistische Entscheidung: Paul Tillich und die sozialdemokratische Junge Rechte in der Weimarer Republik." In *Internationales Jahrbuch der Tillich-Forschung,* vol. 4: *Tillich und der religiöse Sozialismus,* edited by Christian Danz, Werner Schüßler, and Erdmann Sturm, 35–52. Berlin: De Gruyter, 2009.

———. "Strange Encounters: Social Democracy and Radical Nationalism in Weimar Germany." *Journal of Contemporary History* 45 (2010): 253–81.

———. "Zwischen Sozialismus und Faschismus: Nationaler Sozialismus im Europa der Vor- und Zwischenkriegszeit." In *Ideengeschichte als politische Aufklärung: Festschrift für Wolfgang Wippermann zum 65. Geburtstag,* edited by Stefan Vogt et al., 71–107. Berlin: Metropol, 2010.

Walter, Franz. *Nationale Romantik und revolutionärer Mythos: Politik und Lebenswelten im frühen Weimarer Jungsozialismus.* Berlin: Verlag Europäische Perspektiven, 1986.

Winkler, Heinrich August. *Der Weg in die Katastrophe: Arbeiter und Arbeiterbewegung in der Weimarer Republik 1930–1933.* Berlin: Dietz, 1987.

Wippermann, Wolfgang. *Zur Analyse des Faschismus: Die sozialdemokratischen und kommunistischen Faschismustheorien 1921–1945.* Frankfurt a. M.: Diesterweg, 1981.

 9

NATIONALISM, SOCIALISM, AND ORGANIZED LABOR'S RESPONSE TO THE DISSOLUTION OF THE WEIMAR REPUBLIC

William L. Patch Jr.

In the last issue of the theoretical journal of the socialist free unions, Lothar Erdmann reproached the German Social Democratic Party for its failure since 1918 "to educate its followers in the spirit of an active foreign policy" dedicated to revision of the Versailles Treaty; Marxist intellectuals had prevented it from representing the German people's "will to live" and "will to power." Like the "Young Right" faction within the Social Democratic Party (Sozialdemokratische Partei Deutschlands or SPD), Erdmann argued that the party's theoretical Marxism encouraged a passive tendency to wait for economic developments to cause historical change. His essay reflected the most powerful early influence that led this intellectual from a middle-class background to become a socialist: the campaign by Friedrich Naumann to synthesize "national" and "social" values, i.e., a commitment both to patriotism and egalitarian social reform.[1] Detlev Brunner argues that this essay marked the climax of a campaign by leaders of the blue-collar socialist labor federation, the General German Trade Union Federation (Allgemeiner Deutscher Gewerkschaftsbund or ADGB), to embrace nationalist causes. His analysis relies on the concept of generations; older labor leaders made a tactical decision by 1923 to adopt a rhetoric of patriotic self-sacrifice to influence middle-class public opinion and government officials, and they then filled ADGB headquarters with young combat veterans such as Erdmann, who were inspired by the war experience to revere "the nation" in almost mystical terms. For these younger functionaries the rhetoric of patriotic self-sacrifice expressed core values, not merely a public relations strategy. By autumn 1930, according to Brunner, the interaction between senior ADGB leaders and their young advisors yielded a course for the trade unions that diverged widely from the views of most union members, as the ADGB began to blame all economic problems on the Versailles Treaty, to cooperate with Germany's increasingly authoritarian "presidential" governments, and to curry favor with the Nazis after Hitler became chancellor. Some historians judge that the ADGB was compelled to shift course by union members swayed by Nazi propaganda, but Brunner argues like Gerard Braunthal before him that it displayed powerful "oligarchic" tendencies in the sense defined by Robert Michels. All efforts by ADGB leaders to influence middle-class public opinion failed; they succeeded only at alienating their own membership.[2]

This chapter evaluates Brunner's thesis and the health of internal democracy in the blue-collar trade unions from 1930 to 1933. The argument must remain largely conjectural because of the destruction of most union records in 1933. As Siegfried Mielke has observed, all judgments of the ADGB float in the air, because we lack detailed studies of its member unions and the local committees of the umbrella organization.[3] A comparison between the free and smaller Christian trade unions might shed new light, based on the assumption that a divergence in their courses probably reflected the differing political loyalties of the two union bureaucracies, while convergence probably reflected pressure from the membership. The Federation of German Christian Trade Unions (Gesamtverband der christlichen Gewerkschaften Deutschlands or GcG) never grew to more than one-sixth the size of the ADGB nationwide but provided stiff competition in its regional bastions of Rhineland-Westphalia, the Saarland, and Baden-Württemberg. Its predominantly Catholic leadership was reared in an intensely patriotic spirit, and the combat veteran who chaired the Rhineland GcG in the 1920s, Jakob Kaiser, displayed a yearning to reconcile "national" and "social" values that resembled that of Erdmann.[4] Enough evidence survives for the Christian unions to suggest that there was no great upsurge of nationalist sentiment among the membership in the Great Depression; instead, they displayed unprecedented support for socialist economic reforms. Brunner was probably correct that grassroots working-class nationalism cannot explain the key decisions by ADGB leaders from 1930 to 1933, but some of his other arguments are questionable. All labor leaders knew during the Great Depression that their membership desperately wanted the revival of full employment, and that was the leaders' top priority. The membership—like most German economists—had no idea how to revive full employment, however; to criticize union leaders for oligarchic tendencies has little meaning in a situation where creative thinking and novel ideas were needed. Brunner is also misleading when he dismisses all maneuvers by the ADGB in March–April 1933 as an attempt to curry favor with the Nazis. The last-minute attempt to unify the free, Christian, and Hirsch-Duncker unions in April 1933, although doomed to failure, reflected powerful trends in the thinking of union members.

From Conflict to Cooperation among the Labor Federations

The formation of the Brüning cabinet in April 1930 drove a wedge between the free and Christian unions. The ADGB doubtless reflected the views of its membership when it prodded the SPD to resist Brüning's agrarian protectionism and painful measures to balance the budget. When the Reichstag was dissolved in July 1930, the ADGB donated one million marks to the SPD campaign and appealed to all workers to vote for it as the only defender of the democratic republic. Theodor Leipart, who had led the ADGB since 1921, was a historical materialist from his youth, and he and his freethinking speechwriter Erdmann distrusted clerical influence on the German Center Party (Deutsche Zentrumspartei). Leipart told a journalist that the government parties sought "revision of the Weimar constitution [and] greater power for the Reich President," and he discerned "strong tendencies to erect an authoritarian corporatist state."[5] Heinrich Brüning had won the confidence of all GcG leaders, however, while serving as general secretary of their loose umbrella organization with white-collar unions in the 1920s, and he appointed as labor minister the former GcG leader Adam Stegerwald. Christian trade unionists defended Brüning's program as the unavoidable consequence of the world economic crisis. During the campaign, Stegerwald's successor as GcG chair, Bernhard Otte, also argued that Christians who voted SPD betrayed their faith. In September 1930, the GcG described the election outcome as a victory, because the SPD declined from 29.8 percent to 24.5 percent of the vote while the Center Party avoided losses. It thus downplayed the significance of the stunning rise of the Nazi Party to 18.3 percent, following a campaign in which the best defenders of democracy wasted much of their strength attacking each other.[6]

Most ADGB leaders agreed with the SPD's decision after the election to tolerate the Brüning cabinet as "the lesser evil," because a "fascist" government would probably emerge if it fell. The free unions found it much more difficult than the SPD to defend toleration, however. The cabinet announced soon after the election that nominal wages must be reduced to make German exports competitive on the world market, and state arbitrators appointed by Stegerwald began to impose cuts of 6 percent or more whenever a collective labor contract came up for renegotiation. Strikes were almost impossible to sustain in the face of rising unemployment, which inflicted more immediate damage on union organizations than on the parties. The free unions lost 4.7 percent of their five million members in 1930, and the Christian unions 2.1 percent of their 673,000; the rate of loss accelerated in September.[7] Most trade unionists therefore advocated government borrowing to finance large-scale public works, but Brüning had already sought to follow that advice. In May the cabinet had developed a program for 1.5 billion marks in infrastructure investments but could not arrange financing. On the campaign trail in August, Brüning announced a new billion-mark program for public works, but the cabinet could raise only 180 million in loans. The collapse of government credit left trade unionists fearful that nothing could be done to revive employment, and they searched desperately for policy options.[8]

ADGB leaders could think of only two proposals that might create jobs quickly when their National Committee met on 12–13 October 1930: a ceiling of forty hours on the work week to "stretch out" employment among more workers and a moratorium on the payment of war reparations, which should save the government enough money to finance a sizeable public works program. Both proposals were adopted unanimously, including the following motion written by Lothar Erdmann:

> In view of the difficult economic situation of Germany today, our existing reparations payments, whose value has long since exceeded the actual damage caused by the war, represent a burden that puts our social and civic life in dire jeopardy. ... It cannot be denied that the billions Germany must pay to its creditors are one of the causes not only of the frightful unemployment in Germany but also of the disruptions in the world economy. Economics and statesmanship therefore demand the elimination of these hindrances to a healthy development of the world economy.[9]

The last two sentences clothed the resolution with a fig leaf of internationalist sentiment, but the SPD chairman Otto Wels warned the delegates that this language might be confused with rightist propaganda, and that Chancellor Brüning opposed any call for a moratorium because of its disruptive impact on financial markets. The delegates ignored these arguments, however. Detlev Brunner describes this resolution as the beginning of a misguided campaign by the ADGB to support Brüning's foreign policy in the hope of obtaining domestic policy concessions, but it contradicted Brüning's foreign policy at this time. Erdmann's nationalist allies at ADGB headquarters sought to persuade Leipart that most union members shared the anger with the Versailles Treaty revealed in the Nazi electoral success, but they offered no meaningful evidence for that assertion. Most delegates to the National Committee actually assumed that union members were immune to Nazi propaganda, but they were desperate to create jobs.[10]

GcG leaders meanwhile experienced pressure from below to adopt a more critical attitude toward the Brüning cabinet. At the congress of the Christian textile workers in August 1930, Bernhard Otte defended Brüning's program, but all the delegates were angry because of the campaign by employers to slash wages. One mid-ranking functionary declared that "our task as a trade union movement is not to play the role of saviors of the state and nation. Instead we must see to it that the workers do not become beasts of burden."[11] After the Reichstag election, the GcG criticized the cabinet's program sharply, and in early November the congress of the Christian woodworkers' union embraced the demand for the forty-hour week. On 20 November 1930 Brüning defended his program in person to leaders of the Christian labor federation, but the militant chairman of the Christian miners' union, Heinrich Imbusch, replied that it "maintains its independence against the Reich government even when its own friends sit in it. ... Our movement is neither a government defense troop nor an instrument of party politics. In face of the effort to push workers back ..., our movement must not abandon without a fight any position that can and must be defended."[12]

The liberal Hirsch-Duncker unions had only about 160,000 members but took the lead in promoting cooperation among the three labor federations in January 1931, when their general secretary, Ernst Lemmer, invited the ADGB and GcG to discuss a joint protest against war reparations. The ADGB agreed to participate but consulted beforehand with SPD leaders, who argued that rapprochement with France offered the best hope to promote economic recovery with the help of new foreign loans. By the time the leaders of the three labor federations met in February, they were preoccupied with a new campaign by employers to weaken collective bargaining rights. In a major step toward closer cooperation, they sent a joint delegation to President Hindenburg on 26 February 1931, when Leipart declared that the unions had "always sought to persuade their members of the need to make sacrifices in these times and remain calm. But more must happen to alleviate unemployment, so that these state-preserving elements in the trade unions do not become radicalized." In reply, Hindenburg could only promise that the cabinet would discuss these concerns, but Leipart concluded that labor's demands received much more favorable publicity when the three federations acted together.[13] Lemmer resumed the discussion of reparations thereafter, and in May Bernhard Otte informed Leipart that Brüning would now be grateful for a joint declaration by the unions, because the cabinet judged the time ripe for a public anti-reparations campaign. Leipart dropped the idea, however, when he learned that Brüning planned to impose new austerity measures without consulting him; he sent the chancellor a long list of domestic policy demands instead.[14] The GcG sought briefly to defend Brüning's Second Comprehensive Emergency Decree to Secure the Economy and State Finances, published on 5 June 1931, but its members shared the free unions' outrage over its tax hikes and benefits cuts. The Christian unions soon criticized the decree sharply and participated in a joint labor deputation to the chancellor on 15 June, when Otte embraced Leipart's two most urgent demands for amendments and persuaded Brüning to accept them. This was the first time in years that joint action by the three labor federations actually modified government policy.[15]

In July 1931 Germany achieved an unexpected breakthrough in the struggle against reparations with the one-year Hoover Moratorium, but only because the bank crisis had caused a disastrous rise in unemployment. When the free unions convened a national congress on 31 August, Theodor Leipart reported that only 49 percent of union members now worked full time. Leipart focused the congress agenda on the forty-hour week, and he gave labor minister Stegerwald a remarkably cordial welcome and signaled that the ADGB would support the government's foreign policy if it imposed the forty-hour week on at least a few industries. Both Leipart and Professor Emil Lederer, the economist who delivered the keynote policy address, ascribed great importance to reparations as a cause of the world economic crisis and called for their permanent abolition as the precondition for recovery. Brüning had revealed details of the recent economic conferences in Paris and London to Leipart in a face-to-face meeting a few weeks earlier and persuaded him that the foreign policy advocated by the SPD—rapprochement with France—could not yield the new foreign loans for which the SPD hoped.[16] The delegates showed no interest in reparations, so it does not appear that Leipart was responding to nationalist pressure from the membership. Two left-wing Marxists denounced the policy of toleration, calling for resolute class struggle, but the great majority agreed that their arguments amounted to an appeal for a disastrous "civil war." Most speakers simply offered moving accounts of the sufferings of workers in their trade.[17]

On 4 December 1931 Leipart finally issued the joint manifesto against reparations long sought by Ernst Lemmer and thereby earned Chancellor Brüning's gratitude, for whatever that was worth. When Leipart called again for the abolition of reparations a week later at a joint rally with the SPD, Rudolf Breitscheid rebuked him for imitating Nazi slogans in the sharpest clash between SPD and union leaders for many years.[18] Leipart had become anxious to defend the policy of toleration when four delegates to the ADGB National Committee argued in November that organized labor would benefit if Hitler and Hugenberg formed a new government. All ADGB leaders agreed that this strategy would lead to disaster, but such calls proliferated when Brüning imposed new austerity measures in his Fourth Comprehensive Emergency Decree on 8 December 1931. The ADGB economist Hans Arons then advised Leipart that the struggle against reparations offered the best hope to defend toleration. "It is an old and often followed rule of experience," he argued, "that domestic political tensions can be diverted onto foreign policy targets. … Just as Brüning defends his emergency decrees with foreign policy goals, I think the trade unions can in the same manner offer the most persuasive and effective defense of their policy of toleration." Leipart soon tested this theory by telling a journalist that Brüning had been compelled to adopt new austerity measures because the Western powers refused to abolish reparations. There is no evidence, however, that this argument influenced union members; the GcG had publicly denounced reparations since May, but it and the ADGB both lost a painful 12.3 percent of membership in the year 1931.[19]

Leipart's foreign policy line did promote cooperation with the other two labor federations, and the mammoth German Metalworkers' Union (Deutscher Metallarbeiter-Verband) appealed for their merger in late October 1931. Anton Erkelenz of the Hirsch-Duncker unions responded in an open letter that unified trade unions must "embrace workers from all parties" and give "workers who are not socialists a home and a chance to participate." It was even more urgent, he noted, for the unions of the future to guarantee "freedom of religious faith." Finally, they must "conduct a resolute struggle against communist/Bolshevik attempts to foment revolution" and "serve the state, the nation, the Republic, and democracy." Leipart replied on 5 December 1931 that the three labor federations had for years pursued essentially the same goal, "economic democracy," with almost exactly the same methods. He declared somewhat implausibly that the free unions already were completely independent of the SPD, and his statement on religious freedom was also problematic, because he reserved the right for trade unions to attack the Christian churches if they meddled in politics. In view of the ADGB's anticommunist record, Leipart was most believable when he affirmed that the trade union movement must indeed "serve the state, the nation, the Republic, and democracy."[20] Erkelenz, who had already joined the SPD in 1930, applauded this declaration and campaigned thereafter to persuade Hirsch-Duncker colleagues to merge with the ADGB, although he found that many feared a loss of autonomy. GcG leaders refused to discuss merger or even the formation of a joint standing committee, alleging that the Hirsch-Duncker unions considered a merger only because they were on the brink of financial collapse.[21] The GcG supported closer informal cooperation nevertheless and criticized the Fourth Emergency Decree vigorously. When Brüning defended it to the Center Reichstag delegation on 15 December 1931, Heinrich Imbusch replied that "it is useless to preach reason to hungry people." Otte had joined Leipart in a joint deputation to the chancellor the day before, and Leipart reported to the ADGB National Committee that such cooperation offered their only hope to influence public opinion and government policy.[22]

Debates over Economic Policy within Organized Labor

Most trade unionists had no idea how to revive employment, a fact that highlights the limitations of democratic decision-making processes in the Great Depression. Innovative thinking was needed, and it was offered by the ADGB statistician Wladimir Woytinsky. In autumn 1931 new government controls on banking and foreign exchange made it possible for Germany to consider a new monetary policy, and Woytinsky developed the thoughtful "WTB Plan" to expand the money supply to spend two billion marks on public works that would employ one million workers directly. With vigorous support from Lothar Erdmann, Woytinsky gained the backing of all free union leaders by February 1932, but SPD leaders rejected the WTB Plan on the advice of their revered Marxist theoretician, Rudolf Hilferding, who agreed with many liberal economists that it would result in hyperinflation. The free unions possessed no daily newspapers, and the SPD press ignored their plan. Woytinsky later recalled a tense summit conference with the SPD where Hilferding insisted that his plan could not succeed because it contradicted Marx's labor theory of value, and Otto Wels bellowed with rage if anyone questioned Hilferding. This dispute provides some evidence for Erdmann's argument that the Marxism of the SPD encouraged fatalism in practice, but GcG leaders adopted a position similar to Hilferding's under the influence of Stegerwald and Brüning.[23]

The bank crisis of July 1931 did stimulate unprecedented attacks on free enterprise within the Christian unions. Shocking revelations of criminal fraud and gross blunders by business leaders inspired the GcG to demand strong government oversight of the big banks and either the strict regulation or dissolution of the syndicates and trusts. In late October 1931 Heinrich Körner, the vice chairman of the Rhineland GcG, called for "an orderly planned economy" so that the world would never again see mountains of wheat, cotton, and coffee burned while millions suffered privation.[24] Following brutal wage disputes with the Rhenish-Westphalian Coal Syndicate, Heinrich Imbusch appealed in January 1932 for "the transfer of mining to public ownership." He praised the good management of the few government-owned coal mines but focused his argument on the syndicate's political support for the radical right. Imbusch earned thunderous applause when he told miners on 7 February 1932 that "the heavy industrialists are a threat to the nation, they are a state within the state, they display no regard for the common good. … Therefore, we must remove this thorn from the flesh of the German people represented by our most ruthless business-men."[25] All Christian trade unions endorsed the nationalization of the mines by late April, but the Christian miners provoked controversy thereafter by demanding the nationalization of the entire coal, iron, and steel industry. They received vigorous support at the last congress of the Christian unions in September 1932 from Körner and the highest ranking Protestant at GcG headquarters, Friedrich Baltrusch. The key-note address on economic policy by Baltrusch called for public owner-ship of the largest syndicates and trusts and new government agencies to channel investment and regulate prices.[26] The Christian unions were drawing closer to the economic program of the SPD, while the free unions backed away from it to focus in a more pragmatic spirit on the issue of public works to revive employment.

This assault on free enterprise provoked opposition by Theodor Brauer, a professor of economics at Cologne and former aide to Stegerwald. Brauer was a careful student of liberal economics and a pious Catholic, inspired by papal teaching to seek a new era of cooperation between management and organized labor. He celebrated the Central Association of Employers and Employees (Zentralarbeitsgemeinschaft der industriellen und gewerblichen Arbeitgeber und Arbeitnehmer Deutschlands) founded in November 1918 as a great step toward social partnership, and he mourned its dissolution five years later. Brauer's idealistic speeches at postwar congresses of the Christian unions pro-voked disagreement, however, from delegates who experienced con-flict with employers. Friction with union colleagues impelled Brauer to pursue an academic career in 1923, although he always devoted himself to the GcG education program for union functionaries. In 1924 Brauer published a critique of the free and Christian unions that was sympathetic in tone but harsh in substance; he alleged that they had ignored the laws of economics since 1918, launched too many strikes, and pursued an overly ambitious legislative agenda.[27] In March 1932 Brauer returned to the struggle for influence on the Christian unions by declaring that "the issue of nationalizing the mines must under no circumstances be linked with the issue of nationalizing the economy as a whole." The coal mines formed a special case because of the old German legal and Catholic moral tradition that mineral wealth belonged to the community. Any attempt to nationalize all large-scale industry, however, "must result in a sort of police state, whose pressure on human beings would soon become unbearable." The Christian Metalworkers' Union (Christlicher Metallarbeiter-Verband), led by Franz Wieber, also opposed nationalization of the steel industry, and at the last congress of the Christian unions Brauer argued against any expropriations or central state planning.[28] The position of the Christian miners was obviously more popular, however. When the metalworkers held their congress soon thereafter, a young delegate from Essen declared that "capitalism is to blame for our misery. ... Therefore, I demand the nationalization of all large capitalist factories and their transfer to the collective ownership of the workers." Franz Wieber rebuked the speaker, but his own son Georg noted that the "big bourgeoisie" displayed such arrogance as to make calls to nationalize large-scale industry all but irresistible. Imbusch never encountered such challenges at miners' rallies, and his union lost only 7.4 percent of its members in 1932, while losses for the free unions averaged 15 percent.[29]

Brauer described his goal as a "corporatist order" (*berufsständische Ordnung*), a term popularized by the papal encyclical of June 1931, *Quadragesimo anno*, which was interpreted in many different ways.[30] For Brauer it implied that government should delegate some regulatory powers to mixed commissions for each industry made up of equal numbers of employers and trade unionists. His most provocative ideas were that control of unemployment insurance should be transferred to these commissions, so that it ceased to disrupt the national budget, and that the existing National Economic Council should become an upper house of parliament with jurisdiction over labor law and social insurance. He presented these suggestions to a Christian union leadership conference in November 1930, but they provoked many "skeptical remarks." Brauer also discussed them in a book published a year later, but his partner as co-director of the GcG adult education program, Dr. Franz Röhr, commented that "the social order envisioned by Brauer assumes incomparably more reason and civic virtue among individual human beings and their associations than is present among them today." A former aide to Walther Rathenau, Röhr had supported nationalization of the coal mines since 1920 and edited the GcG theoretical journal

since 1923. He had obviously predisposed many Christian trade unionists to regard the Great Depression as a damning judgment on capitalism; Brüning later remembered him as an admirable human being but a
"radical socialist" in all economic questions.[31] Bernhard Otte displayed
more interest in Brauer's ideas than any other GcG leader, but his interpretation of the "corporatist order" to a conference of Catholic scholars
in May 1932 implied little more than a patient campaign to revive
something like the Central Association of Employers and Employees
of November 1918. Jakob Kaiser's close associate at GcG headquarters,
Elfriede Nebgen, later recalled that the idea of a "corporatist order"
was never taken seriously by most Christian trade unionists, except for
Otte. Brauer was evidently losing the policy debate within the Christian
unions when Hitler was appointed chancellor.[32]

Responses to the Collapse of Democratic Institutions

Cooperation between the free and Christian unions intensified after
Franz von Papen replaced Brüning in June 1932. The ADGB declared
that Papen had united all workers against his policy of "class struggle
from above," and the GcG attacked him for seeking to "deprive workers
of their rights again" and restore the dominion of the old ruling class.[33]
The free and Christian unions also adopted the same passive response
when the new cabinet deposed the SPD-Center coalition government in
Prussia on 20 July 1932. Lothar Erdmann urged his superiors to resist,
but the Christian trade unionist who served as the acting prime minister of Prussia, welfare minister Heinrich Hirtsiefer, agreed quickly with
Otto Wels and the leaders of the ADGB and GcG that they must do
nothing to give Papen an excuse to cancel the upcoming Reichstag election. That election left the Reichstag completely paralyzed, however,
because the Nazis achieved 37.4 percent of the vote, and the Communist
Party (Kommunistische Partei Deutschlands or KPD) 14.5 percent.[34]
In September the delegates to the Christian unions' last congress displayed an earnest desire nevertheless to defend the Weimar Republic.
Franz Röhr delivered a ringing defense of the Weimar Constitution
against the proposal by Papen that it should be amended through presidential decree. Two young delegates who would play a major political
role after 1945, Karl Arnold and Johannes Ernst, called for an alliance
with Social Democratic workers, and the chair of the textile workers'
union, Heinrich Fahrenbrach, urged workers' organizations to imitate
the agrarian Green Front; they must all cooperate so that "workers
united can advance their legitimate demands with the same energy."[35]

In August 1932 SPD leaders became suspicious of Leipart and the two ADGB vice chairmen, Peter Grassmann and Wilhelm Eggert, because of press reports that defense minister Kurt von Schleicher was forging a "trade union axis," an alliance of trade unions and paramilitary leagues that would represent the "will of the people" more authentically than did the corrupt political parties. Schleicher had no such plan, however, only an instinct to sow division among his opponents. He inquired of Heinrich Imbusch and Lothar Erdmann about the trade unions' ideas regarding the nationalization of heavy industry, but these feelers led to nothing.[36] Only one of Schleicher's initiatives proved attractive to ADGB leaders—the formation in September of a Reich Institute to Promote Youth Fitness (Reichskuratorium für Jugendertüchtigung) to teach "military sports" to young workers in voluntary labor service brigades. The paramilitary Reich Banner Black-Red-Gold (Reichsbanner Schwarz-Rot-Gold) wanted to participate, but the SPD denounced the program as a thinly veiled attempt to launch illegal rearmament. Erdmann persuaded Leipart and Grassmann to side with the Reich Banner, because he hoped that "military sports" would become popular and compel the SPD to carry out a long overdue revision of its program for national defense.[37] This dispute died away in December, however, when the SPD insisted on "sharpest opposition" to the new Schleicher cabinet and a boycott of the Institute for Youth Fitness, and the ADGB and Reich Banner deferred to its wishes. The SPD and free unions remained tightly bound because of a shared worldview among their functionaries. Two dozen union leaders belonged to the SPD Reichstag delegation; hundreds more held SPD mandates at the state and local level, and most SPD Reichstag delegates belonged to a union. No ADGB leader seriously considered a rupture with the SPD in 1932.[38]

In November 1932 Schleicher gained some goodwill from organized labor by promising to rescind Papen's most offensive decrees on wage policy, implement a public works program, and abandon Papen's idea of imposing authoritarian constitutional amendments through presidential decree. Imbusch and Otte had begun to discuss these concessions with Schleicher before the election of 6 November left the Reichstag hopelessly paralyzed, and they approached Leipart on 9 November. Leipart and Eggert then accepted Schleicher's invitation to a meeting on 28 November, and when the general confirmed the three promises already discussed with the GcG, Leipart cautiously advised that he should become chancellor if Papen was the only alternative.[39] The Christian unions praised Chancellor Schleicher's program and celebrated his appointment as proof that organized labor retained influence, but ADGB leaders avoided public disagreement with the oppositional SPD.[40] Christian trade unionists hoped that Gregor Strasser might persuade Hitler to allow him to join the new cabinet, securing Nazi support for Schleicher's moderate course, and they were dismayed when Strasser abruptly resigned from his party offices on 8 December and left Berlin. They commented that Hitler obviously remained determined to create a violent, one-party dictatorship that would be a catastrophe for Germany.[41]

The Schleicher cabinet scraped together at least 500 million marks for public works, and organized labor applauded this initiative. Most party leaders were prepared in January 1933 to adjourn the Reichstag voluntarily for two or three months so that this program could be implemented, and Leipart and Eggert requested a meeting with Schleicher on 26 January to appeal for the expansion of public works. They were astonished to learn that Schleicher rejected any accommodation with the party leaders and wanted the ADGB to endorse the dissolution of the Reichstag and postponement of new elections until October or November. "That would be something completely different from a breach of the constitution," he insisted. The constitution clearly stated, however, that no more than ninety days could pass between the dissolution of the Reichstag and the first meeting of its elected successor, and Eggert replied immediately that "we do not want the declaration of a state of emergency in any form." Thus ended Schleicher's clumsy attempt to gain the support of organized labor, and he resigned two days later.[42]

The leaders of the three labor federations met when they heard of Schleicher's resignation and agreed that Hindenburg would probably reappoint his favorite, Franz von Papen. They sent the president a telegram to demand that he uphold the Weimar Constitution and repudiate all who advocated a coup d'état, clearly rejecting Papen and Schleicher, but not necessarily a Hitler cabinet authorized to seek a parliamentary majority in new elections.[43] The labor leaders met again on 30 January 1933 to discuss a general strike. They had just agreed to declare that the appointment of Papen would be a "deliberate proclamation of hostilities against all people loyal to the constitution" when they heard with relief that Hitler had been appointed instead. All three labor federations then instructed their followers to observe developments and avoid local initiatives. Leipart told SPD leaders that the Christian unions firmly opposed the new government and would support whatever action the ADGB proposed, a remarkable statement in view of the hostility between the labor federations in 1930. Leipart concluded, however, that a general strike could not succeed because of mass unemployment and the absence of any clear breach of the constitution. The KPD did call for a general strike, but Grassmann reported proudly to SPD leaders on 31 January that trade union discipline held firm. Years later Karl Dörpinghaus recalled that he had made all the necessary preparations for a strike by Christian textile workers on the lower Rhine to protest against the Nazi seizure of power, but his union headquarters vetoed the idea. Thus the leaders of the free and Christian unions adopted the same attitude.[44]

During the Weimar Republic's last election campaign, the free and Christian unions actively supported their traditional partners, the SPD and Center Party. The campaign was soon transformed, however, by massive storm trooper violence. In what may be the only surviving record of a confidential discussion among union leaders in these turbulent weeks, Heinrich Imbusch warned the central committee of the Christian miners' union in early February that a fierce struggle had broken out between "revolutionary" and "reactionary" factions within the NSDAP and that "an attack on the trade-union movement is possible at any time." They agreed that "these elections will determine the future of the trade union movement to the greatest extent," meaning that they must exert themselves to the utmost. Fear and anxiety spread thereafter as a result of incidents such as the assault on Adam Stegerwald at a rally in Krefeld on 22 February 1933 when storm troopers rushed the podium and beat him senseless, the looting of the regional ADGB headquarters in Bitterfeld on 28 February, and most notably the arrest of thousands of KPD functionaries after the Reichstag fire. Physical safety had already become a major concern for free union functionaries during the Reichstag election campaign of July 1932, after Chancellor Papen rescinded the SA ban imposed by Brüning, and the reasons for concern multiplied rapidly in February 1933.[45] Theodor Leipart revealed symptoms of stress when he wrote Wilhelm Keil just before the election that "my concern must be the trade unions primarily, which will perhaps benefit from the fact that I have always distanced myself from party politics." Thus he fantasized that the free unions could survive even if the SPD was suppressed; Hans Mommsen has suggested that an old tendency to exaggerate the importance of trade unions nurtured this fantasy among ADGB leaders.[46] Courageous political activism by many thousands of trade unionists nevertheless helped to keep the Center Party vote largely intact on 5 March in the predominantly Catholic industrial cities of western and southern Germany and the SPD vote in the Protestant cities of northern and central Germany. The Nazis and their nationalist partners gained a 52 percent majority, however, and labor leaders agreed that this outcome deprived them of any justification for a general strike.[47]

Last-Minute Efforts to Unify the Trade Unions

Catholic corporatism nurtured a fantasy among Christian trade unionists resembling Leipart's. The GcG declared on 8 March 1933 that
the time had come to establish "an organic, corporatist social order,
based on the desire for self-administration."[48] Otte and Stegerwald
then invited Theodor Brauer to update the GcG program, since there
appeared to be support for his ideas in the government. Hitler had
expressed fervent admiration for trade unions, if they purged themselves of Marxist influence, and he had endorsed a corporatist upper
house of parliament. The National Socialist Factory Cells Organization
(Nationalsozialistische Betriebszellenorganisation or NSBO) had been
founded with a narrow charter for political agitation, but it was growing rapidly and included many activists who wanted it to become an
effective trade union organization. Vice Chancellor Franz von Papen
surrounded himself with corporatist intellectuals, and GcG leaders had
contact with Heinz Brauweiler, a corporatist legal expert who advised
the new labor minister, Franz Seldte of the Stahlhelm. Otte heard that
Seldte and the NSBO wavered in March 1933 between a pluralist strategy to empower the NSBO and Stahlhelm to compete with the existing
trade unions and the idea of a single, state-sponsored labor organization; the GcG chairman resolved to seek alliance with the "pluralists"
in the government.[49]

Theodor Brauer designed his new GcG program to appeal to all
corporatists in government circles while defending civil liberties. The
preamble to his "Essen Guidelines," adopted by three hundred delegates of the Christian unions on 17 March, declared that the state's
highest duty was to protect the "freedoms guaranteed by law." The
program called for mixed commissions in each industry with equal
representation for workers and employers to supervise job training,
wage levels, and working conditions. Brauer told the conference that
the existing trade unions should be the foundation for this new order,
and he explained in a subsequent editorial that they would survive
as "group organizations" within the *Berufsstand*, authorized to defend
workers' interests; he said nothing about the right to strike, however.
Otte told the Essen conference that it would be a tragic mistake "if
institutions that arose from the free will and resolve of their members,
and which have grown organically from the life of our people, were
forcibly suppressed or compelled to develop in a direction alien to
their character." Stegerwald declared that the new phraseology of corporatism meant the same thing as the Christian unions' old slogans of

"self-administration" and "association between employers and work-ers," i.e., rejection of the idolatry of the state advocated by commu-nism, socialism, and Italian Fascism.[50] Otte sent copies of the Essen Guidelines to Hitler and Seldte, while Brauer joined Franz von Papen's new League of the Cross and Eagle (Bund katholischer Deutscher "Kreuz und Adler") for conservative Catholics. Immediately after the Essen rally, Joseph Goebbels recorded in his diary a visit from unnamed leaders of the Christian unions who wanted to discuss their role in the Third Reich. He responded cordially but wrote that "they will not be able to speak of their following much longer. It's astonishing what all is offering its services to the new state."[51]

Otte's strategy was fundamentally misguided, because the "plural-ists" in the government were losing influence rapidly, and even they thought of competition among rival labor organizations only as a brief transition phase; they planned to give a state-sponsored organiza-tion so many privileges that the older trade unions would soon be deserted by all their members.[52] Only one Nazi functionary had ever truly advocated the solution desired by Otte: Albert Krebs, the editor of the Nazi newspaper in Hamburg and functionary of the white-col-lar union loosely allied with the GcG, the German National Union of Commercial Employees (Deutschnationaler Handlungsgehilfen-Verband or DHV). Krebs founded a network of DHV members who belonged to the NSDAP, and he propagated a strict division of labor and peaceful coexistence between his party and the existing labor unions. He was expelled from the party in May 1932, however, and the only Nazi leader who had ever displayed sympathy for his ideas, Gregor Strasser, broke with Hitler in December. Thereafter all Nazi leaders soon agreed that nothing like a genuine labor union could exist in the Third Reich.[53] Otte displayed great self-confidence nevertheless when he approached Franz von Papen on 1 April to argue that the gov-ernment should appoint a commissar to supervise each existing labor organization. He hoped to arrange for competition on terms in which "the Christian-nationalist current of the trade unions, while retaining voluntary membership, was favored by the state or perhaps gained sole recognition by the state." When a Dutch colleague visited Berlin on 7–8 April, he found Otte remarkably optimistic that the government would follow his advice. Other GcG leaders insisted, however, that the trade unions must merge voluntarily to forestall coercive action by the state, following the advice of Anton Erkelenz, who had sent urgent appeals for merger talks to Stegerwald and Leipart on 1 April.[54] Otte finally agreed to merger talks after Nazis gained control of the DHV on 10 April and expelled its long-time chairman, Hans Bechly. The senior

Nazi leader in that union, Franz Stöhr, advised Otte and Imbusch that a voluntary merger of the blue-collar unions offered their only hope to avoid suppression. Otte and Imbusch visited Goebbels on 11 April to ask whether the government would object if they opened merger talks with the ADGB. Goebbels endorsed the idea but warned that the government could tolerate no "Marxist" unions and expected all workers to participate in a "Day of National Labor" on 1 May, a new official holiday to supplant the internationalist May Day. "If the free unions do not agree to merger by 2 May and obstruct things on 1 May," he concluded, "then they could hardly complain if the People takes matters into its own hands." Otte believed that he had earned Goebbels's respect in this meeting, but Goebbels found the naiveté of the Christian trade unionists highly amusing.[55]

ADGB functionaries had meanwhile become demoralized because of violent attacks against them in scores of cities. The ADGB headquarters in Breslau was pillaged by storm troopers on 8 March 1933, and the Bochum SA invaded the headquarters of the Free Miners' Union on the night of 10–11 March, briefly jailing its chairman, Fritz Husemann. In the following week the public transport workers' union suffered the occupation of fifteen offices in Saxony alone. Union leaders protested vigorously to Hindenburg, Papen, Göring, and regional police officials; they sometimes regained control of the buildings seized but could not prevent new attacks.[56] Under duress the ADGB Central Committee declared on 20 March that the trade unions had always recognized the right of the state to mediate labor disputes and would accept more state oversight. It insisted, however, that "a genuine trade union must be based on the voluntary association of the members, and it must be independent from the employers as well as political parties."[57]

Free union leaders embraced merger talks after Heinz Brauweiler visited Wilhelm Eggert on 6 April, demanding on behalf of Franz Seldte to know whether the ADGB was "finally prepared to participate in the corporatist order planned by the national government." Eggert promised to secure a formal declaration that the ADGB would participate and that it supported the idea of unified trade unions; the ADGB National Committee adopted this resolution on 9 April.[58] The most energetic champion of merger talks was Wilhelm Leuschner, the leader of the free unions of Hesse and former state interior minister, who had recently joined the ADGB Central Committee full time. Leuschner agreed with Lothar Erdmann that the Marxism of the SPD had encouraged fatalism in practice, and Erdmann agreed with him that they should seek the "end of trade unions with differing political orientations," although this must not mean their "politicization in the sense of the NSDAP."[59] On 13 April Leuschner and Leipart received four emissaries from the NSBO who announced that they too sought "unified trade unions" and wished to retain the services of most free union functionaries. They wanted all union leaders to be appointed by the Nazi Party, however, while state officials determined wage levels and working conditions. Leipart responded indignantly that union leaders must work their way up from the humblest offices to earn the confidence of union members and that unions had no purpose if they did not regulate wages and working conditions.[60] Leuschner glimpsed the possibility of a more tolerable outcome when he visited Franz Seldte on 19 April and learned that he had just sent a brief outline of a "corporatist order" for cabinet approval, nominating Theodor Brauer to a small commission to work out the details. Persuaded that the GcG enjoyed real influence, Leuschner initiated merger talks with it and the Hirsch-Duncker unions the next day. He did not understand that Seldte had been excluded from the crucial discussions among Nazi leaders, who had already decided to crush the trade unions on 2 May.[61]

As these merger talks began, Christian trade unionists were torn between a desire to settle old scores with the free unions and a sense of workers' solidarity. At the last congress of the Christian miners' union on 12 March, Imbusch recalled many grievances against the free unions from the Wilhelmian era. "The Social Democrats and Communists are being treated badly today," he concluded. "Well, they have earned this bad treatment through their own behavior. Back then they treated us the same way." Imbusch was far more charitable in his recollections, written in exile, of Fritz Husemann, which describe him as the soul of charity who had promoted good relations between the miners' unions ever since 1922.[62] Jakob Kaiser expressed solidarity more courageously by telling a Cologne rally on 12 April that "the people of the free unions have long been on the path away from the old Marxism and toward the state." The free unions, as well as the Christian, had earned the right to play a major role in the new state by virtue of their conduct since August 1914. Kaiser expressed a willingness to adapt to new political conditions but insisted that it would be "unprincipled [*charakterlos*] to leave a community that I supported yesterday, just because others now have power. And it would be unprincipled … to participate in the defamation of others, just because they are weak or one thinks that the new powers will be pleased." The fragmentary evidence suggests that Kaiser expressed the sentiments of most younger Christian trade unionists.[63]

Leuschner entered the merger talks with a dry summary of the essential features of any genuine labor union, which must include only workers; be independent from the government, employers, and political parties; and enjoy the right to strike.[64] Kaiser presented a draft agreement by Brauer that expressed support for the "new state," which "cannot tolerate class divisions or an internationalism that turns its back on our people." The free, Christian, and Hirsch-Duncker labor federations would contribute to national unity by appointing three representatives each to a "Leadership Ring" to create "unified trade unions." Brauer's draft agreed with the ADGB that unions must be independent of all political parties, but it said nothing about the right to strike and added that the unions "recognize the significance of elemental religious forces and their constructive role in state and society."[65] ADGB leaders responded with more succinct and restrained counterproposals, but the final draft of 28 April retained Brauer's condemnation of class divisions and internationalism, silence about the right to strike, and praise of religious forces. This agreement was endorsed by Leipart, Grassmann, Leuschner, and Franz Spliedt for the ADGB, and Kaiser, Baltrusch, Otte, Stegerwald, and Ernst Lemmer, but it was never ratified. On 24 April Otte had sent an urgent request to Adolf Hitler to receive the negotiators, so they obviously knew that their work meant nothing unless it was endorsed by the highest authority.[66] They apparently agreed that only Brauer spoke a language that might win Hitler's approval, but they left this agreement vague enough that core elements of genuine trade unionism might be salvaged in future negotiations.

Most union activists had already become demoralized and interpreted as a humiliating surrender the declaration by the ADGB National Committee on 19 April that all union members should participate enthusiastically in the official celebration of the "Day of National Labor." Theodor Thomas of the construction workers' union wrote in his diary that everyone at his union headquarters agreed by 11 April that the end was near, and they knew this to be true when their union resolved on 13 April to march in the government parades and wave the monarchist black-white-red flag. On 1 May many thousands of free trade unionists marched in every major city.[67] Christian trade unionists had always opposed the celebration of May Day, and while their leadership greeted the new holiday as a "sign that the Hitler government supports the socially progressive German populace," it said nothing about marching. Kaiser, Imbusch, and Franz Wieber opposed participation as unprincipled, but their front weakened when Wieber died in late April. Otte and Friedrich Baltrusch accepted seats of honor in the reviewing stand for the Berlin parade. Kaiser remained among the ordinary spectators but sadly observed scores of colleagues march, some in new SA uniforms.[68]

On 2 May armed detachments of the SA, SS, and NSBO stormed every free union office, and the Nazi Party boss Robert Ley proclaimed himself the new leader of all German workers. Hundreds of ADGB leaders were imprisoned and/or beaten, all free union property confiscated, and almost all of the four thousand free union functionaries dismissed within a few days or weeks.[69] The Christian and Hirsch-Duncker unions were ignored on 2 May, but the latter group promptly declared its submission to Ley. Ernst Lemmer's communications with high officials focused more on his personal willingness to serve the regime than the future status of labor unions.[70] On 3 May Ley summoned Otte, Baltrusch, Franz Behrens, and Kaiser to demand that they too sign a "voluntary" act of submission. The first three men agreed, but Kaiser refused indignantly and left the room. The three who signed accepted appointment to the Senate of Ley's new German Labor Front (Deutsche Arbeitsfront or DAF), along with Stegerwald, Imbusch, and Brauer. Against the objections of Imbusch and Kaiser, Otte then published a declaration that the DAF had achieved the Christian unions' old dream of unified trade unions purged of Marxism. Otte also promised Christian union functionaries that the DAF would hire no free trade unionists but would retain their services.[71] Some opportunists in the Christian unions sought to exploit the new situation, most notably two mid-ranking Protestant functionaries who wrote the DAF leadership in late May to seek promotion for themselves, while identifying Kaiser as the leader of die-hard Center Party loyalists within the GcG who would never accept the Third Reich. The authors volunteered to draw up lists of union colleagues who should be purged.[72] Heinrich Imbusch later reproached Otte for hindering any discussion of the proper response to the foundation of the DAF; he brought Nazis to every meeting, before whom one could not speak freely, and pinned his hopes on his private discussions with Ley. In mid-May Imbusch fled to the League of Nations mandate territory in the Saarland after Franz Stöhr warned that he would be murdered. He sought to persuade Fritz Husemann to do likewise, but Husemann could not believe that the Nazis would harm him, because he had never done anything but try to help the miners. Imbusch explained that the Nazis "do not want any honest representation of workers' interests. … They do not care whether we have done something wrong. For them it is enough that our existence has become inconvenient." In Luxembourg Imbusch read with great sadness in April 1935 that Husemann had been "shot while trying to escape" from the Esterwegen concentration camp.[73]

The trade unionists' last hope to influence the Third Reich involved the Nazis' desire for international respectability. In June 1933 Otte volunteered to accompany Robert Ley to Geneva to seek recognition of the DAF by the International Labor Organization, and Leuschner was released from prison to join them. Leuschner remained silent when asked about conditions in Germany, however, and Otte soon abandoned as hopeless the effort to defend Ley; Otte apparently confessed to foreign union colleagues in Geneva that the bundles of cash with which Ley financed his drunken revels had been stolen from the trade unions. The socialist and Christian labor internationals soon agreed that the DAF could not be recognized as a labor union, because it was based on compulsory membership, had leaders appointed by the state, and renounced the right to strike. Ley departed abruptly from Geneva on 20 June, denounced Leuschner and Otte for sabotage, ordered Leuschner's return to prison, and expelled all Christian trade unionists from the DAF Senate. In July five hundred Christian union functionaries were dismissed, over 90 percent of the total, and the DAF confiscated all Christian union assets.[74] Among the young nationalists working for the ADGB, there was one spectacular defection to the Nazi Party in April 1933 by Hermann Seelbach, but his case remained isolated. Lothar Erdmann struggled to support his family as a freelance writer and felt torn between admiration of Hitler's foreign policy success and disgust over the persecution of the Jews. He was rounded up with many other former labor leaders in September 1939 and soon died in Sachsenhausen after savage beatings, because he protested when another prisoner was mistreated. Leuschner and Kaiser became the leaders of the trade union wing of the conservative Resistance, and Leuschner was executed in September 1944. Theodor Brauer returned to his teaching duties at the University of Cologne, participated in some of Kaiser's first discussions about organizing a resistance network, and emigrated to the United States in 1937.[75]

Ley's rupture with the Christian trade unions unleashed the aggressive impulses of the SA. In an episode that was unusually well documented but certainly not unique, three storm troopers burst into the Krefeld office of the Christian textile workers' union on the morning of 14 July 1933, beat Jacob Nöhsemes bloody with their truncheons, hung a sign around his neck, and marched him through the city to repeat the sign's message: "I am a louse [*Lump*]! I deceived the workers!" In Essen the Nazis found a more famous victim in early September when the corpulent former Prussian welfare minister Heinrich Hirtsiefer went to police headquarters to complain that his dismissal from government service without a pension exposed him to hunger. As he left, storm troopers hung a sign around his neck to identify him as "The Hungering Hirtsiefer," and they marched him around the city for two hours. He was interned in the Börgermoor concentration camp and beaten repeatedly, until his wife's appeal to President Hindenburg secured his release. Bernhard Otte encountered blacklisting for an "attitude hostile to the state" when he sought to make a new career, and his friends suspected suicide when his car slammed into a tree in October 1933. Ex-functionaries of the free and Christian unions suffered persecution for years, and this shared experience created a strong foundation for unified trade unions after 1945.[76]

Conclusion

Jakob Kaiser later celebrated the Leadership Ring agreement of April 1933 as the foundation for Germany's unified trade unions of the future, a solemn pledge that they would repudiate the free unions' historic alliance with the SPD and anticlericalism. His recollections were sometimes inaccurate, however, and most veterans of the free unions found this document repugnant when they learned of its contents after the war.[77] Deploring the opportunism of the ADGB, Otto Wels persuaded SPD leaders on 26 April 1933 to reaffirm the core ideas of socialism, especially the need for international struggle by the working class to end capitalist oppression and exploitation.[78] It must be questioned, however, whether his Marxist formulas had provided useful guidance in the Great Depression or truly inspired the German labor movement. The ideas shared most widely among trade unionists can be glimpsed in the exchange of open letters between Erkelenz and Leipart in autumn 1931, the speeches at the last congress of the Christian unions, Leipart's indignant lecture to the NSBO leaders who visited him in April 1933, and Kaiser's public defense of free union colleagues, utterances that sought to reconcile "national" and "social" values, i.e., patriotism with a commitment to egalitarian social reform. The functionaries of the three labor federations served their members' interests by forging an alliance during the Great Depression, although "oligarchic" tendencies hindered merger talks until it was far too late to affect the political outcome. The leaders of the ADGB sought in a creative manner to achieve their members' wishes when they embraced the WTB Plan, and GcG leaders adjusted to the changing mood of their members when they called for some nationalization of industry. Until the Reichstag election of March 1933, labor leaders sought to revive parliamentary democracy in alliance with the democratic parties. Thereafter the judgment of ADGB leaders became seriously distorted by fear, while a few Christian trade unionists displayed rank opportunism, and many others were naive. It would be misleading, however, to describe their most questionable decisions in spring 1933 as the logical consequence of strategies adopted already by the year 1930.

William L. Patch Jr. is the Kenan Professor of History at Washington and Lee University. He has published books on *Christian Trade Unions in the Weimar Republic, 1918–1933* (1985) and *Heinrich Brüning and the Dissolution of the Weimar Republic* (1998). His articles include "Fascism, Catholic Corporatism, and the Christian Trade Unions of Germany, Austria, and France" (2005) and "The Legend of Compulsory Unification: The Catholic Clergy and the Revival of Trade Unionism in West Germany after the Second World War" (2007). He is also author of the recently published book *Christian Democratic Workers and the Forging of German Democracy, 1920–1980*.

Notes

1. Lothar Erdmann, "Nation, Gewerkschaften und Sozialismus," *Die Arbeit* 10, no. 3 (March–April 1933): 129–61. See also Ilse Fischer, *Versöhnung von Nation und Sozialismus? Lothar Erdmann (1888–1939): Ein "leidenschaftlicher Individualist" in der Gewerkschaftsspitze* (Bonn: Dietz, 2004), 24–43; Dieter Düding, *Der Nationalsoziale Verein 1896–1903* (Munich and Vienna: Oldenbourg, 1972); and Stefan Vogt, *Nationaler Sozialismus und Soziale Demokratie: Die sozialdemokratische Junge Rechte 1918–1945* (Bonn: Dietz, 2006).

2. See Detlev Brunner, *Bürokratie und Politik des Allgemeinen Deutschen Gewerkschaftsbundes 1918/19 bis 1933* (Cologne: Bund-Verlag, 1992), 223–50, 399–437, 453–73; and Gerard Braunthal, *Socialist Labor and Politics in Weimar Germany: The General Federation of German Trade Unions* (Hamden, CT: Archon Books, 1978), 87–99.

3. See the introduction to Siegfried Mielke and Matthias Frese, eds., *Quellen zur Geschichte der deutschen Gewerkschaftsbewegung im 20. Jahrhundert*, vol. 5: *Die Gewerkschaften im Widerstand und in der Emigration 1933–1945* (Frankfurt a.M.: Bund-Verlag, 1999), 13–14 (hereafter cited as *Gewerkschaftsquellen*, 5); and Peter Jahn, ed., *Quellen zur Geschichte der deutschen Gewerkschaftsbewegung im 20. Jahrhundert*, vol. 4: *Die Gewerkschaften in der Endphase der Republik 1930–1933* (Cologne: Bund-Verlag, 1988), 55–60 (hereafter cited as *Gewerkschaftsquellen*, 4).

4. On the Christian labor movement, see Michael Schneider, *Die Christlichen Gewerkschaften 1894–1933* (Bonn: Verlag Neue Gesellschaft, 1982); Eric Dorn Brose, *Christian Labor and the Politics of Frustration in Imperial Germany* (Washington, DC: Catholic University of America Press, 1985); William Patch, *Christian Trade Unions in the Weimar Republic, 1918–1933: The Failure of "Corporate Pluralism"* (New Haven, CT: Yale University

Press, 1985); Bernhard Forster, *Adam Stegerwald (1874–1945): Christlich-nationaler Gewerkschafter, Zentrumspolitiker, Mitbegründer der Unionsparteien* (Düsseldorf: Droste, 2003); and Erich Kosthorst, *Jakob Kaiser: Der Arbeiterführer* (Stuttgart: Kohlhammer, 1967).

5. See Leipart's interview with John Graudenz, *New York Times*, 6 August 1930, and the ADGB campaign appeal (*Wahlaufruf*) of 16 August 1930 in *Gewerkschaftsquellen*, 4: 119–22. See also Heinrich August Winkler, *Der Weg in die Katastrophe: Arbeiter und Arbeiterbewegung in der Weimarer Republik 1930 bis 1933* (Berlin and Bonn: Dietz, 1987), 125–205; and Ulla Plener, *Theodor Leipart (1867–1947): Persönlichkeit, Handlungsmotive, Wirken, Bilanz—Ein Lebensbild in Dokumenten*, 2 vols. (Berlin: Trafo-Verlag Weist, 2000–2001), 1:35–41, 241–42, 2:392–95; as well as Fischer, *Erdmann*, 17–20, 163–64.

6. Heinrich Imbusch, "Heinrich Brüning" (character sketch written in exile after 1934), in the Landesarchiv Nordrhein-Westfalen, Abteilungen Rheinland, Duisburg (hereafter cited as LA NRW Duisburg), NL Johannes Platte, 14/34–41. See also Otte's circular to the Christian unions of 20 August 1930, in the records of the Gesamtverband der christlichen Gewerkschaften Deutschlands, Bundesarchiv Berlin (BA Berlin), R 9360, 2/108–13, and *Zentralblatt der christlichen Gewerkschaften* 30, no. 19 (1 October 1930): 289. For further information, see William Patch, *Heinrich Brüning and the Dissolution of the Weimar Republic* (Cambridge: Cambridge University Press, 1998), 24–38, 73–77, 89–103.

7. Winkler, *Katastrophe*, 207–35. For an overview of union membership, see Schneider, *Christliche Gewerkschaften*, 452, 767–71, as well as quarterly membership figures and financial records in *Geschäftsbericht des Hauptvorstandes des Gewerkvereins christlicher Bergarbeiter Deutschlands für die Jahre 1930/32* (Essen: Verlag des Gewerkvereins, 1933), 84–86; and the minutes of the *Gewerkverein Hauptvorstand*, 29 November 1930, in the archives of the Deutscher Gewerkschaftsbund, Friedrich Ebert Stiftung, Bonn (hereafter cited as DGB-Archiv, Bonn), NL Imbusch, 2.

8. Patch, *Brüning*, 82–88, 95–96. See also the discussion of unemployment in Zentralverband christlicher Textilarbeiter Deutschlands Hauptvorstand, ed., *Verhandlungen der X. Verbands-Generalversammlung des Zentralverbandes christlicher Textilarbeiter, 3. bis 7. August 1930 zu Dresden* (Krefeld: van Achen, 1930), 94–126, and the report on "Der 19. Verbandstag" of the German Metalworkers' Union, 18–23 August 1930, in *Metallarbeiter-Zeitung* 48, no. 35 (30 August 1930): 275–78, and no. 36 (6 September 1930): 284.

9. Minutes of the ADGB Bundesausschuss, 12–13 October 1930, *Gewerkschaftsquellen*, 4:166–68.

10. Ibid., *Gewerkschaftsquellen*, 4:157–61. See also Brunner, *Bürokratie*, 398–405; Winkler, *Katastrophe*, 225–30; Fischer, *Erdmann*, 173–74; and Heinrich Potthoff, *Freie Gewerkschaften 1918–1933: Der Allgemeine Deutsche Gewerkschaftsbund in der Weimarer Republik* (Düsseldorf: Droste, 1987), 204–6.

11. Zentralverband christlicher Textilarbeiter, *Verhandlungen der X. Verbands-Generalversammlung*, 153–54, 160–62.

12. *Zentralblatt* 30, no. 20 (15 October 1930): 305–6; no. 22 (15 November 1930): 351; and no. 23 (1 December 1930): 357–58.

13. Minutes of the presidential reception, 26 February 1931, in *Akten der Reichskanzlei der Weimarer Republik: Die Kabinette Brüning I und II*, ed. Tilman Koops, 3 vols. (Boppard am Rhein: Boldt, 1982–1990) (hereafter cited as *Kabinette Brüning*), 1:912–15. See also the union leadership conferences of 21 January, 11 February, 20 February, and 10 March 1931, *Gewerkschaftsquellen*, 4:230–33, 241–44, 253–55, 276–77.

14. See the minutes of the ADGB Bundesvorstand, 29 May 1931, and the draft declaration of 30 May 1931, *Gewerkschaftsquellen*, 4:306–12, and Otte's circular to the Christian unions, 1 June 1931, BA Berlin, R 9360, 3/72. See also Patch, *Brüning*, 150–60.

15. See the minutes of ADGB leadership conferences from 10–20 June 1931 in *Gewerkschaftsquellen*, 4:312–46, and the chancellor's reception on 15 June 1931, *Kabinette Brüning*, 2:1194–98, as well as the reports in *Zentralblatt* 31, no. 12 (15 June 1931), 177, and no. 14 (15 July 1931), 209–11; and *Der Bergknappe* 36, no. 25 (20 June 1931): 1–2. For further information, see Patch, *Brüning*, 160–64, 184.

16. Allgemeiner Deutscher Gewerkschaftsbund, *Protokoll der Verhandlungen des 14. Kongresses der Gewerkschaften Deutschlands: Abgehalten in Frankfurt a.M. vom 31. August bis 4. September 1931* (Berlin: Allgemeiner Deutscher Gewerkschaftsbund, 1931), 47–55, 68–72, 94, 149; Leipart's report to ADGB colleagues on his meeting with Brüning on 1 August 1931, *Gewerkschaftsquellen*, 4:369–72. See also the entry for 4 September 1931, in the CD-ROM supplement to Ilse Fischer, *Versöhnung von Nation und Sozialismus? Lothar Erdmann (1888–1939): Auszüge aus den Tagebüchern 1926–1938*, expanded edition (Bonn: Dietz, 2004), 215 (hereafter cited as *Erdmann Tagebücher*); Kaiser's circular to the Christian unions of late July 1931, BA Koblenz, NL Kaiser, 366/4–12; and Patch, *Brüning*, 164–76.

17. ADGB, *14. Kongress der Gewerkschaften*, 99–103, 121–38, 175–79.

18. Winkler, *Katastrophe*, 463–67. See also Heinrich Brüning, *Memoiren 1918–1934* (Stuttgart: Deutsche Verlags-Anstalt, 1970), 471.

19. See the minutes of the ADGB Bundesausschuss, 25 November 1931; Aron's memorandum of 19 December 1931; and Leipart to Otto Nussbaum, 24 December 1931, all in *Gewerkschaftsquellen*, 4:424–36, 461–68. See also the membership table in Schneider, *Christliche Gewerkschaften*, 452.

20. See the abridged version of this exchange in *Grundlagen der Einheitsgewerkschaft: Historische Dokumente und Materialien*, ed. Ulrich Borsdorf, Hans O. Hemmer, and Martin Martiny (Frankfurt a.M.: Europäische Verlagsanstalt, 1977), 196–209, with the Erkelenz quotation on 201, and the complete Leipart article in Plener, *Theodor Leipart*, 2:404–11. See also Erkelenz to Emil Lederer, 29 August 1931, BA Koblenz, NL Erkelenz, 127, and Erkelenz to Alwin Brandes, 23 November 1931, ibid., 136.

21. Erkelenz to Leipart, 7 December 1931, BA Koblenz, NL Erkelenz, 62/227. See also the minutes of the ADGB Bundesvorstand, 2 March 1932, *Gewerkschaftsquellen*, 4:517–18; the minutes of the GcG Vorstand, 18 June 1931, BA Berlin, R 9360, 7/65; and Otte's circular to the Christian unions, 13 October 1931, ibid., 3/127.

22. See the reception of 14 December 1931, *Kabinette Brüning*, 3: 2096–98; ADGB Bundesausschuss, 5 December 1931, *Gewerkschaftsquellen*, 4:444–46; and *Zentralblatt* 32, no. 24 (15 December 1931): 369–74.

23. Wladimir Woytinsky, *Stormy Passage: A Personal History through Two Russian Revolutions to Democracy and Freedom, 1905–1960* (New York: Vanguard Press, 1961), 465–72. See also *Zentralblatt* 32, no. 7 (1 April 1932): 100–101, and no. 9 (1 May 1932): 124. For further information, see Michael Schneider, *Das Arbeitsbeschaffungsprogramm des ADGB: Zur gewerkschaftlichen Politik in der Endphase der Weimarer Republik* (Bonn-Bad Godesberg: Verlag Neue Gesellschaft, 1975), 63–105; Winkler, *Katastrophe*, 432–36, 496–505, 538–41; Fischer, *Erdmann*, 156–59; and Patch, *Brüning*, 215–19, 259–62.

24. See the minutes of a GcG leadership conference attended by Stegerwald, 23 July 1931, BA Berlin, R 9360, 7/58–59, as well as the report in *Zentralblatt* 31, no. 15 (1 August 1931): 227–28, and no. 21 (1 November 1931): 322–23. See also Patch, *Brüning*, 172–81.

25. *Der Bergknappe* 37, no. 4 (23 January 1932): 1, and no. 8 (20 February 1932): 1 (source of quotation). See also Michael Schäfer, *Heinrich Imbusch: Christlicher Gewerkschaftsführer und Widerstandskämpfer* (Munich: Beck, 1990), 232–41.

26. Gesamtverband der Christlichen Gewerkschaften Deutschlands, *Nieder-schrift der Verhandlungen des 13. Kongresses der christlichen Gewerkschaften Deutschlands, Düsseldorf 18.–20. September 1932* (Berlin: Christlicher Gewerkschaftsverlag, 1932), 294–303, 314–17. See also Patch, *Christian Trade Unions*, 177–81.

27. Theodor Brauer, *Krisis der Gewerkschaften*, 2nd ed. (Jena: Gustav Fischer, 1924), 3–11, 17–19, 36–41, 48–53; Forster, *Adam Stegerwald*, 143–46, 201–6, 272–76. See also the recollections of Brauer by Karl Dörpinghaus in "Lebenserinnerungen, I. Teil," 68–69, DGB-Archiv Bonn, NL Dörpinghaus, 2, and by Johannes Albers in "Erinnerungen an meine gewerkschaftliche und politiche Zusammenarbeit mit Jakob Kaiser von 1919 bis 1933," written in 1961, BA Koblenz, NL Kaiser, 215/54–67, esp. 11–12.

28. Theodor Brauer, "Zur Frage der Verstaatlichung des Bergbaus," *Zentralblatt* 32, no. 6 (15 March 1932): 82–85. See also "Reich und Schwerindustrie," and the report of a speech by Karl Schmitz on 10 July 1932, ibid., no. 15 (1 August 1932): 194–95, 203, as well as GcG, *13. Kongress der Christlichen Gewerkschaften*, 376–90.

29. Christlicher Metallarbeiter-Verband, *Protokoll über die Verhandlungen der 13. General-Versammlung des Christlichen Metallarbeiter-Verbandes Deutschlands: Unser Haus Königswinter, 26.–28. September 1932* (Duisburg: Christlicher Metallarbeiter-Verband, 1932), 46, 74–75, 111. For quarterly membership figures in the Christian miners' union, see *Geschäftsbericht des Hauptvorstandes 1930–32*, 84. See also Potthoff, *Freie Gewerkschaften*, 348–49. We lack membership figures from 1932 for most Christian trade unions.

30. See William Patch, "Fascism, Catholic Corporatism, and the Christian Trade Unions of Germany, Austria, and France," in *Between Cross and Class: Comparative Histories of Christian Labour in Europe 1840–2000*, ed. Lex Heerma van Voss, Patrick Pasture, and Jan de Maeyer (Bern: Peter Lang, 2005), 173–201, and Paul Misner, *Catholic Labor Movements in Europe: Social*

Thought and Action, 1914–1965 (Washington, DC: Catholic University of America Press, 2015), 161–230.

31. Reports on the leadership conference of 20–21 November 1930 in *Zentralblatt* 30, no. 23 (1 December 1930): 358–61, and *Der Deutsche*, 22 November 1930, no. 274. See also Theodor Brauer, *Sozialpolitik und Sozialreform* (Jena: Gustav Fischer, 1931); Röhr's book review in *Zentralblatt* 31, no. 24 (15 December 1931): 375–76; "Franz Röhr" in *Wer ist's?*, 9th ed. (Berlin: Degner, 1928), 1282, and Brüning, *Memoiren*, 40–41, 49–50. Brauer sought recognition in 1930 as sole director of the GcG education program, but the Christian miners' union insisted on keeping Röhr as codirector; see the minutes of the Gewerkverein Hauptvorstand, 13 September 1930, DGB-Archiv Bonn, NL Imbusch, 2.

32. Lectures by Brauer and Otte in Josef van der Velden, ed., *Die berufsständische Ordnung: Idee und praktische Möglichkeiten* (Cologne: Katholische Tat, 1932), 53–58, 89–102. See also Elfriede Kaiser-Nebgen to Erich Kosthorst, 19 January 1965, BA Koblenz, NL Kaiser, 247, and Kosthorst, *Jakob Kaiser*, 139–42, as well as Theodor Brauer, "Ende des Kapitalismus?," and rebuttal by Körner, *Zentralblatt* 33, no. 2 (15 January 1933): 13–19.

33. See the GcG declaration of 7 June 1932, *Zentralblatt* 32, no. 12 (15 June 1932): 158, and no. 13 (1 July 1932): 175, as well as the minutes of the ADGB Bundesvorstand, 8 June 1932, and Bundesausschuss, 14 June 1932, in *Gewerkschaftsquellen*, 4:584–97.

34. Otto Wels, "Um den 20. Juli 1932," memoir from late 1933 in *Anpassung oder Widerstand? Aus den Akten des Parteivorstands der deutschen Sozialdemokratie 1932/33*, ed. Hagen Schulze (Bonn-Bad Godesberg: Verlag Neue Gesellschaft, 1975), 4–12 (hereafter cited as *Anpassung oder Widerstand*). See also the joint trade union proclamation of 20 July 1932 and the minutes of the ADGB Bundesausschuss, 21 July 1932, in *Gewerkschaftsquellen*, 4:625–31; as well as entries for the period from 27 July to 10 August 1932 in the *Erdmann Tagebücher*, 240–44. For further information, see Winkler, *Katastrophe*, 646–80, and Brunner, *Bürokratie*, 439–41.

35. GcG, *13. Kongress der christlichen Gewerkschaften*, 76–78, 228–30, 253–54, 323.

36. Schäfer, *Imbusch*, 246–48; Leipart's report to the ADGB Bundesvorstand, 17 August 1932, Erdmann's letter to Erich Marcks, 17 August 1932, and minutes of the ADGB-SPD leadership conference, 26 August 1932, all in *Gewerkschaftsquellen*, 4:650–56. For Schleicher's plans, contrast Axel Schildt, *Militärdiktatur auf Massenbasis? Die Querfrontkonzeption der Reichswehrführung um General von Schleicher am Ende der Weimarer Republik* (Frankfurt a.M.: Campus Verlag, 1981), with the more careful analysis in Heinrich Muth, "Schleicher und die Gewerkschaften 1932: Ein Quellenproblem," *Vierteljahrshefte für Zeitgeschichte* 29 (1981): 189–215, and Henry A. Turner Jr., *Hitler's Thirty Days to Power: January 1933* (Reading, MA.: Addison-Wesley, 1996), 19–29, 79–91.

37. Minutes of the ADGB Bundesvorstand, 26 October and 9 November 1932, and Erdmann to Leipart, 9 November 1932, in *Gewerkschaftsquellen*, 4:734–39, 749–52; minutes of the SPD Parteiausschuss, 10 November 1932, in *Anpassung oder Widerstand*, 72–93; entries for 22 October and 16 November

1932 in the *Erdmann Tagebücher*, 248–49, 252. See also Brunner, *Bürokratie*, 442–52, and Fischer, *Lothar Erdmann*, 180–85.

38. Entry for 18 December 1932 in the *Erdmann Tagebücher*, 254; minutes of the ADGB leadership conferences of 7 October, 8 December, and 21 December 1932 in *Gewerkschaftsquellen*, 4:727, 781–84, 792–93; minutes of the SPD Parteiausschuss, 16 December 1932, in *Anpassung oder Widerstand*, 112–30. See also Braunthal, *Socialist Labor*, 114–41, 175–79, 188–91, and Potthoff, *Freie Gewerkschaften*, 230–37, 245–58.

39. Schäfer, *Imbusch*, 247; minutes of the ADGB leadership conferences of 2–29 November 1932, report by Leipart and Eggert on their meeting with Schleicher, 28 November 1932, and Leipart to Schleicher, 29 November 1932, all in *Gewerkschaftsquellen*, 4:748–50, 766–76.

40. *Zentralblatt* 32, no. 24 (15 December 1932): 309. See also Jakob Kaiser's speech of 12 December 1932, 10–16, BA Koblenz, NL Kaiser, 221; the speech by Heinrich Fahrenbach, *Essener Volkszeitung*, 18 December 1932 (clipping in DGB-Archiv, Bonn, NL Fahrenbrach, 2); and Winkler, *Katastrophe*, 810–19.

41. Kaiser's speech of 12 December 1932, 7–10, BA Koblenz, NL Kaiser, 221; report on Strasser's resignation in *Der Deutsche*, 24 December 1932, no. 302. See also Patch, *Brüning*, 286–88.

42. Baltrusch, "Arbeitsbeschaffung voran!," *Zentralblatt* 33, no. 1 (1 January 1933): 4–5. See also the report on the meeting of Grassmann and Eggert with Schleicher on 26 January 1933, in *Gewerkschaftsquellen*, 4:814–17. For further information, see Turner, *Thirty Days*, 83–108, 118–33.

43. Telegram to Hindenburg by the three labor federations, 28 January 1933, in *Akten der Reichskanzlei der Weimarer Republik: Das Kabinett von Schleicher 1932/33*, ed. Anton Golecki (Boppard am Rhein: Boldt, 1986), 314.

44. Draft declaration by the three labor federations, 30 January 1933, the final version of 31 January, and minutes of the ADGB-SPD conferences of 30 January and 5 February 1933, in *Gewerkschaftsquellen*, 4:823–29, 833–35; minutes of the SPD Parteiausschuss, 31 January 1933, in *Anpassung oder Widerstand*, 148–52; Dörpinghaus, "Lebenserinnerungen, I. Teil," 162, in DGB-Archiv Bonn, NL Dörpinghaus, 2. See also Winkler, *Katastrophe*, 853–75, and Michael Schneider, *Unterm Hakenkreuz: Arbeiter und Arbeiterbewegung 1933 bis 1939* (Bonn: Dietz, 1999), 34–36.

45. Gewerkverein Hauptvorstand, 4 February 1933, Bibliothek des Ruhrgebiets, Bochum, NL Imbusch, 733. See also the GcG Wahlaufruf in *Zentralblatt* 33, no. 4 (15 February 1933): 37–38, as well as the ADGB Wahlaufruf, 15 February 1933, report on the meeting of the ADGB Bundesausschuss, 28 February 1933, and the petition to Hindenburg of 1 March 1933, all in *Gewerkschaftsquellen*, 4:844–45, 850–52. On the Krefeld rally, see the report in the *Kölnische Volkszeitung*, 23 February 1933, no. 54. See also the numerous reports of attacks in Dirk Erb, ed., *Gleichgeschaltet: Der Nazi-Terror gegen Gewerkschaften und Berufsverbände 1930 bis 1933; Eine Dokumentation* (Göttingen: Steindl, 2001), and the analysis of the election campaign in Hermann Beck, *The Fateful Alliance: German Conservatives and Nazis in 1933; The Machtergreifung in a New Light* (New York and Oxford: Berghahn Books, 2008), 89–126.

46. Leipart to Keil, 3 March 1933, in *Gewerkschaftsquellen*, 4:853–54. See also Hans Mommsen, "Die deutschen Gewerkschaften zwischen Anpassung und Widerstand 1930–1944," in *Vom Sozialistengesetz zur Mitbestimmung: Zum 100. Geburtstag von Hans Böckler*, ed. Ulrich Borsdorf and Hans Hemmer (Cologne: Bund-Verlag, 1975), 275–99.

47. Theodor Leipart, "Die deutschen Gewerkschaften 1933," memoir from June 1945 in Plener, *Leipart*, 2:470–77. See also Winkler, *Katastrophe*, 876–88; Wolfgang Jäger, *Bergarbeitermilieus und Parteien im Ruhrgebiet: Zum Wahlverhalten des katholischen Bergarbeitermilieus bis 1933* (Munich: Beck, 1996), 210–318; and Dorit-Maria Krenn, *Die Christliche Arbeiterbewegung in Bayern vom Ersten Weltkrieg bis 1933* (Mainz: Matthias Grünewald, 1991), 293–306, 560–86.

48. *Zentralblatt* 33, no. 6 (15 March 1933): 61.

49. In this respect, see Henry A. Turner, "Hitlers Einstellung zur Wirtschaft und Gesellschaft vor 1933," *Geschichte und Gesellschaft* 2 (1976): 89–117, and Gunther Mai, "Die Nationalsozialistische Betriebszellen-Organisation: Zum Verhältnis von Arbeiterschaft und Nationalsozialismus," *Vierteljahrshefte für Zeitgeschichte* 31 (1983): 573–613. See also Heinz Brauweiler, "Ständestaat und Wirtschaftsvertretung," *Politisches Schrifttum: Monatlicher Literaturbericht* 1, no. 2 (February 1933): 21–26; Dr. Mansfeld to Heinz Brauweiler, 16 March 1933, Stadtarchiv Mönchengladbach (hereafter cited as StA Mönchengladbach), NL Brauweiler, 141. My thanks to Larry Jones for sharing this and other materials that I have used for this chapter. See also Larry Eugene Jones, "The Limits of Collaboration: Edgar Jung, Herbert von Bose, and the Origins of the Conservative Resistance to Hitler, 1933–34," in *Between Reform, Reaction, and Resistance: Studies in the History of German Conservatism from 1789 to 1945*, ed. Larry E. Jones and James Retallack (Oxford and Providence, RI: Berg, 1993), 465–501, and Tim Mason, *Social Policy in the Third Reich: The Working Class and the "National Community"* (Oxford and Providence, RI: Berg, 1993), 73–74.

50. Gesamtverband der christlich-nationalen Gewerkschaften Deutschlands, Hauptgeschäftsstelle, *Die Essener Richtlinien 1933 der christlich-nationalen Gewerkschaften* (Berlin: Christlicher Gewerkschaftsverlag, 1933), 6–35, 46, 51–52, 61–65. See also Brauer, "Gewerkschaft und Berufsstand," *Zentralblatt* 33, no. 8 (15 April 1933): 93–95.

51. Entry of 17 March 1933, in *Joseph Goebbels Tagebücher 1924–1945*, ed. Ralf Georg Reuth, 5 vols. (Munich: Saur, 1992), 2:781. See also Schneider, *Unterm Hakenkreuz*, 68–69. Imbusch recalled in "Bernhard Otte" (LA NRW Duisburg, NL Platte, 14/164–65) that Otte became eager to establish contact with Nazi leaders immediately after the Reichstag election.

52. Memorandum by Walter Schuhmann of the NSBO for Robert Ley and Rudolf Hess, 14 March 1933, in *Ursachen und Folgen vom deutschen Zusammenbruch 1918 und 1945*, ed. Herbert Michaelis and Ernst Schraepler, 29 vols. (Berlin: Wendler, 1958), 9:623–24; Heinz Brauweiler, "Zur Gewerkschaftsfrage," undated memorandum for Seldte from late March or early April 1933, BA Berlin, R 53, 15/20–23.

53. See Albert Krebs, *The Infancy of Nazism: The Memoirs of Ex-Gauleiter Albert Krebs, 1923–1933*, ed. William S. Allen (New York: New Viewpoints, 1976),

and Ronald Smelser, *Robert Ley: Hitler's Labor Front Leader* (Oxford and New York: Berg, 1988), 84–122.

54. "Vermerk" of 1 April 1933, on a visit to Papen by Otte, BA Berlin, R 53, 15/18–19. See also the report by P. J. S. Serrarens on his discussions in Berlin, 7–8 April 1933, Documentation Center for Religion, Culture, and Society at the Catholic University of Leuven, Archives WVA/Box 15/Doc. 40.06 (thanks to Patrick Pasture for sharing this file), as well as letters by Erkelenz to Stegerwald, Leipart, and A. Czieslik on 1 April 1933, BA Koblenz, NL Erkelenz, 136.

55. Heinrich Imbusch, "Hans Bechli" (sic), LA NRW Duisburg, NL Platte, 14/10–12; Goebbels, *Tagebücher*, 2:792–93. See also the reports by Otte on his meetings with Stöhr and Goebbels in two circulars of the Christian textile workers' union, 14 April 1933, in *Gewerkschaftsquellen*, 4:892–96; as well as the report by Otte to the leaders of the Christian labor international, 28 April 1933, Leuven Documentation Center/Archives WVA/Box 15/Doc. 41.01.

56. See ADGB Ortsausschuss Breslau to Vice Chancellor von Papen, 8 March 1933, *Ursachen und Folgen*, 9:621–22; the reports on SA violence and petitions to the authorities, 10–20 March 1933, in *Gewerkschaftsquellen*, 4:856–59, and 5:102–14; and Erb, *Gleichgeschaltet*, 122–79.

57. Leipart to Hitler, 21 March 1933, in *Gewerkschaftsquellen*, 4:865–67.

58. See the two-page summary of a meeting on 6 April 1933 of Dr. Erich Lübbert, Brauweiler, and Eggert, StA Mönchengladbach, NL Brauweiler, 141, and the ADGB declaration of 9 April 1933, in *Gewerkschaftsquellen*, 4:881–82.

59. Fischer, *Lothar Erdmann*, 206 (quoting an undated memorandum from spring 1933). See also Joachim G. Leithäuser, *Wilhelm Leuschner: Ein Leben für die Republik* (Cologne: Bund-Verlag, 1962), 11–30, 38–45, 69–104; Vogt, *Nationaler Sozialismus*, 116–19, 321–36; and Brunner, *Bürokratie*, 153–56.

60. Minutes of the meeting between representatives of the ADGB and NSBO, 13 April 1933, *Gewerkschaftsquellen*, 4:888–92. Otte became alarmed when he heard about this meeting and approached Nazi leaders to demand that they forbid such initiatives by the NSBO; see his report to the Christian labor international on 28 April 1933, Leuven Documentation Center/ Archives WVA/Box 15/Doc. 41.01.

61. Gerhard Beier, ed., "Zur Entstehung des Führerkreises der vereinigten Gewerkschaften Ende April 1933: Eine Dokumentation," *Archiv für Sozialgeschichte* 15 (1975): 365–92, esp. 365–72. See also Goebbels, *Tagebücher*, 17 April 1933, 2:793. On 3 May 1933 Heinz Brauweiler wrote Dr. Mansfeld that he and Seldte had been waiting since March for a cabinet discussion of the trade union issue that never took place; see StA Mönchengladbach, NL Brauweiler, 141.

62. Typescript minutes of the "Gewerkverein Generalversammlung," 12 March 1933, 102–4, DGB-Archiv Bonn, NL Imbusch, 1; see also Imbusch, "Fritz Husemann," LA NRW Duisburg, NL Platte, 14/94–99.

63. Kaiser speech in *Zentralblatt* 33, no. 9 (1 May 1933): 106–11, published in Kosthorst, *Jakob Kaiser*, 271–80. See also the ambivalent statements about

unified trade unions in *Textilarbeiter-Zeitung*, no. 11 (8 March 1933): 2; *Die Rundschau* 21, no. 7 (10 April 1933): 27–29; and *Der Deutsche Metallarbeiter* 34, no. 15 (15 April 1933): 174–76.

64. Beier, ed., "Zur Entstehung," Documents 5–6, esp. 376.

65. Ibid., Doc. 7, 385–87.

66. Ibid., 374–75, 387–92. Compare "Wie sie sich retten wollten," an incomplete version of the final draft published by the DAF in March 1934, in *Gewerkschaftsquellen*, 5:127–28.

67. ADGB declaration of 19 April 1933 and entries from the Thomas diary, in *Gewerkschaftsquellen*, 4:897–98, 915–17. See also Gerhard Beier, *Das Lehrstück vom 1. und 2. Mai 1933* (Frankfurt a.M.: Europäische Verlagsanstalt, 1975), 36–43; Winkler, *Katastrophe*, 921–23, 927–28; and Schneider, *Unterm Hakenkreuz*, 94–100.

68. *Zentralblatt* 33, no. 9 (1 May 1933): 105; memoir by Elfriede Nebgen in January 1963, BA Koblenz, NL Hans Katzer, 303; Heinrich Imbusch, "Franz Wieber," LA NRW Duisburg, NL Platte, 14/237–38. See also Kosthorst, *Jakob Kaiser*, 179–80, and Schneider, *Unterm Hakenkreuz*, 91–93.

69. See Schneider, *Unterm Hakenkreuz*, 101–6, and Erb, *Gleichgeschaltet*, 221–66.

70. Circular to the Hirsch-Duncker unions from Neustedt and Czieslik, mid-May 1933, BA Koblenz, NL Erkelenz, 136/496. See also Lemmer's letters to Ritter von Epp, 18 April 1933; State Secretary Erhard Milch, 28 April 1933; and Robert Ley, 3 May 1933, all in BA Koblenz, Kleine Erwerbung 497, 4.

71. Undated memoir by Kaiser and Nebgen, "Die Auflösung der Gewerkschaften im Jahre 1933," BA Koblenz, NL Kaiser, 362/54–56; Bernhard Otte, "Neue Wege und neue Ziele," *Zentralblatt* 33, no. 10 (15 May 1933): 117–18; circular by the Christian textile workers' union, 30 May 1933, DGB-Archiv, Bonn, NL Fahrenbrach, 2. See also Schneider, *Unterm Hakenkreuz*, 101–2, and Kosthorst, *Jakob Kaiser*, 180–82.

72. Copy of a letter by Karl Dudey and Friedrich Meystre to Ludwig Brucker, 31 May 1933, BA Koblenz, NL Kaiser, 246.

73. Imbusch, "Bernhard Otte," LA NRW Duisburg, NL Platte, 14/164–65, and "Fritz Husemann," ibid., 94–99. See also Schäfer, *Imbusch*, 254–56, and Detlev Peukert and Frank Bajohr, *Spuren des Widerstands: Die Bergarbeiterbewegung im Dritten Reich und im Exil* (Munich: Beck, 1987), 59–72.

74. Jakob Kaiser, "Zur Situation in der früheren deutschen Arbeiterbewegung," memorandum of November 1933 in *Gewerkschaftsquellen*, 5:135–43; Kaiser's recollections of 1933 conveyed in a letter by Elfriede Kaiser-Nebgen to Hans Joachim Reichardt, 20 February 1956, BA Koblenz, NL Kaiser, 413/182–90. See also Patrick Pasture, *Histoire du syndicalisme chrétien international: La difficile recherche d'une troisième voie* (Paris and Montreal: L'Harmattan, 1999), 164–67, and Leithäuser, *Leuschner*, 117–28.

75. See Brunner, *Bürokratie*, 455–59; Fischer, *Erdmann*, 234–66; Leithäuser, *Leuschner*, 157–249; and Elfriede Nebgen, *Jakob Kaiser: Der Widerstandskämpfer*, 2nd ed. (Stuttgart: Kohlhammer, 1970), 52–54.

76. Photostat of a criminal complaint by Nöhsemes, 21 August 1933, DGB-Archiv Bonn, NL Dörpinghaus, 1; Heinrich Imbusch, "Heinrich Hirtsiefer," LA NRW Duisburg, NL Platte, 14/78–79; Brüning, *Memoiren*, 676. See also

William Patch, *Christian Democratic Workers and the Forging of German Democracy, 1920–1980* (Cambridge: Cambridge University Press, 2018), 45–75.

77. See Kaiser's editorials from June 1947 and December 1955 in *Jakob Kaiser: Gewerkschafter und Patriot; Eine Werkauswahl*, ed. Tilman Mayer (Cologne: Bund-Verlag, 1988), 304–7, 641–52. See also Gerhard Beier, "Einheitsgewerkschaft: Zur Geschichte eines organisatorischen Prinzips der deutschen Arbeiterbewegung," *Archiv für Sozialgeschichte* 13 (1973): 207–42; and Wolfgang Schroeder, *Katholizismus und Einheitsgewerkschaft: Der Streit um den DGB und der Niedergang des Sozialkatholizismus in der Bundesrepublik bis 1960* (Bonn: Dietz, 1992), 78–93.

78. Winkler, *Katastrophe*, 923–26.

Bibliography

Beier, Gerhard, ed. "Zur Entstehung des Führerkreises der vereinigten Gewerkschaften Ende April 1933: Eine Dokumentation." *Archiv für Sozialgeschichte* 15 (1975): 365–92.

Brunner, Detlev. *Bürokratie und Politik des Allgemeinen Deutschen Gewerkschaftsbundes 1918/19 bis 1933*. Cologne: Bund-Verlag, 1992.

Erb, Dirk, ed. *Gleichgeschaltet: Der Nazi-Terror gegen Gewerkschaften und Berufsverbände 1930 bis 1933: Eine Dokumentation*. Göttingen: Steindl, 2001.

Fischer, Ilse. *Versöhnung von Nation und Sozialismus? Lothar Erdmann (1888–1939): Ein "leidenschaftlicher Individualist" in der Gewerkschaftsspitze*. Bonn: Dietz, 2004, with CD-ROM supplement, *Auszüge aus den Tagebüchern 1926–1938: Umfassende Edition*.

Forster, Bernhard. *Adam Stegerwald (1874–1945): Christlich-nationaler Gewerkschafter, Zentrumspolitiker, Mitbegründer der Unionsparteien*. Düsseldorf: Droste, 2003.

Patch, William. *Christian Trade Unions in the Weimar Republic, 1918–1933: The Failure of "Corporate Pluralism."* New Haven, CT: Yale University Press, 1985.

———. *Heinrich Brüning and the Dissolution of the Weimar Republic*. Cambridge: Cambridge University Press, 1998.

Plener, Ulla. *Theodor Leipart (1867–1947): Persönlichkeit, Handlungsmotive, Wirken, Bilanz—Ein Lebensbild in Dokumenten*. 2 vols. Berlin: Trafo Verlag, 2000–2001.

Potthoff, Heinrich. *Freie Gewerkschaften 1918–1933: Der Allgemeine Deutsche Gewerkschaftsbund in der Weimarer Republik*. Düsseldorf: Droste, 1987.

Quellen zur Geschichte der deutschen Gewerkschaftsbewegung im 20. Jahrhundert. Vol. 4: *Die Gewerkschaften in der Endphase der Republik 1930–1933*, edited by Peter Jahn, Cologne: Bund-Verlag, 1988.

———. Vol. 5: *Die Gewerkschaften im Widerstand und in der Emigration 1933–1945*, edited by Siegfried Mielke and Matthias Frese. Frankfurt a.M.: Bund-Verlag, 1999.

Schäfer, Michael. *Heinrich Imbusch: Christlicher Gewerkschaftsführer und Widerstandskämpfer*. Munich: Beck, 1990.

Schneider, Michael. *Die Christlichen Gewerkschaften 1894–1933*. Bonn: Verlag Neue Gesellschaft, 1982.

——. *Unterm Hakenkreuz: Arbeiter und Arbeiterbewegung 1933 bis 1939*. Bonn: Dietz, 1999.

Winkler, Heinrich August. *Der Weg in die Katastrophe 1930–1933: Arbeiter und Arbeiterbewegung in der Weimarer Republik,* vol. 3. Berlin: J. W. Dietz, 1987.

 **10**

From Collegiality to the *Führerprinzip*

The 1933 Introduction of the Episcopacy in the Hamburg
Landeskirche

Rainer Hering

"A revolution in the Church" — this is how Heinz Beckmann (1877–1939),
the head pastor of Hamburg's St. Nikolai Church and the leading representative of the politically liberal wing of the Protestant Church, characterized the changes in the Lutheran branch of the church in Hamburg
at the beginning of the Third Reich.[1] The gravity of the Enabling Act
compelled this dyed-in-the-wool democrat to use this stark description
and to record in writing the events that followed. In 1933 the church's
constitution, with its collegial leadership group and a "Senior" as
primus inter pares at its head, in place since the Reformation, was abolished and replaced with a hierarchical episcopacy (*Landesbischofsamt*),
with a state bishop (*Landesbischof*) at its head. The introduction of this
office, with its close alignment and substantive connection to the leadership principle (*Führerprinzip*) introduced throughout the state, flew
in the face of a centuries-old tradition; the *Landesbischof* was endowed
with sweeping legislative and executive authority. Heinz Beckmann
was one of the few who rejected this turn of events. In examining what
he was up against, this chapter poses the following questions: How
did the transition from the Weimar Republic to the Third Reich impact
the Protestant Church? What concrete developments occurred in the
Hamburg *Landeskirche* (territorial church) in the handover of power to
the National Socialists in 1933? What influence did the state have on the
church and how profound were the changes?

The Position of the Church at the End of the Weimar Republic and the Beginning of the Third Reich

With the Weimar Republic Constitution of 11 August 1919, the centuries-old tradition of Protestantism's princely controlled church rule
(*landesherrliches Kirchenregiment*) came to an end. Henceforth, there

would be no more State Church (Article 137). The churches, while still retaining numerous privileges, would now have to independently regulate their own affairs. Furthermore, the church tax, paid by taxpayers to their respective churches, would be collected by the state, which would then subsidize the churches.[2] The Protestant regional churches banded together in 1922 in the German Protestant Church Confederation (Deutschen Evangelischen Kirchenbund); between 1919 and 1930 church congresses (*Kirchentage*), which brought together representatives of church leadership groups, the synod, and church associations, endeavored to uniformly represent Protestantism to the outside world. A national-oriented popular church movement (*volkskirchliche Bewegung*) in Protestantism attempted to realize a new type of ecclesiastical religiosity (*Kirchlichkeit*) on a broader basis "from below" according to democratic principles. The movement succeeded to a certain extent, although not in the way originally intended. The concept of popular nationalism (*Volksbegriff*), as part of the virulent national populist antisemitic movement, took the place of the (new democratic) state, also in church circles.

At the beginning of the Third Reich 95 percent of Germans belonged to one of the Christian churches—there were about 41 million Protestants and approximately 21 million Catholics. Protestantism in the Third Reich was characterized by the opposition between the "German Christians" and the Confessing Church. Various German Christian groups emerged already in the 1920s; for example, in Thuringia, those connected to Siegfried Leffler (1900–83) and Julius Leuthäuser (1900–1942), whose political sympathies lay with the National Socialists. The German Christian religious movement, founded in 1932, published a program under its national leader, Joachim Hossenfelder (1899–1976) that was endorsed by the NSDAP. This "fighting church" (*ecclesia militans*), which saw itself as a unified nationalist church, aimed to stand together with the NSDAP. Its goal was a unified "Aryan" Reichskirche (Reich Church) that would put an end to the confessional and organizational fragmentation of German Protestantism. The German Christian and convinced National Socialist August Jäger (1878–1962), head of church affairs in the Prussian ministry of culture, sought to effect a complete "alignment" (*Gleichschaltung*) of the Protestant Church with National Socialist policies and prescriptions.

Opposed to the discrimination against Christian "non-Aryans," the Young Reformers (*Jungreformatorische*) movement, formed around Martin Niemöller (1892–1984), Walter Künneth (1901–97), and Hans Lilje (1899–1977), emerged in 1933. At first, the group clearly declared its support for the National Socialist state. But to protest against the introduction of the "Aryan paragraph" (first introduced in civil service legislation in April 1933) in the church, the Pastors' Emergency League (Pfarrernotbund), an association of pastors founded to counter discrimination against Christians of Jewish heritage, was formed under the leadership of Martin Niemöller. The first Reich Confessional Synod (Reichsbekenntnissynode) took place at the end of May 1934 in Barmen on the basis of which the Confessing Church (Bekennende Kirche) was organizationally constituted, with a twelve-member brotherhood council (*Brüderrat*); its "Barmen Declaration" clearly distanced itself from the teachings of the German Christians. But the Declaration focused solely on Christian men and women who had been negatively affected by National Socialist racial legislation, not on Jewish men and women. The German Protestant Church saw no reason to be concerned about them.

In the July 1933 church elections, the German Christian religious movement, supported by the NSDAP, received approximately 70 percent of the votes, thereby securing the group's influence; the old leadership remained in office only in the Prussian province of Westphalia and in the "intact" (*intakten*) Lutheran *Landeskirchen* of Hanover, Württemberg, and Bavaria. In September 1933 Hitler's confidante, Ludwig Müller (1883–1945), the army chaplain from Königsberg, was elected *Reichsbischof* of the Protestant Church. At a mass rally, the regional chairman (*Gauobmann*) of the German Christians, Reinhold Krause (1893–1980), openly called for the removal of the Old Testament from the Christian canon and the purging of Pauline theology from the New Testament. This "Berlin Sports Palace Scandal" (*Berliner Sportpalastskandal*) of 13 November 1933 led to closer collaboration between those regional churches that were still "intact" with the Confessing Church's Pastors' Emergency League.

The attempt by newly elected *Reichsbischof* Müller to integrate the *Landeskirchen* into a unified Reichskirche succeeded relatively smoothly in some cases (Oldenburg, Bremen, Lübeck, Eutin, Pfalz, Kurhessen, Mecklenburg) but was defeated by resistance in Bavaria and Württemberg. After a while the National Socialist state lost interest in the churches. The long-term goal of National Socialist ideologues, such as the ideologically influential disassociation proponents (*Distanzierungskräfte*) around Martin Bormann (1900–1945) was the complete ousting of the church from public life. This potentially heated clash was to be postponed, however, until after World War II in light of the German population's preoccupation with war starting in 1941. But the case of the region of Wartheland led by Reich governor (*Reichsstatthalter*) Arthur Greiser (1897–1946) illustrated what the

National Socialists planned for the entire country: Christian churches were to be cut off from all state and outside support, antichurch measures introduced, and all formal church associations forbidden. But the Reich's defeat in the Second World War put an end to those plans.

The Church in Hamburg before 1933

Institutions

In his church regulations of 1529, Johannes Bugenhagen (1485–1558) created the Office of the Superintendent, who supervised the leading pastors and clergymen. When, after 1593, the office was left unoccupied, the Church Council (Kirchenrat) created the position of Senior. The Senior was first voted in by the Church Senate, then by the Church Council starting in 1870, and then by the Church Synod beginning in 1919. As a rule, the head pastor who had served longest in office was chosen as the Senior, who led meetings of the spiritual ministries as *primus inter pares* and presided over the Collegium of Head Pastors.[3]

In Hamburg the separation of church and state began in 1860; this was reflected in the church's constitution ten years later. From that time on the responsibility of the city government (Senate) was limited to the participation of its Lutheran members in the church's newly introduced Patronat, which was responsible for the confirmation of church laws, oversight of Senior and pastor elections, and the appointment of several members to the synod (elected by clergy and laymen), the Church Council, and the parish councils. In 1914 church tax levies, previously collected by church organs, were handed over to state authorities. In March 1919 the Lutheran Senate members handed the Patronat's authority (*Patronatsrecht*) over to the Hamburg *Landeskirche*. With the new church constitution of 1923, valid until 1959, the Lutheran Church in Hamburg independently administered its affairs as a public corporation. As in the political arena, women's electoral rights—both active (running for office) and passive (voting) —were introduced.

The synod was the leading organ of the Hamburg *Landeskirche*. It was composed of representatives of church executive bodies and assemblies (*Konvente*) and elected the Church Council, which performed administrative functions and prepared documents for the synod. The Senior was an ex officio member of the Church Council who supervised the clergy, the chair of the Collegium of Head Pastors, and the collegium as a whole. The Spiritual Ministry included all clergy, although it had only advisory authority over synod resolutions to amend the church constitution. Although the church made no fundamental changes to its constitution during the Weimar Republic, the discussion surrounding the introduction of the episcopacy, with the *Landesbischof* as a replacement for the Senior, was significant. The head pastor of St. Michaelis, Simon Schöffel (1880–1959), supported by his colleague at St. Petri's, Theodor Knolle (1885–1955), had lent his support to this change for both theological and personal reasons. He believed that the episcopacy was a fundamental part of the Lutheran Church and that the term "Senior" did not capture the true essence of church leadership. His own career aspirations also played a role in his thinking. The various discussions concerning the episcopacy in 1925—and again in 1931—were also connected to the attempts by the Catholic Church to establish its own bishop's seat, as well as its claims on the bishopric of Ansgar (801–865).

During the Weimar Republic, in any case, the collegial leadership structure remained in place. Attempts to establish more of a hierarchy in church decision-making structures during this period can be interpreted as a reaction to the introduction of democratic practices in political and church affairs. To counteract the democratization of society and the churches, the pinnacle of the church leadership would have to be restructured and centered on one person alone.

Church Politics

The two leading theological and political orientations inside the Protestant churches in the nineteenth and early twentieth centuries were the post-Enlightenment liberals, who spoke out for more pluralism in the church, and the "positive Christians," who advocated the continuation of Lutheran orthodoxy.[4] This divide in Protestantism was a fundamental fact of German church life that should not be underestimated. These two camps stood in opposition to each other, undermining the ability of the Protestant Church to put forth a consistent public profile. The "positive Christians" dominated throughout Germany and in Hamburg; they represented the internal climate in the church and the orientation of the majority. About four-fifths of the pastors belonged to the nonliberal group; their theological conservatism was already early on connected with political conservatism. Adherence to one of the two groups was a determining factor in the election of pastors. A moderating third "New Church" group, led by Hermann Junge (1884–1953) and Ludwig Heitmann (1880–1953), was less influential in Hamburg. While the "positive Christians" strongly believed in the verbatim interpretation of the Bible and traditional religious beliefs, the liberals accepted the modern interpretation of the Bible as a critical-historical exegesis. The "New Church" adherents attempted to bridge the two groups by connecting religious beliefs and modernist interpretations.[5] The St. Nikolai and St. Katharinen churches were considered "liberal," while St. Jacobi and St. Michaelis were theologically "positive," meaning that the respective head pastors represented these orientations. With Friedrich Rode as head pastor, St. Petri belonged to the "liberal" camp; under Theodor Knolle, it was part of the "positive" group, given that Knolle, along with Simon Schöffel at St. Michaelis, was one of the leading representatives of "positive Christianity." The liberals converged around Heinz Beckmann of St. Nikolai. There were strong substantive disagreements between the two groups, which shifted during the Third Reich into a conflict between German Christians and the confessional movement.

In the church synod, elected for the period between 1930 and 1934, 84 of 160 members were organized in a "positive Christianity" faction and 49 in a liberal faction; 20 members belonged to the "New Church" group and seven remained independent. In the nine-member committees, the "positive" group was represented by five members, the liberal faction by two, and the reformists (New Church) by one; in the six-member committees (e.g., the disciplinary court), there were three "positive" representatives, two liberals, and one reformist. In the Church Council, of the three clergy members, two were "positive Christians" and one a liberal; of the six secular members, three were adherents of "positive Christianity," two were liberals, and one a New Church reformer.

Pastors and Politics

Although there is no comprehensive documentation concerning the clergy's party membership in either the Weimar Republic or the Federal Republic of Germany, their political engagement is at least partially discernable. In the Empire—and afterward—there is a high probability that almost all the pastors were monarchists. It can be inferred from publications throughout Germany that their attitudes and behavior were not as "politically independent" as they often proclaimed. Far more of the clergy were politically engaged, especially in party politics on the political right, ranging from those who distanced themselves from the Weimar Republic to those who were strongly opposed to it, such as members of the German People's Party (Deutsche Volkspartei or DVP) and the German National Peoples' Party (Deutschnationale Volkspartei or DNVP). Some clergymen belonged to the NSDAP already before 1933, including the Hamburg *Landesbischof* Franz Tügel (1888–1946): he joined the party in 1931, acted as NSDAP *Gauredner* and a speaker of the German Christians, and became the latter group's trusted counselor in 1933. The group of religious socialists, in contrast, was numerically very small and insignificant in terms of its influence.[6]

The "Revolution in Hamburg's *Landeskirche*," 1933

Church Political Activities

The transfer of power to the National Socialists was not without its consequences in the Church: In April 1933 the Church Council rein-troduced a prayer petition for the leading political authorities—the Reich president, the Reich government, and the Senate—in Sunday services. The Reich chancellor's birthday was mentioned in a separate petition, which read: "Father, Almighty God, who leads the people according to Thy counsel, look with favor on the German Reich. Bless the Reich President. Convey Thy protection onto the Chancellor of the German Reich. Arm him in this new year of his life with strength from above. Help him to carry the burden of responsibility in his regime and give Thy blessing to the difficult tasks involved in the resurrection of our Fatherland for the good of all our people and in the glory of Thy name."[7] The parishes were requested to bedeck their churches and religious buildings with flags on 20 April 1933.[8] The first day of May was commemorated as the national Labor Day holiday with church services.[9]

The leadership of Senior Karl Horn (1869–1942; St. Jacobi)[10] was criticized in internal church circles in 1933, especially since he had warned against taking part in political activities and joining politi-cal parties. In April 1933 he circulated a confidential memo warning against attempts to bring the churches into line with National Socialist policies (*Gleichschaltungsaktivitäten*), but he toned down his concerns as early as the beginning of May. Forty pastors who were close to the Young Reformers Movement and the German Christians, including later representatives of Hamburg's Confessing Community Bernhard-Heinrich Forck (1893–1963), D. Ludwig Heitmann (1880–1953), Dr. Hermann Junge (1884–1953), and Richard Remé (1875–1944),[11] called for his resignation: "The new age demands an absolute break with the old system and thereby new men in decisive positions of power, those who not only mouth support for these radical changes but who also have internally embraced them."[12]

Senior Horn's position on National Socialism remained ambiva-lent. In the church service celebrating the opening of the new city parliament (*Bürgerschaft*) on 10 May 1933, he characterized Hitler in his sermon as the "God-sent welder of the Reich."[13] Nevertheless, the demands for him to resign were not rescinded; quite to the contrary: since Horn would not immediately resign, Forck, along with fifteen synod members, moved to summon the synod in order to create the episcopacy, elect the *Landesbischof*, and enact a law to invest him with power. Although Horn rejected the criticism directed against him as insincere and invalid, in May he declared himself ready to resign as of 1 July 1933. This despite the fact that he had learned of strong support from Heinz Beckmann, who—although he himself had criticized Horn's leadership—expressed his solidarity with him and counseled him not to resign. But even Beckmann's show of solidarity was not sufficient to keep Horn in office, especially since this was all happening against the background of German Christian threats to intervene in the matter.[14] It was not the German Christians, however, who took the lead in introducing the hierarchical episcopacy in the Hamburg *Landeskirche* by means of an enabling act similar to that of the March 1933 Reich law. Rather, the representatives of the Young Reformers movement and the confessional Lutherans took the initiative here.

The course of these events was not predetermined. In the 22 May Church Council meeting, there were initial misgivings; some thought that the constitutional framework of the planned Reichskirche should be put on hold in order to be able to better integrate existing structures into the new ones. Difficulties involving authority and competencies were foreseen as long as the Senior remained in office. In addition, Hamburg's mayor, Carl Vincent Krogmann (1889–1978), in office since March 1933, registered his protest against the election of a *Landesbischof* in a letter to the Church Council and demanded the agreement of the Hamburg state for such a significant step. At issue was the controversial question of whether the Church Council should resign, given that it had been elected by the parliamentary synod and therefore henceforth no longer had the trust of the public or the state. This question had never been raised during the Weimar Republic. After much consideration it was established that the synod and not the Church Council should issue the desired enabling act—the law itself apparently had not been questioned by anyone—since this would exceed the competency of the council.[15] Two days later, the discussions between the various factions and the Church Council, led by head pastor Theodor Knolle as mediator, yielded an agreement that after the resignation of the Senior a majority vote for a draft law on the episcopacy could be achieved and that Simon Schöffel, who also had the support of the mayor, should be elected to this office.[16]

The Synod of 29 May 1933

On Monday, 29 May 1933 at 4:00 in the afternoon, the 161st synod meeting of Hamburg's Lutheran Protestant Church was convened in the conference room of the city parliament.[17] Present at the meeting were 132 members; vice president of the synod Dr. Wilhelm Fromm (1875–1940)—chair of the St. Nikolai executive committee and Hamburg's Protestant Association, as well as district court director—presided over the session.[18] Because of the importance of this meeting, the chair of the city parliament and Senate representatives were present. On the agenda was the adoption of the law concerning the role and election of the *Landesbischof*.[19]

Bernhard-Heinrich Forck, along with other synod members, had sponsored the draft law, which the Church Council adopted. As the council's representative, head pastor Theodor Knolle explained the details of the law.[20] He referred to the Reich-wide tendency toward unification in German Protestantism that, he argued, should also have an impact on the *Landeskirchen*: "The Landeskirchen should be grateful for the liberation from democratic methods and the resurrection of our people. These new developments are most vigorously symbolized in the leadership principle. In theological reflections since 1918 the idea of the Episcopacy has prevailed over parliamentary methods."[21] Knolle posited a connection with the Office of the Superintendent introduced by Bugenhagen, which he equated with the episcopacy, thereby establishing a historical legitimation for the changes. He clearly distanced himself from the democratic church constitution of 1923, arguing that "its foundational tenets have been destroyed": "Formerly they constructed the constitution from below to above; while now the opposite way is being pursued."[22] At the same time he declared the end of the former roles of the Church Council and the synod—their authorities would be handed over to the episcopacy.[23] The following sentence appears in the text of his speech, though not in the meeting minutes: "The liberation from the un-German, alienating character of the western-style democratic constitution also manifests itself as the liberation of the Church from the parliamentary methods and forms of power that are so foreign to its nature."[24] The individual paragraphs and the law as a whole were unanimously adopted without any discussion:

> Paragraph 1: The office of the Landesbischof of the Lutheran Protestant Church in Hamburg will be established. Paragraph 2: The Landesbischof has full authority [*Gesamtführung*] over the Landeskirche. He represents the Church both internally and externally and speaks in the name of the Church. Paragraph 3: Until final regulations are adopted, all

constitutional rights and functions of the Synod, the Church Council, and the Senior will be transferred to the Landesbischof. The Landesbischof convenes and leads the Action Committee and determines its functions.[25]

Senior Horn thereupon suggested electing Simon Schöffel, synod president and head pastor of St. Michaels, as the first Hamburg *Landesbischof*. The election was carried out by acclamation—there was only one candidate, and he was chosen unanimously in this way.[26] The vice president of the synod greeted Schöffel: "We know that you also are committed with your whole heart to the massive movement that has seized the imagination of our German nation. We know that the Hamburg Senate will welcome you as the highest leader of our Church. We hope that thereby under your leadership the relationship between State and Church will be the best imaginable."[27] With that, Senior Horn, now deprived of power, handed over the official insignia of office to Schöffel.[28]

In his acceptance speech Schöffel gave thanks and promised that he would view the power imbued upon him as "a holy pledge that was handed to me in trust, so that I may lead our Church from the old to the new age and lay the foundation for a new organization."[29] He clearly declared the end of the democratic structures: "The time in which peoples' egos and the individual stood center-stage in all thoughts and actions has seen its day." The church was "still the strongest bulwark against this spirit." Nevertheless, "the parliamentary form of the liberal age furnished the framework on which the building of the church was constructed. And exactly this has become unworkable. If I may venture to give my interpretation of the age to come, then it seems to me that it would now be the time, according to the will of Eternity, to confront a people who have become too prideful with the objective [of realizing] the power of the Eternal itself, the holy will of God. In these times, God demands His justice."[30] Schöffel's words were meant to be the result of theological interpretation.[31] The church was considered to be embarking on an "enormous radical change" "called for by God, set forth by Him in a new age; it is simply our duty to live up to these expectations."[32] He also defended the establishment of the new hierarchical episcopacy: "I also think that the leadership concept, the idea of the spiritual office, must assert itself more strongly in the sense of the Gospels in the new church than it did in the old."[33] Schöffel described democracy as the arrogance of mankind and characterized the leadership principle in the state and in the church as willed by God—thereby implicitly justifying the Third Reich, with all of the attendant consequences.

Schöffel clearly expressed his support for the National Socialist state:

We greet the newly-constructed State and are thankful that it has discovered and proven its own courage and strength so as to pave the way for a new beginning and freedom for our people. We want to work together with this State because we feel that just as we ourselves, so also the State has been born out of the upheaval of the age. We do not want to stand next to the State as an association that conducts its own business, unconcerned about the affairs of others. We know, rather, that the State and the Church belong together in a community of fate, because the people that [the Church] cares for and that [the State] looks after are, after all, the same, and the voice that has called us—the State as well as the Church— is the voice of God.[34]

With that, Schöffel defended the transfer of power to the National Socialists, as well as their actions, by reference to God's own authority. At the same time, he characterized the traditional nation as "willed by God, formed by the Creation and history," emphasizing, however, that "as with all of God's creation, it requires the holy mercy of God if it is to have a beneficial effect; the Church, therefore, is surely devoted to its people, but derives its strength and takes its instructions at the end of the day only from the Gospels."[35] After the election, Hamburg's Protestant youth paid homage to the *Landesbischof* with a torchlight parade.[36] In his address, Schöffel emphasized the close relationship between the state and the church in the Third Reich: "May the Hamburg bishopric never again be eliminated. May we be granted the privilege of being able to build the Fatherland anew. ... May God bless our nation, our Fatherland, our home, and our Church!" He ended his speech with the exclamation "Heil!," which "was echoed amongst the youth a thousandfold."[37]

In only fifty minutes on the afternoon of 29 May 1933, one of the most profound legal changes ever in Hamburg's church history—the creation of the powerful position of *Landesbischof*—was carried out, and not by any formal written set of procedures but by acclamation alone.[38] Hamburg's National Socialist government subsequently appointed Schöffel to the Staatsrat, a powerless advisory body that displaced the city parliament. The democratic components of the church's constitution from 1923 were abolished; all decision-making authority would now rest in the hands of one person—the *Landesbischof*. With this, the leadership principle was embedded in the Lutheran Protestant Church in Hamburg. Again, significant here is that it was not the German Christians—the church group closest to the National Socialists—who spearheaded the introduction of the hierarchical episcopacy and succeeded in passing an enabling act comparable to the Enabling Act of 23 March 1933; rather, the representatives of the

Young Reformers movement and the confessional Lutherans put all of the pieces in place.

Schöffel's Induction into Office on 11 June 1933

The celebratory induction of Hamburg's new *Landesbischof* took place on Trinity Sunday—11 June, a short two weeks after his election, in the Hauptkirche St. Michaelis. Representatives of the Senate who attended were Mayor Dr. Wilhelm Burchard-Motz, who also gave a formal greeting from the Senate, as well as Senators Karl Witt, Hans-Henning von Pressentin (1890–1952), Philipp Klepp (1894–1958), and Dr. Friedrich Ofterdinger (1896–1946); Mayor Krogmann was prevented from attending by the World Economic Conference in London.[39] The participation of the liberal head pastor Beckmann, who gave a vow of the pastors, sparked controversy: Mayor Krogmann, for example, registered his misgivings, since Beckmann was considered to be "a proponent of the liberal and democratic camp." Because Beckmann was relaying a vow and not giving a sermon, Schöffel managed to dispel any concerns.[40] Among external representatives were the *Landesbischöfe* Eduard Völkel (1878–1957, Schleswig), Heinrich Rendtorff (1888–1960, Schwerin), Gerhard Wilhelm Helmut Adolf Theodor Tolzien (1870–1946, Mecklenburg-Strelitz), and Alexander Bernewitz (1863–1935, Braunschweig). Missing was *Reichsbischof* Friedrich von Bodelschwingh (1877–1946), from whom Schöffel quickly distanced himself.[41]

Schöffel preached from the Gospel of Matthew 28:16–20. He established a line of historical continuity with the first Hamburg Bishop Ansgar, in which he placed himself. After Bishop Ansgar and the Reformation, he characterized the existing Protestant bishopric as the third era in the history of Hamburg's church.[42] He emphasized the significance of teaching and pronounced his wish to establish a theological department at the University of Hamburg. Heinrich Wilhelmi (1888–1968) considered the following to be the high point of Schöffel's speech at the induction: "God has given me my bishopric and no one can tear it away from me!," which did not appear in the printed version of the speech. A mere ten months later, Schöffel's acclamation would prove to be an illusion.[43]

Schöffel clearly distanced himself from liberalism, the Enlightenment, and democracy—before he pronounced his vow, he emphasized that it was in the final phase of the Weimar Republic that "the terrible struggle for the downfall and demise of liberalism, the last furious onslaught of Marxism and communism and the counter-thrust of the church in defense and attack" took place.[44] In the introduction to the printed version of his talk, titled "Eternal Truth—Changing Times: The Reorganization of the Hamburg Landeskirche, 1933," he emphasized once again, "Those periods of time built upon the 'I'—such as those of the French Revolution and the Enlightenment—must die. Those periods of time in which life could be understood, developed, and mastered exclusively on the basis of I, the individual, must die."[45] He emphatically praised the changes of the year 1933: "One suddenly can recognize the German nation no longer as the sum of individuals but rather as the creation of God, whose mystery lies in its blood and history."[46]

Simon Schöffel: The First Landesbischof of Hamburg

Simon Schöffel, from Franconia, assumed the position of parish minister in Schweinfurt in 1909; in 1921 he became Dekan. He received his doctorate in 1916 at the University of Erlangen, where he wrote a thesis on the church history of Schweinfurt; in 1918 he received his licentiate of theology, and in 1922 he was bestowed an honorary doctorate in theology from the same institution. In 1921 he was elected to the position of head pastor at St. Michaelis in Hamburg, and after he assumed office in 1922 he was elected chair of the conservative Protestant Parents Association and in 1929 president of the synod. Schöffel was the leading representative of the orthodox "positive Christianity" camp in the church. He was especially engaged in church leadership and in school politics, so that he was positioned early on to have an influence on youth. As an opponent of the separation of church and state, he persevered in the establishment of confessional schools, which was unthinkable in liberal Hamburg. Ever since his transfer to Hamburg, he supported the establishment of the hierarchical episcopacy, whose bishop, in his eyes, would be a guarantor of the purity of church teaching and the preservation of church doctrine.

Schöffel had carefully prepared his acceptance by the National Socialists. He had not taken part in any direct changes in the church but was open to assuming a church office, though he had reservations about this, since quite some time before, on the basis of tradition, he had consented to the election of Heinz Beckmann as the next Senior. Beckmann, however, released him from this commitment in a personal conversation.[47] Schöffel was friends with Carl Vincent Krogmann, the "governing mayor of Hamburg" in the Third Reich; when Krogmann was elected to this office on 8 March 1933, Schöffel had the church bells rung—against the votes of the other head pastors, including Heinz Beckmann. As president of the synod, Schöffel emphatically greeted the new state eight days later; his church, St. Michaelis, was one of the few churches bedecked with flags in the days before. In a letter to the Church Council, Krogmann had declared himself in favor of Schöffel as the first Hamburg *Landesbischof* in the new church hierarchy. Schöffel also belonged to the action committee that had been formed at the beginning of May 1933 at the initiative of Tügel and in agreement with Krogmann. The committee consisted of Horn, Tügel, and Schöffel; Schöffel's task was to prepare the reorganization of the Hamburg *Landeskirche*. After his election as *Landesbischof*, Schöffel appointed a second action committee that included Knolle but not Horn; its task was to work out a new constitution and to foster a relationship between Hamburg's *Landeskirche* and the NSDAP and the state. A day after this second action committee was formed, Tügel was instructed to perform "direct ecclesiastical service for special temporary assignments." Tügel, in light of his close contacts with the NSDAP, had become especially important, since the new *Landesbischof* lacked such connections. In the following month, on 6 July, Tügel was appointed superior councilor of the church (*Oberkirchenrat*).[48]

The elections to church executive committees, very hastily called for by Reich chancellor Hitler on 23 July 1933—in which the German Christians were massively supported by the NSDAP—were a farce, including in Hamburg, since the results were clearly predetermined. Tügel, for the German Christians, and Junge, for the "Gospel and Church" group, had agreed a week before the vote to put together a common electoral list for each parish, whereby the German Christians were to receive at least 51 percent of the seats. In some cases, they received as much as 70 percent. The election to the assemblies on 20 August 1933 took place under the same conditions. This "success" exceeded the actual quantitative significance of the German Christians.[49]

Schöffel began with a restructuring of the church: church districts and assemblies were newly organized and placed under provosts (*Pröpste*); the chair of the church executive committee remained with the pastors. With this he supported his comrade-in-arms in the remodeling of Hamburg's Protestant church: he named his friend Theodor Knolle to the position of general superintendent—an office that had been newly created in July 1933 along the lines of the superintendent's office in the sixteenth century. Bernhard Forck had become Schöffel's very influential right-hand man in Hamburg's church administration, Hermann Junge was named provost that August, and Ludwig Heitmann was appointed to the interim Church Council.[50]

Schöffel was very active at the level of the Reichskirche: in 1933 he unconditionally supported the National Socialist movement and its church politics. Hamburg's Protestant church was one of the three *Landeskirchen* at the end of May that voted against the nomination of Friedrich von Bodelschwingh for *Reichsbischof* and for the election of the German Christian Ludwig Müller. Schöffel's justification: "The church today must storm ahead, not remain quiescent; for this purpose, Müller is the leader we need," and "Bodelschwingh's elevation to the top would mean the death of our Church."[51] When Bodelschwingh was nevertheless initially elected, Schöffel failed to forward Bodelschwingh's traditional Pentecost greeting to Hamburg's pastors, but instead demanded a reconsideration of his election, since Bodelschwingh, according to Schöffel, did not possess the necessary "leadership qualities" of a *Reichsbischof.*[52] Church historian Klaus Scholder (1930–85) argued that Schöffel's "foolhardy theology and reckless intrigues significantly" contributed to the fall of Bodelschwingh and the election of Müller.[53] Müller characterized Schöffel as "a convinced National Socialist" and appointed him to his Spiritual Ministry on 27 September 1933. In this position Schöffel was responsible for the whole of Christian teaching, the relationship with other communities and churches, and the church's missions and external relations. Already during the time between the adoption of the Reich's church constitution on 11 July and the convocation of the National Church Synod on 27 September 1933, Schöffel worked in the Lutheran section of the five-member "interim church leadership" group.

Schöffel, in front of the synod, endorsed in the name of the church "with a joyful yes" the path toward a National Socialist state based on national traditions, blood, and race.[54] As late as the end of November 1933 Schöffel "continued to be convinced of the mission of the faith movement—i.e., the German Christians—in the Third Reich."[55] Hamburg's *Landeskirche* was considered to be reliable in furthering the interests of the Reichskirche. Accordingly, in January 1934 Schöffel introduced censorship into the diocesan newsletters and forbade all clergy from commenting on church politics in church services.[56]

Tensions between the German Christians and Schöffel began as early as the beginning of his time in office as *Landesbischof*. Franz Tügel felt himself pushed into a marginal position by Schöffel's close advisors in the *Landeskirche* administration and ill-used, as his only role was to "iron out" difficulties with the Nazi Party. In October 1933 the semblance of peace between Schöffel and the German Christians in Hamburg came to an end. On 25 November the *Reichsbischof* dismissed Schöffel from his office in the Spiritual Ministry of the German Protestant Church, in part because of the rivalry between him and the more radical Reich leader of the German Christians, Joachim Hossenfelder (1899–1976).

Hamburg's mayor and the Reich governor both began to distance themselves from Schöffel. A newspaper notice in Hamburg placed by the northwest regional leadership of the German Christians characterized Schöffel's removal as a "decisive change in course" that would clear the way for a reconstruction of the German Protestant National Church.[57]

At the end of January 1934 Schöffel criticized the *Reichsbischof's* emergency law, which prohibited disputes and demonstrations within the church under threat of immediate dismissal of the initiators of such actions; this meant that public attacks against the church government and its measures were forbidden. Schöffel characterized the law as "legally untenable, practically unworkable, and completely antithetical to Church doctrine."[58] In Hamburg this criticism mobilized the German Christians, especially Franz Tügel, who, after the break with Müller, no longer had reason to be careful. Schöffel, who was not an NSDAP member, had no direct access to the political establishment despite his position as state counselor; for this he was dependent on Tügel's intervention. In addition, Schöffel had increasingly surrounded himself with people he trusted but who were suspect to the National Socialists, thereby raising suspicion that he wanted to distance himself from the National Socialist state. The German Christians had been trying to breathe some life into their ebbing "movement" since the beginning of 1934, whereby Hamburg, through Tügel's efforts, became the center of German Christian activities in the northern part of the Reich. Tügel, who performed the tasks of a *Staatskommissar* responsible for the church in Hamburg without holding the formal position, represented the interests of the mayor and demanded Schöffel's resignation from the post of Hamburg's *Landesbischof*. Schöffel resigned on 1 March 1934, and Tügel himself took his place. The leader of the German Christians in northwest Germany, Hans Aselmann (1888–1967) and Tügel's deputy in Hamburg's ombudsman's office (*Gauobmannsamt*), Pastor Otto Langmann (1898–1956), had already long before emphatically insisted that Tügel replace Schöffel as *Landesbischof*. State secretary Georg Ahrens (1896–1974) told Schöffel on 22 February that he also expected his resignation, since this had been called for by the *Reichsbischof*. Two days later, Schöffel lost his position as state councilor. At the end of the day, the decisive factor in Schöffel's resignation from the office of *Landesbischof* was the insistence of the synod assembly president, Professor Dr. Heinrich Fabian (1889–1970), NSDAP member and German Christian, who considered Schöffel unfit for the position.[59] After this, Schöffel concentrated on his role as head pastor, adorned himself with the title "*Landesbischof* emeritus," and secured his bishop's pension.[60]

In the 5 March 1934 synod session, Franz Tügel was elected as the new Hamburg *Landesbischof*. In his acceptance speech, which he gave dressed in his NSDAP uniform, he identified himself as a Lutheran and a National Socialist: "I know only *one* enemy: whoever does not want Adolf Hitler's State. With the likes of those I am finished. I owe this not only to my Church, but also to my State, my people, and my wonderful Führer. ... One catchphrase: With Luther and Adolf Hitler for Church and Nation, that both may become *one* heart and *one* soul!" Tügel's address, read out in his brown party uniform, culminated in a sentence that was not on the agenda: "My program is I myself!"[61] In a note to Reich governor Karl Kaufmann (1900–1969), Tügel wrote, "I vow to you, as a true follower of our Führer, to administer my office in the spirit of the Third Reich. ..."[62]

In the newspaper *Luthertum*, which he coedited, Schöffel published a programmatic essay in 1934 titled, "The German *Luthertum* at the Turning-Point," in which he wrote that a new reality had broken through in National Socialism: "*Luthertum* approves of this break-through with the same joy with which Luther once professed the redis-covered Creation to his people." Schöffel saw in the Third Reich the path of the German nation, which would "realize its creative talents": "For us, this path lies in National Socialism." For Schöffel, National Socialism was "the conscious, human executor of God's judgment [in the service of] the German people."[63] In light of the actions against Jews, democrats, and the workers' movement since the beginning of 1933, Schöffel's words, with their reference to the Weimar Republic, are shocking:

> [National Socialism] will have to destroy what turned out to be a long tortuous path to disaster for us and will have to smash it to pieces all along the political line throughout the entire structure of the State. If National Socialism, with its secure instinct, destroys the delusion of lib-eralism, rejects the cause of the bourgeoisie ..., loathes the class struggle, and openly acknowledges that these things are ripe for judgment, then it is correct and the Lutheran will and must from here on in go along with it. What binds us to National Socialism is the innermost heart, the knowl-edge about the judgment that must be. The Lutheran, precisely he, must recognize that the way of the recent past was the way to ruin.[64]

As late as 1934, Schöffel, without any criticism, accepted the goals and methods of National Socialism and justified them theologically. In his hands, the "mission of National Socialism" became the mission of the church: "National Socialism performs this work by tapping into and rousing the deep strengths of the people as they have been given in blood, race, spirit, and history. ... The blood of a strange form of life introduced into the bloodstream of a people poisons them and delivers them over to death."[65] Such a distressing sentence in the context of the time in which it was written unambiguously referred to a racist anti-semitism. Schöffel also verbally used nationalist and National Socialist terminology, thus supporting its acceptance in church circles.[66]

How is Simon Schöffel's behavior to be assessed? Although he was never a member of the NSDAP, he supported the substance of National Socialism to a large degree and approved of a significant part of its ideology. Schöffel showed no signs of political dissent, let alone out-right opposition. He tried to make sure that a (triumphant) National Socialism would serve his own goal of attaining the honor of being named bishop. In doing so, he supported National Socialism consider-ably and accelerated the *Gleichschaltung* of the Protestant Church with the National Socialist state. In 1933 he was successful in his pursuits, until Franz Tügel, using similar methods, managed to have Schöffel relieved of his duties as *Landesbischof*. The Hamburg example makes it clear that several National Socialists got involved in internal politi-cal disagreements in the church; as a result their programs and ideol-ogy attained greater social acceptance among a traditionally Christian bourgeoisie, thus decisively helping National Socialists to enhance their power in society.

In line with his church politics, Simon Schöffel joined the Confessional Community of Hamburg and became a member of its executive committee in 1936. He didn't go so far, however, as to join Martin Niemöller's Pastors' Emergency League, which opposed the application of the Aryan clause in the church; rather, he countered this group with his own distinct and decidedly Lutheran pastors' associa-tion, the "Lutheran Brotherhood." In 1938 Schöffel and his compatriot Knolle prevented Hamburg's Confessional Community from issuing a statement of solidarity with Niemöller, who was in a concentration camp as a personal captive of Hitler. They justified this action with the claim that Niemöller had acted *politically*. Yet in 1934 Schöffel had written, "We must take a stand when it comes to the political path of our people. It is pointless to pretend that faith and politics should not have anything to do with each other."[67] This clearly was meant to refer to statements that supported National Socialism but not to those who criticized it.

After the Allies forced his successor Franz Tügel to resign in July 1945, Simon Schöffel was again voted into the office of *Landesbischof* by acclamation in 1946 and held the post until he retired in December 1954. In his second period in office, Schöffel focused on the training of the upcoming generation of clergy. Schöffel had taught church history and later systematic theology in Hamburg University's General Lecture Series department ever since assuming church office; from 1931 to 1937 he taught in the Religion Teacher Training department, and from 1945 to 1954 at the Church Lecture Series Institution and the Theological College of Hamburg, where he was awarded the title Professor of Theology by the Hamburg Church Council in 1950. Schöffel published numerous academic treatises, including the first and only volume on Hamburg's church history in its early period and the founding of the bishopric by Ansgar between the years 831 and 834; he could not write the planned following two volumes due to the pressures of work. Simon Schöffel was an ambitious theologian and a productive academic. His theology was marked by a strict Lutheran orientation; he was politically conservative and at times subscribed to a body of antidemocratic nationalist ideas.[68]

Critical Voices, 1933

Liberalism Offsides: Heinz Beckmann

In connection with the election of the *Landesbischof*, the more senior liberal head pastor, Heinz Beckmann, was passed over for the position of Senior in the Hamburg church, which flew in the face of all tradition, because he declined to take part in the "1933 Hamburg church revolution."[69] Beckmann was one of the few active democrats in Hamburg's *Landeskirche* in the first half of the twentieth century, a champion of equality for female theologians, and a spokesman for the liberal faction in the synod. He passed his theological exams in 1899 and worked for some time as an assistant editor responsible for regional affairs at the respected liberal Protestant publication *The Christian World*. In 1910 he was named pastor of the Marktkirche in Wiesbaden; ten years later he took over the head pastor's position at Hamburg's St. Nikolai Church, where he was actively engaged until his death.

The talented and highly regarded speaker dedicated himself above all to ethical and religious-philosophical problems; his work touched on manifold borders between theology and literature. One of his central topics was the analysis of the Old Testament. Beckmann worked intensively in the synod and the Church Council. His personal cause was the resolution of the problems of modern urban churches. From 1924 to 1933 he edited the *Hamburgische Kirchenzeitung*, which reached a wide section of church members. He was very involved in school politics, whereby he pursued good relations between the social-democratically influenced Hamburg state and the Lutheran Church. He thereby stood in opposition to the conservative wing of the Protestant Parents Association that was influenced by Simon Schöffel and wanted to take a harder line against the position of the state. In the 1920s Beckmann was especially active in efforts to allow women to sit for both theological exams after their studies and to assume active roles in church service. The ordination of women and their equality of opportunity in pursuing activities alongside pastors, both of which Beckmann also supported, however, could not have mustered the necessary support during this period in Hamburg or in any of the other *Landeskirchen*. With his support, however, it was possible to promulgate a law on female parish assistants in 1927, which facilitated the activities of female theologians, albeit with restricted rights, after they passed their exams. In his own parish, he brought in Margarete Braun (1893–1966) from Wiesbaden in 1926; she passed her second qualifying theological exam in Hamburg and could work as a parish assistant at St. Nikolai.

Another of Beckmann's major concerns was the training of the upcoming generation of theologians to become religious education teachers. He had received an honorary doctorate in theology at Kiel University in 1923 and, in his capacity as head pastor at St. Nikolai, he taught theology in the General Lecture Series department at the University of Hamburg beginning in the 1921–22 winter semester; from 1931 to 1934 he taught the Old Testament to religious education teachers. He gave courses for candidates in theology and ministry (*Predigtamt*) and oversaw their exams. Beckmann looked with great consternation at the National Socialist takeover of power; at the end of one lecture he characterized 30 January 1933 as the end of "the age of culture." After 1933, with the exception of his work as head pastor and in the training of degree candidates, Beckmann had practically no opportunity to be influential in public life.

Judaic Studies Teacher: Walter Windfuhr

Another of Hamburg's clergy who did not take part in the general euphoria of 1933 was pastor Walter Windfuhr (1878–1970), a member of the German National Peoples' Party in the Weimar Republic, who retired in 1933. In 1918 he had viewed the dissolution of the connection between "throne and altar" as a "gift," and, as of 1933, saw the church as "forced into the suffocating clutch of a single political party." He wrote to Schöffel, "It remains the case that, with the best will in the world, I am completely unable to comprehend the capacity of a single political party to be the foundation of our religious community."[70] Windfuhr's views on National Socialism likewise became very clear in a letter that he wrote to a friend on 1 September 1933: "Through its flirtation with National Socialism the Protestant Church has bankrupted itself; toward that end the various shots of morphine in the form of Luther festivals, etc., that feigned to provide new lifeblood to the Church did not help at all. In that moment, when the SA marched through the main door in order to 'conquer' the Church, God fled out the back. Now He has retired to the synagogue as the only religious place not ruled by the swastika."[71]

In November 1933, according to the denunciation of the youth pastor Jürgen Wehrmann (1908–96), Windfuhr was said to have taken the opportunity after a candidate's lecture to criticize the Reichskirche administration, especially Bishop Joachim Hossenfelder, the censorship of the press, and the connection between politics and religion, which he parodied: "I believe in Adolf Hitler, a holy, universal *völkisch* nation, the congregation of Aryans." In his article "The Reichsbischof and Judaism," which appeared at the end of November 1933 in the *Israelitischen Familienblatt*, he refuted the anti-semitic statements that the German Christian *Reichsbischof* Ludwig Müller made on the occasion of the Luther Week celebrations in Eisenach. Hamburg's *Landesbischof* Schöffel demanded the retraction of Windfuhr's article, but by then it had already appeared in print.[72] That fact that a German National Protestant theologian could criticize the *Reichsbischof* already at the beginning of the Third Reich, in which there was great enthusiasm for National Socialism even in church circles, was notably unusual.[73]

Protestantism during the Transfer of Power to National Socialism

The example of Hamburg's *Landeskirche* made it clear that, on an institutional level, Protestantism emphatically welcomed National Socialism in 1933. Only a few theologians or lay religious figures commented critically and only then within a limited public audience. The background to this was the alienation from the Weimar Republic and from democracy as a type of state rule, which, by virtue of its egalitarian measures, had undermined the social status of the church and its office holders. The separation of church and state, the first tentative steps toward gender equality, the increasing opportunities for the laity to have a say in church matters, and the loss of the connection between "throne and altar" all contributed to the fact that the large majority of Protestants and above all their clergy welcomed an autocratic and, at the end of the day, dictatorial rule in politics and society. At the same time, the transfer of power to the National Socialists was used to introduce, once again, authoritarian structures in the church and to restrain, and finally abolish, democratic reforms—above all, the separation of powers, the increased ability of women to have a voice in church affairs, and the new employment opportunities for female theologians. For this, the introduction of the leadership principle in 1933 offered ideal conditions.

The church's attempts to curry favor with the National Socialist dictatorship, however, would not be successful for long. After 1935 the National Socialist state was no longer interested in the political collaboration of the church throughout the Reich. The church's ousting from public life in Hamburg turned out to be relatively mild, due to the Reich governor's neutral, or even indifferent, policies toward the church. After the end of World War II the changes that had been made in the church's internal organization in 1933 were also annulled and the institution's legal status as it was in the Weimar Republic again came into force.

The leading representatives of Hamburg's *Landeskirche* in 1945 recognized no admission of guilt when it came to the Third Reich and offered absolutely no plea for forgiveness from the relatives of National Socialism's victims and all those who suffered. The result of the denazification of the clergy produced no surprises: about half of the pastors—at one time or another—had belonged to the German Christians, about 10 percent were NSDAP members, and some of them fervently embraced the spirit of National Socialism. Only eight pastors—about 5 percent of all the clergy—who had been especially incriminated by their National Socialist leanings were made to retire, and then only on the basis of "health concerns." After only one or two years almost all of them were entrusted with filling temporarily vacant church posts and even received permanent positions at the beginning of the 1950s— their "retirements" were retroactively annulled. Acknowledgment of guilt was never on the agenda; rather, the goal was to protect incriminated individuals. De-nazification in the church was considered a necessary evil, with the main goal of preventing the intervention of the Allied military authorities. Punishment ensued just as rarely as a profession of guilt on the part of the incriminated, who very often even remained defiant. The "Comments of the Regional Synod regarding Contemporary Conditions," publicized on 30 January 1947, highlighted only the existing emergency situation in Hamburg "in order not to imply guilt through silence." No mention of the Third Reich and its victims was anywhere to be found.[74]

Rainer Hering is director of the Landesarchiv Schleswig-Holstein in Schleswig and teaches modern history and archival science at the Universities of Hamburg and Kiel. His extensive publications include *Die Konstruierte Nation: Der Alldeutsche Verband 1890 bis 1933* (2003) and *"Aber ich brauche die Gebote..."*: *Helmut Schmidt, die Kirchen und die Religion* (2012), as well as numerous articles on different aspects of the history of the Lutheran Church in modern German history. Hering is also a specialist on the history of Hamburg and Schleswig-Holstein.

Notes

Parts of this chapter have been previously published in Rainer Hering, "Nationalistisch und hierarchiebewusst: Evangelische und Katholische Kirche," in *Hamburg im Dritten Reich*, ed. Forschungsstelle für Zeitgeschichte in Hamburg (Göttingen: Wallstein Verlag, 2005).

 1. Rainer Hering, *Heinz Beckmann und die "Hamburgische Kirchenrevolution"* (hereafter *Kirchenrevolution*) (Hamburg: Archiv des Kirchenkreises Hamburg-Ost, 2009), 53.
 2. See *Ökumenische Kirchengeschichte*, vol. 3: *Von der Französischen Revolution bis 1989*, ed. Hubert Wolf (Darmstadt: Wissenschaftliche Buchgesellschaft, 2007).
 3. See Hans Georg Bergemann, *Staat und Kirche in Hamburg während des 19. Jahrhunderts* (Hamburg: Wittig, 1958), 47–92.
 4. See Rainer Hering, "Auf dem Weg in die Moderne? Die Hamburgische Landeskirche in der Weimarer Republik," *Zeitschrift des Vereins für Hamburgische Geschichte* 82 (1996): 127–66, esp. 145–49.
 5. See Rainer Hering, *Das Führerprinzip in der Hamburger Kirche: Vor 70 Jahren; Amtseinführung des ersten Hamburger Landesbischofs am 11. Juni 1933* (Hamburg: Archiv des Kirchenkreises Alt-Hamburg, 2003), 23–33.
 6. For specific details, see Hering, "Auf dem Weg," 127–66, esp. 145–49. See also Rainer Hering, "Protestantismus vor der Moderne: Die Hamburger Landeskirche 1860 bis 1933," in *Andocken: Hamburgs Kulturgeschichte 1848 bis 1933*, ed. Dirk Hempel and Ingrid Schröder (Hamburg: Dobu, 2012), 52–74.
 7. Fürbitte, April 1933, Staatsarchiv Hamburg, (hereafter cited as StA Hamburg), 363-3 Senatskommission für die Angelegenheiten der Religionsgesellschaften, A 145, 2–4.
 8. Verordnung April 1933, *Gesetze, Verordnungen und Mitteilungen aus der Hamburgischen Kirche 1933*, 15.
 9. Verordnung April 1933, StA Hamburg, 363-3 Senatskommission für die Angelegenheiten der Religionsgesellschaften, A 146, 2–3.
10. See Rainer Hering, "Horn, Karl Albert Ernst Friedrich Theodor," in *Biographisch-Bibliographisches Kirchenlexikon*, vol. 16, ed. Friedrich Wilhelm Bautz and Traugott Bautz (Herzberg/Nordhausen: Bautz, 1999), 733–43.
11. On Junge, see Iris Groschek, *Gemeindechronik der Erlöserkirche Borgfelde: "Jesus Christus gestern und heute und derselbe auch in Ewigkeit"* (Hamburg:

Archiv des Kirchenkreises Alt-Hamburg, 2000), esp. 68–73; on Forck, see Michael Reiter, *Christliche Existenz und sozialer Wandel in der ersten Hälfte des 20. Jahrhunderts: Eine Hamburger Kirchengemeinde in den politischen Auseinandersetzungen der Weimarer Republik und des Dritten Reiches* (Phil. diss. University of Hamburg, 1992), esp. 66–68, 98–100, 170–75; on Heitmann, see Rainer Hering, "Heitmann, Ferdinand Carl Ludwig," in *Biographisch-Bibliographisches Kirchenlexikon*, vol. 16, ed. Friedrich Wilhelm Bautz and Traugott Bautz (Herzberg/Nordhausen: Bautz, 1999), 649–67.

12. Heinrich Wilhelmi, *Die Hamburger Kirche in der nationalsozialistischen Zeit 1933–1945* (Göttingen: Vandenhoeck and Ruprecht, 1968), 51; see also 46–54.

13. Ibid., 50.

14. Ibid., esp. 46–54; see also Hering, "Horn," esp. 736–37, as well as the press release of 24 May 1933 in the records of the Landeskirchliches Archiv der Nordkirche (hereafter cited as LKA Nordkirche), Kiel, 32.01, 573/ 7. Heinz Beckmann describes his support of the Senior and his motives for doing so in his memoirs; see Hering, *Kirchenrevolution*, 53, 56.

15. Minutes of the meeting of the Church Council, 22 May 1933, LKA Nordliche, Kiel, 32.01 573/1. See also Krogmann to the president of the Church Council, Heinrich Schröder (1867–1938), 22 May 1933, ibid., 573/3. Krogmann wrote, "As I have heard, today the Church Council intends to name a Landesbischof and to equip him with dictatorial powers. I must energetically object to this action and request that the appointment of a Landesbischof be carried out only with the agreement of the Land government."

16. Minutes of the meeting of the Church Council, 24 May 1933, LKA Nordkirche, Kiel, 32.01, 573/4.

17. See the minutes of the 161st meeting of the synod, 29 May 1933, LKA Nordkirche, Kiel, 30.01, 247. For the printed version, see *Ewige Wahrheit— wandernde Zeit: Die Neugestaltung der Hamburgischen Landeskirche 1933*, ed. Vorläufiger Landeskirchenrat der Evangelisch-lutherischen Kirche im Hamburgischen Staate (Hamburg: Kirchenrat, 1933), 9–31.

18. On Fromm, see *Gesetze, Verordnungen und Mitteilungen aus der Hamburgischen Kirche 1940*, 89; Wilhelm Heydorn, *"Nur Mensch sein!" Lebenserinnerungen 1873 bis 1958*, ed. Iris Groschek and Rainer Hering (Hamburg-München: Dölling und Galitz, 1999), 485.

19. Minutes of the 161st meeting of the synod, 29 May 1933, LKA Nordkirche, Kiel, 30.01, 247/1–2.

20. Ibid., 3–5.

21. Ibid., 3–4.

22. Ibid., 4.

23. Ibid., 5.

24. Manuscript of the speech by Theodor Knolle, 29 May 1933, LKA Nordkirche, Kiel, 32.01, 573/19. See also Rainer Hering, *Die Bischöfe Simon Schöffel, Franz Tügel* (Hamburg: Verein für Hamburgische Geschichte, 1995), 11, and Wilhelmi, *Hamburger Kirche*, 54–59.

25. *Gesetze, Verordnungen und Mitteilungen aus der Hamburgischen Kirche 1933*, 36a.
26. Minutes of the 161st meeting of the synod, 29 May 1933, LKA Nordkirche, Kiel, 30.01 Landeskirchenrat Kanzlei, 247/6–7.
27. Ibid., 8.
28. Ibid., 8–9.
29. Ibid., 10.
30. Ibid., 12.
31. Ibid., 12–13.
32. Ibid., 13.
33. Ibid., 15.
34. Ibid., 15–16.
35. Ibid., fol. 16.
36. *Hamburger Fremdenblatt*, no. 148A (30 May 1933); *Hamburger Nachrichten*, no. 248 (30 May 1933), with photo.
37. *Ewige Wahrheit*, 32–34, here 33.
38. Schöffel attained office again by acclamation in 1946; he remained in office until 1954. See Hering, *Bischöfe*, 38–40.
39. See Schöffel to Krogmann, 6 June 1933, LKA Nordkirche, Kiel, 32.01, 573/35, and Schöffel to the Landeskirchenrat, 10 June 1933, ibid., 573/28.
40. Ibid., 573/37. See also Krogmann to Knolle, 7 June 1933, ibid., 573/39, and Schöffel to Krogmann, 10 June 1933, ibid., 573/38–39. See also Wilhelmi, *Hamburger Kirche*, 57.
41. For press reports, see *Hamburger Nachrichten*, no. 268 (12 June 1933); *Hamburger Tageblatt*, no. 134 (12 June 1933); *Hamburger Fremdenblatt*, no. 160 (12 June 1933). See also Hering, *Bischöfe*, 29–30.
42. *Ewige Wahrheit*, 38–58; see also Rainer Hering, *Theologie im Spannungsfeld von Kirche und Staat: Die Entstehung der Evangelisch-Theologischen Fakultät an der Universität Hamburg 1895 bis 1955* (Berlin and Hamburg: Reimer, 1992), esp. 82–97.
43. As quoted in Wilhelmi, *Hamburger Kirche*, 58.
44. *Ewige Wahrheit*, 59–61; here 61.
45. Ibid., 5–8; here 5–6.
46. Ibid.
47. This follows from Beckmann's note. Schöffel was not counted among the candidates. See Hering, *Kirchenrevolution*, 59–60.
48. Hering, *Bischöfe*, 29, 37, and 75–76; see also Wilhelmi, 43–54. Schöffel's state-friendly engagement paid off: from August 1933 until February 1934 he was a member of the Hamburg State Council (*Staatsrat*), which was supposed to advise the Senate on issues of state business; he could thereby add "Hamburg State Councillor" to the list of his professional titles. See Hering, *Bischöfe*, 29, 33.
49. See Wilhelmi, 77–86; Groschek, *Gemeindechronik*, 54–55; Reiter, 101–4; *100 Jahre Apostelgemeinde Hamburg-Eimsbüttel* (Hamburg: Apostelgemeinde, 1990), 61; and Günther Severin, *Jahre einer Gemeinde: Eilbek 1872–1943* (Hamburg: Gemeinde, 1985), 523–26.
50. Wilhelmi, *Hamburger Kirche*, 82.

51. Klaus Scholder, *Die Kirchen und das Dritte Reich,* vol. 1: Vorgeschichte und Zeit der Illusionen 1918–1934 (Frankfurt a.M., Berlin, and Vienna: Popyläen, 1977), 443.
52. Ibid.
53. Ibid., 479.
54. Ibid., 623.
55. Ibid., 720.
56. Hering, *Bischöfe,* 29–32. See also Scholder, *Kirchen,* 419–20, 435–37, 584–85.
57. Hering, *Bischöfe,* 31.
58. Ibid.
59. Hering, *Bischöfe,* 76–78. See also Wilhelmi, *Hamburger Kirche,* 93–118; 126–41.
60. Gehaltskarte 1936 for Simon Schöffel, LKA Nordkirche, Kiel, 32.03, 11.
61. Hering, *Bischöfe,* 51, emphasis in original. See also *Gesetze, Verordnungen und Mitteilungen aus der Hamburgischen Kirche 1934,* 29–30, and Franz Tügel, *Mein Weg 1888–1946: Erinnerungen eines Hamburger Bischofs,* ed. Carsten Nicolaisen (Hamburg: Wittig, 1972), 435; and Wilhelmi, *Hamburger Kirche,* esp. 143–44.
62. Tügel to Kaufmann 12 March 1934, LKA Nordkirche, Kiel, 32.01, 573.
63. Simon Schöffel, "Das deutsche Luthertum an der Wende der Zeit," *Luthertum* 45 (1934): 1–11, here 3.
64. Ibid., 5–6.
65. Ibid., 7–8.
66. Ibid., 1–11. See also Hering, *Bischöfe,* 34–36.
67. Schöffel, *Das deutsche Luthertum,* 3.
68. Hering, *Bischöfe,* 9–47.
69. Hering, *Kirchenrevolution.* See also Rainer Hering, "Die letzten beiden Hauptpastoren an der Hamburger Hauptkirche St. Nikolai am Hopfenmarkt: Heinz Beckmann und Paul Schütz," *Auskunft* 16 (1996), 27–47; Rainer Hering, "Beckmann, Heinrich Jakob Hartwig," in *Biographisch-Bibliographisches Kirchenlexikon,* vol. 17, ed. Friedrich Wilhelm Bautz and Traugott Bautz (Herzberg/Nordhausen: Bautz, 2000), 60–94; and Rainer Hering, "Liberale Theologen: Heinz Beckmann über Otto Baumgarten und Christian Chalybaeus: Edition und Kommentierung von zwei Texten aus dem Jahr 1934," forthcoming in *Zeitschrift für Schleswig-Holsteinische Kirchengeschichte* 3 (2018).
70. Windfuhr to Schöffel, 30 August 1933, Personalakte Walter Windfuhr, LKA Nordkirche, Kiel, 32.3.01.
71. Archiv der Evangelischen Kirche in Hessen und Nassau, Darmstadt, 44/126; as quoted in Scholder, *Kirchen,* 664–65.
72. Windfuhr to Schöffel 28 November 1933, Personalakte Walter Windfuhr, LKA Nordkirche, Kiel, 32.3.01, 65–67; Schöffel to Windfuhr, 30 November 1933, ibid., 73–75; and Walter Windfuhr, "Reichsbischof und Judentum," *Israelitisches Familienblatt,* no. 48 (30 November 1933).
73. On Windfuhr, see Rainer Hering, "'Sprache und Kultur des Judentums im Nationalsozialismus: Walter Windfuhrs Lehrtätigkeit an der Hamburger Universität," *Zeitschrift des Vereins für Hamburgische Geschichte* 80

(1994), 141–51, and Rainer Hering, "Windfuhr, Walter," in *Biographisch-Bibliographisches Kirchenlexikon*, vol. 13, ed. Friedrich Wilhelm Bautz and Traugott Bautz (Herzberg/Nordhausen: Bautz, 1990–1998), 1365–75. See also Henry Wassermann, *False Start: Jewish Studies at German Universities during the Weimar Republic* (Amherst, NY: Prometheus, 2003), 113–36.

74. Rainer Hering, "'Einer antichristlichen Dämonie verfallen': Die evangelisch-lutherischen Kirchen nördlich der Elbe und die nationalsozialistische Vergangenheit," in *Nordlichter: Geschichtsbewußtein und Geschichtsmythen nördlich der Elbe*, ed. Bea Lundt (Cologne, Weimar, and Vienna: Böhlau, 2004), 355–70.

Bibliography

Besier, Gerhard. *Kirche, Politik und Gesellschaft im 20. Jahrhundert: Enzyklopädie deutscher Geschichte*, no. 56. Munich: De Gruyter Oldenbourg, 2000.

———. *Die Kirchen und das Dritte Reich: Spaltungen und Abwehrkämpfe 1934–1937.* Berlin: Propyläen, 2001.

Bockermann, Dirk, et al. *Freiheit gestalten: Zum Demokratieverständnis des deutschen Protestantismus;Kommentierte Quellentexte 1789–1989.* Göttingen: Vandenhoeck and Ruprecht, 1996.

Brakelmann, Günter. *Evangelische Kirche und Judenverfolgung: Drei Einblicke.* Schriften der Hans Ehrenberg Gesellschaft, no. 7. Waltrop: Spenner, 2001.

Conway, John S. *Die nationalsozialistische Kirchenpolitik 1933–1945:Ihre Ziele, Widersprüche und Fehlschläge.* Munich: Kaiser, 1969.

Frauenforschungsprojekt zur Geschichte der Theologinnen, ed. *"Darum wagt es, Schwestern ..." Zur Geschichte evangelischer Theologinnen in Deutschland.* Historisch-Theologische Studien zum 19. und 20. Jahrhundert, no. 7. Neukirchen-Vluyn: Neukirchener, 1994.

Gailus, Manfred. *Protestantismus und Nationalsozialismus: Studien zur nationalsozialistischen Durchdringung des protestantischen Sozialmilieus in Berlin.* Industrielle Welt, no. 61. Cologne: Böhlau, 2001.

Gailus, Manfred, and Wolfgang Krogel, eds. *Von der babylonischen Gefangenschaft der Kirche im Nationalen: Regionalstudien zu Protestantismus, Nationalsozialismus und Nachkriegsgeschichte 1930 bis 2000.* Berlin: Wichern 2006.

Gotto, Klaus, and Konrad Repgen, eds. *Kirche, Katholiken und Nationalsozialismus.* Mainz: Matthias-Grünewald, 1980.

Greschat, Martin, and Jochen-Christoph Kaiser, eds. *Christentum und Demokratie im 20. Jahrhundert.* Konfession und Gesellschaft, no. 4. Stuttgart, Berlin, and Cologne: Kohlhammer, 1992.

Hausammann, Susi, Nicole Kuropka, and Heike Scherer, eds. *Frauen in dunkler Zeit: Schicksal und Arbeit von Frauen in der Kirche zwischen 1933 und 1945; Aufsätze aus der Sozietät Frauen im "Kirchenkampf."* Schriftenreihe des Vereins für Rheinische Kirchengeschichte, no. 118. Cologne: Habelt, 1996.

Hering, Rainer. *Die Bischöfe Simon Schöffel, Franz Tügel.* Hamburgische Lebensbilder in Darstellungen und Selbstzeugnissen, no. 10. Hamburg: Verlag Verein für Hamburgische Geschichte, 1995.

——. "Auf dem Weg in die Moderne? Die Hamburgische Landeskirche in der Weimarer Republik." *Zeitschrift des Vereins für Hamburgische Geschichte* 82 (1996): 127–66.

——. "Säkularisierung, Entkirchlichung, Dechristianisierung und Formen der Rechristianisierung bzw: Resakralisierung in Deutschland." In *Völkische Religion und Krisen der Moderne: Entwürfe "arteigener" Glaubenssysteme seit der Jahrhundertwende*, edited by Stefanie von Schnurbein and Justus H. Ulbricht, 120–64. Würzburg: Königshausen and Neumann, 2001.

——. *Das Führerprinzip in der Hamburger Kirche: Vor 70 Jahren; Amtseinführung des ersten Hamburger Landesbischofs am 11. Juni 1933."* Veröffentlichungen des Archivs des Kirchenkreises Alt-Hamburg, no. 18. Hamburg: Hamburg Archiv des Kirchenkreises Alt-Hamburg, 2003.

——. *Heinz Beckmann und die "Hamburgische Kirchenrevolution."* Veröffentlichungen des Archivs des Kirchenkreises Hamburg-Ost, no. 1. Hamburg: Hamburg Archiv des Kirchenkreises Hamburg-Ost, 2009.

——. "Konservative Ökumene. Hochkirchliche und liturgische Strömungen im deutschen Protestantismus des 20. Jahrhunderts." In *Preußische Katholiken und katholische Preußen im 20. Jahrhundert*, edited by Richard Faber und Uwe Puschner, 63–86. Würzburg: Königshausen and Neumann, 2011.

——. "Protestantismus vor der Moderne. Die Hamburger Landeskirche 1860 bis 1933." In *Andocken: Hamburgs Kulturgeschichte 1848 bis 1933*, edited by Dirk Hempel and Ingrid Schröder, 52–74. Hamburg: Dobu, 2012.

——. "Christen und Juden im 20. Jahrhundert." *Blätter für deutsche Landesgeschichte* 149 (2013): 311–26.

——. "Liberale Theologen: Heinz Beckmann über Otto Baumgarten und Christian Chalybaeus; Edition und Kommentierung von zwei Texten aus dem Jahr 1934." Forthcoming in *Zeitschrift für Schleswig-Holsteinische Kirchengeschichte* 3 (2018).

Hering, Rainer, and Inge Mager, eds. *Hamburgische Kirchengeschichte in Aufsätzen*. Kirchliche Zeitgeschichte (20. Jahrhundert), part 5. Hamburg: Hamburg University Press, 2008.

Kreutzer, Heike. *Das Reichskirchenministerium im Gefüge der nationalsozialistischen Herrschaft*. Schriften des Bundesarchivs, vol. 56. Düsseldorf: Droste, 2000.

Meier, Kurt. *Die Deutschen Christen: Das Bild einer Bewegung im Kirchenkampf des Dritten Reiches*. Göttingen: Vandenhoeck and Ruprecht, 1964.

——. *Der evangelische Kirchenkampf*. 3 vols. Göttingen: Vandenhoeck and Ruprecht, 1976–84.

——. *Kreuz und Hakenkreuz*. Munich: Deutscher Taschenbuch Verlag, 1992.

Mensing, Björn. *Pfarrer und Nationalsozialismus: Geschichte einer Verstrickung am Beispiel der Evangelisch-Lutherischen Kirche in Bayern*. Arbeiten zur Kirchlichen Zeitgeschichte, Series B, vol. 26. Göttingen: Vandenhoeck and Ruprecht, 1998.

Nowak, Kurt, *Evangelische Kirche und Weimarer Republik: Zum politischen Weg des deutschen Protestantismus zwischen 1918 und 1932*. Göttingen: Vandenhoeck and Ruprecht, 1981.

Overlack, Victoria. *Zwischen nationalem Aufbruch und Nischenexistenz: Evangelisches Leben in Hamburg 1933–1945.* Forum Zeitgeschichte 18. München-Hamburg: Dölling und Galitz, 2007.

Scholder, Klaus. *Die Kirchen und das Dritte Reich.* 2 vols. Frankfurt a.M., Berlin, and Vienna: Popyläen, 1977; Berlin: Siedler, 1985.

Ustorf, Werner. *Sailing on the Next Tide: Missions, Missiology, and the Third Reich.* Studien zur interkulturellen Geschichte des Christentum, no. 125. Frankfurt a.M.: Peter Lang, 2000.

Wilhelmi, Heinrich. *Die Hamburger Kirche in der nationalsozialistischen Zeit 1933–1945.* Arbeiten zur Geschichte des Kirchenkampfes, vol. 5. Göttingen: Vandenhoeck and Ruprecht, 1968.

✚ 11

FRIEDRICH VON BODELSCHWINGH AND THE PROTESTANT APPEASEMENT OF THE NAZI REGIME, 1933–34

Edward Snyder

On 11 August 1933 Friedrich von Bodelschwingh, a well-known and respected Lutheran pastor from the eastern Westphalian city of Bielefeld, invited a small number of prominent theologians, including Dietrich Bonhoeffer, to convene later that month at his Bethel community to draft a new theological confession. Like many Protestants, Bodelschwingh was growing increasingly concerned that the German Christians, a pro-Nazi faction of Protestants, would use their recent victories in church elections to introduce the Aryan Paragraph into the church. The paragraph excluded clergy who were "not of Aryan descent" from the church and represented the first time that Protestant leaders in Germany were directly confronted with antisemitic legislation.

The purpose of the meeting was to draft a confession that clearly resisted the efforts of the German Christians. The resulting document, however, fell far short of this goal. Worried about the consequences of confronting the regime directly over its efforts to control the church, the pastors at Bethel revised the final draft to remove or water down nearly all of the confrontational language. Distraught over the attitudes of his fellow pastors, Bonhoeffer left Bethel without signing the confession. Moments like this are nevertheless noteworthy because they both involve famous resistance figures like Dietrich Bonhoeffer and Martin Niemöller and symbolize important moments of conflict between German Protestants and the Nazi regime. As a result, they have repeatedly drawn the interest of scholars of modern German history. Individuals like Bonhoeffer are, however, the exception to the rule. The Bethel Confession and efforts to resist the regime failed to meet their potential because the vast majority of Protestants in Germany sought accommodation rather than resistance, especially in the aftermath of the Nazi assumption of power in January 1933.

No figure within German Protestantism symbolizes this attitude better than Friedrich von Bodelschwingh. A popular conservative pastor, Bodelschwingh nevertheless deeply disapproved of the regime's policies with respect to the church. The attitudes of the German Christians and their aggressive efforts to seize control of the provincial churches on behalf of the regime especially horrified him. As a result, he reluctantly agreed to run for the position of Reich Bishop as part of a newly created German Protestant Reich Church (Deutsche Evangelische Reichskirche). Although he won the election by a narrow margin in the spring of 1933, he resigned one month later under heavy pressure from the regime. Despite this nasty encounter with the regime, Bodelschwingh cautiously avoided voicing any direct criticism of the state and its policies. Rather, he made a concerted effort to reach out to important figures within the state and the German Christian movement in the hopes of avoiding additional confrontations and reconciling the two groups.

Utilizing Bodelschwingh's private papers in the Hauptarchiv der von Bodelschwingh'schen Anstalten, Bethel in Bielefeld, this chapter explores the ways in which Protestants sought to reconcile the church with the state between May 1933 and the summer of 1934. It argues that in the aftermath of the Reich Bishop election, Bodelschwingh devoted himself to preventing a permanent fracture of the church and further estrangement from the state. He took clear steps within his home community of Bethel to eliminate the potential for public disagreements with pro-Nazi groups and used his position of prominence within the church to act as a moderating influence, such as his efforts to water down the confrontational language of the Bethel Confession. When the church still appeared to be on a course of imminent conflict with the state, Bodelschwingh went so far as to reach out to the largely inept and unpopular Reich Bishop, Ludwig Müller, and offered to serve as his unofficial adviser. Ultimately, Bodelschwingh's actions during this period are important because they illustrate how a large segment of German Protestantism understood themselves as neither protestors nor collaborators during the first years of the regime's existence. Despite deep misgivings about the regime's policies toward the churches, they believed it was more important to preserve unity within the church and to avoid an open confrontation with the state at all costs, even if it meant seeking accommodation with the regime.

The Reich Bishop Election: May 1933

Within the greater context of the Nazi seizure of power, the Protestant Church has always occupied a unique position, as it marked the first time in this process that the Nazis ran into stiff opposition that ultimately resulted in failure. Unlike the Catholic Church, which was highly centralized, the Protestant Church in Germany was organized into provincial churches called *Landeskirchen* that traced their origins back to the sixteenth century. During the nineteenth century, the boundaries of these churches changed dramatically, as territorial changes resulted in the consolidation of smaller churches with larger ones. Nevertheless, each provincial church maintained its own governing bureaucracy through the end of World War I.[1]

In the aftermath of 1918 a large number of Protestants who had identified closely with the Empire worried about the impact of a secular republic on the interests of the church. As a result, Protestants focused their efforts on finding ways to maintain political representation during the 1920s. To this end, several Protestant leaders proposed the creation of a single German Protestant Reich Church, but they ultimately failed because of confessional differences between the Reformed (Calvinist) and Lutheran traditions. Not until the German Christians revived the idea during the early 1930s did it gain serious traction.[2] The group's leader, Joachim Hossenfelder, clearly stated multiple times in 1932 and 1933 that the establishment of a Reich Church was one of the group's top priorities. The Nazis, for their part, were more than happy to encourage and facilitate these efforts, as a single Reich Church would be significantly easier to manipulate than numerous, smaller provincial churches.

Hitler and the German Christians, however, had little interest in the complex debates over theological confessions and church governance that would go into the creation of a single church structure. For them, the only thing that mattered was the office of Reich Bishop, the head of the church. By gaining control of the Reich Bishop, the German Christians believed they could implement an "ecclesiastical *Führerprinzip*" modeled closely after the Nazi regime.[3] As Hossenfelder wrote in 1933, the German Christians did not envision a church that would be "a state within a state" but rather a church that would "recognize" the "supremacy" of National Socialism.[4]

On 25 April 1933 Hitler officially appointed Ludwig Müller, a German Christian military chaplain based in Königsberg, as his plenipotentiary for church affairs to ensure that the state remained actively involved in the drafting of the new constitution for the Reich Church.[5] Furthermore, Hitler sought to use Müller to exercise control over the German Christians, whose rhetoric and propaganda were becoming increasingly more radical, and to wrestle the leadership of the group away from Hossenfelder. Ultimately, the German Christians made it clear that Müller was the only person they would accept as the new Reich Bishop.[6]

Although Protestant leaders were open to the idea of a Reich Church, the growing influence of the German Christians and Müller alarmed them greatly. Rather than total integration with the state, they wanted to ensure that the church continued "to enjoy political and legal independence." To this end, a group of prominent pastors, led by Berlin pastor and World War I veteran Martin Niemöller, joined together in May 1933 to form the Young Reformers Movement as a way to push back against the German Christians.[7] On the surface, the Young Reformers seemed to share several important beliefs in common with the German Christians. Both movements were extremely nationalistic, with "almost unlimited enthusiasm" for Hitler and the Third Reich.[8] Statements like Article 11 of the Young Reformers' Appeal demanding the "joyful affirmation of the new German state" could just as easily have come from the German Christians. Yet the two groups differed sharply over the role of the state and outside groups in creating the new church.[9] The Young Reformers firmly rejected the demands of the German Christians for an election to determine the selection of the Reich Bishop. Instead, they believed a committee of pastors should appoint the Bishop.

Given the interest of both Hitler and Müller in instituting the *Führerprinzip* within the church, the Reich Bishop quickly became the focal point of the conflict between the German Christians and the Young Reformers, whose primary goal was to find someone who would undoubtedly place the interests of the church ahead of those of the state.[10] They quickly settled on Friedrich von Bodelschwingh, a man whom historians have repeatedly described in overwhelmingly positive language. Klaus Scholder, for example, writes that Bodelschwingh's "piety was genuine" and that he was "by nature rather shy." Scholder contends that Bodelschwingh, despite not being a natural born leader, nevertheless "possessed undaunted courage" in accepting the nomination.[11]

When compared to Müller, whom historians frequently characterize as intellectually uncurious and little more than a Nazi pawn, Bodelschwingh was undoubtedly the better choice to lead the church.[12] However, characterizations like those of Scholder's are also exaggerated and overly apologetic. As his interaction with the regime demonstrates, Bodelschwingh was more often timid than shy, and despite his piety he was still a conservative nationalist. Thus the "undaunted courage" Bodelschwingh demonstrated did not translate into a confrontation with the state over its church policies.

Even though Bodelschwingh was not a member of the Nazi party and did not want the state to intervene in church affairs, he nevertheless held a largely favorable view of the new state. Like many Protestants, Bodelschwingh was deeply suspicious of the Weimar Republic and anxious about the church's position in a nominally secular state. In September 1933 he remarked that despite the real concerns he had about German Christian theology, there were also aspects of their agenda with which he could "literally [*wörtlich*] agree." Specifically, he "largely agreed with the practical goals" of the group, "especially when I see the things from the East." Given these concerns, he added that a "dictatorship was the only solution" for the problems faced by the state.[13] Coming to power in alliance with the conservatives, Bodelschwingh believed that the church would once again have a "secure" place in German society.[14] Marxist socialism, the most "dangerous opponent" of the church, was almost totally removed from "public life," and the "influence" of "Jewish literati," the church's "deadly enemy," was "broken."[15] Thus, Bodelschwingh never intended for his candidacy for Reich Bishop to symbolize a major confrontation with the state. Rather, he believed the Nazi rise to power created "wide possibilities for a politically and socially united Volk" to move ahead "unimpeded" by anything associated with the Weimar Republic.[16] Taken together, his reflections and statements from early 1933 demonstrate that he was relatively enthusiastic about the Nazi rise to power and believed that a dictatorship was the only solution to Germany's problems.[17]

When Bodelschwingh first learned that the Young Reformers wanted to nominate him for the position of Reich Bishop, he furiously attempted to discourage his candidacy. He clearly understood that his nomination would invite controversy and thus force him to become politically active in opposition to the state. In a letter to August Marahrens, a close friend and the well-respected bishop of the Hanoverian State Church, Bodelschwingh wrote that he "did not understand church politics" and that he "belonged neither to the German Christians nor to the National Socialist Party." As a result, he told Marahrens that he felt he could not "take a step" through which he would "hurt the Church."[18] Reading the writing on the wall, Bodelschwingh understood that simply by virtue of not being a party member, his candidacy would potentially drive the church into further conflict with the state.

In addition to Marahrens, Bodelschwingh also reached out to Ludwig Müller and, unlike most of his colleagues within the church, actually came away from the meeting impressed as Müller explained how he would use the vast infrastructure of the party and state to benefit the church. Reflecting upon this initial encounter, Bodelschwingh wrote that Müller appeared to be "agile, adaptable," and "warm hearted." Furthermore, the "openness" with which he stated his opinions gave him a "winning" personality.[19] As long as Müller promised to use his connections with the state to benefit the church without actually interfering in its affairs, Bodelschwingh was willing to accept Müller's nomination.

Only after additional conversations did Bodelschwingh realize that Müller intended to go well beyond what he discussed during the initial meeting. Müller made it clear over the course of several meetings in late May with Marahrens and Hermann Albert Hesse that his ultimate goal was to entwine the new church completely with the Nazi state. Furthermore, according to Bodelschwingh, two other leading representatives of the German Christians, Karl Fezer and Emmanuel Hirsch, even went so far as to make "threatening" statements about the future of Bethel if Bodelschwingh became Bishop.[20] Ironically, despite the horrified reactions of Marahrens and Hesse to these meetings, Bodelschwingh came away feeling "relieved" because he believed the German Christians had engineered a fait accompli that would help him escape the nomination. Early on the morning of 25 May, as he traveled by train to Berlin following an urgent phone call the night before from Marahrens, Bodelschwingh drafted a "rejection" letter with respect to the nomination. But as Marahrens explained to him upon his arrival, the situation was now so dire that for the sake of the church rejection was simply impossible.

Bodelschwingh insisted on one final meeting with Müller as a precondition to accepting the nomination. His concern, again, was that the Reich Bishop was more of a political than spiritual position and that it would force him to confront the state over its church policies. Müller, however, horrified Bodelschwingh when he reiterated that under his leadership the church would have a "close reliance" on the Nazi Party and that he would reorganize the church bureaucracy to mirror the structure of the party. Once again Bodelschwingh attempted to reason with Müller as he sought a plausible way to avoid the nomination. He even went so far as to propose nominating Karl Fezer as a compromise candidate, which Müller flatly rejected.[21] By the end of the day, Bodelschwingh understood that he would have to accept the nomination of the Young Reformers.

On 26 May the two candidates were finally put to a vote, and after three rounds of voting, Bodelschwingh secured a majority large enough to elect him.[22] The vote, however, revealed deep divisions among Protestant leaders over the ramifications of rejecting Müller. Notably, two of the most influential provincial bishops, Theophil Wurm from

Württemberg and Hans Meiser from Bavaria, were particularly concerned about the fallout of the election. Wurm claimed his support of Müller was a vote in protest of the decision to hold the election before the completion of a church constitution. He also noted, however, that Fezer's "disturbing information" about Bodelschwingh influenced his vote. Specifically, Wurm raised concerns about the implications of the election on his relationship with the state.[23] Meiser, on the other hand, was the newly elected bishop of the largest Lutheran provincial church and was therefore "anxious to cultivate good relations" with the state.[24] While he ultimately voted for Bodelschwingh after Niemöller explained the urgency of the situation, his support was tepid. He quickly abandoned Bodelschwingh after the election.

The lack of support from major Lutheran leaders like Wurm and Meiser ultimately doomed Bodelschwingh to failure as Reich Bishop. Bodelschwingh wrote that he was struck by the "clouds of doubt" hanging over many of the officials who congratulated him after the election. Despite their votes for Bodelschwingh, a large number of pastors maintained strong reservations about his prospects for success and wondered if Müller would have been the better choice. As one pastor wrote, it seemed as if Bodelschwingh was elected more out of "fear" of Müller than anything else.[25] Furthermore, many younger Protestants resented Bodelschwingh's election because they believed he was representative of the old guard in the church and that the election result was an attempt to stymie the youth and dynamism of the German Christians.[26]

Within the larger context of *Gleichschaltung*, Bodelschwingh's election held extraordinary significance because it was the first time Hitler's efforts failed. As a result, the party adopted more aggressive tactics in coordination with the German Christians to force out Bodelschwingh. Through a coordinated and overwhelming propaganda campaign, the German Christians, with the help of the regime, played on many of the concerns of those who feared a confrontation with the state. At the same time, Hermann Kapler, one of Bodelschwingh's staunchest allies, resigned from his position as head of the Prussian Church on 6 June. This allowed the party to take advantage of a clause in a 1931 treaty that allowed for the "possibility of consulting the civil government" before making a new appointment to ensure that the new head of the church would be a staunch Nazi. On 23 June, August Jäger became the new head of the church. In addition to sealing Bodelschwingh's demise as Reich Bishop, Jäger's appointment would have ominous consequences as he also supported introducing the infamous Aryan Paragraph into the church bylaws. The Lutheran bishops could have formed a "united front against the obviously unlawful state intervention" and stopped Jäger, but they were "more concerned to finally get rid of Bodelschwingh."[27] They could not fathom the idea of a confrontation with the state over the Reich Bishop. Facing pressure from both the state and within the church, Bodelschwingh submitted his resignation on 24 June 1933, only one month after his election.[28]

The Vischer Controversy

While Bodelschwingh was embroiled in the Reich Bishop controversy, a second crisis broke out back home in Bethel. Like the conflict with the German Christians and Ludwig Müller, this crisis also involved a direct confrontation with the regime. Wilhelm Vischer, a docent with the Theological School at Bethel, became the target of a Nazi-led campaign to oust him from the school's faculty after Vischer publicly discussed the Jewish philosopher Martin Buber. Once again Bodelschwingh responded by trying to avoid direct confrontation with the party while seeking an outcome that would ultimately accommodate the wishes of the state.

The controversy surrounding Wilhelm Vischer began on 30 April 1933, when he gave a lecture before the Lippe *Brüderkonferenz* in which he discussed Martin Buber's thoughts on the Old Testament and anti-semitism.[29] When coupled with comments he supposedly made about the party's antisemitism and Hitler, it quickly led to a potentially explosive confrontation between Bethel's leaders and the party. Although the party was not particularly dominant in Lippe at the time Vischer made his comments, it nevertheless wielded a considerable amount of influence. In the elections of 15 January 1933, the party became the head of a ruling coalition, and during the winter semester of 1932–33 a large portion of the student body at the Bethel Theological School demonstrated increasing enthusiasm for Nazi ideology. As a result, Vischer's comments did not pass unnoticed, and pro-Nazi student groups immediately went on the offensive to oust him from the school's faculty.[30] SS men and students who had never had class with Vischer now claimed to be offended by his teachings and insisted that they would never take another class with him. Furthermore, even the docent group at the school contained enthusiastic party members such as Hans-Wilhelm Schmidt, an instructor of systematic theology who was "flags flying" for the party. Schmidt's presence was particularly stifling because it meant that not even within the docent group could one express one's opinion.[31]

While the party's public campaign against Vischer placed Bethel under intense pressure, an even greater threat emerged in the form of Hans Löhr, both the chief of the interior at the Gilead hospital on the Bethel campus and the local party leader of Bielefeld. As Gottfried Michaelis notes, he was easily the "most powerful man" in the area, who could "in a wink, mobilize the SA against the theological school and the entire institution."[32] On 19 May Löhr wrote to Wilhelm Brandt, the director of the theological school, demanding that Vischer be "suspended" until a state investigation could be completed. Failure to comply, Löhr indicated, would require him to make the "unpleasant and painful" decision to arrest Vischer. He concluded his letter by warning Vischer's colleagues against making any public "declarations of solidarity."[33] As the conflict dragged on through the end of the year, Löhr continued to express his disapproval if not hatred for Vischer when he wrote to Brandt: "I characterize Vischer not only as nationally untrustworthy, but primarily as nationally corruptive."[34] Löhr was so determined to oust Vischer that he frequently failed to observe proper administrative boundaries and procedures.[35]

For someone who desperately wanted to avoid conflict with the state, the Vischer controversy could not have come at a worse time for Bodelschwingh. Combined with the Reich Bishop conflict, it had the effect of casting Bethel as a "nest of resistance against the new state." The state-controlled press seized on both controversies, creating "especially strong" tension among the student body. Bethel's leaders were particularly concerned about the potentially radicalizing effect of the commotion on the pro-Nazi student groups on campus. In a letter to Gerhard Stratenwerth on 15 June they noted that over the past few weeks these groups had become particularly active and vocal. "It could suddenly flare up here, so that it would mean an endangerment of public security after the groups speak."[36] To an outside observer, Bethel appeared to be a powder keg one spark away from exploding.

The so-called Vischer affair dragged on for several months, with Vischer being placed on leave in May 1933. While he continued to hold discussion sessions at his private residence, he never returned to Bethel in any official capacity. When considering the timing of the controversy and the other events surrounding it, the general historical consensus of Bodelschwingh's role is that he was nothing short of heroic. Gottfried Michaelis, for example, adamantly argues that it would be nothing short of absurd to have expected Bodelschwingh to protest actively the party's attempt to remove Vischer:

> Should one have also pounded his fist on the table, brought a case before the courts, made the affair public, a protest march of confessional students through the streets of Bielefeld, called on foreign countries? Loud Illusions! Power was unfairly distributed. All the power lay with the

party. Bodelschwingh had only the word, with which to quietly convince, but fanatics do not care to let themselves be convinced. Courts in the modern sense were not established until after World War II. The press was closed off: nothing was permitted to be printed against the will of Goebbels.[37]

By taking a passive approach and avoiding direct intervention on behalf of Vischer, Michaelis believes Bodelschwingh pursued the only possible course of action at that time. In the same vein, Heinrich Bödeker writes, "The noble-minded Pastor Friedrich von Bodelschiwngh could not rescue Vischer and keep him in the theological school, although he tried everything in his power."[38] Like Michaelis, he portrays Bodelschwingh as someone doomed to fail as he fought overwhelming odds.

An examination of Bodelschwingh's actions during the controversy, however, once again demonstrates that his primary goal was to avoid a direct confrontation with the state. For example, on 18 May 1933, a group of theological students at Bethel gathered at an assembly to protest against Vischer. As Jürgen Kampmann indicates, historians often point to this episode as an example of how Bodelschwingh led the defense of the embattled Vischer.[39] Notes taken by the various student assemblies in attendance, though, indicated that Bodelschwingh barely participated in the assembly, let alone came to Vischer's defense. In the minutes Otto Witt recorded for the group of seniors of the Bethel student body, he indicated that Bodelschwingh not only failed to assume leadership of the assembly but also spoke only once at the beginning of the event.[40] Using a separate transcript from the student organization of Isenstedt-Frotheim (Kirchenkreis Lübbecke), Kampmann argues that Bodelschwingh publicly sought to distance himself from Vischer during his brief comments, stating that he looked "upon their collaboration as co-workers … with love and thankfulness."[41] By describing their relationship as "co-workers," Bodelschwingh "suspended his personal contact until that point with Vischer as a voluntary co-worker." During the assembly Bodelschwingh also refrained from making any public statement in support of Vischer's teaching at Bethel.

These actions become even more noteworthy in light of Bodelschwingh's departure halfway through the assembly. He left with the rest of the Docent College.[42] Using the Isenstedt-Frotheim minutes, Kampmann argues that the timing of Bodelschwingh's departure was especially damning because it came shortly after a series of Nazi student groups walked out of the assembly in protest.[43] Thus, Bodelschwingh never assumed a leading role in defending Vischer from the Nazi-led attacks. Even though he had multiple opportunities to shield Vischer, he once again believed it was more important to avoid confrontation and backed down. As Kampmann writes, Bodelschwingh's strategy during the crisis was "not to take the strongly growing wind from the sail, but rather cautiously to take the sail from the wind."[44]

When taken together, these two conflicts between the church and the state marked the initial confrontations of the *Kirchenkampf*. For the first time, Hitler's efforts at the consolidation of power had not gone according to plan, and the party made it abundantly clear it would not stand idly by and allow the church to have any autonomy within Nazi society. During these early weeks, Protestant leaders had many opportunities to voice their disapproval of the state's actions, but the church leadership, influenced as it was by the Lutheran theory of the state, could not fathom the idea of a Reich Church estranged from the state, let alone in open conflict with it. In this respect, Bodelschwingh's actions were representative of the vast majority of Lutheran pastors. Despite the increasing aggression and hostility of the state, Bodelschwingh could not bring himself to challenge it, preferring instead to avoid open confrontation by retreating back to Bethel and letting the storm blow over.

The Aryan Paragraph

As the opening salvos in the *Kirchenkampf*, the Reich Bishop conflict, and the Vischer controversy clearly revealed, the new regime would not hesitate to use all the tools at its disposal to attack aggressively anyone who did not voluntarily fall in line. Yet despite these violent encounters, Bodelschwingh continued to pursue a course of action that ultimately sought reconciliation and accommodation with the state. His writings and actions through the end of 1933 clearly demonstrate that he wanted to preserve the church's autonomy from growing state control, although Bodelschwingh limited his understanding of autonomy to spiritual matters. As long as the church remained confessionally independent, he was content to allow the state to play a role in maintaining the church-political bureaucracy.

To this end, Bodelschwingh devoted much of his energy following his resignation as Reich Bishop to reconciling the church with the state while preventing further splintering between Calvinists, Lutherans, and the German Christians. Although he retreated back to Bethel following his resignation on 24 June 1933, he nevertheless remained very active in the debates and conflicts over the future of the church in Germany, which appeared to be in a state of dire crisis. Describing services held by German Christians and their opponents on 2 July 1933,

Klaus Scholder wrote that "anyone who had been to services held by each side this Sunday … would hardly have thought that this was still one church."[45]

With Bodelschwingh gone, August Jäger, a key figure in Bodelschwingh's decision to resign, continued his efforts to coordinate the Prussian Church by dismissing all of its leaders, including Otto Dibelius, a strong supporter of Bodelschwingh.[46] At the same time, Müller worked to bring the Federation of Protestant Churches (Evangelischer Kirchenbund) under his control. This was significant not only because it represented a grab for power by Müller but also because it robbed the committee responsible for drafting the new constitution of its legitimacy. Upon seizing control of the federation, Müller reconstituted the committee so that it consisted of Jäger, four Lutheran bishops, four German Christians, and one representative from both the Young Reformers and the Prussian Church.[47] Such an arrangement allowed Müller, and by extension the state, to control the constitutional process completely.

In the middle of all this, Bodelschwingh immediately began writing to state and religious leaders to express his concerns about Jäger's aggressive actions. In late June he wrote to leading German Christians in order to voice his fears that Jäger, and by extension the state, were rapidly infringing on the church's spiritual autonomy. Amazingly, despite having just directly experienced the aggressive, nasty side of the new state through its relentless propaganda onslaught, Bodelschwingh nevertheless maintained a very conciliatory attitude toward the state and the German Christians. He limited his criticism to securing the church's "inner being" from the state's influence and almost always coupled critical comments with praise for the state's efforts to revitalize the nation. For example, in a letter to Joachim Hossenfelder on 29 June he wrote, "The church thanks the state, since it is ready to give space and privilege to the forces coming from the Gospel during the reorganization of German nature and German history. So the church, with the eternal goods which it administers, can be a strong supporter of the state. However, that is only possible if its internal liberty is not touched."[48] Despite his deep concern about the state's increased influence over the restructuring of church bureaucracies, Bodelschwingh's strong statements of praise for the new regime almost drowned out his critical comments.

The same themes are also clearly evident in a letter Bodelschwingh wrote on the same day to Friedrich Werner, the newly appointed Prussian Church president following Jäger's reorganization. The letter contained many of the same themes and concerns that he raised with

Hossenfelder but was noticeably different in that Bodelschwingh also directly addressed the impact of the German Christian–led propaganda campaign on the cohesion of the Protestant community. While he understood the state wanted to help create a more "beautiful relationship" with the church through its incorporation, in reality he argued it was creating a "condition of deeper and perhaps longer lasting division." Of particular concern to him was the state's tendency to use its influence within the church bureaucracy to ensure that German Christians received leading positions. He argued that in its efforts to promote German Christian candidates, the party provided them with overwhelming support through the press and radio. Ultimately, Bodelschwingh feared this would create the impression that those Protestants who did not belong to the German Christian movement were "second tier." Thus, through its constant intervention, the state threatened to shatter the inner cohesion and unity of the church itself.[49]

When the German Christians won an overwhelming victory in church elections held on 23 July, Bodelschwingh grew even more concerned about the future direction of the church. Therefore, he contacted his former rival Müller in a long letter on 29 July that echoed many of the concerns he had already voiced to Hossenfelder and Werner. He criticized the German Christians' propaganda, which portrayed the movement as the "SA of Jesus Christ," as too militaristic while also voicing disapproval of its stated mission to "eliminate biological, social and spiritual distress." He reiterated his concerns about the state's strong backing of the movement, arguing that since many people only voted in the election because of the state's heavy use of propaganda, the German Christians' victory was not a proper reflection of "reality."[50]

Despite these concerns and his harsh criticism of the German Christian movement, however, Bodelschwingh made it clear that he did not want to exclude them from the church, which would have been equally as disastrous for the future of German Protestantism. Therefore, as was his tendency, Bodelschwingh almost always offered a conciliatory remark following a criticism. For example, after criticizing the group's militancy, he nevertheless noted that "one is thankful for the powerful desire to create something new in the church." With a "dynamic and popular (*volkstümliche*) message," he told Müller that "we are one with you" in the movement's drive to "bring with new strength" this message to the people.[51] Excluding the German Christians from the church was never an option in Bodelschwingh's mind.

By this point, however, other Protestant leaders did not share Bodelschwingh's optimism about the possibility of maintaining unity under the leadership of the German Christians. With both the Prussian

Church and the Federation of Protestant Churches under the state's control, the newly reconstituted constitutional committee completed its draft of a new constitution on 11 July 1933. With this task now complete, the state also announced that new church elections would be held eight days later on 23 July.[52] With little time to lose, the German Christians once again used their support from the state to embark on a massive propaganda campaign. Despite claiming to favor "free and unpartisan" elections, the state made no secret of its support for Müller.[53] The climax of this support came on 22 July when, at Müller's urging, Hitler gave a radio address in which he showered the German Christians with praise, stating that "the German Christian movement has consciously taken its stand on the ground of the National Socialist state—not in an enforced submission but in a living affirmation."[54] With such strong support from the state, many church leaders feared that supporting the Young Reformers Movement's list of candidates would be interpreted as an act of open resistance. Therefore, they frequently merged the oppositional list of candidates with those of the German Christians (to the distinct advantage of the latter) in order to preempt the need for a vote. In the actual event of the elections, the German Christians won more than two-thirds of the seats. Notably, however, the only provincial synod of the Prussian Church to reject the German Christians was Bodelschwingh's home province of Westphalia.[55]

In the wake of this defeat, several prominent Protestants, led most notably by Martin Niemöller and Karl Barth, firmly believed that unity within the church was impossible. Furthermore, they began to speak openly about the need for an entirely new confession. In the pages of a new journal called *Junge Kirche*, Niemöller articulated sixteen theses to express his concerns, writing, "Is there theologically a basic difference between Reformation doctrine and what the German Christians proclaim? We fear: Yes! They say: No! This lack of clarity must be removed by a modern confession."[56] Following Niemöller's call to action, leading Protestants began the "practical community work" of organizing to draft a new confession. Since they wanted to avoid attracting attention as much as possible, the effort depended on the "initiative of individual pastors" who eschewed a formal organizational structure as much as possible. Given his role in the Reich Bishop election and his general reputation among his fellow pastors, Bodelschwingh naturally "assumed the role of a personal and spiritual focus."[57] As a result, he exercised a significant amount of influence over the initial process.

To this end, on 11 August 1933, Bodelschwingh invited "a small circle of younger theologians" to Bethel to work together to begin drafting the new confession.[58] This group included not only Dietrich

Bonhoeffer and Hermann Albert Hesse, the former editor of the *Kirchliches Jahrbuch*, but also Bethel scholars Georg Merz and Wilhelm Vischer.[59] As Bodelschwingh's close associate Gerhard Stratenwerth noted in a letter to Martin Niemöller, the original purpose of the work at Bethel was so that the German Christians "could show if they stood on the same ground of the confession."[60] Bodelschwingh's primary concern, however, remained finding common ground with the German Christians in order to prevent further division within the church. Consequently, he used his leading role within the group to exercise a moderating influence over the meeting and prevent the confession from becoming too confrontational.

In the end, the pastors at Bethel produced a nearly thirty-page document that almost exclusively addressed confessional and theological questions. However, the sixth and final chapter stood out as arguably the most significant because it discussed themes with clear political significance. In its original state, the Bethel Confession not only spelled out a new theological confession but also leveled clear and unmistakable criticism against the state. Thus its authors had taken a clear step into the realm of politics. For example, in the section entitled "*Kirche und Volk*" the authors concluded that "the *Volk* is not the church. However the people, who belong to both, are bound to each with insoluble solidarity. They share in the guilt of the *Volk*. They are at the same time members of God's people, whose citizenship is in heaven."[61] Although the pastors acknowledged a close relationship between the church and the common racial community promoted by the Nazis, they nevertheless insisted that they were two distinct entities. By stating that ultimately one's "citizenship is in heaven," the authors argued that one's primary allegiance was to God and the church, not Hitler and the Third Reich.

The following section, "*Kirche und Staat*," was even more explicit in its efforts to highlight this distinction. The pastors proclaimed that all "world authority is ordered by God" and that "everyone" must be "obedient" to this order. Furthermore, all worldly authority belonged undeniably in the "realm of death" and not in the "realm of the holy."[62] One of the church's tasks, they argued, was to mediate the relationship between these two spheres of authority. In so doing, they made it clear that the different types of authority claimed by each institution were by no means synonymous. Moreover, they claimed the authority of the church, derived from God, was superior to that of any political institution. Making an unambiguous reference to the situation of the Protestant Church in Nazi Germany, they insisted that "the church can never merge with worldly authority … it can never be built within a state."[63] Between these two sections it was undeniable that the pastors at Bethel initially intended for the document to be more than a new theological confession.

The Confession's commentary on the relationship between church and state was unambiguously critical of the new regime's attitude toward the church. These remarks, however, paled in comparison to the pointed attack it made on the party's antisemitism. In the section titled "*Die Kirche und die Juden*," the pastors at Bethel directly addressed the efforts of the German Christians to introduce Nazi racial ideology into the church. Drafted primarily by Vischer with strong support from Bonhoeffer, the document stated that "the community that belongs to the church is not confirmed through blood, and therefore also not through race, but rather through the Holy Spirit and baptism."[64] The statement could not have been any clearer and directly addressed the concerns of many pastors regarding the efforts of the state to shape major theological issues within the church.

This section could not have been timelier. As the pastors were drawing up their new confession, the German Christians were actively working to introduce the so-called Aryan Paragraph into the church. August Jäger was particularly aggressive within the Prussian Church, using the German Christians' newly won power within the church to secure passage of a law introducing the Aryan Paragraph in the church on 5 September 1933, the first time the church's general synod convened under the control of the German Christians.[65]

For a small handful of pastors, most notably Dietrich Bonhoeffer, the section addressing antisemitism was also the most important. Unlike the vast majority of his Protestant colleagues, Bonhoeffer had recognized the threat posed by the Nazis from the moment they seized power. He experienced the new regime's antisemitism personally when his twin sister Sabine asked him to preside at the funeral of her father-in-law, who was Jewish. After consulting with a colleague of his for advice, he declined Sabine's request, a decision that would ultimately haunt him.[66] At the same time, however, Bonhoeffer also recognized the Aryan Paragraph as a direct assault on the church. Nowhere in the scriptures did it say anything about denying someone the right to receive the sacrament of baptism. As John Moses writes, "To demand in 1933 that the church should refuse to baptize Jews and admit them to full membership of the church, including the pastorate, was a blatant theological absurdity."[67] Thus, for Bonhoeffer it was impossible for the church to ignore this direct assault on its theological integrity.

In its original form, therefore, the Bethel Confession had the potential to be a significant symbol of opposition to the Third Reich. Although it fell short of outright resistance in large part because its authors limited their criticism of the state solely to matters that pertained to the church, it nevertheless confronted the state over its attempt to force the church under its control. At the same time, it directly criticized the regime's racial ideology, which would become a central aspect of life in the Third Reich. Yet the Bethel Confession never fulfilled this potential. Just as Bonhoeffer believed it was important to use the document to articulate clear opposition to the state, Bodelschwingh, the leading organizer of the conference, firmly believed it should find common ground with the German Christians in order to prevent further fracturing within the church. For him, the Bethel Confession needed to generate broad support among all German Protestants. Thus, once the authors completed their initial draft, Bodelschwingh sent a copy of the document to twenty other pastors and religious leaders for "examination and collaboration."[68] To Bonhoeffer's dismay, he wrote that he understood the goal of the confession was "to find a basis for discussion with the German Christians."[69] As a result, Bodelschwingh completely sapped the Bethel Confession of its potential to be an important document of Christian opposition to the new state. The revisions he solicited "water[ed] down" the criticisms to the point that Bonhoeffer abruptly left Bielefeld without signing the final document.[70]

Bonhoeffer was particularly "annoyed" with Bodelschwingh's revisions to the section dealing with the church's relationship with the Jews. As Gerlach notes, the revised version adopted a strikingly more "negative" tone, as "God was no longer devoted to Israel" but rather was simply "not rejecting Israel."[71] Also absent in the final version was the pointed language that the church would stand with Jews in the face of persecution and reject efforts to turn converted Christians into second-class members of the church. Rather, after Bodelschwingh's revisions, the confession now stated only that the church would "grant all the rights" to converted Christians that it had also "granted to Gentile Christians."[72]

Once it became clear that the Bethel Confession would not contain a statement that clearly rejected the Aryan Paragraph, Bonhoeffer drafted his own pamphlet titled "The Aryan Paragraph in the Church" to influence debates within the Prussian Church. Unlike the vast majority of his colleagues, Bonhoeffer understood very early that even though it only affected "two percent of the nearly eighteen thousand Protestant pastors in Germany," it still represented an existential threat to an independent Protestant church in Germany.[73] Following the completion of the pamphlet in August 1933, Bonhoeffer also collaborated with Martin Niemöller on a second declaration that stated, "Whoever agrees with such a breach of the confession thereby excludes himself from the community of the church. Therefore, we demand that this law, which separates the Protestant Church of the Old Prussian Union from the Christian Church, be rescinded without delay."[74] It was becoming increasingly clear that as a result of the Aryan Paragraph, the church was becoming irreparably fractured.

In order to gain further support for their statement, Bonhoeffer and Niemöller once again sent it to Bodelschwingh for further distribution. Bodelschwingh, however, continued to fear the consequences of a break within the church and the conflict with the state that would ensue. Therefore, just as he had done with the Bethel Confession one month earlier, he edited the pointedly phrased protests of Bonhoeffer and Niemöller to dilute their criticisms.[75] In a letter to Müller on 11 September 1933, Bodelschwingh included a very similarly worded protest. However, notably absent was the statement that supporters of the Aryan Paragraph were automatically "excluded" from the church. Furthermore, Bonhoeffer's "demand" that the law be rejected was rephrased by Bodelschwingh to read "urgently request."[76] Throughout the controversy surrounding the Aryan Paragraph, Bodelschwingh firmly believed a division within the church posed a significantly greater threat to its future than the adoption of a theologically blasphemous law.

The Formation of the Confessing Church and Further Accommodation with the Regime

With the introduction of the Aryan Paragraph into the Prussian Church in September 1933, the writing on the wall was clear, as the divisions within the church began to calcify. Under the leadership of Niemöller, those pastors who rejected the agenda of the German Christians gathered together to form the Pastors' Emergency League (Pfarrernotbund), an organization that would eventually evolve into the Confessing Church. Although the group still acknowledged Bodelschwingh in the original draft of the league declaration as a focal point and leader of the opposition, it was clear that they were beginning to leave him behind.[77] While he acknowledged the urgency of the moment and rejected the Aryan Paragraph, he nevertheless "doubted whether the radical formulation of the commitment was in fact the right way."[78] The league dropped its direct reference to him in the final draft of its declaration after Bodelschwingh stated he did not want to be associated with "even one group."[79]

In the short term, the formation of the Pastors' Emergency League successfully pressured the German Christians to temper their rhetoric and agenda. On 27 September 1933, at the Wittenberg Synod, they "quietly dropped" the Aryan Paragraph from their agenda.[80] Over the next several weeks, however, the increased opposition to the German Christians resulted in a dramatic radicalization of their rhetoric that culminated with the disastrous Sports Palace rally in Berlin on 13 November. While many leaders of the group spoke, the most conse-quential speech was given by Reinhold Krause, a staunch supporter of the Aryan Paragraph. Krause called for Protestants to "complete the völkisch mission of Martin Luther in a second German Reformation." He demanded the creation of a "German Volkskirche that leaves room for the whole range of the truly German [*artgemäss*] experience of God, and that is also in its external form as utterly German as one would expect it to be in the Third Reich." This church would expunge the Old Testament of its "stories of cattle-dealers and pimps." The new church, he proclaimed, would "return to the heroic Jesus."[81]

The Sports Palace rally would prove to be a high-water mark for the German Christians, as they would never again enjoy the amount of power and influence they possessed before the event. Concerned about the public uproar over Krause's speech, the state quickly distanced itself from the movement. The Pastors' Emergency League, however, was deeply alarmed.[82] On 14 November 1933, its leaders recruited Bodelschwingh to contact Reich president Paul von Hindenburg regarding the dire situation in the church.[83] While Bodelschwingh suc-ceeded in arranging a meeting with Hindenburg on 16 November, it was nothing short of a failure. According to his notes, the two spent more time discussing military battles during the Napoleonic Wars than the current state of the church in Germany.[84] When the two finally got around to discussing the church, Bodelschwingh failed to accomplish anything significant. He told Hindenburg that he had "anxious con-cerns" about the content of Müller's preaching and asked him "if he would like to" and "if the opportunity presented itself" say a word in defense of the church's autonomy.[85] Although Hindenburg did not say anything "definite" regarding the request, Bodelschwingh was confi-dent that he "took the subject again close to his heart."[86] Whereas he needed to be forceful and direct with Hindenburg about the state of affairs within the church, he was too awestruck to push him. Even after the meeting concluded, Bodelschwingh remarked that "one saw noth-ing of the room, only the man. He is spiritually very fresh, his speech slow and strong. His old face deeply crenate, but still full of life."[87] Never one to assert himself against political authority, Bodelschwingh was overwhelmed by Hindenburg's presence and clearly still viewed him as a great conservative and military hero. Consequently, he never pushed Hindenburg for a concrete commitment to speak out on behalf of the church.

While Bodelschwingh met with Hindenburg, Müller was desperately trying to restore his power and prestige in the humiliating aftermath of the Berlin rally. To this end, on 12 December 1933, he reached a secret agreement with Baldur von Schirach to merge the Protestant Youth Foundation with the Hitler Youth.[88] He went even further on 4 January 1934 by issuing a decree that not only reinstituted the Aryan Paragraph but also prohibited the clergy from making any political statements.[89] While Müller hoped that these decrees would restore his authority within the church, the only thing he succeeded in accomplishing was galvanizing his opposition to draft a new confession that would become the Confessing Church.

Throughout all of this, Bodelschwingh refused to follow the lead of Niemöller's group. Still committed to finding consensus within the church, he instead reached out to the embattled Müller. On 21 December 1933—between the secret agreement with Schirach and the declarations of 4 January—Bodelschwingh met with Müller to discuss the state of the church. Amazingly, however, Bodelschwingh placed absolutely no pressure on Müller to clean up the mess he had made over the previous six months. Furthermore, when Müller brought up the affair with the Protestant Youth Group, Bodelschwingh never challenged his explanation of events. Instead, he emphasized that it was "urgently necessary" not to "push the German Christians into a fruitless opposition."[90] By extending an offer of "parole" to the group, Bodelschwingh believed he could help guide them back to the larger church in a way that would be acceptable to pastors like Niemöller and Bonhoeffer. He even went so far as to say that while he would not engage in "official collaboration," he stood ready to "serve with advice."[91] Essentially, Bodelschwingh offered to help Müller in the capacity of an unofficial adviser.

Amazingly, Müller actually appears to have taken Bodelschwingh up on his offer by opening up about his vision for the future of the church. According to Thomas Martin Schneider, Müller began to rethink his church policy in light of his recent failures. Instead of trying to create an independent church that was "freely, closely cooperating" with the state, he instead began to focus on an "integration of the church in the state" through a ministry of church affairs.[92] Schneider argues that during their conversation on 21 December 1933, Müller discussed this idea for the first time with someone who was not part of his inner circle. In the end, he argues that Müller genuinely appeared to trust Bodelschwingh, as the latter's notes on the meeting indicate that the two also talked extensively about spiritual matters. While Müller was not entirely "free of scruples"—for example he did not tell Bodelschwingh that August Jäger was to head the ministry—the conversation was enough to convince Bodelschwingh that there was still an opportunity to bring the two sides together.[93] After meeting with Müller, Bodelschwingh thought he could bring Jäger and Karl Koch together for a serious conversation that would resolve the issues dividing the two sides.

Ultimately, Bodelschwingh's conversations with Müller were important because they indicated the approach he would adopt with the state over the next few years. While many of his closest friends and colleagues would become leading members of the Confessing Church, Bodelschwingh continued to search for a way to prevent a total break with the state. In March 1934 he addressed more than twenty thousand people at the Westphalian Confessing Synod in Dortmund and stressed the importance of not forming a new church that would oppose the state.[94] At the same time, Bodelschwingh even went so far as to meet with Rudolf Diehl, the head of the Prussian secret police, at which time he spoke openly with Diehl about the actions of the Pastors' Emergency League. He believed that the church could still work closely with the state, lamenting to Diehl that the church "missed its great hour" as a result of the conflict over the German Christians. Interestingly, he remarked that the church could have been extremely useful in helping the state to fight "the only fight which it has to fight … against Catholicism."[95] These efforts to help maintain open communication channels would eventually culminate in the summer of 1935 when Bodelschwingh, to the dismay of his friends in the Confessing Church, began advising Hans Kerrl, the head of the new ministry for ecclesiastical affairs. In this capacity he actively advised Kerrl to work with moderate members of the Confessing Church because they would be more willing to work with the state than the church's more radical leaders.[96] By 1935, Bodelschwingh was focused on neutralizing the more radical members of the Confessing Church out of the fear that they were going to drive German Protestantism into open conflict with the state.[97]

Conclusion

Throughout the *Kirchenkampf*, Bodelschwingh was naturally sympathetic to the grievances articulated by the Confessing Church. Like all of his colleagues, he was horrified by the radical rhetoric and policies of the German Christians and disapproved of the state's efforts to interfere in the church's internal affairs. However, unlike Bonhoeffer and Niemöller, Bodelschwingh sought to avoid any actions that would potentially result in conflict with the state. Like many of his Lutheran colleagues, Bodelschwingh's understanding of the state was heavily shaped by Lutheran theology, which proclaimed that the state was ordained by God. Thus, for him, challenging the state was akin to challenging God. At the same time, as someone who deeply disapproved of the Weimar government and lamented the fall of the Empire in 1918, Bodelschwingh also saw much potential for collaboration with the new Nazi state. While he disapproved of the state's efforts to coordinate the church, a far worse fate for the church in Bodelschwingh's eyes would be open conflict with the regime. In this respect, Bodelschwingh is symbolic of the majority of German Protestants. Although the vast majority of scholarship on German Protestantism during the Third Reich is devoted to either the German Christians or the Confessing Church, it is extremely important to remember that the majority of German Protestants were nonaligned. Like Bodelschwingh, they wanted more than anything to avoid fighting with the new state.

Throughout the course of the Third Reich, Bodelschwingh's interaction with the regime was shaped primarily by this concern. It explains why he desperately wanted to avoid accepting the nomination for Reich Bishop in May 1933, why he watered down the Bethel Confession to eliminate its biting criticism of the state, and why he voluntarily went to state officials and offered to advise them on church policies. His collaboration with the Reich ministry of ecclesiastical affairs greatly upset the leaders of the Confessing Church and led to them becoming slowly estranged from Bodelschwingh. As always, for Bodelschwingh, and the many Protestants like him, the greatest tragedy would be a church estranged from the state. Unfortunately, the very policies he pursued to promote reconciliation resulted in further dividing the very church he hoped to unify.

Edward Snyder is an assistant professor of history at Chowan University in Murfreesboro, North Carolina. He is the author of "The Bodelschwingh Initiative: A Transcontinental Examination of German Protestant Attitudes towards Poverty and Deviancy, 1880–1933," in *The Welfare State and the "Deviant" Poor in Europe, 1870–1933* (2014), and "Eugenics and Conservative Social Policy in the Weimar Republic: Friedrich von Bodelschwingh and the Bethel Institutions," in *The German Right in the Weimar Republic: Studies in German Conservatism,*

Nationalism, and Antisemitism (2014). He is currently preparing his doctoral dissertation on Bodelschwingh and the Bethel Institutions for publication.

Notes

1. For a more extensive discussion of the history of the Protestant Church before 1918, see Klaus Scholder, *The Churches and the Third Reich*, vol. 1: *Preliminary History and the Time of Illusions, 1918–1934*, trans. John Bowden (Philadelphia: Fortress Press, 1988), esp. 21–24. For a more concise history of the immediate background to the *Kirchenkampf*, see J. R. C. Wright, *"Above Parties": The Political Attitudes of the German Protestant Church Leadership, 1918–1933* (New York: Oxford University Press, 1974).
2. Wright, *"Above Parties,"* 29.
3. Doris Bergen, *Twisted Cross: The German Christian Movement in the Third Reich* (Chapel Hill: University of North Carolina Press, 1996), 8.
4. Joachim Hossenfelder, "Richtlinien der Glaubensbewegung 'Deutsche Christen,'" 26 May 1932, in *Die Bekenntnisse und grundsätzlichen Äusserungen zur Kirchenfrage des Jahres 1933*, ed. Kurt Dietrich Schmidt (Göttingen: Vandenhoeck and Ruprecht, 1934), 135–36.
5. "Hitler beruft Ludwig Müller zu seinem Bevollmächtigen für die evangelische Kirche," 25 April 1933, in *Dokumente zur Kirchenpolitik des Dritten Reiches*, vol. 1: *Das Jahr 1933*, ed. Carsten Nicolaisen and Georg Kretschmar (Munich: Chr. Kaiser Verlag, 1971), 42–43.
6. Wright, *"Above Parties,"* 125–26.
7. Scholder, *Churches and the Third Reich*, 1:320–21.
8. Ibid., 321.
9. "Der Aufruf der Jungreformatorischen Bewegung," May 1933, in *Die Bekenntnisse*, ed. Schmidt, 145–46.
10. Scholder, *Churches and the Third Reich*, 1:325.
11. Ibid.
12. See for example John A. Moses, *The Reluctant Revolutionary: Dietrich Bonhoeffer's Collision with Prusso-German History* (New York: Berghahn Books, 2014), 118.
13. Brüderrats-Sitzung, 4 September 1933, Hauptarchiv der von Bodelschwinghschen Anstalten Bethel, Bielefeld (hereafter cited as HAB Bielefeld), N-A-060, 43–45.
14. Friedrich von Bodelschwingh, "Dreißig Tage an einer Wegwende deutscher Kirchengeschichte," HAB Bielefeld, 2/39–177, 1. For a published version of the essay along with accompanying documents on the Reich Bishop controversy, see Friedrich von Bodelschwingh, *Dreißig Tage an einer Wegwende deutscher Kirchengeschichte: Erinnerungen des ersten Reichsbischofs*, ed. Carsten Nicolaisen and Thomas Martin Schneider (Bielefeld: Bethel-Verlag, 2013).
15. Bodelschwingh, "Dreißig Tage," 1.
16. Ibid.

17. Wilhelm Brandt, *Friedrich von Bodelschwingh, 1877–1946: Nachfolger und Gestalter* (Bielefeld: Verlagshandlung der Anstalt Bethel, 1967), 183. See also Matthias Benad, "Bethels Verhältnis zum Nationalsozialismus," in *Zwangsverpflichtet: Kriegsgefangene und zivile Zwangsarbeiter(-innen) in Bethel und Lobetal, 1939–1945*, ed. Matthias Benad, and Regina Mentner (Bielefeld: Bethel Verlag und Verlag für Regionalgeschichte, 2002), 28.

18. Bodelschwingh to Marahrens, 23 May 1933, in the unpublished Nachlass of August Maharens, Landeskirchliches Archiv der Evangelisch-lutherischen Landeskirche Hannovers, L2 Nr. 4a, vol. 1.

19. Bodelschwingh, "Dreißig Tage an einer Wegwende deutscher Kirchengeschichte," HAB Bielefeld, 2/39–177, 6–7. See also Thomas Martin Schneider, *Reichsbischof Ludwig Müller: Eine Untersuchung zu Leben, Werk und Persönlichkeit* (Göttingen: Vandenhoeck and Ruprecht, 1993), 110.

20. Bodelschwingh, "Dreißig Tage," 18–19.

21. Ibid., 24–25.

22. Ibid., 27, 31.

23. Theophil Wurm, *Erinnerungen aus meinem Leben* (Stuttgart: Quell-Verlag, 1953), 88–89.

24. Wright, "*Above Parties*," 133.

25. Lagrange to Stratenwerth, 10 June 1933, HAB Bethel, 2/39–5.

26. Hoffman to Bodelschwingh, 21 June 1933, HAB Bethel, 2/39–6. See also Bodelschwingh's response on 4 July 1933.

27. Scholder, *Churches and the Third Reich*, 1:355.

28. See also Schneider, *Reichsbischof Ludwig Müller*, 129–38.

29. Nazi activists seized on Vischer's approval of Buber. Regarding anti-semitism, the party accused him of stating that if the Nazis persecuted Jews, the Jews should respond in kind. At the same time, they also took a quotation from Vischer out of context, arguing that he called Hitler a "*balkanese*" instead of Nordic. For more on Vischer's comments, see his reply to the National Socialist accusations from 21 May 1933 in HAB Bethel, 2/41–66.

30. Gottfried Michaelis, *Der Fall Vischer: Ein Kapitel des Kirchenkampfes* (Bielefeld: Luther Verlag, 1994), 32–34, 37–38.

31. Ibid., 35.

32. Ibid.

33. Löhr to Brandt, 19 May 1933, HAB Bethel, 2/41–66.

34. Löhr to Brandt, 30 Nov. 1933, ibid., 2/41–66.

35. Michaelis, *Der Fall Vischer*, 41.

36. Letter to Stratenwerth, 15 June 1933, HAB Bethel, 2/41–66.

37. Michaelis, *Der Fall Vischer*, 58.

38. Heinrich Bödeker, "Das Sommersemester 1933: Die Vertreibung von Wilhelm Vischer," in *Kirchliche Hochschule Bethel: 1905–1980*, ed. Gerhard Ruhbach (Bethel, Bielefeld: Kirchliche Hochschule Bethel: 1980), 95.

39. Jürgen Kampmann, "Friedrich von Bodelschwinghs Rolle im west-fälischen Kirchenkampf," in *Bethels Mission (2): Bethel im Spannungsfeld von Erweckungsfrömmigkeit und öffentlicher Fürsorge: Beiträge zur Geschichte der v. Bodelschwinghschen Anstalten Bethel*, ed. Matthias Bendad, Kerstin

Winkler, Beiträge zur Westfälischen Kirchengeschichte, no. 20 (Bielefeld: Luther Verlag, 2001), 127.

40. Protokoll der Studentenversammlung, 18 May 1933, HAB Bethel, 2/41–66.
41. Kampmann, "Bodelschwinghs Rolle im westfälischen Kirchenkampf," 127–29.
42. Protokoll der Studentenversammlung, 18 May 1933, HAB Bethel, 2/41–66.
43. Kampmann, "Friedrich von Bodelschwinghs Rolle im westfälischen Kirchenkampf," 129.
44. Ibid., 132.
45. Scholder, *Churches and the Third Reich*, 1:370.
46. Otto Dibelius, *In the Service of the Lord: The Autobiography of Bishop Otto Dibelius*, trans. Mary Ilford (New York: Holt, Rinehart and Winston, 1964), 144. For Dibelius's description of the Reich Bishop election, see 141–43. Kampmann, "Friedrich von Bodelschwinghs Rolle im westfälischen Kirchenkampf," 125–46
47. Scholder, *Churches and the Third Reich*, 1:363.
48. Bodelschwingh to Hossenfelder, 29 June 1933, HAB Bethel, 2/39–44.
49. Bodelschwingh to Werner, 29 June 1933, HAB Bethel, 2/39–44.
50. Bodelschwingh to Müller, 29 July 1933, ibid., 2/39–51.
51. Ibid.
52. "Gesetz über die Verfassung der Deutschen Evangelischen Kirche," 14 July 1933, in *Dokumente zur Kirchenpolitik des Dritten Reiches, vol. 2: Vom Beginn des Jahres 1934 bis zur Errichtung des Reichsministeriums für kirchlichen Angelegenheiten am 16. Juli 1935*, ed. Carsten Nicolaisen (Munich: Chr. Kaiser Verlag, 1975), 107–9. For the full text of the constitution, see 185–90.
53. "Runderlass Staatssekretär Pfundtners an die Landesregierungen," 18 July 1933, in *Dokumente zur Kirchenpolitik*, ed. Nicolaisen, 2:110–11. See also "Presseanweisungen des Propagandaministeriums," 17 July 1933, ibid., 113.
54. Dibelius, *In the Service of the Lord*, 144. Reich Bishop Kampmann, "Friedrich von Bodelschwinghs Rolle im westfälischen Kirchenkampf," 125–46. Ernst Christian Helmreich, *The German Churches under Hitler: Background, Struggle, and Epilogue* (Detroit: Wayne State University Press, 1979), 142. See also "Rundfunkansprache Hitlers am Vorabend der Kirchenwahlen," Bayreuth, 22 July 1933, in *Dokumente zur Kirchenpolitik*, ed. Nicolaisen, 2:119–21.
55. Helmreich, *German Churches under Hitler*, 143.
56. Martin Niemöller, "Die Jungreformatorische Bewegung und die Kirchenpolitik: 16 Thesen," *Junge Kirche* 1 (1933): 99–101. See also Scholder, *Churches and the Third Reich*, 1:454.
57. Scholder, *Churches and the Third Reich*, 1:455.
58. Circular by Bodelschwingh, 11 August 1933, in *Dokumente zur Bonhoeffer-Forschung, 1928–1945*, ed. Jørgen Glenthøj (Munich: Chr. Kaiser Verlag, n.d. [1969]), 105.
59. Scholder, *Churches and the Third Reich*, 1:456.
60. Stratenwerth to Niemöller, 18 August 1933, in Dietrich Bonhoeffer, *Gesammelte Schriften*, ed. Eberhard Bethge, 6 vols. (Munich: Chr. Kaiser Verlag, 1959–74), 2:82.

61. "Das Betheler Bekenntnis. 1933" in Bonhoeffer, *Gesammelte Schriften*, ed. Bethge, 2:112–13.

62. Ibid., 113.

63. Ibid.

64. Ibid., 83, 116.

65. Initially, the law was proposed by Reinhold Krause, a German Christian leader and close advisor of Müller, at the synod of the Provincial Church of Brandenburg, held before the General Synod. Krause would also achieve notoriety a few months later when he made a similar speech at the Berlin Sports Palace rally in November.

66. Elizabeth Sifton and Fritz Stern, *No Ordinary Men: Dietrich Bonhoeffer and Hans von Dohnanyi, Resisters against Hitler in Church and State* (New York: New York Review Books, 2013), 33–34.

67. Moses, *Reluctant Revolutionary*, 150.

68. Circular from Bodelschwingh, 26 August 1933, in Bonhoeffer, *Gesammelte Schriften*, 2:90–91. See also Wolfgang Gerlach, *And the Witnesses Were Silent: The Confessing Church and the Persecution of the Jews*, trans. Victoria J. Barnett (Lincoln: University of Nebraska Press, 2000), 28

69. Circular from Bodelschwingh, 26 August 1933, in Bonhoeffer, *Gesammelte Schriften*, 2:91.

70. Bodelschwingh to Müller, 11 September 1933, HAB Bethel, 2/39–51; See also Gerlach, *And the Witnesses Were Silent*, 33.

71. Ibid., 28.

72. "Das Bekenntnis der Väter und die bekennende Gemeinde (Das sog. Bethler Bekenntnis)," in *Die Bekenntnisse*, ed. Schmidt, 128.

73. Gerlach, *And the Witnesses Were Silent*, 29–31. For the text of the pamphlet, see "Der Arierparagraph in der Kirche," Flugblatt from August 1933, in Bonhoeffer, *Gesammelte Schriften*, ed. Bethge, 2:62–9.

74. Dietrich Bonhoeffer and Martin Niemöller, "Erklärung," in Bonhoeffer, *Gesammelte Schriften*, 2:70–71.

75. Gerlach, *And the Witnesses Were Silent*, 33.

76. Bodelschwingh to Müller, 11 September 1933, HAB Bethel, 2/39–51.

77. See "Die Notbund-Verpflichtung," in *Texte zur Geschichte des Pfarrernotbundes*, ed. Wilhelm Niemöller (Berlin: Verlag Walter de Gruyter & Co., 1958), 26–27.

78. Scholder, *Churches and the Third Reich*, 1:483. See also Jürgen Schmidt, *Martin Niemöller im Kirchenkampf* (Hamburg: Leibnitz-Verlag, 1971), 125.

79. Wilhelm Niemöller, *Pfarrernotbund: Die Geschichte einer kämpfenden Bruderschaft* (Hamburg: Wittig, 1973), 17.

80. J. S. Conway, *The Nazi Persecution of the Churches, 1933–1945* (Vancouver: Regent College Publishing, 2001), 49.

81. Reinhard Krause, "Speech at the Sports Palace in Berlin," in *A Church Undone: Documents from the German Christian Faith Movement, 1932–1940*, trans. Mary M. Solberg (Minneapolis: Fortress Press, 2015), 249–62, esp. 256–58, 260.

82. Bergen, *Twisted Cross*, 89.

83. Scholder, *Churches and the Third Reich*, 1:555. The league also asked Karl Barth to meet with Hitler, but this meeting never occurred.

84. "Aufzeichnungen Bodelschwinghs über seinen Empfang beim Reichspräsidenten," 16 November 1933, in *Dokumente zur Kirchenpolitik*, ed. Nicolaisen, 2:173.
85. Ibid., 174.
86. Ibid.
87. Ibid.
88. Ibid.
89. Ibid., 72.
90. Notes from conversation with Reich Bishop Müller in Hannover, 21 December 1933, HAB Bethel, 2/39–51.
91. Ibid.
92. Schneider, *Reichsbischof Ludwig Müller*, 180.
93. Ibid., 183.
94. Friedrich von Bodelschwingh, "Rein, frei und fest!," in *Rheinische Bekenntnissynoden im Kirchenkampf: Eine Dokumentation aus den Jahren 1933–1945*, ed. Joachim Beckmann (Neukirchen-Vluyn: Newkirchener Verlag, 1975), 119. See also Klaus Scholder, *Churches and the Third Reich*, vol. 2: *The Year of Disillusionment: 1934, Barmen and Rome* (Philadelphia: Fortress Press, 1988), 73–75, and Carsten Nicolaisen, "Fritz von Bodelschwingh als Kirchenpolitiker," in *Friedrich von Bodelschwingh d. J. und die Betheler Anstalten: Frömigkeit und Weltgestaltung*, ed. Matthias Benad (Stuttgart: Verlag W. Kohlhammer, 1997), 90–91.
95. "Aufzeichnung Pastor von Bodelschwinghs über eine Unterredung mit Ministerialrat Diels," 24 February 1934, in *Dokumente zur Kirchenpolitik*, ed. Nicolaisen, 2:61–64.
96. Bodelschwingh to Kerrl, 6 December 1935, and 30 January 1936, both in HAB 2/39–46.
97. Thomas Martin Schneider, "Kollaboration oder Vermittlung im Dienste des Evangeliums? Zum Verhältnis Friedrich von Bodelschwinghs zum Reichminister für kirchliche Angelegenheiten," in *… und über Barmen hinaus: Studien zur Kirchlichen Zeitgeschichte…*, ed. Joachim Mehlhausen (Göttingen: Vandenhoeck and Ruprecht, 1995), 314.

Bibliography

Beckmann, Joachim, ed. *Rheinische Bekenntnissynoden im Kirchenkampf: Eine Dokumentation aus den Jahren 1933–1945.* Neukirchen-Vluyn: Newkirchener Verlag, 1975.

Benad, Matthias. "Bethels Verhältnis zum Nationalsozialismus." In *Zwangsverpflichtet: Kriegsgefangene und zivile Zwangsarbeiter(-innen) in Bethel und Lobetal 1939–1945*, edited by Matthias Benad and Regina Mentner, 27–66. Bielefeld: Bethel Verlag und Verlag für Regionalgeschichte, 2002.

Bergen, Doris. *Twisted Cross: The German Christian Movement in the Third Reich.* Chapel Hill: University of North Carolina Press, 1996.

Bödeker, Heinrich. "Das Sommersemester 1933: Die Vertreibung von Wilhelm Vischer." In *Kirchliche Hochschule Bethel: 1905–1980*, edited by Gerhard Ruhbach, 89–97. Bethel-Bielefeld: Kirchliche Hochschule Bethel, 1980.

Bodelschwingh, Friedrich von. "Rein, frei und fest!" In *Texte zur Geschichte des Pfarrernotbundes*, edited by Wilhelm Niemöller. Berlin: Verlag Walter de Gruyter & Co., 1958.

———. *Dreißig Tage an einer Wegwende deutscher Kirchengeschichte: Erinnerungen des ersten Reichsbischofs*, edited by Carsten Nicolaisen and Thomas Martin Schneider, Bielefeld: Bethel-Verlag, 2013.

Bonhoeffer, Dietrich. *Gesammelte Schriften: Zweiter Band*. Edited by Eberhard Bethge. Munich: Chr. Kaiser Verlag, 1959.

Brandt, Wilhelm. *Friedrich von Bodelschwingh, 1877–1946: Nachfolger und Gestalter*. Bielefeld: Verlagshandlung der Anstalt Bethel, 1967.

Conway, John S. *The Nazi Persecution of the Churches, 1933–1945*. Vancouver: Regent College Publishing, 2001.

Dibelius, Otto. *In the Service of the Lord: The Autobiography of Bishop Otto Dibelius*. Translated by Mary Ilford. New York: Holt, Rinehart and Winston, 1964.

Gerlach, Wolfgang. *And the Witnesses Were Silent: The Confessing Church and the Persecution of the Jews*. Translated by Victoria J. Barnett. Lincoln: University of Nebraska Press, 2000.

Glenthøj, Jørgen, ed. *Dokumente zur Bonhoeffer-Forschung, 1928–1945*. Munich: Chr. Kaiser Verlag, n.d. [1969].

Helmreich, Ernst Christian. *The German Churches under Hitler: Background, Struggle, and Epilogue*. Detroit: Wayne State University Press, 1979.

Kampmann, Jürgen. "Friedrich von Bodelschwinghs Rolle im westfälischen Kirchenkampf." In *Bethels Mission (2): Bethel im Spannungsfeld von Erweckungsfrömmigkeit und öffentlicher Fürsorge; Beiträge zur Geschichte der v. Bodelschwinghschen Anstalten Bethel*, edited by Matthias Bendads and Kerstin Winkler, Beiträge zur Westfälischen Kirchengeschichte, no. 20, 125–46. Bielefeld: Luther Verlag, 2001.

Michaelis, Gottfried. *Der Fall Vischer: Ein Kapitel des Kirchenkampfes*. Bielefeld: Luther Verlag, 1994,

Moses, John A. *The Reluctant Revolutionary: Dietrich Bonhoeffer's Collision with Prusso-German History*. New York: Berghahn Books, 2014.

Nicolaisen, Carsten, "Fritz von Bodelschwingh als Kirchenpolitiker." In *Friedrich von Bodelschwingh d. J. und die Betheler Anstalten: Frömigkeit und Weltgestaltung*, edited by Matthias Benad, 82–100. Stuttgart: Verlag W. Kohlhammer, 1997.

———. ed. *Dokumente zur Kirchenpolitik des Dritten Reiches*, vol. 2: *Vom Beginn des Jahres 1934 bis zur Errichtung des Reichsministeriums für kirchlichen Angelegenheiten am 16. Juli 1935*. Munich: Chr. Kaiser Verlag, 1975.

Nicolaisen, Carsten, and Georg Kretschmar, eds. *Dokumente zur Kirchenpolitik des Dritten Reiches*, vol. 1: *Das Jahr 1933*. Munich: Chr. Kaiser Verlag, 1971.

Niemöller, Wilhelm. *Pfarrernotbund: Die Geschichte einer kämpfenden Bruderschaft*. Hamburg: Wittig, 1973.

Schmidt, Jürgen. *Martin Niemöller im Kirchenkampf*. Hamburg: Leibnitz-Verlag, 1971.

Schneider, Thomas Martin. *Reichsbischof Ludwig Müller: Eine Untersuchung zu Leben, Werk und Persönlichkeit.* Göttingen: Vandenhoeck and Ruprecht, 1993,
——. "Kollaboration oder Vermittlung im Dienste des Evangeliums? Zum Verhältnis Friedrich von Bodelschwinghs zum Reichminister für kirchliche Angelegenheiten." In *… und über Barmen hinaus: Studien zur Kirchlichen Zeitgeschichte…*, edited by Joachim Mehlhausen, 305–17. Göttingen: Vandenhoeck and Ruprecht, 1995.
Scholder, Klaus. *Churches and the Third Reich.* Translated by John Bowden. 2 vols. Philadelphia: Fortress Press, 1988.
Sifton, Elizabeth, and Fritz Stern. *No Ordinary Men: Dietrich Bonhoeffer and Hans von Dohnanyi, Resisters against Hitler in Church and State.* New York: New York Review Books, 2013.
Solberg, Mary A. *A Church Undone: Documents from the German Christian Faith Movement, 1932–1940.* Minneapolis: Fortress Press, 2015.
Wright, J. R. C. *"Above Parties": The Political Attitudes of the German Protestant Church Leadership, 1918–1933.* New York: Oxford University Press, 1974.
Wurm, Theophil. *Erinnerungen aus meinem Leben.* Stuttgart: Quell-Verlag, 1953.

 **12**

In Search of Allies

Catholic Conservatives, the Alliance of Catholic Germans, and
the Nazi Regime, 1933–34

Larry Eugene Jones and Kevin P. Spicer

One of the major challenges awaiting Adolf Hitler upon his appointment as chancellor on 30 January 1933 was the reconciliation of
Germany's Catholic population to Nazi rule. For although Catholics
constituted approximately a third of Germany's population, they
had proven remarkably resistant to Nazi penetration throughout the
Weimar Republic and continued to withstand the appeal of Nazism
well into the first months of the Third Reich.[1] If Hitler and his Nazi
minions were ever to achieve their goal of forging a sense of national
unity that transcended the classical divisions of class, confession, and
region, then full and total integration of German Catholics into the
fabric of the Nazi *Volksgemeinschaft* would remain one of their most
pressing tasks. Here, however, the initiative came not just from Hitler
and the leaders of the new Nazi state but also from Catholic conservatives who, for the most part, had not belonged to either of Weimar's two
Catholic parties, the German Center Party (Deutsche Zentrumspartei)
or the Bavarian People's Party (Bayerische Volkspartei or BVP), but had
generally sought allegiance with various right-wing organizations in a
common crusade to overthrow the Weimar Republic and replace it with
a more authoritarian form of government.[2] Between 8 and 10 percent
of Germany's seventeen million Catholics would fall into this category,
although some remained loyal to Weimar's Catholic parties and did not
openly participate in the politics of Germany's anti-republican right.
But the collapse of Weimar democracy and the installation of a new
government in which Catholic conservatives, most notably vice chancellor Franz von Papen, were prominently represented, would enable
them to break out of the political isolation in which they had found
themselves throughout the Weimar Republic and to place themselves
in the service of Germany's new political order.

The following chapter will examine the efforts of Catholic conservatives allied to the new vice chancellor to build bridges between the

regime and German Catholics who greeted the establishment of the Nazi order with a mixture of disbelief, bitterness, and estrangement. It will focus in particular on the two organizations that Papen's supporters launched in the first year of the Third Reich, the League of Catholic Germans Cross and Eagle (Bund katholischer Deutscher "Kreuz und Adler" or BKA) and its successor the Alliance of Catholic Germans (Arbeitsgemeinschaft Katholischer Deutscher or AKD), and explore the obstacles they faced in their efforts to reconcile German Catholics to Nazi rule. It will devote particular attention to the role that Papen and these two organizations played as mediators between the church and state in the critical months that followed Hitler's appointment as chancellor. In this respect, the chapter will explore in detail the way in which officials of the Catholic Church and Nazi regime responded to the aspirations of the Catholic conservatives who fueled the ambitions and activities of these two organizations to the point where by the spring of 1934 regime police officials began to harbor suspicions that prominent Catholic conservatives affiliated with Papen were part of a larger conspiracy to remove Hitler from power. Accordingly, the essay will conclude with an analysis of the factors that led to the AKD's dissolution and the persecution of some of its most prominent leaders in the aftermath of the Röhm Purge in the summer of 1934.

In the New Reich

In the Weimar Republic, Catholic conservatism recruited the bulk of its adherents from one of three groups: the Catholic nobility in the Rhineland, Westphalia, Silesia, and Bavaria; the Catholic intelligentsia; and elements of the clergy, particularly within the religious orders. After 1918 they had gravitated either toward the right-wing German National People's Party (Deutschnationale Volkspartei or DNVP), where they became actively involved in the DNVP's Reich Catholic Committee (Reichskatholikenausschuß der DNVP)[3] and paramilitary organizations like the Stahlhelm or abstained from partisan political activity altogether. A few, like Franz von Papen, Baron Engelbert von Kerckerinck zur Borg, and Prince Alois zu Löwenstein-Wertheim, remained loyal to the Center but experienced little success in returning the party to the tried-and-true principles that had inspired its founding in the early 1870s. Yet regardless of their political affiliation after 1918, all had deep reservations about the system of parliamentary democracy that Germany had inherited from the November Revolution; favored a reorganization of the state, society, and economy along corporatist lines; and advocated, if not for a restoration of the monarchy, then at least for the establishment of a more authoritarian political order that would no longer be so dependent upon the sovereign will of the people.[4]

By the beginning of the 1930s Germany's Catholic conservatives were in complete disarray. The DNVP's Reich Catholic Committee had virtually collapsed in the summer of 1929 as the result of a conflict with party chairman Alfred Hugenberg over the concordat between the Vatican and the Prussian state government. In the spring and summer of 1931 the DNVP launched a determined effort to revive the party's Reich Catholic Committee under the leadership of Julius Doms.[5] It is highly unlikely, however, that all of this energy succeeded in overcoming the deep-seated antipathy that the former leaders of the Reich Catholic Committee felt toward Hugenberg, in part because its position as the preeminent organization on the Catholic right was soon challenged by the emergence of a new organization calling itself the Alliance of Catholic Germans that made its public debut with an appeal supporting Hitler in the 1932 presidential elections. In its initial iteration, the AKD was an ostensibly bipartisan association of right-wing Catholics whose leadership lay in the hands of the Stahlhelm's Edgar Schmidt-Pauli, the NSDAP's Baron Carl von Schorlemer, and Georg Lossau from the Catholic Association for National Policy (Katholische Vereinigung für nationale Politik).[6] But this organization was immediately dismissed by the leaders of both the Stahlhelm and DNVP as a Nazi front organization whose real purpose was to win right-wing Catholics over to the NSDAP.[7] The situation on the Catholic right was confused even further by the appointment of one of their own, Franz von Papen, as chancellor in early June 1932 and by the sharp rejection that his appointment received from the Center, the party to which he had belonged. For while Papen proudly reaffirmed his embrace of the Catholic conservative philosophy of the state and political leadership,[8] his ascendancy to the chancellorship did little to help Germany's Catholic conservatives break out of the political isolation in which they had found themselves since the founding of the Weimar Republic. If anything, Papen's break with the Center only underscored just how far out of step Catholic conservatives were with the vast majority of Germany's politically active Catholics.

As one of the principal spokesmen for the non-Nazi elements of the governmental coalition, Papen placed great emphasis in the campaign for the 1933 Reichstag elections upon the importance of Christian-conservative values in shaping the polices of the new order that was to take the place of the old, defunct democratic state.[9] In the meantime,

Christian conservatives worked behind the scenes and very much on their own initiative to launch a new organization, initially calling itself the Greater German League of Conservative Catholics (Großdeutscher Bund konservativer Katholiken).[10] Here the principal impetus came from Emil Ritter, a journalist and Catholic pedagogue with ties to the People's Association for a Catholic Germany (Volksverein für das katholische Deutschland) that dated back to the early twentieth century.[11] Unlike many Catholic conservatives who found it difficult to accept the fall of the old monarchical order, Ritter remained loyal to the Center throughout the 1920s and worked closely with Joseph Joos to keep the party from falling completely under the influence of its left wing. Ritter supported the Brüning experiment in government by presidential decree as a necessary response to the economic crisis that had descended upon Germany at the beginning of the 1930s, and in May 1932 he assumed editorship of *Germania*, the Center Party's national newspaper. As editor of *Germania*, Ritter came into regular contact with Papen, and when the Center refused to support Papen after his appointment as chancellor in early June 1932, Ritter both resigned as editor of *Germania* and left the Center.[12] For Ritter, as someone who had dedicated his entire life to cultivating a sense of Catholic unity that transcended partisan political divisions, the Center's rejection of Papen was part of a larger crisis of political Catholicism that required new forms of political organization.[13] At the same time, Ritter harbored deep-seated misgivings about National Socialism. In an article written in December 1932 for the fifth edition of the *Staatslexikon* of the Görres Society (Görres Gesellschaft), Ritter highlighted in what was for the most part a balanced account of National Socialism, its history, and its ideas some of the fundamental differences between the basic values of Christianity and those of the Nazi movement on matters such as marriage and the family, the confessional school, and the legal status of the church. For Ritter, National Socialism was essentially a political phenomenon whose claim that it was a party with a worldview or *Weltanschauung* was spurious at best. And from a political perspective, Ritter concluded, the challenge was to integrate the valuable elements that existed in National Socialism into the service of the state and nation, a challenge that would oblige the National Socialists to moderate the tone of their radicalism and to adopt a more responsible attitude toward the burning issues that confronted the German people.[14]

Under Ritter's tutelage the new organization quickly reorganized itself as the League of the Cross and Eagle. The League of the Cross and Eagle, whose founding was announced with great fanfare in early April 1933,[15] did not portray itself as a new political party but as "an independent organization of Catholic Germans who out of profound national conviction and religious obligation have placed themselves at the service of the national and social renewal of the Reich." According to its statutes, the BKA's purpose was "to mobilize the vital forces [*Lebens- und Formkräfte*] that existed in the Catholic Church for the German future, to help overcome the liberal-democratic and Marxist ethos, and to revive the Christian-conservative and imperial traditions of German Catholics." In this respect, the league would "meet its obligations to the political necessities of the day by cooperating in a corporatist reform of German public life, the creation of a state system based upon leadership and responsibility, and the [territorial and administrative] reorganization of the German Reich."[16] Though skeptical about Papen's political acumen and his ability to hold the Nazis in check, Ritter quickly recruited the vice chancellor as the organization's patron, or *Schirmherr*, in an obvious attempt to insulate it as much as possible from the threat of Nazi interference.[17] From Papen's perspective, the most pressing imperative was to integrate the forces of political Catholicism into the structure of the Nazi state as smoothly and as expeditiously as possible[18] It was with this in mind that Papen would take the lead in negotiating a concordat with the Holy See in the late spring and early summer of 1933.[19] At the same time, however, Papen was anxious to build up a political base of his own after the dismal performance of the Combat Front Black-White-Red (Kampffront Schwarz-Weiß-Rot) in the March 1933 Reichstag elections and no doubt hoped that the BKA would help him consolidate his own position within the Nazi regime. Careful not to arouse the suspicions of Hitler and his political entourage, Papen went to great lengths to reassure the chancellor of the loyalty and good intentions that lay behind his willingness to serve as the BKA's patron. Writing to Hitler in late April 1933, Papen declared,

> I am of the opinion that the ties of German Catholicism to the party political formations of the liberal era must disappear. At the same time, it is of greatest importance that German Catholics are brought into the closest possible relationship to the government of national renewal. The aim of this thoroughly nonpartisan union [*überparteilicher Zusammenschluß*] of conservative Catholics must be to find ways to extricate German Catholicism from outmoded party forms and make this preeminently important sector of our population of service to your government. As you yourself know, Herr Reich Chancellor, many difficulties stand in the way of this goal. The best way of solving them is the path of the League of the Cross and Eagle.[20]

For Papen, the League of the Cross and Eagle had three specific objectives: "to free German Catholicism from the outmoded party forms of the liberal era, to eliminate doctrinaire misunderstandings in the cultural program of the NSDAP, and to create a common front of both Christian confessions in the spiritual renewal of the Reich." All of this presupposed a reform of Germany's federal structure that at one and the same time respected the needs of a powerful central government and the tried-and-true traditions of the individual German states. Moreover, the "melting together" of the German people could succeed only by replacing the conflict that had sown so much disunity in the German nation with a new corporate structure capable of bringing all estates and professions into a dynamic synthesis. But none of this, Papen concluded, was a product of the moment. All of these ideas were deeply rooted in the German national spirit. Only now they were borne by a truly revolutionary wave, a wave that since 1918 had gone hand in hand with the broad movement of National Socialism.[21]

If Papen was responsible for setting the project's political course in accordance with the policies and objectives of the new regime, the *rector spiritus* behind it was Ildefons Herwegen, abbot of the famous Benedictine monastery at Maria Laach.[22] Profoundly nationalistic and disdainful of parliamentary democracy, Herwegen saw in the National Socialist quest for Germany's national regeneration a complement to his own longing for the spiritual renewal of German Catholicism. Hopeful that Catholics would gain access to the new regime despite the anti-Christian diatribes of Alfred Rosenberg and other Nazi ideologues, Herwegen threw his full support behind the project and made the abbey at Maria Laach available for the new organization's first leadership conference in the fourth week of April 1933.[23] Papen's efforts on behalf of the BKA also received strong support from Albert Schmitt, the abbot at the Benedictine abbey in Grüssau in Silesia.[24] Yet, for all of the support he received from these quarters, Papen faced formidable obstacles in his quest to unite Germany's Catholic conservatives behind the banner of the BKA. For not only had the founding of the BKA met with a cool response from prominent representatives of Germany's Catholic aristocracy, such as Ferdinand von Lüninck, the newly appointed provincial governor of Westphalia,[25] but Doms and the leaders of the DNVP's Reich Catholic Committee also decided against affiliating themselves with the BKA after extensive deliberations at the end of March and beginning of April.[26] Additionally, the BKA experienced considerable difficulty in developing an organizational foothold in Bavaria, where the Center's Bavarian counterpart, the Bavarian People's Party, and other Catholic institutions had managed to withstand Nazi pressure better than the Center and were therefore less vulnerable to the BKA's agitation.[27] Yet with all of the fanfare that had accompanied its founding in April 1933, the League of the Cross and Eagle was never able to attract the broad base of popular support for which its founders had hoped. For all intents and purposes its support was restricted to individual members of the Catholic aristocracy in Westphalia and Silesia and to representatives of the Catholic intelligentsia who had always stood outside the orbit of organized political Catholicism before the Nazi seizure of power. The organizational malaise that afflicted the BKA was in fact so pervasive that its official founding, which was scheduled to take place in Berlin in May, had to be postponed,[28] and on 1 July Ritter formally resigned as its general secretary in order to reassume editorship of *Germania* in a step that carried Papen's full blessing.[29]

Papen and the Alliance of Catholic Germans

The high hopes that Papen had placed in the League of the Cross and Eagle remained unfulfilled. The inertia that had taken grip of the BKA had less to do with the lassitude of Papen's leadership than with the fact that by the summer of 1933 the strain in relations between the regime and the Catholic Church had by and large abated. The church's decision to lift its ban on Catholic membership in the Nazi Party and Nazi paramilitary organizations, the acquiescence of the Center and Bavarian People's Party in the passage of the Enabling Act, and the signing and ratification of the Reich Concordat between the regime and the Holy See had all helped to create what Germany's Catholic conservatives hoped would mark the beginning of a new era in church-state relations. Nowhere was the sense of elation to which this had given rise among those who had championed the ideas of the League of the Cross and Eagle more evident than at the Third Sociological Congress of the Catholic Academic League (Katholischer Akaemiker-Verband) that took place at Maria Laach from 20 to 23 July 1933 on the theme of "Das nationale Problem im Katholizismus: Die Neuordnung von Gesellschaft und Staat im Lichte des Reichsgedankens."[30] Catholic conservatives were particularly elated over the signing of the concordat with the Vatican and rejoiced over the death to which it had condemned political Catholicism in Germany.[31] All of this would suggest that the goals of the League of the Cross and Eagle had been accomplished and that the organization, having served its purpose, was no longer needed. But it soon became clear that whatever relief church leaders may have felt over the relaxation of political tensions following the conclusion of the Reich Concordat was unwarranted. For by the early fall of 1933 a bitter conflict between the church and the regime had erupted over the status of ancillary Catholic organizations for youth, students, women, and charity. What was at stake was whether or not these organizations enjoyed protection from the regime under Article 31 of the treaty with the Vatican.[32]

The Nazi assault upon the institutions of Catholic associational life severely challenged the unity of the Catholic conservatives in their approach to National Socialism and undercut their efforts to build a bridge between Germany's Catholic population and the Nazi regime. As this conflict drew to a head in the fall of 1933, the regime became increasingly suspicious not just of the church but also of the Catholic conservatives, who seemed intent on creating for themselves a political base within the new Nazi state. In late September Hitler's personal secretary Rudolf Hess ordered the dissolution of the League of the Cross and Eagle and its absorption into a new Catholic umbrella organization entitled the Alliance of Catholic Germans.[33] The new organization was in no way whatsoever a direct successor of the association of the same name that Lossau, Schmidt-Pauli, and Schorlemer had launched at the beginning of 1932 in support of Hitler's candidacy for the Reich presidency but was a much more broadly conceived coalition of Catholics who were prepared to place their talents at the service of the new regime.[34] Despite the fact that Papen served as *Schirmherr* of the new organization and Count Roderich Thun as its general secretary, the AKD stood much more directly under the control of the regime than any of its predecessor organizations with a national leadership committee composed of three proven Nazis: Hans Dauser, Hermann von Detten, and Rudolf zur Bonsen.[35] The goal of this organization, as a press communiqué released in October explained, was essentially twofold. On the one hand, it sought to solicit support for National Socialist ideas among German Catholics and to work for a clear relationship between church, state, and party, while on the other it would engage special committees, or *Arbeitsausschüsse*, to examine the relationship between the National Socialist and Catholic worldviews with the goal of facilitating Catholic acceptance of National Socialist political and ideological hegemony.[36]

If the founding of the League of the Cross and Eagle in the spring of 1933 had been driven by Papen's desire to create for himself a power base within the structure of the Nazi state, the primary purpose of the Alliance of Catholic Germans was to expedite the *Gleichschaltung* of German Catholics into the associational life of the Third Reich. In this respect the campaign for the Reichstag elections that were scheduled to take place on 12 November 1933 would play a critical role. For the

Nazis, the elections were seen as an opportunity to provide Hitler with the plebiscitary mandate that would further legitimate his claim to the leadership of the German nation, and from their perspective it was imperative that the Catholic Church and its leaders do their part in mobilizing their faithful in support of the regime. The person to whom this task fell was, of course, Hitler's reliable sycophant, Franz von Papen. Speaking at an AKD rally in Cologne three days before the election, Papen exhorted his fellow Catholics to join the National Socialists in the liquidation of the liberal era and the rescue of Germany's Christian culture from the cabal of sinister forces, both domestic and international, that currently besieged it.[37] But Papen was more than the public face of the AKD in its efforts to mobilize German Catholics in the support of Hitler's regime; he was also working behind the scenes to overcome the bitterness that many high-ranking church officials felt toward the regime as a result of the anti-Christian polemics of Nazi ideologue Alfred Rosenberg and his circle, the harassment and arrests of Catholic priests in the first six months of 1933, and lingering differences between the church and state over the status of the institutions of Catholic associational life.

The AKD and the German Catholic Bishops

On 29 October 1933 Papen wrote to Cardinal Adolf Bertram, archbishop of Breslau and head of the Fulda Bishops' Conference, to request "an official statement" by the German bishops on participation in the Reichstag elections that were scheduled to take place on 12 November. He reminded Bertram that the Protestant Reich Bishop, Ludwig Müller, had already issued a similar statement and that it would be only fitting to ensure peace in the land for the Catholic bishops to follow Müller's example.[38] Papen also assured the cardinal that he and other AKD leaders were working diligently to ensure that Catholics voted in support of the government.[39] In a separate effort, Hans Schemm, the Bavarian state minister for education and culture, approached Passau diocesan officials and asked them to coordinate a joint public statement by the German bishops in favor of the list of NSDAP candidates in the upcoming Reichstag elections and to approve a referendum to withdraw Germany from the League of Nations.[40] Although the German bishops received these requests, months of repressive action against Catholic associations and youth organizations whose existence the state questioned as a result of the lack of clarity in Article 31 of the Reich Concordat left the German hierarchy doubting the intentions of the Hitler government and divided over how to respond. The passage of a recent forced sterilization law scheduled to go into effect on 1 January 1934 only made the bishops' reservations more pressing.

In the face of such difficulties, Conrad Gröber, Archbishop of Freiburg, maintained an enthusiastic optimism about the future of church-state relations, sharing that a statement about the election "could not be avoided."[41] Taking the lead, Cardinal Bertram created a draft statement in which he acknowledged the strain in church-state relations while encouraging Catholics to express loyalty to Germany when making electoral decisions.[42] The tone of Bertram's draft did not please many of his peers. Even the ultraconservative bishop of Passau, Sigismund Felix Freiherr von Ow-Felldorf, deemed Bertram's draft too conciliatory, offering that it might cause the faithful to vote "Yes" without sufficient consideration of the church's difficult situation.[43] The individual responses of the bishops soon revealed their disagreement on the approach and left them to issue separate statements.[44] Although the majority reflected hope in the future and support for the government, some included references to ongoing church-state tensions.[45] The most critical version, eventually adopted by his fellow Bavarian bishops, came from the pen of Cardinal Michael von Faulhaber, archbishop of Munich and Freising, who listed specific infractions against the Concordat by the state and called on Catholics "to advocate for peace among peoples and for equal rights of the German people."[46] Such ambiguous phrasing led the Gestapo to confiscate copies of the statement and ban priests from publicly reading it during Mass.[47] Despite the lack of enthusiasm by the church hierarchy, 92.1 percent of the German electorate voted in favor of the NSDAP candidate slate—the only slate on the ballot—while 95.1 percent voted for Germany to leave the League of Nations.[48] Overall, it was a great success for Hitler and the Nazi Party.

On the eve of the election, Papen wrote to his confidant Abbot Albert Schmitt of Grüssau: "The statement on the election by Cardinal Bertram was a half-measure and that of the Bavarian bishops was completely impossible." However, Papen did confess that he was pleased by the support Archbishop Gröber had shown for the election.[49] Gröber would soon lend his support to another cause: the founding of the AKD, an organization he enthusiastically greeted in a statement in which he described the AKD members as an "elite" that will "demonstrate the usefulness of convinced Catholics for the new Reich."[50] Although Gröber was the only member of the Catholic hierarchy to declare his support publicly for the AKD, he was not alone in his enthusiasm. In private correspondence with Cardinal Bertram, Monsignor

Paul Steinmann, who was administering the Berlin diocese following the death of its first bishop Christian Schreiber, professed that there was "nothing to object to" in the AKD, although he argued that it was important for the AKD to allow clergy to contribute to its work by infusing it with the "necessary religious spirit."[51] Cardinal Bertram expressed a greater reserve when Papen announced the founding of the AKD by emphasizing that it had been established without any "prior common understanding with the German bishops" and insisting that the AKD acknowledge that "the Catholic population wholeheartedly and gratefully recognized everything that the new Reich had achieved."[52] The most significant objection to the AKD came not from the German Catholic hierarchy but from a Catholic layperson who sent an anonymous letter to Thun, the general secretary of the AKD, in which the author challenged the AKD's push to align Catholicism with the National Socialist glorification of "blood and race" and the regime's efforts to nazify (*vernationalsozialisern*) the church and its members.[53]

The lack of clear pronouncement of the German episcopacy on the AKD left the majority of the Catholic laity uncertain whether or not they should support its endeavors. The former Center Party leader of Silesia, Count Hans von Praschma, voiced such a concern to Cardinal Bertram explaining that the "aims and operating approaches" of the AKD were "still not clear," even though some clergy in his area eagerly supported it.[54] In his reply, Bertram agreed with Praschma's assessment but also admitted that he was not ready to reject the Alliance, since numerous situations could arise in which it might serve a mediating role. Still, Bertram feared that the AKD came close to crossing a line by endeavoring to speak for the church, a role traditionally reserved to the Catholic hierarchy alone.[55] A few weeks later, Franz Rudolf Bornewasser, the bishop of Trier, would express a similar uneasiness in direct correspondence with the AKD leader for his region.[56]

To assert its authority and to prove its effectiveness in the Nazi state, the AKD began a campaign soon after the elections on 12 November to win over Catholic youth for the Hitler Youth.[57] It is unclear whether this initiative originated with the AKD leadership or from somewhere in the NSDAP. What was clear is that the Nazi Party wanted to be the primary influence in the lives of Germany's youth. Already in late July 1933, Baldur von Schirach, the Reich Youth leader, had forbidden double membership in both the Hitler Youth and all denominational youth groups, forcing parents to decide whether to allow their children to remain in a church-based youth group or to join the Hitler Youth.[58] Then vice-chancellor Papen, working together with the regional AKD leaders, spearheaded a separate effort to dismantle the Catholic youth groups and to entrust the care of Catholic youth to the Hitler Youth.[59] Their strategy was to personally approach chancery officials in each diocese to encourage this process. At least four dioceses expressed openness to the request.[60] Such conciliatory thinking was not shared by everyone. During a meeting with the leaders of various Catholic youth groups, Monsignor Ludwig Wolker, the head of Germany's Catholic Young Men's Association, spoke against making any sudden moves while also expressing his dismay over the lack of unity among diocesan chancery officials to act decisively against the effort. According to Wolker, there were four conditions that had to be met before any further steps could be taken: "(1) that a representative of the Catholic organizations be added to the leadership of the Hitler Youth; (2) that [attendance at] Sunday Mass be guaranteed for Hitler Youth members; (3) that a monthly religious lecture be included in the educational program of the Hitler Youth; and (4) that a division of teachers who would offer instruction in the Catholic faith be established in the Hitler Youth." Yet, even if these steps were taken, Wolker doubted that Schirach would honor any promises that he made to the church. Still Wolker understood that "no one wanted the situation to escalate into a *Kulturkampf*."[61] Yet, some bishops were prepared for a fight. Writing to Cardinal Bertram, Bishop Bornewasser expressed his disgust over Papen's machinations and argued that the moment had come for "the bishops to stand together and put the AKD in its place."[62]

After receiving the opinions of his fellow bishops, Cardinal Bertram informed the members of the German episcopate that the church would not soon be placing its young men and women under the Hitler Youth.[63] This was a bold decision, especially for Bertram whose record under National Socialism reveals an individual who disliked questioning state authority, for less than a month later, Bertram's Protestant counterpart, Reich Bishop Müller, would surrender the entire Protestant youth to Schirach's care.[64] Bertram's decision did not also mean any respite from the agitation of the AKD on this issue. In the 22 February 1934 edition of the AKD's *Mitteilungsblatt*, the headline read: "The AKD Supports a Transfer of the Religious Youth-Sports Organizations to the Hitler Youth." A few pages later, the newsletter offered a glowing report on St. Stephen's parish in Konstanz in the Freiburg diocese where in May 1933 the pastor, on his own accord, had turned over members of the Youth and Young Men's associations to the Hitler Youth.[65] Two days following the publication of the *Mitteilungsblatt*, Thun presented Archbishop Gröber with a memo from Schirach to Papen promising to allow the Catholic youth to fulfill their religious duties following "the necessary incorporation of the Catholic Youth organizations into the

Hitler Youth."[66] It was clear that Papen and the AKD were not prepared to let this situation rest.[67] The following month, Gröber reported to Eugenio Pacelli, the Vatican secretary of state, that "the situation was extremely tense."[68] Nevertheless, Bertram and his fellow bishops held firm in their refusal to abandon their youth to the Hitler Youth. Church-state tensions over this issue continued to deteriorate long after the AKD had been disbanded and would not be formerly resolved until 6 February 1939, when the Gestapo officially ordered the dissolution of the Catholic Young Men's Association.[69]

Eclipse of the AKD

On 14 January 1934, at a time when the campaign against the Catholic youth organizations was reaching a fever pitch, Papen delivered a speech in Gleiwitz to members of the Silesian AKD. Papen enjoyed close ties to the Catholic nobility in Silesia, and his visit had been arranged with the help of Count Nikolaus von Ballestrem, an influential Catholic noble who had officially broken with the Center in October 1932,[70] and the independent-minded abbot of Grüssau, Albert Schmitt.[71] Papen opened his speech by responding to allegations that the Austrian episcopacy had made in its pastoral letter from 21 December 1933 in which it had criticized National Socialism's extreme nationalism and racial ideology.[72] Papen reminded Catholics of the strong support they had given Hitler and his government in the recent Reichstag elections and castigated the Austrian bishops for their "unusual interference" in an "inner German affair." Then, in one of the rare moments where he ever addressed Nazi antisemitism and the so-called Jewish question in public, Papen argued that Germans had a right to maintain the purity of their race and stressed that "in no way whatsoever did that aspiration stand in contradiction to our Catholic faith." Papen rejected the objections of the Austrian bishops to "radical antisemitism" and reminded his audience that over the past several years the very bishops who were criticizing Hitler for his antisemitism had "justifiably and repeatedly opposed the excesses of Jewry in all areas of public life." At the same time, Papen acknowledged that while "we condemn exaggerations in the Jewish question," there was "nothing in the principle [of antisemitism] to dispute from the Catholic perspective."[73]

The real purpose of Papen's speech, however, was not to clarify the Catholic position on the Jewish question but to underscore what he saw as the fundamental compatibility of the basic values of the Christian faith with those of National Socialism. In this respect, Papen argued that the construction of the Third Reich was perfectly compatible with the ideas and principles embodied in Pius XI's encyclical "Quadragesimo Anno" and that, in fact, no European country could claim a social, economic, and political order that was more consistent with the fundamentals of the Catholic faith than Germany itself. Papen cited the regime's commitment to end the conflict between capital and labor, to "deproletarianize" the proletariat, to create a new and more organic social order, and to prevent the Bolshevization of the West as proof of the way in which its goals coincided with those of the Catholic Church.

> We German Catholics [Papen concluded] want to support Adolf Hitler and his government with all our soul and conviction. … In this historical movement German Catholicism must find its way out of negation, out of the ghetto, to take an active part in the founding of the Third Reich, for it is only by dedicating ourselves unconditionally to this great task that we will be justified in demanding that which we from the perspective of Catholic thought find indispensable. For it is upon our shoulders that the responsibility for the future of Germany and the Christian culture of the west rests.[74]

Papen's speech was broadcast over the radio not just in Silesia but also in southern and western Germany and was published in its entirety in *Germania* and the *Schlesische Volkszeitung*.[75] This stood in conspicuous contrast to the silence of the official Catholic press and the church hierarchy on Papen's speech. At the same time, the ideological warriors or *Glaubenskrieger* in Heinrich Himmler's SS could only have been outraged at the way in which Papen had equated the values of the Catholic Church with those of the Nazi regime.[76] No less a student of these events than Ludwig Volk has described Papen's Gleiwitz speech as his "political swansong" that only underscored how isolated he had become not just within the cabinet but also from Germany's Catholic establishment.[77] The vast majority of German Catholics showed little enthusiasm for Papen's feeble attempt to represent their interests in the face of the repression of their beloved church associations and organizations. At the same time, Papen's Gleiwitz speech reflected poorly on the AKD and severely strained its relations with the Catholic hierarchy. As Wilhelm Berning, the bishop of Osnabrück, expressed it, if the AKD worked against the "institutions and organizations that are promoted and supported by the bishops …, then it will find neither support from the Catholic bishops nor trust from the Catholic *Volk*."[78] To be sure, Gröber from Freiburg continued to voice support for Papen and the AKD and was willing to "speak up for it at all costs,"[79] while various members of the hierarchy continued to offer audiences for the

AKD's regional leaders.[80] But Papen remained concerned that outside of Gröber none of Germany's Catholic bishops had endorsed the AKD's efforts on behalf of better relations between the church and the Nazi regime and appealed in vain to high-ranking clerics like Cardinal Karl Joseph Schulte, the bishop of Cologne, to publicly endorse the AKD and its work.[81]

Perhaps the most significant consequence of Papen's Gleiwitz speech was the effect it had upon the vice chancellor's relationship with leaders of the Nazi movement. For not only had Papen and the AKD failed to deliver the Catholic youth into the hands of the Hitler Youth but, in attempting to defend Hitler's Reich against the Austrian bishops' charges and in trying to appease Catholics, Papen had chosen words that hardened Nazis viewed as critical of their movement's ideology, especially its racial antisemitism. Complicating the situation even further was an "Aufruf zum Abwehrkampf" the AKD had published in the May 1934 issue of its *Mitteilungsblatt*. As in the past, the AKD sharply criticized the German Faith Movement, a loosely structured neo-pagan effort supported by the SS in an attempt to supplant Christianity with the worship of German nationalism and a return to a pre-Christian German religion. In this respect, the AKD was particularly critical of those individual party members who sought to supplement Christian teaching with Nazi ideology. At the same time, however, the AKD also warned the church not to use religion to disguise politically motivated protests against the state by exploiting the term *Kulturkampf*. The AKD proclaimed to both the church and the state that it had been entrusted with "the task of nipping in the bud [*im Keime zu verhindern*] all attempts to disturb the harmony of church and state" and that it would "direct its attack with the same intensity and the same decisiveness against any dangerous tendency on either side."[82] To the militant anti-Christians and guardians of their party's ideological purity at the upper echelons of the SS, such remarks were tantamount to heresy and could only be seen as a clear affront to the ideas and aspirations of the Nazi movement.[83]

In essence, what the AKD sought to do was to insinuate itself as the mediator in any church-state dispute involving Catholicism. That this, in the eyes of most Nazi officials, was presumptuous and constituted an open challenge to Nazi hegemony in all matters related to religion and the intellectual welfare of the German nation was clear to everyone involved. And no issue in church-state relations was more contentious than the status of Catholic organizations for youth, women, and young men. The Nazis were so concerned about the threat of an open break between the church and state that in May 1934 Rudolf Hess, deputy leader of the Nazi Party, announced the establishment of the Department for Cultural Peace (Abteilung für kulturellen Frieden) as a special agency in the NSDAP headquarters. As the head of the new agency Hess selected Hermann von Detten, a member of the Nazi Party who had served in the AKD leadership since the organization's founding in the fall of 1933 but who now resigned his posts in the AKD in order to devote himself fully to the responsibilities of his new office.[84] Whatever Hitler's motives might have been in orchestrating these developments, they did little to alleviate the crisis that had developed in the regime's relationship with the Catholic Church over differing interpretations of the protection that Article 31 of the Reich Concordat supposedly afforded Catholic youth and student organizations. Relations between the church and regime had in fact deteriorated to such a point that the bishops were in the process of drafting a pastoral letter that would have been read from the pulpit in all German churches on 1 July 1934 that categorically rejected Nazi claims of spiritual primacy and accused the regime of fostering a neo-pagan crusade against more than a thousand years of Christian culture in Germany.[85]

The very fact that Germany's Catholic bishops were on the verge of going public with their dissatisfaction with the regime's policies meant that the AKD had not only failed to persuade church officials to go along with the incorporation of Catholic youth organizations into the Hitler Youth but also in its larger mission to build a bridge between Catholicism and National Socialism, between the cross and the swastika. From the perspective of the regime, the AKD had become superfluous and no longer served any meaningful purpose. By this time, however, the fate of the AKD had become inextricably linked with the larger crisis that gripped Germany in the early summer of 1934, the crisis in Hitler's relations with SA chief of staff Ernst Röhm and Hitler's two-pronged strike against the SA leadership and conservatives in the vice chancery and elsewhere who had had the temerity to plot for the overthrow of the Hitler dictatorship. It was an accident that the so-called "Night of the Long Knives" of 30 June 1934 should claim among its victims two prominent Catholics: Erich Klausener, the Berlin leader of the Catholic Action (Katholische Aktion) and Adalbert Probst, the recently appointed Reich leader of the German Youth Force (Deutsche Jugendkraft). In the course of the action the SS occupied the vice chancery, shot Papen's press secretary Herbert von Bose, and confiscated the records of the AKD from an office that Thun had shared with Baron Wilhelm von Ketteler. Thun himself was arrested later that evening but was subsequently released after spending only a few hours in Gestapo custody.[86]

The events of 30 June–2 July 1934 sealed the fate of the AKD. Papen would submit his resignation as vice chancellor and accept reassignment to Vienna in a move that only confirmed his moral bankruptcy and left many of his erstwhile associates deeply embittered by what they saw as a feeble act of betrayal.[87] Thun would try to avert the AKD's dissolution with impassioned appeals to Hitler and Papen in which he reassured them of the organization's loyalty to the goals and aspirations of the Nazi state and stressed the important role the AKD had to play in achieving those goals.[88] But none of this would prove to any avail. On 19 September 1934 the AKD officially dissolved itself in a move to which Papen gave his full blessing. The AKD, Papen wrote in a post mortem thanking all of those who had unselfishly dedicated themselves to its goal and aspirations, had accomplished a great historical mission in "fusing together the spiritual forces of our nation and in grounding the future of the Third Reich on the eternal and blessed prophesy of Christianity."[89]

Conclusion

Papen's rosy epitaph notwithstanding, the resumé of the League of the Cross and Eagle and the Alliance of Catholic Germans was quite disappointing. The BKA, a creation of Catholic intellectuals and clerics who sought to infuse the new Nazi state with the spirit and values of Christianity, never got off the ground and found itself stymied by the indifference and hostility of the regime. The AKD, on the other hand, was the political creation of Franz von Papen, who hoped that it would somehow provide him with the political base he needed to assert himself as a member of the national government. But the AKD never succeeded in gaining the confidence of Germany's Catholic episcopacy or overcoming the deep-seated mistrust that the leaders of the Catholic Church in both Germany and the Vatican harbored toward the new Nazi regime. And without the support of the Catholic bishops, the AKD was to prove worthless to Papen and his Nazi masters in bringing the Catholic youth into the Nazi fold or in almost any other issue where there was a conflict between the interests of the church and those of the Nazi state. Although the founders of the AKD had launched their organization in order to mediate more effectively between church and state, in virtually every case where there was a conflict between church and state, Papen and the AKD sided with the regime. The AKD's much vaunted "Aufruf zum Abwehrkampf" from May 1934 and its outspoken defense of Christian cultural values were part of an attempt to reassert its independence from the state but ended up inflaming the anti-Catholic sentiments of prominent Nazi leaders. As a result, the AKD remained isolated from the two institutions it had hoped to influence, the Catholic Church and the Nazi state. The crisis in church-state relations that drew to a head in the early summer of 1934 revealed just how superfluous the AKD had become. This was a conflict that could be resolved only through direct negotiations between the two protagonists; there was no longer any room for a self-proclaimed mediator like the AKD. The official dissolution of the AKD several months later only underscored what had already become a well-established fact of political life in the Third Reich, namely that organizations like the AKD that sought to defend specific interests within the framework of the Nazi state had no place in Hitler's new order.

Larry Eugene Jones is professor of history at Canisius College in Buffalo, New York, where he specializes in the history of modern Germany and the Holocaust. He also edited *The German Right in the Weimar Republic: Studies in the History of German Conservatism, Nationalism, and Antisemitism* (2014). He is the author of *Hitler versus Hindenburg: The 1932 Presidential Elections and the End of the Weimar Republic* (2016) and is currently working on a new book tentatively titled *The German Right, 1918–1930: Political Parties, Organized Interests, and Patriotic Associations in the Struggle against Weimar Democracy.*

Kevin P. Spicer, CSC, is the James J. Kenneally Distinguished Professor of History at Stonehill College in Easton, Massachusetts. He is the author of *Hitler's Priests: Catholic Clergy and National Socialism* (2008) and *Resisting the Third Reich: The Catholic Clergy in Hitler's Berlin* (2004), and editor of *Antisemitism, Christian Ambivalence, and the Holocaust* (2007). Together with Martina Cucchiara, he recently translated, edited, and wrote the introduction for *The Evil That Surrounds Us: The World War II Memoir of Erna Becker-Kohen* (2017). He is currently working on a study concerning the relationship of Jews and Catholics in Germany from 1918 to 1945.

Notes

1. For a concise overview, see Rudolf Morsey, "Die katholische Volksminderheit und der Aufstieg des Nationalsozialismus 1930–1933," in Rainer Bendel, ed., *Die katholische Schuld? Katholizismus im Dritten Reich—*

Zwischen Arrangement und Widerstand (Münster, Hamburg, and London: LIT Verlag, 2002), 43–55.

2. For a more precise definition of Catholic conservatives and an analysis of their role in the transition from the Weimar Republic to the Third Reich, see Larry Eugene Jones, "Franz von Papen, Catholic Conservatives, and the Establishment of the Third Reich," *Journal of Modern History* 83 (2011): 272–318, esp. 273–75. For a comprehensive history of Catholic conservatism from its origins in the late nineteenth century to the end of the Weimar Republic, see Christoph Hübner, *Die Rechtskatholiken, die Zentrumspartei und die katholische Kirche in Deutschland bis zum Reichskonkordat von 1933: Ein Beitrag zur Geschichte des Scheiterns der Weimarer Republik*, Beiträge zu Theologie, Kirche und Gesellschaft im 20. Jahrhundert, vol. 24 (Berlin: LIT Verlag, 2014), esp. 612–791.

3. For further details, see Larry Eugene Jones, "Catholics on the Right: The Reich Catholic Committee of the German National People's Party, 1920–33," *Historisches Jahrbuch* 126 (2006): 221–67.

4. For a fuller statement of the Catholic conservative ideology, see Papen's speech "Der Staat von heute und der Einsatz der konservativen Kräfte Deutschlands," in *Wechselburger Tagung 1927*, ed. Hauptausschuß der katholischen Adelsgenossenschaften Deutschlands (Munich, n.d. [1927], 6–11.

5. Doms's efforts are well documented. For example, see his petition to Cardinal Adolf von Bertram, chairman of the Fulda Bishops Conference, 20 July 1931, appended to his letter to Cardinal Secretary of State Eugenio Pacelli, 24 July 1931, United States Holocaust Memorial Museum, Washington, DC (hereafter cited as USHMM), RG-76 001M, Reel 10, Pos. 606, Fasc. 118, as well as the report by Martin Spahn, "Die politische Lage und der deutsche Katholizismus: Vortrag auf dem Parteitag in Stettin am 20.9.1931," Bundesarchiv Koblenz (hereafter cited as BA Koblenz), NL Spahn, 280.

6. On the founding of the AKD, see the appeal "An alle katholischen Deutschen!" signed by Schmidt-Pauli, Schorlemer, and Lossau in the maiden issue of the *Deutsche Volksblatt: Kampfblatt der rechtsgerichteten Katholiken*, January 1932, no. 1, as well as Wagner to Duesterberg, 23 February 1932, Bundesarchiv Berlin (hereafter cited as BA Berlin), R 72/63.

7. For the reaction of the Stahlhelm, see Wagner to Duesterberg, 23 February 1932, BA Berlin, R 72, 307/63, and the memo for Wagner, 4 July 1932, ibid., 307/48; for that of the DNVP, see Doms to Karlewski, 16 January 1932, ibid., 307/68, and Hugenberg to Wagner, 19 January 1932, ibid., 307/74–75.

8. Franz von Papen, "Konservative Staatsführung," *Volk und Reich* 6 (1932): 585–89.

9. Franz von Papen, "Die Sammlung der christlich-konservativen Kräfte," *Die Kampffront: Pressedienst der Kampffront Schwarz-Weiß-Rot* 1, no. 7 (1 March 1933): 1–2. For a recent assessment of Papen's accomplishments as the leader of the non-Nazi elements in the Hitler cabinet, see André Postert, "Das Ende der konservativen Ambitionen: Franz von Papen und die Vizekanzlei im Sommer 1934," *Historisches Jahrbuch* 134 (2014): 259–88.

10. For further details, see the two letters from Max ten Hompel to Watter, 3 March 1933, and Papen, 23 March 1933, both in the Nordrhein-Westfälisches Staatsarchiv, Münster, NL ten Hompel, 185.

11. On the Volksverein, see Gotthard Klein, *Der Volksverein für das katholische Deutschland 1890–1933: Geschichte, Bedeutung, Untergang* (Paderborn: Ferdinand Schöningh, 1996).

12. Ritter, "Mein Ziel und meine Wege," in the archives of the Kommission für Zeitgeschichte, Bonn (hereafter cited as KfZ Bonn), NL Ritter, C1/8–28, here 010–19. For a scholarly biography of Ritter, see Martin Dust, *"Unser Ja zum neuen Deutschland": Katholische Erwachsenbildung von der Weimarer Republik zur Nazi-Diktatur* (Frankfurt a.M.: Peter Lang, 2007), 373–508, esp. 406–25.

13. Emil Ritter, "Zur Lage des politischen Katholizismus in Deutschland," *Schweizerische Rundschau* 33, no. 9 (1 December 1932): 824–35, esp. 830–35.

14. Emil Ritter, "Nationalsozialismus," in *Staatslexikon*, ed. by Hermann Sacher, 5th ed. (Freiburg in Breisgau: Herder, 1932), 5:1750–63, esp. 1760–62.

15. "Deutsch-katholisch-konservativ! Aufruf des Bundes 'Kreuz und Adler' an die katholischen Deutschen," *Neue Preußische (Kreuz-Zeitung)*, 5 April 1933, no. 95.

16. Draft of "Satzungen des Bundes Kreuz- und Adler," n.d. [March 1933], appended to Glasebock to Lüninck, 20 March 1933, Vereinigte Westfälische Adelsarchive, Münster (hereafter cited as VWA Münster), NL Ferdinand Freiherr von Lüninck, 714.

17. Ritter, "Mein Ziel und meine Wege," n.d. [1946], KfZ Bonn, NL Ritter, C1/20.

18. Papen's remarks at a ministerial conference, 15 March 1933, BA Berlin, R 43 II, 1263/52–59. Papen's role as a mediator between Catholicism and the Nazi regime from 1933 to 1945 has been explored in some detail in the recent Papen biography by Reiner Möckelmann, *Franz von Papen: Hitler ewiger Vasall* (Darmstadt: Philipp von Zabern Verlag, 2016), 290–363.

19. The literature on Papen's role in negotiating the Reich Concordat with the Vatican is far too extensive to be cited here. Among others, see Georg Denzler, "Franz von Papen (1878–1969): Katholik, Zentrumspolitiker, Konkordatspromotor und Nationalsozialist," in *Das Reichskonkordat 1933: Forschungsstand, Kontroversen, Dokumente*, ed. Thomas Brechenmacher (Paderborn: Ferdinand Schöningh, 2007), 55–69, esp. 60–64.

20. Papen to Hitler, 28 April 1933, BA Berlin, R 53, 99/8–9.

21. Papen, "Konservative Revolution," *Kreuz und Adler Führerbriefe*, ed. Emil Ritter, May 1933, no. 1, KfZ Bonn, NL Ritter, A9.

22. On Herwegen, see Marcel Albert, "Ildefons Herwegen (1874–1946)," in *Kölner Theologen: Von Rupert von Deutz bis Wilhelm Nyssen*, ed. Sebastian Cüppers (Cologne: J. P. Bachem, 2004), 357–87. On Maria Laach and its place in the religious life of German Catholics, see Richard Faber, "Politischer Katholizismus: Die Bewegung von Maria Laach," in *Religions- und Geistesgeschichte der Weimarer Republik*, ed. Hubert Cancik (Düsseldorf: Patmos Verlag, 1982), 136–58.

23. On the leadership conference in Maria Laach, see *Kreuz und Adler Führerbriefe*, May 1933, no. 1, 14, KfZ Bonn, NL Ritter, A9.

24. On the politics of Abbot Schmidt, see Brigitte Lob, *Albert Schmitt O.S.B., Abt in Grüssau und Wimpfen: Sein kirchenpolitisches Handeln in der Weimarer Republik und im Dritten Reich* (Cologne, Weimar, and Vienna: Bohlau Verlag, 2000), esp. 127–31, 194–200. See also Schmidt to Papen, 3 February and 2–8 March 1933, BA Berlin, R 53, 77/128, 132–33, as well as the extensive correspondence between Papen and Schmitt, 24 June 1933–8 June 1934, BA Berlin, R 58. 8048/237–75.

25. Ritter to Hertling, 10 March 1933, BA Berlin, R 53, 75/206.

26. In this respect, see Spahn to Lüninck, 27 March 1933, BA Koblenz, NL Spahn, 93, and Spahn to Ritter, 3 April 1933, ibid., 20.

27. Ritter, "Bericht über die Organisationsreise des geschäftsführenden Vorsitzenden vom 7.–20. Mai 33," KfZ Bonn, NL Ritter, A9.

28. Ibid.

29. On Ritter's resignation, see his letter to Joos, 14 March 1955, KfZ Bonn, NL Ritter, C4/42.

30. For the best contemporary accounts of the Maria Laach congress, see Wilhelm Spael, "Die dritte soziologische Sondertagung des Katholischen Akademikerverbandes in Maria Laach: Die nationale Aufgabe im Katholizismus—Idee und Aufbau des Reiches; Bericht und Würdigung," *Im Schritt der Zeit: Sonntagsbeilage der Kölnischen Volksszeitung*, 30 July 1933, no. 25, as well as the briefer report by Baron Friedrich August von der Heydte, "Die Katholiken im neuen Deutschland: Dritte soziologische Tagung des Katholischen Akademikerverbandes in Maria-Laach vom 21. bis 23. Juli 1933," *Die schönere Zukunft* 8, no. 47 (20 August 1933): 1131–33. On the significance of this conference, see Klaus Breuning, *Die Vision des Reiches: Deutscher Katholizismus zwischen Demokratie und Diktatur* (Munich: Hueber, 1969), 207–10, and Jones, "Papen, Catholic Conservatives, and the Third Reich," 295–98.

31. For example, see Emil Ritter, *Der Weg des politischen Katholizismus in Deutschland* (Breslau: Bergstadtverlag Wilh. Gottl. Korn, 1934), 301.

32. For further details of the conflict, see Klaus Scholder, *The Churches and the Third Reich*, vol. 1: *Preliminary History and the Time of Illusions 1918–1934*, trans. John Bowden (Philadelphia, PA: Fortress Press, 1988), 493–519; Ludwig Volk, *Das Reichskonkordat vom 20. Juli 1933: Von den Ansätzen in der Weimarer Republik bis zur Ratifizierung am 10. September 1933* (Mainz: Matthias Grünewald, 1972), especially 151–68; and Hubert Wolf, *Pope and Devil: The Vatican's Archives and the Third Reich*, trans. Kenneth Kronenberg (Cambridge, MA: Harvard University Press, 2010), 126–78.

33. On the dissolution of the BKA, see the circular from Thun, October 1933, KfZ Bonn, NL Ritter, A9, as well as AKD *Mitteilungsblatt*, no. 1 (22 November 1933), ibid., A11.

34. Papen to Bertram, 3 October 1933, in *Akten deutscher Bischöfe über die Lage der Kirche 1933–1945*, ed. Bernhard Stasiewski and Ludwig Volk, 6 vols. (Mainz: Matthias Grünewald, 1968–85), vol 1: *1933–1934*, ed. Bernhard Stasiewski (Mainz: Matthias Grünewald, 1968), 403, n.1.

35. AKD, "Merkblatt mit Auszug aus den Satzungen," n.d. (October 1933), KfZ Bonn, NL Ritter, A11.

36. See Thun's address on the AKD to the Rhenish-Westphalian nobility in *Protokoll der ordentlichen Generalversammlung des Rheinisch-Westfälischen Vereins kath: Edelleute am 24. Februar 1934 in Münster i. Westf.* (Münster, 1934), 6–10, in VWA Münster, NL Fredinand von Lüninck, 809. For a brief overview of the AKD and its history, see Herbert Gottwald, "Arbeitsgemeinschaft Katholischer Deutscher (AKD)," in *Lexikon zur Parteiengeschichte: Die bürgerlichen und kleinbürgerlichen Parteien und Verbände in Deutschland (1789–1945),* 4 vols., ed. Dieter Fricke (Leipzig: VEB Bibiographisches Institut, 1983), 1:118–23.

37. Franz von Papen, *Der 12. November 1933 und die deutschen Katholiken: Rede gehalten in der Arbeitsgemeinschaft katholischer Deutscher in der Messehalle zu Köln am 9. November 1933* (Münster: Aschendorff Verlagsbuchhandlung, n.d. [1933]), esp. 11–15.

38. Papen to Bertram, 29 October 1933, Archiwum Archidiecezji we Wrocław (hereafter cited as AA Wrocław), IA 25 z/55, n.f.

39. For example, see Hermann von Detten, "Ziele und Aufgaben der Arbeitsgemeinschaft kath. Deutscher und die Wahl am 12. November," Bürgerverein zu Paderborn, 10 November 1933, in Erzbistumsarchiv Paderborn (hereafter cited as EBA Paderborn), Gen. XVIII, 23. In a similar vein, see Count Eugen von Quadt zu Wykradt und Isny, "Der Katholik im neuen Staat," *Germania,* 9 November 1933, no. 309, and "Arbeitsgemeinschaft kath. Deutscher Wahlaufruf zum 12. November," ibid., 1 November 1933, no. 301.

40. Faulhaber to Bavarian Bishops, 31 October 1933, in *Akten deutscher Bischöfe,* ed. Stasiewski, 1:426–30, here 426.

41. Gröber's position discussed in Faulhaber to German Bishops, 31 October 1933, in *Akten deutscher Bischöfe,* ed. Stasiewski, 1:425.

42. Bertram to German Bishops, 30 October 1933, in *Akten deutscher Bischöfe,* ed. Stasiewski, 1:423.

43. Ow-Felldorf (handwritten note) on Bertram to the German Episcopates, 30 October 1933, in *Akten deutscher Bischöfe,* ed. Stasiewski, 1:424, n.1.

44. "Wahlaufruf zur Volksabstimmung am 12. November 1933," Archiv für Christlich-Demokratische Politik, Sankt Augustin, NL Edmund Forschbach, I-199, 012/3. The Holy See was well informed over the situation of the church in Germany and was greatly displeased at the lack of unity among the German bishops. For example, see Kaas to Gröber, 12 December 1933, in *Akten deutscher Bischöfe,* ed. Stasiewski, 1:482–84.

45. The Breslau and Cologne church provinces issued a revised version of Bertram's initial draft. The Bavarian bishops issued a joint statement based upon Faulhaber's draft. Some dioceses chose not to issue a statement. For a more detailed discussion of the debate among the bishops on the election of 12 November, see Ludwig Volk, *Der bayerische Episkopat und der Nationalsozialismus 1930–1934* (Mainz: Matthias Grünewald, 1966), 148–62.

46. Faulhaber to the Bavarian Episcopates, 31 October 1933, in *Akten deutscher Bischöfe,* ed. Stasiewski, 1:426–30, here 427. On Faulhaber and the AKD in Munich, see Brigitte Zuber, "Die Arbeitsgemeinschaft katholischer

Deutscher (AKD) in München und Kardinal Faulhaber," *theologie.geschichte* 9 (2014), accessed at http://universaar.uni-saarland.de/journals/index.php/ tg/article/viewArticle/849/892.

47. Faulhaber to the Bavarian State Chancellery, 18 November 1933, in *Akten deutscher Bischöfe*, ed. Stasiewski, 1:456–60.

48. Ian Kershaw, *Hitler 1998–1936: Hubris* (New York: W. W. Norton, 1999), 495.

49. Papen to Schmitt, 11 November 1933, BA Berlin, R 58, 8048/267.

50. Conrad Gröber, "Das Wort der kirchlichen Autorität," in AKD *Mitteilungsblatt*, no. 1 (22 November 1933), Historisches Archiv des Erzbistums Köln, Generalia I 23.75; also KfZ Bonn, NL Ritter, A11. Count Thun personally asked Gröber to write this welcoming statement. See Thun to Gröber, 17 November 1933, in *Akten der deutschen Bischöfe*, ed. Stasiewski, 1:461, n.1.

51. Steinmann to Bertram, 4 October 1933, AA Wrocław, IA 25 z/55.

52. Bertram to Papen, 7 October 1933, in *Akten deutscher Bischöfe*, ed. Stasiewski, 1:403–5, here 404.

53. "Ein treuer Sohn der Kirche" to Bertram, 3 November 1933, and "Offener Brief" to Thun, middle of October 1933, both in AA Wrocław, IA 25z/55.

54. Praschma to Bertram, 23 October 1933, AA Wrocław, IA 25 z/55.

55. Bertram to Praschma, 13 November 1933, Bistumsarchiv Fulda (hereafter cited as BA Fulda), 270–12/Fasz. 82.

56. Bornewasser to Reichert, 11 December 1933, Bistumsarchiv Trier Abt. 134–137 AKD.

57. The events of the struggle between the Catholic Youth Organizations and the Hitler Youth are discussed in greater detail in Remigius Bäumer, "Die 'Arbeitsgemeinschaft katholischer Deutscher' im Erzbistum Freiburg: Der Versuch eines 'Brückenschlags' zum Nationalsozialismus," *Freiburger Diözesan Archiv* 104 (1984): 281–313, here 289–98.

58. Decree of the Reich Youth Leader Schirach, 29 July 1933, in *Katholische Jugend in der NS-Zeit unter besonderer Berücksichtigung des Katholischen Jungmännerverbandes: Daten und Dokumente*, ed. Heinrich Roth (Düsseldorf: Altenberg, 1959), 99.

59. On this point, see Bornewasser to Bertram, 24 November 1933, in *Akten deutscher Bischöfe*, ed. Stasiewski, 1:463–64.

60. The dioceses were not named. See Bertram to German Bishops, 22 November 1933, in *Akten deutscher Bischöfe*, ed. Stasiewski, 1:462.

61. Minutes of a private discussion in Freiburg on the position of the Catholic associations in the new Germany, 15 November 1933, in *Akten deutscher Bischöfe*, ed. Stasiewski, 1:467–73, here 468.

62. Bornewasser to Bertram, 24 November 1933, in *Akten deutscher Bischöfe*, ed. Stasiewski, 1:463–64.

63. Bertram to German bishops, 27 November 1933, in *Akten deutscher Bischöfe*, ed. Stasiewski, 1:478–80.

64. Scholder, *Churches and the Third Reich*, 1:575–78.

65. AKD *Mitteilungsblatt*, no. 4 (22 February 1934), Diözesanarchiv Rottenburg (hereafter DA Rottenburg), G 1.5–Nr. 138, also in KfZ Bonn, NL Ritter, A 11.

66. Thun to Gröber, 24 February 1934, with the letter from Schirach to Papen, 20 February 1934 as an enclosure, in *Akten deutscher Bischöfe*, ed. Stasiewski, 1:607–08.

67. The *Deutsche Presse* in Prague described Papen as one who "in less than a few hours became a convinced National Socialist." *Deutsche Presse*, 19 April 1934, AA Wrocław IA 25z/55.

68. Gröber to Pacelli, 2 March 1934, in *Akten deutscher Bischöfe*, ed. Stasiewski, 1:611–14, here 613.

69. Roth, ed. *Katholische Jugend in der NS-Zeit*, 45. On Catholic youth under National Socialism, see Karl-Werner Goldhammer, *Katholische Jugend Frankens im Dritten Reich: Die Situation der katholischen Jugendarbeit unter besonderer Berücksichtigung Unterfrankens und seiner Hauptstadt Würzburg* (Frankfurt a.M.: Peter Lang, 1987); Gisbert Kranz, *Jugend unterm Hakenkreuz: Erinnerungen eines ganz normalen Katholiken* (Augsburg: St. Ulrich, 2007); and Barbara Schellenberger, *Katholische Jugend und Drittes Reich: Eine Geschichte des Katholischen Jungmännerverbandes 1933–1939 unter besonderer Berücksichtigung der Rheinprovinz* (Mainz: Matthias Grünewald, 1975).

70. Ballestrem, "Meine Stellung zur Politik des Zentrums," 19 October 1932, BA Koblenz, NL Hans Graf von Praschma, 32/6–11.

71. Papen used his trip to Silesia also as an opportunity to meet privately with the Association of the Catholic Nobility of Silesia (Vereinigung katholischer Edelleute Schlesiens) in an attempt to enlist its support for the AKD. For further information, see Lob, *Albert Schmitt O.S.B.*, 191–94.

72. Pastoral letter of the Austrian bishops, 21 December 1933, in *Ecclesiastica: Archiv für Zeitgenössische Kirchengeschichte* 17 (28 April 1934): 121–25.

73. "Die christlichen Grundsätze des dritten Reiches: Rede des Vizekanzlers von Papen in Gleiwitz am 14. Januar 1934," VWA Muenster, NL Lünick, Oberpräsident: Kirche und Politik, 1934–35.

74. Ibid.

75. AKD *Mitteilungsblatt*, no. 3 (22 January 1934), KfZ Bonn, NL Ritter, A 11.

76. On the anti-Christian hysteria of Himmler and the SS leadership, see Wolfgang Dierker, *Himmlers Glaubenskrieger: Der Sicherheitsdienst der SS und seine Religionspolitik 1933–1941* (Paderborn: Ferdinand Schöningh, 2002), 139–70.

77. Ludwig Volk, "Der österreichische Weihnachtsbrief 1933: Zur Vorgeschichte und Resonanz," in *Politik und Konfession: Festschrift für Konrad Repgen zum 60. Geburtstag*, ed. Dieter Albrecht, Hans Günter Hockerts, Paul Mikat, and Rudolf Morsey (Berlin: Dunker and Humblot, 1983), 405.

78. Berning to Klein, 24 January 1934, EBA Paderborn, Generalvikariat XVIII, 23. See also the report on "Die Tätigkeit der AKD" from the Catholic Press Agency in Berlin, 16 March 1934, Archiv des Bistums Augsburg, BO 2616.

79. Gröber to Brombacher, 1 February 1934, in *Akten deutscher Bischöfe*, ed. Stasiewski, 1:531–32, here 532. As late as June 1934, some dioceses were still giving permission to their clergy to work with the AKD. For example, see Ordinariat to Weidner (Stadtpfarramt Hanau), 4 June 1934, BA Fulda, 270–12–Fasz. 44.

80. For example, see "Gespräche zwischen Dauser und Faulhaber," *Abendblatt*, 28 February 1934, Archiv des Erzbistums München und Freising, NL Faulhaber, 8057; Schulte to Bertram, 27 March 1934, AA Wrocław, IA 25z/55; "AKD im Saargebiet," *Saarbrücker Landeszeitung*, 11 April 1934, Politisches Archiv des Auswärtiges Amt, Berlin, R72348; and "Aus der AKD," AKD *Mitteilungsblatt* 5 (15 March 1934), DA Rottenburg G1.5–Nr. 138, also in KfZ Bonn, NL Ritter, A 11.

81. Papen to Schulte, 23 March 1934, BA Berlin: R 58, 8048/84–85.

82. "Die AKD zur Lage: Aufruf zum Abwehrkampf!," AKD *Mitteilungsblatt*, no. 6 (15 May 1934), DA Rottenburg G1.5–Nr. 138, also KfZ Bonn, NL Ritter, A 11. The appeal was also published in various newspapers. For example, see "Klarheit im Weltschauungskampf! Ein Aufruf der AKD zur kultur-politischen Lage," *Germania*, 19 May 1934, no. 137.

83. For a sample of the anti-Catholic paranoia that existed at the highest levels of the SS leadership, see the "Lagebericht" on the "Katholische Bewegung" from the Reichsführer SS, Chef des Sicherheitsamt, May–June 1934, in Friedrich Zipfel, *Kirchenkampf in Deutschland 1933–1945: Religionsverfolgung und Selbstbehauptung der Kirchen in der nationalsozialistischen Zeit* (Berlin: De Gruyter, 1965), 272–326, esp. 281–91.

84. "Eine 'Abteilung für den kulturellen Frieden' bei der Reichsparteileitung," AKD *Mitteilungsblatt*, no. 6 (15 May 1934), DA Rottenburg G1.5–Nr. 138, also in KfZ Bonn, NL Ritter, A 11.

85. *Gemeinsamer Hirtenbrief der am Grabe des hl. Bonifatius versammelten Oberhirten der Diözesen Deutschlands* (n.p., n.d. [1934]), esp. 7–12. There are various printed copies of this letter. The copy to which this note refers is to be found in KfZ Bonn, NL Ritter, A11.

86. Affidavit by Thun, 18 April 1946, defense exhibit P-47 in the case against Papen, in *Trial of the Major War Criminals before the International Military Tribunal, Nuremberg 14 November 1945–October 1946*, 42 vols. (Nuremberg, 1949), 40:563–65. On the events in the vice chancery, see Rainer Orth, *"Der Amtssitz der Opposition"? Politik und Staatsumbaupläne im Büro des Stellvertreters des Reichskanzlers in den Jahren 1933–1934* (Cologne, Weimar, and Vienna: Böhlau Verlag, 2016), 495–503.

87. For example, see the verdict of Fritz Günther von Tschirschky, *Erinnerungen eines Hochverräters* (Stuttgart: Deutsche Verlags-Anstalt, 1972), 231–39.

88. Thun to Hitler, 18 July 1934, and to Franz von Papen Jr., 18 July 1934, both in the Russisches Staatliches Militärarchiv, Moscow, NL Papen (Fond 703), 54/18–20.

89. AKD, *Mitteilungsblatt*, no. 8 (20 September 1934), KfZ Bonn, NL Ritter, A9.

Bibliography

Albert, Marcel. "Iledefons Herwegen (1874–1946)." In *Kölner Theologen: Von Rupert von Deutz bis Wilhelm Nyssen*, edited by Sebastian Cüppers, 357–87. Cologne: J. P. Bachem Verlag, 2004.

Bäumer, Remigius. "Die 'Arbeitsgemeinschaft katholischer Deutscher' im Erzbistum Freiburg: Der Versuch eines 'Brückenschlags' zum Nationalsozialismus." *Freiburger Diözesan Archiv* 104 (1984): 281–313.

Breuning, Klaus. *Die Vision des Reiches: Deutscher Katholizismus zwischen Demokratie und Diktatur.* Munich: Hueber, 1969.

Denzler, Georg. "Franz von Papen (1878–1969): Katholik, Zentrumspolitiker, Konkordatspromotor und Nationalsozialist." In *Das Reichskonkordat 1933: Forschungsstand, Kontroversen, Dokumente,* edited by Thomas Brechenmacher, 55–69. Paderborn: Ferdinand Schöningh, 2007.

Dierker, Wolfgang. *Himmlers Glaubenkrieger: Der Sicherheitsdienst der SS und seine Religionspolitik 1933–1941.* Paderborn: Ferdinand Schöningh, 2002.

Dust, Martin. *"Unser Ja zum neuen Deutschland": Katholische Erwachsenbildung von der Weimarer Republik zur Nazi-Diktatur.* Frankfurt a.M.: Peter Lang, 2007.

Faber, Richard. "Politischer Katholizismus: Die Bewegung von Maria Laach." In *Religions- und Geistesgeschichte der Weimarer Republik,* edited by Hubert Cancik, 136–58. Düsseldorf: Patmos, 1982.

Goldhammer, Karl-Werner. *Katholische Jugend Frankens im Dritten Reich: Die Situation der katholischen Jugendarbeit unter besonderer Berücksichtigung Unterfrankens und seiner Hauptstadt Würzburg.* Frankfurt a.M.: Peter Lang, 1987.

Hübner, Christoph. *Die Rechtskatholiken, die Zentrumspartei und die katholische Kirche in Deutschland bis zum Reichskonkordat von 1933: Ein Beitrag zur Geschichte des Scheiterns der Weimarer Republik,* Beiträge zu Theologie, Kirche und Gesellschaft im 20. Jahrhundert, vol. 24. Berlin: LIT Verlag, 2014.

Jones, Larry Eugene. "Catholics on the Right: The Reich Catholic Committee of the German National People's Party, 1920–33." *Historisches Jahrbuch* 126 (2006): 221–67.

——. "Franz von Papen, Catholic Conservatives, and the Establishment of the Third Reich." *Journal of Modern History* 83 (2011): 272–318.

Klein, Gotthard. *Der Volksverein für das katholische Deutschland 1890–1933: Geschichte, Bedeutung, Untergang.* Paderborn: Ferdinand Schöningh, 1996.

Kranz, Gisbert. *Jugend unterm Hakenkreuz: Erinnerungen eines ganz normalen Katholiken.* Augsburg: St. Ulrich, 2007.

Lob, Brigitte. *Albert Schmidt O.S.B., Abt in Grüssau und Wimpfen: Sein kirchenpolitisches Handeln in der Weimarer Republik und im Dritten Reich.* Cologne, Weimar, and Vienna: Bohlau Verlag, 2000.

Möckelmann, Reiner. *Franz von Papen: Hitler ewiger Vasall.* Darmstadt: Philipp von Zabern Verlag, 2016.

Morsey, Rudolf. "Die katholische Volksminderheit und der Aufstieg des Nationalsozialismus 1930–1933." In *Die katholische Schuld? Katholizismus im Dritten Reich—Zwischen Arrangement und Widerstand,* edited by Rainer Bendel, 43–55. Münster, Hamburg, and London: LIT Verlag, 2002.

Orth, Rainer. *"Der Amtssitz der Opposition"? Politik und Staatsumbaupläne im Büro des Stellvertreters des Reichskanzlers in den Jahren 1933–1934.* Cologne, Weimar, and Vienna: Böhlau Verlag, 2016.

Postert, André. "Das Ende der konservativen Ambitionen: Franz von Papen und die Vizekanzlei im Sommer 1934." *Historisches Jahrbuch* 134 (2014): 259–88.

Roth, Heinrich, ed. *Katholische Jugend in der NS-Zeit unter besonderer Berücksichtigung des Katholischen Jungmännerverbandes: Daten und Dokumente.* Düsseldorf: Altenberg, 1959.

Schellenberger, Barbara. *Katholische Jugend und Drittes Reich: Eine Geschichte des Katholischen Jungmännerverbandes 1933–1939 unter besonderer Berücksichtigung der Rheinprovinz.* Mainz: Matthias Grünewald, 1975.

Scholder, Klaus. *The Churches and the Third Reich.* Vol. 1: *Preliminary History and the Time of Illusions 1918–1934.* Translated by John Bowden. Philadelphia, PA: Fortress Press, 1988.

Stasiewski, Bernhard, ed. *Akten deutscher Bischöfe über die Lage der Kirche 1933–1945,* 6 vols. Vol. 1, *1933–1934.* Mainz: Matthias Grünewald, 1968. Edited by Bernhard Stasiewski and Ludwig Volk. Mainz: Matthias Grünewald, 1968–1985.

Tschirschky, Fritz Günther von. *Erinnerungen eines Hochverräters.* Stuttgart: Deutsche Verlags-Anstalt, 1972.

Volk, Ludwig. *Der bayerische Episkopat und der Nationalsozialismus 1930–1934.* Mainz: Matthias Grünewald, 1966.

———. *Das Reichskonkordat vom 20. Juli 1933: Von den Ansätzen in der Weimarer Republik bis zur Ratifizierung am 10. September 1933.* Mainz: Matthias Grünewald, 1972.

———. "Der österreichische Weihnachtsbrief 1933: Zur Vorgeschichte und Resonanz." In *Politik und Konfession: Festschrift für Konrad Repgen zum 60. Geburtstag,* edited by Dieter Albrecht, Hans Günter Hockerts, Paul Mikat, and Rudolf Morsey, 393–414. Berlin: Duncker and Humblot, 1983.

Wolf, Hubert. *Pope and Devil: The Vatican's Archives and the Third Reich.* Translated by Kenneth Kronenberg. Cambridge, MA: Harvard University Press, 2010.

Zipfel, Friedrich. *Kirchenkampf in Deutschland 1933–1945: Religionsverfolgung und Selbstbehauptung der Kirchen in der nationalsozialistischen Zeit.* Berlin: De Gruyter, 1965.

Zuber, Brigitte. "Die Arbeitsgemeinschaft katholischer Deutscher (AKD) in München und Kardinal Faulhaber." *theologie.geschichte* 9 (2014), http://universaar.uni-saarland.de/journals/index.php/tg/article/viewArticle/849/892.

 **13**

German Youth between Euphoria and Resistance

Political Coercion and the Coordination of German Youth

André Postert

"Youth Festivities"

On 24 June 1933, the day of the summer solstice, the NS regime launched the first of its celebrated "Youth Festivities." Nearly everywhere, hundreds of thousands of boys and girls gathered on public squares, lawns, and open-air stages for ritual celebrations with flags, songs, "fire incantations," and campfires to hail the rebirth of the nation. These festivals were to bear witness to the vitality of the new state and to affirm that the young generation stood solidly behind National Socialism. For the first time since Hitler had been appointed Reich chancellor, the Hitler Youth (Hitlerjugend or HJ) was deployed nationwide. In Hanover, Reich Youth leader Baldur von Schirach rose to speak in person: "Here we stand united before the flaming fire to express the indomitable will and spirit of German youth … who today have seized youth leadership in the entire German Reich. Today's celebration, my comrades, is symbolic for all the youths of Germany, for this youth in its entirety is engaged in change and transformation, too."[1]

Since its founding at the Nazi Party Congress in Weimar in 1926, the Hitler Youth had asserted its right to represent all the young people of Germany. In doing this, it laid claim to carry on the traditions of the youth movement after World War I and the longing for the "ethnic community" or *Volksgemeinschaft* that had always embodied the promise of unification and unity. During the 1920s, young people tended to organize themselves into clubs; approximately half of all German male youth held some sort of club membership. It seemed to contemporaries as if the youth was every bit as fragmented as German society as a whole. Clubs, organizations, groups, and leagues of various tendencies and spheres vied for popularity. For nearly all protagonists of the German youth movement, it was beyond a doubt that this division—if the state and the nation were to recover again—had to be overcome, and the youth needed to be repatriated. The ethnic community was more of a mythical ideal than a pragmatic project, but it existed in the thinking of the German youth as much as in the German public in general. Indeed, the HJ had advocated its unity promise with totalitarian rigor from the beginning. In 1934, Baldur von Schirach stated in retrospect, "The organization of the HJ declares itself as the only and singular representation of the German youth. This is its totalitarian claim. As the NSDAP is Germany's only political party, so the HJ is the only German youth organization."[2]

Indeed, during the summer solstice of 1933 something until then unique could be observed. For the first time it appeared as if the "solidarity of the youth" was not merely an empty phrase devoid of content—as during the Weimar Republic—but had, in fact, come within reach in the new state. Not only Hitler Boys (Hitlerjungen) and BDM-Girls (Bund Deutscher Mädel or BDM) had been deployed for the propaganda celebration. At times, school classes under the guidance of teachers, sports and gymnastics clubs, choral groups, and groups of Protestant—and to a somewhat lesser degree, Catholic—youth, as well as members of smaller youth leagues, could be spotted. In some locations, members of the Stahlhelm Youth (Stahlhelm Jugend) acted as stewards. Inappropriate literature—the so-called *Schmutzliteratur*, including the writings of Marxist and Jewish authors—was solemnly burned.[3] Although in many cases the gatherings had to be canceled due to inclement weather, the "Youth Festivities" turned out to be a decisive propaganda success for the Reich Youth Leadership (Reichsjugendführung or RjF), established in 1933, and its chief, Baldur von Schirach. The NS dictatorship impressively demonstrated that, apparently, it could depend on the support of many young people. With their evening "fire incantations," the HJ drew on traditions of the youth movement: Johann Wolfgang von Goethe, Georg Stammler, and Heinrich George were also recited as well as obvious National Socialist poets.[4] The propaganda show was an important link in a sequence of activities staged by the Nazi regime from the very beginning to court and win the support of German youth.

On the one hand, the "Youth Festivities" were a demagogic spectacle, no less so than others and, of course, not a reflection of societal reality: although many youths participated, not all of them did so voluntarily as they had been subjected to pressure in classrooms and organizations beforehand. By the end of June, the Social Democrat and Communist youths of Germany had already been forced into the underground, and Jewish organizations had been excluded from participation. On the other hand, it would be a mistake to construe the image of youthful enthusiasm that was visible in so many places throughout the country if the "Youth Festivities" were seen as little more than a clever propaganda ploy or as the result of state coercion. To the contrary, in the year of the so-called "seizure of power" or *Machtergreifung*, HJ membership had risen to two million. Even in the eyes of contemporaries, this growth was spectacular. One cannot possibly understand this success without taking into consideration the genuine euphoria of large parts of the younger generation. The reason the Nazi regime was able to prevail against its political opponents in the initial phase of the Third Reich was that it was supported by a significant part of the population. As in the case of the "Youth Festivities," the regime continuously strove to assure itself of youth's support and, alternatively, to create a scenario of intimidation against all those who chose to keep their distance and rejected the new times. On a small scale, what happened in the German youth movement only mirrored the logic of the large-scale National Socialist seizure of power.

Political Youth Organizations

According to general understanding, the "political coordination" or *Gleichschaltung* of the youth associations in Germany was preceded by a bold action: on 5 April 1933, a brigade of HJ leaders under the aegis of Karl Nabersberg occupied the Reich Committee of German Youth Associations (Reichsausschuss der deutschen Jugendverbände or RddJ) in Berlin. The field office, an office building at Alsenstrasse in the embassy quarter, was stormed, and records were confiscated.[5] At the time of the Weimar Republic, the umbrella organization coordinated public youth work and gathered approximately nine million youths of different organizations under its aegis; the largest group consisted of sports and gymnastics clubs, followed in number by the Christian youth organizations, then by the party youth as well as the leftist labor union youth, and, finally, by the free youth leagues. From the RjF's viewpoint, the umbrella organization was a "true democratic construct" that needed to be occupied and deactivated before the monopoly claim of the HJ could be successfully asserted.[6] By the same token, the state field offices of the RddJ had been occupied throughout the country. As a result, the largest and most important umbrella organization in the German youth movement had been effectively neutralized. Reich youth leader Baldur von Schirach unscrupulously exploited the opportunities afforded by the Reichstag fire decree of 28 February and Enabling Act of 24 March 1933 to confiscate records that provided information about addresses and likely whereabouts of individuals who had been active in the German youth movement before the Nazis assumed power.[7]

As of 22 April 1933, Social Democratic, Communist, and Jewish youth organizations were expelled from the RddJ. The general manager, Hermann Maass, a Social Democrat, was dismissed. Ludwig Vogt, chairman of the umbrella organization, reluctantly accepted Schirach's claim to leadership. A few days later, Schirach repeated the procedure at the Reich Organization of German Youth Hostels whose two thousand hostels came under the authority of the NS state from then on. The final liquidation of the RddJ followed in July.[8] Hitler rewarded the radical procedure by appointing Schirach "Youth Leader of the German Reich" on 17 July. As such, Schirach now "headed all the organizations of male and female youth as well as the youth organizations of adult organizations."[9] From then on, the establishment of new clubs and organizations required his consent, which he granted only in rare cases.

Doubtlessly, the youth from the left spectrum were the first to find themselves confronted with the repercussions of the "takeover": following the Reichstag election on 5 March, youth houses of the Socialist Labor Youth were occupied in many places and without further ado converted into office buildings for the NSDAP, the SA, and the HJ. Even so, the NS Youth continued to reside in small cellar rooms or houses that were little more than shacks, but at least in the metropolitan cities of Cologne, Hamburg, and Berlin they succeeded in establishing headquarters from which they could recruit and organize propaganda marches through the inner cities.[10] The leftist progeny, until then organized in the Socialist Labor Youth (Sozialistische Arbeiterjugend or SAJ) and the Communist Youth Organization of Germany, tried to defend themselves against the destruction of their structures with leaflets and sabotage but, in the end, without success.

The leading politician of the SAJ, Erich Ollenhauer, opposed violent opposition in any form whatsoever. In April 1933 he pleaded instead for the dissolution and reorganization of the SAJ in a "completely legal" form, a concept that appeared illusory to most. The following month Ollenhauer and the SPD's exile executive relocated to Prague. In the meantime, the dispute over the possibility of retreating into the underground and just how this was to be managed had severely limited the Labor Youth's opportunities for action from the very beginning. Already in mid-March the SAJ and other left-wing youth organizations had been proscribed in several German states such as Bavaria, Baden, and Württemberg.[11] In terms of the size of their membership, the left-wing party organizations had not been impressive during the final phase of the Weimar Republic, particularly in contrast to the paramilitary youth divisions of the Reich Banner Black-Red-Gold (Reichsbanner Schwarz-Rot-Gold). Structures proved too unstable and groups too quarrelsome among themselves for successful resistance, all the more so because in the spring of 1933 the Hitler Youth had begun to attract left-wing youth and young workers.[12] The fact that the majority of the SAJ districts had already dissolved themselves before they were officially banned has been explained by historians as an attempt on the part of the SAJ to "protect its members from persecution."[13] It is debatable, however, whether this serves as sufficient explanation in and of itself. From the Free Labor Union Youth (Freie Gewerkschaftsjugend), whose organization had been largely crushed in the spring, as well as from the youth divisions of the Reich Banner, more and more of Germany's socialist youth found their way into the ranks of the HJ.[14] In any event, the greater challenge to the National Socialists lay less in the courageous but, in the final analysis, largely ineffective resistance by Germany's working-class youth than in the large bourgeois organizations that remained organizationally as well as structurally intact and that continued to define the everyday life of German youth during the National Socialist seizure of power.

However, as had become apparent during the Nazi assault against the RddJ, vehement protest from this side was unlikely. Schirach's success against the bourgeois youth organizations was not so much the result of his own action as from the erosion and weakness of his bourgeois competitors. Children and youth, especially from the bourgeois-conservative milieu, had flocked to the HJ in droves ever since spring. Here one found a deep-seated skepticism about the Weimar party system that greatly enhanced the new regime's appeal after the Reichstag election on 5 March. First and foremost, it was the national-conservative youth organizations and the paramilitary Defense Youth (Wehrjugend) that suffered the greatest losses. All of this followed a similar pattern. Against the background of a mass exodus of members, disputes erupted everywhere about how they should cooperate with the HJ and effectively paralyzed local chapters that already found themselves in the midst of dissolution. The National Socialists immediately took advantage of this opportunity by implying to their often no less antidemocratic competitors that they were being infiltrated by Marxists and that they had not been sufficiently sincere about their participation in the National Revolution.[15]

In the summer of 1933, the dissolution and incorporation of the larger national youth organizations in almost all of the German states, among them the youth divisions of the DNVP—the Bismarck Youth

League (Bismarckjugend der DNVP) and Combat Ring of Young German Nationalists (Kampfring junger Deutschnationaler)—followed in quick succession, while the Young German Order (Jungdeutscher Orden) and its "Grand Master" Artur Mahraun did their best to resist prohibition. As an example of the self-conformity of the Defense Youth, the Stahlhelm deserves particular attention. The children of Stahlhelm loyalists had been organized into two groups: the younger ones for the most part in the Scharnhorst League (Scharnhorst, Bund der Jungmannen) and the ones over eighteen in the Young Steel Helmet (Jungstahlhelm). The latter were subordinated to the SA leadership at the beginning of July after an agreement with Stahlhelm leader Franz Seldte, who also served as Reich secretary of labor in Hitler's cabinet.[16] By this time, many of the Stahlhelm chapters had already disintegrated or were close to it. According to a subsequent agreement, approximately ten to fifteen thousand members of the Scharnhorst League were to be integrated into the HJ by 30 September in the "spirit of comradery" and without "undue duress."[17] In this case, too, many youths had by now joined the HJ, arbitrarily. In December the HJ area leader "North Sea" was able to announce truthfully that the dissolution of the Steel Helmet youth groups had been made possible by complete "cooperation between the incorporated and the current comrades of the Hitler Youth" and that the transfer had now been completed with the caveat that members of the former Scharnhorst League were permitted to continue wearing their uniforms for a short while.[18] HJ leaders, however, expressed concern that "all of a sudden there had been an enormous influx of youth that had been raised in an entirely different political spirit."[19] Years later badges and uniform items from dissolved organizations were still displayed despite the fact that this had been banned.[20]

Another example of the fact that the political coordination of bourgeois youth organizations had been preceded by an erosion of their membership basis could be seen in the fate of the giant employee union with its main seat in Hamburg, the German National Union of Commercial Employees (Deutschnationaler Handlungsgehilfen-Verband or DHV). Already in the early Weimar Republic the organization had promoted the political radicalization of its own youth on a massive scale through ideological education and social work in a *völkisch* spirit. By early 1933 a substantial portion of its apprentices—in large part as a consequence of high youth unemployment—demonstrated an affinity for the Hitler movement. As a result, the youth groups and culture functionaries of the DHV found themselves in opposition to the union leadership, which in the late Weimar Republic followed a somewhat national-conservative course. Alfred Krebs, a DHV functionary and NSDAP member, reported to Hitler in 1930 that an estimated three-quarters of the youth in the union were sympathetic to National Socialism.[21] It thus comes as no surprise that the DHV youth placed itself under the control of the Nazi youth organizations on their own initiative without ever consulting the organization's leadership and long before the DHV's "coordination" into the German Labor Front (Deutsche Arbeitsfront or DAF). This included the hiking club Wayfaring Journeymen (Fahrende Gesellen), which in the last years of the Weimar Republic had called for the liquidation of democracy in favor of a new Reich with an aristocratic authority.[22] In April 1933, the leadership of the Hiking League (Wanderbund) decided to disband. At first, the DHV was baffled by the exodus of its youth groups and apprentices but then began to actively promote it. For those in authority there remained little alternative but, as in the case of Swabia, to cooperate with the HJ area leaders in advocating "by any means possible the incorporation of all DHV apprentice members into the Hitler Youth. … The aim of this incorporation," as the statement announcing this event claimed, "is the strengthening of the state-affirming youth front against all professional and confessional fragmentation tendencies in the German youth."[23] At the end of 1933, the large-scale incorporation of other bourgeois clubs and political youth groups took place, as in the case of young girls with the absorption of the Young Luise Club (Jung-Luisenbund) and the "Little Cornflowers" ("Kornblümchen"), both affiliated with the Queen Luise League and hostile to the republic.[24] By the end of the year, the divestiture of party youth organizations as well as the Defense Youth had been completed nearly everywhere. As an HJ leader in Württemberg exclaimed, "Out of what were once small groups there has emerged the mighty brown ribbons of German youth who … are marching today. Even if in the beginning the Hitler Youth had to fight for respect and recognition, it has become 'the' German youth, the state youth."[25]

Gymnasts and Sport Youth

By 30 April 1933, organized Social Democrat and labor union workers' sports had been banned throughout the entire country. At this point the youth elements of the German labor movement and leftist milieu fell back on sports clubs or founded camouflage clubs of their own that were prohibited as soon as they were discovered and identified as such.[26] For the organized youth of Germany, sports clubs had presented the most important factor already during the Weimar Republic.

Although by no means unpolitical, the clubs had escaped seizure by the RjF during the first phase of the Nazi takeover. This had two reasons. In the first place, organized sports had already been targeted for state-sponsored conformity. The Reich Sports leader, Hans von Tschammer und Osten, was expressly appointed to this position and pursued personal ambitions of his own that did not automatically concur with the HJ's monopolistic claim. Secondly, the sports clubs were not in direct political competition with the HJ, a fact that might have accounted for why they were only second or third in Reich Youth leader Schirach's list of priorities.

From the beginning, the leadership of the Hitler Youth stressed that its mandate to "unify German youth" also gave it priority in the field of organized sports. The representatives of the German Gymnastic Federation (Deutsche Turnerschaft or DT)—the most important sports organization within the RddJ—had demonstrated their loyalty and subservience almost immediately following the Nazi assumption of power. Edmund Neuendorff, a racist and antisemitic pedagogue as well as high-ranking functionary in the DT, led the campaign for political conformity. Prior to the Fifth German Sports Festival in Stuttgart, celebrated as the "Festival of the German People" and "Epiphany of the Nation" in the spring of 1933, he had asked Hitler to appoint him its patron.[27] Furthermore, Neuendorff supported Schirach's efforts to force the dissolution of various sports groups within the HJ. Neuendorff also believed that it would be possible for the NS Youth Organization to upgrade sports as a pre-military defense program in accordance with an educational mandate from the state. In 1933 he played a leading role in the publication of *Der Deutsche Jungendienst*, a remarkable volume in which various pedagogues and sports representatives contributed their own ideas regarding pre-military fitness in the Third Reich. This manual was primarily directed toward sports clubs and young boys who had not yet joined the NS Youth Organization. Their slogan, also embraced by sports functionaries throughout the country, left little room for interpretation: "The boys hail the new Reich. They pledge allegiance and reckless abandon."[28]

The "Youth Festivities" of 24 June 1933 afforded Baldur von Schirach and the RjF an excellent opportunity to align sports clubs throughout the country more closely with the HJ. Sports organizations were instructed to contact the NS offices about the implementation of the opening ceremony.[29] In the larger cities, the torso of the RddJ, the regional branches which had been staffed with HJ leaders, coordinated the integration of sports groups and gymnasts into the ranks of the Hitler Youth. Adolescent club members received the uniforms,

caps, badges, and flags of the NS youth organization. While marching through the inner city and during the subsequent festivities, club
members were no longer distinguishable from members of the Hitler
Youth and the League of German Girls. The attendant propaganda
skillfully managed to produce uniformity even where sports clubs and
the HJ had not yet officially melted into one. It still remained unclear,
however, as to how the two-sided relationship between the HJ and the
sports clubs would develop in the future. Schirach himself kept a low
profile, perhaps out of respect for the Reich Sports leader Neuendorff,
but this did not prevent numerous sports clubs from joining the Hitler
Youth on their own. In Thuringia the HJ regional leadership reached
an agreement with local sports organizations in October 1933. Club
members were to be admitted to the NS Youth Organization, while at
the same time HJ members were encouraged to join the sports clubs.
This agreement stipulated that the sports clubs would assume sole
responsibility for physical fitness whereas the HJ would be responsible
for political education.[30] In several Thuringian cities and small towns,
reciprocal transfers were celebrated during fall vacation and in the
winter months.[31] Such agreements were a regional phenomenon, but in
Schirach's view they were simply a temporary answer to a problem that
still required a solution for the entire Reich. What this suggests is that
political coordination was not imposed on the clubs and their members
exclusively from above but that local and regional leaders frequently
anticipated what was happening throughout the Reich as a whole.

It was not until 1934 that a solution for the entire Reich was
achieved. Schirach declared 1934 to be the year of "Education and Inner
Orientation." The HJ was to sharpen its profile through physical exercise and pre-military training, including the use of firearms, as well
as terrain sports and sporting events.[32] A leading functionary of the
German Gymnastic Organization, Thilo Scheller, announced in March
1934 that "we ... will soon be working in the larger *Volksgemeinschaft*.
The Reich Sports leader will transfer us to the Hitler Youth within the
next few days."[33] This, however, did not take effect until November. By
then, children and youths desiring to join a sports club had to belong
to the NS youth organization in order to be accepted. To be sure, sports
clubs were not forbidden, but at this point they could only conduct
their activities in close conjunction with the HJ. With the participation
of the population, the incorporation of the gymnasts and the sports
youth into the Hitler Youth in the fall of 1934 was accompanied by
celebrations in small towns and villages.[34] In larger cities this was celebrated by the speeches of party officials and mass demonstrations.[35]
From this point on, the HJ combined the two tasks of ideological educa-

tion and physical fitness, that is, defense sports for the boys and gymnastics, ballet, and dancing for the girls. The sports activities were "not [to be] an end to themselves as it is unavoidably the case in gymnastics and sports clubs." Instead, the youth needed to be forged into a force "joyous in contest, ideologically steadfast, and physically strong."[36]

The RjF's conception that service in the Hitler Youth would supersede and replace club-oriented sports did not materialize immediately. In fact, youths who joined the NS youth organization so that they could belong to a club did not always show up for HJ service. The RjF lacked the means to coerce children and youths into performing service for the Hitler Youth and rightly feared that their organization would lose popularity if direct force were applied. The consequence of this situation was foreseeable: progressively, the NS youth organization consisted more and more of nominal and passive members who felt little commitment to the larger goals of the movement. At this point, signs of fatigue that the leaders of the Nazi youth movement had not anticipated were becoming increasingly apparent.

Incorporation of the *Bündisch* Youth

From the perspective of the RjF, the destruction of the so-called *bündisch* youth movement was every bit as important as the dissolution of the party youth organizations and the incorporation of the sports clubs. The *bündisch* youth movement followed in the tradition of the Wandervogel and Pathfinder movements of the Weimar Republic and was anything but an ideologically coherent entity. To the contrary, it was a conglomerate of disparate organizations, groups, and assemblages of one kind or another with a reformist wing of new scouts and the so-called "Boys Groups" (Jungenschaften), and a nationalist, if not racist, wing that was ideologically aligned with the German right. In between these two wings was a large block that included Christian-oriented organizations such as the Organization New Germany (Bund Neudeutschland) and groups closely tied to bourgeois institutions. The history of Germany's organized youth in the late Weimar Republic was marked by fusions and secessions along all possible fronts.

The *bündisch* youth movement constituted the fourth-largest factor in Germany behind the denominational, political, and sporting clubs. Nevertheless, it carried the distinction of having profoundly influenced the lifestyle of not just German youth but also that of the HJ with its treasury of song, poetry, attire, and nature-oriented activity. By the beginning of March 1933, the most important youth leagues had consolidated themselves into the so called Greater German Confederation (Großdeutscher Bund or GB) in an attempt to resist encroachment by the NS Youth Organization. Unable to find a common ground on which they could unite, the leaders of groups as diverse as the German Pathfinder Organization (Deutscher Pfadfinderbund), the German Irregular Voluntary Corps (Deutsche Freischar), and the Young Charge (Jungsturm) had only one common goal: to somehow survive Hitler's state. With a membership estimated at fifty thousand, the Greater German Confederation was under the tutelage of retired vice admiral Adolf von Trotha, who had been in charge of various youth organizations during the Weimar Republic. His goal was to secure cooperation with Hitler's government in preserving the independence of the Greater German Confederation through his ties to conservative politicians. Neither Hitler nor Reich Youth leader Schirach, however, was interested in a coexistence of the NS Youth and *bündisch* youth groups.

The Greater German Confederation had been an elitist project from the very beginning, and quite an artificial one at that. Ordinary members of the youth organizations that belonged to it frequently marched with the swastika flag or sang Nazi songs as they marched through the streets. In the Weimar Republic, many of these organizations—but particularly those that identified themselves with Germany's political right—had linked their demands for the *Volksgemeinschaft* to revolutionary slogans and the ideas from the *völkisch* cults. The willingness to commit one's self to the new order was especially pronounced among this cadre of German youth, and its affinity for National Socialism was apparent early in the history of the organization. At the Greater German Confederation youth camp in Grunewald in April 1933, participants frequently decorated their tents with flags bearing the swastika. Several eminent leaders of the *bündisch* youth had recommended to their followers that they should take the plunge and join the HJ rather than allow themselves to be steered by the "political reactionaries" into the Greater German Confederation.[37] Elements of the German Free Corps' leadership, among them the chemist Hermann Kügler and future Halle professor Ernst Raupach, had already gone over to the Hitler Youth, while others such as Helmuth Kittel represented a National Socialist wing within the Greater German Confederation and torpedoed the federal leadership in its efforts to preserve *bündisch* autonomy. A short while later, NS youth leaders were able to point with justification to the fact that "the members of the smaller organizations were defecting to the Hitler Youth" in droves.[38] Many ordinary members called for their leaders to cooperate with the representatives of the new order, although only a few were advocating integration into the HJ or the political coordination of the German youth movement with the Nazi state. Occasionally, however, as in the case of the Irregular Voluntary Corps of the Young Nation (Freischar Junger Nation) in Mecklenburg, entire groups embraced the Hitler Youth and joined it enthusiastically.[39] It was against the background of these developments that the confederation leadership under Trotha declared its loyalty to the National Socialist regime at the end of March 1933 in an attempt to avert the ban of the Greater German Confederation while simultaneously accommodating the demands of its members. The tactically motivated maneuver, however, did not work. On 17 June—the same day that Schirach was appointed Youth Leader of the German Reich—the GB was incorporated into the HJ by Schirach's official order.[40] Instead of securing its survival, the GB's hierarchical organizational structure only facilitated Schirach's seizure of the many *bündisch* organizations belonging to the Greater German Confederation.

Admiral von Trotha had reluctantly consented to the GB's incorporation into the Hitler Youth not only because the defection of GB members to the Hitler Youth foreshadowed his organization's complete disintegration but also because the conservatives in Hitler's government failed to support him in his struggle with Schirach and because many within the Greater German Confederation itself were urging voluntary liquidation.[41] Trotha and his faithful had been steering a national-conservative course and learned that an adage that had been frequently applied to conservatism held true here as well, namely that skepticism about democracy paired with citizenship in the German nation prevented an honest desire for autonomy from developing into real opposition. As the GB federal leadership told its members, "The Reich Chancellor has not revoked … the enacted ban on the Greater German Confederacy. The decree of the Chancellor as the order of sovereignty is binding on us. … The resolution demanded of us will be difficult for many. But we recognize that the battle for Germany that is being fought today will be decided by a higher judge."[42]

The majority of German youth organizations voluntarily integrated themselves into the Hitler Youth during the course of the summer. For the most part, it was not even necessary to order their prohibition. Among those organizations that joined the HJ at the beginning of June were the Nerother Organization, the Forest Scouts, the German Falconry, the Wandervogel Organization, and the Kyffhäuser Youth.[43] Youth groups that declined voluntary liquidation were eventually prohibited. The *Reichsschaft* of German Pathfinders, which the NS regime had spared dissolution out of consideration for scouts abroad, was suspended in May 1934 on the grounds that scouting "had become a haven for young people who held a hostile disposition toward the new state."[44] Interesting special cases existed in the *völkisch* faction, for example, in the case of the Artam League (Bund Artam). At the end of the 1920s the Artam League had mobilized several thousand youths with the aim of resettling rural farmland. The brew of *völkisch* ideology, esotericism, and rural romanticism was closely related to the ideology of the National Socialists. In 1933 the so called Artamans were able to maintain a certain degree of autonomy from the Hitler Youth until its last remaining branch in Mecklenburg was integrated into the HJ in October 1934: "Not as the recently converted will the Hitler Youth accept them with a wry look. No! As old fighters and combatants for Germany's youth and future will the Hitler Youth joyfully welcome into their ranks the modest workers of the soil."[45] The organization was a germ cell for the later HJ Farmland Service (Landdienst). Its leader, Albert Wojirsch, joined the social office of the RjF.[46]

The *bündisch* youth movement did not immediately cease to exist simply because former *bündisch* youths now wore HJ uniforms or marched under the swastika. It was not uncommon for units of the former *bündisch* youth movement to use Nazi youth organizations to continue its old traditions. Numerous HJ units, primarily those in the countryside and in small towns, frequently managed to escape the uninterrupted control of the RjF. In the spring of 1933 Reich authorities in Berlin began to establish the administration and structures of the Nazi youth organization. This process was tedious and confusing. *Bündisch* groupings were able to act with amazing independence, all the more so because they were no longer embedded in organizations like the Greater German Confederation. For example, a fairly sizable Young Volk (Jungvolk) unit in Ulm — Young District 120 (Jungbann 120) — was placed under the leadership of Karl Ruth, an old *bündisch* leader. Under Ruth's protective wing, Young Pathfinders, Wandervogel, and other *bündisch* groups as well as individual members of the Scharnhorst Youth were able to continue their nature-oriented traveling (Fahrtenwesen) and communal life of the Weimar era. Their newspaper *Totila* was neither decorated with the swastika nor was any message of greetings to the "Führer and Reich Chancellor" Hitler to be found in its pages. The Young District 120 carried on in this form over an amazing two and a half years before Ruth was finally deposed and replaced by a veteran Young Volk leader in 1936. Ruth, in the meantime conscripted for military service, was forbidden to have any further contact with children and youth. The Young District 120 was divided up, and new units were created.[47]

This was by no means the only example of where *bündisch* life continued under the cloak of the Hitler Youth. For the most part, however, this phenomenon is not to be regarded as a form of political opposition. Many *bündisch* youths had enthusiastically joined the ranks of the Hitler Youth after the Nazi assumption of power in January 1933. Others held on to the rites, symbols, songs, and poems of the *bündisch* youth movement in the face of political coordination and without questioning the aims of the *Volksgemeinschaft*. *Bündisch* members who, for example, modeled themselves after Eberhard Koebel and his German Boys Organization (Deutsche Jungenschaft) continued to exist within as well as outside the bounds of the Hitler Youth even after 1933.[48] They had not entirely disappeared but continued to move about covertly and, in part, illegally. Yet aside from some impressive exceptions, this did not provide a genuine motif for resistance. This was the decisive factor that accounted for the step-by-step destruction of the *bündisch* youth, even though it may not have occurred immediately everywhere. As a young HJ fealty leader from Württemberg announced to his mayor at the end of 1933, "The ... statistics for the year 1933 registered an unimaginable boost for the National Socialist Youth. Today, now this youth ... has become the youth of the state. All youth organizations have been dissolved or immersed in the H.J. The great work of unification is in the making."[49]

Incorporation and Resistance of Christian Youth

Without a doubt, the first phase of the Nazi "takeover" of German youth organizations turned into an enormous success for the RjF. Still, in sharp contrast to the propaganda slogans of its leadership, German youth did not entirely identify with the HJ in either 1933–34 or subsequent years. This was due almost entirely to the resistance of Christian youth organizations that did not—or at least not entirely—accept the Hitler Youth's claim to an absolute monopoly over Germany's youth organizations.

No sooner had the German Center Party (Deutsche Zentrumspartei) been dissolved in the summer of 1933 than the Nazi regime initiated a massive action against Catholic youth organizations. Demands for the dissolution of Catholic youth clubs and for their integration into the Nazi youth movement had already been raised.[50] In the interim the police, acting on instructions from Schirach, occupied and closed down staffed offices. Records were confiscated.[51] On several occasions the state governments issued bans against the denominational youth organizations, sometimes against wearing uniforms or badges, at other times against singing or merely gathering in public places. First and foremost, sports served as an effective instrument to limit the scope of their operations. In September 1933 all youth organizations except the sports clubs were permanently banned from conducting physical training.[52] In this case, too, it took some time before the directive took effect. The Protestant and the Catholic youth organizations frequently continued to practice sports as usual. Occasionally Christian youth groups defied the control of authorities by disguising themselves as groups from the Hitler Youth or League of German Girls and by flying swastika flags. By the end of 1933, this kind of behavior had become so pervasive that the state youth leader of Baden, Friedrich Kemper, called upon authorities to conduct an intensive investigation.[53]

The NS Youth sought to cause as much trouble as possible for the confessional sports clubs, even in the more mundane trivialities of everyday life, as, for example, when the HJ suddenly requisitioned gymnasiums to make it impossible for the confessional sports clubs to hold meetings of their dance groups.[54] In the late summer of 1933, Hitler Boys, goaded by the speeches of their leaders, ransacked Catholic youth houses, ran amok in recreational camps, and attacked youth groups in broad daylight. But the ban on Catholic youth organizations that had been issued earlier that summer had to be rescinded inasmuch as it threatened to strain relations with the Vatican. Article 31 of the Reich Concordat, which had been signed on 20 July, protected organizations that were essential to the missionary work of the church from the threat of dissolution by the state. Hitler feared that a move against these organizations would provoke resistance among Germany's Catholic population, with the result that Schirach and the leadership of the Hitler Youth had no alternative but to observe the regulations of the Concordat. The most important Catholic youth organization was the Catholic Young Men's Association of Germany (Katholischer Jungmännerverband Deutschlands or KJVD) with an estimated 365,000 young men organized in approximately 6,100 clubs. Protected by the Reich Concordat, the KJVD continued to exist well into the 1930s despite considerable restrictions on its activities. Although its youth groups portrayed themselves as self-confident and independent, they too were obliged to commit themselves in public to the new order: "For we are just as German as everyone else and adhere to Volk and Fatherland as loyally as anyone else. ... Just as we are closely linked to the Volk, so we stand in the state of Adolph Hitler ... who has placed so much trust in the German youth."[55] It was not until February 1939 that the Young Men's Association was prohibited by Heinrich Himmler's Directive for the Protection of Volk and State.

From the beginning, the NS regime pursued a two-pronged strategy with respect to the Christian youth organizations: the animosity, bans, and repression of Christian youth groups were accompanied by appeals wooing the support of Christian youth. Almost certainly, the sense of "national renewal" that seemed to be sweeping Germany after years of crisis also struck a responsive chord in the ranks of the Christian youth organizations. In processions by the Catholic Storm Horde (Sturmschar), the *bündisch*-style-oriented hiking club within the KJVD, swastika flags could be seen and were not—as contemporary photographs clearly prove—a "fleeting illusion based in the deceit of the Nazi regime" as Catholics later maintained.[56] In fact, Baldur von Schirach had planted the seed of false hope among Christian youth leaders when he threatened to "dissolve and proscribe only those denominational youth organizations that dared to oppose the revolutionary will of the German youth in whatever form."[57]

In light of this statement, many clubs were encouraged to believe that their existence was not endangered as long as they professed their commitment to the new state order. At the "Youth Festivities" at the end of June 1933, it became evident that in many places Christian youth groups—often voluntarily with only a few under pressure—willingly followed the regime's expectations.[58] In numerous cities, Christian youth groups took part in the ritual summer solstice celebrations. Protestant clubs proved particularly susceptible in this regard. Much of this stemmed from the development of Protestantism itself. For example, the influence of the "German Christians" (Deutsche Christen) and those clergymen who supported a fusion of Protestant doctrine and Nazi ideology reached its zenith in the year following Hitler's appointment as chancellor. Protestant youth, even more so than Catholic youth, began a large-scale exodus to the HJ that spring. Time and time again Protestant youth clubs in the Rhineland and elsewhere voluntarily disbanded since, as they themselves quickly came to realize, the "extreme exodus" rendered their work impossible.[59] In the Reich Organization of Protestant Young Men's Clubs (Reichsverband der Evangelischen Jungmännerbünde), the second-largest Protestant umbrella organization with approximately 265,000 male members, church representatives and youth leaders had difficulty arguing against the demand for the unification of the German youth since they themselves had embraced the *Volksgemeinschaft* and its vision of a German nation that transcended the divisions of social class, confession, and region. Approximately 20 percent of the Christian Pathfinders of Germany (Christlicher

Pfadfinderschaft Deutschlands or CPD) joined the Hitler Youth in the summer of 1933. In Württemberg and Frankfurt am Main, for example, Protestant youth leaders had sought to reach an agreement with the HJ about dividing up tasks and areas of activity.

But efforts to develop a framework for coexistence stood virtually no chance of success under the conditions of the dictatorship.[60] It was against the background of these developments that the Reich Bishop Ludwig Müller mapped out the terms of an agreement with Schirach in the fall of 1933 that took effect on 19 December and provided for the corporative integration of the Protestant Youth Office (Evangelische Jugendwerk) into the Hitler Youth. This umbrella organization included all the larger Protestant organizations such as the CPD. All Protestant children and youth were "to be integrated into the Hitler Youth and its subdivisions" and "to wear the service dress of the Hitler Youth according to their affiliation. ..."[61] After having banned the simultaneous membership in a Nazi youth organization and a denominational organization at the beginning of August, the RjF took the next important step in the political coordination of Christian youth when the Protestant Reich Church formally recognized the Hitler Youth as the "embodiment of the state idea" entrusted with the "uniform state-political education" of German youth through National Socialism.[62] It became obvious, however, that integration would not proceed as smoothly as hoped when just before Christmas there were public protest demonstrations in several cities. Youths who had not joined the HJ during the promotional campaign of the preceding months refused to enter the ranks of the NS Youth.[63] In the following year Reich Youth pastor Karl Friedrich Zahn was given the task of reorganizing the Protestant Youth Office in order to expedite the integration of Protestant youth organizations into the Nazi youth movement. His predecessor, Erich Stange, had been accused of "sabotaging the desired conciliation" and had been relieved of his position at the beginning of 1934 and expelled from the NSDAP.[64] Zahn, on the other hand, proved to be a true party loyalist: "Due to Reich Bishop and Youth Leader, the Church and the Youth have taken a big step toward each other. The [Protestant] Church joyfully lets its youth march under the flags of the Third Reich, and from now on the Hitler Youth will no longer see in the Church and its youth work an enemy, but a good friend."[65]

Implementing the integration agreement, however, proved to be more difficult than anticipated inasmuch as it was frequently circumvented, not adhered to, or openly attacked. Speakers for the Protestant Youth Office embarked upon a confrontational course at the begin-

ning of 1934 when they argued that the umbrella organization constituted an "independent organization" and therefore "had nothing
to do with the Church as such." Reich Bishop Müller was not in a
position to control the situation,[66] while Otto Riethmüller, on the other
hand, was quick to assert himself. Since 1928 Riethmüller had assumed
responsibility for the Protestant Reich Organization of Female Youths
(Evangelischer Reichsverband weiblicher Jugend or ERwJ) which was
one of the most important Protestant youth organizations with approximately three hundred thousand members. At the end of December
Riethmüller had—in what he described as a "grave hour"—composed
a circular in which he accepted the regime's claim for responsibility
over the training of the youth while at the same time expressing opposition to the Protestant youth's integration in the HJ. As Riethmüller
wrote, "We really want the unity of the German youth—a joyous inter-
relationship of the entire youth in the service of the new Germany!
However, after renewed, thorough investigation we do not consider
the … way … viable in practice. It will not achieve any unification of
the German youth, prevents truly educational work, and gradually
destroys all independent Protestant youth work, with which not even
the German Reich can dispense."[67] Similar protests also came from
other quarters; for example, from the CPD Reich Leadership, which
declared in a memorandum that it "was not willing to bow to a clerical
claim to power for integration into the Hitler Youth."[68]

On 4 January 1934 Reich Bishop Müller reacted to these protests
with a "gag order" that prohibited demonstrations as well as the printing and distribution of pamphlets and circulars. In the weeks that followed, the first voluntary dissolutions and integrations took place. In
the Düsseldorf administrative district, where Protestantism tended to
be weak, Protestant youth organizations were prohibited from meeting or demonstrating together, although the organizations themselves
were not banned. Pursuant to an agreement with the local HJ leadership, the affected clubs released all members under the age of eighteen
on 7 February so that they could be absorbed into the NS Youth.[69]
This particular procedure took place in similar ways at different times
according to location and administrative district. Throughout much of
western and northern Germany the Hitler Youth was able to register
a series of important triumphs in the spring of 1934. However, wher-
ever Protestantism was more deeply rooted in the local population,
the integrative process proved to be much more tedious. In Thuringia
the HJ had carried on its crusade "against denominational reaction"
and its "youth parties"[70] ever since the winter of 1933. In Saxony, the
heartland of the German Christians, there were particularly intense

conflicts in the summer of 1934. In many cases, clergy refused to allow HJ leaders access to club membership lists. Young Protestant activists wrote pamphlets or circulars, left notices in showcases, and demanded that the leaders of the HJ acknowledge Protestant youth work. Acting on their own initiative, low-ranking HJ leaders infiltrated youth groups and private discussions by clergymen in order to accumulate evidence of "subversive activities." In one report from HJ battalion leader Karl Linke in Dresden, the statement by the clergyman that "We claim the complete totality as coming from Christ" had been underlined several times by the HJ leaders.[71] The oppositional wind was so strong that HJ activists felt obliged to issue their own pamphlets. "Everywhere, pamphlets are being circulated to stir up hatred," wrote another HJ leader. "Despise these blasphemers who exclude themselves from the ethnic community! Destroy the pamphlets that are meant to stir up hatred."[72] In desperation, worried parents turned to teachers because they feared that the HJ would have a negative influence on the religious beliefs of their children.[73] A situation report from Saxony highlighted not only the distribution of pamphlets and graffiti on public office buildings but also the craftiness of Protestant youth groups that, after having been dissolved, either continued their existence behind the back of Nazi youth organizations or reestablished themselves under new names. As resistance to the incorporation of Protestant youth groups into the Hitler Youth stiffened, reports about these activities assumed an even more radical tone. For example, as one report read, "The information about sabotage and wreaking havoc are mounting daily throughout the country. ... It is absolutely necessary that appropriate measures be taken against those unscrupulous agitators and saboteurs who want to prevent the unification of German youth and that those who show such disrespect for their *Volk* should suffer severe punishment."[74]

There can be little doubt in the light of the existing documentation that Germany's Christian youth—Catholic as well as Protestant—demonstrated the will to resist and the courage to stand up against the regime and its youth leaders. The political coordination of the Christian youth did not occur overnight but was a slow process replete with conflicts that continued well into the 1930s. But the National Socialists were able to exclude rival groups more and more from the public eye or, in some cases, completely eliminate them. As a general rule, this occurred earlier to Protestant youth groups and only later to Germany's Catholic youth. Over time, uniforms and flags of Christian youth and camps, hiking, and pilgrimages organized by Christian youth organizations became increasingly marginal phenomena in the youth culture of the Third Reich. Spheres of resistance continued to exist, but Christian youth work was forced back into church sanctuaries and the realm of pastoral ministry. As Richard Reckewerth, an HJ area leader in Halle, reported—perhaps prematurely and with an all too obvious intent—at the end of 1934, "The monumental work of the formal organizational unification of the German youth and its power and uniform coordination in the Hitler Youth ... was finally complete."[75]

Conclusion

Just as living conditions for adults had undergone a dramatic transformation during the Nazi seizure of power, so had that of the young people. Up until 1934 the political coordination of the German youth had progressed smoothly with the exception of the denominational organizations. A colorful mosaic composed of countless organizations, groups, leagues, and circles had been shattered and the components newly reassembled into a monopoly. Although the Nazi regime never succeeded in achieving complete ideological saturation or even the organizational integration of all German children and youth, the unification of the young generation was more than empty propaganda. In the first year after the Nazi assumption of power, the male and female membership of the Hitler Youth grew to two million; by the end of 1934 the figure stood at almost 3.6 million.[76] As in the case of German society as a whole, the broad spectrum of divergent forces can also be discerned within the ranks of German youth. At the beginning the Nazi regime relied upon repression and bans of workers' youth organizations while at the same time offering new opportunities for their members to become involved in the activities of the Nazi youth movement.[77] With "Let go of everything old" as its cultural-political battle cry,[78] the Hitler Youth sought to mobilize the emotions of German youth against such sclerotic authorities as school, church, bureaucracy, and employers. Youth, in turn, did not respond passively inasmuch as a substantial segment of German youth euphorically celebrated the Nazi assumption of power. However, alongside this euphoria there existed skepticism and various forms of rebellion, particularly within the ranks of the denominational organizations. Whereas a large segment of German adolescents voluntarily found their way into the HJ and while many youth organizations chose political self-conformity after March 1933, others reacted with caution or resistance. As a result, the political coordination of the youth organizations proceeded in a confusing manner, often more dynamically than controlled and marked by a wide range of behavioral patterns. Still, the core question remains: what enabled the Hitler Youth in just a few months to transform itself into the most powerful youth organization in all of Germany and into the dominating entity in many young peoples' lives? Whoever seeks to explain this development will necessarily have to make choices. Older studies have given center stage to politics and have concentrated their analyses on the regime's actions, particularly on those of Reich Youth leader Baldur von Schirach and the RjF leadership. These studies focused their attention on the repressive character of politics "from above," committed to crushing any and all resistance in establishing the regime's totalitarian claim to power. The foundation for the political coordination of German youth was always violence, propaganda, and the ruthless suppression of all resistance. In this narrative, youth appears as an actor only rarely and remains for the most part a kind of passively moving mass wedged between the structures and contentions of a dictatorship organizing itself for the exercise of its power. This image, however, falls short and is in need of correction.

Without taking into consideration the passionate euphoria with which large parts of the younger generation greeted the establishment of the Third Reich, it is impossible to comprehend the lightning-speed at which the Hitler Youth transformed itself into the mass organization of German youth. Whoever stood apart or refused to participate seemed destined to be excluded from an epochal transition in the history of the German nation. Just how vigorously older representatives of the youth movement were committed to National Socialism can be seen in a volume published in 1934 and edited by the popular Nazi author Will Vesper under the title *Deutsche Jugend: 30 Jahre Geschichte einer Bewegung*. Here important spokesmen and role models of bourgeois youth offered testimony to the Nazi dictatorship: Knud Ahlhorn of the Free Germans, Hermann Mitgau and Werner Kindt of the Wandervogel, Arnold Littmann and Wilhelm Flitner of the *bündisch* youth, Thilo Scheller as a representative of the gymnastics youth, and Guida Diehl of the German Christian New Land Organization (Neulandbund).[79] If the concept of the *Volksgemeinschaft* served as a point of reference for the more mature spokesmen of the German youth movement, this was no less true in the case of its younger adherents as well. The political coordination of German youth organizations took many different forms from violent pursuit, cooperative initiatives, and voluntary subordination by clubs and organizations—forced dissolution here, voluntary self-coordination there. The common thread in almost all of this was that the political coordination of Germany's youth organizations had been preceded by the large-scale exodus of their members and the erosion of their popular base. As the demand for the "unification of the youth" found widespread acceptance both ideo-logically and organizationally, and as the defection of ever-increasing numbers of German youth to the HJ seemed to legitimate the project of a political *Volksgemeinschaft*, youth clubs and organizations found them-selves forced more and more on the defensive until they voluntarily acquiesced in their coordination into the Nazi youth movement. This process was not centralized or directed from above. On the contrary, it proceeded chaotically in diverse ways on regional as well as local levels, eventually becoming a process in its own right. The RjF in Berlin as well as its HJ district leaders throughout Germany only needed to hold in place what in practice had already taken shape at the local level and on its own momentum.

It was against the background of these developments that high-rank-ing National Socialists began to use the term *Staatsjugend* to describe the NS youth organization, even though this term was not completely accurate until the enactment of the Hitler Youth laws in December 1936. From a purely formal point of view, the Hitler Youth was and contin-ued to be a party formation in every sense of the word, although as an arm of the RjF it was also entrusted with far-reaching responsibility for the education, training, and physical fitness of German youth. At first, the regime relied upon the principle of voluntary participation even as pressure on parents and in schools began to mount. Only if children and youth joined the HJ of their own free will, claimed Reich Youth leader von Schirach, would the junior organization appear legitimate as a "Foundation of the Youth for the State."[80] The fact that the Hitler Youth had not been founded solely on federal political coordination from above but had grown out of the initiative and euphoria of youth itself would distinguish it from other fascist and authoritarian youth organi-zations throughout Europe.[81] Nonetheless, the revolutionary momen-tum that had characterized the Hitler Youth during the Nazi assumption of power had begun to die down by the middle of the 1930s. For the first time in the history of the movement, membership growth stagnated in 1935. With the implementation of the "compulsory youth service" in 1939, the Hitler Youth was ultimately transformed into an organization based on constraint and the use of force. By then the HJ had developed into a gigantic apparatus that no longer relied on youthful enthusiasm and euphoria but on indoctrination, surveillance, and control.[82]

André Postert is currently a research associate at the Hannah Arendt Institute for the Research on Totalitarianism in Dresden. He is the author of *Von der Kritik der Parteien zur außerparlamentarischen Opposition: Die jungkonservative Klub-Bewegung in der Weimarer Republik* *und ihre Auflösung im Nationalsozialismus* (2014); "Das Ende der konservativen Ambitionen: Franz von Papen und die Vizekanzlei im Sommer 1934," *Historisches Jahrbuch* (2014); and most recently *Hitlerjunge Schall: Die Tagebücher eines jungen Nationalsozialisten* (2016). He is currently working on a publication on the Hitler Youth from 1933 to 1945 and on a book about toys and play in Germany from 1900 to 1945.

Notes

1. Speech by Baldur von Schirach, 24 June 1933, quoted in Kurt Maßmann, *Hitlerjugend—Neue Jugend! Vom Wege der Jugend in die deutsche Zukunft* (Breslau: F. Hirt, 1933), 66–69, here 66.
2. Baldur von Schirach, *Die Hitler-Jugend: Idee und Gestalt* (Berlin: "Zeitgeschichte," 1934), 69.
3. "Feiern im Märkgräferland, Baden," *Baseler Nachrichten*, 25 June 1933, no. 171. A respective statement by the municipal district office (*Bezirksamt*) Lörrach to the Baden ministry of the interior in Karlsruhe, 28 June 1933, Landesarchiv Baden-Württemberg, Stuttgart (hereafter cited as LABW Stuttgart), STAF B719/1, merely established that the report about practice throws of hand grenades had been a false report by the enemy abroad.
4. Obergebiet IV. Hitlerjugend (Hj.), *Solstice: Feier der Hitlerjugend*, ed. Eberhard Eckardt (Leipzig and Gera: "Junger Wille," 1934).
5. In this respect, see Michael Buddrus, *Totale Erziehung für den totalen Krieg: Hitlerjugend und die nationalsozialistische Jugendpolitik*, 2 vols. (Munich: K. G. Saur, 2003), 1:1191, and Ernst Klee, *Das Personenlexikon zum Dritten Reich: Wer war was vor und nach 1945* (Frankfurt a.M: Fischer Taschenbuch. 2005), 427, as well as the contemporary report in "Die Geschäftsstelle des Reichsausschusses der Deutschen Jugendverbände," *Das junge Deutschland* 24, no. 4 (April 1930): 211–12.
6. Georg Usadel, *Entwicklung und Bedeutung der nationalsozialistischen Jugendbewegung*, Deutschlands Erwachen: Bücher der Kraft und des Lebens für unsere Zukunft (Bielefeld and Leipzig: Velhagen and Klasing, 1934), 57.
7. Eva Kraus, "Das Deutsche Jugendherbergwerk und seine Gleichschaltung durch die Hitlerjugend (1909–1933)" (PhD diss., Universität Paderborn, 2011), 142.
8. Ibid., 199–215.
9. Wolff's Telegraphisches Büro on the appointment of Baldur von Schirach as Youth Leader of the German Reich, 17 June 1933, in *Die Hitler-Jugend 1933 bis 1945: Programmatik, Alltag, Erinnerungen. Eine Dokumentation*, ed. Jakob Benecke (Weinheim and Basel: Juventa, 2013), 100.
10. On the occupation of the Workers' Youth in Cologne, see issues of *Der Westdeutsche Beobachter* for 14 April, 2 May, and 28 June 1933.
11. Wolfgang Uellenberg-van Dawen, *Gegen Faschismus und Krieg: Die Auseinandersetzungen sozialdemokratischer Jugendorganisationen mit dem Nationalsozialismus* (Essen: Klartext, 2014), 167–75.

12. Winfried Speitkamp, *Jugend in der Neuzeit: Deutschland vom 16. Bis zum 20. Jahrhundert* (Göttingen: Vandenhoeck and Ruprecht, 1998), 229.
13. Franz Osterrath, "Sozialistische Arbeiterjugend," in *Die deutsche Jugendbewegung 1920 bis 1933; Die bündische Zeit; Quellenschriften*, ed. Werner Kindt, Dokumentation der Jugendbewegung III (Cologne and Düsseldorf: Diederichs-Verlag, 1974), 1011–25.
14. Uellenberg-van Dawen, *Gegen Faschismus und Krieg*, 177–79.
15. Wolfgang Krabbe, *Die gescheiterte Zukunft der ersten Republik: Jugendorganisationen bürgerlicher Parteien im Weimarer Staat* (Opladen: Verlag für Sozialwissenschaften, 1995), 195.
16. Further documents on the two organizations may be found in BA Berlin, R72/1891 and 1892, as well as in ibid., R72/479, and 482:2.
17. The "Scharnhorst League" was integrated into the HJ. See the regulatory statutes in *Der Thüringer Sturmtrupp*, 1 October 1933, no. 1.
18. See Joachim Tautz, *Militaristische Jugendpolitik in der Weimarer Republik: Die Jugendorganisationen des Stahlhelm, Bund der Frontsoldaten; Jungstahlhelm und Scharnhorst, Bund deutscher Jungmannen* (Regensburg: Roderer, 1998), 457.
19. The state commissioner of Baden about the establishment of leader schools in the state of Baden, 8/10/1933, LABW Stuttgart, STAF 8719/1.
20. "Traditionsarmabzeichen," in *Gebietsbefehl Sachsen*, 1936, no. 1, 11.
21. George L. Mosse, "Die deutsche Rechte und die Juden," in *Entscheidungsjahr 1932: Zur Judenfrage in der Endphase der Weimarer Republik*, 2nd ed., ed. Werner E. Mosse (Tübingen: J. C. B. Mohr, 1966), 226.
22. Heinz Dähnhardt, "Die Liquidation der Demokratie," in *Der fahrende Gesell* 20, no. 3 (April 1932): 42–45.
23. Agreements between the leadership of district #20 of the Hitler Youth and the DHV State Youth leader Swabia, 7 December 1933, Staatsarchiv Ludwigsburg (hereafter cited as StA Ludwigsburg), PL 509, Bü 25.
24. "Gegen die Parteien der Jugend," *Der Thüringer Sturmtrupp*, 1 October 1933, no. 1.
25. Non-Com HJ-Battalion Leader III to the mayor's office and the municipal council Brackenheim, 29 December 1933, StA Ludwigsburg, PL 509, Bü. 7.
26. Uellenberg-van Dawen, *Gegen Faschismus und Krieg*, 180–82. As a local example for the prohibition of a camouflage club, see "Spielsperre für Heidenauer Sport-Club: Amtliche Bekanntmachung des Gaues Ostsachsen," *Der Freiheitskampf*, 28 June 1933, no. 148.
27. Radio speech by Neuendorff, "Zukunftsaufgaben des deutschen Sports," *Der Freiheitskampf*, 31 August 1933, no. 31. See also Elk Franke, "Der Sport nach 1933: Äußere Gleichschaltung oder innere Anpassung?," in *Die Berliner Universität in der NS-Zeit*, 2 vols., ed. Rüdiger vom Bruch (Wiesbaden: Steiner, 2005), 2:243–56.
28. *Deutscher Jungendienst: Handbuch*, ed. Deutscher Jungendienst (Potsdam: Voggenreiter, 1933), esp. 6.
29. "Anordnung der Thüringer Staatskommissars über die Durchführung des Festes der Jugend," *Thüringer Staatszeitung*, 16 June 1933, no. 139.
30. "Zusammenschluss der Turn-und Sportjugend mit der HJ. Durchführungsbestimmungen," *Der Thüringer Sturmtrupp*, October 1933, no. 2.

31. "Übernahme der Altenburger Turnerjugend in die HJ," *Der Thüringer Sturmtrupp*, December 1933, no. 5.
32. Reichsjugendführung, ed., *HJ im Dienst: Ausbildungsvorschrift für die Ertüchtigung der deutschen Jugend* (Berlin: Bernard and Graefe, 1935), 6.
33. Thilo Scheller, "Volksgemeinschaft," *Turnerjugend*, 1934, no. 3, edition A.
34. Quoted from a myriad of recorded sources on this topic, here the club news (*Vereinsmitteilungen*) of the Turngemeinde Pirna e. V., 9, no. 11 (November 1934).
35. "Hitler-Jugend und Sportjugend eins," *Der Freiheitskampf*, 19 November 1934, no. 322, 9.
36. "Der Führer des Gebietes 16/Sachsen HJ, Weltanschauliche Schulung u. körperliche Ertüchtigung," in Hitler-Jugend, Gebiet Sachsen, *Die Gefolgschaft*, no. 6: *Bann und Jungbann-Sportfeste 1935* (n.p., 1935), 1.
37. Christoph Schubert-Weller, *Hitlerjugend: Vom "Jungsturm Adolf Hitler" zur Staatsjugend des Dritten Reiches* (Weinheim: Juventa, 1993), 108.
38. Usadel, *Entwicklung und Bedeutung der nationalsozialistischen Jugendbewegung*, 56.
39. *Niederdeutsche Beobachter*, 17 May 1933. For the larger context, see Hermann Langer, *"Im gleichen Schritt und Tritt": Die Geschichte der Hitlerjugend in Mecklenburg von den Anfängen bis 1945* (Rostock: Ingo Koch Verlag, 2001), 30–33.
40. *Wille und Werk: Pressedienst der deutschen Jugendbewegung*, 6, no. 25 (June 1933): 1. See also Arno Klönne, *Jugend im Dritten Reich: Die Hitlerjugend und ihre Gegner* (Cologne: Papyrossa Verlag GmbH, 2003), 22.
41. Schubert-Weller, *Hitlerjugend*, 109–11.
42. "Befehl Großdeutscher Bund, 26 June 1933," in *Die Pfadfinder in der deutschen Jugendgeschichte*, part 2.1: *Quellen und Dokumente aus der Zeit bis 1945*, ed. Kurt Seidelmann (Hanover: Schroedel, 1980), 258–59.
43. *Der Freiheitskampf*, 29 June 1933, no. 149.
44. Heydrich, "Verfügung des geheimen Staatskriminalamtes," 26 May 1934, in Arno Klönne, *Jugendliche Opposition im "Dritten Reich"* (Dresden: Sächsische Landeszentrale für politische Bildung, 2005), 42–43.
45. "Die Artamanen der Hitler-Jugend eingegliedert," in *HJ im Vormarsch*, 26 October 1934, no. 9.
46. Ibid.
47. See among other items the documents in Stadtarchiv Ulm, NL Goetz Lauser, 34b.
48. See Matthias von Hellfeld, *Bündische Jugend und Hitlerjugend, Zur Geschichte von Anpassung und Widerstand 1930–1939*, Archiv der deutschen Jugendbewegung, vol. 3 (Cologne: Verlag Wissenschaft und Politik, 1987).
49. Fealty leader of the HJ to the Mayor Ebert of the Township of Möckmühl, 23 January 1934, StA Ludwigsburg, PL 509, Bü 7.
50. "Katholische Jugend will zur HJ," by a Catholic priest in *Essener Nationalzeitung*, 2 November 1933.
51. Statement by the head of the diocese about the police action against the Catholic youth organizations, n.d., Historisches Archiv des Erzbistums Köln, Gen. 1, 23.11.4, Teil II. See also Hans-Christian Brandenburg, *Die*

Geschichte der HJ: Wege und Irrwege einer Generation (Cologne: Verlag Wissenschaft und Politik, 1968), 152–54.

52. Friedrich Kemper, youth leader of the State of Baden, "Guidelines for the Youth Work of the State of Baden," 8 December 1933, LABW Stuttgart, STAF B719/1.

53. Ibid.

54. BdM 471/121 to Vicar Heberle, Gundelsheim, 6 March 1934, StA Ludwigsburg, StAL PL 509, Bü 7.

55. Katholische Jungmännerbund, ed., *Wer kämpft mit uns?* (n.p., n.d.), 4, in "Chronik der Sturmschar Wesel," Archiv des Jugendhauses Düsseldorf.

56. Franz-Josef Krehwinkel, "Sturmschar unter dem NS-Regime," in *Sie hielten stand: Sturmschar und Katholischer Jungmännerverband Deutschlands*, ed. Bernd Börger and Hans Schroer (Düsseldorf: Verlag Haus Alternberg, 1989), 99.

57. Baldur von Schirach on his tasks as Youth Leader of the German Reich, 24 June 1933, in *Jugend unter der NS-Diktatur: Eine Dokumentation*, ed. Karl Heinz Jahnke (Rostock: Koch, 2003), 56–59.

58. "Evangelische Jugend beteiligt sich an den Sonnwendfeiern," *Essener Nationalzeitung*, 23 June 1933.

59. Dekan Schöttler to the Westbund in Wuppertal-Barmen, 14 November 1933, in Archiv des CVJM-Westbundes, Wuppertal, 37–15 (CVJM Köln-Süd).

60. Dieter von Lersner, *Die evangelischen Jugendverbände Württembergs und die Hitler-Jugend 1933/34*, Arbeiten und Geschichte des Kirchenkampfes, vol. 4 (Göttingen: Vandenhoeck and Ruprecht, 1958), 36.

61. Agreement between Schirach and the Reich leader of the Protestant Youth Office of Germany, Ludwig Müller, on the incorporation of the Protestant youth organizations into the Hitler Youth, 19 December 1933, in Benecke, *Hitler-Jugend*, 108.

62. Ibid.

63. Schubert-Weller, *Hitlerjugend*, 144.

64. *Der Thüringer Sturmtrupp*, January 1934, no. 2.

65. Karl Friedrich Zahn, *Kirche und Hitlerjugend* (Berlin: Zentralverlag, 1934), 15.

66. Report of a discussion between the Saxon ministry of the interior and the local group leader of the Evangelischen Jugendwerk Eberhard, 11 January 1934, Sächsisches Hauptstaatsarchiv Dresden (hereafter cited as SHStA Dresden), 10736: Ministerium des Innern, No. 22522.

67. O. Rietmüller, "An die Eltern unserer evangelischen Jugend," n.d., flyer circulated by the Evangelischer Reichsverband weiblicher Jugend, ibid.

68. "Unsere Stellung zur Jugend," 12 November 1933, quoted in Günter Brakelmann, *Kreuz und Hakenkreuz: Christliche Pfadfinderschaft und National-sozialismus in den Jahren 1933/1934* (Kamen: Hartmut Spenner, 2013), 168.

69. "Volksparolen," 2 December 1933 and 3 January 1934, in *Dokumentation zur Geschichte der Stadt Düsseldorf 1935–1945* (Düsseldorf: Pädagogisches Institut der Landeshauptstadt Düsseldorf, 1983), 131.

70. "Sie sind gar bald verloren," *Der Thüringer Sturmtrupp*, December 1933, no. 6.

71. Transcript sent to Battalion Leader Karl Linke, 10 January 1934, SHStA Dresden, 10736: Ministerium des Innern, No. 22522.
72. HJ-Battalion Leader IV, signed Battalion Leader Süß, n.d., ibid.
73. Report by the principal of the city *Gymnasium* in Halle, 23 May 1933, Stadtarchiv Halle, Schulverwaltungsamt, no. 556, vol. 1.
74. Gebietsführung des Gebietes Sachsen in der HJ, "Denkschrift über die Eingliederung der ev. Jugend in die Hitlerjugend," n.d., ibid.
75. Hitler-Jugend Gebiet Mittelland, ed., *Werden. Sein. Wollen* (Berlin, 1934), 2.
76. Buddrus, *Totale Erziehung*, part 1, 288.
77. Fritz Hippler, *Jugend fordert: Junge Generationen zwischen Gestern und Morgen* (Berlin: Gerhard Stalling, 1934), 32–43.
78. Ernst Lahmann, "Werbelied," in *Das Gesicht der Hitler-Jugend: Den Freunden der Schöneberger Jugend zum 1–jährigen Bestehen des Bannes 278* (Berlin: Richter, 1934).
79. Will Vesper, *Deutsche Jugend: 30 Jahre Geschichte einer Bewegung* (Berlin: Holle and Co., 1934).
80. Schirach, *Idee und Gestalt*, 71ff.
81. Ibid.
82. André Postert, "Freiwilligkeit und Verpflichtung: Widersprüche der nationalsozialistischen Jugendorganisation in ihrer Entwicklung," *Totalitarismus und Demokratie* 12 (2015): 186–207.

Bibliography

Benecke, Jakob, ed. *Die Hitler-Jugend 1933 bis 1945: Programmatik, Alltag, Erinnerungen; Eine Dokumentation*. Weinheim and Basel: Juventa, 2013.

Brandenburg, Hans-Christian. *Die Geschichte der HJ: Wege und Irrwege einer Generation*. Cologne: Verlag Wissenschaft und Politik, 1968.

Buddrus, Michael. *Totale Erziehung für den totalen Krieg: Hitlerjugend und die nationalsozialistische Jugendpolitik*, 2 vols. Munich: K. G. Saur, 2003.

Franke, Elk. "Der Sport nach 1933: Äußere Gleichschaltung oder innere Anpassung?" In *Die Berliner Universität in der NS-Zeit*, edited by Rüdiger vom Bruch, 2 vols. Wiesbaden: Steiner, 2005, 2:243–56.

Hellfeld, Matthias von. *Bündische Jugend und Hitlerjugend: Zur Geschichte von Anpassung und Widerstand 1930–1939*, Archiv der deutschen Jugendbewegung, vol. 3. Cologne: Verlag Wissenschaft und Politik, 1987.

Jahnke, Karl Heinz, ed. *Jugend unter der NS-Diktatur: Eine Dokumentation*. Rostock: Koch, 2003.

Klee, Ernst. *Das Personenlexikon zum Dritten Reich: Wer war was vor und nach 1945*. Frankfurt a.M: Fischer Taschenbuch. 2005.

Klönne, Arno. *Jugend im Dritten Reich: Die Hitlerjugend und ihre Gegner*. Cologne: Papyrossa Verlag GmbH, 2003.

———. *Jugendliche Opposition im "Dritten Reich."* Dresden: Sächsische Landeszentrale für politische Bildung, 2005.

Krabbe, Wolfgang. *Die gescheiterte Zukunft der ersten Republik: Jugendorganisationen bürgerlicher Parteien im Weimarer Staat.* Opladen: Verlag für Sozialwissenschaften, 1995.

Kraus, Eva. "Das Deutsche Jugendherbergwerk und seine Gleichschaltung durch die Hitlerjugend (1909–1933)." PhD diss. Universität Paderborn, 2011.

Krehwinkel, Franz-Josef. "Sturmschar unter dem NS-Regime." In *Sie hielten stand. Sturmschar und Katholischer Jungmännerverband Deutschlands,* edited by Bernd Börger and Hans Schroer, 95–117. Düsseldorf: Verlag Haus Alternberg, 1989.

Langer, Hermann. *"Im gleichen Schritt und Tritt": Die Geschichte der Hitlerjugend in Mecklenburg von den Anfängen bis 1945.* Rostock: Ingo Koch Verlag, 2001.

Lersner, Dieter von. *Die evangelischen Jugendverbände Württembergs und die Hitler-Jugend 1933/34,* Arbeiten und Geschichte des Kirchenkampfes, vol. 4. Göttingen: Vandenhoeck and Ruprecht, 1958.

Mosse, George L. "Die deutsche Rechte und die Juden." In *Entscheidungsjahr 1932: Zur Judenfrage in der Endphase der Weimarer Republik,* 2nd ed., edited by Werner E. Mosse, 183–249. Tübingen: J. C. B. Mohr, 1966.

Osterrath, Franz. "Sozialistische Arbeiterjugend." In *Die deutsche Jugendbewegung 1920 bis 1933: Die bündische Zeit; Quellenschriften,* edited by Werner Kindt, Dokumentation der Jugendbewegung III, 1011–25. Cologne and Düsseldorf: Diederichs-Verlag, 1974.

Postert, André. "Freiwilligkeit und Verpflichtung: Widersprüche der national-sozialistischen Jugendorganisation in ihrer Entwicklung." *Totalitarismus und Demokratie* 12 (2015): 186–207.

Schubert-Weller, Christoph. *Hitlerjugend: Vom "Jungsturm Adolf Hitler" zur Staatsjugend des Dritten Reiches.* Weinheim: Juventa, 1993.

Seidelmann, Kurt. *Die Pfadfinder in der deutschen Jugendgeschichte,* part 2.1: *Quellen und Dokumente aus der Zeit bis 1945.* Hanover: Schroedel, 1980.

Speitkamp, Winfried. *Jugend in der Neuzeit: Deutschland vom 16. Bis zum 20. Jahrhundert.* Göttingen: Vandenhoeck and Ruprecht, 1998.

Tautz, Joachim. *Militaristische Jugendpolitik in der Weimarer Republik: Die Jugendorganisationen des Stahlhelm, Bund der Frontsoldaten; Jungstahlhelm und Scharnhorst, Bund deutscher Jungmannen.* Regensburg: Roderer, 1998.

Uellenberg-van Dawen, Wolfgang. *Gegen Faschismus und Krieg: Die Auseinandersetzungen sozialdemokratischer Jugendorganisationen mit dem Nationalsozialismus.* Essen: Klartext, 2014.

 14

"German Youth, Your Leader!"

How National Socialism Entered Elementary Schools in 1933

Katharine Kennedy

On 9 May 1933 Reich interior minister Wilhelm Frick convened the Nazi education ministers from the German states and told them of his intention to transform German schooling, with the overall goal of educating children to identify "completely and inseparably" with the state. Frick emphasized that fulfillment of this goal would require "years of strenuous work," and he warned, in the meantime, against "hasty experimentation."[1] At the time, there was no plan for overhauling education,[2] and Frick's prediction that changes would take years may have been even more accurate than he realized. For example, it was only in 1939 that the Third Reich's ministry of education completed adoption of a new national curriculum and new readers for elementary schools (*Volksschulen*). Weimar-era curricula and textbooks largely remained in use until the late 1930s, with education ministries periodically issuing reminders that schools should continue using the old books and that parents should continue buying them.[3] Nonetheless, even as Frick anticipated a long path to nazified education, his warning to the education ministers suggests that the states, which had always had purview over German schooling, were in fact undertaking what Frick called "hasty experiments."[4] This chapter shows that, despite the delayed adoption of national textbooks and curricula, National Socialism, largely through initiatives from the states, began reshaping the rhythms and content of schooling during the months of the *Machtergreifung,* and that, furthermore, these scattered, rapid, and zealous early initiatives were more likely to present unvarnished Nazi ideology than were the more carefully vetted textbooks and curricula adopted several years later. The discussion that follows will argue not only that schooling has a place in the narrative of the *Machtergreifung* but that educational initiatives reflected the exhilaration as well as the turmoil and brutality that marked the spring of 1933.

This chapter addresses two paths through which National Socialism entered classrooms in 1933, focusing on elementary schools, which educated most German children. The first path involved curricular disruption; various states suspended their usual history curricula at the beginning of the 1933–34 school year and replaced them with nazi-fied narratives of Germany's recent history. Implemented in thousands of classrooms, these curricula delegitimized the Weimar Republic and exalted National Socialism. Hastily published supplementary booklets for use in the classroom supported these curricula. Two of the earliest of these booklets, published to support Bavaria's replacement history curricula, set forth themes of the *Machtergreifung* period, offering both a child-oriented leadership cult and coarse, hateful attacks on Jews, socialists, and others designated by the Nazis as threats to Germans and Germanness.

A second way that National Socialism entered schools was through the adoption of Nazi symbols, rituals, and festivals. While local initiatives and directives from the states often introduced Nazi symbols, orders from Frick's interior ministry sought to centralize and regularize ritual practice. Initiative for the observance of new holidays came from Berlin. In contrast with the replacement history curricula and supplemental booklets, which were used only temporarily, Nazi rituals and holidays became defining aspects of the school day and the school year, encouraging an aestheticized and festive attachment to National Socialism.

Replacement History Curricula

In 1933, controlling the narrative about the previous twenty years of German history quickly emerged as an educational priority, and it was for this purpose that the earliest curricular interventions took place. Beginning in late March, ministries of education in the states began introducing special curricula, devoted to the period since 1914, to replace the existing history curricula for one or more months in the summer and/or fall of 1933. Hans Schemm issued the first replacement curriculum on 27 March for Bavaria, just eleven days after his appointment as Bavarian minister of education and six weeks before Frick's speech to the ministers of education. Other states, including Württemberg, Hamburg, Saxony, Baden, Hesse, and Thuringia, followed with their own replacement curricula. The discussion that follows considers the content and goals of three of these replacement curricula, those adopted for Bavaria, Württemberg, and Hamburg.

The hastily produced Bavarian lesson plan was designed, with age-appropriate adaptations, for pupils at all grade levels and in all school types, for use when the Bavarian school year began on 27 April.[5] This newly prescribed course of instruction was to last at least four to six weeks. History instruction at the time, in Bavaria and elsewhere, generally received no more than two hours each week, beginning in the fifth grade and continuing until the final year of school, usually the eighth grade.[6] In Bavaria's sixth grade, for example, time for the replacement curriculum came at the expense of the year's usual subject, "Topics from the history of our people through the end of the Thirty Years' War."[7] Schemm, a former elementary school teacher and the founding leader of the National Socialist Teachers League, was directly involved in creating this curriculum. He titled it "Awakening of the Nation" and described it as a "principle of instruction" that was to influence lessons not just in history but across the curriculum. The lofty goals announced for this special curriculum were to introduce children to the "significance and greatness of the historical events of the National Revolution," to instill "a feeling for the people's honor and strength," and "to mobilize in every boy and girl sacred feelings of love of fatherland and conscientious fulfillment of duty." Teachers were expected to approach this course "with warmth and enthusiasm," and the course was to conclude with a celebration featuring speeches, patriotic songs, and flags.[8] The stated goals of Württemberg's replacement curriculum, issued on 23 May, resembled those for Bavaria.

As in Bavaria, a celebration would conclude the course and mark the beginning of summer vacation.[9] Hamburg's program lasted longer, from late May until mid-December, but it was required only in the two upper grades of the elementary school. The goals of Hamburg's course were more explicitly political: "Especially in history instruction, the primacy of politics must supplant the autonomy of pedagogy." Study of recent history was to contribute to Germans' "political education," and lessons were to distinguish clearly between "friend and enemy." Although Hamburg had long been a center of progressive education, every teacher was expected to hold a positive view of National Socialism.[10] Compared with Weimar-era history curricula, which usually simply listed topics to be covered, the replacement curricula of 1933 were thoroughly propagandistic, providing the "correct" interpretation of events. The Hamburg curriculum was explicit in asserting that "today, propaganda and education work together."[11] With its open discussion of "friends and enemies" and its use of propaganda, the Hamburg curriculum came closest to articulating the political goals of the curricula changes. Despite the patriotic language found in some of these statements of purpose, the content of the curricula leaves no doubt that their intention was to contribute to the Nazis' consolidation of power by condemning every aspect of the Weimar Republic, including especially the people associated with it.

Beginning with the end of the First World War, these curricula fully embraced the "stab-in-the-back" myth, offering no suggestion that the German military lost the war. Among the culprits in Germany's defeat, according to the Bavarian curriculum, were "alien Marxist informers," "leaflets with black-red-gold borders," repeated strikes, and disintegration on the home front.[12] The Hamburg curriculum used the phrase "stab-in-the-back" and blamed, among others, "shirkers, smugglers, hoarders, and war profiteers."[13] Although the stab-in-the-back myth was widely accepted in the Weimar Republic, it was generally not present in Weimar-era history books and curricula for elementary schools.[14] A rare area of agreement between the new curricula and their Weimar-era predecessors was their shared condemnation of the Treaty of Versailles and subsequent reparations. It was common, both in history textbooks published before 1933 and in the replacement curricula to refer to the "dictated peace."[15] The 1933 curricula for Bavaria, Hamburg, and Württemberg all claimed that the Versailles Treaty and reparations led to German "enslavement," again echoing language found in some Weimar-era history books.[16]

What really distinguished the 1933 curricula, however, were their relentless attacks on the republic, associating it with an endless list of political, economic, social, and cultural ills. According to the Bavarian curriculum, the republic represented "Germany under Marxist leadership" and destruction both of Germany's middle class and its rural population. The German people were "bleeding" due to the Dawes Plan and the Young Plan, and they were subject to "enormous tax burdens." "Marxist teachings" led to "destruction of faith in God," and youth organizations educated children for "cowardice and betrayal of the fatherland." As unemployment rose, a few profiteers were said to enjoy tremendous luxury, while the Social Democrats betrayed the workers.[17] Similarly, Württemberg's replacement curriculum criticized the republic for fostering internationalism, class struggle, pacifism, materialism, and "exaggerated individualism." All of this led to "the spiritual downfall of the German people," "impoverishment of the German middle class," and widespread unemployment.[18] The Hamburg curriculum titled its section on the republic "Germany in Chains" and divided this section with subheadings such as "People without Honor," "People without Space," "People without Armaments," "The Plundering of the Reich," and "Servitude to Reparations."[19] Furthermore, the Hamburg curriculum claimed that "unlimited equality of rights" enabled "Jewish influence over all public life."[20] In the three replacement curricula discussed here, this was the only reference to Jews or Jewishness. All three curricula, however, by presenting the entire history of the Weimar Republic as one of unmitigated failure and harm for the German people, sought to destroy any remaining allegiance to the republic and all sympathy for the republic's supporters.

As presented in these curricula, this narrative of failed leadership, economic collapse, and "spiritual downfall" set the stage for Germany's rebirth under National Socialism. All emphasized the struggles of the movement's early years and the sacrifice of its martyrs. The Bavarian curriculum referred to the resilience of Hitler and his fellow "freedom fighters" after the "tragic" setback on 9 November 1923 and then to "hundreds of SA men butchered by Reds."[21] While the Bavarian curriculum culminated with the growth of the Nazi "freedom movement" and what it called the Nazis' "enormous" electoral successes in 1932, it neglected to mention the percentage of the votes received by the Nazis in any of these elections, and it had nothing to say about how Hitler became chancellor. Without its usual commentary, the curriculum simply referred to 30 January 1933 as a date of historical significance and stated, "Hitler becomes chancellor."[22]

Unlike Bavaria's curriculum, which offered little discussion of the Nazis' program or goals other than holding out the prospect of "faith in God, honor, freedom, and strength," Württemberg's curriculum included a section called "National Socialism's World of Ideas." The list included central themes in National Socialist ideology: nationalism, race, *Volksgemeinschaft*, the *Führerprinzip*, and the will to military power. In addition, like many supporters of National Socialism at the time, this list affirmed Christianity. This discussion of Nazi thought also reprised National Socialism's opposition to liberalism, individualism, and parliamentary government.[23] Hamburg's curriculum addressed National Socialist ideology by including mention of the party's twenty-five-point program and urging teachers to offer persuasive instruction about "fundamental ideas pertaining to *Volk*, race, culture, state, and church." Since Hamburg's curriculum appeared after those for Bavaria and Württemberg, it included such recent developments as the Day of Potsdam, the Enabling Law, and the *Gleichschaltung* law.[24]

These hastily written and implemented curricula were impatient and uncompromising in their efforts to legitimate and validate Nazi rule and to instill hostility toward the Weimar Republic and everyone associated with it. Through this message, these curricula were among the enablers of the climate of fear, intolerance, and brutality experienced by many during the *Machtergreifung* period. The effects of these curricula are difficult to evaluate; it is clear, however, that their authors were seri-

ous about implementation. Several of the curricula included requirements that school assignments and exams incorporate topics from the
new curriculum and that school inspectors and school directors submit
reports on pupils' performance. Hans Schemm asked school inspectors
to provide evidence of "exacting and thorough implementation" of the
new guidelines.[25]

Meanwhile, after the appearance of most of the state replacement
curricula, Minister Frick issued his own guidelines on 20 July in an
effort to encourage a common, centralized approach to history instruction. While acknowledging the importance of the past two decades,
Frick's guidelines focused instead on a racialized view of antiquity,
crediting the Nordic race with achievements by the Persians, Hittites,
Greeks, and Romans but blaming racial mixing or "blood of alien
races" for the decline of these civilizations. With an eye to secondary
schools, Frick acknowledged the limited amount of time available in
elementary schools and the need to focus there on "the personalities
of great leaders" and on recent events.[26] While Frick's guidelines had
a less direct and immediate effect on instruction than did the curricula
imposed by the states, they did influence themes of history instruction
in the following years, as adoption of new comprehensive curricula
was delayed.

Supplementary Booklets

Among the most direct and immediate tools for bringing National
Socialism to schoolchildren were the many booklets intended to supplement existing schoolbooks. Beginning in 1933, major textbook publishers as well as smaller regional publishers issued these inexpensive
booklets, which frequently made their way into classrooms without
the scrutiny and review traditionally applied during official textbook
adoption. Although it is often difficult to know if, when, and where
these booklets were actually used, two of the very earliest booklets,
published under the auspices of Hans Schemm in May 1933, were
widely used in Bavaria, and possibly elsewhere, in the 1933–34 school
year. Intended to support Bavaria's replacement history curriculum
and, according to Schemm, to give German youth "an accurate picture
of the greatness of our time," the booklets inaugurated what was to
become a series called *Der junge Staat*. The booklets clearly indicate that
they were commissioned by the Bavarian ministry of education and
that Hans Schemm, the series publisher, was personally involved in
their creation. Although use of the booklets was not required, Schemm

announced their publication on 12 May and encouraged their use in Bavaria.[27] The first booklet was a biography of Hitler, titled *Deutsche Jugend, Dein Führer!,* and the second was called *Aufbruch der Nation: Geschichte des deutschen Volkes von 1914 bis 1933.* Both booklets were sixty-one pages long and appeared initially in editions of at least two hundred thousand, with additional printings following in 1933. The title page of *Deutsche Jugend* identifies "leading individuals of the National Socialist Teachers League" as its authors, while Hans Roder, an associate of Schemm's in the ministry of education, wrote *Aufbruch.* Providing illustrations for both booklets was Philipp Rupprecht, who signed his drawings "Fips" and was known as the illustrator of *Der Stürmer,* where his work included scurrilous antisemitic drawings.[28] Although both booklets appear to have been widely used in Bavarian schools in 1933, the next year a new series of supplementary booklets, called *Die Fahne hoch,* came into use in Bavarian schools. By 1935 the booklets in this later series were still widely used, but none of the Bavarian provinces listed the earlier volumes of *Der junge Staat* among texts adopted in their schools. While texts about National Socialism certainly had a central role in the booklets of the *Fahne hoch* series, Nazis and their organizations were generally depicted as friendly, happy, and adventuresome, in contrast with the focus on destiny and conflict in the earlier booklets of the *Machtergreifung* period.[29]

That the first volume in *Der junge Staat* series would be devoted to Hitler is, of course, unsurprising. By 1933, the Hitler myth was well developed, and that spring Hitler emerged as the leading symbol of the nation, embodying rebirth and the focus of widespread euphoria. The image of Hitler as a man of destiny, altogether different from the discredited leaders of the republic, readily filled a leadership vacuum evident in Weimar-era teaching materials.[30] Republican efforts to undermine monarchism included the removal of images of Kaiser Wilhelm and other German royalty from schoolrooms and textbooks, but no individuals replaced them as representatives of the nation. A review of forty-five illustrated frontispieces in Weimar-era readers reveals that none depicted a German leader, past or present. Although several offered a picture of Goethe and some Protestant readers featured Jesus, the more usual frontispieces depicted children in idyllic rural settings.[31] Even in the body of these books, which were the most widely used in elementary schools, texts or images that celebrated President Ebert or Hindenburg were not common. In a group of thirty-five Weimar-era readers for the upper grades, only one included a presidential picture, in this case a full-page image of Hindenburg.[32] In 1929 a school official in Brandenburg argued that the "time has come when our reading books for elementary schools can no longer exclude pictures of the Reich president,"[33] but few new readers appeared in the republic's troubled final years. The books that remained in use in the early 1930s, including the first years of the Third Reich, contained little that celebrated the republic's leaders, including Hindenburg.

Deutsche Jugend, Dein Führer!, a child-oriented contribution to the Hitler cult, tells the story of Hitler's life, from his birth until the Day of Potsdam, emphasizing Hitler's destiny to lead, his heroism, and his role as a unifier, all while reminding readers that he was a man of the people. On 12 May 1933 Hans Schemm announced that this booklet was suitable for use in Bavaria's elementary schools beginning in the fourth grade.[34] The story of Hitler's childhood up until his departure for Vienna receives special focus and fills the first third of this booklet. Based largely on Hitler's own account in the first pages of *Mein Kampf*, *Deutsche Jugend* embellishes the story, filling in some of the gaps in Hitler's account but amplifying Hitler's own claims to be a long-awaited leader destined for greatness.[35] Philipp Rupprecht's illustrations also depict early signs of Hitler's leadership ability. One of the first pictures shows young Adolf giving orders to the compliant family dog, and a few pages later Hitler demonstrates his speaking skills to a group of neighborhood boys.[36] The text explains: "Leadership qualities manifested themselves very soon in the boy Hitler. Often one of his rousing speeches would have an educational effect on his comrades. Soon the other boys had to acknowledge his obvious superiority." When Hitler and his friends played war games, his side always won. With regard to his playmates, "He commanded them. They followed him." According to *Deutche Jugend*, the foundations of Hitler's "later life as Führer" and, indeed, evidence of his "genius" were apparent in Hitler's childhood, even as he enjoyed boyhood games and pranks.[37]

Complicating efforts to portray Hitler not only as an exceptional talent but also as a model child were his difficult relationship with his father and his terrible performance at the Linz *Realschule*. Rupprecht's drawing of the infant Hitler with his admiring parents humanizes the harsh father. *Deutsche Jugend* does mention Hitler's rejection of his father's insistence that his son should prepare for a career in the civil service and explains Hitler's poor performance in school as the boy's strategy for winning his father's support for his plan to become an artist.[38] Even compared with *Mein Kampf*, *Deutsche Jugend* minimizes the extent and duration of Hitler's bad grades. Like *Mein Kampf*, *Deutsche Jugend* claims that a serious illness, which was actually an invention or an exaggeration, caused Hitler to end his schooling, obscuring the reality of his inadequate performance at two *Realschulen*.

Elsewhere, however, drawing on Hitler's earlier success in elementary school, *Deutsche Jugend* praises Hitler as a "gifted pupil."[39] The section of *Deutsche Jugend* about Hitler's childhood concludes with the deaths of his parents and the insistence that, despite adversity, his "soul and conscience" remained intact."[40]

World War I, which added heroism to the emerging Hitler myth, pervades the second part of *Deutsche Jugend*. Treatment of the Vienna years is brief, but it emphasizes Hitler's hostility toward social democrats and Jews, who became the "fundamental evil at the center of his political thought."[41] The section about Vienna also describes Hitler as a simple construction worker. Although this comes from *Mein Kampf*, there is no evidence that Hitler actually held such a job.[42] Absent from *Deutsche Jugend* is any mention of Hitler's repeated failure to gain admission to art school.

The narrative about Hitler's enlistment in the Bavarian army and his participation in the early weeks of the war follows *Mein Kampf*, with Rupprecht's drawings depicting Hitler's joy at his enlistment and his earnest valor at the front. *Deutsche Jugend* describes Hitler's role as a dispatch runner as "the most dangerous" of assignments.[43] Another drawing shows Hitler's receipt in 1918 of the Iron Cross First Class. *Deutsche Jugend* offers readers a fictitious tale claiming that Hitler received this award for cleverly and single-handedly capturing a basement full of French soldiers. Hitler's war ended in a military hospital in eastern Germany, where he fully embraced the stab-in-the-back myth and allegedly decided to become a politician.[44] The final third of *German Youth*, devoted to Hitler's leadership of the Nazis and rise to power, reinforces, especially through pictures, the notion of Hitler as a transcendent, heroic leader. In several pictures a large image of Hitler dominates crowds of small followers. In one of these images, Hitler, saluting against the background of a large swastika, seems to be suspended between earth and sky, and in the second, Hitler, again in front of a large swastika, is illuminated by a bright beam from above, while an enraptured crowd, their faces small, listens in the shadows.[45] Freedom and unity, themes by no means unique to National Socialism, are woven through the story of Hitler's rise to power. The final words of the text, concluding with a description of the Day of Potsdam, invoke the "blessings of a united, free, proud Germany"[46]; a picture follows of Hitler and Hindenburg shaking hands, with the Garrison Church behind them and the swastika and the iron cross flanking the name Potsdam. As leader of a movement that claimed to be about liberation from a host of enemies and problems, Hitler emerged as the "savior from all peril."[47]

The second volume in the *Der junge Staat* series, *Aufbruch der Nation*, closely follows the structure of Schemm's 27 March curriculum, offering a nazified version of Germany's history from the First World War until 1 May 1933. The introduction addresses both educators and pupils as the audience for this booklet and makes it clear that the intent is to flesh out the 27 March curriculum, with the goal of "anchoring" the younger generation as "the sustainers of the nation." The reading level of *Aufbruch* is more advanced than that of *Deutsche Jugend*, making it less suitable for younger children to read themselves, but the intent was that the booklet would inform instruction at various grade levels. The introduction also reiterates the involvement of the National Socialist Teachers League (Nationalsozialistischer Lehrerbund) and notably of Hans Schemm, with a reminder that he served both as Bavarian education minister and as Reich leader of the league. While repeating the Bavarian replacement curriculum's language about treasonous Marxists, enslaved Germans, and martyred freedom fighters, *Aufbruch* injected antisemitic language reminiscent of that found in *Mein Kampf* and Hitler's speeches of the early 1920s, in contrast to the absence of any references to Jews that characterized Hitler's speeches in 1933 and many Nazi textbooks of the mid- to late 1930s.[48] Vitriolic, dehumanizing attacks, mostly on Jews and Marxists, permeate the text, along with grandiose claims about the "world historical" role of National Socialism. Largely absent are the friendly, helpful Nazis ubiquitous in later Nazi schoolbooks. While *Deutsche Jugend* reflected the euphoria focused on Hitler in 1933, *Aufbruch* is more reflective of the terror of those months. According to *Aufbruch*, Marxism "infected" Germany at the end of the World War, and the revolution "was entirely under Jewish leadership." Demeaning images of a communist and a Jew show them literally stabbing the back of a German soldier. Many who had honorably served their country were said to have lost their lives to "dehumanized hordes."[49] In Bavaria, the "Jewish Galician Eisner" displaced the "venerable, glorious Wittelsbach dynasty."[50] *Aufbruch* blames "the Jew [Hugo] Preuss" for the Weimar Constitution, which, the booklet claims, subjected the German people to predation by "countless political parties."[51]

Turning to the German inflation, the booklet claims that "human parasites from around the world" devoured the German economy, like "flies on carrion." "International finance," led by "world Jewry," took possession of the remnants of German wealth. Furthermore, "the activities of Jewish bloodsuckers during the inflation were not just tolerated but supported and encouraged by the Marxist government." Jews "smirked" at Germany's difficulties and celebrated their own success in gaining control of the "fate of the German people."[52] Referring to "the Marxist November criminal and his Jewish manipulator," *Aufbruch* explicitly sets forth the Nazi notion of an all-controlling Jewish conspiracy, blamed for most of Germany's problems.[53]

According to *Aufbruch*, Marxist youth organizations, with the help of "Jewish elements" from Moscow, had furthered the "infection" of the German people. Hitler, however, understood that Germany could recover from its cultural, moral, economic, and political degeneration only after "overcoming Marxism and Judaism."[54] Meanwhile, young "men in brown shirts" faced violent deaths at the hands of "red bandits" who were motivated by "animalistic Marxism" and supported by "Jewish-influenced big city newspapers."[55] The final chapter of *Aufbruch*, called "100 Days of the Third Reich," includes early measures taken to remove communists, socialists, and Jews from German civil society.[56] Although Marxists and Jews, often seen as working in tandem, were the main targets of the venom exuded by this little book, *Aufbruch* did not spare other groups, accusing the Russian army of "Asiatic barbarism" in World War I and using crude, racist language to refer to French colonial troops.[57]

In contrast to the many images of threatening, conspiratorial enemies found in the pages of *Aufbruch*, the booklet presented the promise of National Socialism as liberation and virtue. As also stated in the Bavarian replacement curriculum, the pillars of the "new Germany" were to be "faith in God, honor, freedom, and strength."[58] After harshly condemning the Republic, *Aufbruch* called National Socialism "the strongest freedom movement in history."[59] Hitler assumes a messianic role; chosen by God, he was endowed with "special gifts and abilities."[60] The German people, in the first one hundred days of Hitler's rule, were already experiencing "a true redemption," but *Aufbruch* assured readers that "not only the German people, but the entire world has awaited this German son."[61] A product of zealous supporters of the Third Reich from the heavily Nazi region of upper and middle Franconia, *Aufbruch* brought to Bavarian classrooms an unfiltered view of the hate-filled, delusional Nazi worldview during the violence, chaos, and fervor of the spring of 1933.[62] *Aufbruch* exposed teachers and pupils to unrestrained racism and especially to crude, venomous antisemitism. This contrasts with the supplementary booklets that appeared a year later in 1934, including some for Bavaria. While thoroughly nazified, these texts tended to associate National Socialism with adventure, comradery, and festivity, often through stories describing activities of the Hitler Youth or Labor Service. Jews and antisemitism were largely absent.[63] Similarly, when in 1935 the ministry of education announced the contents of the first volume of the national reader for grades five and six, it contained stories such as "We Build a Street," written by a Labor Service man, and a poem about a proud *Jungvolk* flag bearer, but no mention of Jews.[64]

Although the earliest curricular interventions used history instruction to bring Hitler and National Socialism into the classroom, there were other early efforts to stitch National Socialism into the curriculum, including calls for the integration of "heredity and racial studies," especially in science, German, history, and geography courses in the final grade of elementary school. Beginning with a decree in Prussia on 13 September 1933 and continuing with similar initiatives in other states during the following weeks and months, these orders generally did not specify a course of study but rather urged instruction in areas such as "heredity studies, racial studies, racial hygiene, family studies, and the politics of population."[65] Frick's speech of 9 May had given some direction to these efforts. In racial studies, according to Frick, pupils were to learn to distinguish the physical and mental characteristics of different races and especially to understand the dangers to "German blood" of "racially alien blood, especially Jewish and colored blood." Racial studies should also, Frick continued, assert the dominant role of the "Nordic race" throughout Western civilization. Heredity studies were to promote reproduction by people perceived as hereditarily strong while discouraging or preventing reproduction by those with "physical deformities" or "mental weakness."[66]

Of the instructions on racial studies issued by the states in 1933, the Hamburg guidelines issued in December were notable for developing these dangerous fictions into something resembling a course of study. Hamburg's guidelines contained a chilling discussion of "possible solutions to the Jewish question." While the guidelines dismissed pogroms as "thoroughly reprehensible," they concluded that the best option was "clear, legal separation between the host people and the visiting people." The Hamburg guidelines also endorsed the Nazi sterilization law as a means of preventing the reproduction of the "hereditarily less able and the racially less valuable."[67] The short-term effects of these measures on instruction are difficult to determine, but in January 1935, Minister Bernhard Rust, who had become Reich education minister in 1934, issued more detailed guidelines for instruction in heredity and racial studies, and he required their adoption in schools throughout the Reich.[68]

Rituals and Holidays

Rituals and holidays provided a second path through which National Socialism quickly became present in German schools and in German society more broadly. The Weimar Republic, having largely failed to build consensus in support of new national festivals and symbols, left a symbolic vacuum readily filled by the Nazis, who eliminated or appropriated Weimar practices and introduced their own rituals and symbols. Rituals and holidays could define the rhythms of the school day and school year independent of the introduction of new curricula and textbooks, which, despite the rapid appearance of the supplemental history curricula and booklets, was usually slow.

Local and regional initiatives typically introduced the Hitler greeting and the swastika flag in 1933, but national guidelines governing schools' use of these key Nazi symbols were issued only in the spring of 1934. Perhaps the most ubiquitous Nazi ritual, which lacked a Weimar antecedent, was the Hitler greeting or salute, consisting of the outstretched right arm and accompanied by the phrase "Heil Hitler." By the summer of 1933, this greeting, which injected Hitler into all official interactions, was practiced in most schools. Interior Minister Frick, in an order issued on 13 July, made the Hitler salute mandatory for government officials; several states then quickly followed with requirements that pupils and teachers exchange the salute at the beginning and end of class.[69] By the spring of 1934, a series of further orders originating from Berlin established uniform requirements for use of the Hitler salute in schools. In typical elementary schools, where a single teacher stayed with a class for the entire day, the Hitler salute would take place at the beginning and end of the morning and afternoon sessions. These policies also made the Hitler salute optional for "non-Aryan" children, heightening their sense of exclusion from a national community structured around loyalty to Hitler.[70]

Coinciding with the rapidly growing presence in schools of the swastika flag was the elimination of the black-red-gold flag of the republic, although this flag had never become a ubiquitous presence in Weimar-era schools. Having gained its status as the republic's official flag only after contentious debate, the black-red-gold flag faced determined opposition throughout the republic's history, especially from parties on the right of the political spectrum, which favored the imperial black-white-red flag.[71] Although supporters of the republic and of the black-red-gold flag had intended that the flag would contribute to national integration, mention of the flag in Weimar-era textbooks and curricula was rare.[72] In Braunschweig the education ministry had ordered each school to acquire the new national flag in 1921, but in 1928 there were still schools that had not complied with this order.[73] In Prussia, policy called for display of the black-red-gold flag at schools only on Constitution Day and other special occasions.[74]

The new Nazi government moved quickly to banish the black-red-gold flag, replacing it on 7 March 1933 with not one flag but two: the black-white-red tricolor and the swastika flag of the Nazi party. The swastika and the swastika flag already featured prominently in the early supplementary booklets and replacement history curricula issued in the spring of 1933.[75] In Hamburg, beginning on 1 July 1933, all pupils and teachers were required to attend a ceremony every Monday morning for the raising of the swastika flag, "the symbol of our new Germany."[76] By early 1934 the Reich ministry of the interior decreed that all schools in Germany were required to hold flag ceremonies at the beginning and end of all school vacations, raising or lowering both flags of the Reich. All pupils were to attend and to sing one stanza each of the national anthem and the "Horst Wessel Song" whenever flags were raised or lowered.[77]

Pictures of Hitler became a usual feature in classrooms beginning in the spring of 1933. On 20 March the Prussian ministry of education ordered the display of Hitler's picture along with that of Hindenburg. Other states took steps to regulate and encourage the acquisition and display of these pictures. In Württemberg, there was insistence that the images be "dignified" and "tasteful."[78] Although display of classroom portraits of the republic's leaders had been far from universal, the Reich ministry of the interior ordered the removal of all pictures of people "who participated in the November Revolution of 1918."[79] This had the effect of banishing pictures of former president Friedrich Ebert while allowing pictures of Hindenburg.

Despite some regional differences in timing and details, by the summer of 1933 the Hitler salute, the swastika flag, and pictures of Hitler and Hindenburg were regular fixtures at schools, having easily supplanted and delegitimized the contested symbols of the republic. The limited presence of and support for the republic's symbols simplified their elimination. Although Nazi symbols were also common in public spaces, their presence in schools helped to give National Socialism, even in the turmoil of 1933, a veneer of legitimacy and normality in addition to projecting power.

The first three national holidays that the Nazis designated, namely Heroes' Memorial Day (*Heldengedenktag*), the National Celebration of Labor (*Feiertag der nationalen Arbeit*), and the Harvest Festival

(Erntedanktag), were all adaptations of existing observances. In each case, the ministries of propaganda and interior specified how holidays should be observed, and for which ideological ends.[80] Each of these three holidays emphasized a central Nazi theme: sacrifice for nation (Heroes' Memorial Day), *Volksgemeinschaft* (Celebration of Labor), and blood and soil (Harvest Festival). While states and localities took the initiative in introducing Nazi symbols, the impetus for these revamped holidays came from the national ministries in Berlin.

Observances of a National Day of Mourning (Volkstrauertag), held in memory of those who died in World War I, had begun in 1925, but years of discussion among the states had failed to reach agreement on an acceptable date for the holiday. Most states opted for the fifth Sunday before Easter, while some held their commemoration in the fall.[81] For states in the former group, the holiday fell on 12 March in 1933, but the Nazis did not thoroughly reconfigure it that year. Baden's republican minister of education, writing on 20 January 1933, urged teachers to include lessons on the day before the holiday that addressed the "significance" of the Day of Mourning.[82] In contrast, the following month, Prussia's Nazi minister of education Bernhard Rust issued a message that anticipated the transformation of the holiday in 1934. While remembering the fallen, children should develop a "military disposition" and love of fatherland worthy of the previous generation. Through "sacred reverence for the greatness of their sacrifice," children were to become convinced "that they themselves must be ready to commit themselves, with body and soul, to their fatherland."[83] The next year, 1934, the holiday received a new name, Heroes' Memorial Day, and Goebbels's propaganda ministry staged the main events, incorporating banners of the SA, the "Horst Wessel Song," a wreath-laying by President Hindenburg, and a long parade.[84] The observances in schools were to include solemn lectures, songs, and choral readings in a setting decorated with swastikas and possibly featuring a ceremonial fire.[85] As Rust had proposed, the ceremony was to urge children to emulate the fallen soldiers by preparing to sacrifice their own lives, with the promise of becoming heroes.

Perhaps the most egregious Nazi appropriation of a holiday was the transformation of 1 May from an international celebration of labor and the working class into a national endorsement of a supposedly classless *Volksgemeinschaft* composed of Germans performing work of all types. The National Celebration of Labor became a national holiday in 1933 as the Nazis were destroying working-class organizations, but participation by schoolchildren was limited in many areas because school was not in session on 1 May. Nonetheless, schools received detailed instructions for ceremonies, including, where possible, listening on the radio to the festivities in Berlin. The program prescribed for schools in Baden was to convince children that, when they finished school, the national state would value them equally, whether they pursued manual or intellectual work.[86]

In 1933 the Nazis also designated the Harvest Festival, observed on 1 October, a national holiday, with a focus on honoring German farmers and German identification with blood and soil. Churches and rural communities had previously held harvest festivals, but the Nazis transformed the celebrations into a major national holiday that featured parades of costumed peasants, outdoor festivals and dances, speeches, and church services.[87] Teachers were to accompany their pupils and supervise their attendance at these events. Prior to the holiday, schools were to sponsor their own events, including relevant speeches and possibly visits to farms in the vicinity. As the Nazi May Day was designed to obscure class differences, so the Harvest Festival was contrived to create ties between town and country.[88] The Reich interior ministry urged schools to distribute an eight-page pamphlet to pupils titled *Blut und Boden: Die Grundlagen der deutschen Zukunft*. Hitler's picture appeared on the cover with the caption, "Our Führer Adolf Hitler: Champion of the Concept of Blood and Soil." The booklet makes two main points to demonstrate the peasantry's connection with blood and soil and, indeed, with Germany's survival. First, the peasantry served as the "life source of the German people" because rural birthrates were higher than urban birthrates. Second, the peasantry provided food: "Without the work of our farmers, the entire German people would starve." The pamphlet includes several images of farmhouses and farmers at work, but otherwise provides no information about the segment of the population extolled here.[89]

In addition to these three national holidays and ongoing observance of traditional religious holidays, many other observances and festivities punctuated school calendars in 1933. All of these occasions required allotting at least one hour of a school day for special speeches and commemorations, and some of these observances required cancellation of classes for at least part of a day. In most cases, initiative came from the Reich ministry of the interior, but in others, states ordered celebrations. Among these occasions were the tenth anniversary of the death of Albert Leo Schlageter on 26 May, the anniversary of the signing of the Treaty of Versailles on 28 June, the anniversary of the liberation of Vienna on 11 September, Hindenburg's birthday on 2 October, and the anniversary of the founding of the German Empire on 18 January.[90] All of these events were to be instrumentalized to validate National

Socialism, often by embedding it in Germany's past. Mother's Day, with the support of the florist industry and some conservative groups that advocated large families, had gained some recognition during the late Weimar years, but the Nazis quickly appropriated the "German Mother's Day" in May 1933, requiring schools to include lessons on the day before Mother's Day in support of the Nazi movement's ideas about family and *Volksgemeinschaft*. The more specific instructions for Mother's Day in 1934 asked the German people to express "their commitment to the racially pure, hereditarily healthy, and child-rich German family."[91] In 1933 Nazi ministries required schools to organize many festivals and commemorations and to use these events to embed Nazi ideology in German festive culture and history. Narratives that promoted national and ethnic identity were introduced into classrooms, accompanied by flags and parades, along with the promise of a break in the regular schedule of classes.

Although the Nazi authorities proved to be adept at appropriating existing holidays for their own purposes, one Weimar-era holiday that came to an abrupt and expected end in 1933 was Constitution Day. From the republic's inception, required participation in annual Constitution Day observances had been part of an effort to instill in pupils feelings of attachment and loyalty to the republic and its constitution. While the scale of festivities varied from place to place, they included speeches, music, dramatic presentations, displays of black-red-gold flags, slide shows, and sometimes sports events. Regular classes were canceled on Constitution Day, and schools were required to encourage children to participate in decorating and other preparations. Often, however, supporters of the holiday were disappointed that the festivities lacked "joyful resonance" with the general population.[92] Hostile parents forbade their children from participating in Constitution Day events, even though some of these families faced legal proceedings for violating school attendance laws.[93] In the early 1930s, Constitution Day observances suffered from reduced budgets and diminishing popular support, and in 1932 Franz von Papen deposed the pro-republic Prussian government three weeks before the 11 August holiday.[94] On Constitution Day in 1932, Josef Goebbels could write with confidence in his diary: "final Constitution Day."[95] In the summer of 1933, Nazi ministers of education made the end of Constitution Day official. These announcements were terse, but no explanation was needed since Germany's new leaders had thoroughly undermined the Weimar Constitution.[96] As further expression of their contempt for the Weimar Constitution, they ended the practice of distributing copies of the constitution to pupils when they completed their required schooling, as required by Article

148 in the document's text. In Prussia, the order to end distribution of the constitution came as early as March 1933. In place of the rejected constitution, some states, including Bavaria and Hamburg, ordered distribution of copies of the Treaty of Versailles, fulfilling a goal of conservatives that dated back to 1919.[97]

In the spring of 1933, the new Nazi state, represented in educational matters by Wilhelm Frick's ministry of the interior and the newly empowered Nazi ministers of education, readily undertook the dismantling of explicitly republican symbols, such as the black-red-gold flag and Constitution Day, while continuing to allow, and even promote, the use of Weimar-era schoolbooks and curricula, in part because they contained little advocacy for and representation of the republic. Despite Frick's desire for centralized nazification of schooling, impetus for many of the early changes came from the states. Like many aspects of the *Machtergreifung*, the first interventions in schools' curricula were abrupt but incomplete, zealous but impermanent. Although the Reich ministry brought some uniformity to Nazi rituals and holidays observed in schools and sustained these practices throughout most of the Third Reich, new ad hoc curricula and textbooks overlay, supplemented, and only partially supplanted those already in existence. These hastily compiled supplemental history curricula harshly denounced all aspects of the Weimar Republic, contributing to the multifaceted campaign to legitimate Nazi rule by discrediting the republic and republicans. The first supplemental booklets issued for Bavaria depicted, in words and images, the racial state, the cult of the leader, the abandonment of civility, and the obsession with national community that would characterize the Third Reich, all while projecting the anger, vengefulness, and exhilaration characteristic of the period of the *Machtergreifung*.

Katharine Kennedy is the Charles A. Dana Professor of History at Agnes Scott College in Decatur, Georgia. Her research focuses on the content of German primary education, with an emphasis on textbooks and curricula, from the Empire to the Third Reich. She has published articles on various aspects of this subject, and she is completing the manuscript for a book tentatively titled *Schooling Germans, 1890–1945: Lessons about God, Home, and Fatherland*.

Notes

1. Wilhelm Frick, *Kampfziel der deutschen Schule* (Langensalza: Hermann Beyer, 1933), 6–7.

2. Delia Nixdorf and Gerd Nixdorf, "Politisierung und Neutralisierung der Schule in der NS-Zeit," in *Herrschaftsalltag im Dritten Reich*, ed. Hans Mommsen and Susanne Willems (Düsseldorf: Schwann, 1988), 230.

3. In this respect, see Prussia, Ministerium für Wissenschaft, Kunst und Volksbildung, *Zentralblatt für die gesamte Unterrichtsverwaltung in Preussen* (hereafter cited as *Zentralblatt*) (Berlin: Weidmannsche Buchhandlung) 75 (1933): 121; 76 (1934): 139; Württembergisches Kultministerium, *Amtsblatt des Württembergischen Kultministeriums* (hereafter cited as *Amtsblatt Württemberg*) (Stuttgart: Ernst Klett), 26 (1933): 61; 27 (1934): 77; and Sächsisches Ministerium für Volksbildung, *Verordnungsblatt des Sächsischen Ministeriums für Volksbildung* (hereafter cited as *Verordnungsblatt Sachsen*), (Dresden: N. C. Heinrich), 15 (1933): 87.

4. Frick, *Kampfziel*, 21.

5. Franz Kühnel, *Hans Schemm: Gauleiter und Kultusminister (1891–1935)* (Neustadt/Aisch: Schmidt, 1985), 307.

6. *Richtlinien des Preussischen Ministeriums für Wissenschaft, Kunst und Volksbildung für die Lehrpläne der Volksschulen* (Breslau: Ferdinand Hirt, 1931), 73; *Lehrpläne für die Volks- und Mittelschulen in Württemberg* (Stuttgart: Ernst Klett, 1928), 83; "Lehrordnung für die bayerischen Volksschulen," in Bayerisches Staatsministerium für Unterricht und Kultus, *Amtsblatt des Bayerischen Staatsministeriums für Unterricht und Kultus* (hereafter cited as *Amtsblatt Bayern*) (Munich: Kastner and Callwey), 60 (1926): 137–39.

7. "Lehrordnung für die bayerischen Volksschulen," 166.

8. *Amtsblatt Bayern*, 67 (1933): 31, 35–36. See also Kühnel, *Hans Schemm*, 308–11.

9. *Amtsblatt Württemberg*, 26 (1933): 44–45.

10. "Hamburg: Die Landesunterrichtsbehörde Hamburg nimmt Stellung zum Geschichtsunterricht," *Pädagogisches Zentralblatt* 13 (1933): 535.

11. Ibid.

12. *Amtsblatt Bayern*, 67 (1933): 32.

13. "Hamburg," 531.

14. See, for example, Ludwig Eckl, *Teubners Sachkunde für Volksschulen, Fachband I Geschichte*, Teil III (Leipzig: B. G. Teubner, 1930), 35, and Bernhard Kumsteller, *Geschichtsbuch für die deutsche Jugend für Volksschulen* (Leipzig: Quelle and Meyer, 1932), 42–43.

15. *Amtsblatt Württemberg*, 26 (1933): 46; and "Hamburg," 531. See also Kumsteller, *Geschichtsbuch*, 44.

16. *Amtsblatt Bayern*, 67 (1933): 32; *Amtsblatt Württemberg*, 26 (1933): 46; "Hamburg," 533. See, for example, *Merkbuch für den Unterricht in der Geschichte, Achtes Schuljahr*, ed. Bezirkslehrer-Verein München (Munich: Max Kellerer, 1924), 38.

17. *Amtsblatt Bayern*, 67 (1933): 32–34.

18. *Amtsblatt Württemberg*, 26 (1933): 47–48.

19. "Hamburg," 531–33.

20. Ibid., 532–33.

21. *Amtsblatt Bayern*, 67 (1933): 32–33.

22. Ibid., 33–35.

23. *Amtsblatt Württemberg*, 26 (1933): 48–49.

24. "Hamburg," 534.

25. *Amtsblatt Bayern*, 67 (1933): 36. See also Dorte Gernert, *Schulvorschriften für den Geschichtsunterricht im 19./20. Jahrhundert* (Cologne: Böhlau, 1994), 189, as well as *Amtsblatt Württemberg*, 26 (1933): 46, and *Verordnungsblatt Sachsen*, 15 (1933): 34.

26. *Zentralblatt*, 75 (1933): 197–99.

27. Gernert, *Schulvorschriften*, 191–92.

28. See *Deutsche Jugend, Dein Führer!* (Sulzbach/Oberpfalz: W. Regele, 1933); and Hans Roder, *Aufbruch der Nation: Geschichte des deutschen Volkes von 1914 bis 1933* (Sulzbach/Oberpfalz: W. Regele, 1933), 3, as well as Benedikt Lochmüller, *Hans Schemm*, vol. 2 (Munich: Deutscher Volksverlag, 1935), 381–82.

29. *Volksschulwesen—Lehr- und Lernmittel—Lehrmittelverzeichnis 1920–1942*, 4 January 1936, Bayerisches Hauptstaatsarchiv, Munich, MK 42567. See also Hans Stanglmaier, ed., *Die Fahne hoch: Ergänzungsbogen zum Lesebuch, 2. und 3. Schülerjahrgang* (Munich: Josef Kösel & Friedrich Pustet, 1934), 24; and J. Prestel, ed., *Die Fahne hoch: Ergänzungsbogen zum Lesebuch, 6. und 7. Schülerjahrgang* (Munich: Josef Kösel & Friedrich Pustet, 1934), 6–7.

30. See Ian Kershaw, *The "Hitler Myth": Image and Reality in the Third Reich* (Oxford: Oxford University Press, 1987), 53–56, and David Welch, "'Working towards the Führer': Charismatic Leadership and the Image of Adolf Hitler in Nazi Propaganda," in *Working toward the Führer: Essays in Honour of Sir Ian Kershaw*, ed. Anthony McElligott and Tim Kirk (Manchester: Manchester University Press, 2003), 94–95.

31. See, for example, *Ferdinand Hirts Deutsches Lesebuch für das 5. bis. 8. Schuljahr, Ausgabe B.* (Breslau: Ferdinand Hirt, 1925), frontispiece; and *Lesebuch für die evangelischen Schulen der Rheinprovinz: Ausgabe für den Regierungsbezirk Düsseldorf, III. Teil* (Bielefeld: Velhagen and Klasing, 1931), frontispiece, as well as Wilhelm Cremer and Oskar Wahnelt, eds., *Brandenburgisches Lesebuch, Dritter Teil, 1. Band* (Bielefeld: Velhagen and Klasing, 1927), frontispiece.

32. *Vaterländisches Lesebuch für Schleswig-Holstein*, Teil II (Langensalza: Julius Beltz, 1927), 391.

33. *Lesebücher-Gedichtssammlungen für evangelischen Schulen*, 12 February 1929, Brandenburgisches Landeshauptarchiv, Potsdam, Rep 2A II Gen 1411.

34. Gernert, *Schulvorschriften*, 190.

35. Kershaw, *Hitler Myth*, 23–35.

36. *Deutsche Jugend*, 8, 17.

37. Ibid., 16.

38. Ibid., 9–11.

39. Ibid., 11, 14, 18. See also Christian Hartmann et al., eds., *Hitler, Mein Kampf. Eine kritische Edition*, vol. 1 (Munich: Institut für Zeitgeschichte, 2016), 109, 122–25, as well as Ian Kershaw, *Hitler: 1889–1936: Hubris* (New York: W. W. Norton, 1998), 19–20.

40. *Deutsche Jugend*, 20.

41. Ibid., 24–26.

42. Ibid., 22–24. See also Hartmann, et al., eds., *Hitler, Mein Kampf*, 142.

43. *Deutsche Jugend*, 29–32.

44. Ibid., 34–37. See also Kershaw, *Hitler*, 96.

45. *Deutsche Jugend*, 49, 53.

46. Ibid., 58.

47. Ibid., 52, 59.

48. Kershaw, *Hitler Myth*, 233–34. See also Claudia Koonz, *The Nazi Conscience* (Cambridge, MA: Belknap Press of Harvard University Press, 2003), 20, 253.

49. Roder, *Aufbruch der Nation*, 16, 19–20.

50. Ibid., 16–17, 20–21.

51. Ibid., 27.

52. Ibid., 27, 31.

53. Ibid., 28.

54. Ibid., 28–29, 35.

55. Ibid., 37

56. Ibid., 60–61.

57. Ibid., 13, 24, 25.

58. Ibid., 44.

59. Ibid., 28.

60. Ibid., 28.

61. Ibid., 49, 53–54.

62. See Ian Kershaw, *Popular Opinion and Political Dissent in the Third Reich: Bavaria 1933–1945* (New York: Oxford University Press, 1983), 25–26.

63. See, for example, *Die Fahne hoch. 6. und 7. Schülerjahrgang*, 45–46, and *Ferdinand Hirts Ergänzungshefte zu deutschen Lesebüchern*, Drittes Heft (Breslau: Ferdinand Hirt, 1934), 19.

64. *Deutsches Lesebuch für Volksschulen. 5. und 6. Schuljahr. VIII* (Bielefeld: Velhagen and Klasing 1936), 372–74; and "Alphabetisches Verzeichnis vom Kernteil des Reichslesebuches für das 5. und 6. Schuljahr," *Deutsche Volkserziehung* 3 (1936): 60–55. See also Katharine Kennedy, "'Black-Red-Gold Enemies': Catholics, Socialists, and Jews in Elementary Schoolbooks from *Kaiserreich* to Third Reich," in *German History from the Margins*, ed. Neil Gregor, Nils Roemer and Mark Roseman (Bloomington: Indiana University Press, 2006), 156.

65. *Zentralblatt*, 75 (1933): 244; *Amtsblatt Württemberg*, 26 (1933): 121, and Baden, Ministerium für Kultus und Unterricht, *Amtsblatt des Badischen Ministeriums des Kultus und Unterrichts* (hereafter cited as *Amtsblatt Baden*), 71 (1933): 178–79. See also Ottwilm Ottweiler, *Die Volksschule im Nationalsozialismus* (Weinheim: Beltz, 1979), 14.

66. Frick, *Kampfziel*, 12–14.

67. Hans-Joachim Schumann, *Die nationalsozialistische Erziehung im Rahmen amtlicher Bestimmungen* (Langensalza: Beltz, 1938), 9. See also Reiner Lehberger and Hans-Peter Lorent, eds., *"Die Fahne hoch": Schulpolitik und Schulalltag in Hamburg unterm Hakenkreuz* (Hamburg: Ergebnisse Verlag, 1986), 28.

68. *Deutsche Wissenschaft, Erziehung und Volksbildung*, 1935: 43–46.

69. *Amtsblatt Baden*, 71 (1933): 117–18, and *Amtsblatt Württemberg*, 26 (1933): 86; and *Verordnungsblatt Sachsen*, 15 (1933): 53. See also Tilman Allert, *The Hitler Salute: On the Meaning of a Gesture* (New York: Metropolitan Books, 2008), 38.

70. *Zentralblatt*, 76 (1933): 43–44; 76 (1934): 128, and *Amtsblatt Baden*, 71 (1933): 205. See also Max Liedtke, ed., *Handbuch der Geschichte des Bayerischen Bildungswesens*, vol. 3 (Bad Heilbrunn: Julius Klinkhardt, 1997), 3:187.

71. Bernd Buchner, *Um nationale und republikanische Identität: Die deutsche Sozialdemokratie und der Kampf um die politischen Symbole in der Weimarer Republik* (Bonn: J. H. W. Dietz Nachf., 2001), 45.

72. Two rare exceptions are Wilhelm Michel, "Die Verfassung des deutschen Freistaats," in *Hessisches Lesebuch: Die weite Welt* (Giessen: Emil Roth, 1925), 288–91, and Eugen Baumgartner, "Der 18. Mai 1848 und 1923 in der Paulskirche zu Frankfurt am Main," in *Lesebuch für die Volksschulen Badens: Deutsches Land und Volk* (Lahr i.B: Moritz Schauenburg, 1928), 177–80.

73. *Ministerialblatt für das braunschweigische Unterrichtswesen*, 1928, 37.

74. *Zentralblatt*, 71 (1929): 247–48; 76 (1934): 44; and *Amtsblatt Baden*, 71 (1933): 206.

75. Roder, *Aufbruch der Nation*, 30, 37, 41, 45; and *Deutsche Jugend*, 47, 49. See also *Amtsblatt Bayern*, 75 (1933): 35; *Amtsblatt Württemberg*, 26 (1933): 49; and "Hamburg," 534.

76. Lehberger and Lorent, eds., *"Die Fahne hoch,"* 19.

77. *Amtsblatt Baden*, 72 (1934): 67–68.

78. *Amtsblatt Württemberg*, 26 (1933): 37. See also Ottweiler, *Volksschule*, 16.

79. *Zentralblatt*, 75 (1933): 150; *Amtsblatt Baden*, 71 (1933): 109. See also Lehberger and Lorent, eds., *"Die Fahne hoch,"* 21.

80. [Alois] Kluger, *Die Deutsche Volksschule im Grossdeutschen Reich* (Breslau: Ferdinand Hirt, 1940), 45–46, reprinted as *Die Volksschule im NS-Staat*, ed. Hans Jürgen Apel and Michael Klöckner (Cologne: Böhlau, 2000).

81. Fritz Schellack, *Nationalfeiertage in Deutschland von 1871 bis 1945* (Frankfurt a.M: Peter Lang, 1990), 230–46, 262–76.

82. *Amtsblatt Baden*, 71 (1933): 13.

83. *Zentralblatt*, 75 (1933): 64. See also Schellack, *Nationalfeiertage*, 284–85

84. *Zentralblatt*, 76 (1934): 75. See also Schellack, *Nationalfeiertage*, 297–98.

85. Herbert Breuer, ed., *Die völkische Schulfeier* (Bochum: Ferdinand Kamp, 1937), 65–87.

86. *Amtsblatt Baden*, 71 (1933): 48. See also Schellack, *Nationalfeiertage*, 287–92.

87. Schellack, *Nationalfeiertage*, 293–95, 312–15.

88. *Amtsblatt Baden*, 71 (1933): 149.

89. Karl Motz, *Blut und Boden: Die Grundlagen der deutschen Zukunft* (Berlin: Zeitgeschichte Verlag, 1933).

90. *Amtsblatt Baden*, 71 (1933): 64–65, 135–36, 149; (1934): 1; *Zentralblatt*, 75 (1933): 166; and *Verordnungsblatt Sachsen*, 23 (1933): 21.

91. *Zentralblatt*, 76 (1934): 129; (1933): 141–42. See also Karin Hausen, "Mother's Day in the Weimar Republic," in *When Biology Became Destiny: Women in Weimar and Nazi Germany*, ed. Renate Bridenthal, Atina Grossmann, and Marion Kaplan (New York: Monthly Review Press, 1984), 131–43.

92. *Allgemeines Schulblatt: Vereinsblatt des Allg. Lehrervereins im Reg. Bez. Wiesbaden*, 29 July 1929, no page. See also Gernert, *Schulvorschriften*, 211–13, 220–23, 241; Pamela E. Swett, "Celebrating the Republic Without Republicans: The *Reichsverfassungstag* in Berlin, 1929–32," in *Festive Culture in Germany and Europe from the Sixteenth to the Twentieth Century*, ed. Karin Friedrich (Lewiston: Edwin Mellen, 2000), 282–95; and Buchner, *Um nationale und republikanische Identität*, 329–39, as well as *Richtlinien Preussen*, 1931: 49–50.

93. *Zentralblatt*, 72 (1930): 26–27, 41–42; 74 (1932): 130.

94. *Zentralblatt*, 73 (1931): 199; 74 (1932): 197. See also Swett, "Celebrating the Republic," 295–302; Schellack, *Nationalfeiertage*, 258–59; and Buchner, *Um nationale und republikanische Identität*, 344–45.

95. Elke Fröhlich, ed., *Die Tagebücher von Joseph Goebbels*, Teil 1, Vol. 2/II (Munich: KG Saur, 2004), 337.

96. *Zentralblatt*, 75 (1933): 196; and *Amtsblatt Baden*, 71 (1933): 118.

97. *Amtsblatt Württemberg*, 26 (1933): 61. See also Ottweiler, *Volksschule*, 17; Lochmüller, *Hans Schemm*, 2:365; Lehberger and Lorent, eds., *"Die Fahne hoch,"* 32, and Rainer Bendick, *Kriegserwartung und Kriegserfahrung: Der Erste Weltkrieg in deutschen und französischen Schulgeschichtsbüchern (1900–1939/45)* (Pfaffenweiler: Centaurus, 1999), 274–75.

Bibliography

Dithmar, Reinhard, and Wolfgang Schmitz, eds. *Schule und Unterricht im Dritten Reich*. Ludwigsfelde: Ludwigsfelder Verlagshaus, 2001.

Eilers, Rolf. *Die nationalsozialistische Schulpolitik: Eine Studie zur Funktion der Erziehung im totalitären Staat*. Cologne: Westdeutscher Verlag, 1963.

Frick, Wilhelm. *Kampfziel der deutschen Schule*. Langensalza: Hermann Beyer, 1933.

Gies, Horst. *Geschichtsunterricht unter der Diktatur Hitlers*. Cologne: Böhlau, 1992.

Herrmann, Ulrich, ed. *"Die Formung des Volksgenossen": Der "Erziehungsstaat" des Dritten Reiches*. Weinheim: Beltz, 1985.

Keim, Wolfgang. *Erziehung unter der Nazi-Diktatur*, vol. 1: *Antidemokratische Potentiale, Machtantritt und Machtdurchsetzung*. Darmstadt: Wissenschaftliche Buchgesellschaft, 1995.

Kennedy, Katharine. "'Black-Red-Gold Enemies': Catholics, Socialists, and Jews in Elementary Schoolbooks from *Kaiserreich* to Third Reich." In *German History from the Margins*, edited by Neil Gregor, Nils Roemer, and Mark Roseman, 146–64. Bloomington: Indiana University Press, 2006.

Kershaw, Ian. *Popular Opinion and Political Dissent in the Third Reich: Bavaria 1933–1945*. Oxford: Oxford University Press, 1983.

———. *The "Hitler Myth": Image and Reality in the Third Reich*. Oxford: Oxford University Press, 1987.

Koonz, Claudia. *The Nazi Conscience*. Cambridge, MA: Belknap Press of Harvard University Press, 2003.

Kühnel, Franz. *Hans Schemm: Gauleiter und Kultusminister (1891–1935).* Neustadt/Aisch: Schmidt, 1985.

Lehberger, Reiner, and Hans-Peter de Lorent, eds. *"Die Fahne hoch": Schulpolitik und Schulalltag in Hamburg unterm Hakenkreuz.* Hamburg: Ergebnisse Verlag, 1986.

Nixdorf, Dalia, and Gerd Nixdorf. "Politisierung und Neutralisierung der Schule in der NS-Zeit." In *Herrschaftsalltag im Dritten Reich,* edited by Hans Mommsen and Susanne Willems, 225–303. Düsseldorf: Swann, 1988.

Ottweiler, Ottwilm. *Die Volksschule im Nationalsozialismus.* Weinheim: Beltz, 1979.

Schellack, Fritz. *Nationalfeiertage in Deutschland von 1871 bis 1945.* Frankfurt a.M.: Peter Lang, 1990.

Scholtz, Harald. *Erziehung und Unterricht unterm Hakenkreuz.* Göttingen: Vandenhoeck and Ruprecht, 1985.

 # Conclusion

REAFFIRMING THE VALUE OF POLITICAL HISTORY

Hermann Beck and Larry Eugene Jones

In an intriguing article that appeared in *History and Memory* in the winter of 2005, Helmut Walser Smith invoked the metaphor of the "vanishing point" to frame his discussion of the Nazi seizure of power and its place in modern German history. The concept of the vanishing point comes from the history of painting and refers to the efforts of European artists from the fifteenth and sixteenth centuries to master the problem of perspective. More specifically, the vanishing point—or what Leo Batista Alberti called the "centric point" in his classic treatise *On Painting* from 1436—refers to the point on "a flat plane [where] the lines of a three-dimensional image ... converge," thus determining "the relative size of all other objects on the canvas" in a "mathematically precise fashion." While Smith readily concedes that "history is not a Renaissance canvas with a vanishing point," he nevertheless suggests that the "painterly metaphor" has had a place in historical writing that goes back at least to Voltaire's *Age of Louis XIV* but that has also experienced a rebirth with the rise of the new social and cultural histories of the 1960s and 1970s. "When taken seriously," Smith writes, "the painterly metaphor helps us consider the place of facts in a larger image; it allows us to see what is in the foreground and what is placed out of view. It also enjoins us to consider these things from an analytical position that does not necessarily privilege our present perspective, or reduce perspective to a putative political ideology. Instead, the metaphor suggests that while we now see certain historical forces with greater clarity, the price of this clarity is a necessary blindness in other spheres."[1]

In periods marked by great trauma, Smith goes on to argue, the narrative tropes that have traditionally governed the writing of history since the middle of the nineteenth century—and here Smith makes specific reference to Hayden White's *Metahistory* as the *locus classicus* of the narrative argument—are so overwhelmed by the sheer force and weight of the trauma that it requires the power of a single image rather than a narrative trope rooted in the poetic imagination to render that trauma palpable. The events of January 1933 were, in Smith's mind, of such enormous magnitude and consequence that they would become a vanishing point in the historical imagination of those who wrestled with its implications and thus served as a point of reference from which all that had preceded and all that followed would be seen and interpreted. This was true of no less a historian than Friedrich Meinecke, the dean of the German historical profession and the octogenarian author of the 1946 classic *Die Deutsche Katastrophe*.[2] The same held true for that first wave of German historians such as Hajo Holborn, Hans Kohn, and Hans Rosenberg who had immigrated to the United States in the aftermath of Hitler's accession to power and brought their respective talents to bear on the rise of National Socialism.[3] In Germany the tone was set in the 1960s by two monumental works by Karl Dietrich Bracher, the first on the collapse of the Weimar Republic and the second on the National Socialist seizure of power.[4] Bracher's work indisputably established the events of January 1933 as the vanishing point of modern German history. The cohort of German historians that rose to prominence in the late 1960s and 1970s and that included the likes of Hans Mommsen, Gerhard Schulz, and Heinrich August Winkler would continue to interpret the events that came to make up the broader tapestry of twentieth-century German and European history through the lens of 1933.[5] Much of this literature, however, tended to focus less on the triumph of National Socialism than on the reasons for the failure of Weimar democracy and thus served as a barometer for the success or failure of Germany's second and ultimately more durable experiment in democratic government.

The value of 1933 as a vanishing point in modern German history is further enhanced by the fact that the events of January 1933 did not have to end the way they did. By no means was Hitler's appointment as chancellor the only way in which the crisis of Weimar democracy could have been resolved. As Harold James reminds us in an essay from 1990, the collapse of Weimar democracy and Hitler's installation as chancellor represent "two logically separate processes" that require fundamentally different analytical strategies.[6] Too often the two have been conflated to produce the mistaken conclusion that the latter was the inevitable or historically necessary consequence of the former without adequately examining the historical record of what transpired in the events that led up to the formation of the Hitler cabinet.[7] The situation in Germany after the November 1932 Reichstag elections, after all, was extraordinarily fluid, and there is no compelling reason to believe that Hitler's appointment as chancellor was the only way in which the political deadlock in Berlin could have been broken. It was, in fact, not until after Franz von Papen's fateful meeting with Hitler on 4 January 1933 that the idea of a Hitler chancellorship gained any traction whatsoever, and the negotiations that eventually culminated in the formation of the Hitler cabinet were fraught with all sorts of difficulties and very nearly collapsed on several occasions right up until the very moment of the cabinet's installation. All of this suggests that the outcome of the negotiations that began with the meeting between Hitler and Papen was far from certain, with the DNVP party chairman Alfred Hugenberg equivocating right up until the very moment that Hindenburg invited the new cabinet into his office for its official presentation on the morning of 30 January.[8] What Bracher, Mommsen, Schulz, and Winkler as authors of the most authoritative texts on the last months of the Weimar Republic and the transition to the Nazi dictatorship shared in common despite whatever differences there might have been in their respective analyses of these events was the conviction that in the final analysis it was the decisions and actions of individual historical actors such as Hindenburg, Papen, Hugenberg, and Kurt von Schleicher that ultimately determined how these negotiations played out.[9] To argue, therefore, that the end result of these negotiations was somehow predetermined by the force of long-term cultural or structural factors that had been at work in German history since at least the eighteenth century if not earlier is to misread or ignore the dynamic that was at work on the ground.

In no way whatsoever does this argument ignore or downplay the role that long-term structural and cultural factors have played in shaping the context in which historical actors such as those mentioned above pursued their respective objectives. It simply stresses the importance of situating a theory of human agency within the analysis of those factors in order to develop a proper understanding of the balance between the action of individuals and the context within which they operate. This is the goal of the first two contributions to this volume, each on an individual who was very much at the center of events in the transition from Weimar democracy to the Third Reich. Kurt von Schleicher is prominently mentioned in virtually all of the secondary literature as one of those who was most responsible for Hitler's appointment as chancellor. In his chapter on Schleicher, Larry Eugene Jones argues that Schleicher was an uncompromising opponent of Hitler from the time that he first took notice of the Nazi party leader in the early 1920s. But Schleicher's efforts to contain the dynamism of the Nazi movement by bringing it into the government on the assumption that this would somehow "tame" the Nazis and force them to behave more responsibly ended in disaster and left Germany's conservative elites with no viable alternative but to accept Hitler's appointment as chancellor. Part of Schleicher's plan, as Joseph Bendersky argues in his chapter on the famous German legal expert Carl Schmitt, was to enlist Schmitt's assistance in drafting a series of proposals that would have made it possible for the national government to dissolve the Reichstag yet continue to govern without calling for new elections in a measure that would have effectively insulated the exercise of executive authority from the agitation in the streets. But the success or failure of Schleicher's "taming strategy" ultimately depended upon his ability to develop a broad base of support capable of holding the Nazis in check. By the beginning of 1933, however, Hindenburg had grown weary of Schleicher's intrigues and had become increasingly receptive to the influence of those who now supported a Hitler chancellorship as the only way out of the impasse in which the German state found itself. This turn of events was an unmitigated defeat not just for Schleicher but also for Schmitt, who had hoped that his proposals for a declaration of a state of emergency could have kept Hitler at bay but who now found himself obliged to accommodate himself to the new regime as expeditiously as possible.

Schleicher's miscalculations as the architect of the "taming strategy" for containing the threat of Nazism clearly paved the way for Hitler's appointment as chancellor. Schmitt, on the other hand, had actually very little to do with the events that eventually culminated in Hitler's appointment but quickly reconciled himself to the realities of Nazi power and contributed in no small way to the legal normalization of the Nazi state. The next two chapters approach the Nazi seizure of power from the perspective of political Catholicism, a force that had strongly opposed the Nazis and that would now be among the first casualties of the totalitarian state. Martin Menke's chapter on the end of the German Center Party (Deutsche Zentrumspartei) focuses on its party chairman Ludwig Kaas. A prelate in the Catholic Church who had been elevated to the position of party chairman at the end of 1928, Kaas was unequivocally committed to the republican system of government as embodied in the Weimar Constitution of 1919. As party chairman, Kaas embraced the principle of *Sammlung* as a way both to unite the divergent forces within the Center and to foster a broadly based coalition of different political forces in support of Germany's beleaguered republican system. But Kaas, argues Menke, was largely ineffective as the party's leader and lacked the will and determination to stand up against Hitler's totalitarian aspirations. At no point was this more apparent than in the period after Hitler's appointment as chancellor when Kaas quietly encouraged members of the party's delegation to the Reichstag to support the Enabling Act rather than put themselves and their families at risk. In other words, Kaas is a perfect example of a German leader who lacked the moral resolve to resist Hitlerism at a point in time when it still might have made a difference. Kaas's behavior stands in sharp contrast to that of the leaders of the Center's sister party, the Bavarian People's Party (Bayerische Volkspartei or BVP). Heinrich Held, the Bavarian minister president, and his supporters in Munich did their best to prevent the coordination or *Gleichschaltung* of the Bavarian government into the structure of the new Nazi state. Only the overt threat of force and the physical intimidation of leading government and party officials as well as the less-than-intrepid behavior on the part of Bavaria's representatives in Berlin finally forced Held to recognize that he had no alternative but to flee Germany for the sake of his own safety. In contrast to Kaas and the leaders of the German Center Party, Held and his supporters in the Bavarian People's Party tried to resist up to the point where it became obvious that resistance was pointless and not worth the enormous price it would entail.

Historians of the later Weimar Republic and the establishment of the Third Reich have long been struck by the role that Germany's conservative elites played in this transition. Fritz Fischer and Hans-Ulrich Wehler, for example, were among the first to have posited a direct line of continuity from the politics of Germany's conservative elites at the end of the Second Empire to the role that they played in the destruction of the Weimar Republic and the installation of the Hitler regime in 1933.[10] The common thread through all of this was their unmitigated hostility to democracy and the political enfranchisement of the German working class. This was a theme to which Bracher, Mommsen, and to a lesser degree Winkler would return in their respective studies on the end of Weimar, with Mommsen going so far as to issue a blanket indictment of Germany's elites for having done their best to sabotage Germany's experiment in democracy until the outbreak of the world economic crisis provided them with the opportunity to finish the project. Here Mommsen has detected a "hollowing out" of the moral substance of the culture of Germany's traditional elites that left them increasingly susceptible to the appeal of Nazism and incapable of resisting it once Hitler was in power.[11] Like Mommsen, Bracher and Winkler not only sought to understand the structural factors that had led to the paralysis of Weimar democracy and the rise of Nazism but also to situate a theory of human agency within the analysis of those factors. All of this carried the discussion of the role that Germany's elites had played in the destruction of the Weimar Republic and the establishment of the Third Reich significantly further than the more simplistic arguments of Fischer and Wehler.

The role of Germany's elites in Hitler's rise to power is only part of the problem. No less important is the way in which those elites responded to the new circumstances that had been created by Hitler's assumption of power. This topic, like that of elite responsibility for the establishment of the Third Reich, requires a sense of nuance and discernment. Here it is important to avoid simplistic arguments that often ignore the concrete difficulties that individuals and institutions faced with the establishment of the Third Reich. Human motivation is extremely complex, and it is not always easy to determine the extent to which individuals acted out of self-interest, ideological empathy, a sense of relief and euphoria, career anxiety, the fear for physical safety, or any one of a multitude of other factors that might have affected an individual's response to the realities of Nazi power. Nowhere was this more apparent than in the case of Germany's business elite. In his chapter on big business and the Nazi revolution, Peter Hayes acknowledges that few of Germany's business leaders supported the Nazi Party before 1933 and that most were skeptical of the Hitler cabinet when it assumed office. But with a few notable exceptions, the leaders of the German business community quickly set aside their reservations about Hitler to place "pragmatism over principle" and align their priorities with those of the new regime. The first casualties of this pragmatism were the Jews, who were moved out as unobtrusively as possible from managerial positions in the firms where they had worked, often for a decade or more. In some cases, banks that had a conspicuously high number of Jewish employees even tried to anticipate governmental ordinances by dismissing Jewish employees before they felt state pressure to do so.

The response of big business to the birth of the Third Reich only confirms what Hans Mommsen had identified as the "hollowing out" of the ethical culture of Germany's bourgeois elites. A further example of this can be seen in the way in which ordinary Germans reacted to the wave of violence that was visited upon German Jewry in the spring of 1933. This is, as Hermann Beck argues in his chapter on anti-Jewish violence in the wake of the Reichstag fire, a frequently overlooked episode in the series of events that led up to the November pogrom of 1938 and the mass murder of European Jewry in World War II. But what is equally disturbing, as Beck's analysis illustrates, is the revelation that high-level officials in the Saxon ministry of the interior and various Reich ministries falsified evidence, minimized the extent of the attacks, intimidated victims, and occasionally even went so far as to fabricate phony charges against victims in order to shield the perpetrators from possible repercussions. While this could be attributed to the antisemitic prejudices within the ranks of the German civil service or to a misplaced patriotism that sought to avert damage to the reputation of the Reich, there is no doubt that the principal motivation behind this behavior was the desire of German civil servants to please their new masters in government. Bruce Campbell offers a different perspective on the role of violence in the Nazi seizure of power in his chapter on the SA. Campbell argues that the use of violence was an integral part of the NSDAP's strategy, employed during its consolidation of power, to intimidate and silence those who might have had the temerity to challenge Germany's new rulers. In this respect, Campbell goes beyond conventional discussions of SA violence by developing a psychological profile of the SA rank and file to explain the function of violence as a technique of "primary male group" bonding. But, as Campbell also shows, the use of violence caused serious problems for Hitler and the leaders of the new state, particularly as they tried to normalize relations with Germany's traditional elites.

Brief and sporadic as it sometimes was, the SA reign of terror in the spring of 1933 nevertheless played a critical role in intimidating Germany's traditional elites and securing their acquiescence to the new regime's policies. In its own way, the fact that so few of those in a position to do so, including high-ranking officials in the Catholic and Lutheran Churches, spoke out against the violence against Jews or the regime's use of violence in silencing its opponents or persecuting Jews offers yet another example of the lack of civil courage—or moral resolve—on the part of Germany's conservative elites, some of whom simply accepted such outrages as the price they were willing to pay for the restoration of order.[12] The same ambivalence, though in a markedly different form, can also be seen on the German left. In his chapter on the circle of socialist thinkers associated with the *Neue Blätter für den Sozialismus*, Stefan Vogt explores the ideology and political strategy of a group of intellectuals who stood on the right wing of the Social Democratic Party (Sozialdemokratische Partei Deutschlands or SPD). Arguing that patriotism served as the common denominator that united the German people, this group claimed that the Nazi movement contained respectable socialist and nationalist elements that could be weaned away from the NSDAP in favor of a more mature response to the crisis of German capitalism. In the final analysis, however, such an assessment of Nazism proved far too optimistic and severely handicapped the intellectuals who wrote for the *Neue Blätter für den Sozialismus* in formulating an effective strategy for the containment of the Nazi threat. A counterpoint to this was to be found in the reaction of organized labor. In his chapter on the demise of the German labor movement, William Patch argues that German labor leaders, regardless of their specific ideological orientation, were alarmed at the rise of Nazism and reacted to Hitler's appointment as chancellor with a mixture of disbelief and apprehension. But, as Patch clearly demonstrates, organized labor was anything but passive in its response to the threat that the new regime posed to its very existence. After the Reichstag elections of 5 March 1933, the leaders of the German labor movement took the momentous step of trying to overcome the ideological differences that had split their ranks since before World War I by entering into negotiations that sought to bring the socialist, Christian, and liberal unions together into a single union or *Einheitsgewerkschaft*. The hope was that this would strengthen organized labor's position vis-à-vis the Nazi state. But this ran straight into the face of the regime's determination to deprive the German labor movement of any independent representation whatsoever. The ubiquitous threat and use of violence by the regime, in conjunction with the establishment of paramilitary auxiliaries that subjected everyone in the German labor movement to its brutal force, would prove decisive in the defeat of organized labor and its subsequent incorporation into the structure of the Nazi state.

The acceptance of violence by German elites was part of the price they were willing to pay for what they imagined would be a restoration of the old order. This is simply another example of the "hollowing out" of the ethical culture of Germany's bourgeois elites. The same can be said, perhaps even more evocatively, of the leadership of Germany's Protestant establishment. As Rainer Hering demonstrates in his chapter on the leadership changes in the Hamburg state church, or *Landeskirche*, in the first months of the Third Reich, church leaders were only too eager to curry favor with the new regime. This, Hering argues, had little to do with fear or intimidation but represented an enthusiastic response on the part of church leaders in Hamburg and throughout the rest of the Reich to the transfer of power to the Nazis and the opportunity it presented for undoing the reforms that had been introduced in the wake of the November Revolution and for restoring authoritarian structures in the church administration along the lines of Hitler's much celebrated *Führerprinzip*. Edward Snyder, in his chapter on Friedrich von Bodelschwingh's short-lived tenure as Reich Bishop of the German Lutheran Church, approaches church-state relations at the beginning of the Third Reich from a different perspective. As the director of the Bethel Institutes in Bielefeld, Bodelschwingh was one of Germany's most prominent Protestant leaders and was especially well known for his work in the field of social reform. Although Bodelschwingh was sympathetic to much of what he found in the

National Socialist program, he was apprehensive about what the Nazi seizure of power and particularly the agitation of the German Christians meant for the future of church-state relations in the Third Reich. To the great disappointment of those who had hoped that he might take up the church's struggle against the German Christians and the regime's religious policies, Bodelschwingh shied away from a direct confrontation with the Nazi state and resigned as Reich Bishop after only six months in office.

A distinctly different dynamic was at work in the case of German Catholics. With few exceptions, Germany's Catholic population greeted Hitler's assumption of power with great trepidation. Both the Catholic Church and Germany's two Catholic parties, the German Center Party and the Bavarian People's Party, had opposed the rise of Nazism and were viewed as politically suspect by the leaders of the new regime. From the perspective of Franz von Papen, a devout Catholic and vice chancellor in the Hitler cabinet, the fact that Catholics made up a third of the German population made it imperative that they be included in the process of national reconciliation that Hitler and his government had made their first order of business. But this was easier said than done. As Larry Jones and Kevin Spicer demonstrate in their chapter on the Alliance of Catholic Germans (Arbeitsgemeinschaft Katholischer Deutscher or AKD), Papen's efforts to facilitate this process through the founding of the AKD failed to attract the support of a skeptical Catholic hierarchy, aroused the regime's deepest suspicions, and were ignominiously abandoned in the aftermath of the Röhm Purge. As much as Papen and AKD leaders tried to allay Catholic fears of a new *Kulturkampf*, the Catholic Church felt profoundly threatened by the specter of a Nazi revolution and assumed a distinctly defensive stance in its relations with the regime. This stood in sharp contrast to the Protestant experience, where church leaders and the church faithful seemed much more disposed to an accommodation with the state that would allow them to serve two masters.

For the most part, German Protestants seemed to join in the mood of national jubilation that accompanied the installation of the Hitler cabinet and the rapid consolidation of power in the months that followed. In this respect, the Nazis were able to draw upon well-established traditions that made it appear as if the new regime represented the fulfillment of national hopes and aspirations. This was particularly true in the case of the German youth movement, as André Postert demonstrates in his chapter on the Hitler Youth (Hitlerjugend or HJ) and its absorption of the panoply of German youth organizations that confronted the Nazis when they first assumed power in 1933. The German youth movement, as Postert reminds us, had been extremely diverse before 1933 and represented a wide range of political and ideological viewpoints. Many of these organizations, but particularly those that had been demonstratively apolitical, joined the HJ in a burst of enthusiasm that made coercion, except in the case of those organizations that had been linked to the German left, all but unnecessary. A key ingredient of the Nazi appeal to youth was its embrace of the *Volksgemeinschaft* and its commitment to creating a genuine national community that transcended the divisions of class, confession, and region. Katharine Kennedy approaches the Nazi struggle to win over German youth from a different perspective by examining Nazi efforts to reshape the elementary school curricula and to introduce new materials for classroom instruction that not only highlighted nazified narratives of Germany's recent past but extolled the virtues of the racial state and celebrated the idea of the *Volksgemeinschaft*. It is perhaps most surprising that Nazi efforts to reform the curricula encountered little resistance from parents, students, or teachers, as all seemed to welcome a closer alignment of elementary and secondary education with the objectives of the Nazi regime.

* * *

This volume opened with a series of questions on the causes and consequences of the National Socialist seizure of power from the last months of the Weimar Republic to the Röhm Purge in the summer of 1934. It was never the purpose of this book to address, let alone answer, all of these questions. The goal of this book has been to provide an overview—or what the Germans call a *Bestandsaufnahme*—of the current state of research on the Nazi seizure of power with an eye toward identifying those areas of research in which much has been accomplished and those in which important work is yet to be done. In the field of political history, the most important work by far remains that of Karl Dietrich Bracher. His books *Die Auflösung der Weimarer Republik* and *Die nationalsozialistische Machtergreifung* remain classics that are as remarkable for their breadth as they are for their insights and interpretation. To be sure, these works appeared a half century ago, and much has since appeared that amplified or qualified certain aspects of his overall thesis. But the essential outlines of Bracher's synthesis remain the same, and it is unlikely that this will change. Bracher does, however, touch upon two themes that stimulate further discussion not only in this collection but in future research on the topic: the question of human agency, including the question of personal responsibility and the role of German elites in Hitler's installation as chancellor and in the subsequent consolidation of power. The chapters by Larry Jones, James Bendersky, Martin Menke, and Edward Snyder all address aspects of this question and in so doing serve as a reminder that the decisions and actions of individuals such as Schleicher, Schmitt, Kaas, and Bodelschwingh do count and do carry causal agency, an argument that flies in the face of the more deterministic models of historical explanation that view the establishment of the Third Reich as the inevitable consequence of long-term structural and cultural determinants that took precedence over the decisions and behavior of individual historical actors.

This is not to dispute what has become a point of consensus among students of the late Weimar Republic and the establishment of the Third Reich, namely that the impetus behind the sequence of events that marked the transition from Weimar democracy to the Third Reich came from Germany's conservative elites. Here one is tempted to ask to what extent is Hans Mommsen correct in arguing that the complicity of Germany's elites in the transition from the Weimar Republic to the Third Reich reflected the "hollowing out" of the ethical culture of Germany's traditional elites. Or was this the result of other factors more practical in nature and less global in scope? In answering this question, it is every bit as important to understand how German elites responded to the Nazis in power as it is to understand the role that they played in the installation of the Hitler cabinet in the first place. The precise modalities of this question have never been fully explored, and it remains a topic that warrants further investigation. Peter Hayes's chapter on German big business and the Nazi revolution is clearly a step in the right direction, and it serves as a model of the discerning analysis that should be focused on other sectors of Germany's conservative establishment. In this respect, the chapters by Rainer Hering and Eduard Snyder provide interesting new insights on how the leaders of the Evangelical-Lutheran Church reacted to the realities of Nazi power, while the chapter by Larry Jones and Kevin Spicer sheds interesting new light on the efforts of the Catholic Church to preserve its independence from both the regime and Papen's proxies in the AKD. While recent work has shown the contempt with which the Nazis viewed their conservative allies in the period after Hitler's assumption of power,[13] there is still much that can be learned about this relationship in the months and years that followed.

A closely related problem was the role and function of violence in the establishment of the Nazi dictatorship, if for no other reason that it placed a severe strain on Hitler's alliance with elements of Germany's conservative elites. Violence has long been a matter of considerable interest in studies of the Third Reich but has just begun to receive its due attention in recent scholarly literature on the Weimar Republic.[14] By cataloguing early abuses with particular emphasis on the reaction of civil servants, Hermann Beck's chapter on Nazi anti-Jewish violence focuses attention on aspects of the first months of the Third Reich that has largely escaped serious scholarly attention. Bruce Campbell's chapter on the role of the SA in the Nazi seizure of power focuses attention on the use of violence to coerce consensus and intimidate opponents of the regime. While recent research has indicated that anti-Jewish violence in the winter and spring of 1933 emanated from below despite efforts by the Nazi party leadership to halt it,[15] the only way to determine whether violence in other spheres of life was the result of uncoordinated spontaneous actions from below or mandated by the upper echelons of the Nazi party leadership is through local and regional studies that examine the precise mechanisms by which the Nazis secured their power outside of Berlin, Munich, and other metropolitan centers.[16] Both Winfried Becker's chapter on the end of political Catholicism in Bavaria and William Patch's chapter on the destruction of the German labor movement, on the other hand, address the use of violence from the perspective of its victims, in the first case the leaders of the Bavarian government and their supporters in the Bavarian People's Party and in the second the leaders of the German trade union movement.

In a similar vein, André Postert's chapter on the incorporation of German youth organizations into the Hitler Youth stresses the role that coercion and the threat of violence played in making this possible. Postert also reminds us that this was not the product of violence alone but that propaganda and ideology also played a critical role in securing the integration of the German youth movement into the organizational structure of the NSDAP. Here Postert addresses a theme that has echoes in several other contributions to this volume, namely those of Stefan Vogt and Katharine Kennedy. Vogt illustrates that a group of intellectuals who considered themselves part of the political left identified common denominators with National Socialism, such as patriotism and anticapitalism, that would allow them to work with the Nazi movement. Kennedy shows that the National Socialists employed a comprehensive strategy to steer the hearts and minds of Germany's youth into acceptable ideological channels by institutionalizing their creed into school curricula. Both Vogt and Kennedy make it clear that National Socialism could draw upon a deeply felt nationalism that encompassed virtually the entire political spectrum from the right wing of the SPD to the German Nationalists. Both contributions reflect the increasingly important role that the analysis of propaganda and ideology have played in much of the recent scholarly literature on continuities between the pre-Nazi right and the Third Reich.[17]

At stake here is the question of whether propaganda and ideology function as independent variables in the process of historical change or can only be understood as part of a larger context shaped by material interests and their struggle for political power. In other words, which is primary: culture or politics? A further question along this line of inquiry involves the role and agency of individual historical actors. Do their actions have agency, or are these individuals simply playing roles that have already been determined by the cultural and structural forces that shape the context within which they operate? At a point in history when so much was at stake as on 30 January 1933, it is important to sort out as far as possible the precise way in which the cultural, social, economic, and political determinants of historical change intersected with each other to create an environment that suddenly invested the actions of specific historical actors with so much more causal agency than they otherwise would have possessed. Without making a claim to having resolved this conundrum, this volume and the individual contributions contained within it have sought instead to pose the foregoing questions for the sake of future historical inquiry and to point out possible paths that such research might eventually take.

Hermann Beck is professor of history at the University of Miami. He is author of *The Origins of the Authoritarian Welfare State in Prussia: Conservatives, Bureaucracy, and the Social Question, 1815–1870* (1995, 1998) and *The Fateful Alliance: German Conservatives and Nazis in 1933; The Machtergreifung in a New Light* (2008, 2010), and he has published numerous articles in leading American and European journals, including the *Historische Zeitschrift, The Journal of Modern History,* and *The Journal of Contemporary History*. He recently completed a book-length manuscript on "Before the Holocaust: Anti-Semitism and the Reaction of German Society during the Nazi Seizure of Power."

Larry Eugene Jones is professor of history at Canisius College in Buffalo, New York, where he specializes in the history of modern Germany and the Holocaust. He also edited *The German Right in the Weimar Republic: Studies in the History of German Conservatism, Nationalism, and Antisemitism* (2014). He is the author of *Hitler versus Hindenburg: The 1932 Presidential Elections and the End of the Weimar Republic* (2016) and is currently working on a new book tentatively titled *The German Right, 1918–1930: Political Parties, Organized Interests, and Patriotic Associations in the Struggle against Weimar Democracy.*

Notes

1. Helmut Walser Smith, "The Vanishing Point of German History: An Essay on Perspective," *History and Memory* 17 (2005): 270.
2. On Meinecke's struggle with Germany's Nazi past, see Nicolas Berg, "Tragedy, Fate, and Breach: Friedrich Meinecke's *The German Catastrophe* (1946) and the Paradoxes of 'National-Historical' Interpretation," in Berg, *The Holocaust and the West German Historians: Historical Interpretation and Autobiographical Memory*, trans. and ed. Joel Golb (Madison: University of Wisconsin Press, 2015), 17–46.
3. See the insightful essay by Kenneth D. Barkin, "German Émigré Historians in America: The Fifties, Sixties, and Seventies," in *An Interrupted Past: German-Speaking Refugee Historians in the United States after 1933*, ed. Hartmut Lehmann and James J. Sheehan (Cambridge, 1991), 149–69, esp. 158–63.
4. Karl Dietrich Bracher, *Die Auflösung der Weimarer Republik: Eine Studie des Machtverfalls in der Demokratie*, 3rd ed. (Villingen-Schwarwald: Ring-Verlag, 1960); and "Stufen der Machtergreifung," in Karl Dietrich Bracher, Wolfgang Sauer, and Gerhard Schulz, *Die nationalsozialistische Machtergreifung: Studien zur Errichtung des totalitären Herrschaftssystems in Deutschland 1933/34* (Cologne and Opladen: Westdeutscher Verlag, 1960), 31–219.
5. In addition to Bracher, *Auflösung*, 644–732, see Hans Mommsen, *The Rise and Fall of Weimar Democracy*, trans. Elborg Forster and Larry Eugene Jones (Chapel Hill and London: University of North Carolina Press, 1996), 490–544; Gerhard Schulz, *Von Brüning zu Hitler: Der Wandel des politischen Systems in Deutschland 1930–1933* (Berlin: de Gruyter, 1992), 1028–49; and Heinrich August Winkler, *Weimar 1918–1933: Die Geschichte der ersten Deutschen Demokratie* (Munich: C. H. Beck, 1993), 557–94.
6. Harold James, "Economic Reasons for the Collapse of the Weimar Republic," in *Weimar: Why Did German Democracy Fail*, ed. Ian Kershaw (New York: St. Martin's, 1990), 30.
7. Larry Eugene Jones, "Why Hitler Came to Power: In Defense of a New History of Politics," in *Geschichtswissenschaft vor 2000: Perspektiven der Historiographiegeschichte, Geschichtstheorie, Sozial- und Kulturgeschichte; Festschrift für Georg G. Iggers zum 65. Geburtstag*, ed. Konrad H. Jarausch, Jorn Rüsen, and Hans Schleicher (Hagen: Magrit Roman Medienverlag, 1991), 256–76.
8. For the most authoritative statement of this argument, see Henry Ashby Turner, Jr., *Hitler's Thirty Days to Power: January 1933* (Reading, MA: Addison-Wesley, 1966), 163–83. See also Eberhard Kolb, *Was Hitler's Seizure of Power on January 30, 1933, Inevitable?*, with a comment by Henry Ashby Turner Jr. (Washington, DC: German Historical Institute, 1970), as well as Larry Eugene Jones, "'The Greatest Stupidity of My Life': Alfred Hugenberg and the Formation of the Hitler Cabinet, January 1933," *Journal of Contemporary History* 27 (1992): 63–87.

9. See the sources cited above in note 5.

10. See Fritz Fischer, *From Kaiserreich to the Third Reich: Elements of Continuity in German History, 1871–1945*, trans. Roger Fletcher (1986), and Hans-Ulrich Wehler, *Entsorgung der deutschen Vergangenheit: Ein polemischer Essay zum "Historikerstreit"* (Munich: Beck, 1988).

11. This is a consistent theme in Mommsen's work. For its earliest formulation, see Hans Mommsen, "Hitlers Stellung im nationalsozialistischen Herrschaftssystem," in *Der "Führerstaat": Mythos und Realität; Studien zur Struktur und Politik des Dritten Reiches/The "Führer State": Myth and Reality; Studies on the Structure of Politics of the Third Reich*, ed. Gerhard Hirschfeld and Lothar Kettenacker (Stuttgart: Allen and Unwin, 1981), 43–72. For a return to this argument, see Hans Mommsen, "Die deutschen Eliten und der Mythos des nationalen Aufbruchs von 1933," *Merkur: Deutsche Zeitschrift für europäisches Denken* 38 (1984): 97–102, and "Die nationalsozialistische Machteroberung: Revolution oder Gegenrevolution," in *Europäische Sozialgeschichte: Festschrift für Wolfgang Schieder*, ed. Christof Dipper, Lutz Klinkhammer, and Alexander Nützenadel (Berlin: Duncker and Humblot, 2000), 41–56.

12. In this respect, see Heinrich August Winkler, "German Society, Hitler and the Illusion of Restoration 1930–33," *Journal of Contemporary History* 11 (1976): 1–16.

13. See the recent publications by Hermann Beck, "Konflikte zwischen Deutschnationalen und Nationalsozialisten während der Machtergreifungszeit," *Historische Zeitschrift* 292 (2011): 645–81, and "The Anti-Bourgeois Character of National Socialism," *Journal of Modern History* 88 (2016): 572–610.

14. For example, see Robert Gerwarth, "The Central European Counter-Revolution: Paramilitary Violence in Germany, Austria, and Hungary after the Great War," *Past and Present* 200 (2008): 175–209, as well as the more specialized contributions by Benjamin Ziemann, *Front und Heimat: Ländliche Kriegserfahrungen im südlichen Bayern 1914–1923* (Essen: Klartext, 1997), and Mark Jones, *Founding Weimar: Violence and the German Revolution of 1918–1919* (Cambridge: Cambridge University Press, 2016).

15. For further information, see Hermann Beck, "Anti-Semitic Violence 'From Below': Attacks and Protestant Church Responses in Germany in 1933," *Politics, Religion, and Ideology* 14 (2013): 395–412, as well as Beck, *The Fateful Alliance: German Conservatives and Nazis in 1933* (New York and Oxford: Berghahn Books, 2008), 182–88.

16. In this respect, see the classic study by William S. Allen, *The Nazi Seizure of Power: The Experience of a Single German Town, 1922–1945*, rev. ed. (New York: Franklin Watts, 1984), as well as the contributions to the literature on this topic in Thomas Schnabel, ed., *Die Machtergreifung in Südwestdeutschland; Das Ende der Weimarer Republik in Baden und Württemberg 1928–1933* (Stuttgart: Kohlhammer, 1986), as well as Joachim Paschen, *Hamburg zwischen Hindenburg und Hitler; Die nationalsozialistische Machteroberung in einer roten Festung* (Bremen: Edition Temmen, 2013), and Andreas Wagner, *"Machtergreifung in Sachsen": NSDAP und staatliche Verwaltung 1930–1935* (Cologne, Weimar, and Vienna: Böhlau Verlag, 2004).

17. In particular, see Geoff Eley, *Nazism as Fascism: Violence, Ideology, and the Ground of Consent in Germany 1930–1945* (London and New York: Routledge, 2013), 59–90.

Bibliography

Allen, William S. *The Nazi Seizure of Power: The Experience of a Single German Town, 1922–1945*, rev. ed. New York: Frankin Watts, 1984.

Barkin, Kenneth D. "German Émigré Historians in America: The Fifties, Sixties, and Seventies." In *An Interrupted Past: German-Speaking Refugee Historians in the United States after 1933*, edited by Hartmut Lehmann and James J. Sheehan, 149–69. Cambridge: Cambridge University Press, 1991.

Beck, Hermann. *The Fateful Alliance: German Conservatives and Nazis in 1933; The Machtergreifung in a New Light*. New York and Oxford: Berghahn Books, 2008.

———. "Konflikte zwischen Deutschnationalen und Nationalsozialisten während der Machtergreifungszeit." *Historische Zeitschrift* 292 (2011): 645–81,

———. "The Antibourgeois Character of National Socialism." *Journal of Modern History* 88 (2016): 572–609.

Berg, Nicolas. *The Holocaust and the West German Historians: Historical Interpretation and Autobiographical Memory*. Translated and edited by Joel Golb. Madison: University of Wisconsin Press, 2015.

Bracher, Karl Dietrich. *Die Auflösung der Weimarer Republik: Eine Studie des Machtverfalls in der Demokratie*, 3rd ed. Villingen-Schwarzwald: Ring-Verlag, 1960.

Bracher, Karl Dietrich, Wolfgang Sauer, and Gerhard Schulz. *Die nationalsozialistische Machtergreifung: Studien zur Errichtung des totalitären Herrschaftssystems in Deutschland 1933/34*. Cologne and Opladen: Westdeutscher Verlag, 1960.

Eley, Geoff. *Nazism as Fascism: Violence, Ideology, and the Ground of Consent in Germany, 1930–1945*. London and New York: Routledge, 2013.

Eschenburg, Theodor. "The Role of Personality in the Crisis of the Weimar Republic: Hindenburg, Brüning, Groener, Schleicher." In *Republic to Reich: The Making of the Nazi Revolution*, edited by Hajo Holborn, 3–50. New York: Pantheon Books, 1972.

Gerwarth, Robert. "The Central European Counter-Revolution: Paramilitary Violence in Germany, Austria, and Hungary after the Great War." *Past and Present* 200 (2008): 175–209.

James, Harold. "Economic Reasons for the Collapse of the Weimar Republic." In *Weimar: Why Did German Democracy Fail?*, edited by Ian Kershaw, 30–57. New York: St. Martin's Press, 1990.

Jones, Larry Eugene. "Why Hitler Came to Power: In Defense of a New History of Politics." In *Geschichtswissenschaft vor 2000: Perspektiven der Historiographiegeschichte, Geschichtstheorie, Sozial- und Kulturgeschichte; Festschrift für Georg G. Iggers zum 65. Geburtstag*, edited by Konrad H. Jarausch, Jörn Rüsen, and Hans Schleier, 256–76. Hagen: Magrit Rottmann Medienverlag, 1991.

———. "'The Greatest Stupidity of My Life': Alfred Hugenberg and the Formation of the Hitler Cabinet, January 1933." *Journal of Contemporary History* 27 (1992): 63–87.

Jones, Mark. *Founding Weimar: Violence and the German Revolution of 1918–1919.* Cambridge: Cambridge University Press, 2016.

Kolb, Eberhard. *Was Hitler's Seizure of Power on January 30, 1933, Inevitable?* With a comment by Henry Ashby Turner Jr. Washington, DC: German Historical Institute, 1970.

Mommsen, Hans. "Hitlers Stellung im *nationalsozialistischen* Herrschaftssystem." In *Der "Führerstaat": Mythos und Realität; Studien zur Struktur und Politik des Dritten Reiches/The "Führer State": Myth and Reality; Studies on the Structure of Politics of the Third Reich,* edited by Gerhard Hirschfeld and Lothar Kettenacker, 43–72. Stuttgart: Allen and Unwin, 1981.

———. "Die deutschen Eliten und der Mythos des nationalen Aufbruchs von 1933." *Merkur: Deutsche Zeitschrift für europäisches Denken* 38 (1984): 97–102.

———. *The Rise and Fall of Weimar Democracy.* Translated by Elborg Forster and Larry Eugene Jones. Chapel Hill and London: University of North Carolina Press, 1996.

———. "Die nationalsozialistische Machteroberung: Revolution oder Gegenrevolution." In *Europäische Sozialgeschichte: Festschrift für Wolfgang Schieder,* edited by Christof Dipper, Lutz Klinkhammer, and Alexander Nützenadel, 41–56. Berlin: Duncker and Humblot, 2000.

Paschen, Joachim. *Hamburg zwischen Hindenburg und Hitler: Die nationalsozialistische Machteroberung in einer roten Festung.* Bremen: Edition Temmen, 2013.

Schnabel, Thomas, ed. *Die Machtergreifung in Südwestdeutschland: Das Ende der Weimarer Republik in Baden und Württemberg 1928–1933.* Stuttgart: Kohlhammer, 1986.

Schulz, Gerhard. *Von Brüning zu Hitler: Der Wandel des politischen Systems in Deutschland 1930–1933.* Berlin: de Gruyter, 1992.

Smith, Helmut Walser. "The Vanishing Point of German History: An Essay on Perspective." *History and Memory* 17 (2005): 269–95.

Turner, Henry Ashby, Jr. *Hitler's Thirty Days to Power: January 1933.* Reading, MA: Addison-Wesley, 1966.

Wagner, Andreas. *"Machtergreifung in Sachsen": NSDAP und staatliche Verwaltung 1930–1935.* Cologne, Weimar, and Vienna: Böhlau, 2004.

Wehler, Hans-Ulrich. *Entsorgung der deutschen Vergangenheit: Ein polemischer Essay zum "Historikerstreit."* Munich: Beck, 1988.

Winkler, Heinrich August. "German Society, Hitler and the Illusion of Restoration 1930–33." *Journal of Contemporary History* 11 (1976): 1–16.

———. *Weimar 1918–1933: Die Geschichte der ersten deutschen Demokratie.* Munich: Beck, 1993.

Ziemann, Benjamin. *Front und Heimat: Ländliche Kriegserfahrungen im südlichen Bayern 1914–1923.* Essen: Klartext, 1997.

✚ Index

CPSIA information can be obtained
at www.ICGtesting.com
Printed in the USA
BVHW041721111220
595479BV00012B/439